Princess Jellyfish 03

Akiko Higashimura

DEAREST READERS!

OH MY GOODNESS!
RECENTLY, THE AMOUNT OF
30-SOMETHING-YEAR-OLD WOMEN
AROUND ME WHO ARE ORGANIZING
AMARS IS RAPIDLY INCREASING!
AMARS KARAOKE,
AMARS BUS TOUR,
AMARS CAMPING TRIP,
AMARS MOUNTAIN CLIMBING...
THEY'RE HARD AT WORK SEEING
HOW FAR AND WIDE THEY CAN
EXPAND THEIR SCOPE OF
ACTIVITIES WITH *JUST* WOMEN!
IT SEEMS *SO* FUN!
A GUY FRIEND SAID,
"THAT SEEMS FUN, LET ME JOIN!"
BUT I HEARD HE GOT TURNED
DOWN IN ONE SECOND!
IS THIS REALLY OKAY?!

-AKIKO HIGASHIMURA

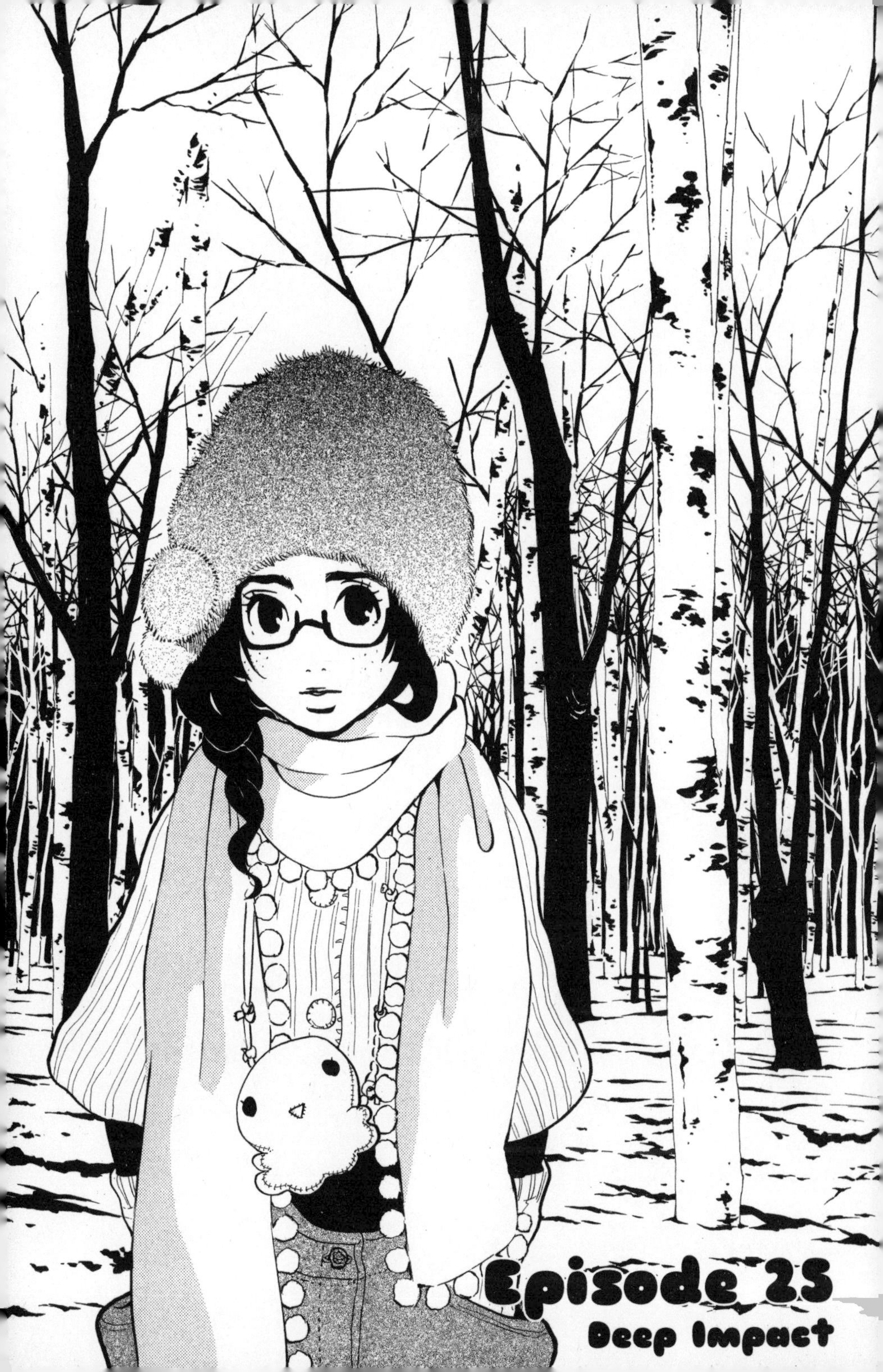
Episode 25
Deep Impact

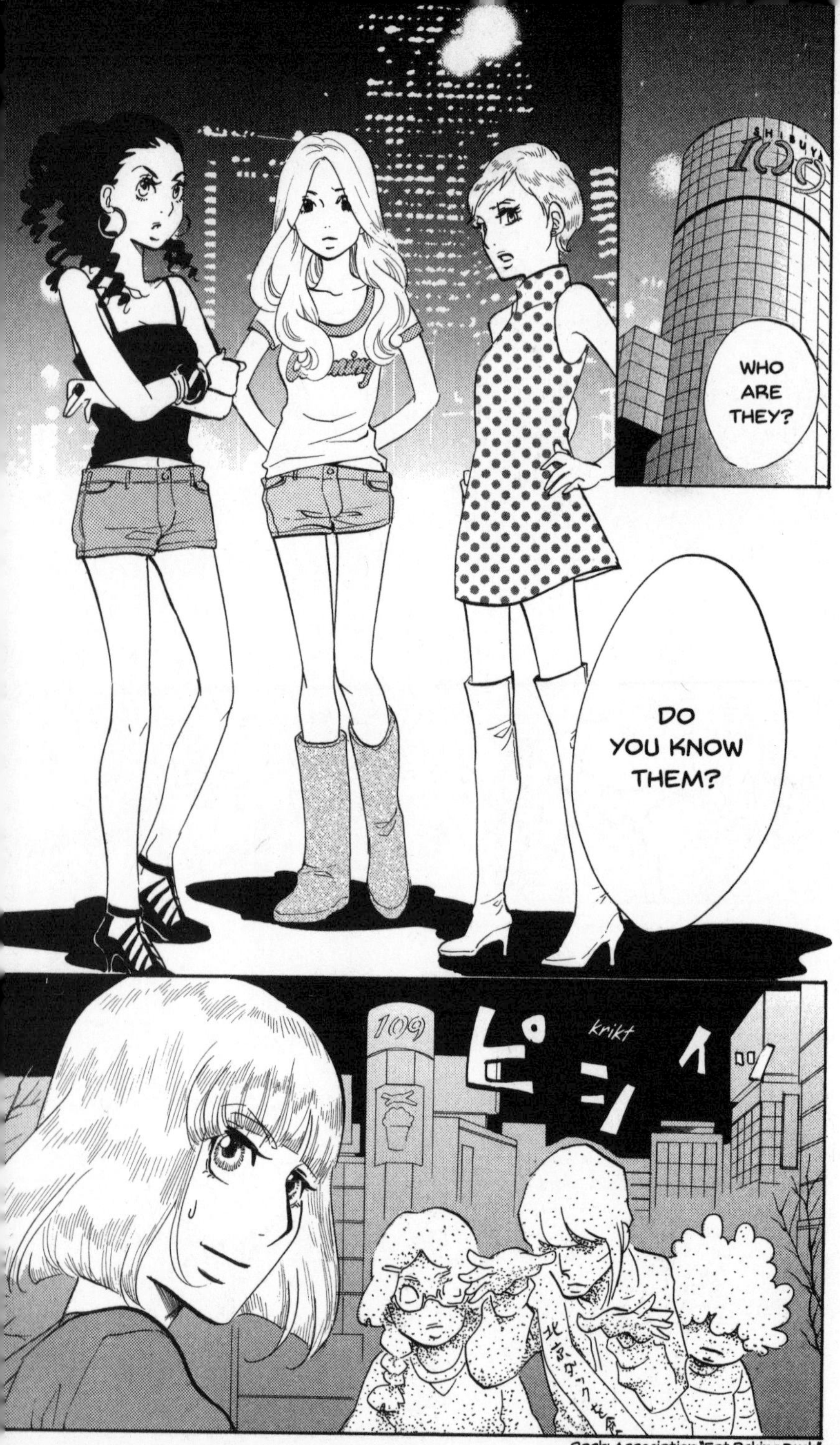
SHIBUYA 109
WHO ARE THEY?
DO YOU KNOW THEM?
109
ピシィ
krikt
Sash: Association "Eat Peking Duck"

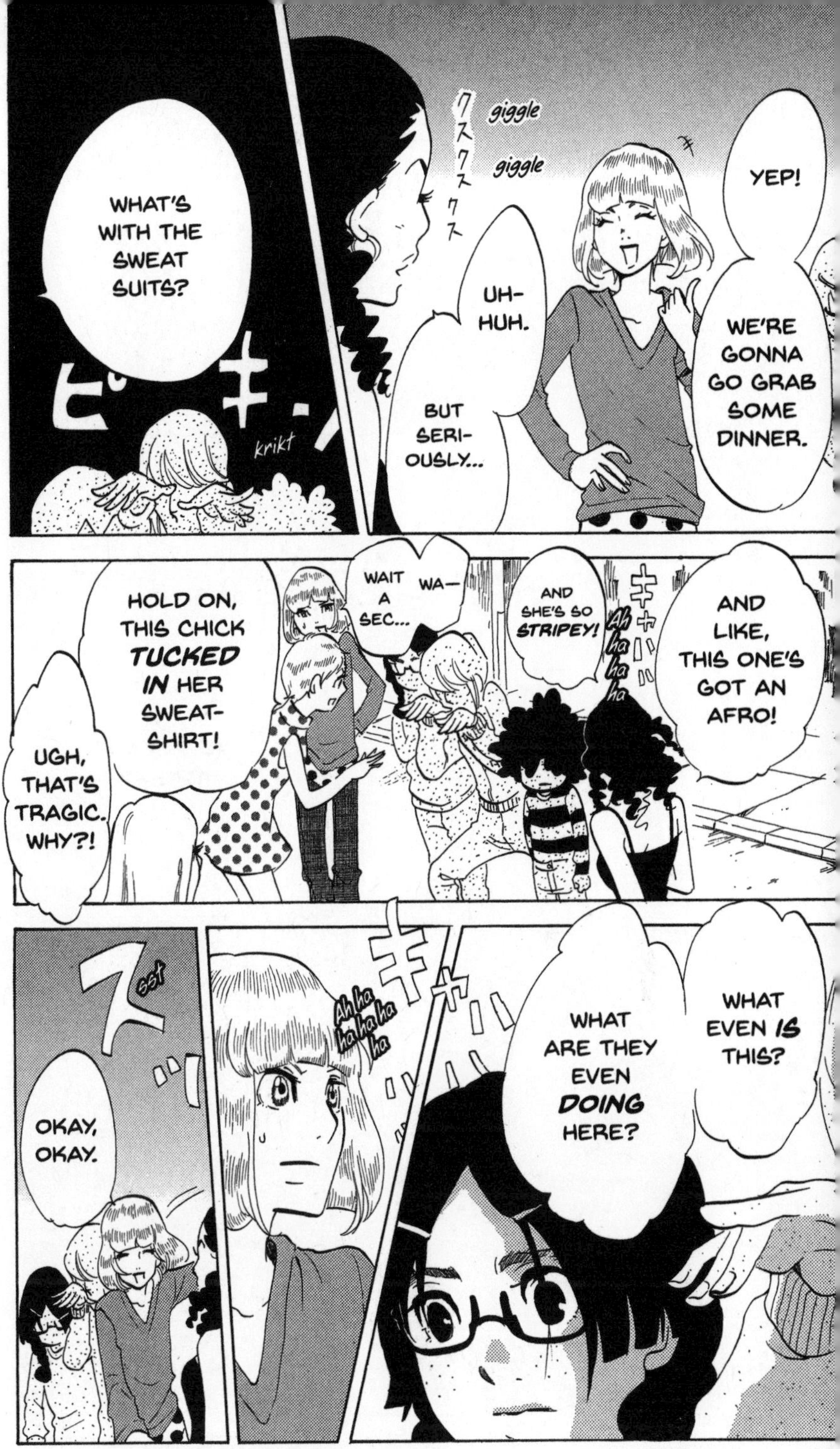
YEP!
WE'RE GONNA GO GRAB SOME DINNER.
クスクスクス
giggle
giggle
UH-HUH.
BUT SERI-OUSLY...
WHAT'S WITH THE SWEAT SUITS?
ピキ
krikt
AND LIKE, THIS ONE'S GOT AN AFRO!
キャハハ
Ah ha ha ha
AND SHE'S SO STRIPEY!
WA—
WAIT A SEC...
HOLD ON, THIS CHICK TUCKED IN HER SWEAT-SHIRT!
UGH, THAT'S TRAGIC. WHY?!
WHAT EVEN IS THIS?
WHAT ARE THEY EVEN DOING HERE?
キャハハ
Ah ha ha ha ha
ス
sst
OKAY, OKAY.

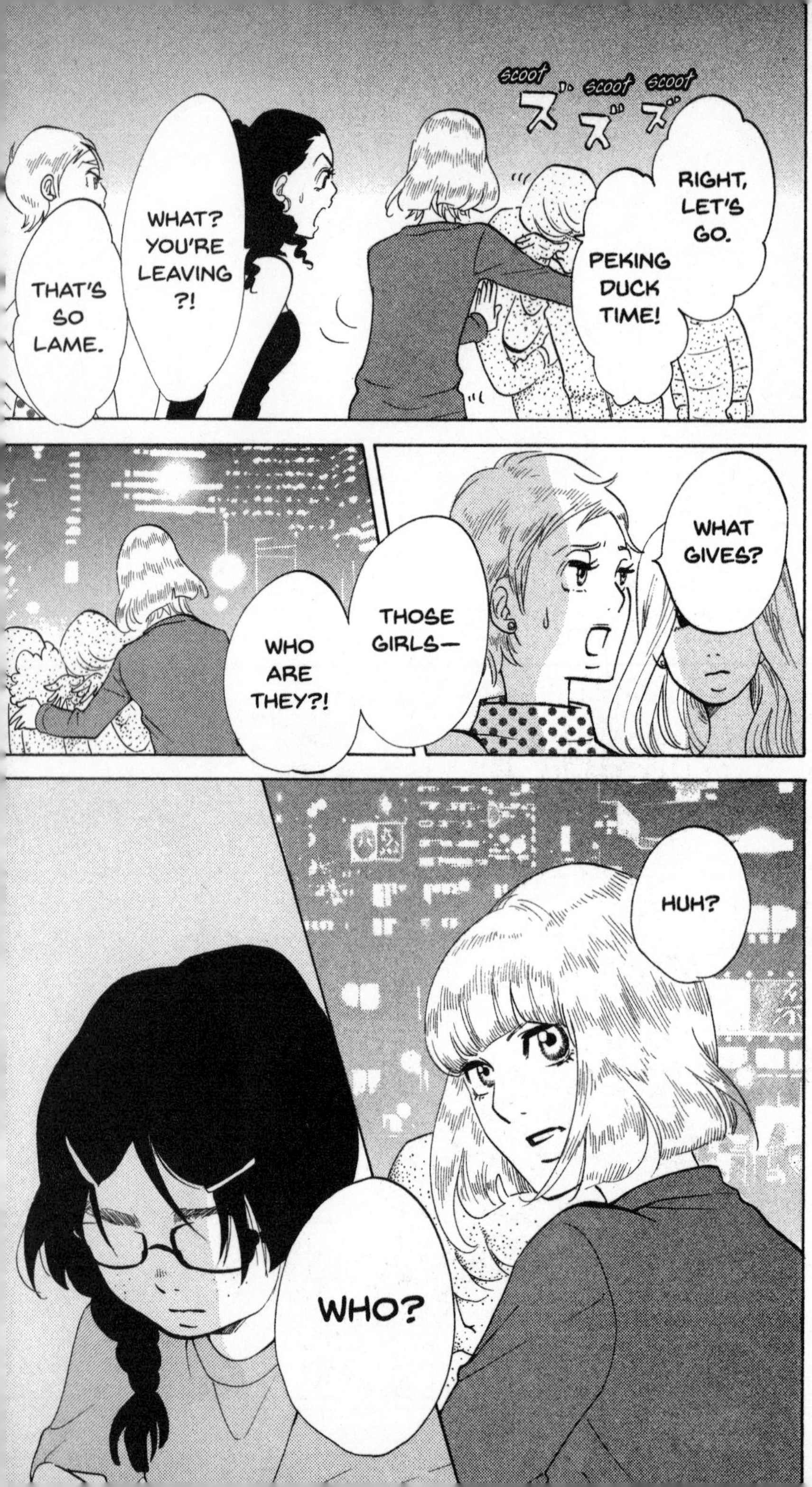
scoot scoot scoot
ズズズ
RIGHT, LET'S GO.
PEKING DUCK TIME!
WHAT? YOU'RE LEAVING?!
THAT'S SO LAME.
WHAT GIVES?
THOSE GIRLS—
WHO ARE THEY?!
HUH?
WHO?

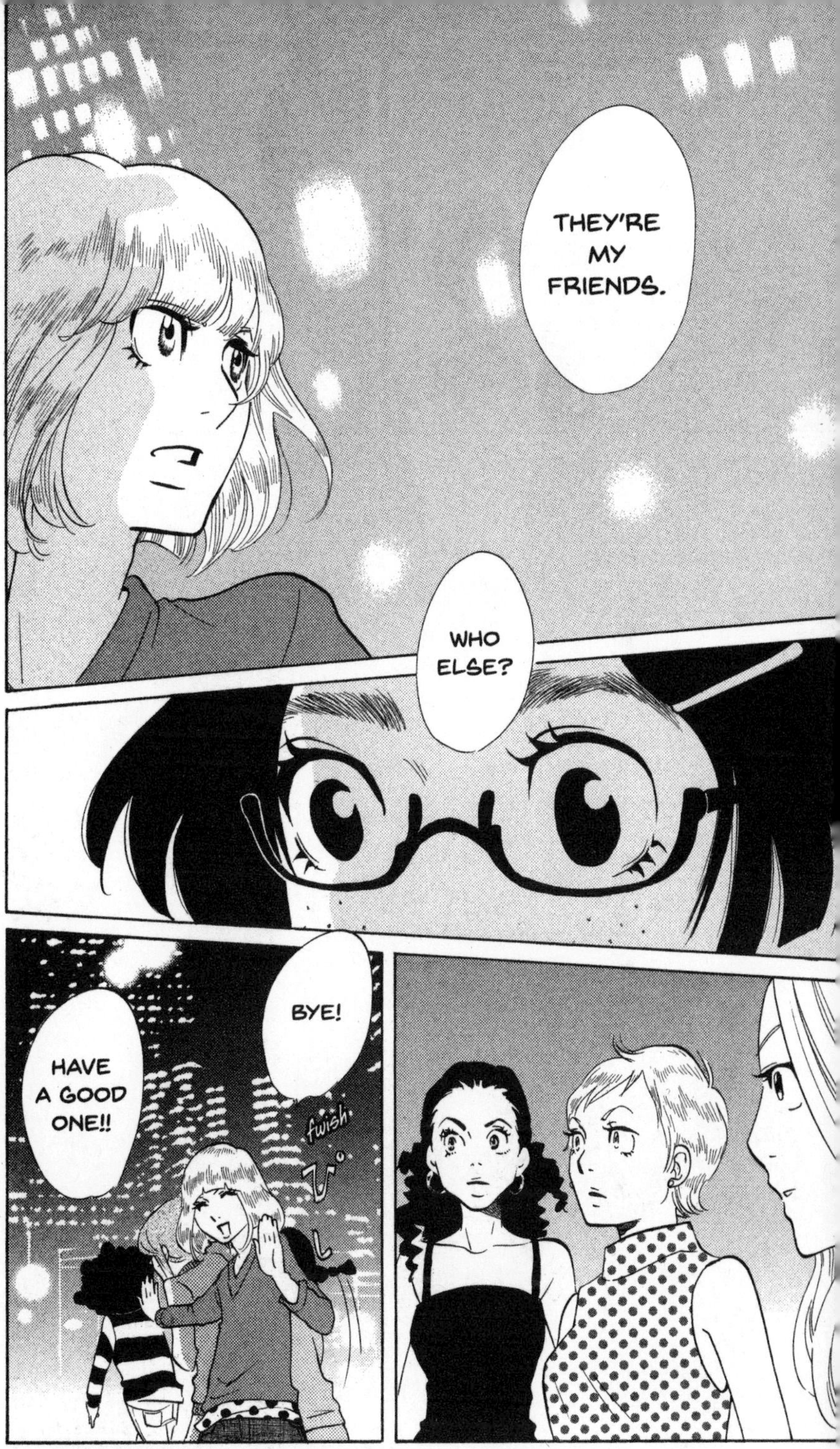
THEY'RE MY FRIENDS.
WHO ELSE?
BYE!
HAVE A GOOD ONE!!
fwish

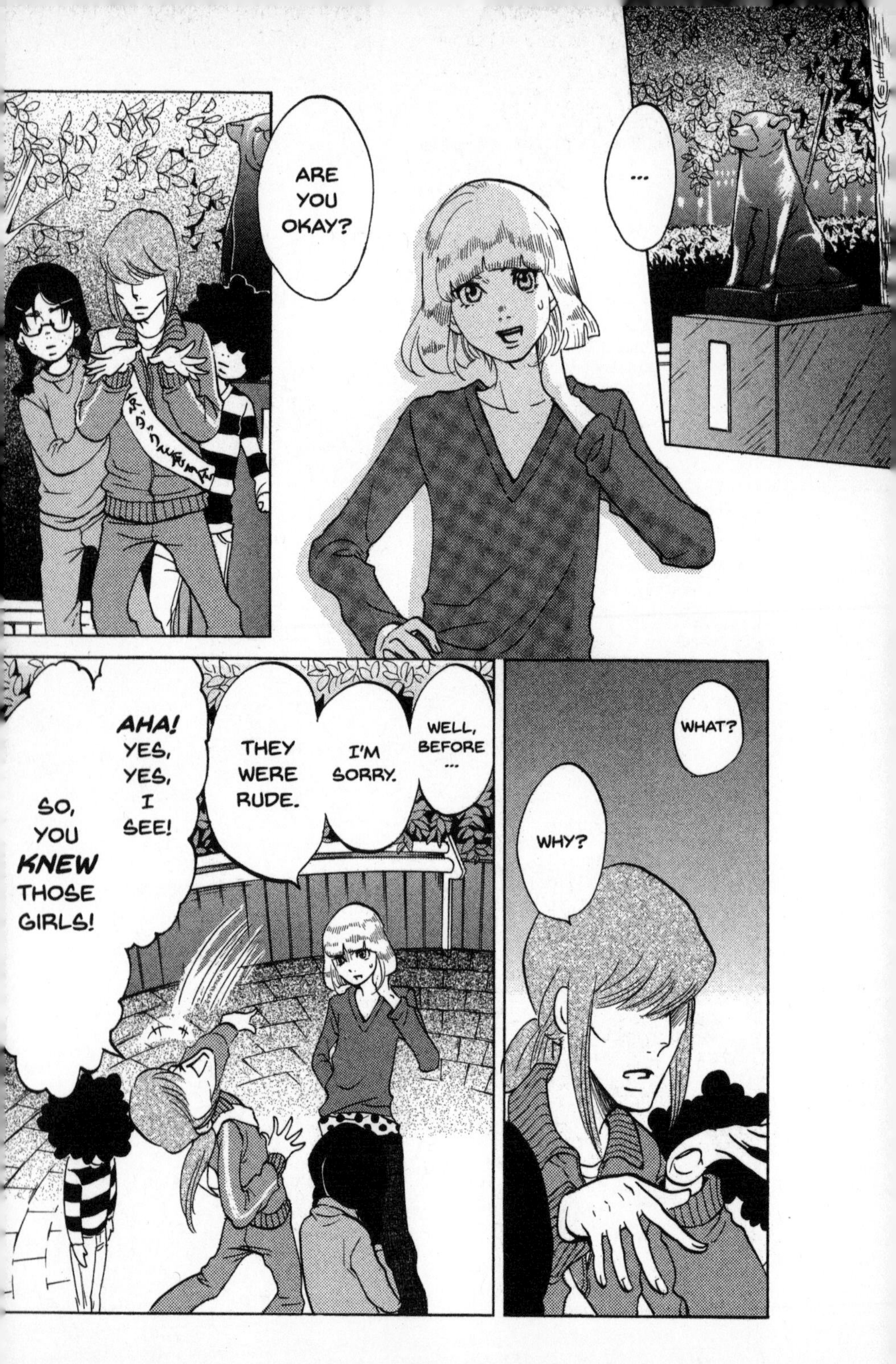
...
ARE YOU OKAY?
WHAT?
WHY?
WELL, BEFORE ...
I'M SORRY.
THEY WERE RUDE.
AHA! YES, YES, I SEE!
SO, YOU KNEW THOSE GIRLS!

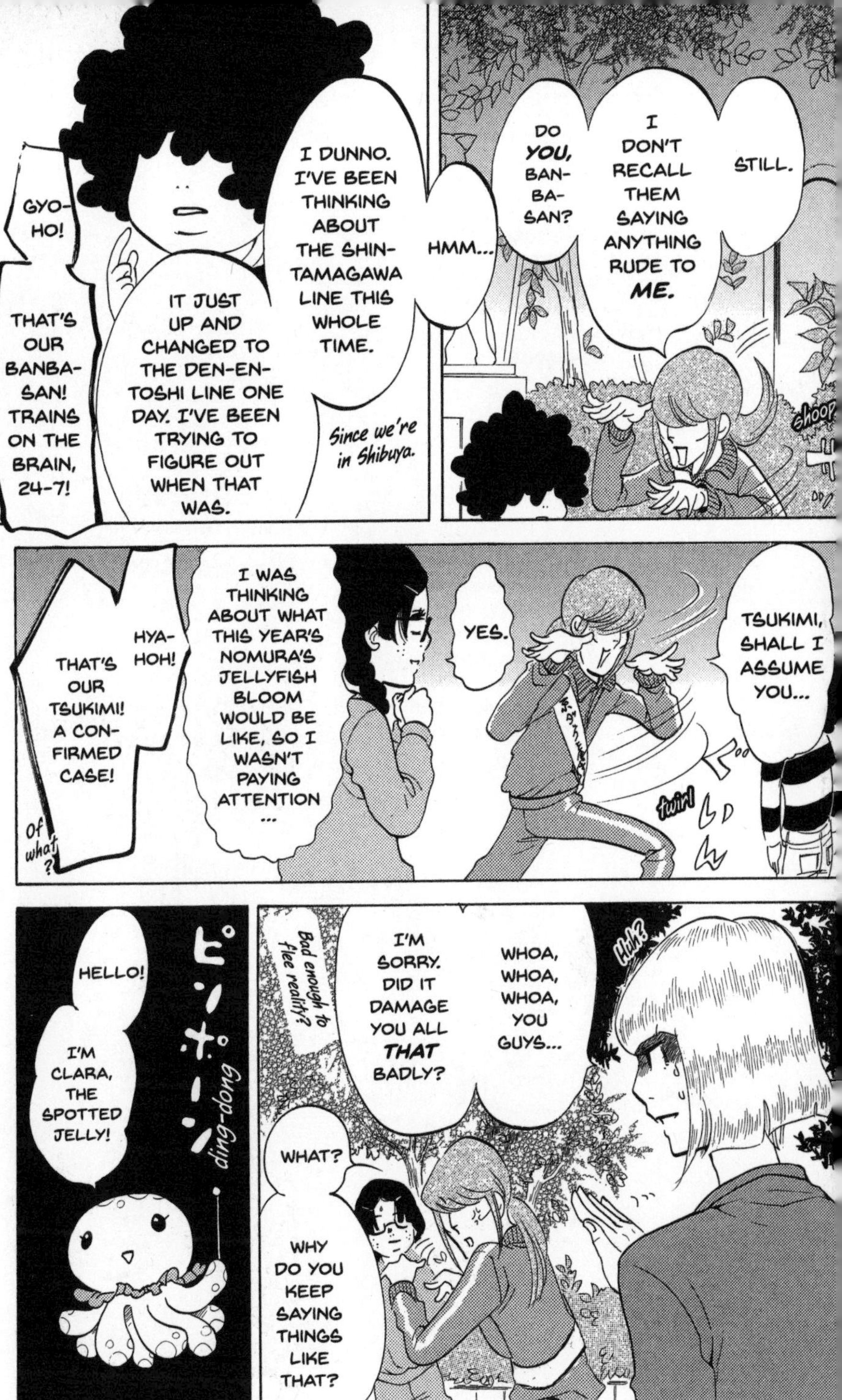
STILL.
I DON'T RECALL THEM SAYING ANYTHING RUDE TO ME.
DO YOU, BANBA-SAN?
HMM...
shoop
I DUNNO. I'VE BEEN THINKING ABOUT THE SHIN-TAMAGAWA LINE THIS WHOLE TIME.
IT JUST UP AND CHANGED TO THE DEN-EN-TOSHI LINE ONE DAY. I'VE BEEN TRYING TO FIGURE OUT WHEN THAT WAS.
Since we're in Shibuya.
GYO-HO!
THAT'S OUR BANBA-SAN! TRAINS ON THE BRAIN, 24-7!
TSUKIMI, SHALL I ASSUME YOU...
twirl
YES.
I WAS THINKING ABOUT WHAT THIS YEAR'S NOMURA'S JELLYFISH BLOOM WOULD BE LIKE, SO I WASN'T PAYING ATTENTION...
HYA-HOH!
THAT'S OUR TSUKIMI! A CON-FIRMED CASE!
Of what?
Huh?
WHOA, WHOA, WHOA, YOU GUYS...
I'M SORRY. DID IT DAMAGE YOU ALL THAT BADLY?
Bad enough to flee reality?
WHAT?
WHY DO YOU KEEP SAYING THINGS LIKE THAT?
ding-dong
HELLO!
I'M CLARA, THE SPOTTED JELLY!

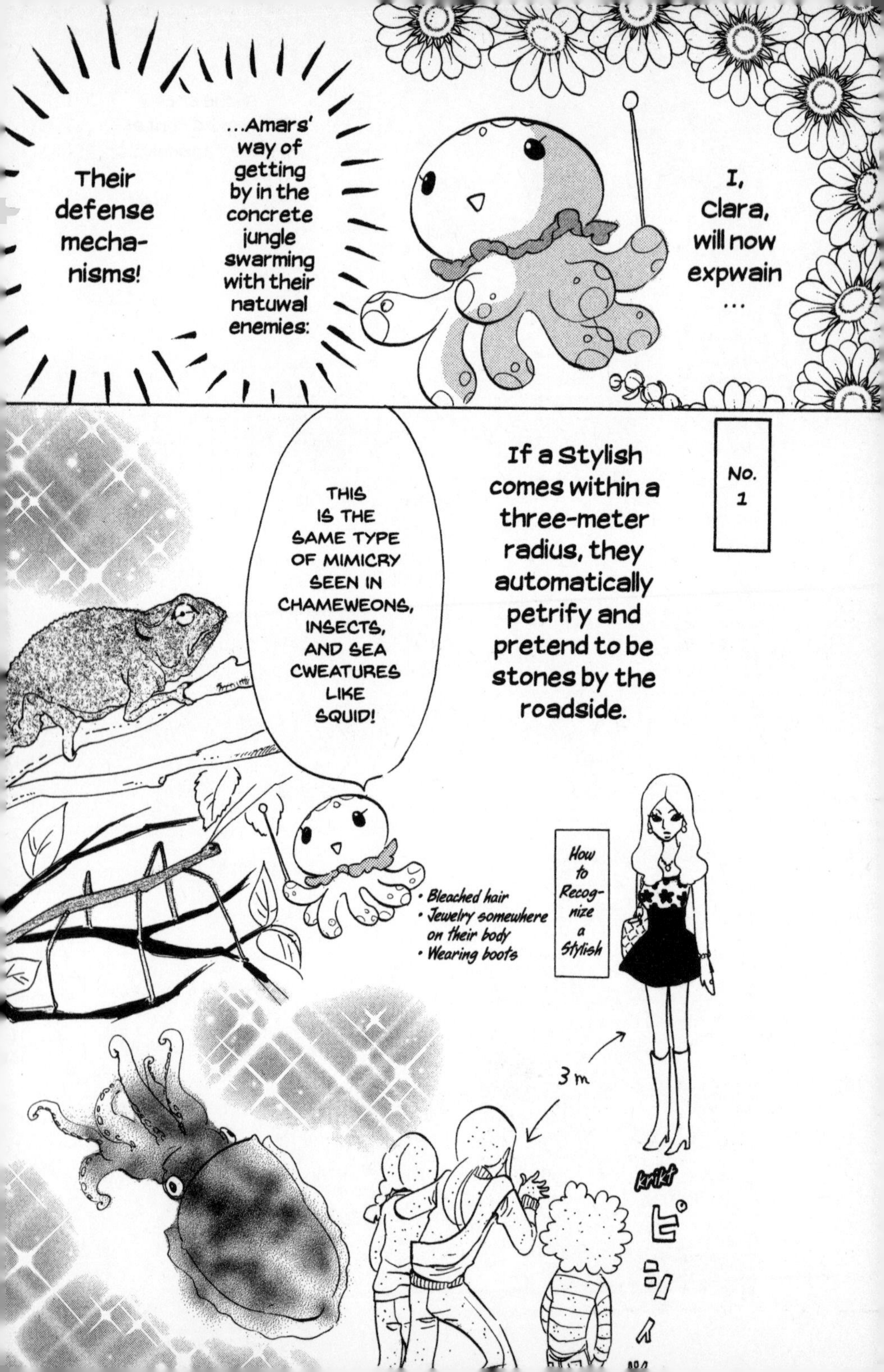
I, Clara, will now expwain ...
...Amars' way of getting by in the concrete jungle swarming with their natuwal enemies:
Their defense mechanisms!
No. 1
If a Stylish comes within a three-meter radius, they automatically petrify and pretend to be stones by the roadside.
THIS IS THE SAME TYPE OF MIMICRY SEEN IN CHAMEWEONS, INSECTS, AND SEA CWEATURES LIKE SQUID!
How to Recognize a Stylish
• Bleached hair
• Jewelry somewhere on their body
• Wearing boots
3 m
krikt

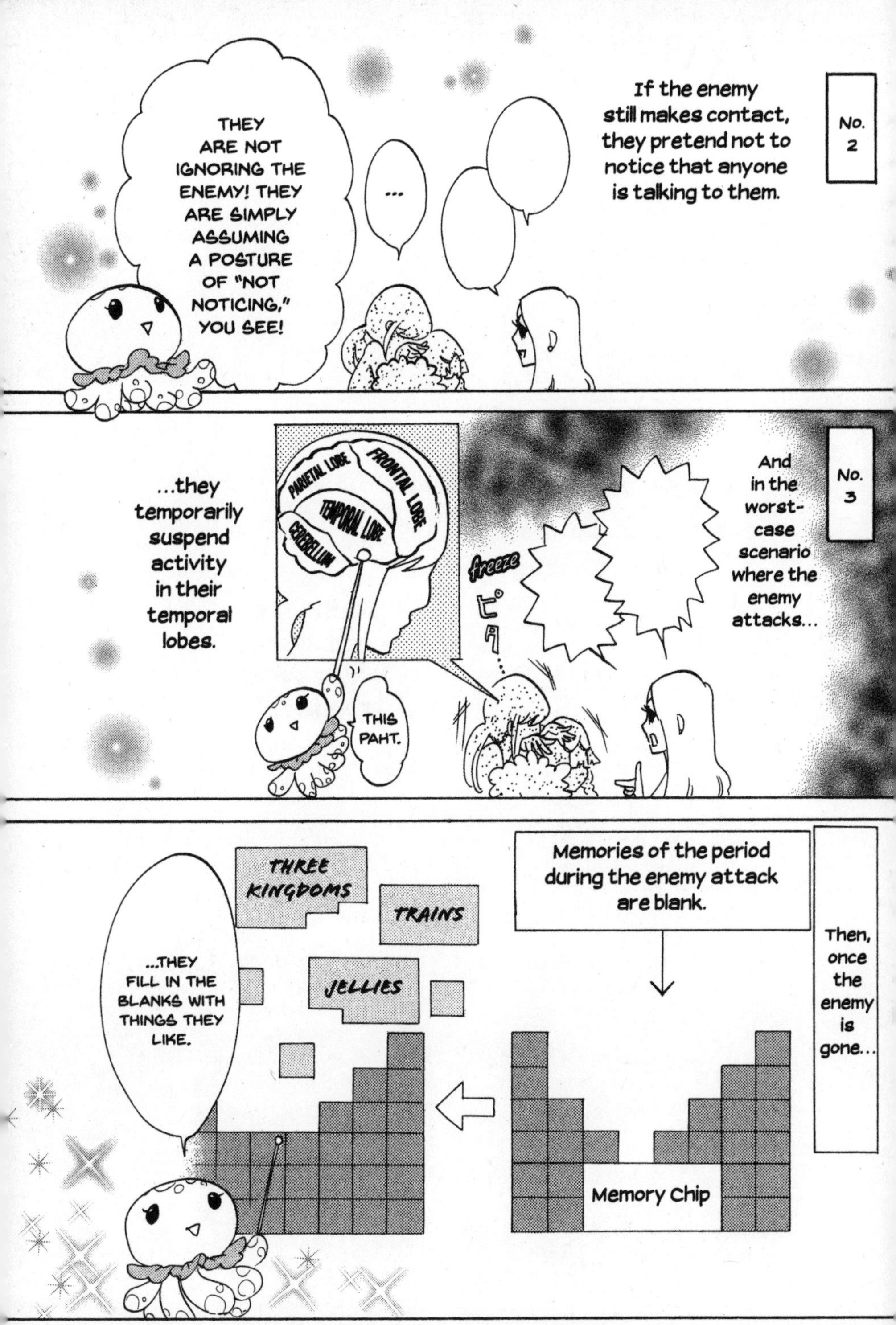
No. 2
If the enemy still makes contact, they pretend not to notice that anyone is talking to them.
...
THEY ARE NOT IGNORING THE ENEMY! THEY ARE SIMPLY ASSUMING A POSTURE OF "NOT NOTICING," YOU SEE!
No. 3
And in the worst-case scenario where the enemy attacks...
freeze
ピタ...
...they temporarily suspend activity in their temporal lobes.
PARIETAL LOBE
FRONTAL LOBE
TEMPORAL LOBE
CEREBELLUM
THIS PAHT.
Then, once the enemy is gone...
Memories of the period during the enemy attack are blank.
Memory Chip
THREE KINGDOMS
TRAINS
JELLIES
...THEY FILL IN THE BLANKS WITH THINGS THEY LIKE.

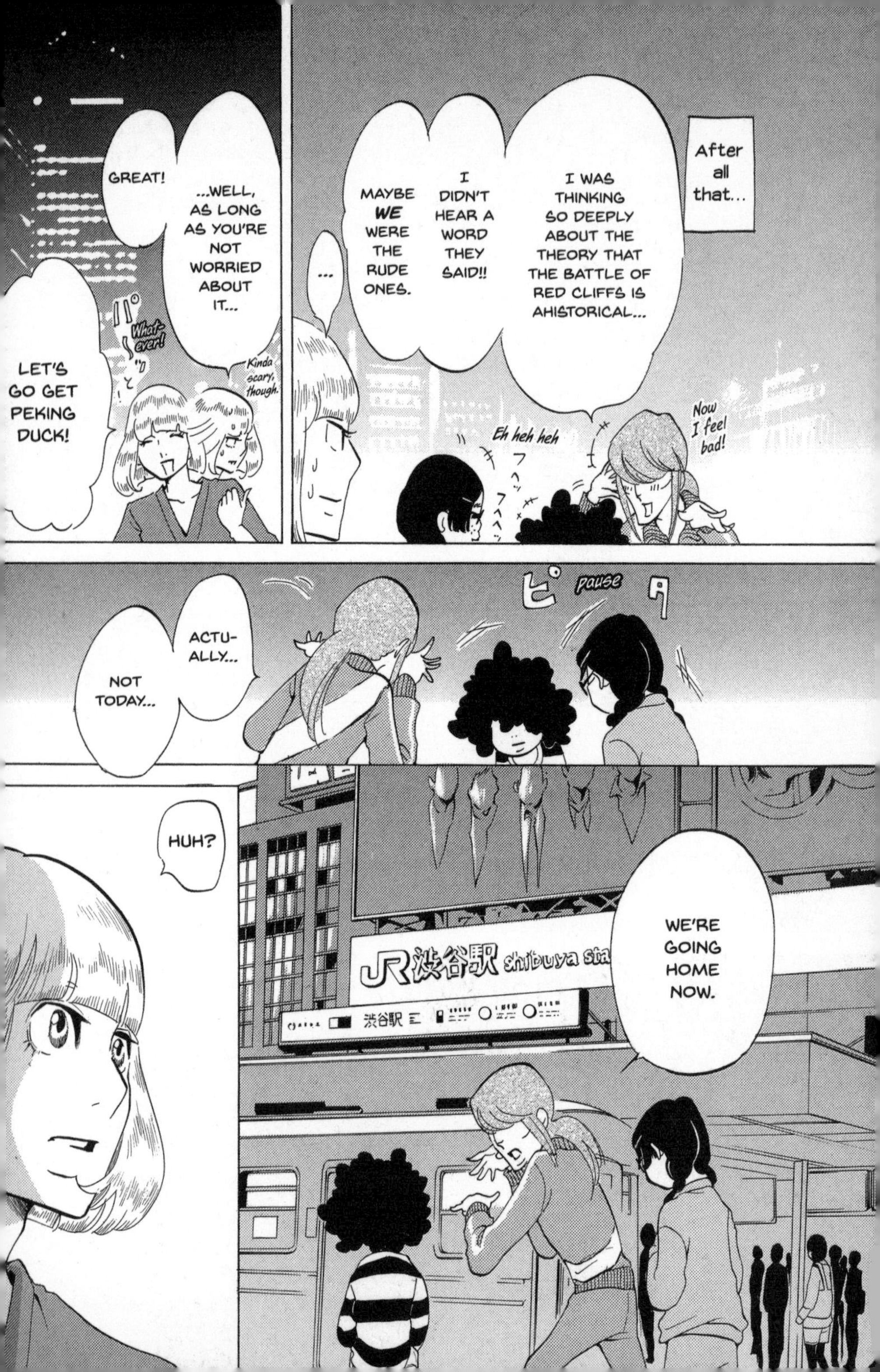
After all that...
I WAS THINKING SO DEEPLY ABOUT THE THEORY THAT THE BATTLE OF RED CLIFFS IS AHISTORICAL...
Now I feel bad!
Eh heh heh
I DIDN'T HEAR A WORD THEY SAID!!
MAYBE WE WERE THE RUDE ONES.
...
...WELL, AS LONG AS YOU'RE NOT WORRIED ABOUT IT...
GREAT!
Kinda scary, though.
What-ever!
LET'S GO GET PEKING DUCK!
pause
ACTU-ALLY...
NOT TODAY...
WE'RE GOING HOME NOW.
JR渋谷駅 shibuya sta
渋谷駅
HUH?

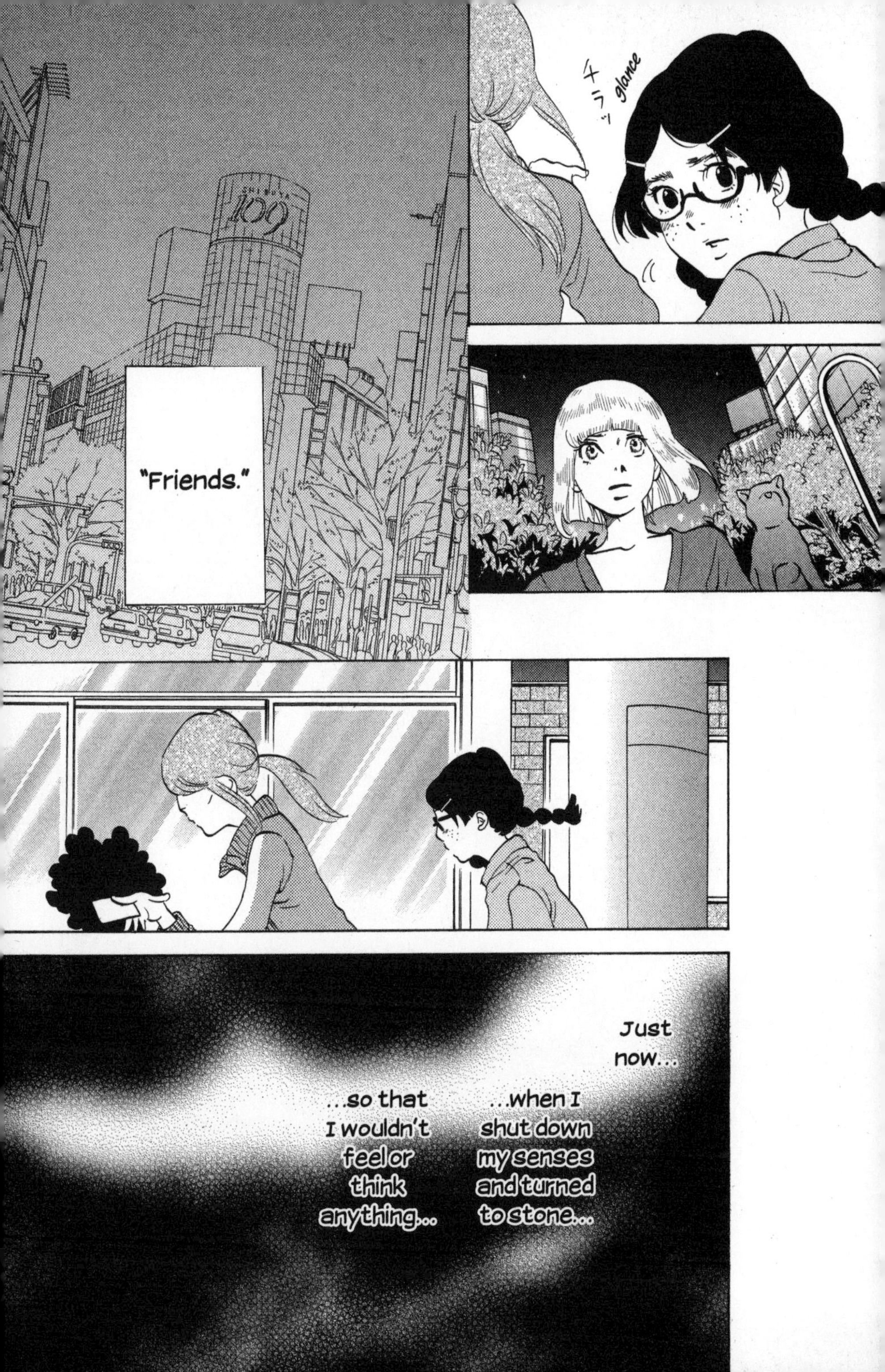
チラッ glance
"Friends."
Just now...
...when I shut down my senses and turned to stone...
...so that I wouldn't feel or think anything...

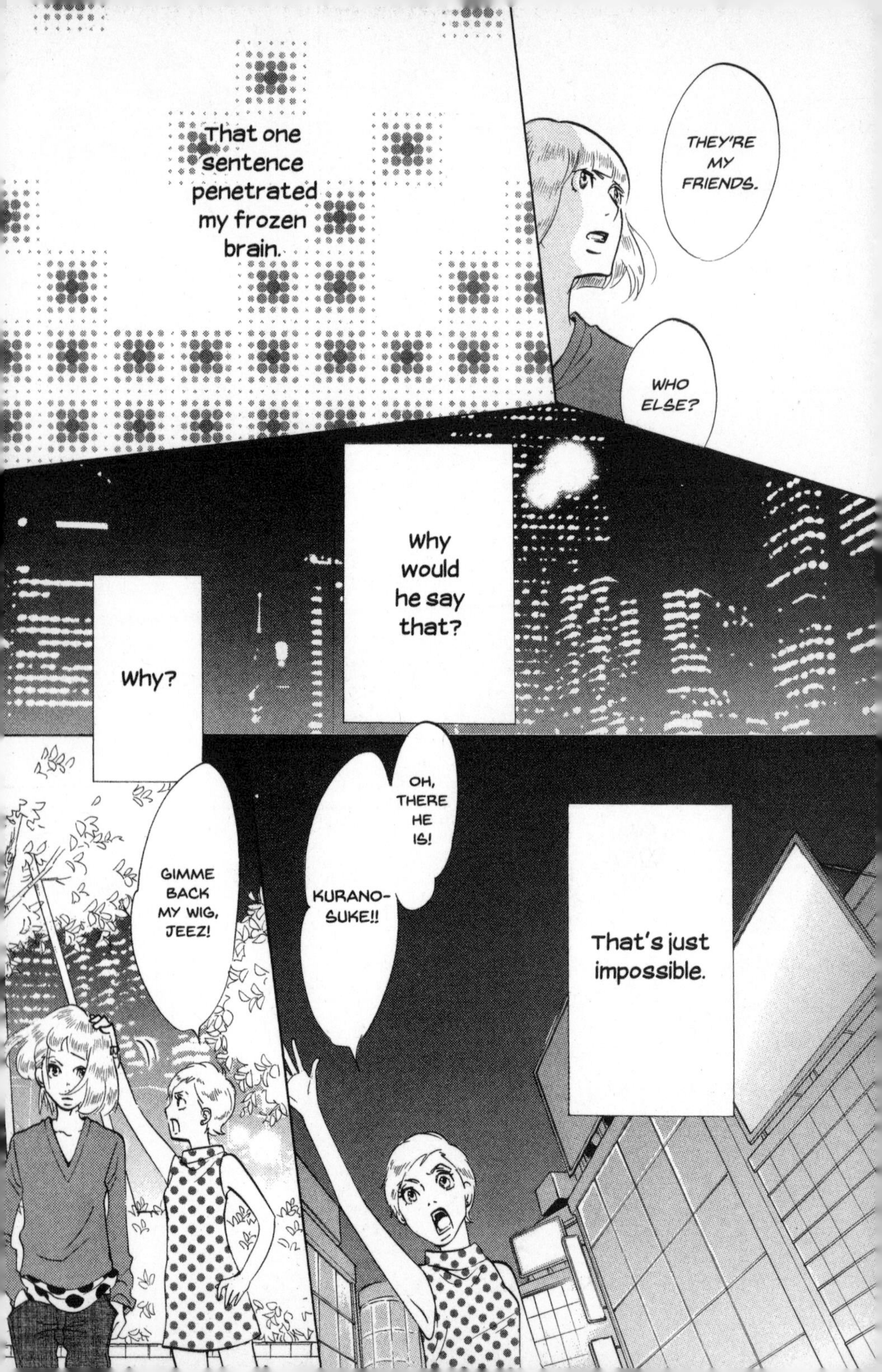
THEY'RE MY FRIENDS.
WHO ELSE?
That one sentence penetrated my frozen brain.
Why would he say that?
Why?
That's just impossible.
OH, THERE HE IS!
KURANO-SUKE!!
GIMME BACK MY WIG, JEEZ!

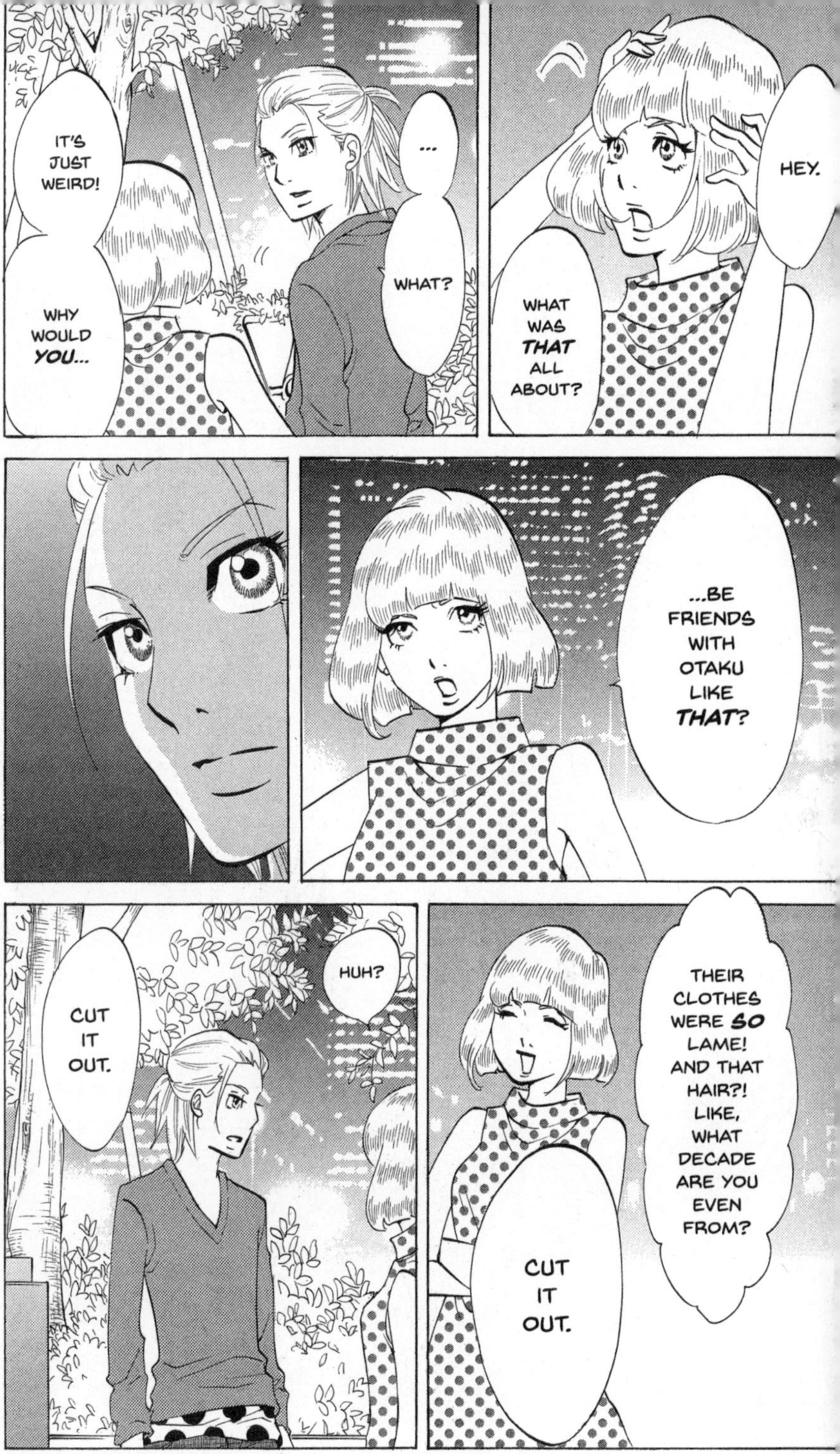
HEY.
WHAT WAS THAT ALL ABOUT?
...
WHAT?
IT'S JUST WEIRD!
WHY WOULD YOU...
...BE FRIENDS WITH OTAKU LIKE THAT?
THEIR CLOTHES WERE SO LAME! AND THAT HAIR?! LIKE, WHAT DECADE ARE YOU EVEN FROM?
CUT IT OUT.
HUH?
CUT IT OUT.

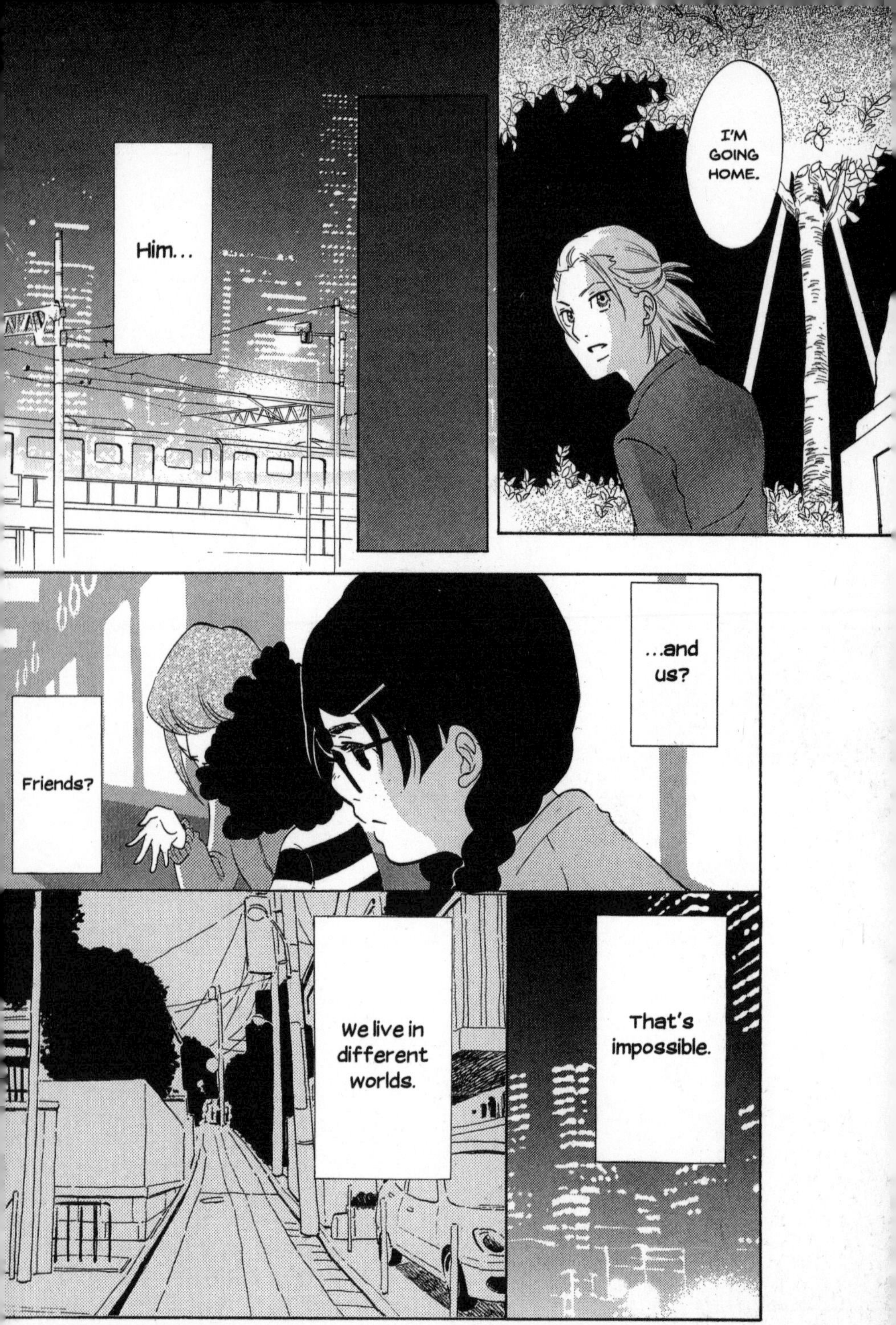
I'M GOING HOME.
Him...
...and us?
Friends?
That's impossible.
We live in different worlds.

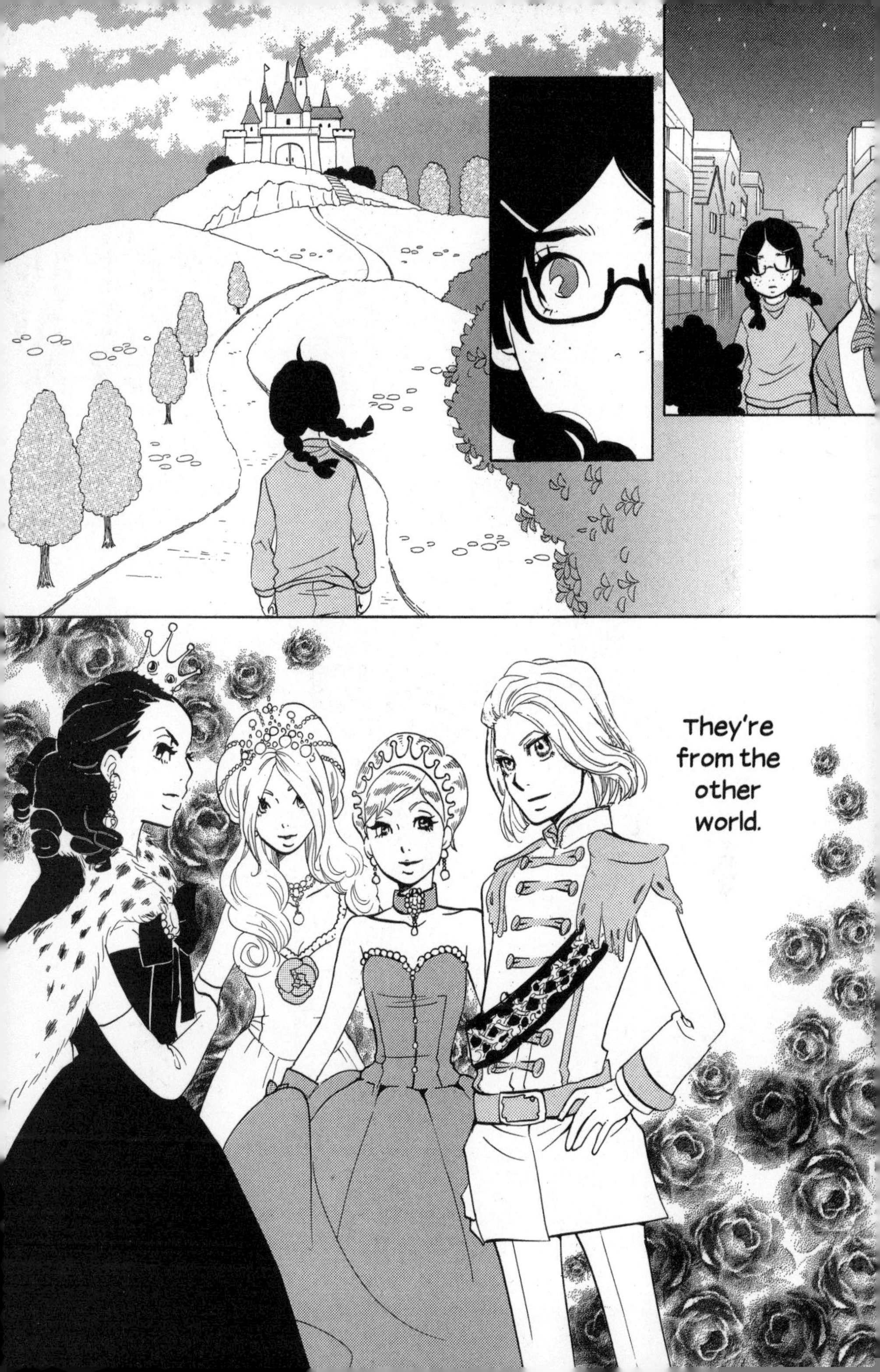
They're from the other world.

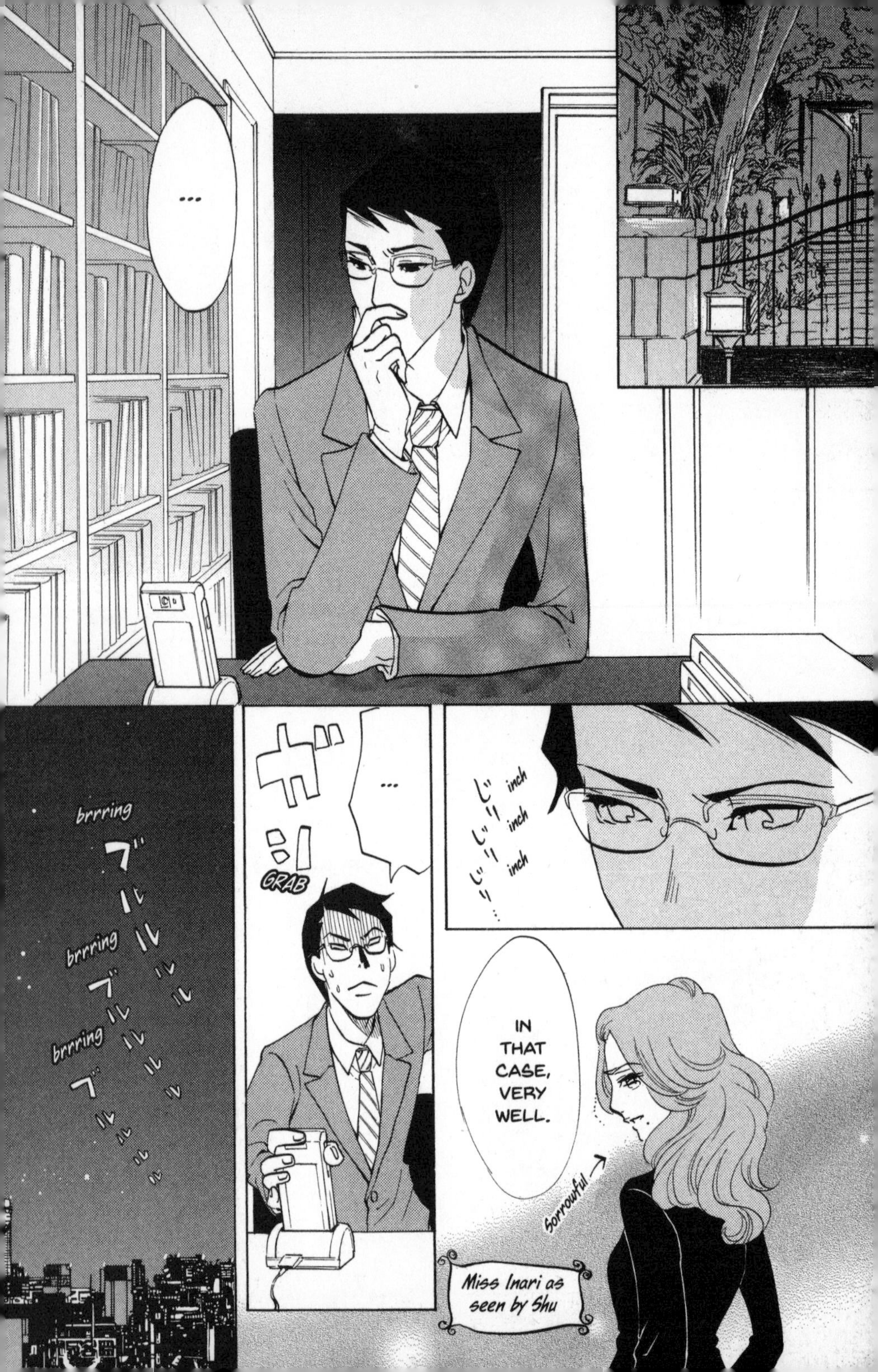
...
じりじりじり…
inch inch inch
IN THAT CASE, VERY WELL.
Sorrowful
Miss Inari as seen by Shu
...
ガバッ
GRAB
brrring brrring brrring
ブルルル ブルルル ブルルル

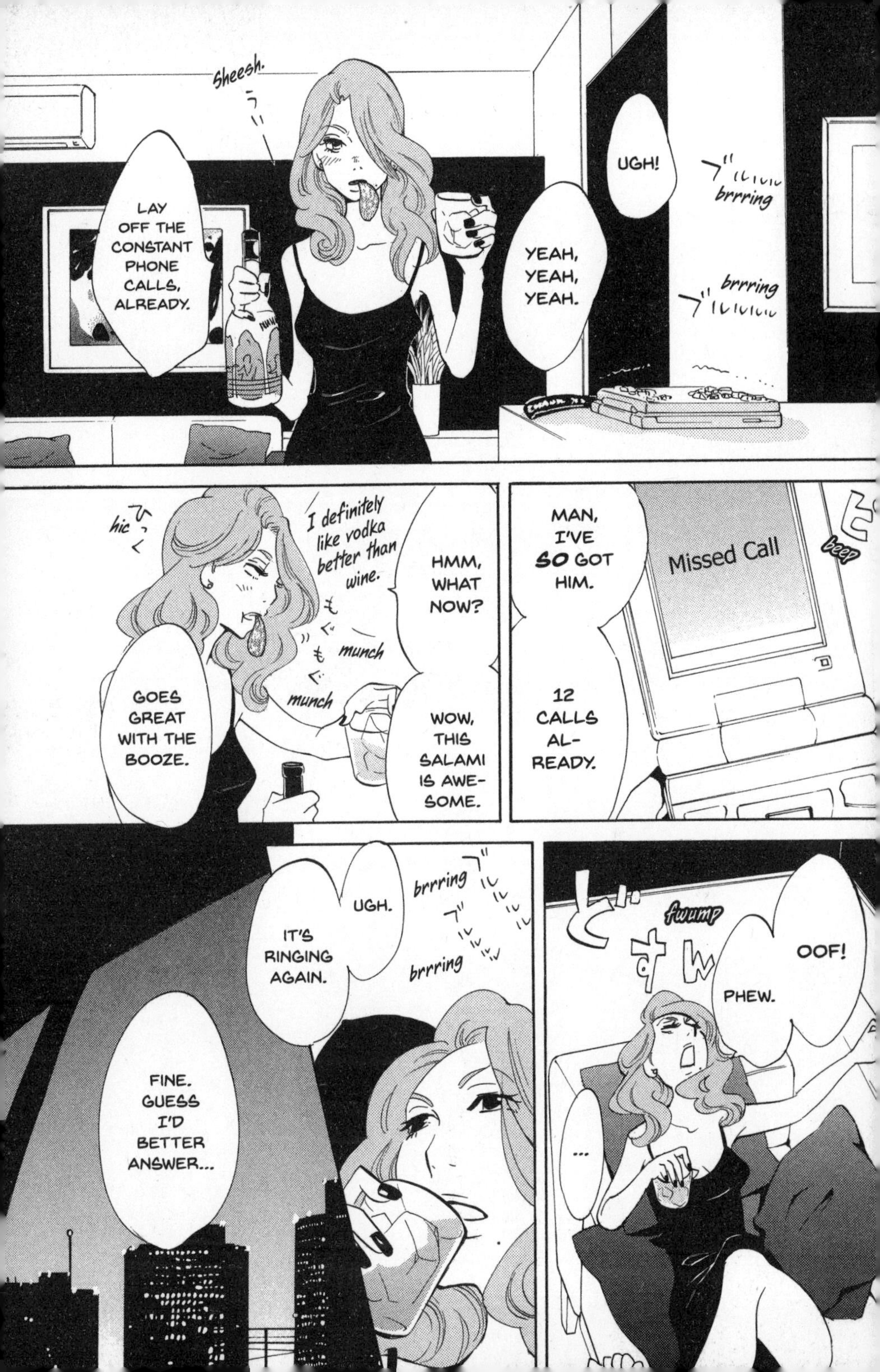
UGH!
brrring
YEAH, YEAH, YEAH.
brrring
Sheesh.
LAY OFF THE CONSTANT PHONE CALLS, ALREADY.
beep
Missed Call
MAN, I'VE SO GOT HIM.
12 CALLS AL- READY.
HMM, WHAT NOW?
I definitely like vodka better than wine.
hic
munch
munch
WOW, THIS SALAMI IS AWE- SOME.
GOES GREAT WITH THE BOOZE.
fwump
OOF!
PHEW.
...
brrring
UGH.
IT'S RINGING AGAIN.
brrring
FINE. GUESS I'D BETTER ANSWER...

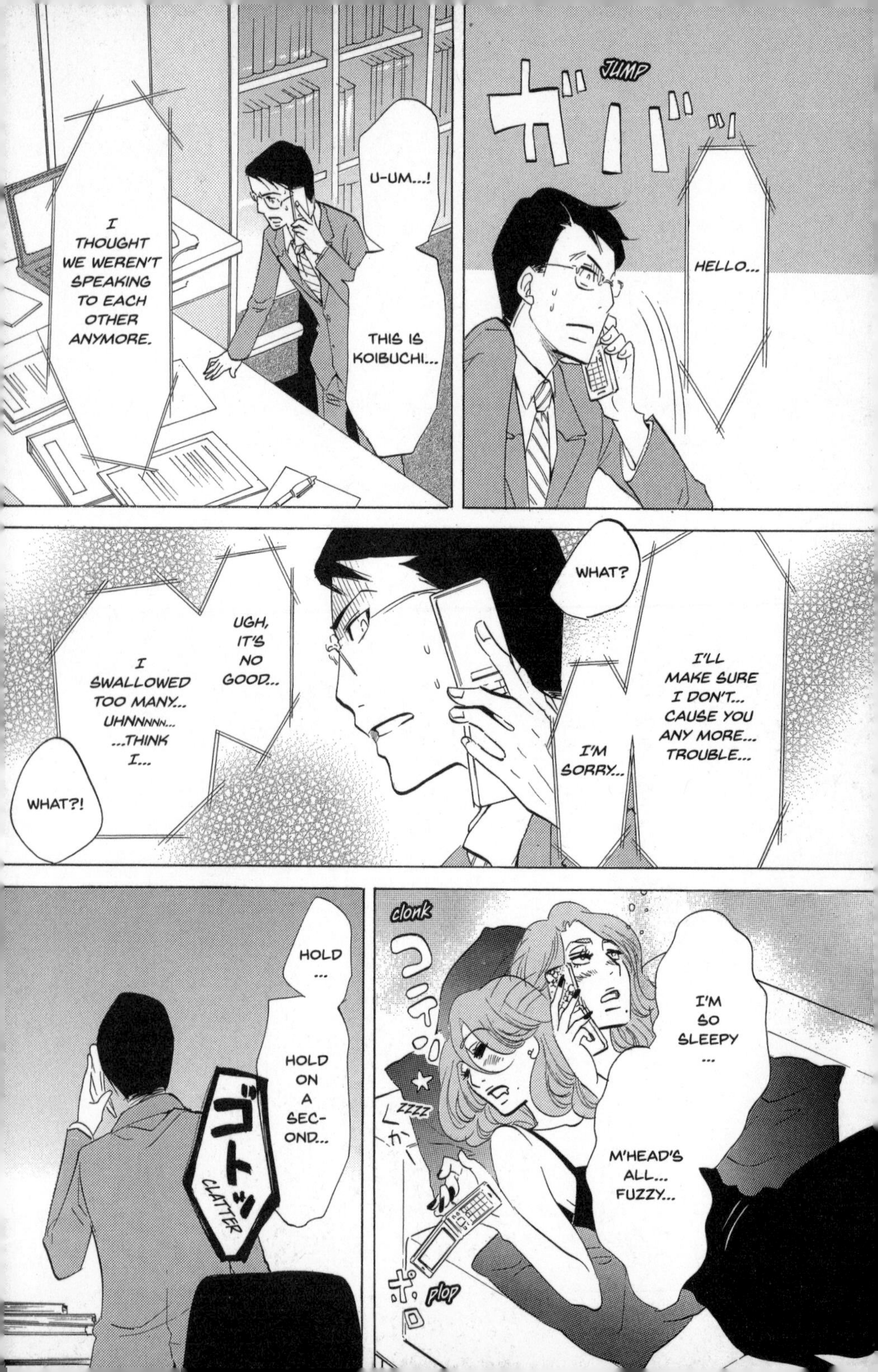
JUMP
HELLO...
U-UM...!
THIS IS KOIBUCHI...
I THOUGHT WE WEREN'T SPEAKING TO EACH OTHER ANYMORE.
WHAT?
I'LL MAKE SURE I DON'T... CAUSE YOU ANY MORE... TROUBLE...
I'M SORRY...
UGH, IT'S NO GOOD...
I SWALLOWED TOO MANY... UHNNNNN... ...THINK I...
WHAT?!
clonk
I'M SO SLEEPY ...
M'HEAD'S ALL... FUZZY...
zzzz
plop
HOLD ...
HOLD ON A SEC-OND...
CLATTER

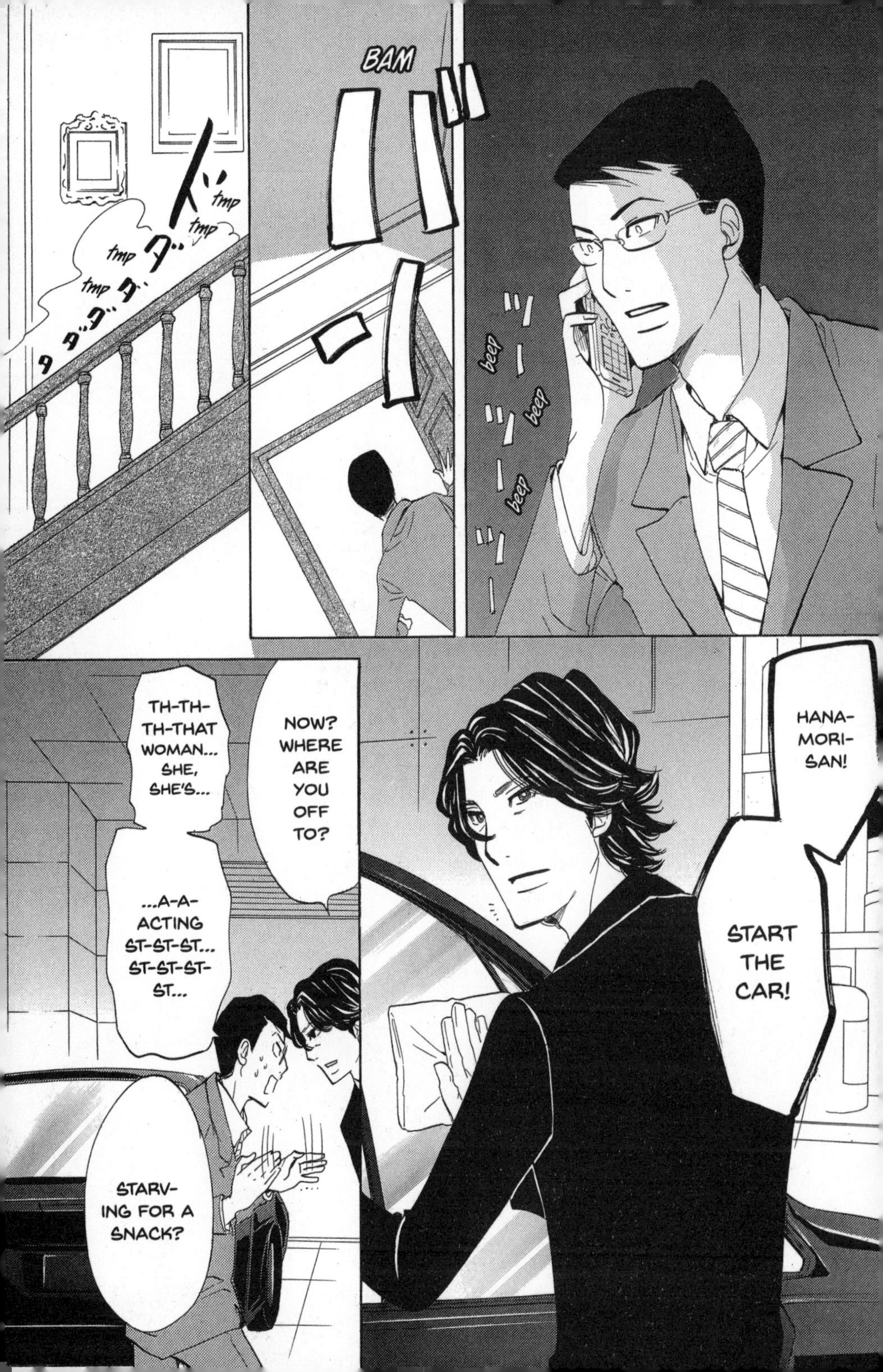
beep
beep
beep
BAM
tmp
tmp
tmp
tmp
HANA-MORI-SAN!
START THE CAR!
NOW? WHERE ARE YOU OFF TO?
TH-TH-TH-THAT WOMAN... SHE, SHE'S...
...A-A-ACTING ST-ST-ST... ST-ST-ST-ST...
STARV-ING FOR A SNACK?

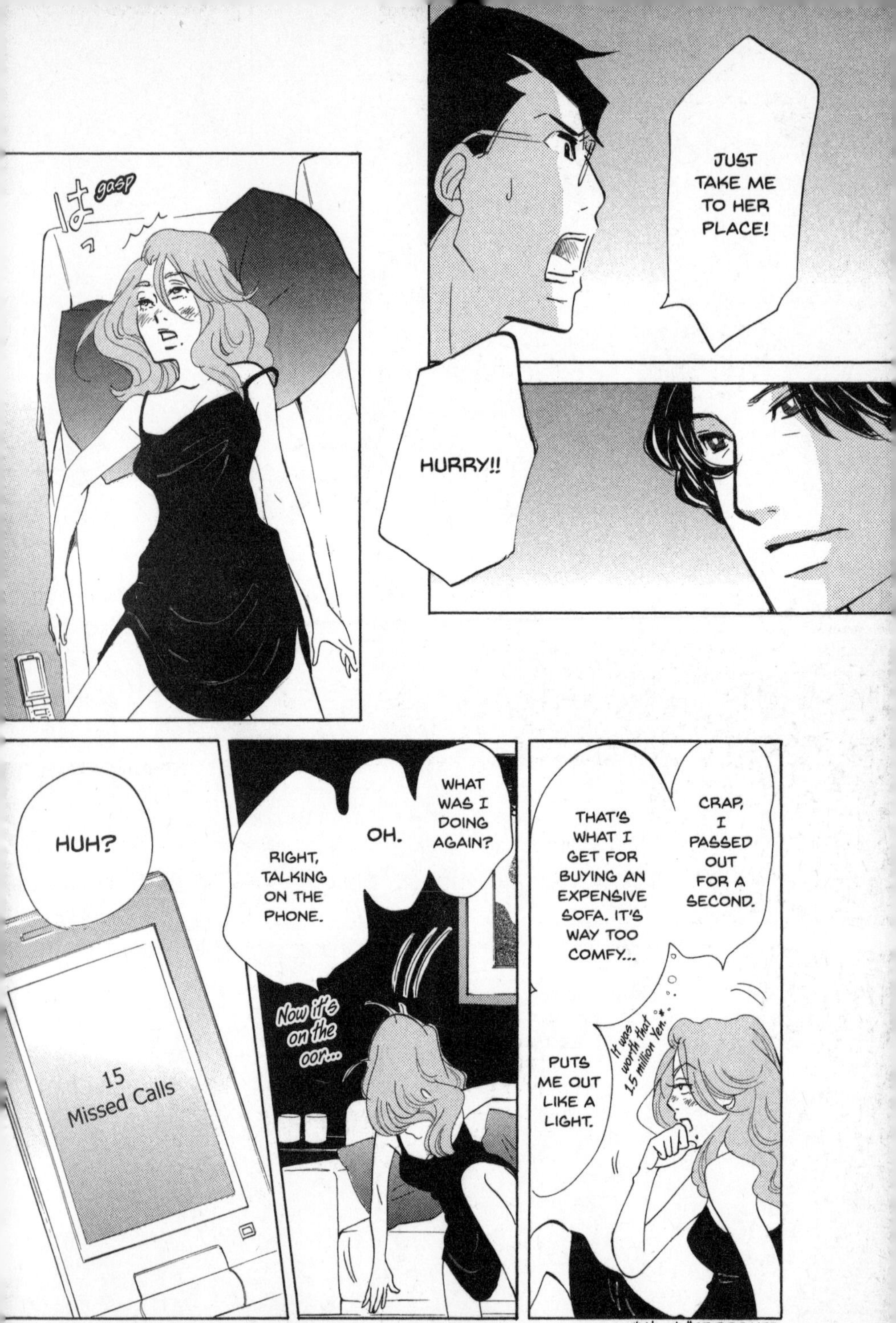
JUST TAKE ME TO HER PLACE!
HURRY!!
は gasp
CRAP, I PASSED OUT FOR A SECOND.
THAT'S WHAT I GET FOR BUYING AN EXPENSIVE SOFA. IT'S WAY TOO COMFY...
It was worth that 1.5 million Yen.*
PUTS ME OUT LIKE A LIGHT.
WHAT WAS I DOING AGAIN?
OH.
RIGHT, TALKING ON THE PHONE.
Now it's on the oor...
HUH?
15 Missed Calls

*About $15,000 USD.

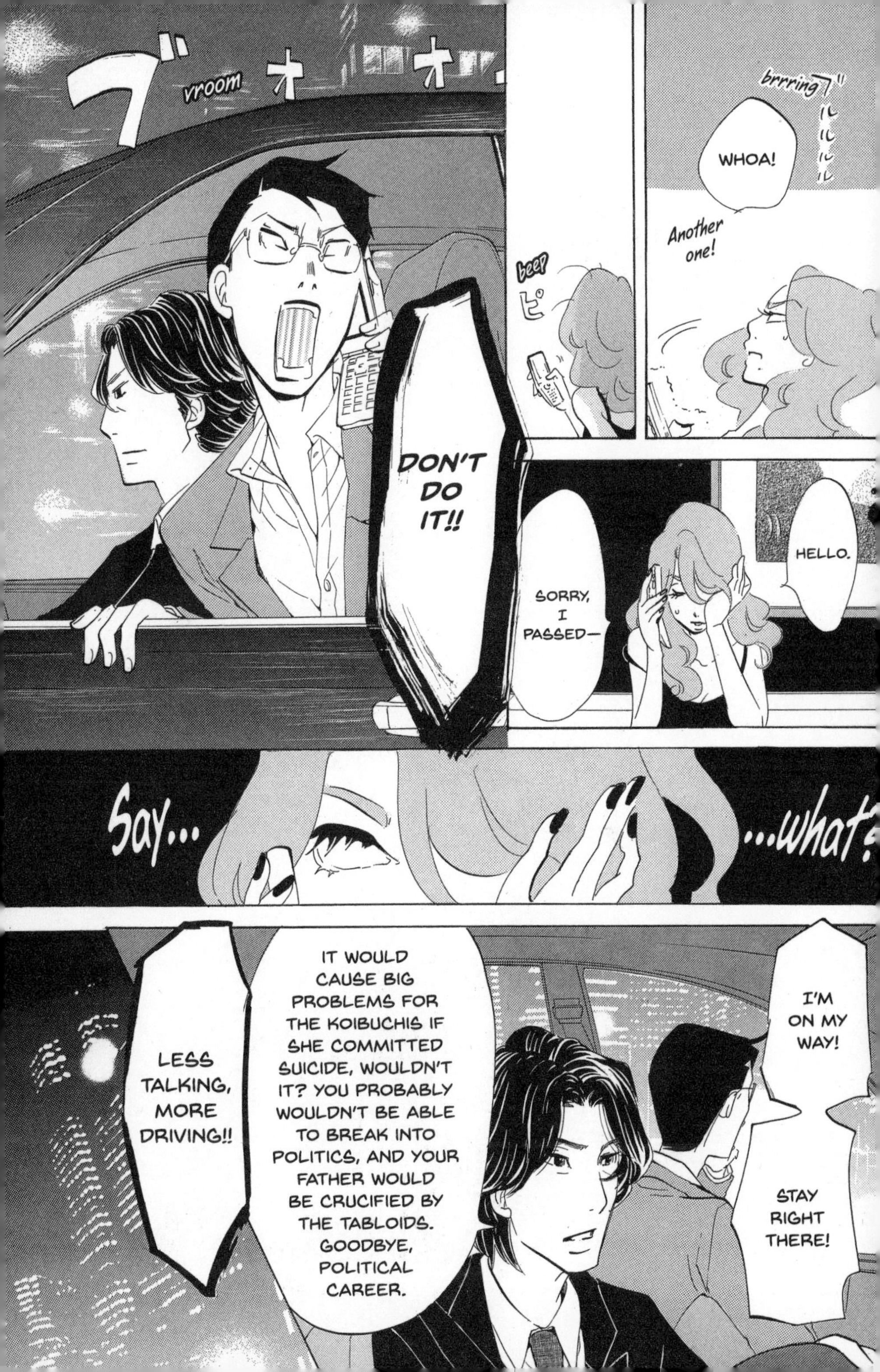
brrring
WHOA!
Another one!
beep
HELLO.
SORRY, I PASSED—
vroom
DON'T DO IT!!
Say...
...what?
I'M ON MY WAY!
STAY RIGHT THERE!
IT WOULD CAUSE BIG PROBLEMS FOR THE KOIBUCHIS IF SHE COMMITTED SUICIDE, WOULDN'T IT? YOU PROBABLY WOULDN'T BE ABLE TO BREAK INTO POLITICS, AND YOUR FATHER WOULD BE CRUCIFIED BY THE TABLOIDS. GOODBYE, POLITICAL CAREER.
LESS TALKING, MORE DRIVING!!

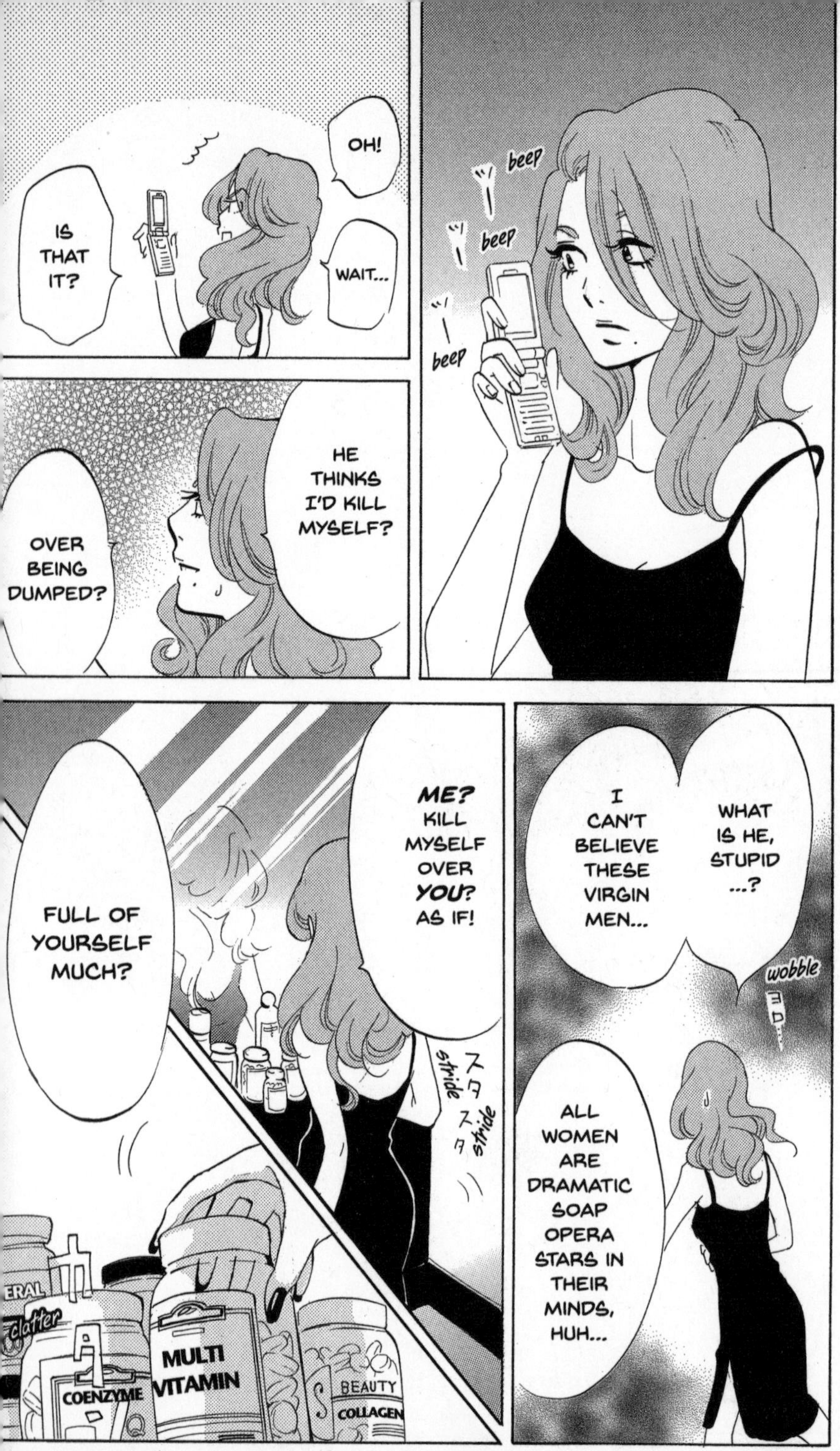
beep
beep
beep
OH!
WAIT...
IS THAT IT?
HE THINKS I'D KILL MYSELF?
OVER BEING DUMPED?
WHAT IS HE, STUPID ...?
I CAN'T BELIEVE THESE VIRGIN MEN...
ヨロ…
wobble
ALL WOMEN ARE DRAMATIC SOAP OPERA STARS IN THEIR MINDS, HUH...
ME? KILL MYSELF OVER YOU? AS IF!
スタ
stride
スタ
stride
FULL OF YOURSELF MUCH?
clatter
ERAL
COENZYME
MULTI VITAMIN
BEAUTY
COLLAGEN

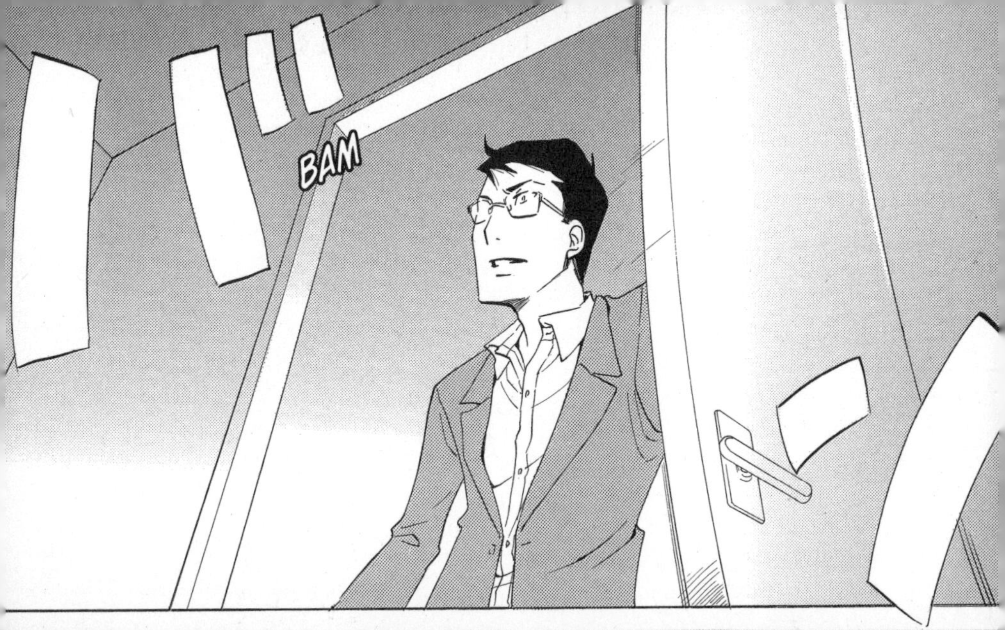
BAM
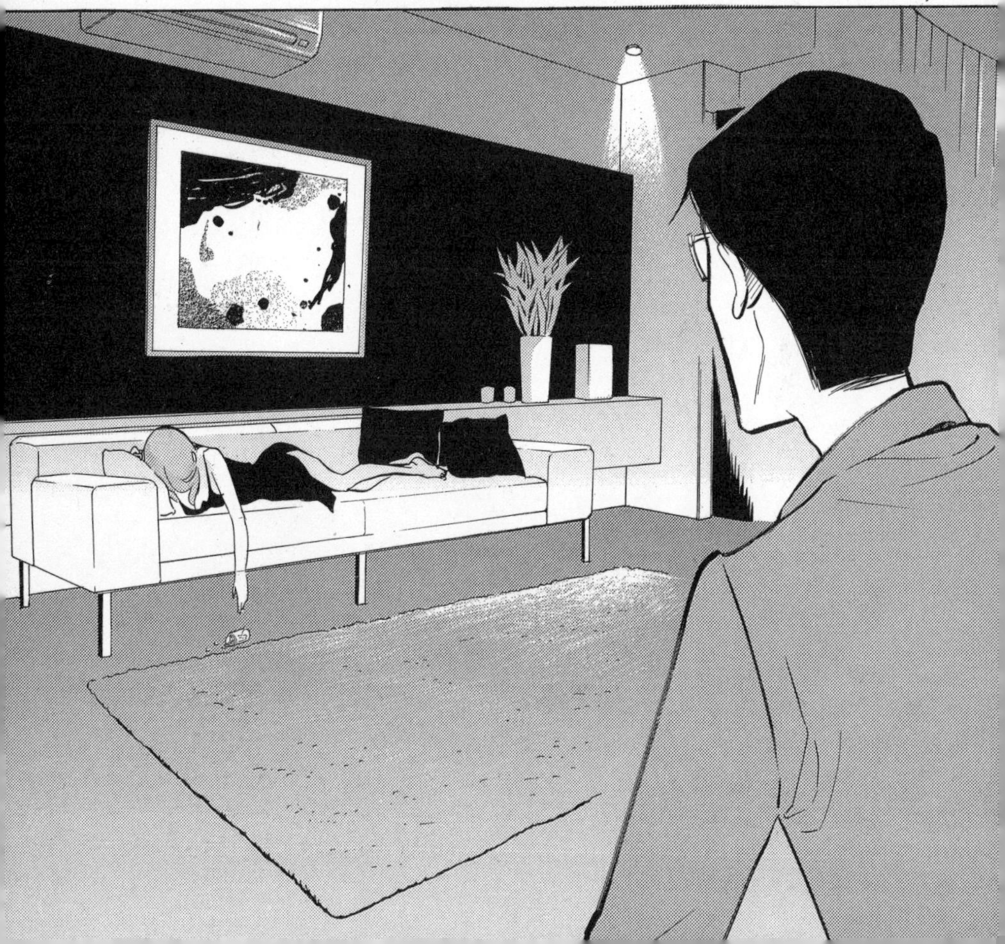

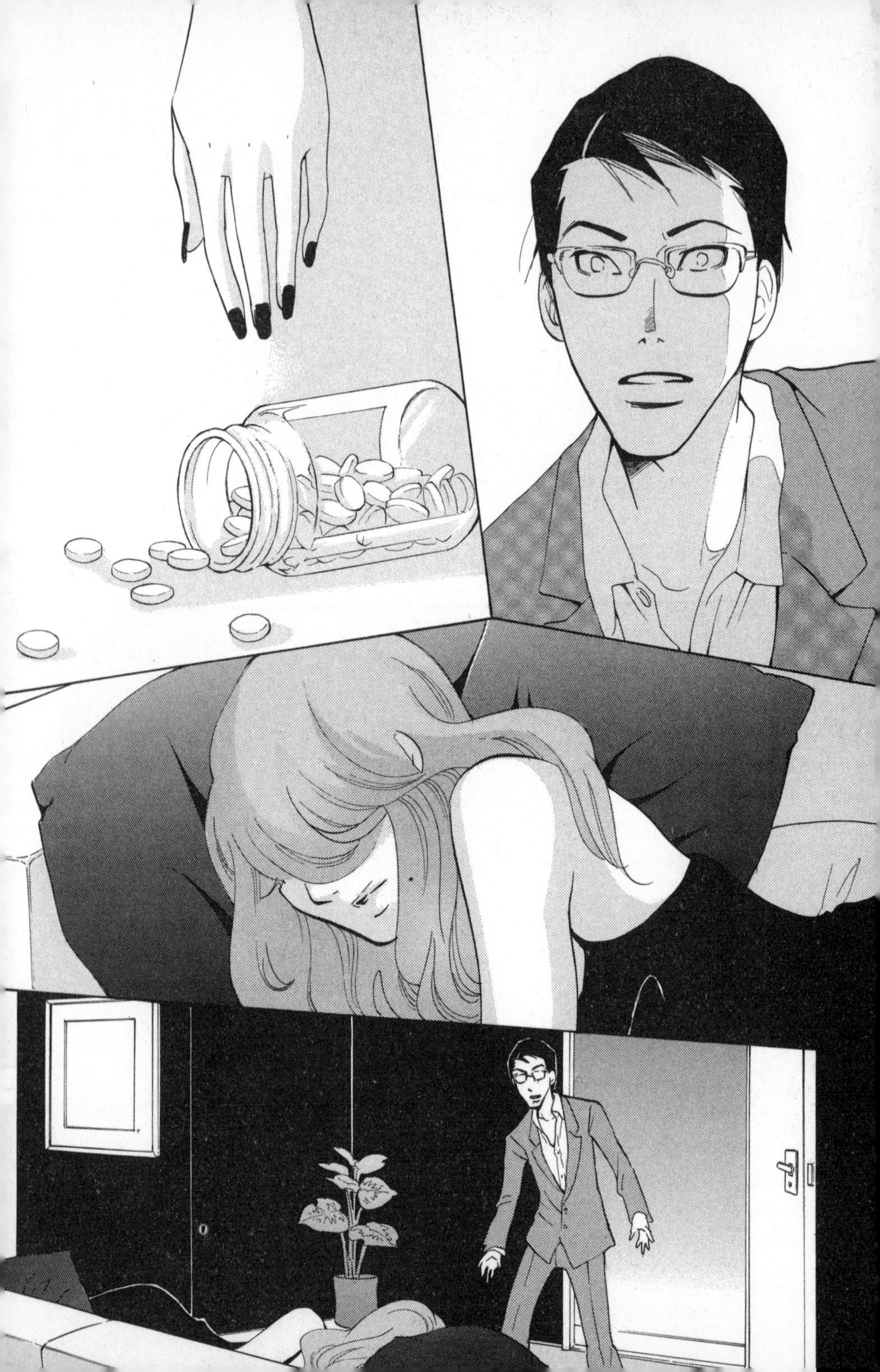

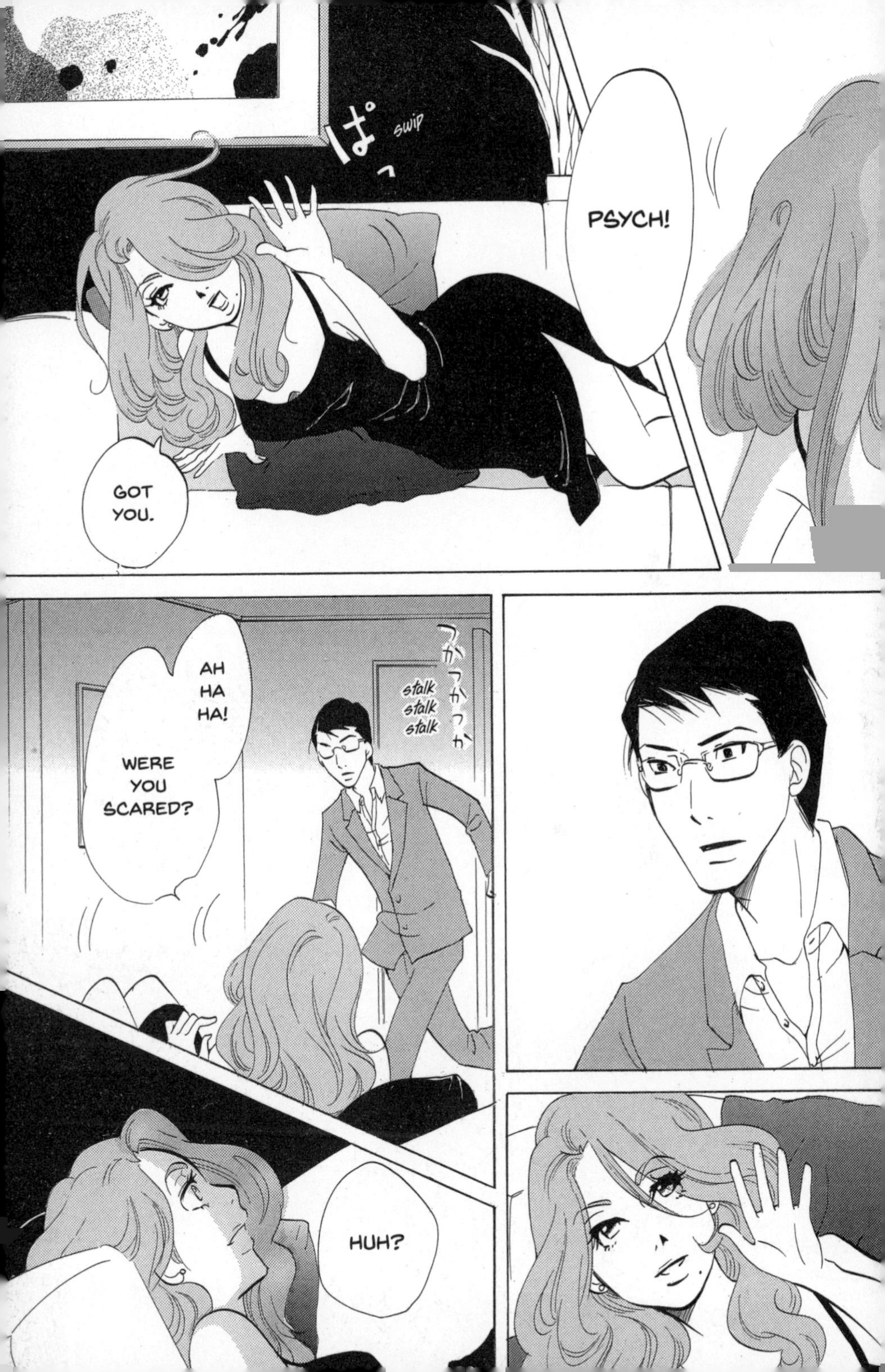
PSYCH!
ぱっ
swip
GOT YOU.
つかつかつか
stalk stalk stalk
AH HA HA!
WERE YOU SCARED?
HUH?

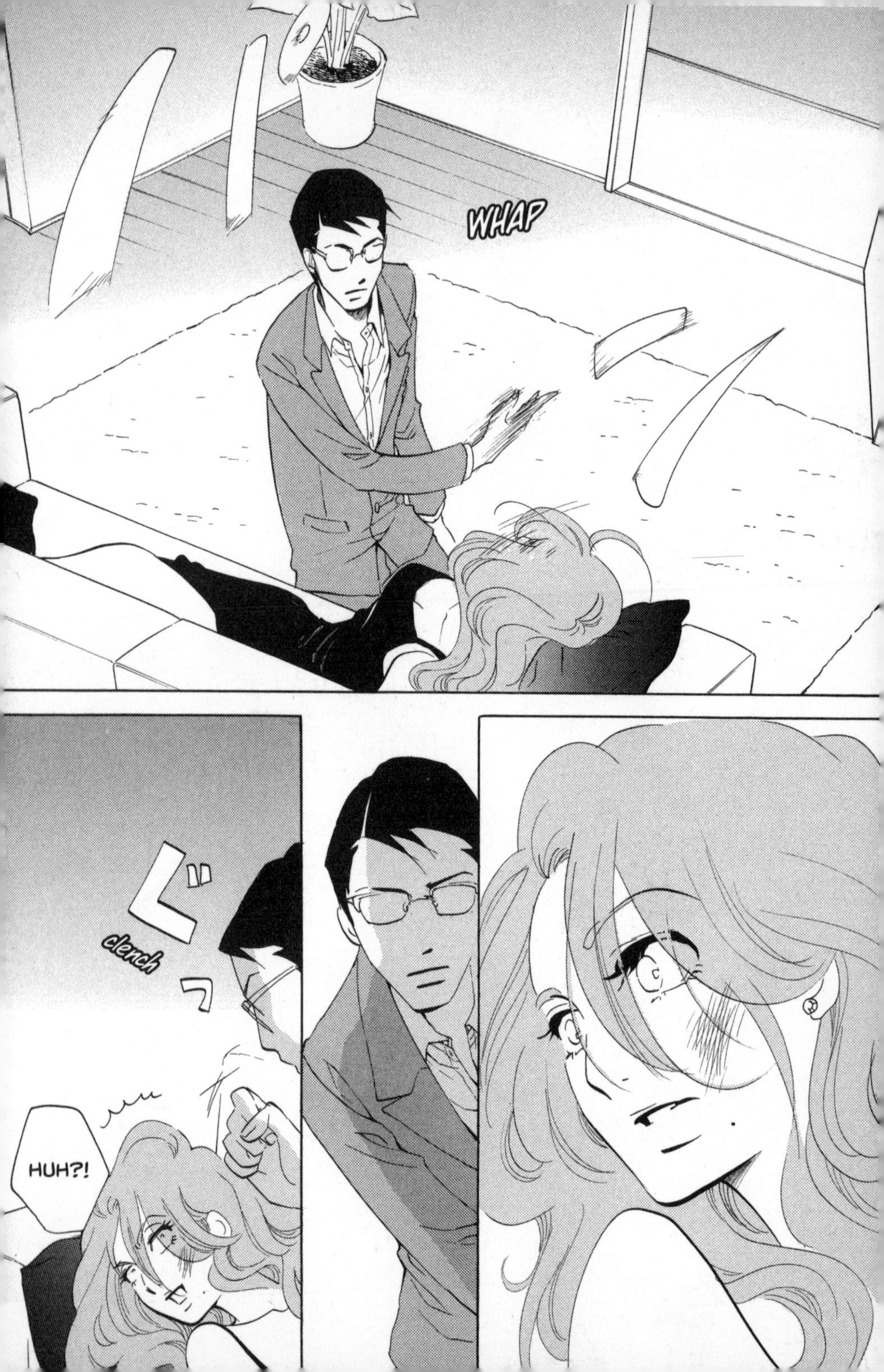
WHAP
clench
HUH?!

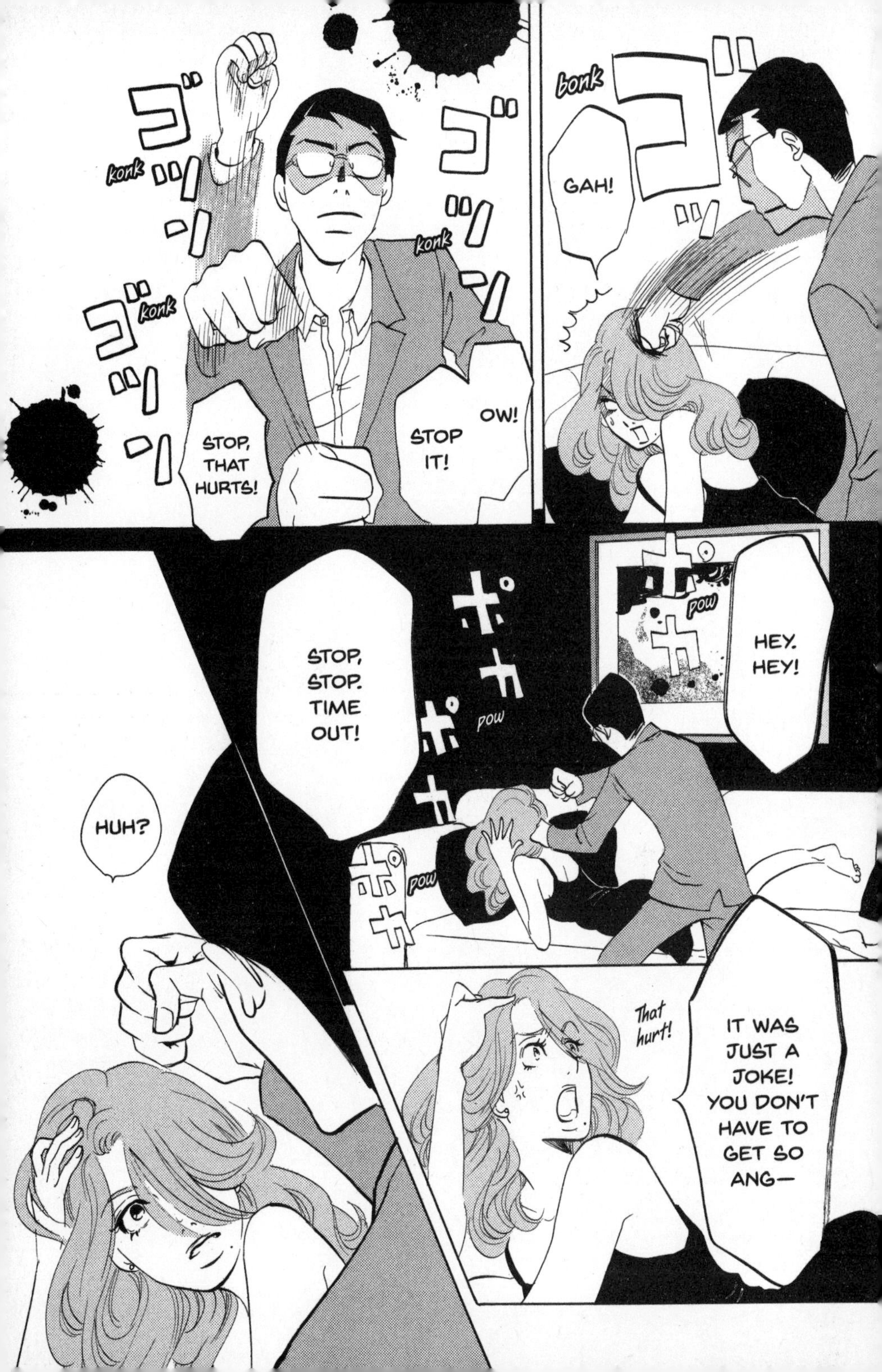
bonk
GAH!
konk
OW!
STOP IT!
konk
konk
STOP, THAT HURTS!
HEY. HEY!
pow
pow
pow
STOP, STOP. TIME OUT!
HUH?
IT WAS JUST A JOKE! YOU DON'T HAVE TO GET SO ANG—
That hurt!

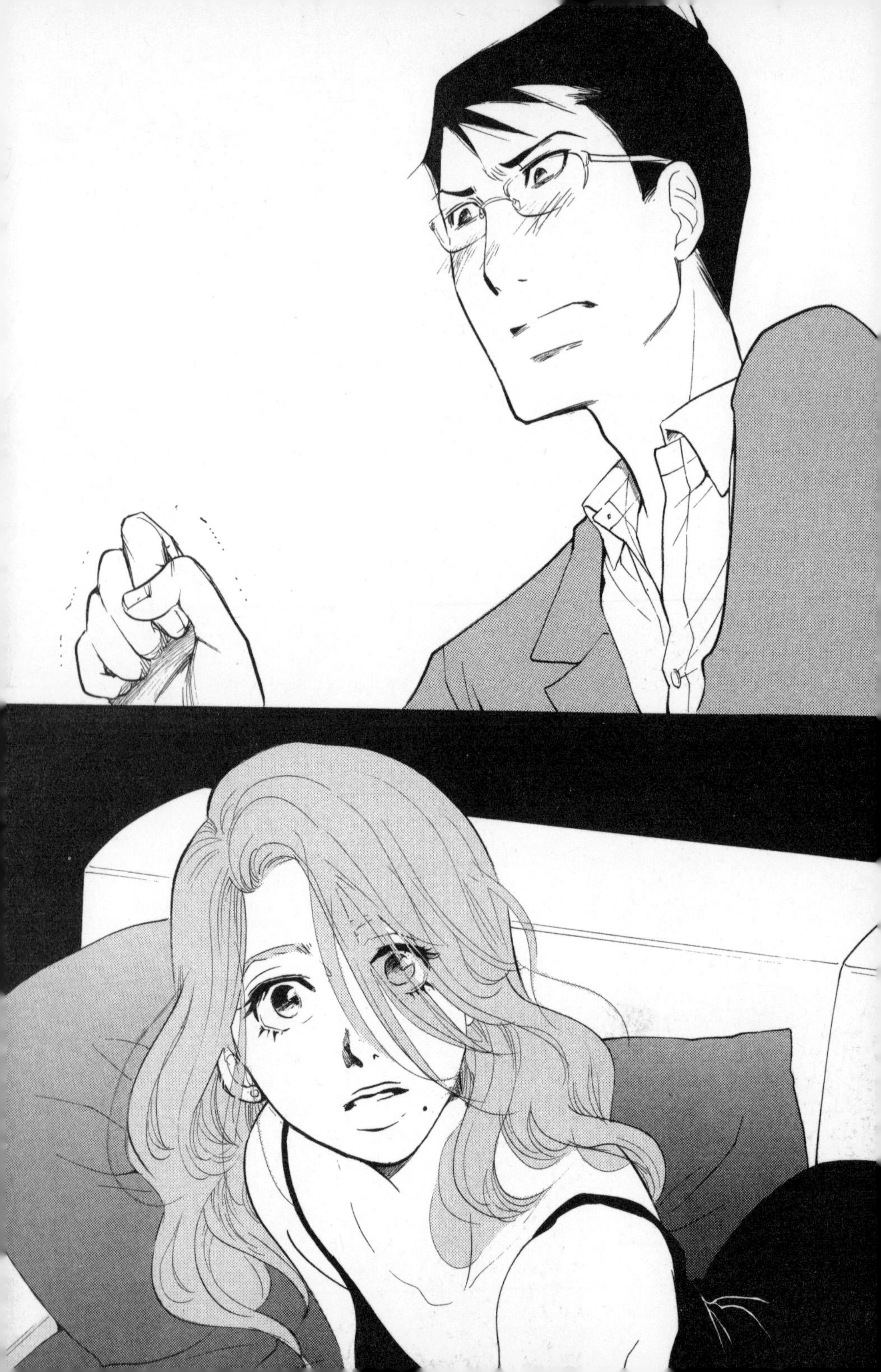

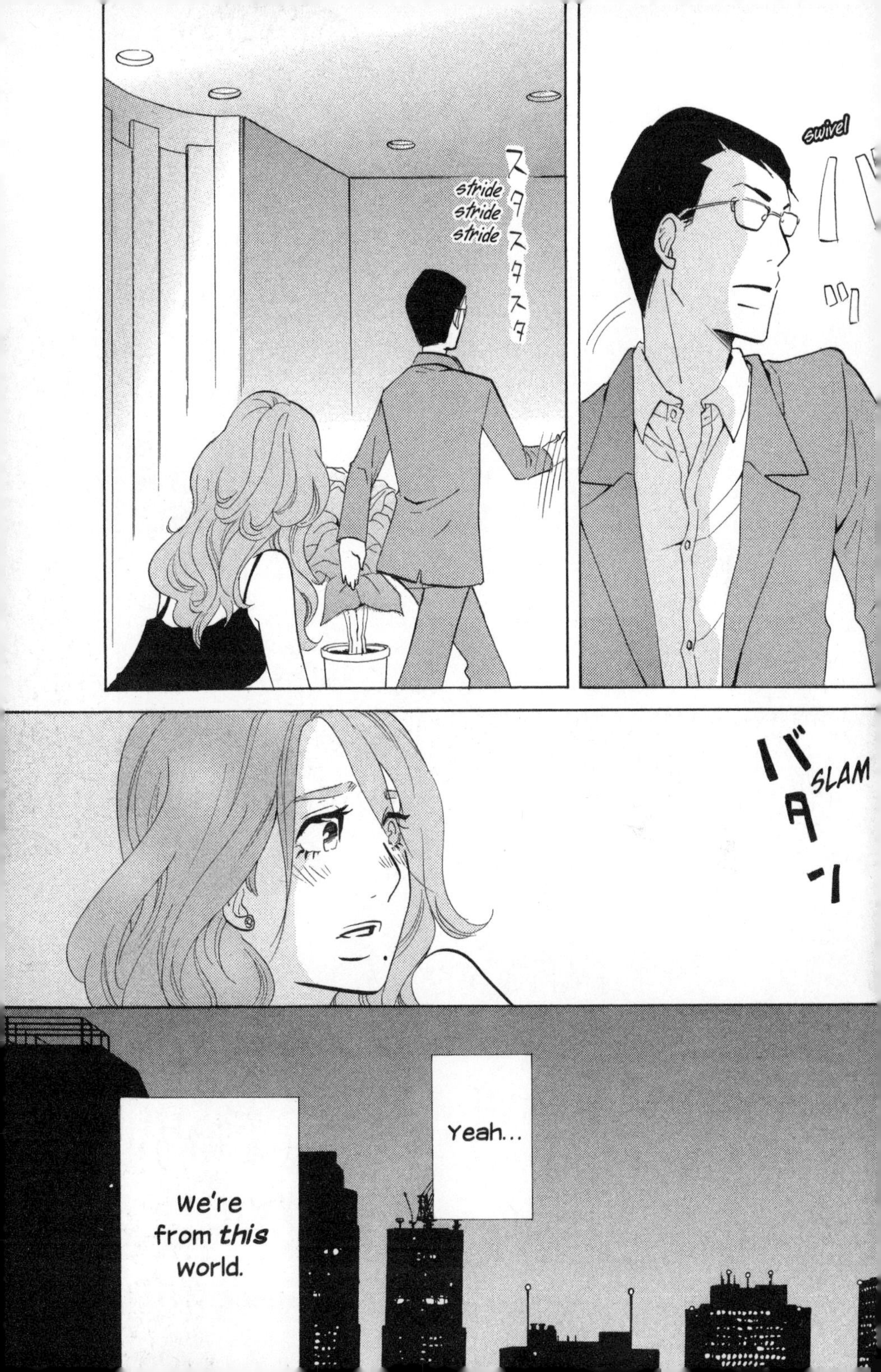
swivel
stride
stride
stride
スタスタスタ
SLAM
Yeah...
We're from *this* world.

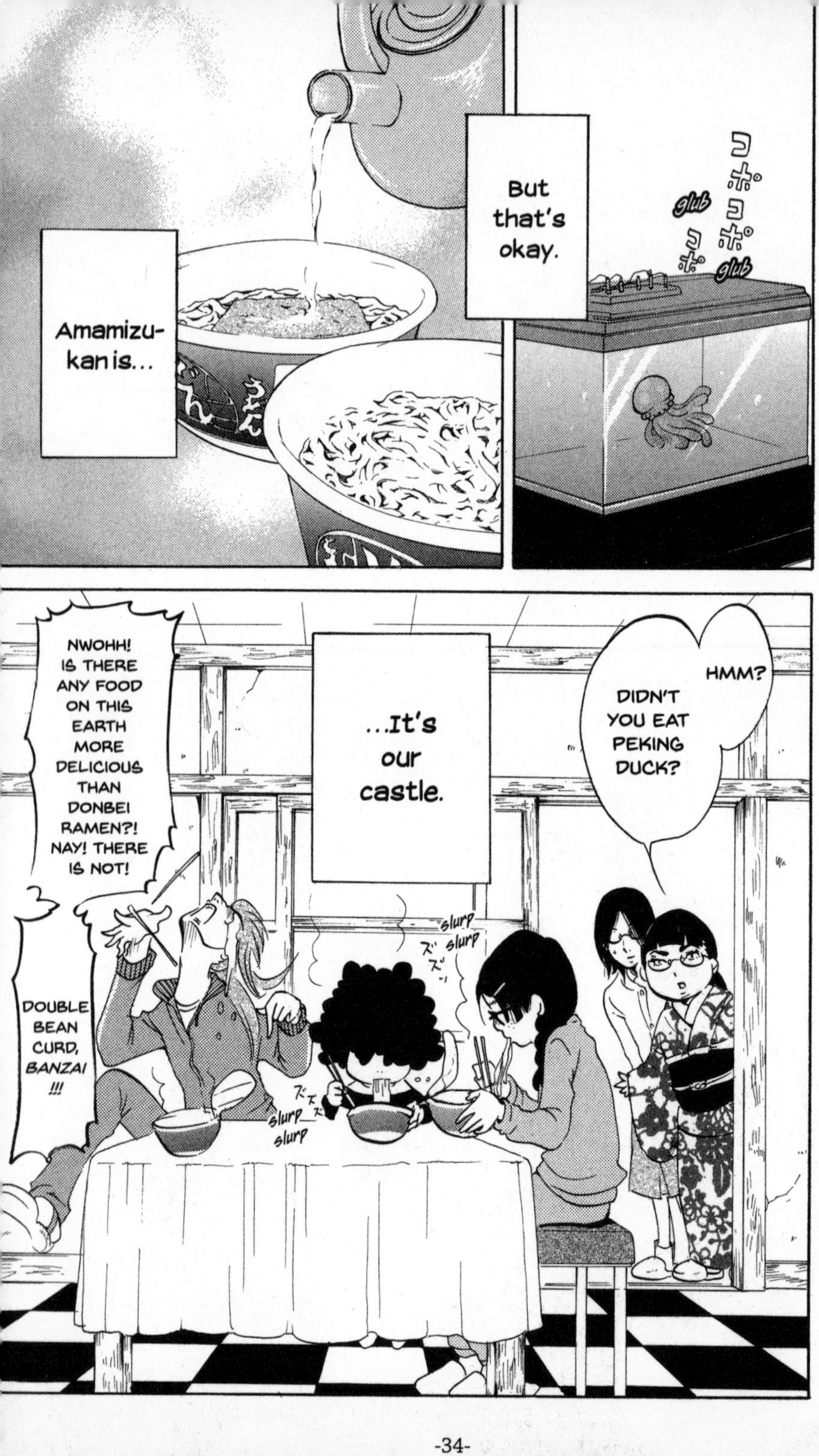

But that's okay.
コポコポ
glub
コポ
glub
Amamizu-kan is...
HMM?
DIDN'T YOU EAT PEKING DUCK?
...It's our castle.
slurp slurp
ズズ
NWOHH! IS THERE ANY FOOD ON THIS EARTH MORE DELICIOUS THAN DONBEI RAMEN?! NAY! THERE IS NOT!
DOUBLE BEAN CURD, BANZAI !!!
slurp slurp

Episode 26
Rock Me Hamlet!

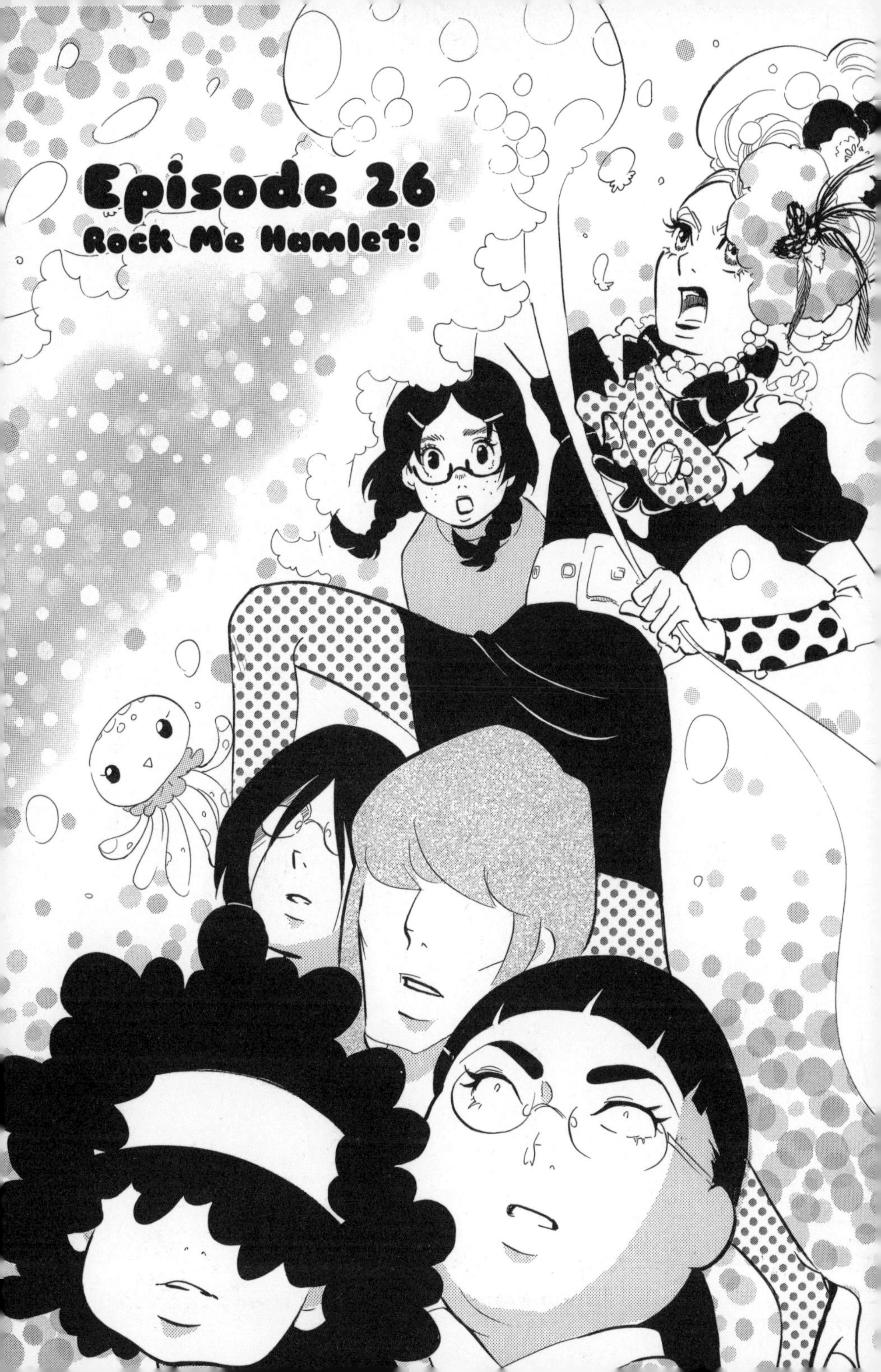

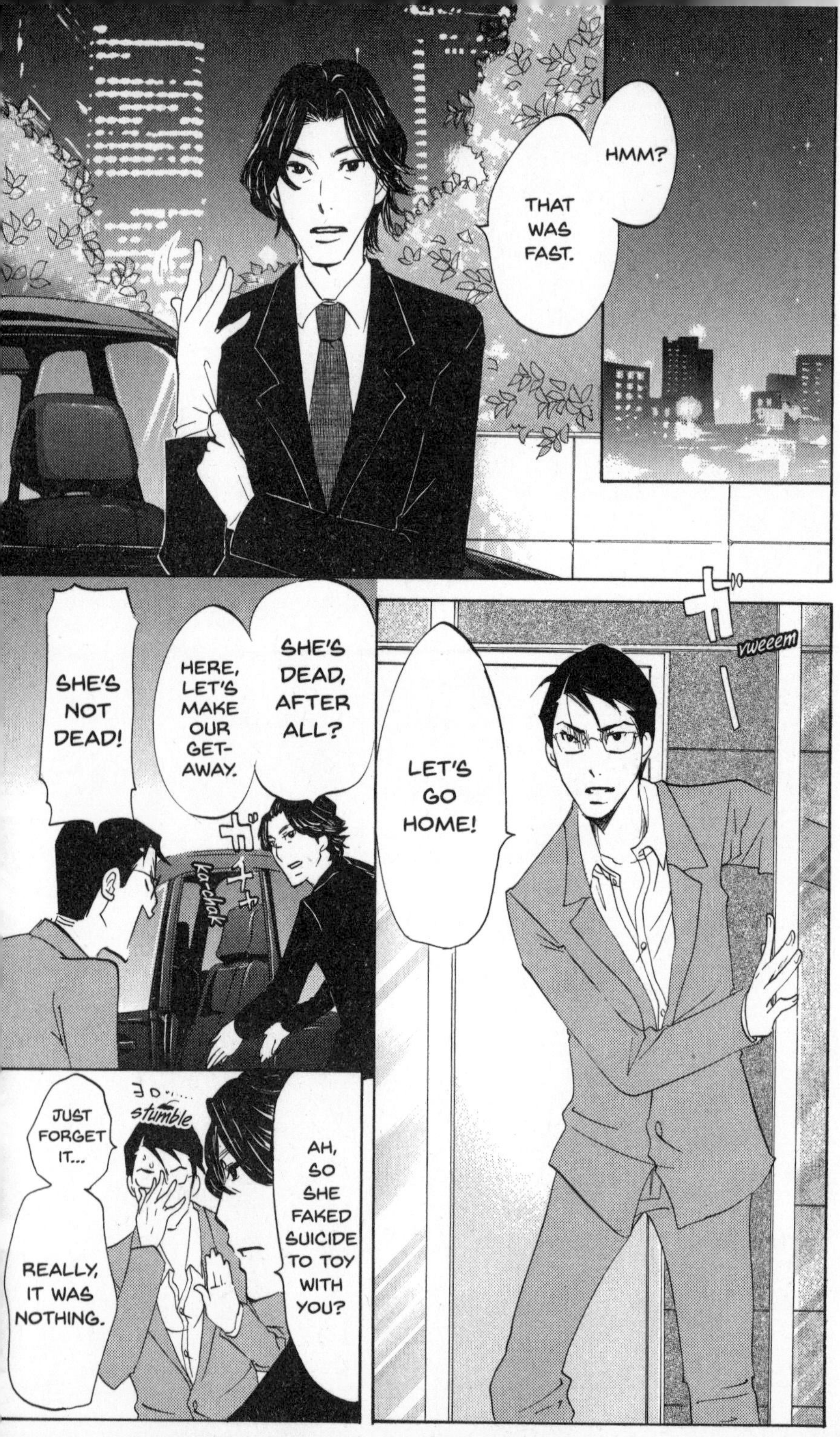

HMM?
THAT WAS FAST.
vweeem
LET'S GO HOME!
SHE'S DEAD, AFTER ALL?
HERE, LET'S MAKE OUR GET-AWAY.
SHE'S NOT DEAD!
Ka-chak
AH, SO SHE FAKED SUICIDE TO TOY WITH YOU?
stumble
JUST FORGET IT...
REALLY, IT WAS NOTHING.

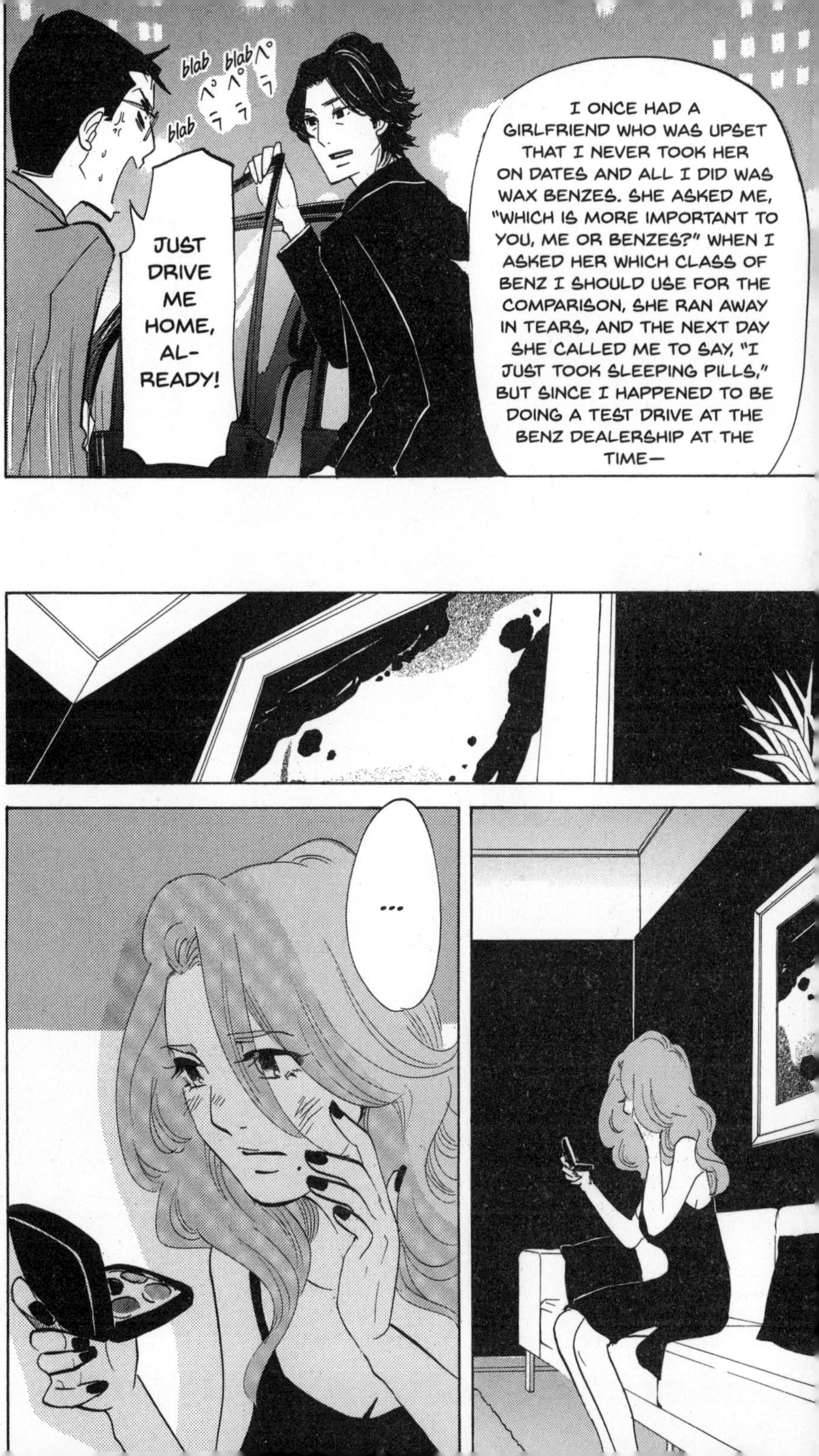
I ONCE HAD A GIRLFRIEND WHO WAS UPSET THAT I NEVER TOOK HER ON DATES AND ALL I DID WAS WAX BENZES. SHE ASKED ME, "WHICH IS MORE IMPORTANT TO YOU, ME OR BENZES?" WHEN I ASKED HER WHICH CLASS OF BENZ I SHOULD USE FOR THE COMPARISON, SHE RAN AWAY IN TEARS, AND THE NEXT DAY SHE CALLED ME TO SAY, "I JUST TOOK SLEEPING PILLS," BUT SINCE I HAPPENED TO BE DOING A TEST DRIVE AT THE BENZ DEALERSHIP AT THE TIME—
blab blab
ペラペラ
blab
ペラペラ
JUST DRIVE ME HOME, AL-READY!
...

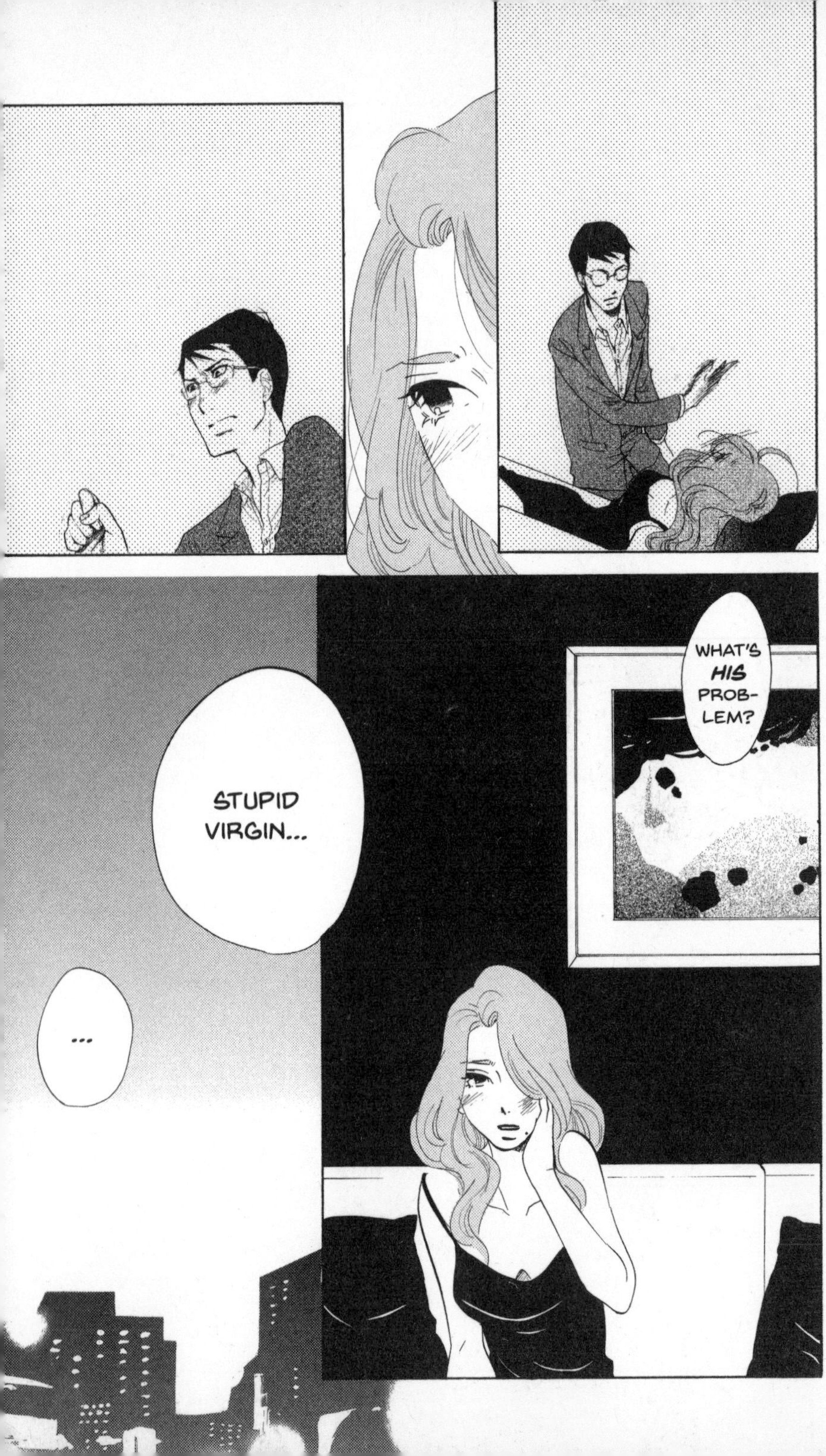
WHAT'S **HIS** PROB-LEM?
STUPID VIRGIN...
...

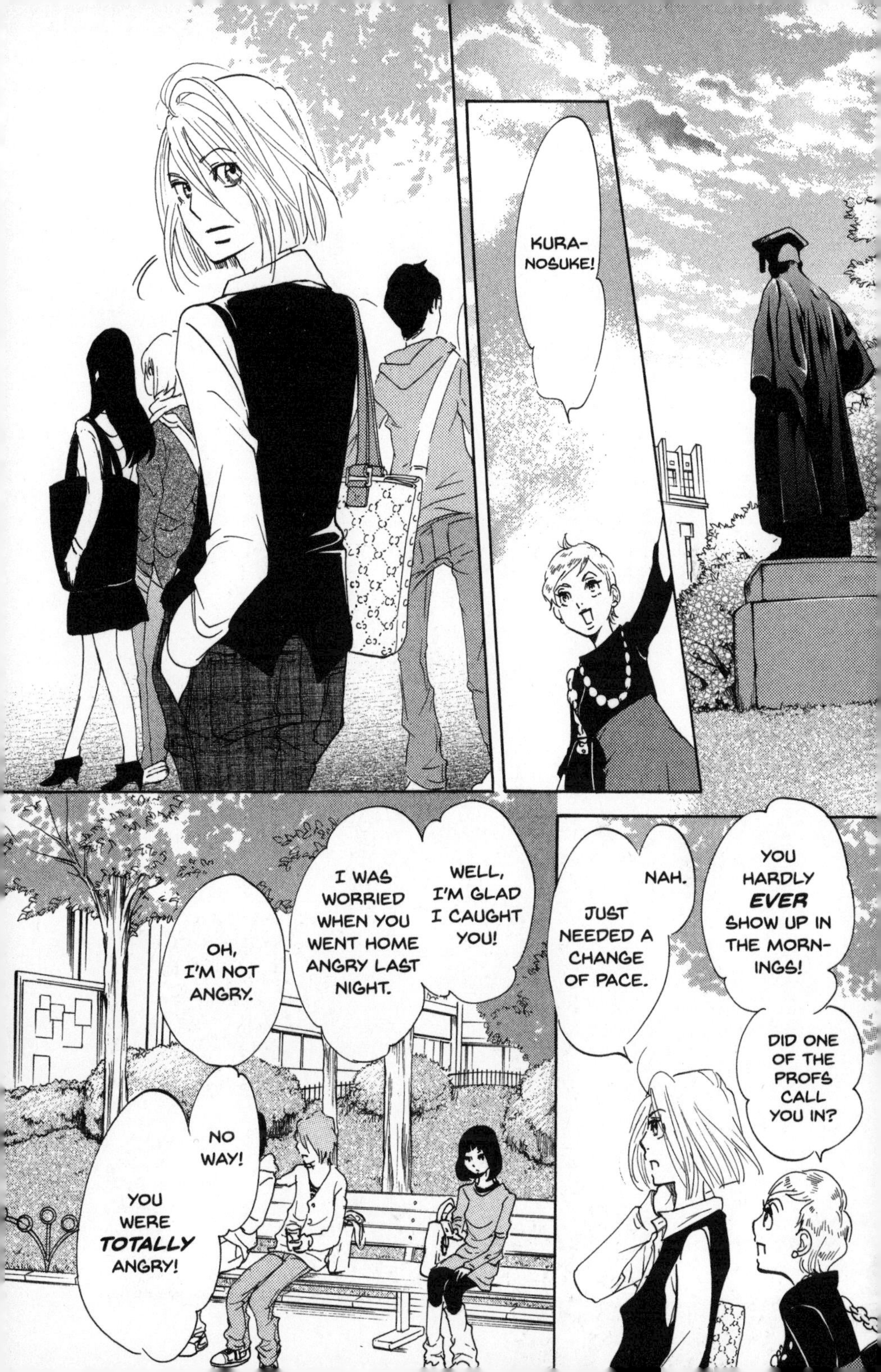
KURA-NOSUKE!
YOU HARDLY EVER SHOW UP IN THE MORN-INGS!
DID ONE OF THE PROFS CALL YOU IN?
NAH.
JUST NEEDED A CHANGE OF PACE.
WELL, I'M GLAD I CAUGHT YOU!
I WAS WORRIED WHEN YOU WENT HOME ANGRY LAST NIGHT.
OH, I'M NOT ANGRY.
NO WAY!
YOU WERE TOTALLY ANGRY!

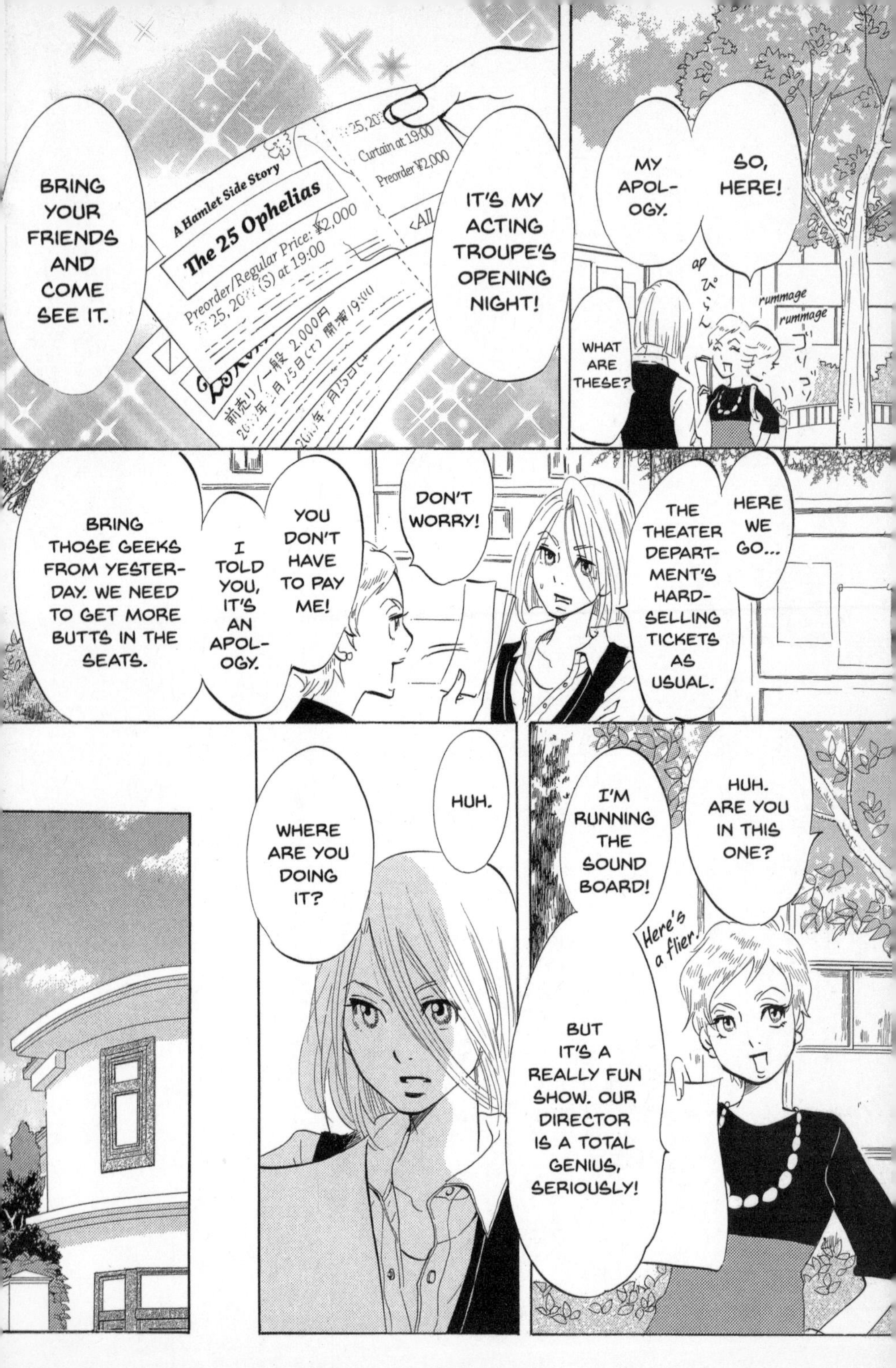
SO, HERE!
MY APOLOGY.
ap
ぴらん
rummage
rummage
ゴソゴソ
WHAT ARE THESE?
IT'S MY ACTING TROUPE'S OPENING NIGHT!
Curtain at 19:00
Preorder ¥2,000
A Hamlet Side Story
The 25 Ophelias
Preorder/Regular Price: ¥2,000
BRING YOUR FRIENDS AND COME SEE IT.
HERE WE GO...
THE THEATER DEPARTMENT'S HARD-SELLING TICKETS AS USUAL.
DON'T WORRY!
YOU DON'T HAVE TO PAY ME!
I TOLD YOU, IT'S AN APOLOGY.
BRING THOSE GEEKS FROM YESTERDAY. WE NEED TO GET MORE BUTTS IN THE SEATS.
HUH. ARE YOU IN THIS ONE?
I'M RUNNING THE SOUND BOARD!
Here's a flier.
BUT IT'S A REALLY FUN SHOW. OUR DIRECTOR IS A TOTAL GENIUS, SERIOUSLY!
HUH.
WHERE ARE YOU DOING IT?

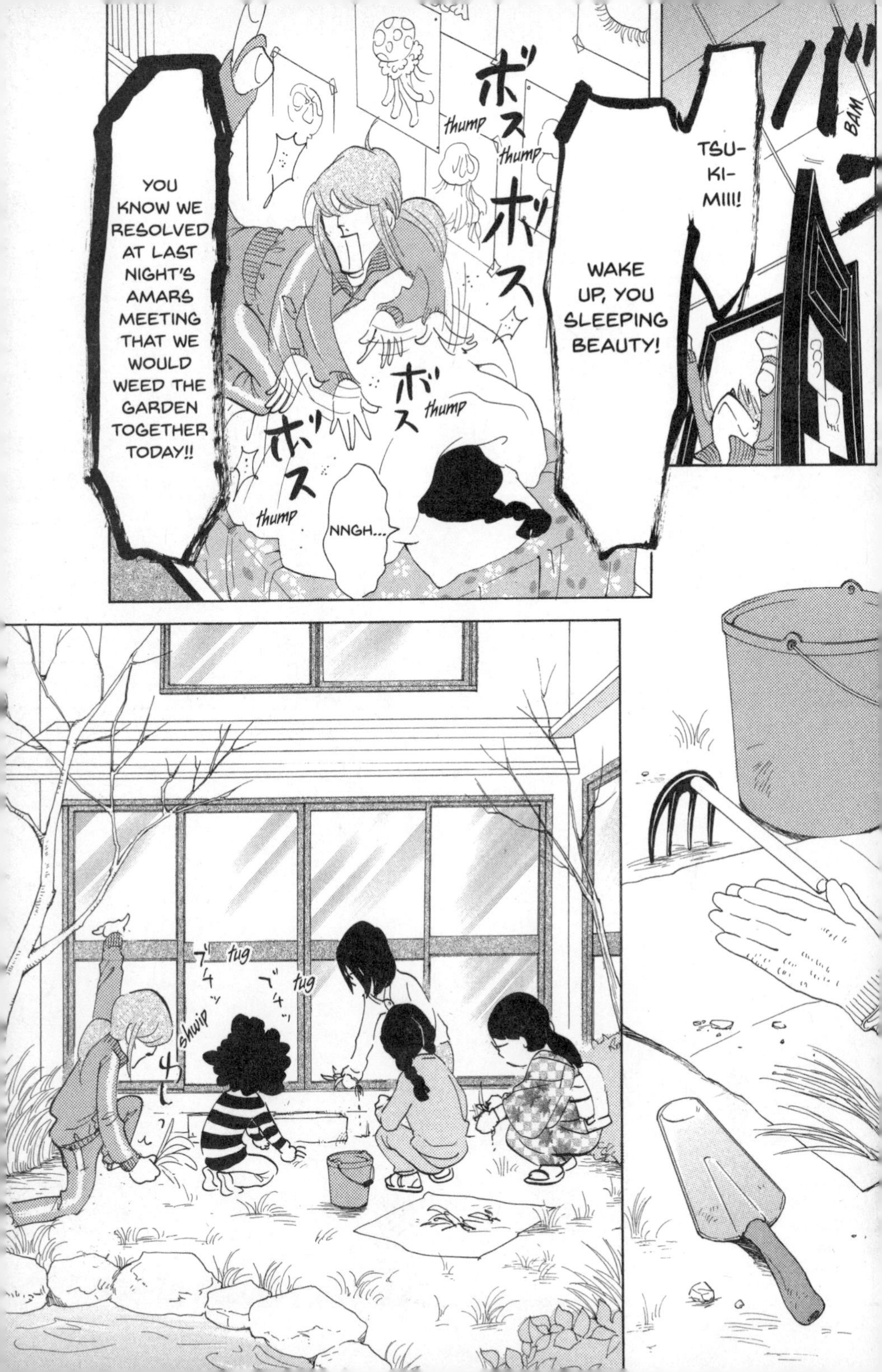
バン
BAM
TSU-KI-MIII!
WAKE UP, YOU SLEEPING BEAUTY!
YOU KNOW WE RESOLVED AT LAST NIGHT'S AMARS MEETING THAT WE WOULD WEED THE GARDEN TOGETHER TODAY!!
ボス
thump
thump
ボス
thump
thump
NNGH...
tug
tug
shwip

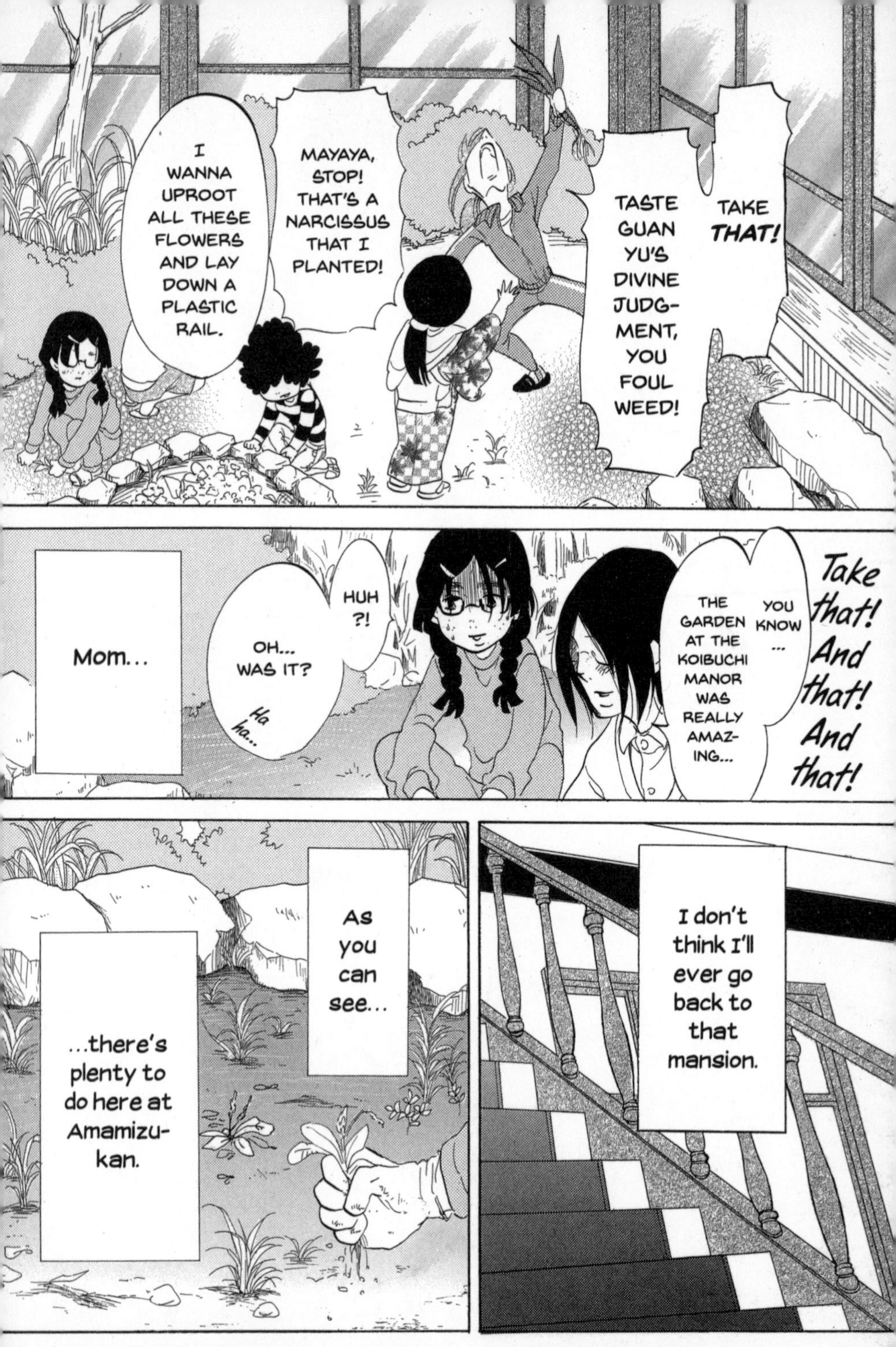
TAKE THAT!
TASTE GUAN YU'S DIVINE JUDGMENT, YOU FOUL WEED!
MAYAYA, STOP! THAT'S A NARCISSUS THAT I PLANTED!
I WANNA UPROOT ALL THESE FLOWERS AND LAY DOWN A PLASTIC RAIL.
Take that! And that! And that!
YOU KNOW ...
THE GARDEN AT THE KOIBUCHI MANOR WAS REALLY AMAZING...
HUH ?!
OH... WAS IT?
Ha ha...
Mom...
I don't think I'll ever go back to that mansion.
As you can see...
...there's plenty to do here at Amamizukan.

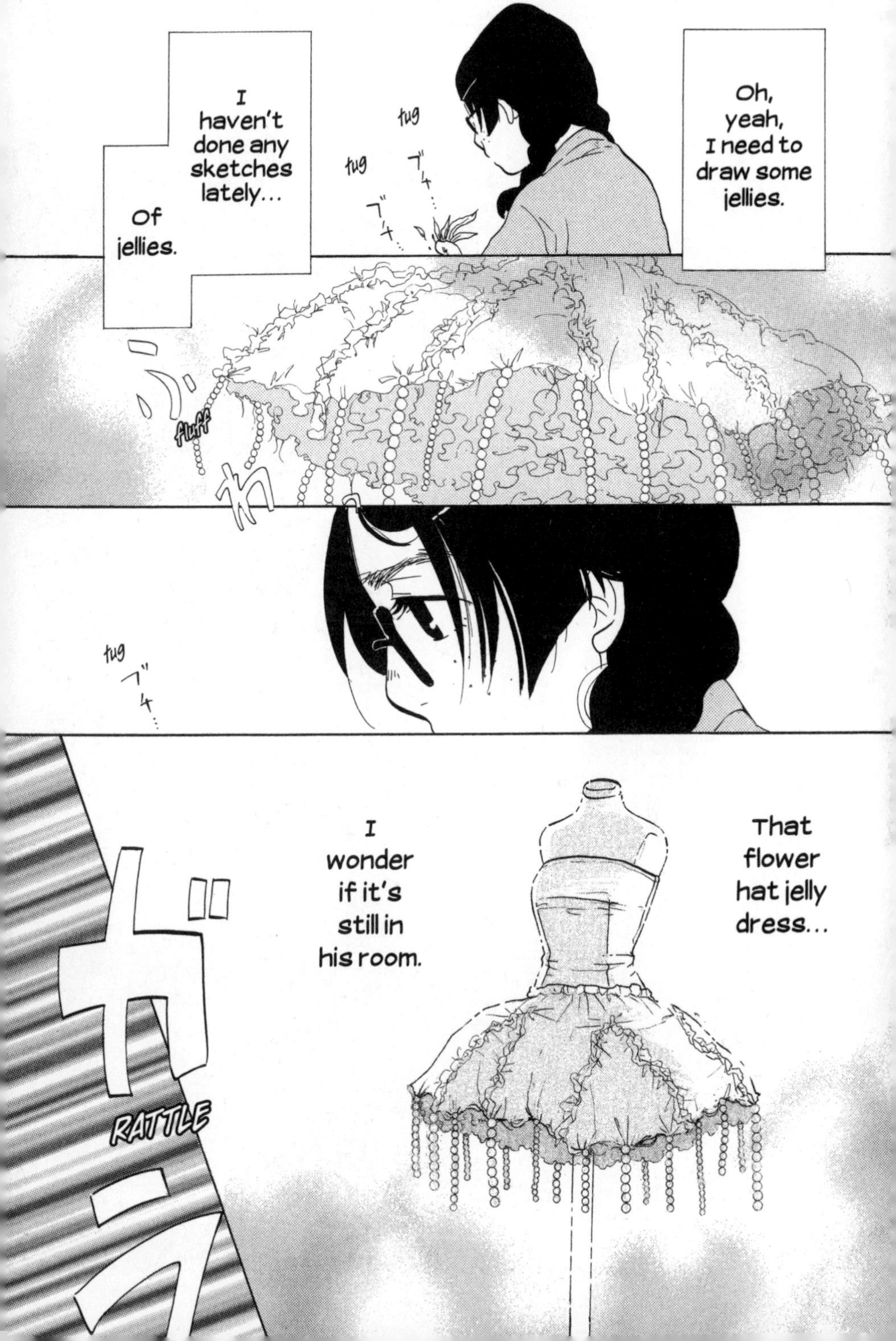

Oh, yeah, I need to draw some jellies.
I haven't done any sketches lately...
Of jellies.
tug
tug
fluff
tug
That flower hat jelly dress...
I wonder if it's still in his room.
RATTLE

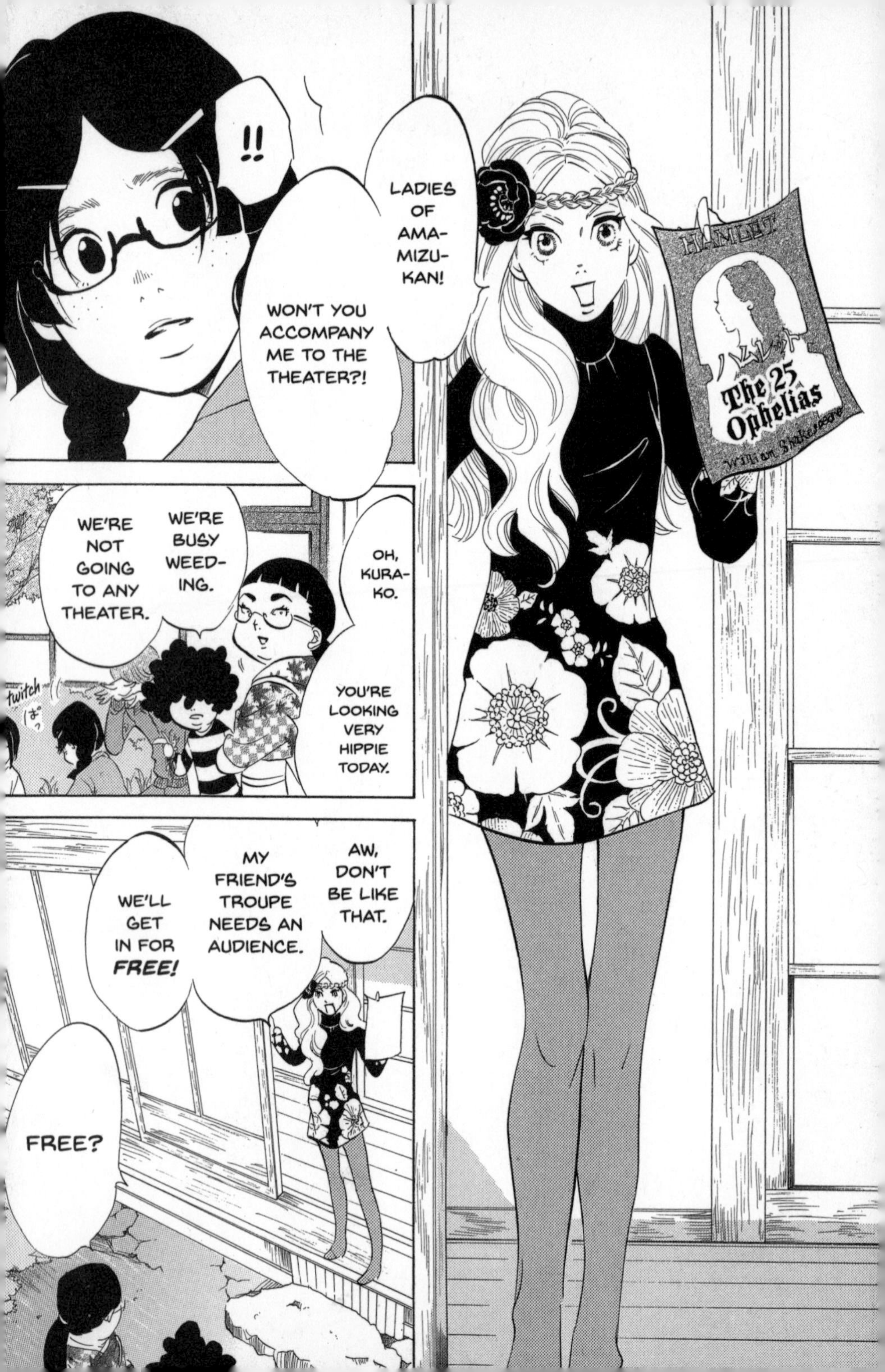
LADIES OF AMA-MIZUKAN!
WON'T YOU ACCOMPANY ME TO THE THEATER?!
HAMLET
The 25 Ophelias
William Shakespeare
!!
OH, KURA-KO.
YOU'RE LOOKING VERY HIPPIE TODAY.
WE'RE BUSY WEEDING.
WE'RE NOT GOING TO ANY THEATER.
twitch
AW, DON'T BE LIKE THAT.
MY FRIEND'S TROUPE NEEDS AN AUDIENCE.
WE'LL GET IN FOR ***FREE!***
FREE?

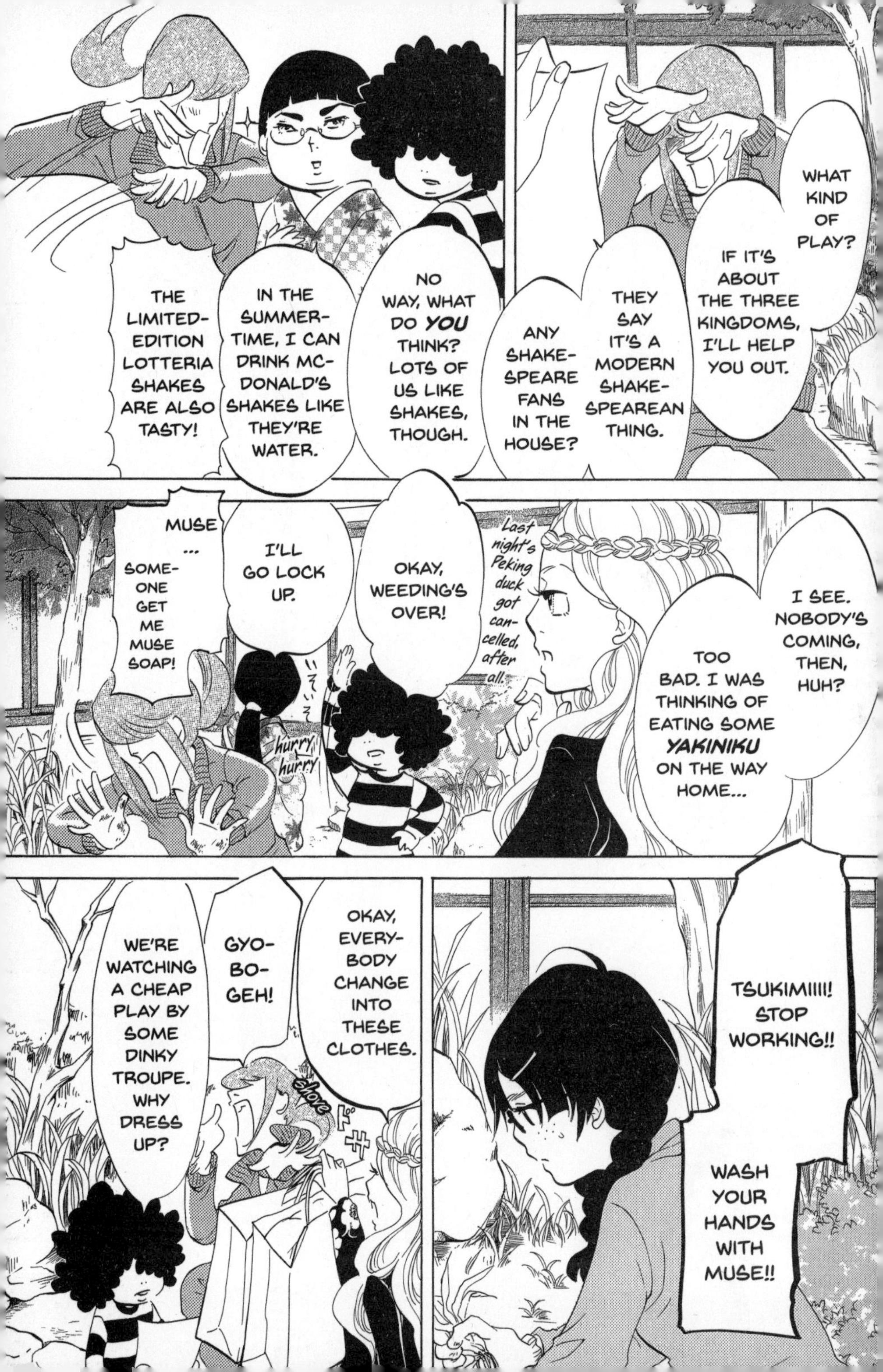
WHAT KIND OF PLAY?
IF IT'S ABOUT THE THREE KINGDOMS, I'LL HELP YOU OUT.
THEY SAY IT'S A MODERN SHAKESPEAREAN THING.
ANY SHAKESPEARE FANS IN THE HOUSE?
NO WAY, WHAT DO *YOU* THINK? LOTS OF US LIKE SHAKES, THOUGH.
IN THE SUMMERTIME, I CAN DRINK MCDONALD'S SHAKES LIKE THEY'RE WATER.
THE LIMITED-EDITION LOTTERIA SHAKES ARE ALSO TASTY!
I SEE. NOBODY'S COMING, THEN, HUH?
TOO BAD. I WAS THINKING OF EATING SOME *YAKINIKU* ON THE WAY HOME...
Last night's Peking duck got cancelled, after all.
OKAY, WEEDING'S OVER!
I'LL GO LOCK UP.
hurry hurry
MUSE... SOMEONE GET ME MUSE SOAP!
TSUKIMIIII! STOP WORKING!!
WASH YOUR HANDS WITH MUSE!!
OKAY, EVERYBODY CHANGE INTO THESE CLOTHES.
shove
GYO-BO-GEH!
WE'RE WATCHING A CHEAP PLAY BY SOME DINKY TROUPE. WHY DRESS UP?

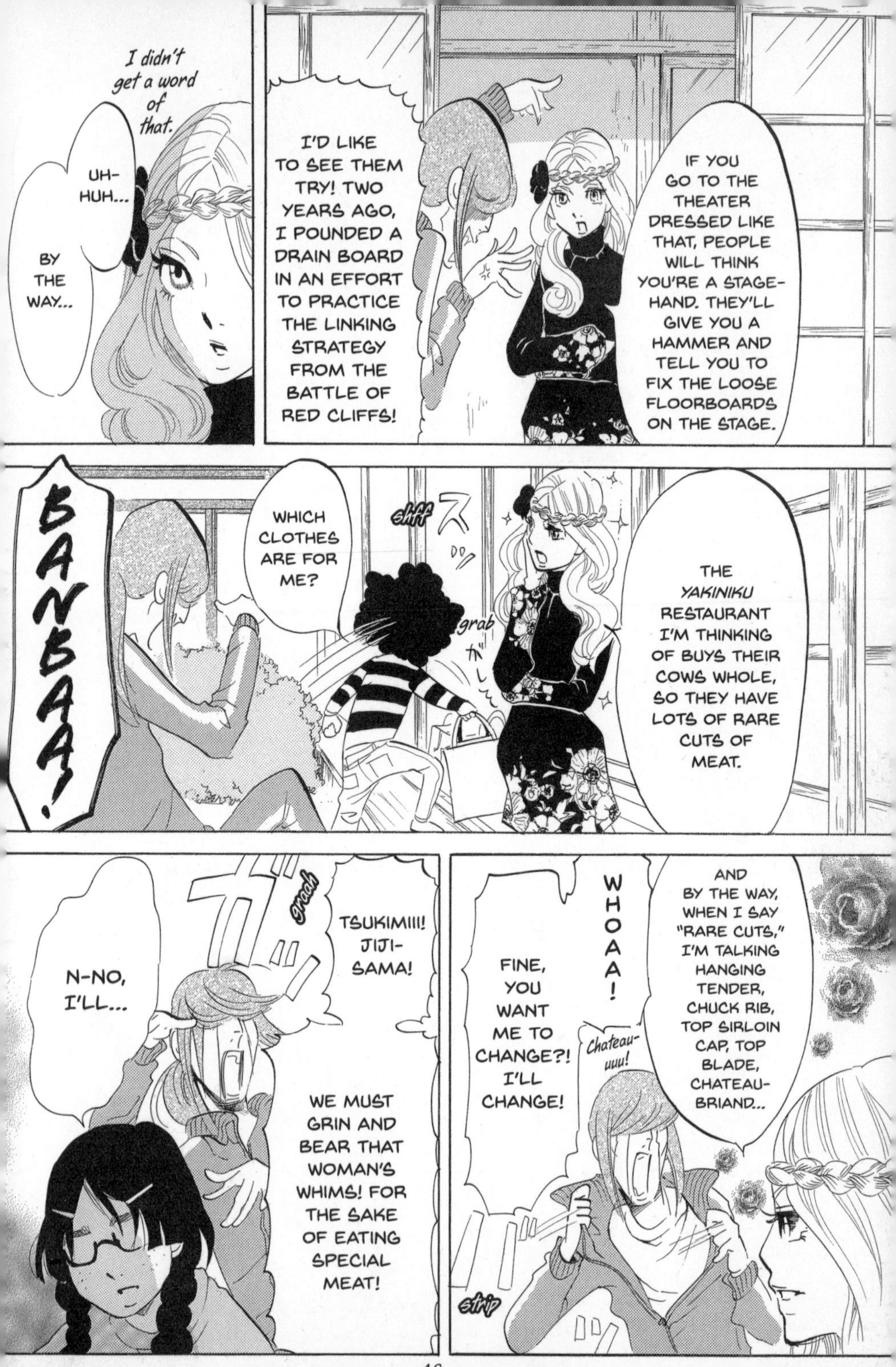
IF YOU GO TO THE THEATER DRESSED LIKE THAT, PEOPLE WILL THINK YOU'RE A STAGE-HAND. THEY'LL GIVE YOU A HAMMER AND TELL YOU TO FIX THE LOOSE FLOORBOARDS ON THE STAGE.
I'D LIKE TO SEE THEM TRY! TWO YEARS AGO, I POUNDED A DRAIN BOARD IN AN EFFORT TO PRACTICE THE LINKING STRATEGY FROM THE BATTLE OF RED CLIFFS!
I didn't get a word of that.
UH-HUH...
BY THE WAY...
THE YAKINIKU RESTAURANT I'M THINKING OF BUYS THEIR COWS WHOLE, SO THEY HAVE LOTS OF RARE CUTS OF MEAT.
shff
WHICH CLOTHES ARE FOR ME?
grab
BANBAA!
AND BY THE WAY, WHEN I SAY "RARE CUTS," I'M TALKING HANGING TENDER, CHUCK RIB, TOP SIRLOIN CAP, TOP BLADE, CHATEAU-BRIAND...
WHOAAA!
FINE, YOU WANT ME TO CHANGE?! I'LL CHANGE!
Chateau-uuu!
strip
TSUKIMIII! JIJI-SAMA!
grach
WE MUST GRIN AND BEAR THAT WOMAN'S WHIMS! FOR THE SAKE OF EATING SPECIAL MEAT!
N-NO, I'LL...

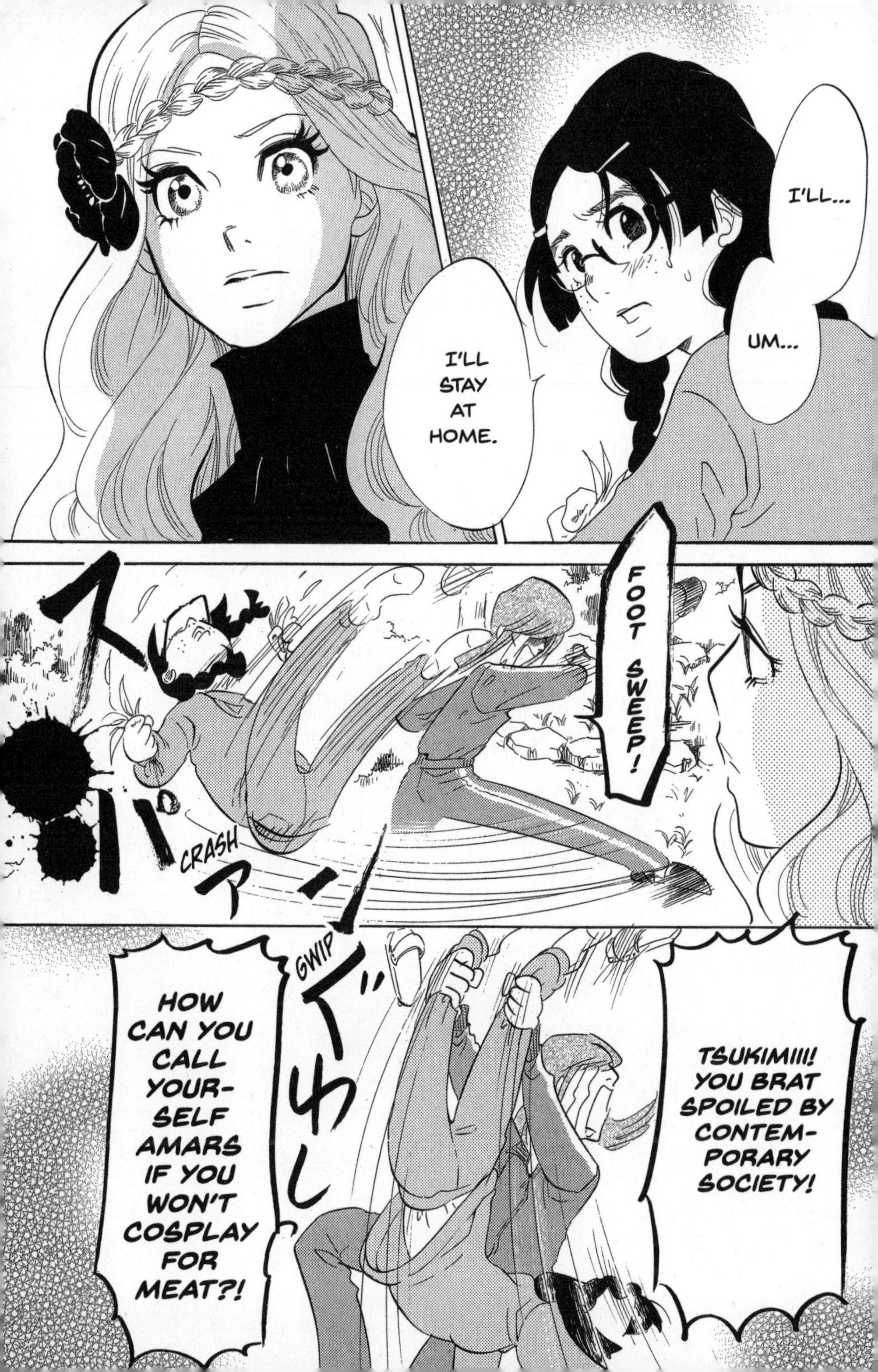
I'LL...
UM...
I'LL STAY AT HOME.
FOOT SWEEP!
CRASH
TSUKIMIII! YOU BRAT SPOILED BY CONTEM-PORARY SOCIETY!
GWIP
HOW CAN YOU CALL YOUR-SELF AMARS IF YOU WON'T COSPLAY FOR MEAT?!

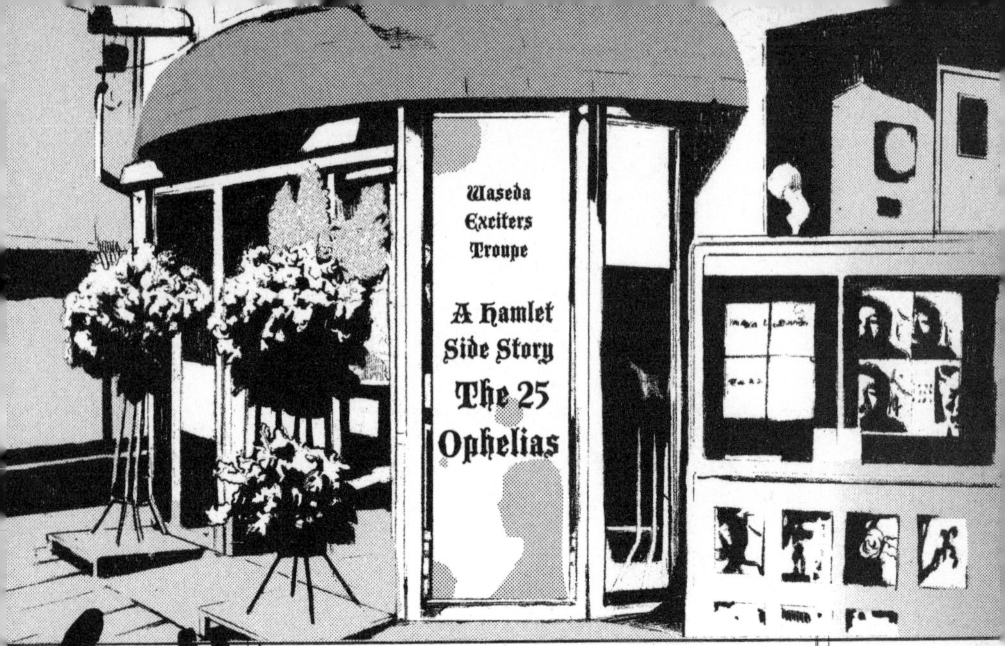
Waseda
Exciters
Troupe
A Hamlet
Side Story
The 25
Ophelias

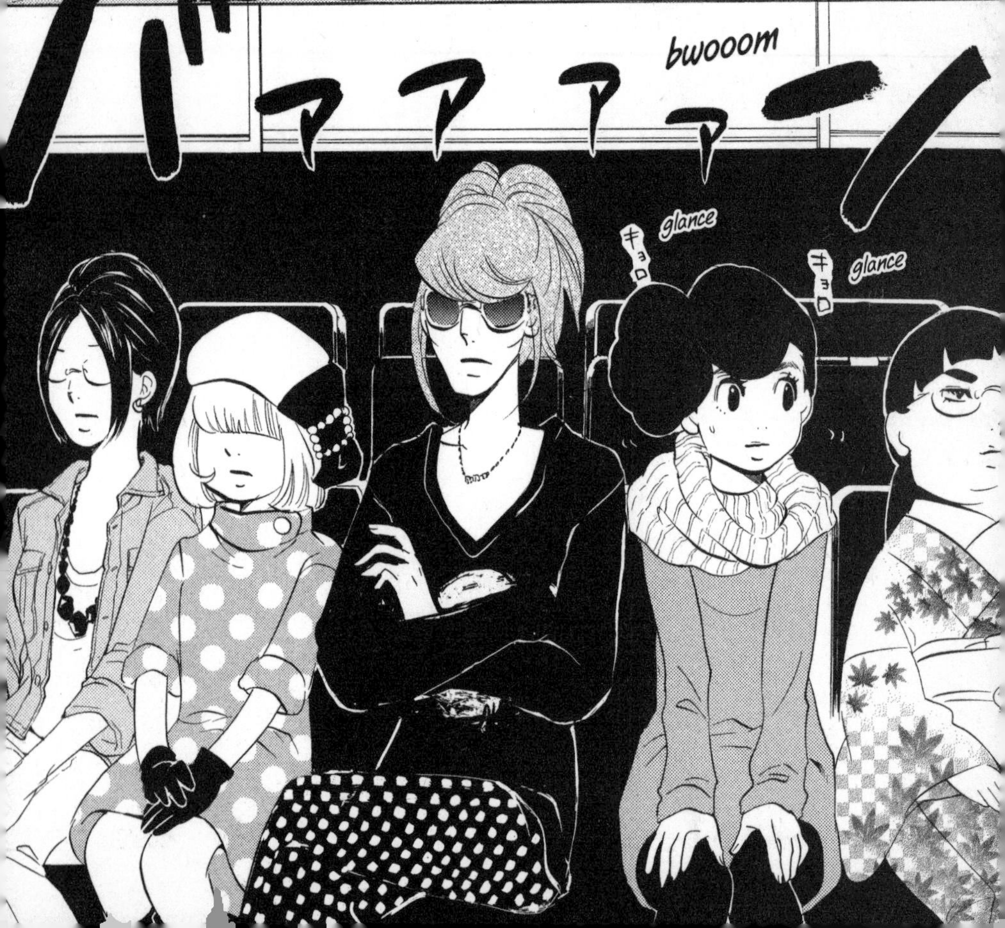
バァァァーン
bwooom
キョロ
glance
キョロ
glance

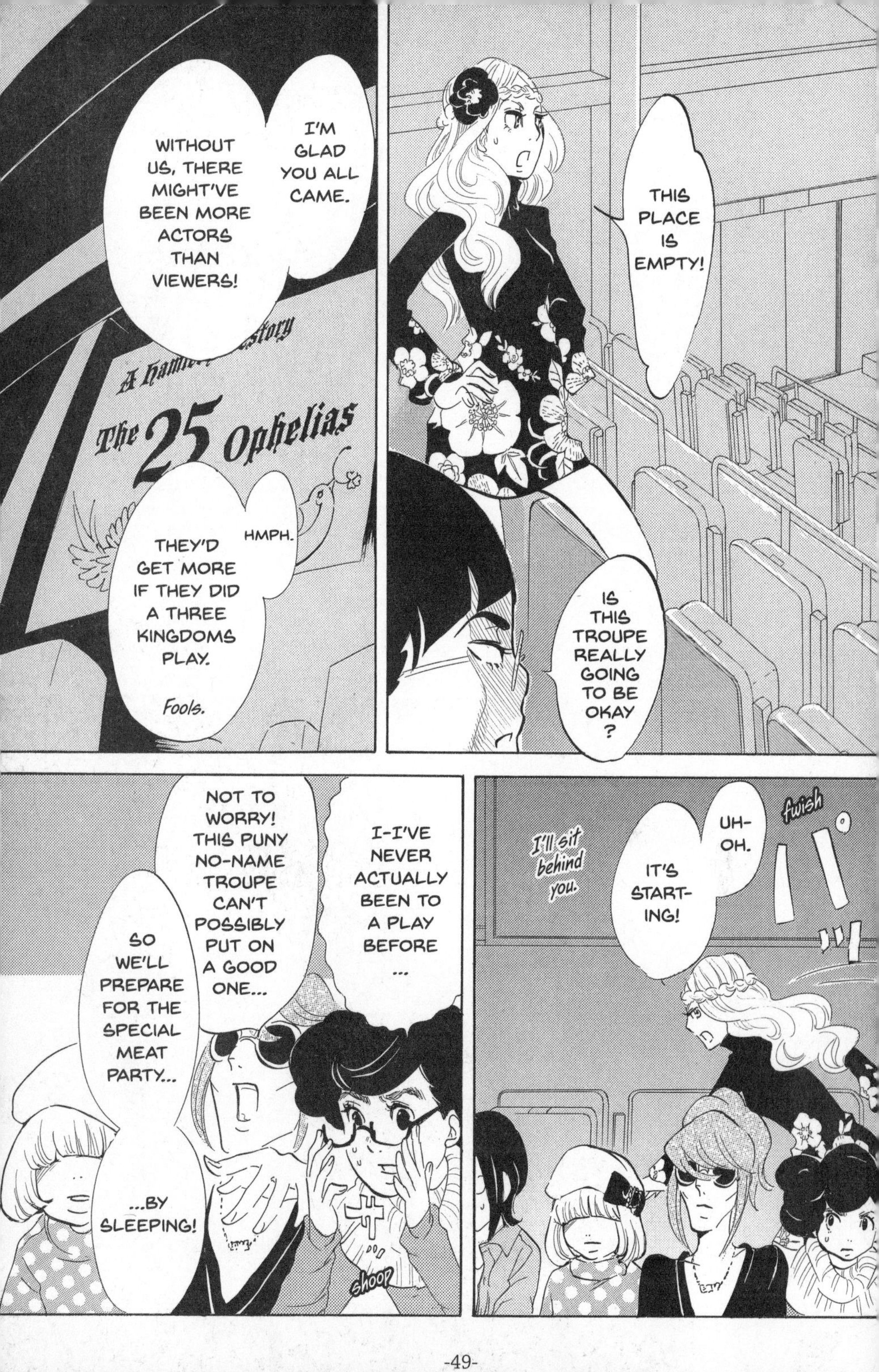
THIS PLACE IS EMPTY!
IS THIS TROUPE REALLY GOING TO BE OKAY ?
I'M GLAD YOU ALL CAME.
WITHOUT US, THERE MIGHT'VE BEEN MORE ACTORS THAN VIEWERS!
The 25 Ophelias
HMPH.
THEY'D GET MORE IF THEY DID A THREE KINGDOMS PLAY.
Fools.
fwish
UH-OH.
IT'S START-ING!
I'll sit behind you.
I-I'VE NEVER ACTUALLY BEEN TO A PLAY BEFORE ...
NOT TO WORRY! THIS PUNY NO-NAME TROUPE CAN'T POSSIBLY PUT ON A GOOD ONE...
SO WE'LL PREPARE FOR THE SPECIAL MEAT PARTY...
...BY SLEEPING!
shoop

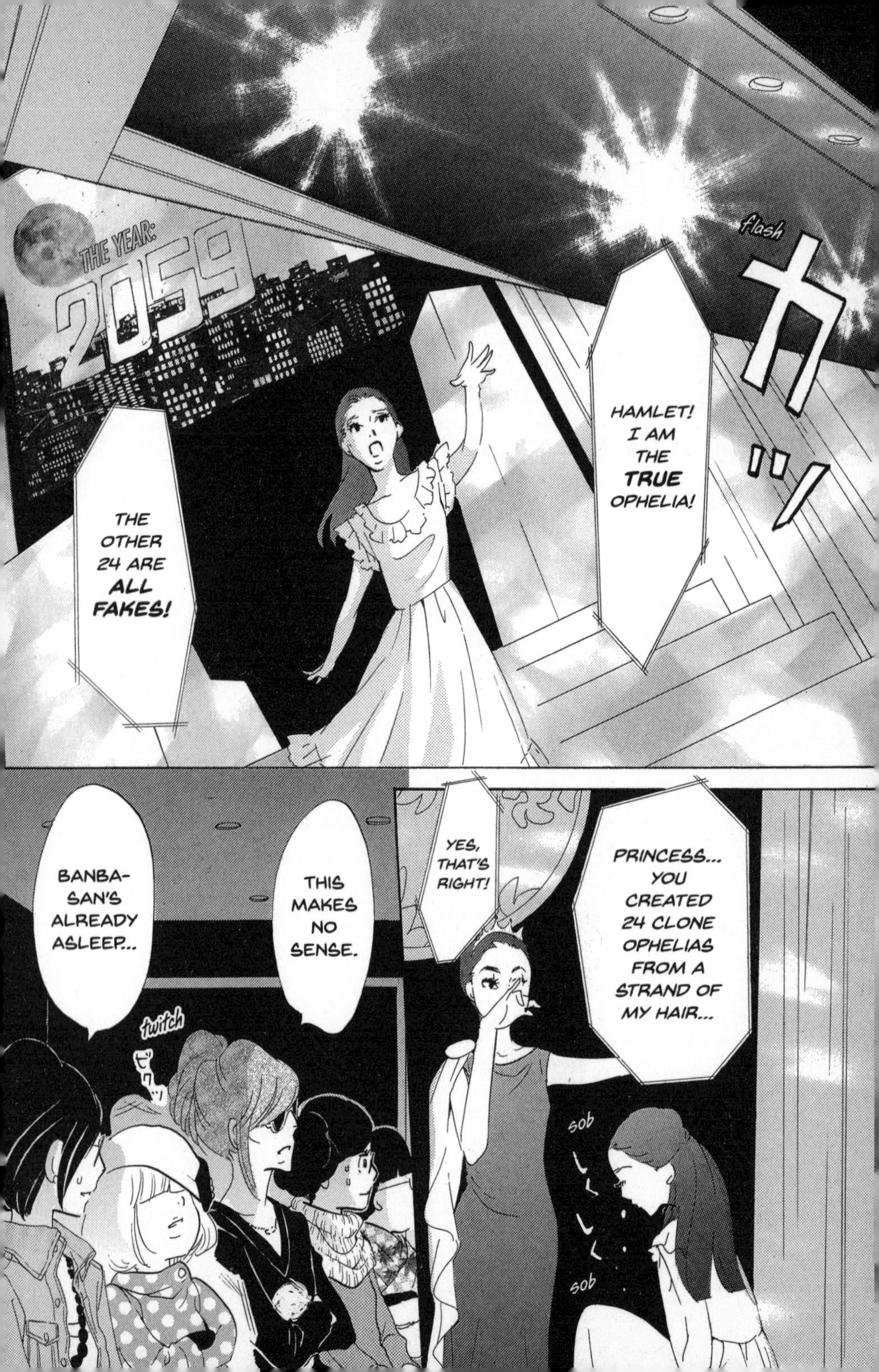
flash
カッ
HAMLET! I AM THE TRUE OPHELIA!
THE OTHER 24 ARE ALL FAKES!
THE YEAR: 2059
PRINCESS... YOU CREATED 24 CLONE OPHELIAS FROM A STRAND OF MY HAIR...
YES, THAT'S RIGHT!
sob
しくしく
sob
THIS MAKES NO SENSE.
twitch
ビクッ
BANBA-SAN'S ALREADY ASLEEP...

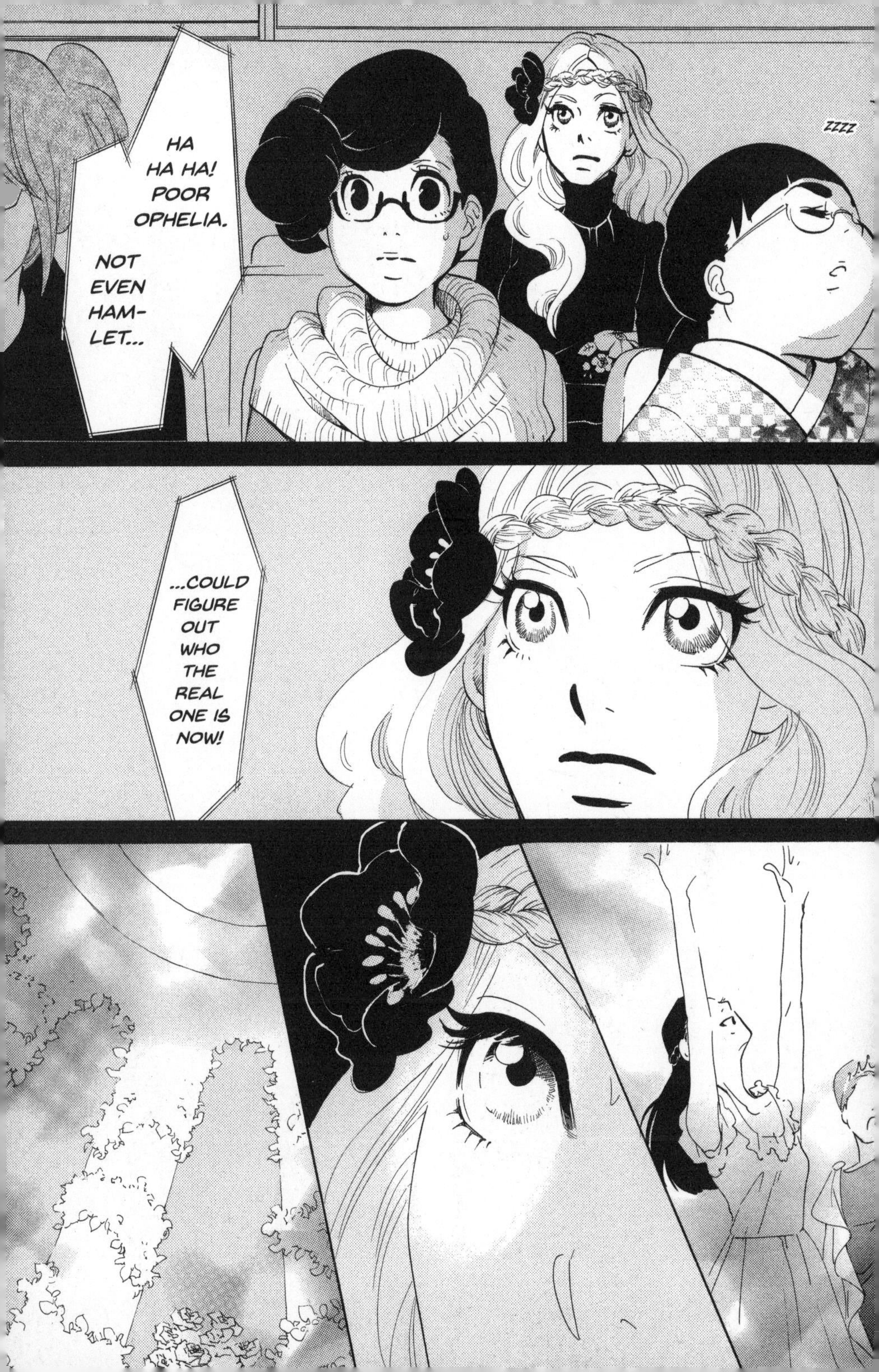
ZZZZ
HA HA HA! POOR OPHELIA.
NOT EVEN HAM-LET...
...COULD FIGURE OUT WHO THE REAL ONE IS NOW!

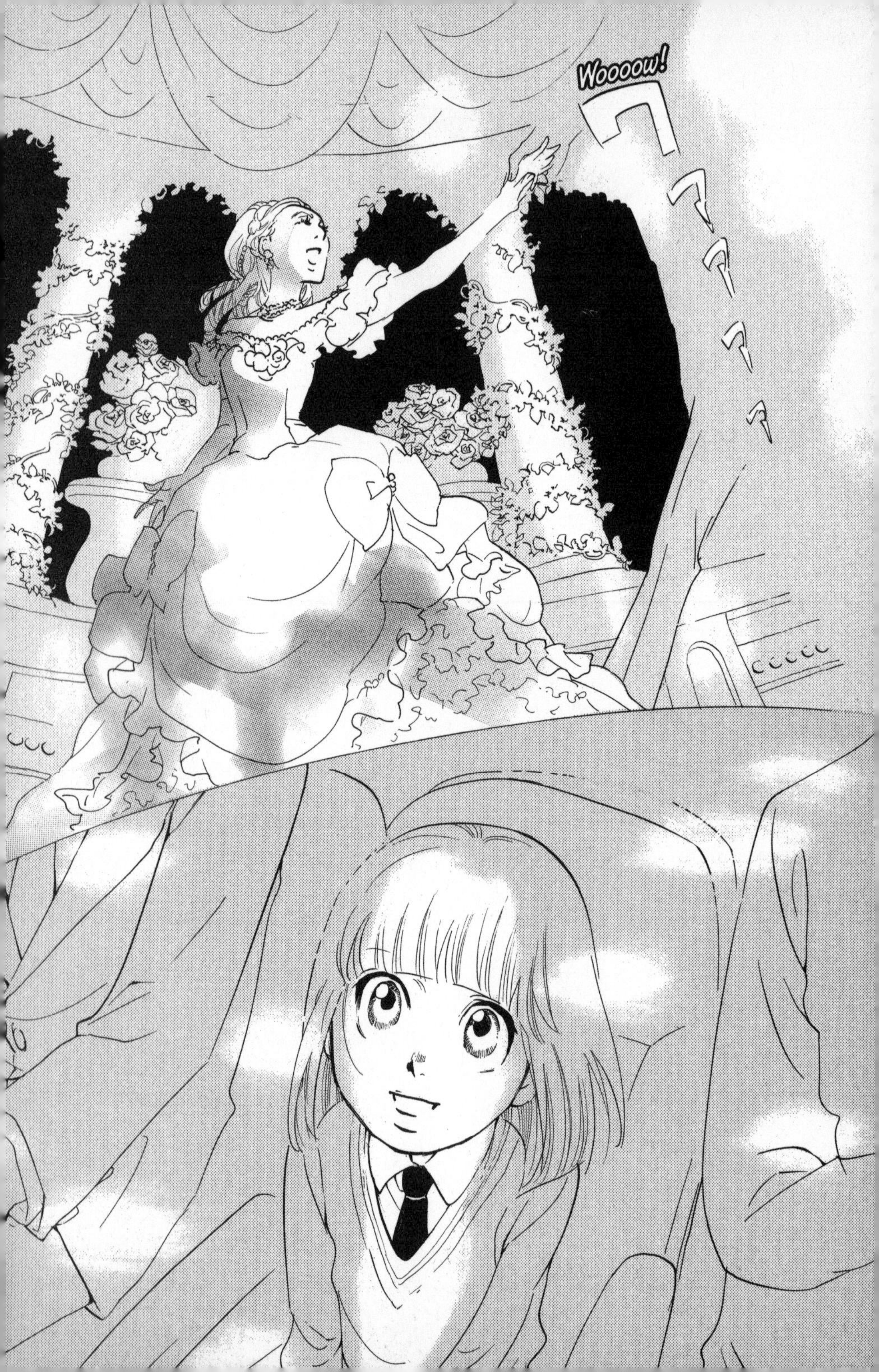
Woooow!

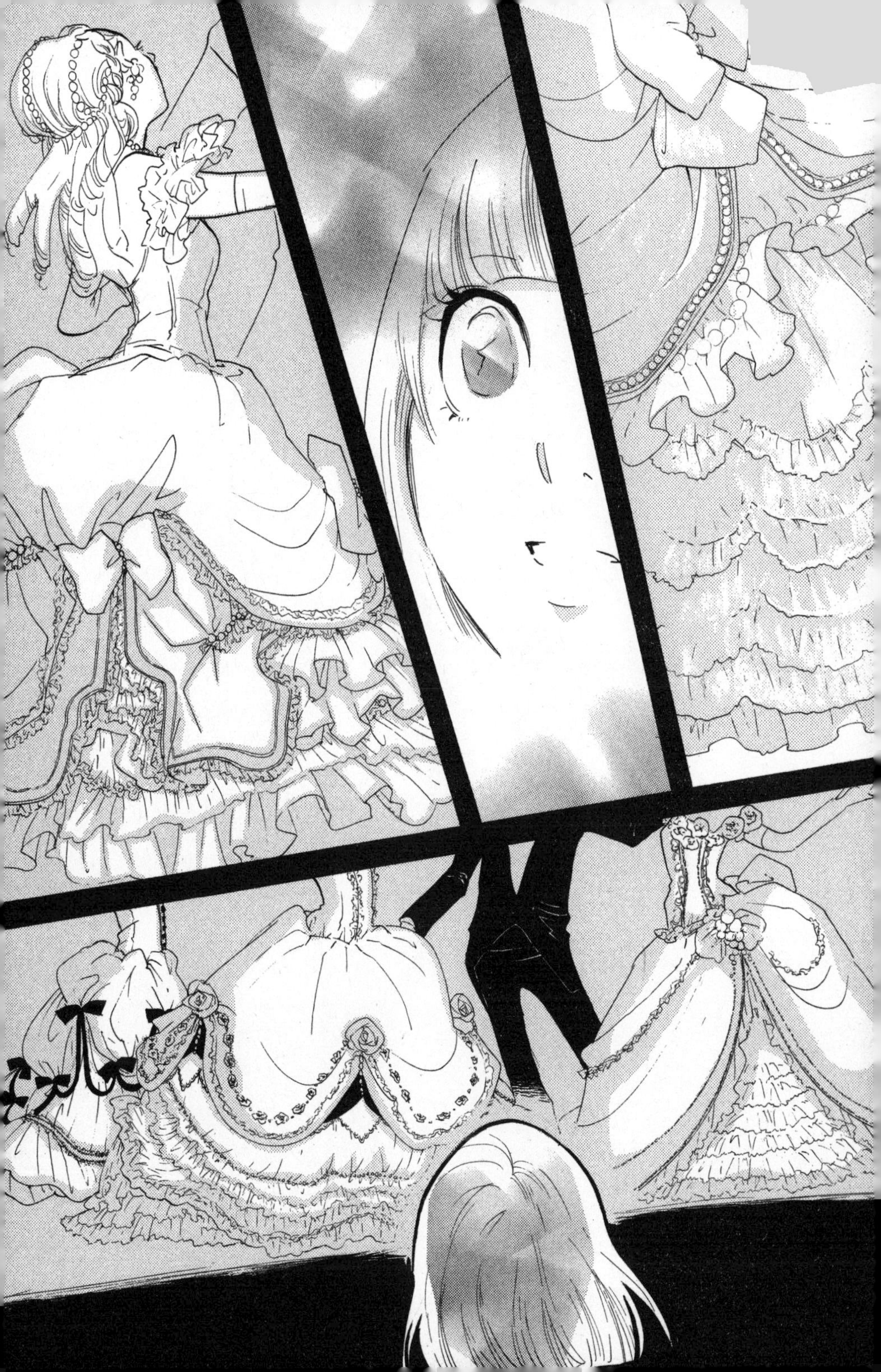

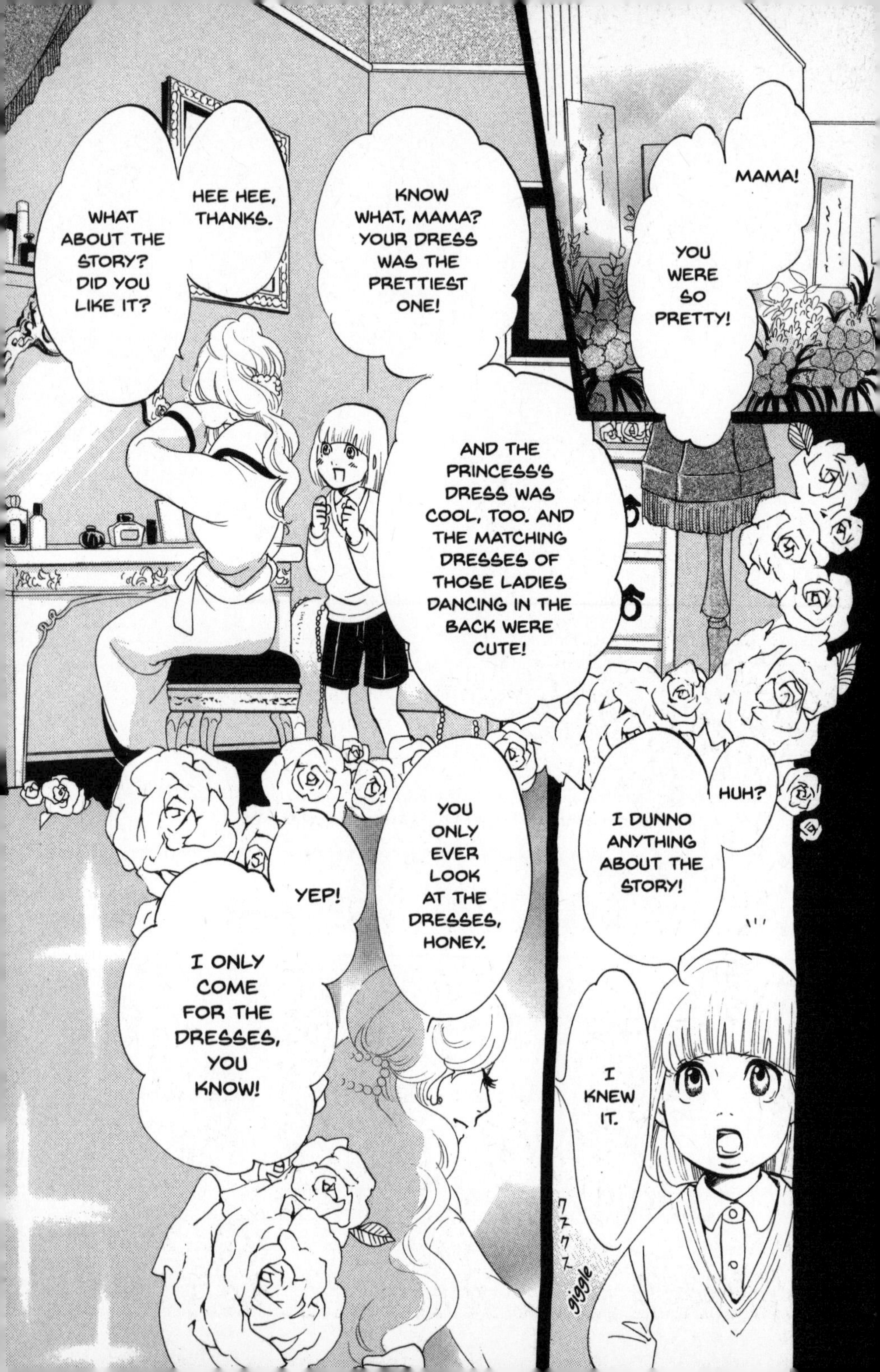
MAMA!
YOU WERE SO PRETTY!
KNOW WHAT, MAMA? YOUR DRESS WAS THE PRETTIEST ONE!
AND THE PRINCESS'S DRESS WAS COOL, TOO. AND THE MATCHING DRESSES OF THOSE LADIES DANCING IN THE BACK WERE CUTE!
HEE HEE, THANKS.
WHAT ABOUT THE STORY? DID YOU LIKE IT?
HUH?
I DUNNO ANYTHING ABOUT THE STORY!
I KNEW IT.
giggle
YOU ONLY EVER LOOK AT THE DRESSES, HONEY.
YEP!
I ONLY COME FOR THE DRESSES, YOU KNOW!

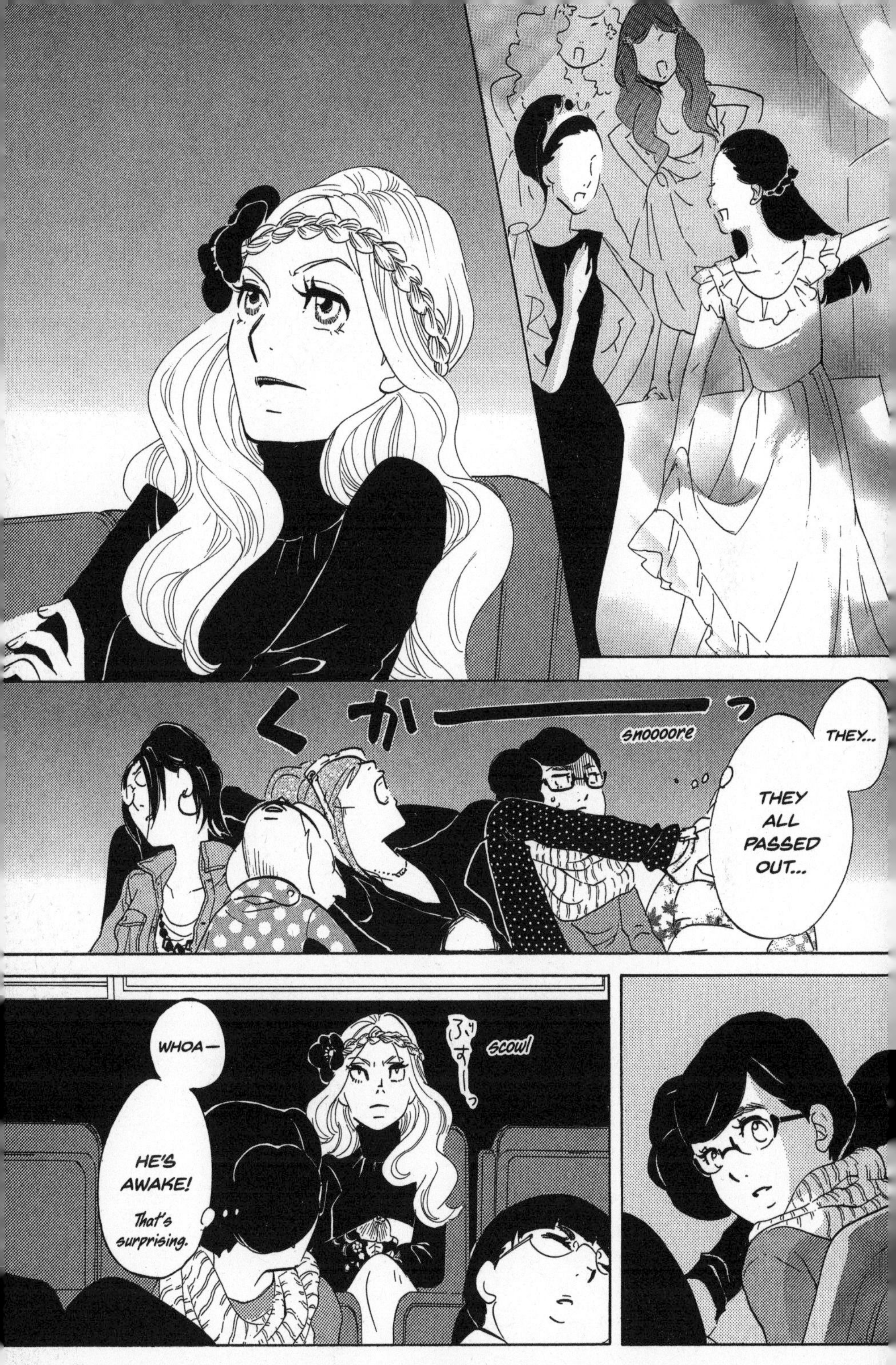
THEY...
THEY ALL PASSED OUT...
くかーーーっ
snoooore
ふすーっ
scowl
WHOA—
HE'S AWAKE!
That's surprising.

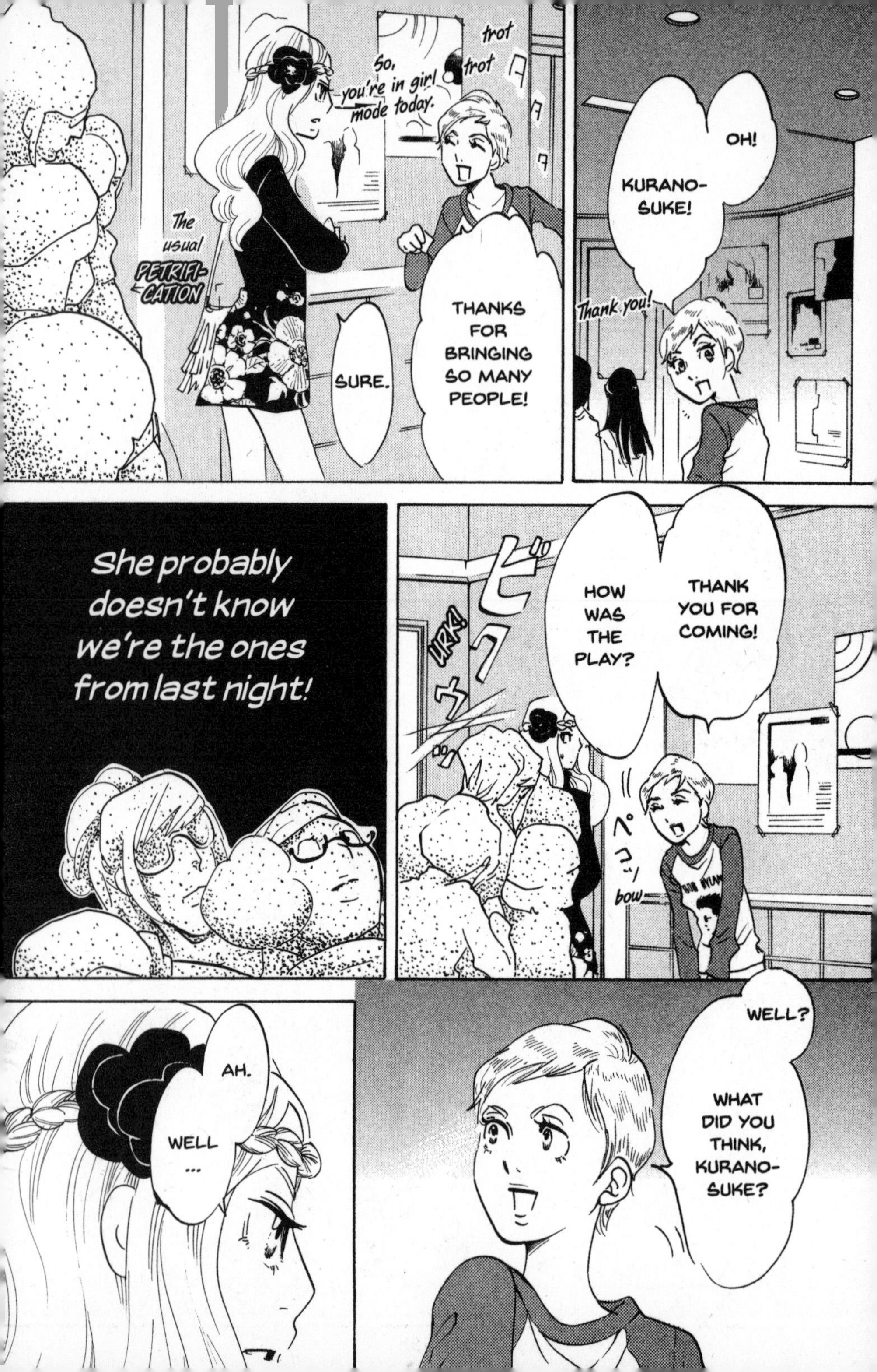
OH!
KURANO-SUKE!
Thank you!
trot trot
So, you're in girl mode today.
THANKS FOR BRINGING SO MANY PEOPLE!
SURE.
The usual PETRIFICATION
THANK YOU FOR COMING!
HOW WAS THE PLAY?
URK!
bow
She probably doesn't know we're the ones from last night!
WELL?
WHAT DID YOU THINK, KURANO-SUKE?
AH.
WELL ...

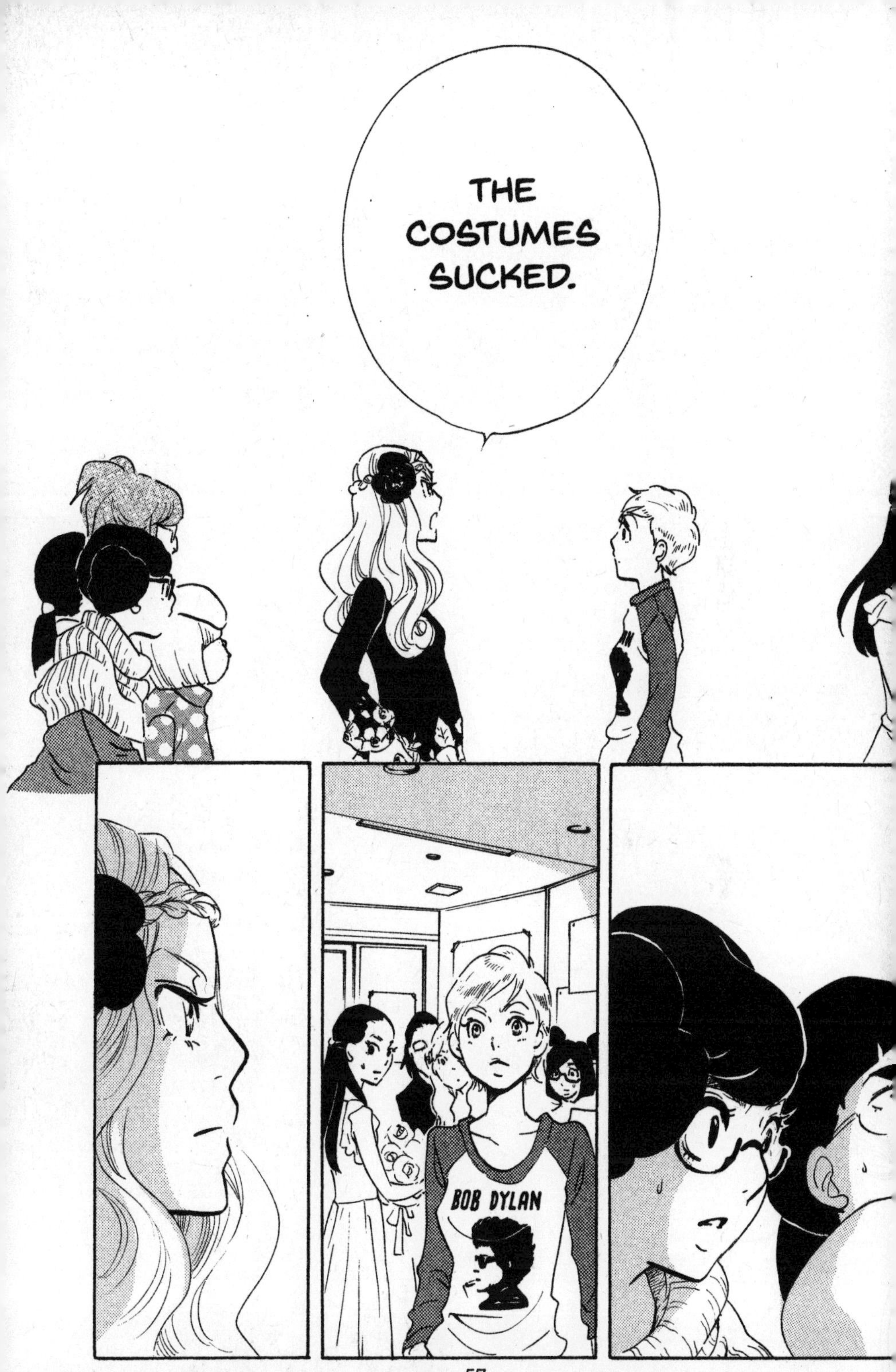
THE COSTUMES SUCKED.
BOB DYLAN

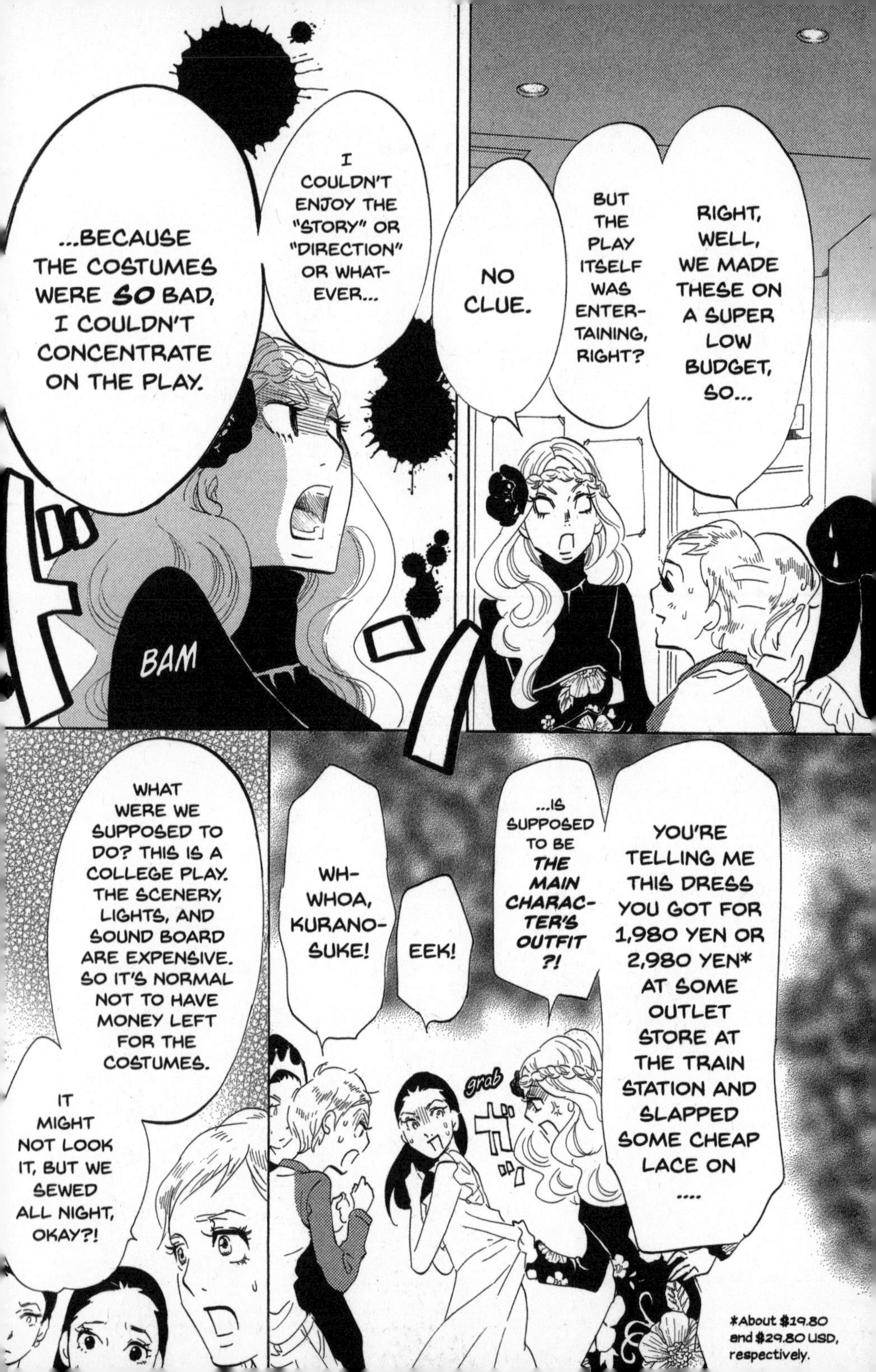
RIGHT, WELL, WE MADE THESE ON A SUPER LOW BUDGET, SO...
BUT THE PLAY ITSELF WAS ENTERTAINING, RIGHT?
NO CLUE.
I COULDN'T ENJOY THE "STORY" OR "DIRECTION" OR WHATEVER...
...BECAUSE THE COSTUMES WERE **SO** BAD, I COULDN'T CONCENTRATE ON THE PLAY.
BAM
YOU'RE TELLING ME THIS DRESS YOU GOT FOR 1,980 YEN OR 2,980 YEN* AT SOME OUTLET STORE AT THE TRAIN STATION AND SLAPPED SOME CHEAP LACE ON ....
...IS SUPPOSED TO BE *THE MAIN CHARACTER'S OUTFIT* ?!
grab
EEK!
WH- WHOA, KURANOSUKE!
WHAT WERE WE SUPPOSED TO DO? THIS IS A COLLEGE PLAY. THE SCENERY, LIGHTS, AND SOUND BOARD ARE EXPENSIVE. SO IT'S NORMAL NOT TO HAVE MONEY LEFT FOR THE COSTUMES.
IT MIGHT NOT LOOK IT, BUT WE SEWED ALL NIGHT, OKAY?!

*About $19.80 and $29.80 USD, respectively.

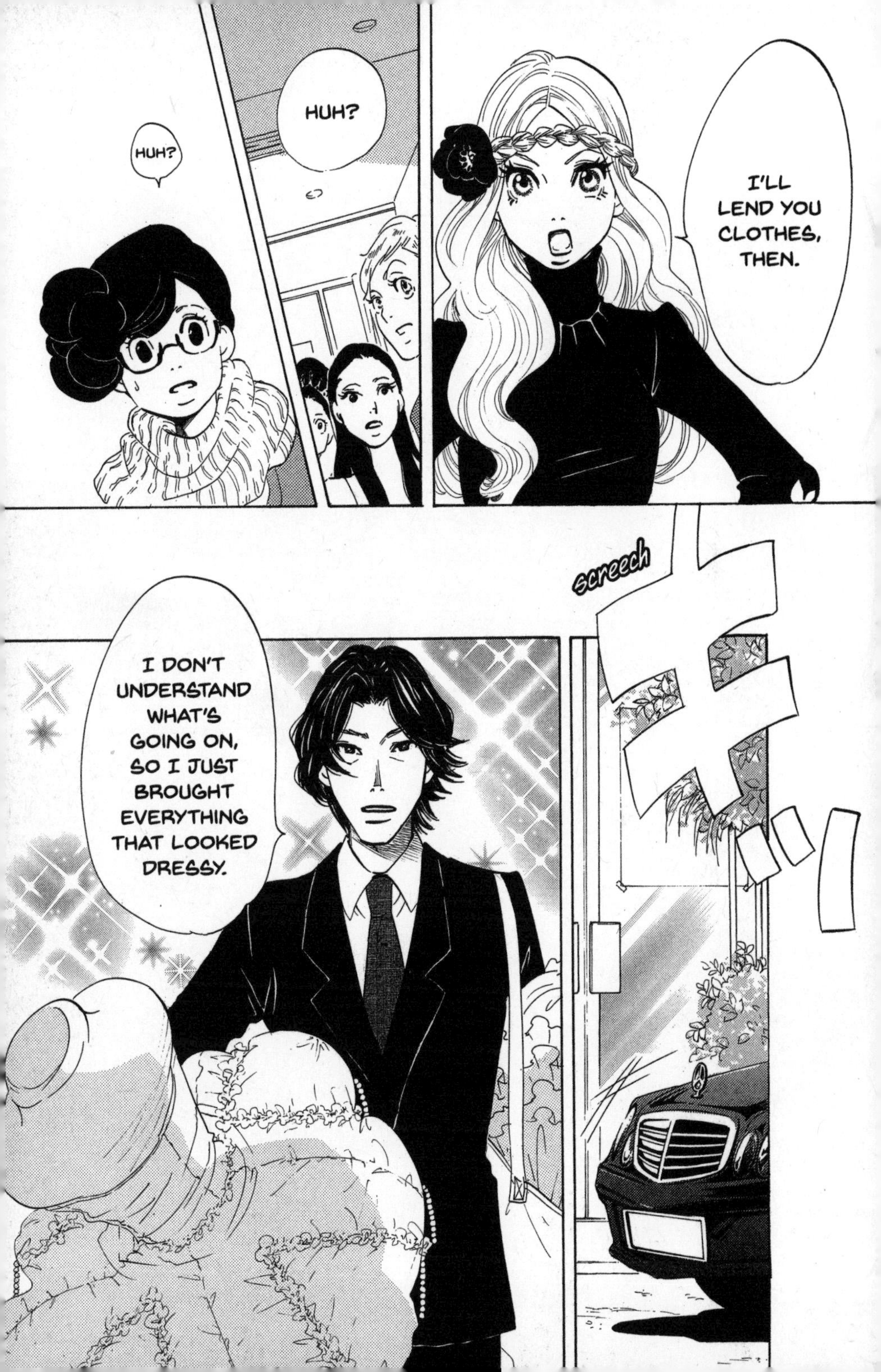
I'LL LEND YOU CLOTHES, THEN.
HUH?
HUH?
screech
I DON'T UNDERSTAND WHAT'S GOING ON, SO I JUST BROUGHT EVERYTHING THAT LOOKED DRESSY.

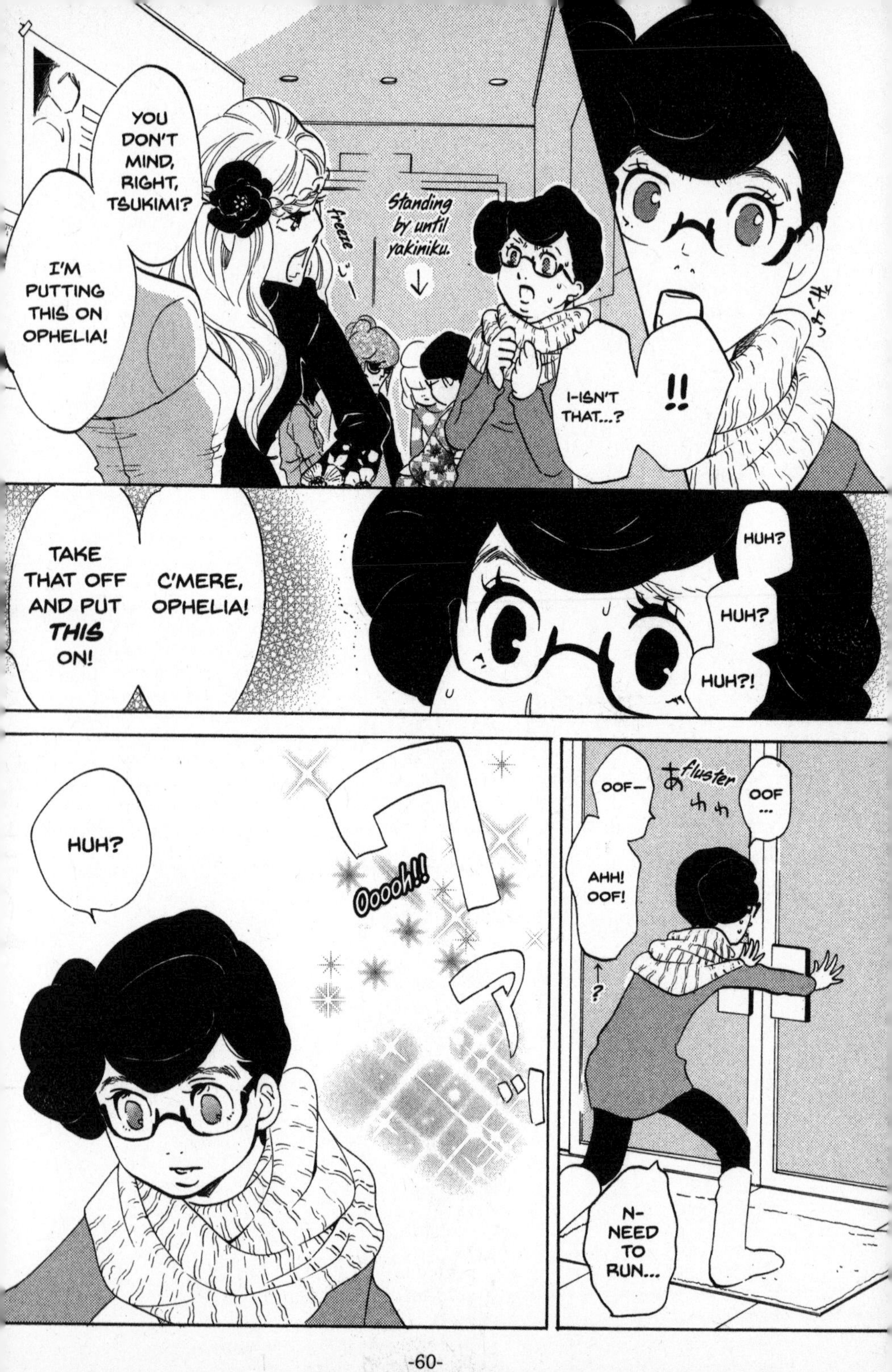
!!
I-ISN'T THAT...?
Standing by until yakiniku.
freeze
YOU DON'T MIND, RIGHT, TSUKIMI?
I'M PUTTING THIS ON OPHELIA!
HUH?
HUH?
HUH?!
C'MERE, OPHELIA!
TAKE THAT OFF AND PUT THIS ON!
OOF ...
fluster
OOF—
AHH! OOF!
?
N-NEED TO RUN...
Ooooh!!
HUH?

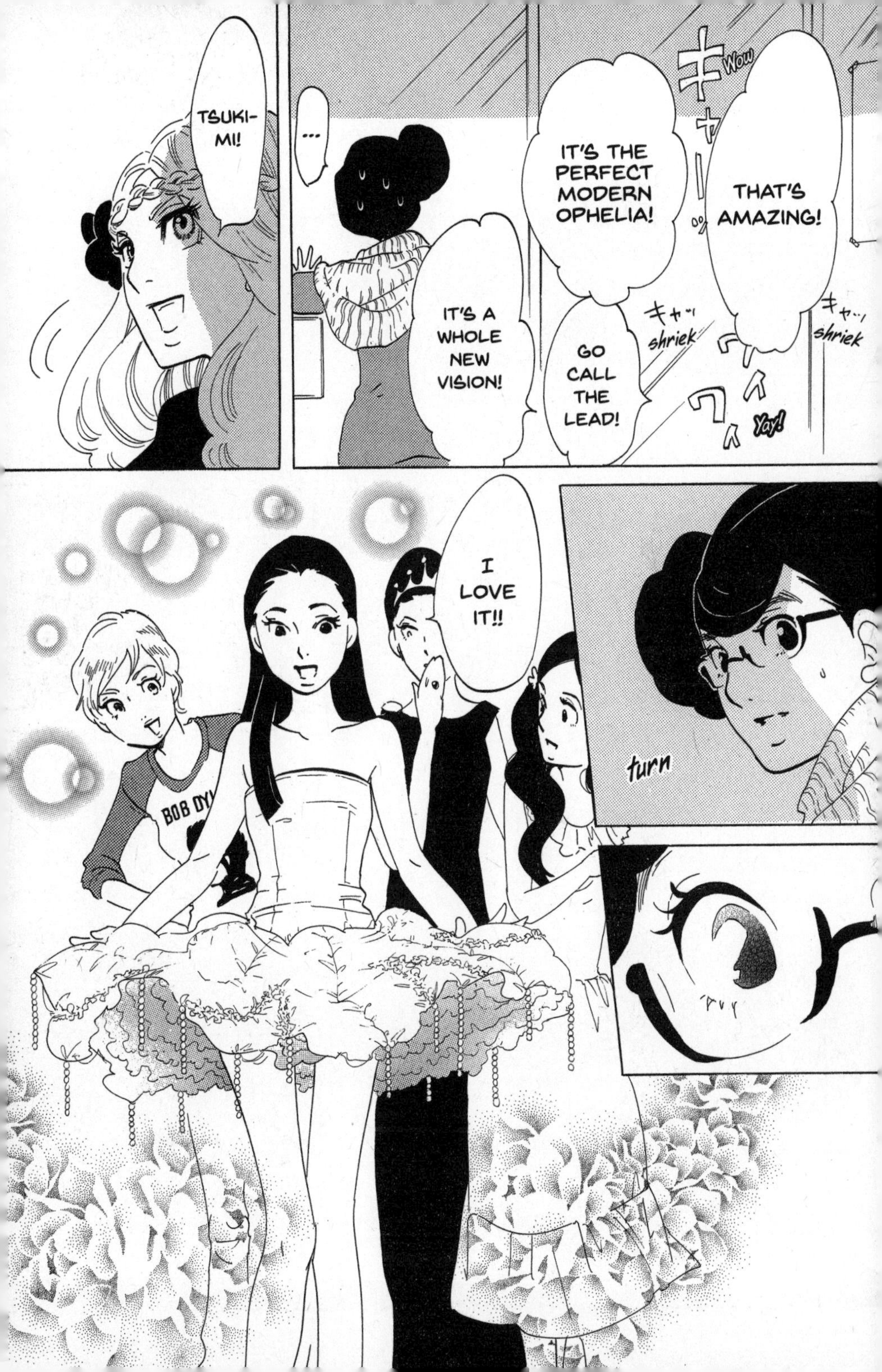
キャー Wow
THAT'S AMAZING!
キャッ shriek
IT'S THE PERFECT MODERN OPHELIA!
ワァイワァイ Yay!
GO CALL THE LEAD!
キャッ shriek
IT'S A WHOLE NEW VISION!
...
TSUKI-MI!
turn
I LOVE IT!!
BOB DY

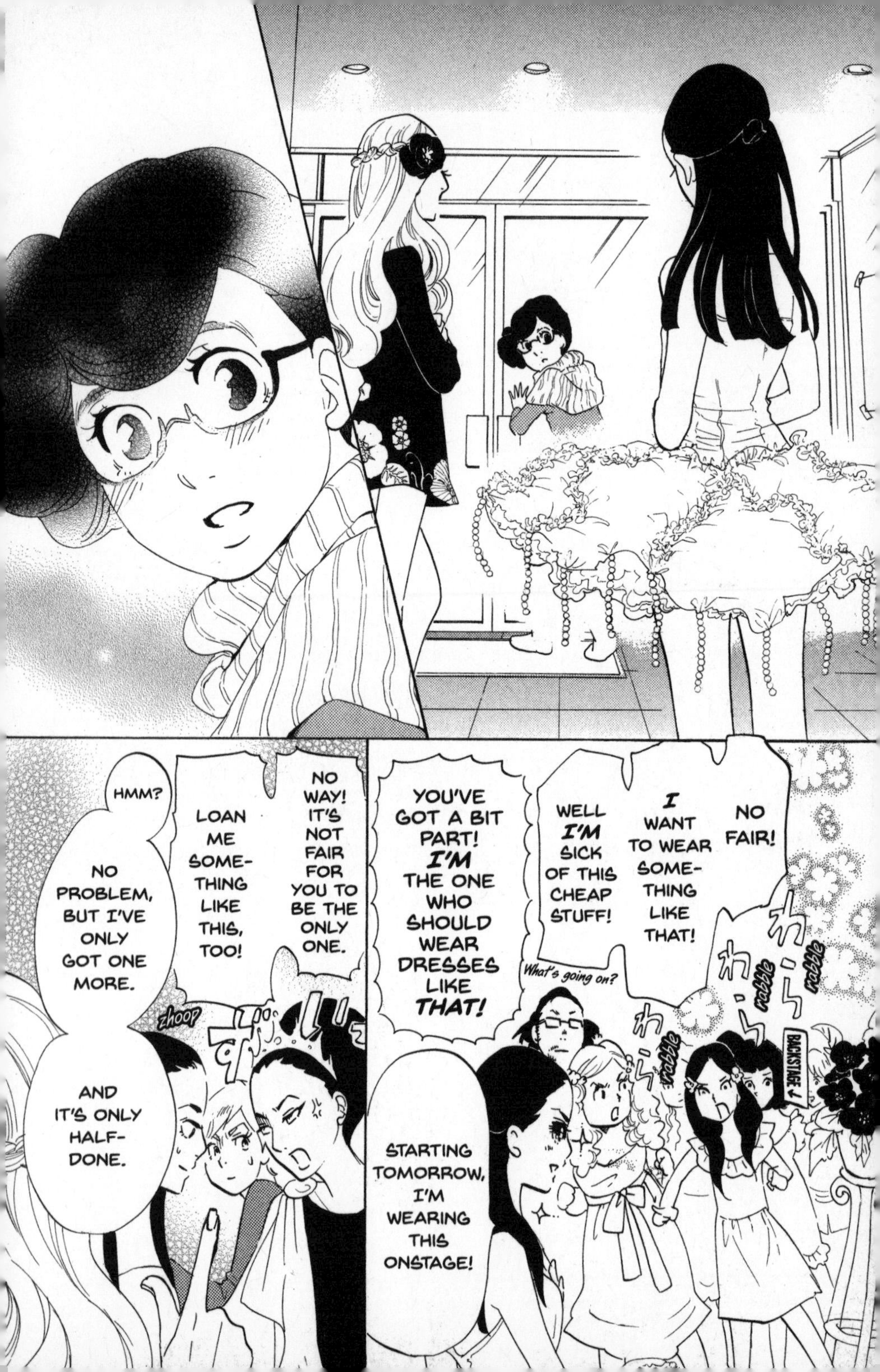
NO FAIR!
I WANT TO WEAR SOMETHING LIKE THAT!
rabble
rabble
WELL I'M SICK OF THIS CHEAP STUFF!
YOU'VE GOT A BIT PART! I'M THE ONE WHO SHOULD WEAR DRESSES LIKE THAT!
What's going on?
rabble
BACKSTAGE
STARTING TOMORROW, I'M WEARING THIS ONSTAGE!
NO WAY! IT'S NOT FAIR FOR YOU TO BE THE ONLY ONE.
LOAN ME SOMETHING LIKE THIS, TOO!
HMM?
NO PROBLEM, BUT I'VE ONLY GOT ONE MORE.
zhoop
AND IT'S ONLY HALF-DONE.

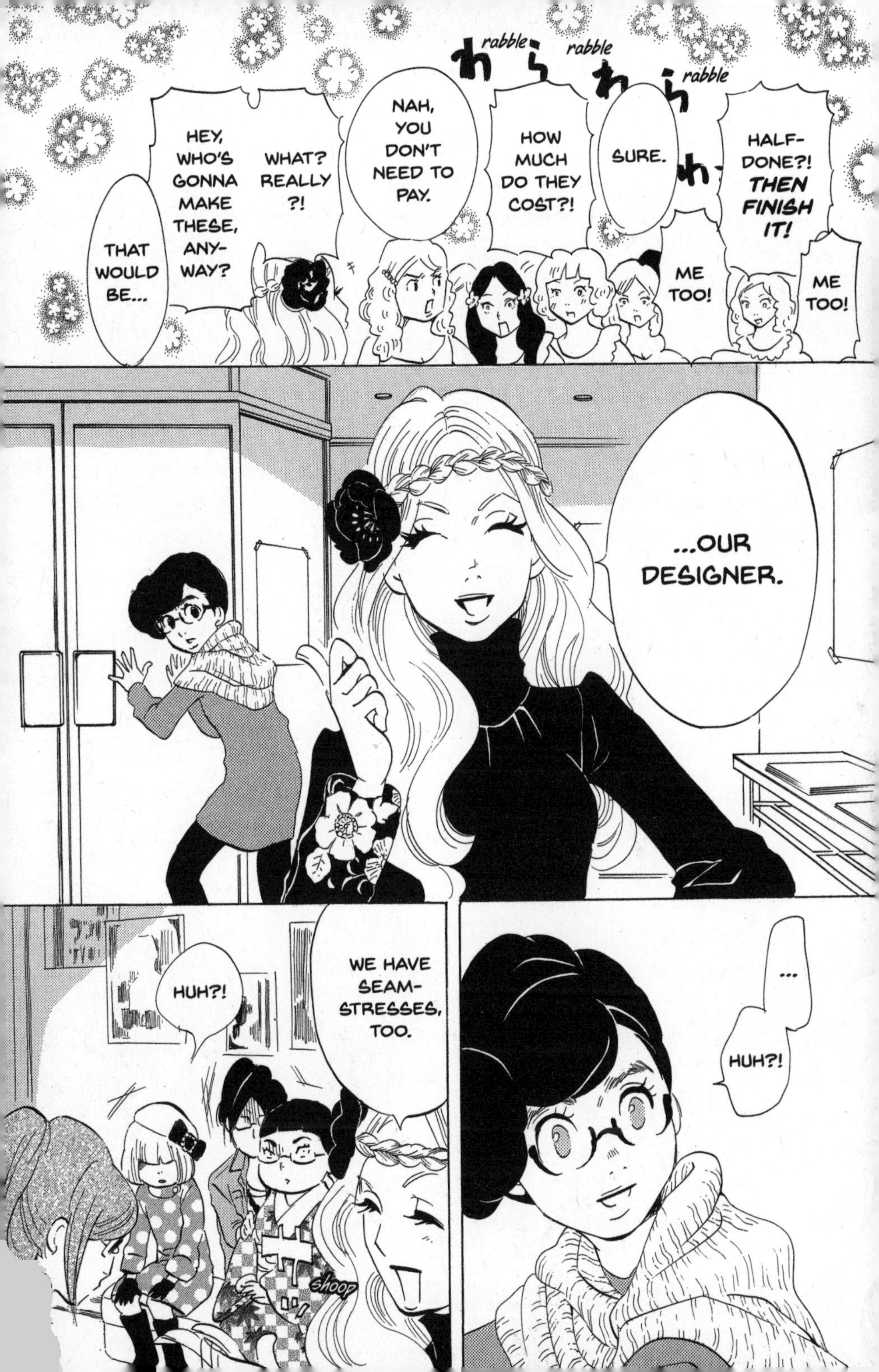
わらわら rabble rabble rabble
HALF-DONE?! THEN FINISH IT!
ME TOO!
SURE.
ME TOO!
HOW MUCH DO THEY COST?!
NAH, YOU DON'T NEED TO PAY.
WHAT? REALLY?!
HEY, WHO'S GONNA MAKE THESE, ANYWAY?
THAT WOULD BE...
...OUR DESIGNER.
...
HUH?!
WE HAVE SEAMSTRESSES, TOO.
HUH?!
shoop

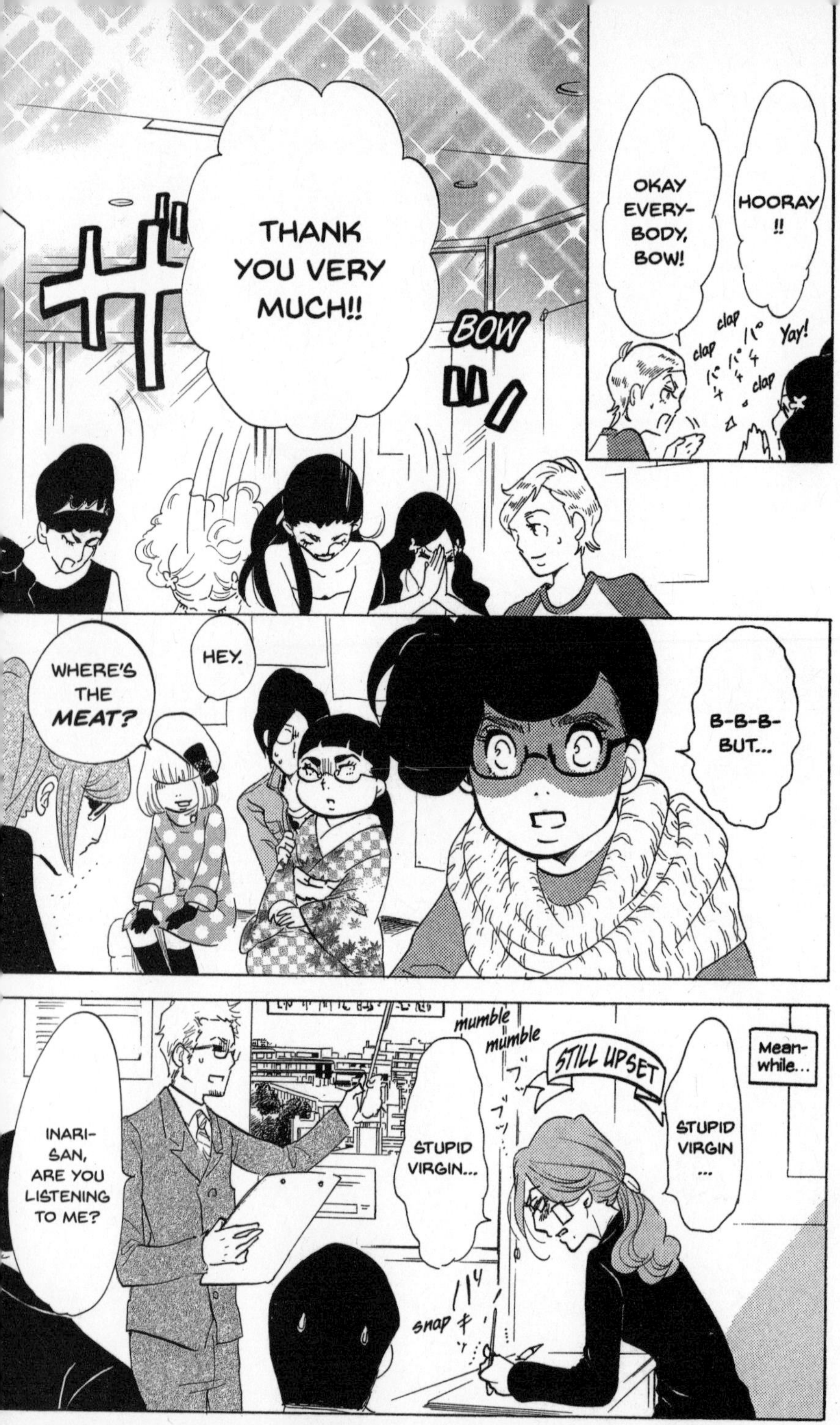
HOORAY!!
OKAY EVERY-BODY, BOW!
Yay!
clap clap
clap
THANK YOU VERY MUCH!!
BOW!!
B-B-B-BUT...
HEY.
WHERE'S THE MEAT?
Mean-while...
STUPID VIRGIN...
STILL UPSET
mumble mumble
STUPID VIRGIN...
INARI-SAN, ARE YOU LISTENING TO ME?
snap

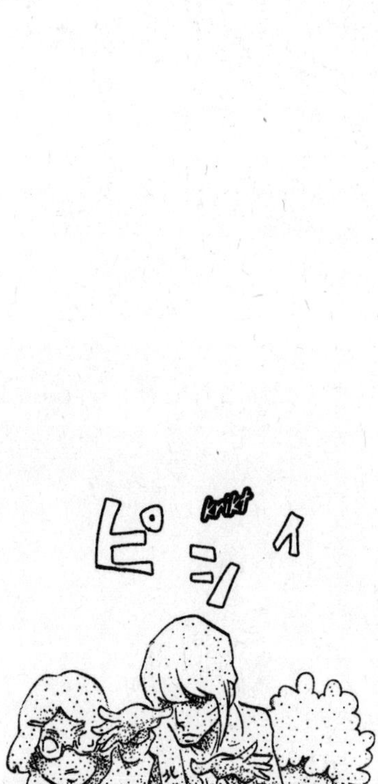
ピシィ
krikt

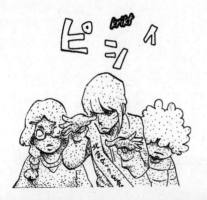

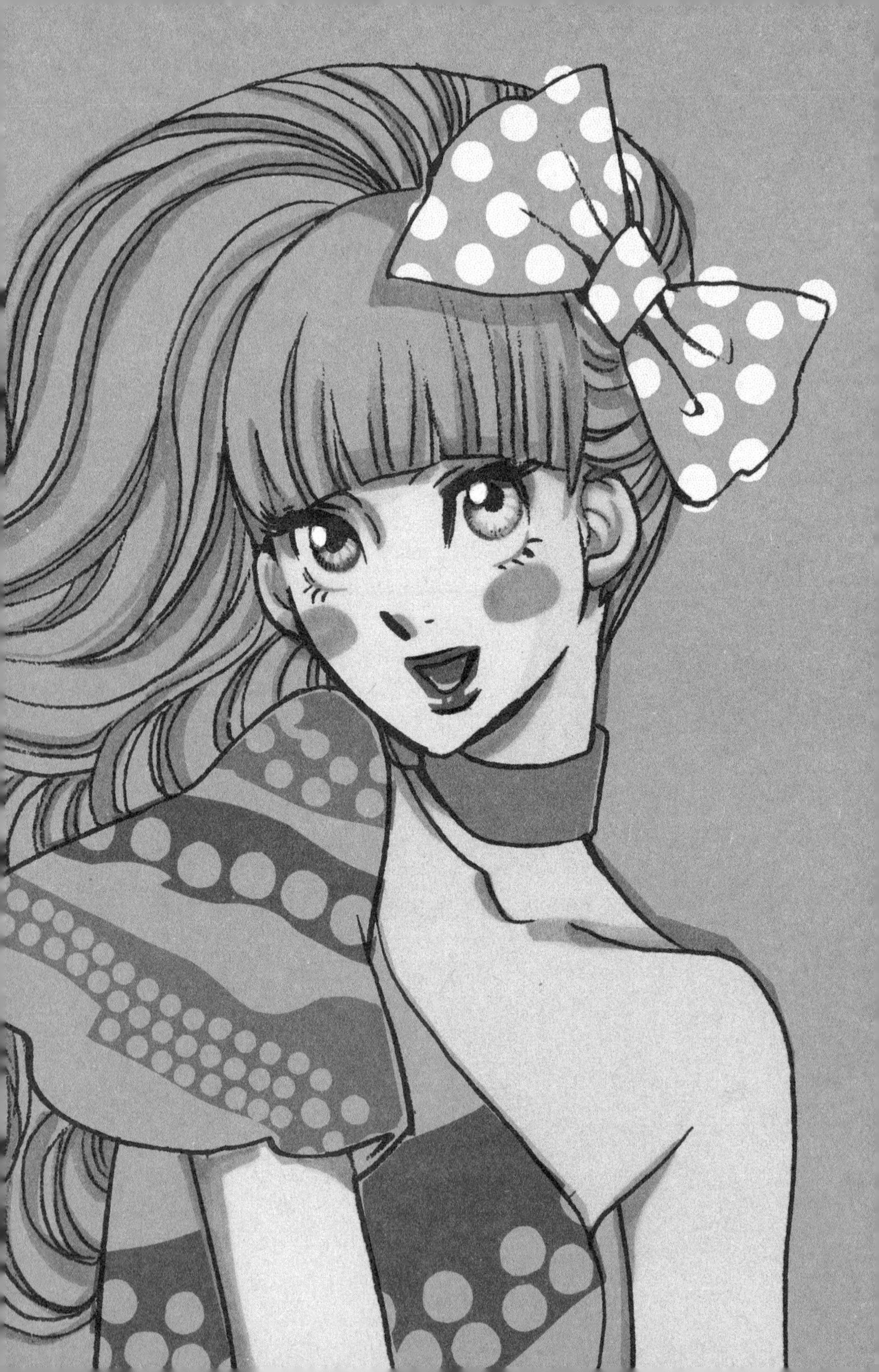

Episode 27
The Big Blue

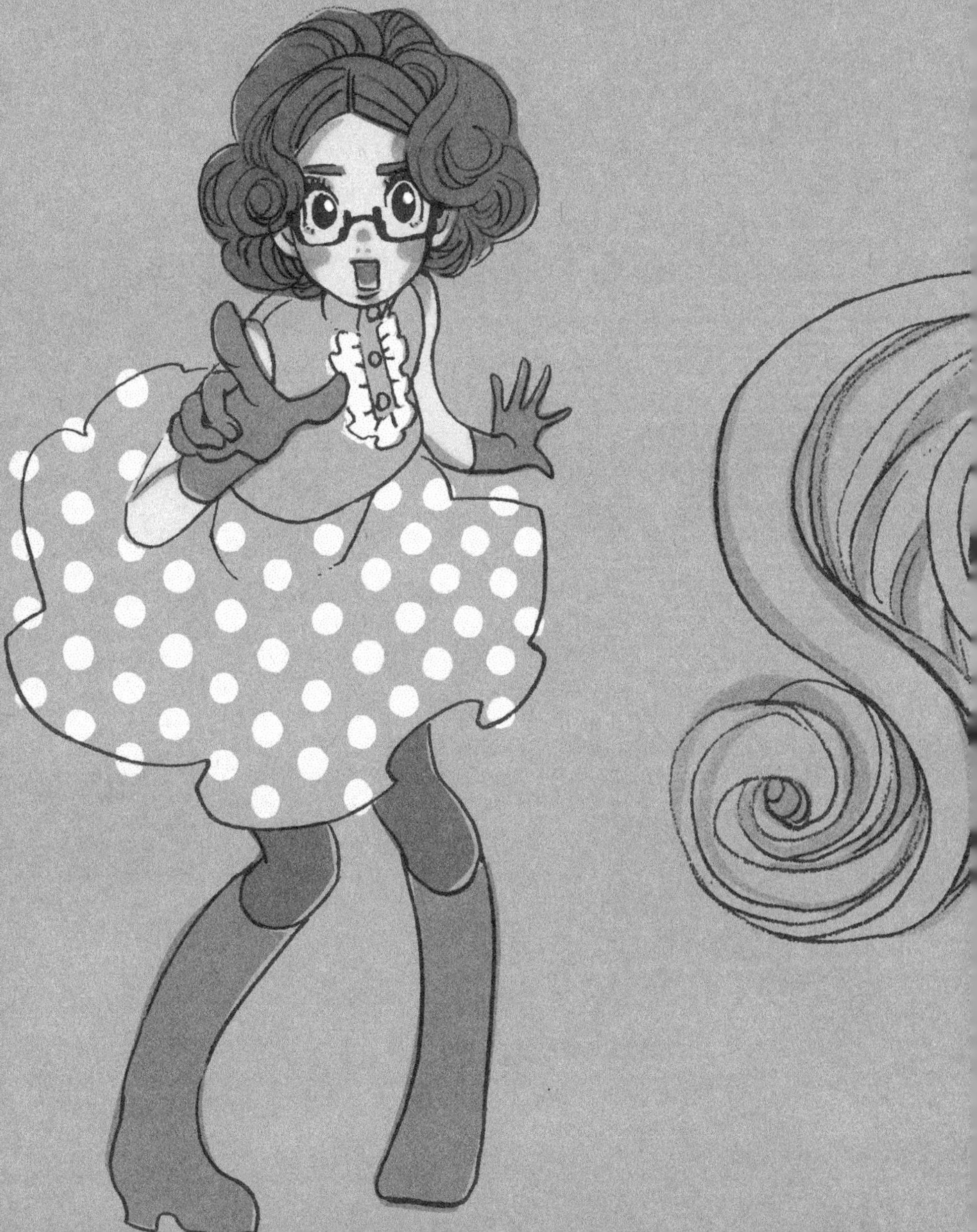

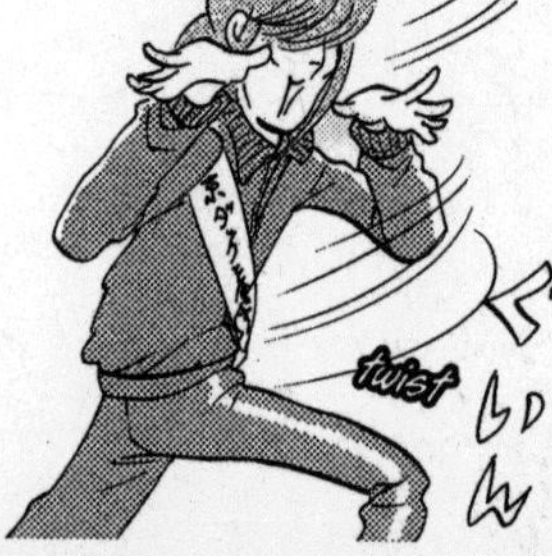
ぐいん
twist

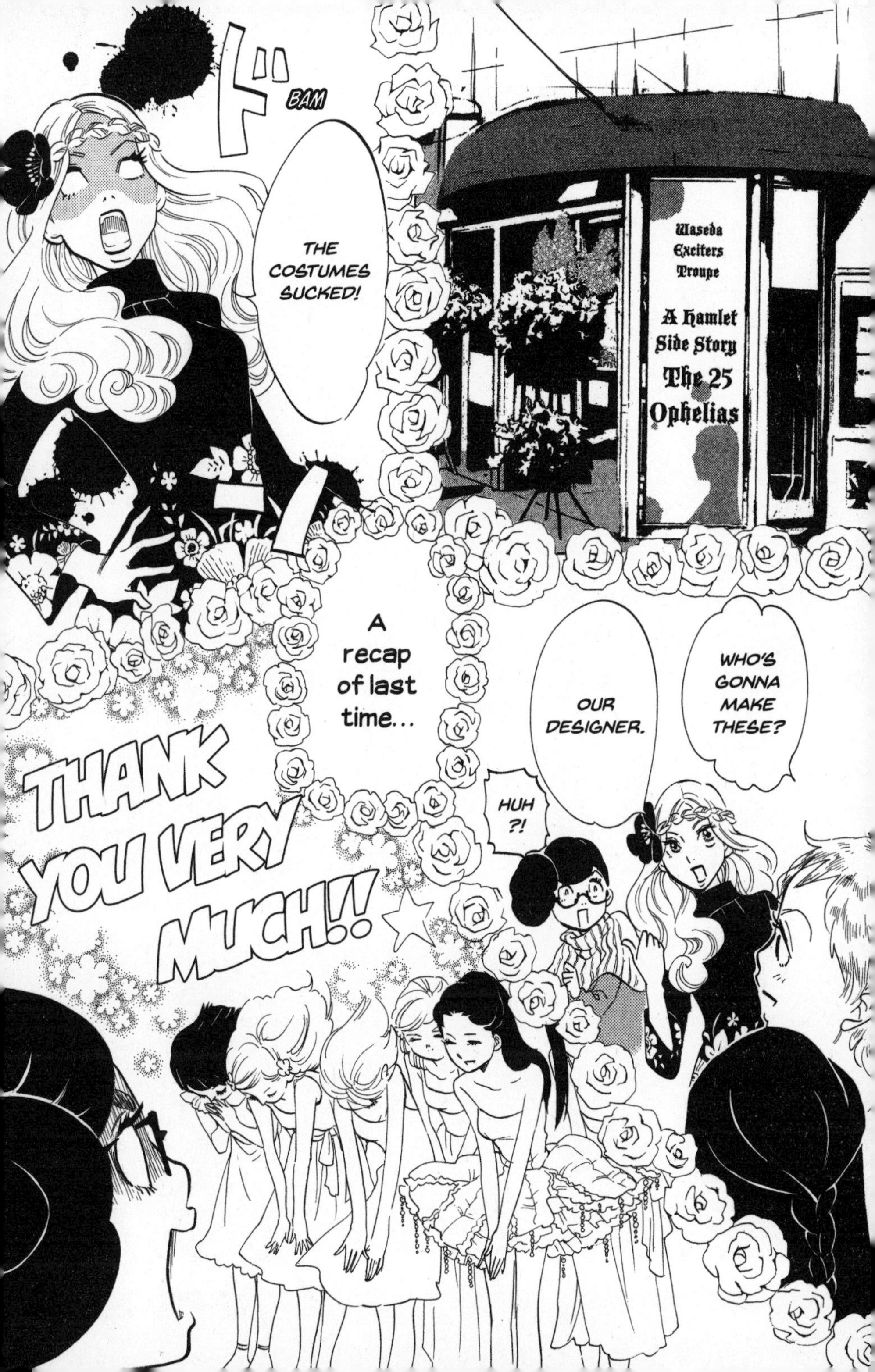
Waseda Exciters Troupe
A Hamlet Side Story The 25 Ophelias
BAM
THE COSTUMES SUCKED!
A recap of last time...
WHO'S GONNA MAKE THESE?
OUR DESIGNER.
HUH?!
THANK YOU VERY MUCH!!

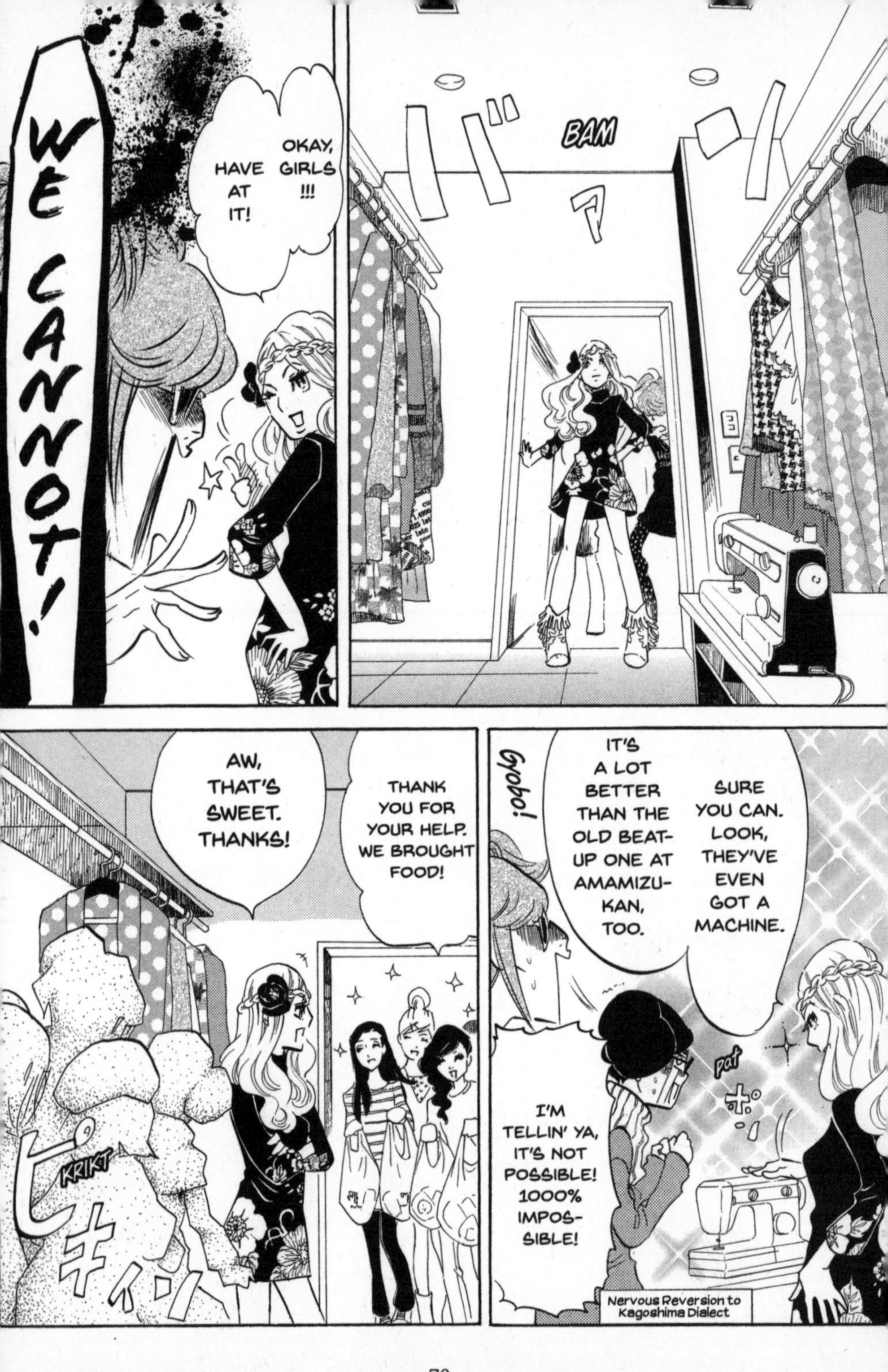
BAM
OKAY, GIRLS!!! HAVE AT IT!
WE CANNOT!
SURE YOU CAN. LOOK, THEY'VE EVEN GOT A MACHINE.
IT'S A LOT BETTER THAN THE OLD BEAT-UP ONE AT AMAMIZU-KAN, TOO.
Gyobo!
pat
I'M TELLIN' YA, IT'S NOT POSSIBLE! 1000% IMPOS-SIBLE!
Nervous Reversion to Kagoshima Dialect
THANK YOU FOR YOUR HELP. WE BROUGHT FOOD!
AW, THAT'S SWEET. THANKS!
KRIKT

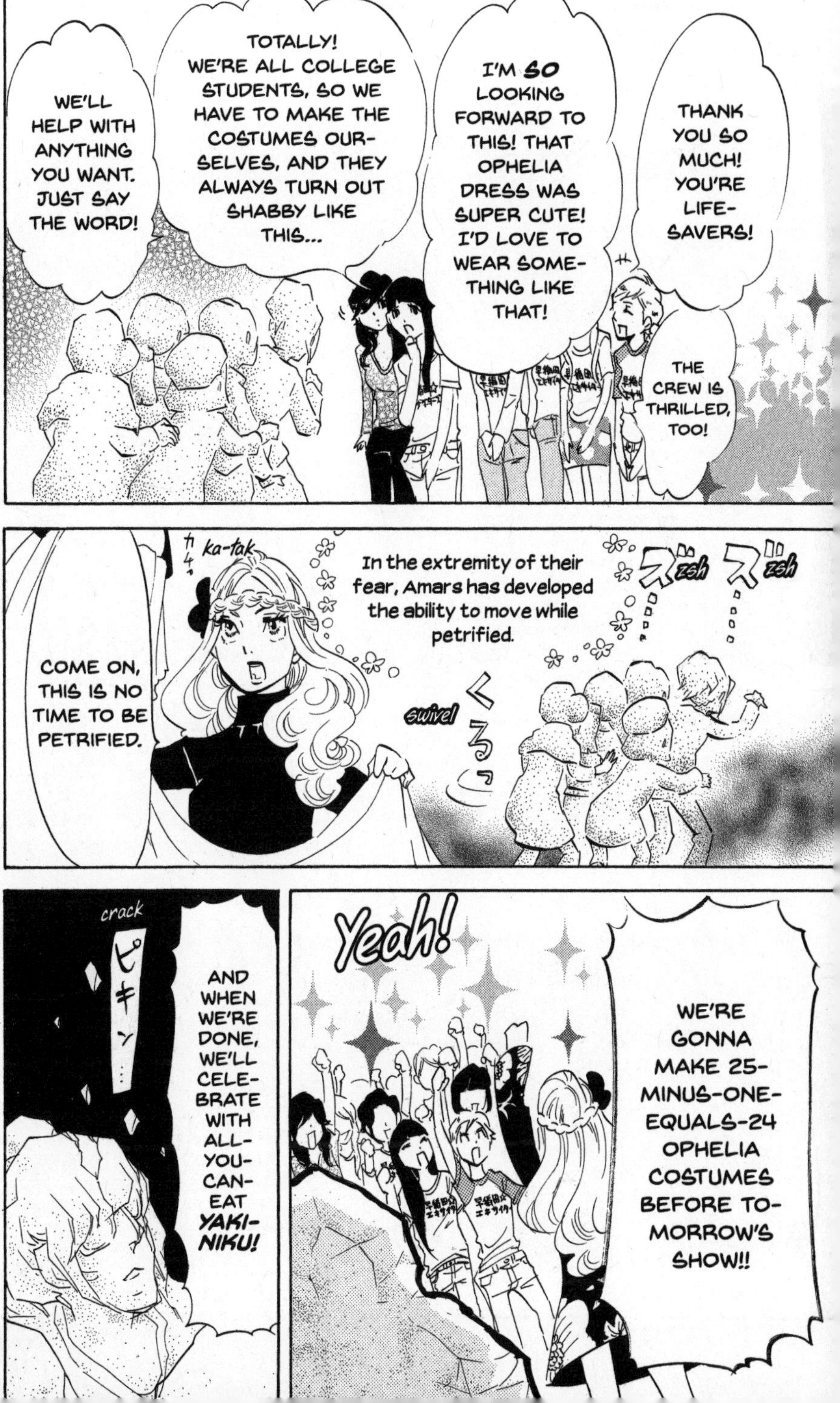
THANK YOU SO MUCH! YOU'RE LIFE-SAVERS!
THE CREW IS THRILLED, TOO!
I'M **SO** LOOKING FORWARD TO THIS! THAT OPHELIA DRESS WAS SUPER CUTE! I'D LOVE TO WEAR SOMETHING LIKE THAT!
TOTALLY! WE'RE ALL COLLEGE STUDENTS, SO WE HAVE TO MAKE THE COSTUMES OURSELVES, AND THEY ALWAYS TURN OUT SHABBY LIKE THIS...
WE'LL HELP WITH ANYTHING YOU WANT. JUST SAY THE WORD!
zsh
zsh
In the extremity of their fear, Amars has developed the ability to move while petrified.
ka-tak
swivel
COME ON, THIS IS NO TIME TO BE PETRIFIED.
WE'RE GONNA MAKE 25-MINUS-ONE-EQUALS-24 OPHELIA COSTUMES BEFORE TOMORROW'S SHOW!!
Yeah!
AND WHEN WE'RE DONE, WE'LL CELEBRATE WITH ALL-YOU-CAN-EAT ***YAKINIKU!***
crack

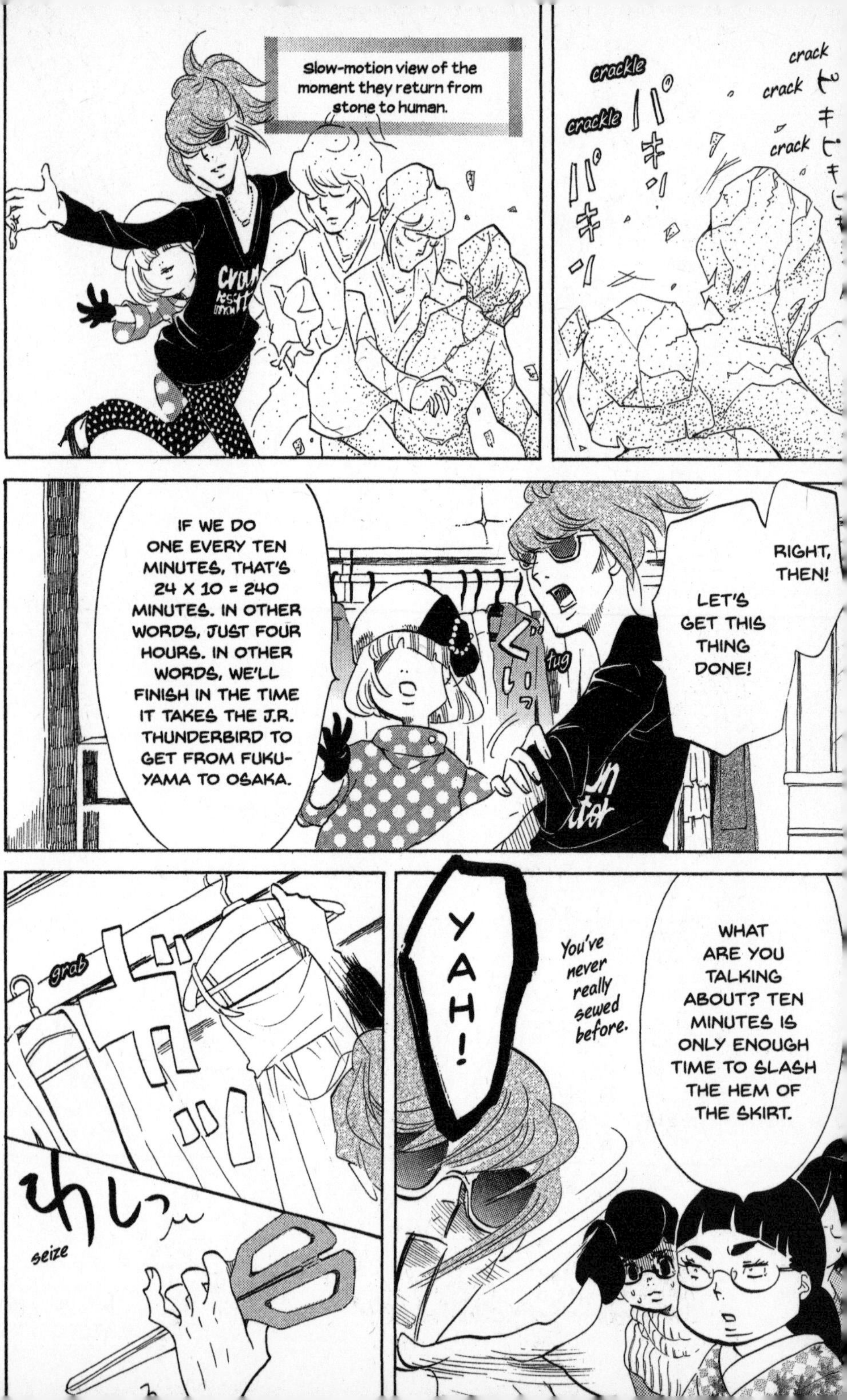
crackle
crackle
crack
crack
crack
Slow-motion view of the moment they return from stone to human.
RIGHT, THEN!
LET'S GET THIS THING DONE!
tug
IF WE DO ONE EVERY TEN MINUTES, THAT'S 24 X 10 = 240 MINUTES. IN OTHER WORDS, JUST FOUR HOURS. IN OTHER WORDS, WE'LL FINISH IN THE TIME IT TAKES THE J.R. THUNDERBIRD TO GET FROM FUKUYAMA TO OSAKA.
WHAT ARE YOU TALKING ABOUT? TEN MINUTES IS ONLY ENOUGH TIME TO SLASH THE HEM OF THE SKIRT.
You've never really sewed before.
YAH!
grab
seize

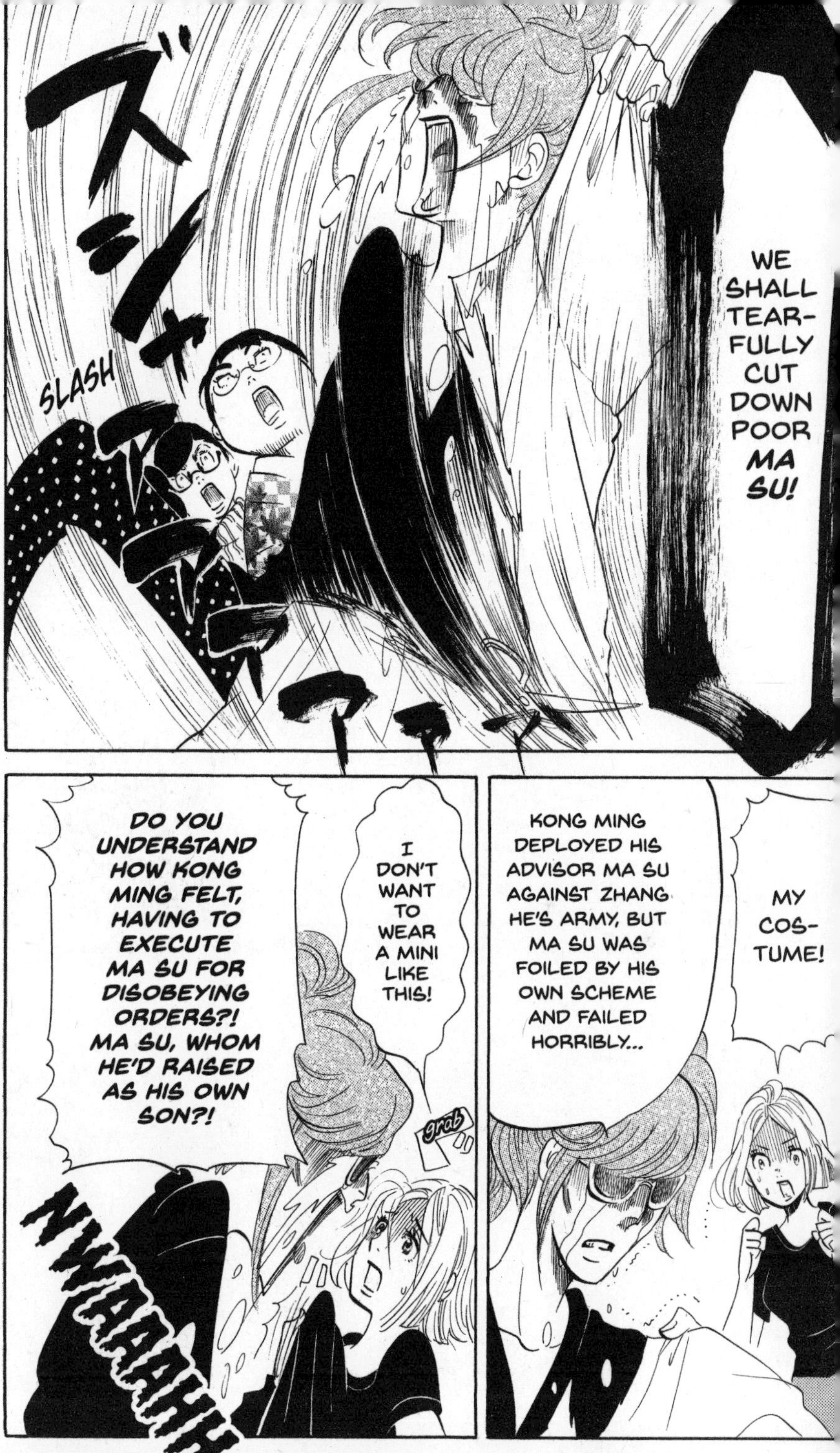
WE SHALL TEARFULLY CUT DOWN POOR MA SU!
ズシャ
SLASH
MY COSTUME!
KONG MING DEPLOYED HIS ADVISOR MA SU AGAINST ZHANG HE'S ARMY, BUT MA SU WAS FOILED BY HIS OWN SCHEME AND FAILED HORRIBLY...
I DON'T WANT TO WEAR A MINI LIKE THIS!
DO YOU UNDERSTAND HOW KONG MING FELT, HAVING TO EXECUTE MA SU FOR DISOBEYING ORDERS?! MA SU, WHOM HE'D RAISED AS HIS OWN SON?!
grab
NWAAAHH

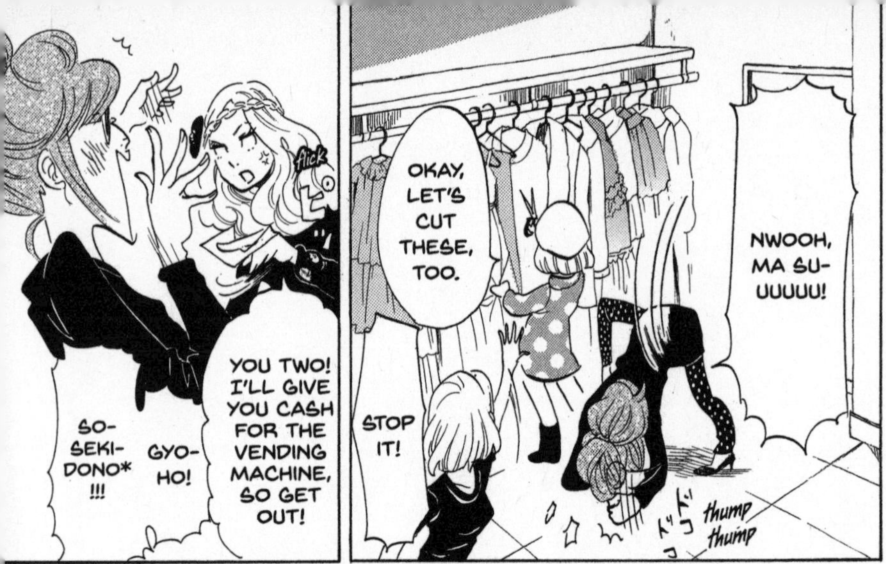
NWOOH, MA SU-UUUUU!
OKAY, LET'S CUT THESE, TOO.
STOP IT!
thump thump
YOU TWO! I'LL GIVE YOU CASH FOR THE VENDING MACHINE, SO GET OUT!
GYO-HO!
SO-SEKI-DONO* !!!
flick

Novelist Natsume Soseki's portrait was on the 1,000 Yen note from 1984 - 2004.

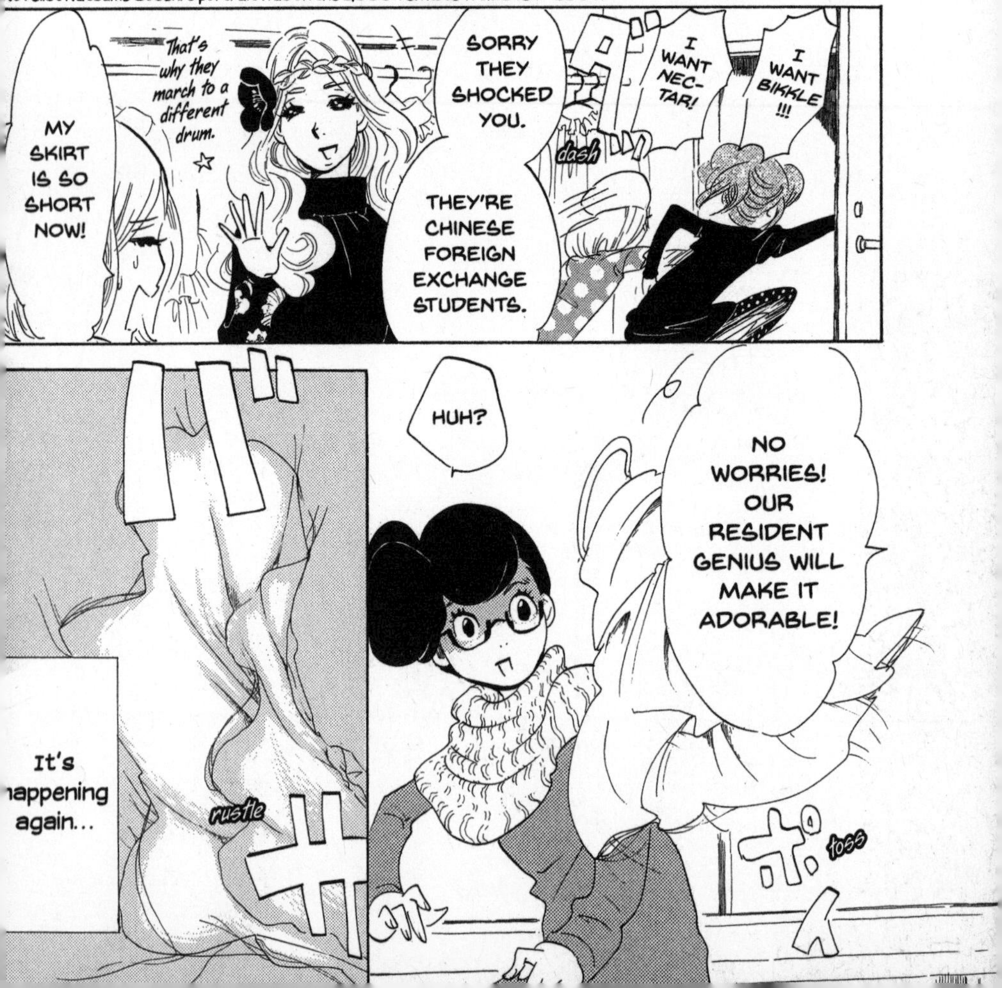
I WANT BIKKLE !!!
I WANT NEC-TAR!
dash
SORRY THEY SHOCKED YOU.
THEY'RE CHINESE FOREIGN EXCHANGE STUDENTS.
That's why they march to a different drum.
MY SKIRT IS SO SHORT NOW!
NO WORRIES! OUR RESIDENT GENIUS WILL MAKE IT ADORABLE!
HUH?
toss
It's happening again...
rustle

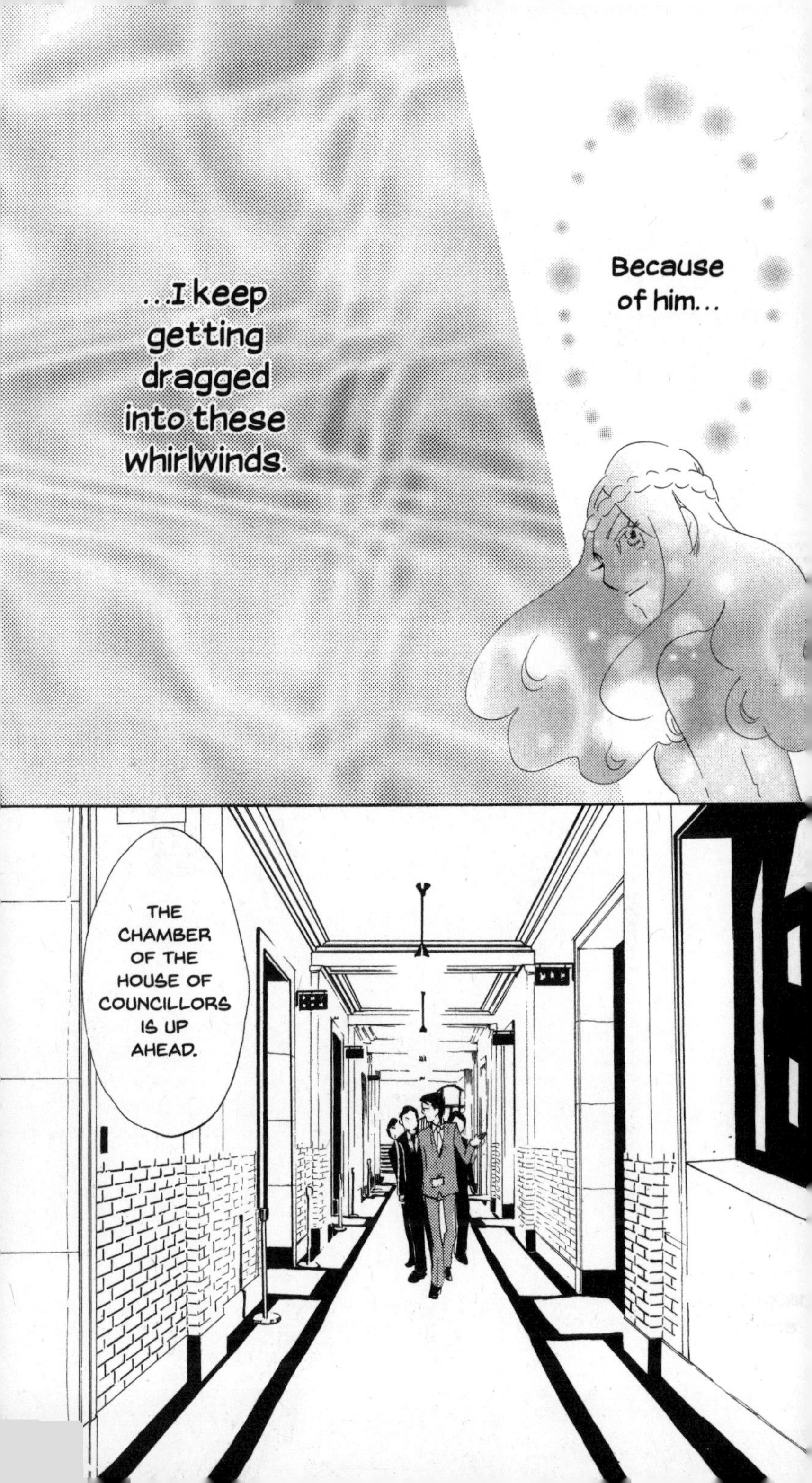
Because of him...
...I keep getting dragged into these whirlwinds.
THE CHAMBER OF THE HOUSE OF COUNCILLORS IS UP AHEAD.

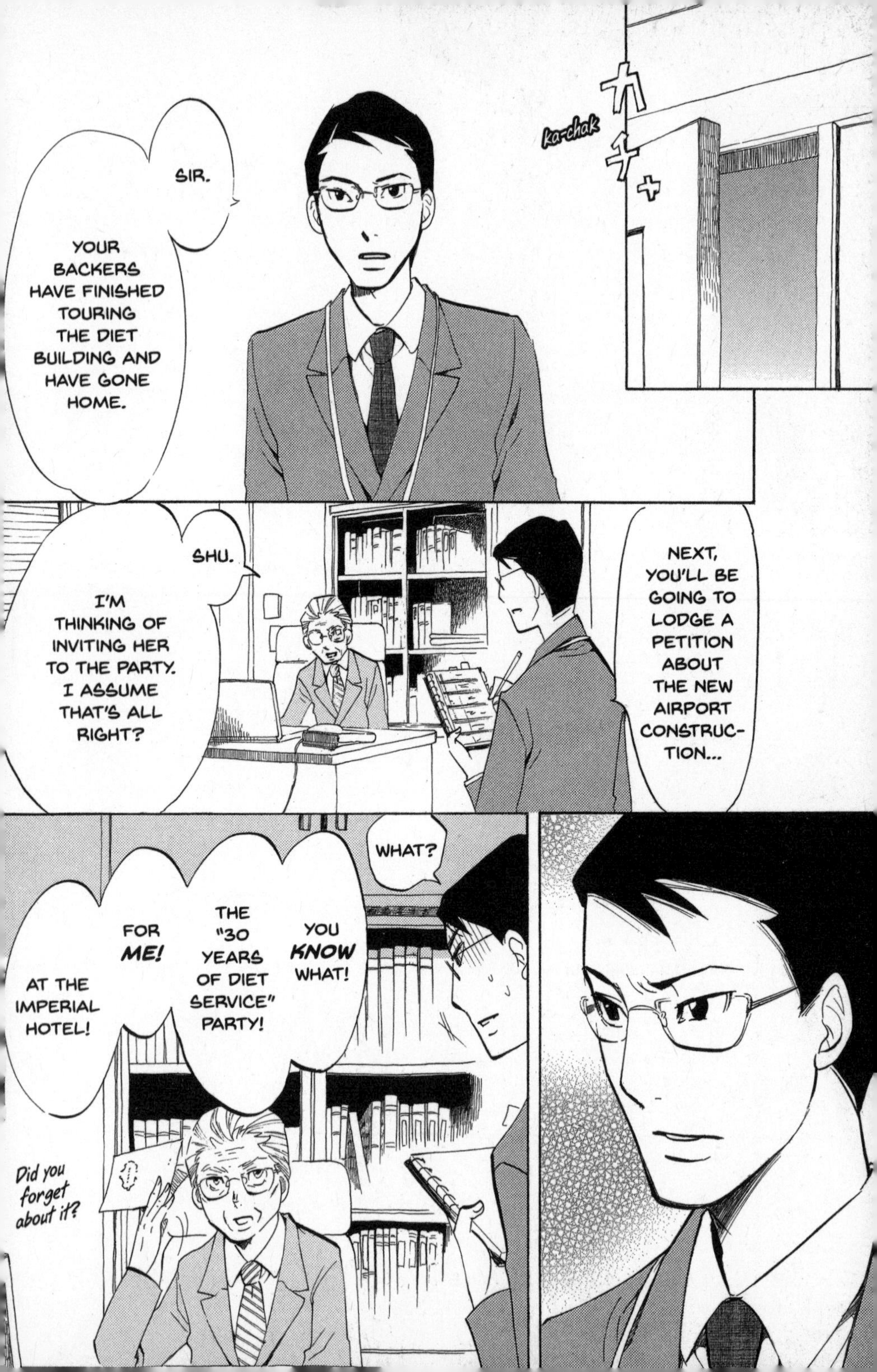
カチャ
ka-chak
SIR.
YOUR BACKERS HAVE FINISHED TOURING THE DIET BUILDING AND HAVE GONE HOME.
NEXT, YOU'LL BE GOING TO LODGE A PETITION ABOUT THE NEW AIRPORT CONSTRUC-TION...
SHU.
I'M THINKING OF INVITING HER TO THE PARTY. I ASSUME THAT'S ALL RIGHT?
WHAT?
YOU KNOW WHAT!
THE "30 YEARS OF DIET SERVICE" PARTY!
FOR ME!
AT THE IMPERIAL HOTEL!
Did you forget about it?

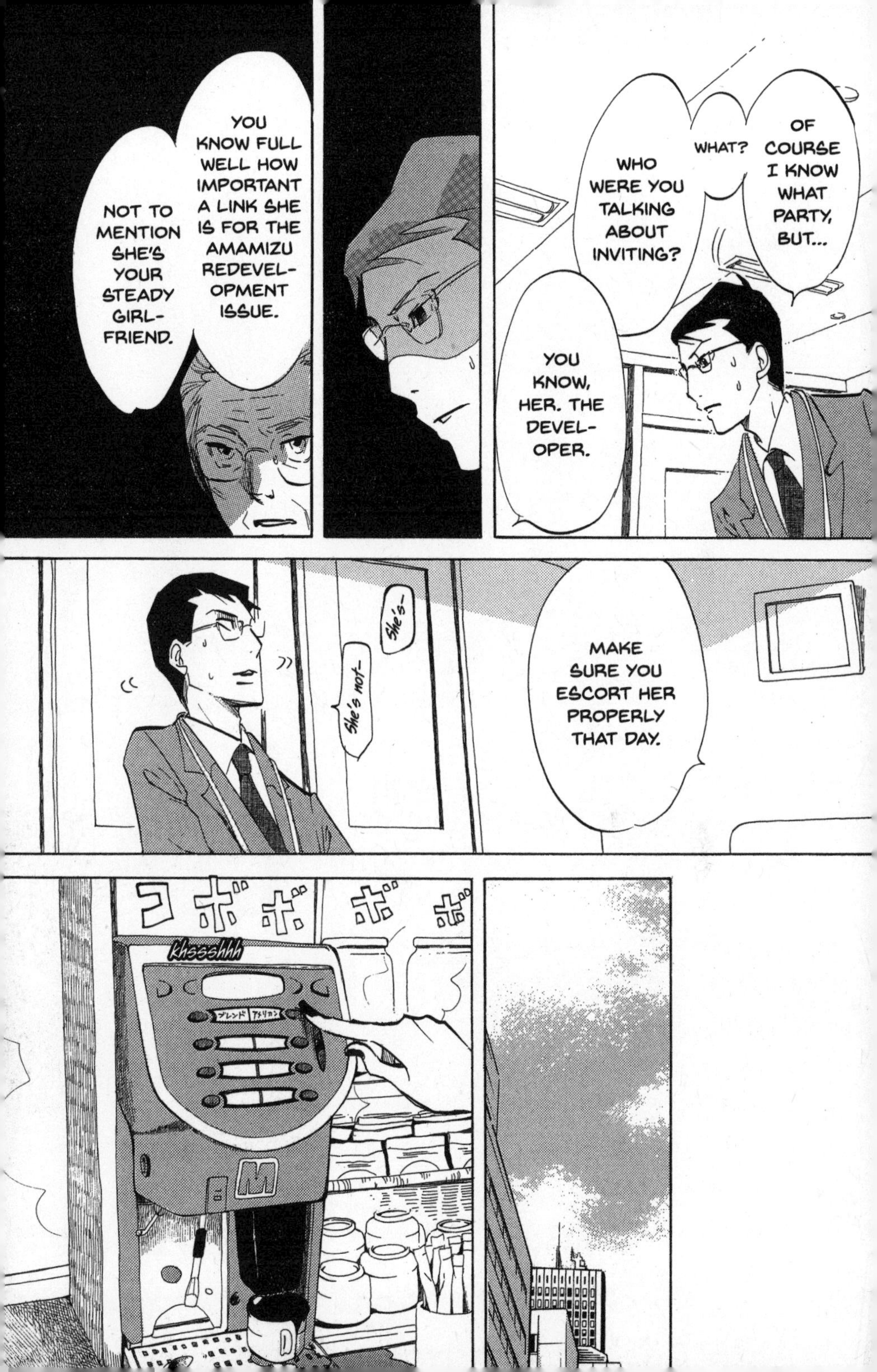
OF COURSE I KNOW WHAT PARTY, BUT...
WHAT?
WHO WERE YOU TALKING ABOUT INVITING?
YOU KNOW, HER. THE DEVEL-OPER.
YOU KNOW FULL WELL HOW IMPORTANT A LINK SHE IS FOR THE AMAMIZU REDEVEL-OPMENT ISSUE.
NOT TO MENTION SHE'S YOUR STEADY GIRL-FRIEND.
MAKE SURE YOU ESCORT HER PROPERLY THAT DAY.
She's-
She's not-
コポポポポ
khssshhh
ブレンド アメリカン

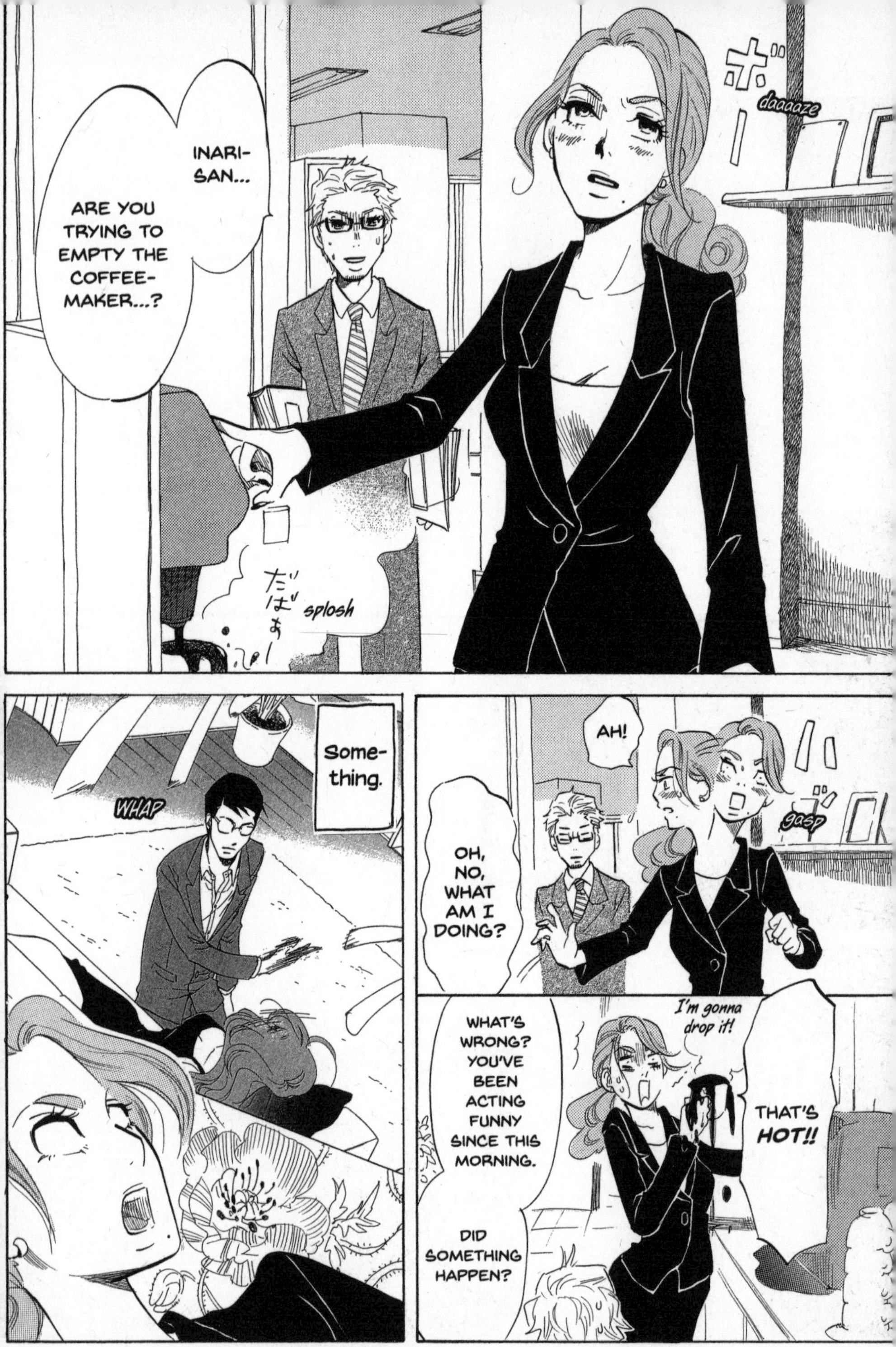
daaaaze
INARI-SAN...
ARE YOU TRYING TO EMPTY THE COFFEE-MAKER...?
splosh
AH!
gasp
OH, NO, WHAT AM I DOING?
THAT'S HOT!!
I'm gonna drop it!
WHAT'S WRONG? YOU'VE BEEN ACTING FUNNY SINCE THIS MORNING.
DID SOMETHING HAPPEN?
Some-thing.
WHAP

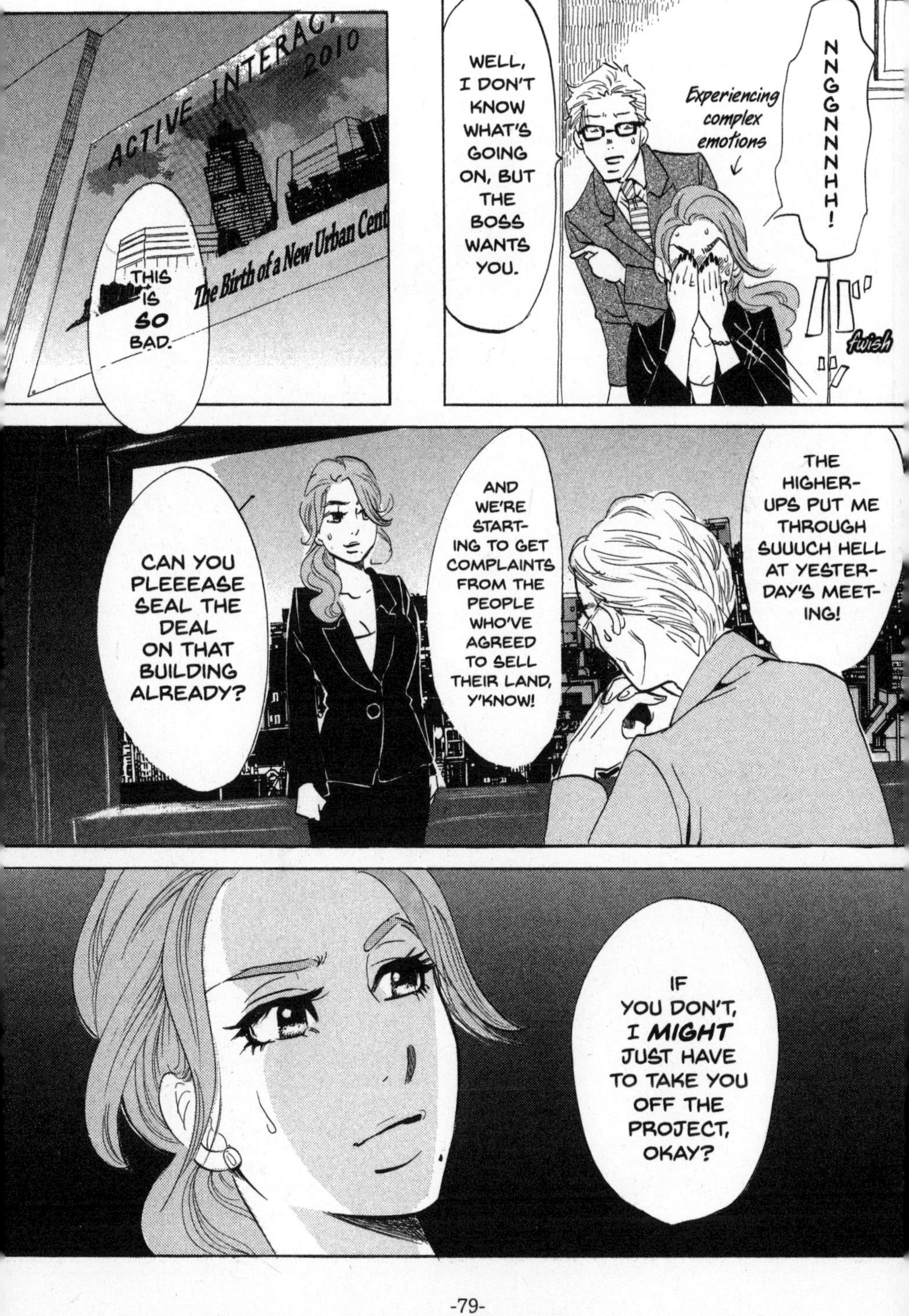
NNGGNNNHH!
Experiencing complex emotions
fwish
WELL, I DON'T KNOW WHAT'S GOING ON, BUT THE BOSS WANTS YOU.
ACTIVE INTERAC
2010
The Birth of a New Urban Cent
THIS IS SO BAD.
THE HIGHER-UPS PUT ME THROUGH SUUUCH HELL AT YESTER-DAY'S MEET-ING!
AND WE'RE START-ING TO GET COMPLAINTS FROM THE PEOPLE WHO'VE AGREED TO SELL THEIR LAND, Y'KNOW!
CAN YOU PLEEEASE SEAL THE DEAL ON THAT BUILDING ALREADY?
IF YOU DON'T, I MIGHT JUST HAVE TO TAKE YOU OFF THE PROJECT, OKAY?

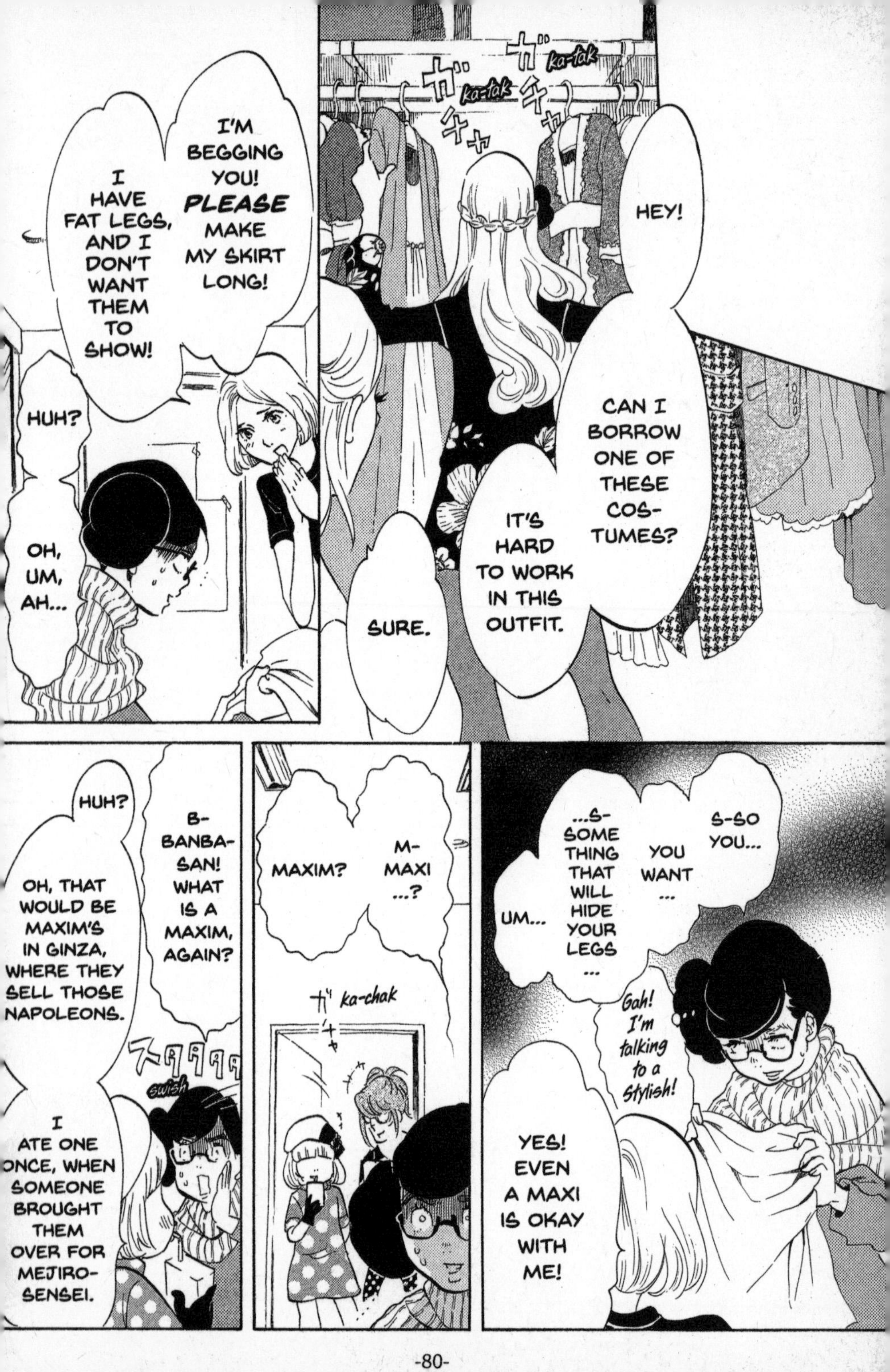
ka-tak
ka-tak
HEY!
CAN I BORROW ONE OF THESE COS-TUMES?
IT'S HARD TO WORK IN THIS OUTFIT.
SURE.
I'M BEGGING YOU! PLEASE MAKE MY SKIRT LONG!
I HAVE FAT LEGS, AND I DON'T WANT THEM TO SHOW!
HUH?
OH, UM, AH...
S-SO YOU...
YOU WANT ...
...S-SOME THING THAT WILL HIDE YOUR LEGS ...
UM...
Gah! I'm talking to a stylish!
YES! EVEN A MAXI IS OKAY WITH ME!
M-MAXI ...?
MAXIM?
ka-chak
B-BANBA-SAN! WHAT IS A MAXIM, AGAIN?
HUH?
OH, THAT WOULD BE MAXIM'S IN GINZA, WHERE THEY SELL THOSE NAPOLEONS.
swish
I ATE ONE ONCE, WHEN SOMEONE BROUGHT THEM OVER FOR MEJIRO-SENSEI.

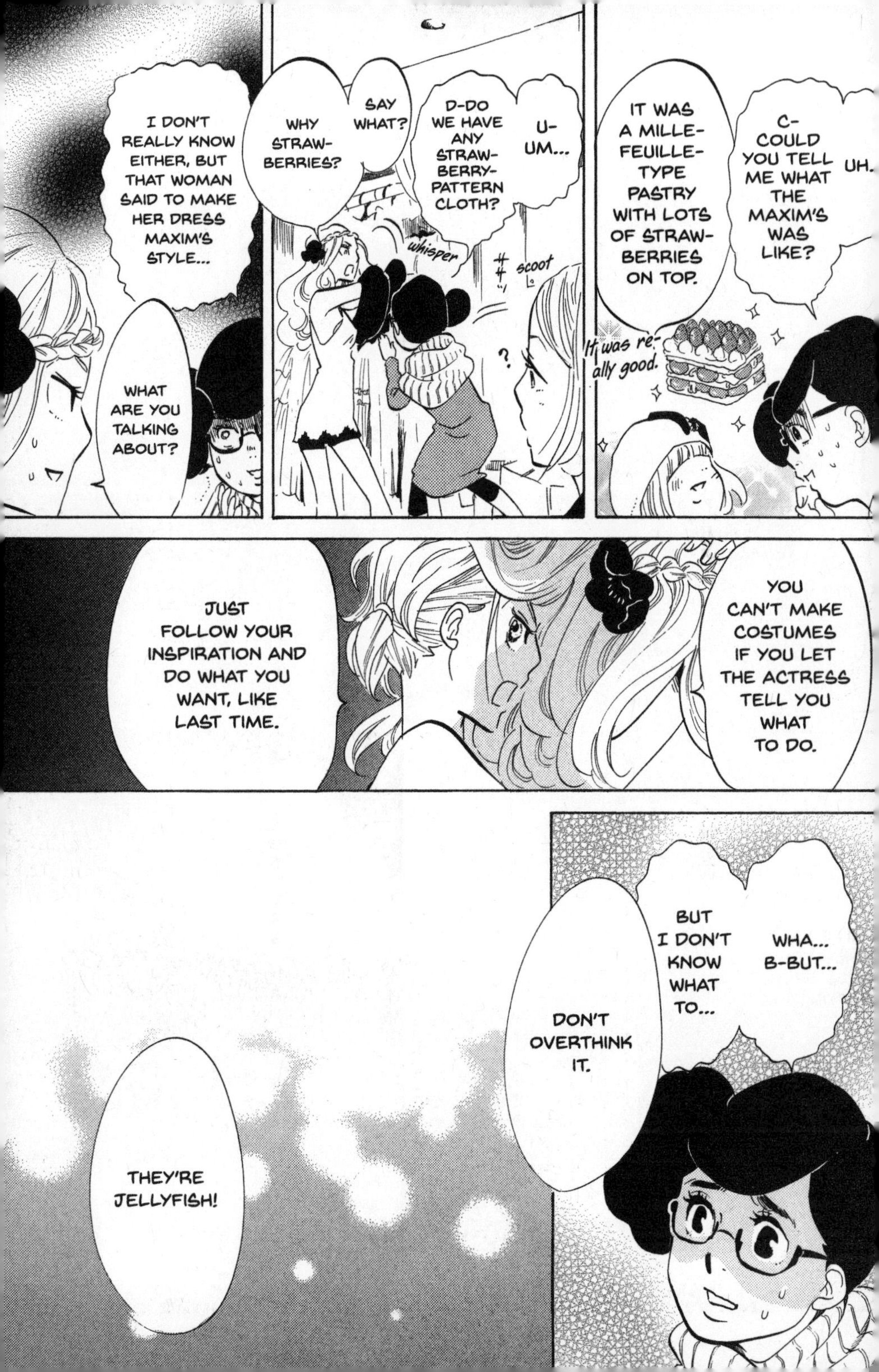
UH.
C-COULD YOU TELL ME WHAT THE MAXIM'S WAS LIKE?
IT WAS A MILLE-FEUILLE-TYPE PASTRY WITH LOTS OF STRAWBERRIES ON TOP.
It was really good.
U-UM...
D-DO WE HAVE ANY STRAWBERRY-PATTERN CLOTH?
SAY WHAT?
WHY STRAWBERRIES?
whisper
scoot
I DON'T REALLY KNOW EITHER, BUT THAT WOMAN SAID TO MAKE HER DRESS MAXIM'S STYLE...
WHAT ARE YOU TALKING ABOUT?
YOU CAN'T MAKE COSTUMES IF YOU LET THE ACTRESS TELL YOU WHAT TO DO.
JUST FOLLOW YOUR INSPIRATION AND DO WHAT YOU WANT, LIKE LAST TIME.
WHA... B-BUT...
BUT I DON'T KNOW WHAT TO...
DON'T OVERTHINK IT.
THEY'RE JELLYFISH!

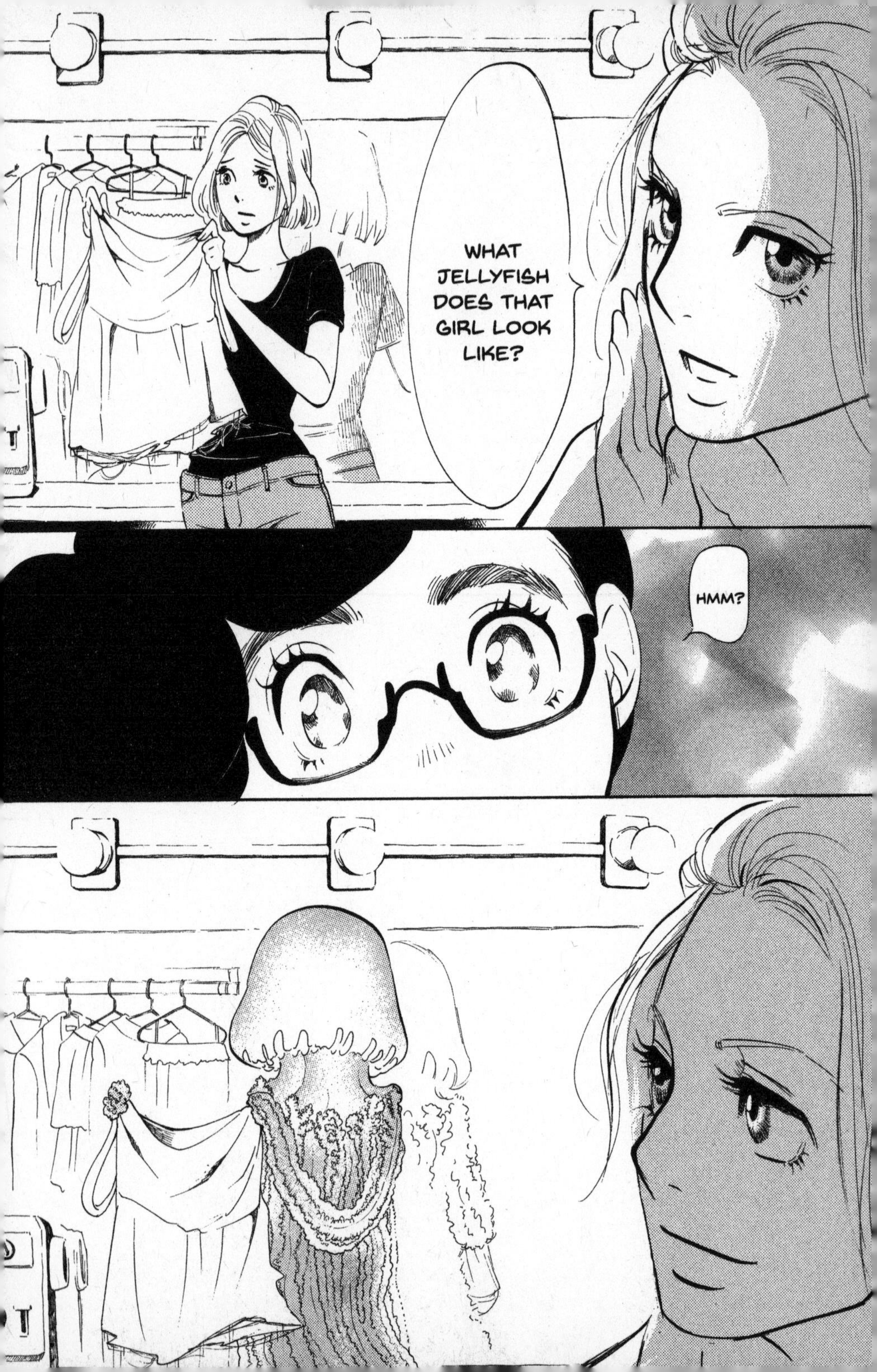
WHAT JELLYFISH DOES THAT GIRL LOOK LIKE?
HMM?

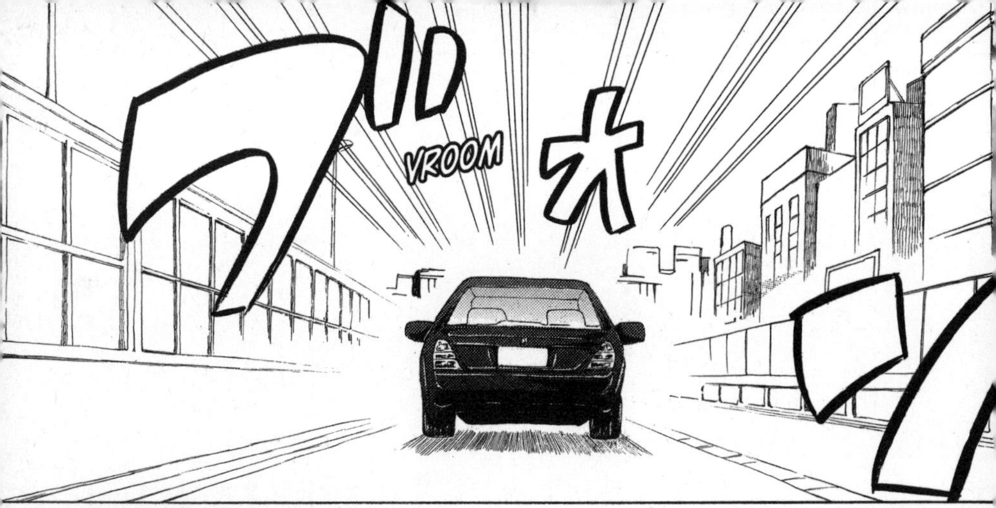
VROOM

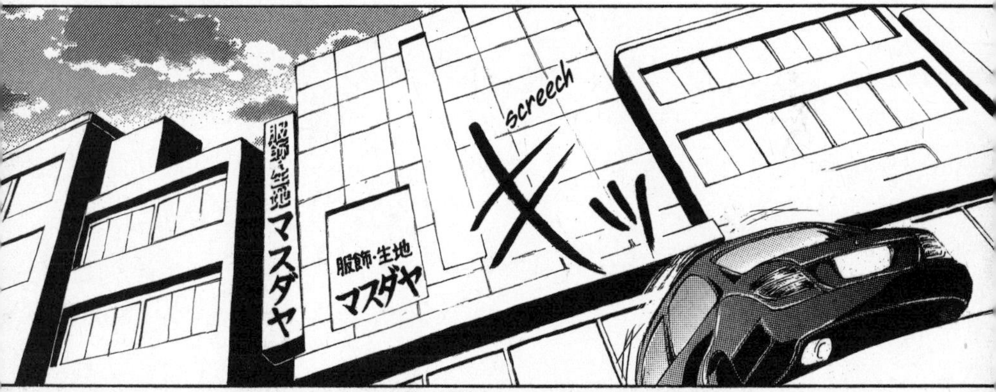
服飾・生地 マスダヤ
服飾・生地 マスダヤ
screech

Sign: Masudaya Fashion & Fabrics

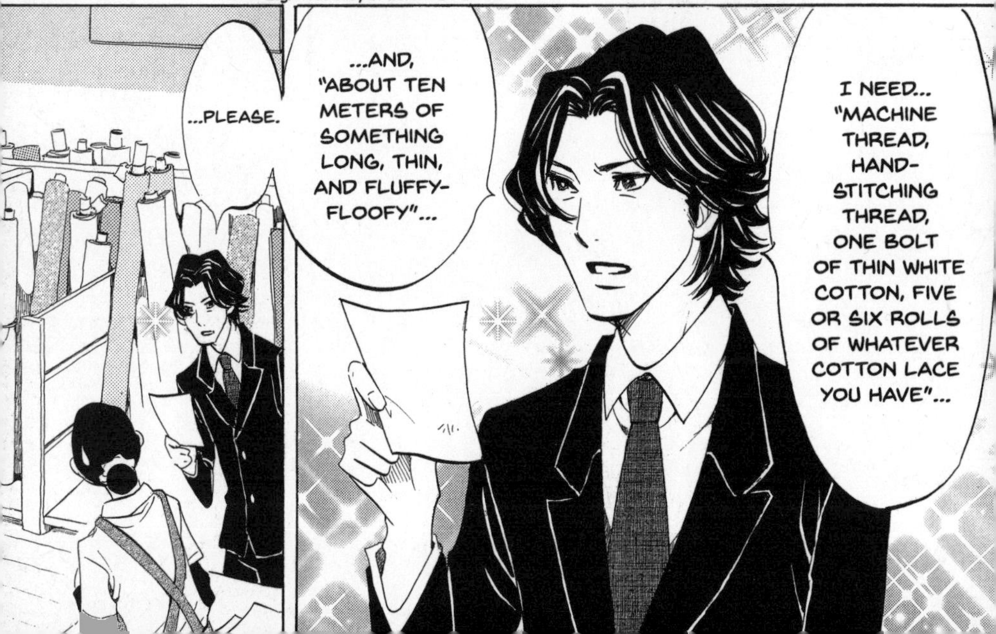
I NEED... "MACHINE THREAD, HAND-STITCHING THREAD, ONE BOLT OF THIN WHITE COTTON, FIVE OR SIX ROLLS OF WHATEVER COTTON LACE YOU HAVE"...
...AND, "ABOUT TEN METERS OF SOMETHING LONG, THIN, AND FLUFFY-FLOOFY"...
...PLEASE.

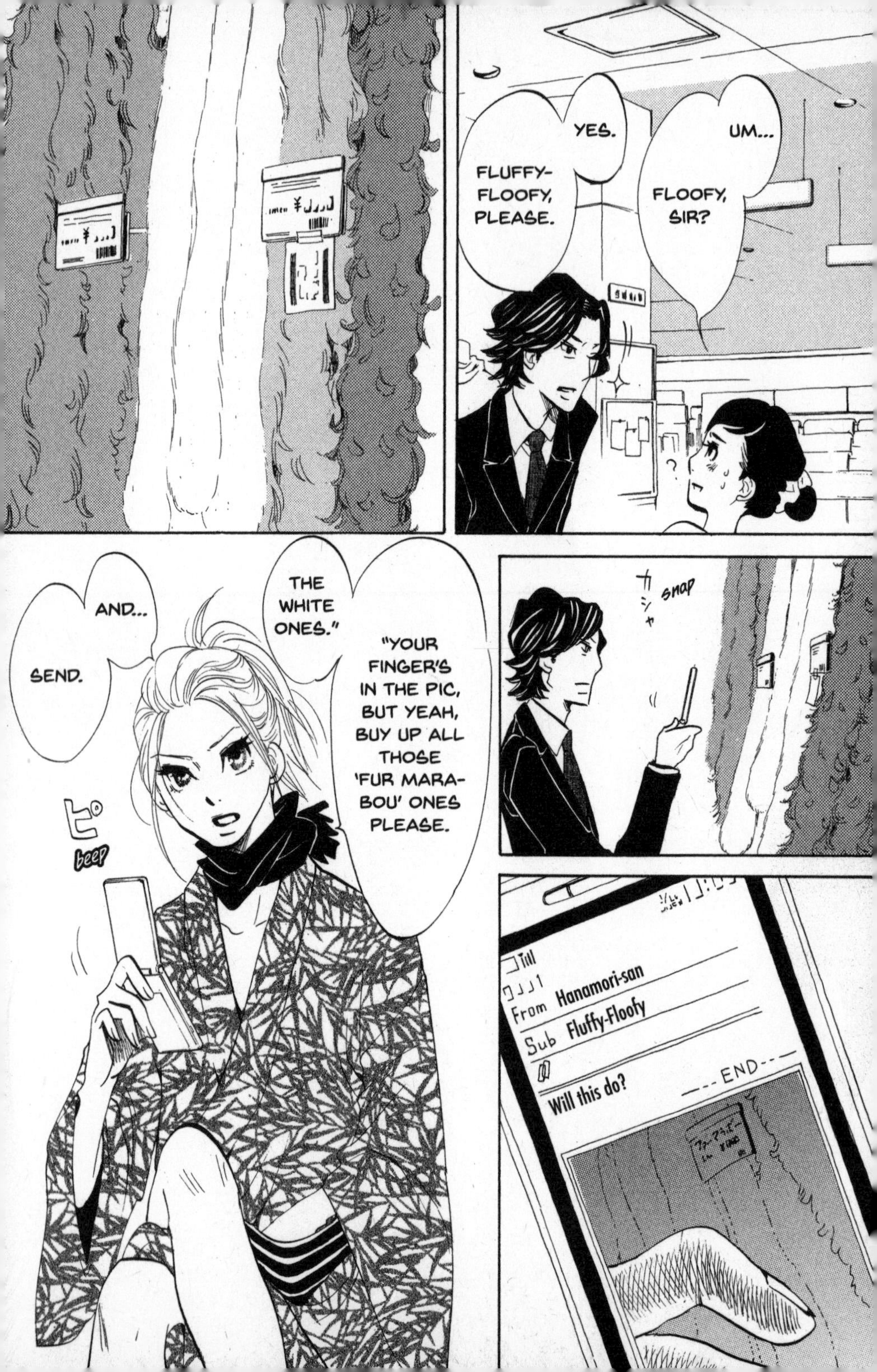
UM... FLOOFY, SIR?
YES. FLUFFY-FLOOFY, PLEASE.
カシャ snap
From Hanamori-san
Sub Fluffy-Floofy
Will this do?
---END---
"YOUR FINGER'S IN THE PIC, BUT YEAH, BUY UP ALL THOSE 'FUR MARABOU' ONES PLEASE.
THE WHITE ONES."
AND... SEND.
ピ beep

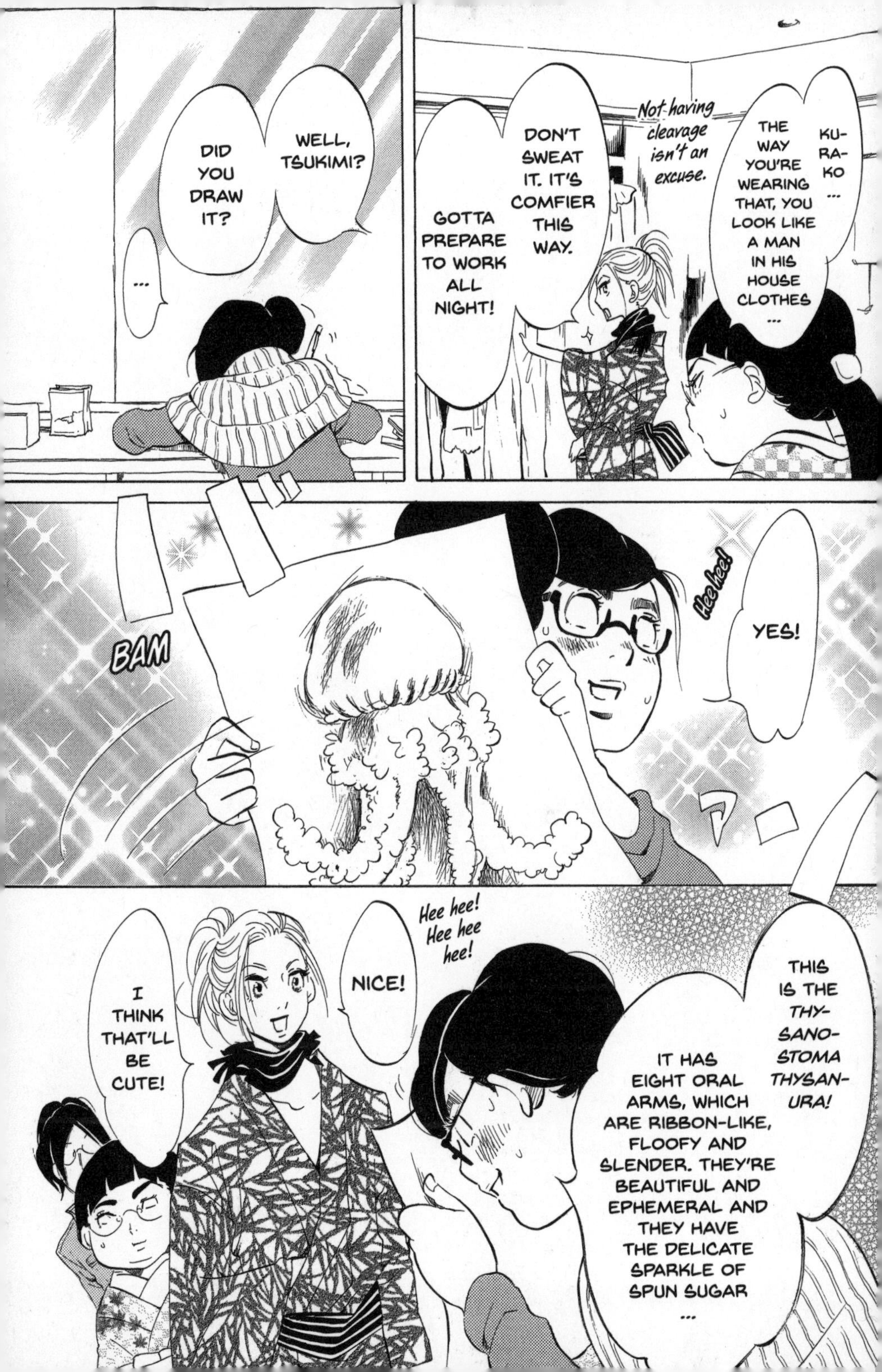
KU-RA-KO ...
THE WAY YOU'RE WEARING THAT, YOU LOOK LIKE A MAN IN HIS HOUSE CLOTHES ...
Not having cleavage isn't an excuse.
DON'T SWEAT IT. IT'S COMFIER THIS WAY.
GOTTA PREPARE TO WORK ALL NIGHT!
WELL, TSUKIMI?
DID YOU DRAW IT?
...
YES!
Hee hee!
BAM
THIS IS THE THY-SANO-STOMA THYSAN-URA!
IT HAS EIGHT ORAL ARMS, WHICH ARE RIBBON-LIKE, FLOOFY AND SLENDER. THEY'RE BEAUTIFUL AND EPHEMERAL AND THEY HAVE THE DELICATE SPARKLE OF SPUN SUGAR ...
Hee hee! Hee hee hee!
NICE!
I THINK THAT'LL BE CUTE!

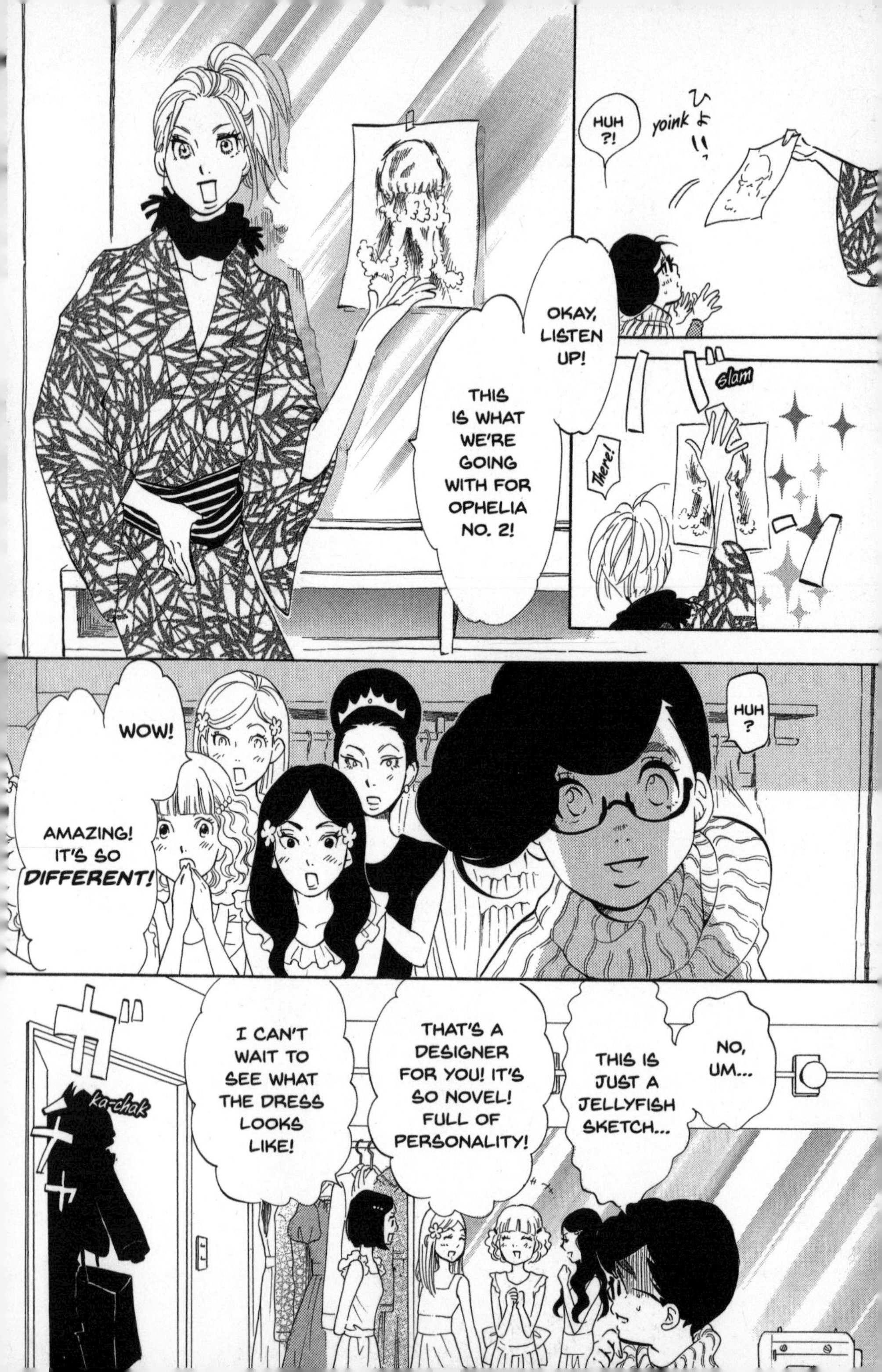
HUH ?!
yoink
ひょ!!
slam
There!
OKAY, LISTEN UP!
THIS IS WHAT WE'RE GOING WITH FOR OPHELIA NO. 2!
HUH ?
WOW!
AMAZING! IT'S SO DIFFERENT!
NO, UM...
THIS IS JUST A JELLYFISH SKETCH...
THAT'S A DESIGNER FOR YOU! IT'S SO NOVEL! FULL OF PERSONALITY!
I CAN'T WAIT TO SEE WHAT THE DRESS LOOKS LIKE!
ka-chak

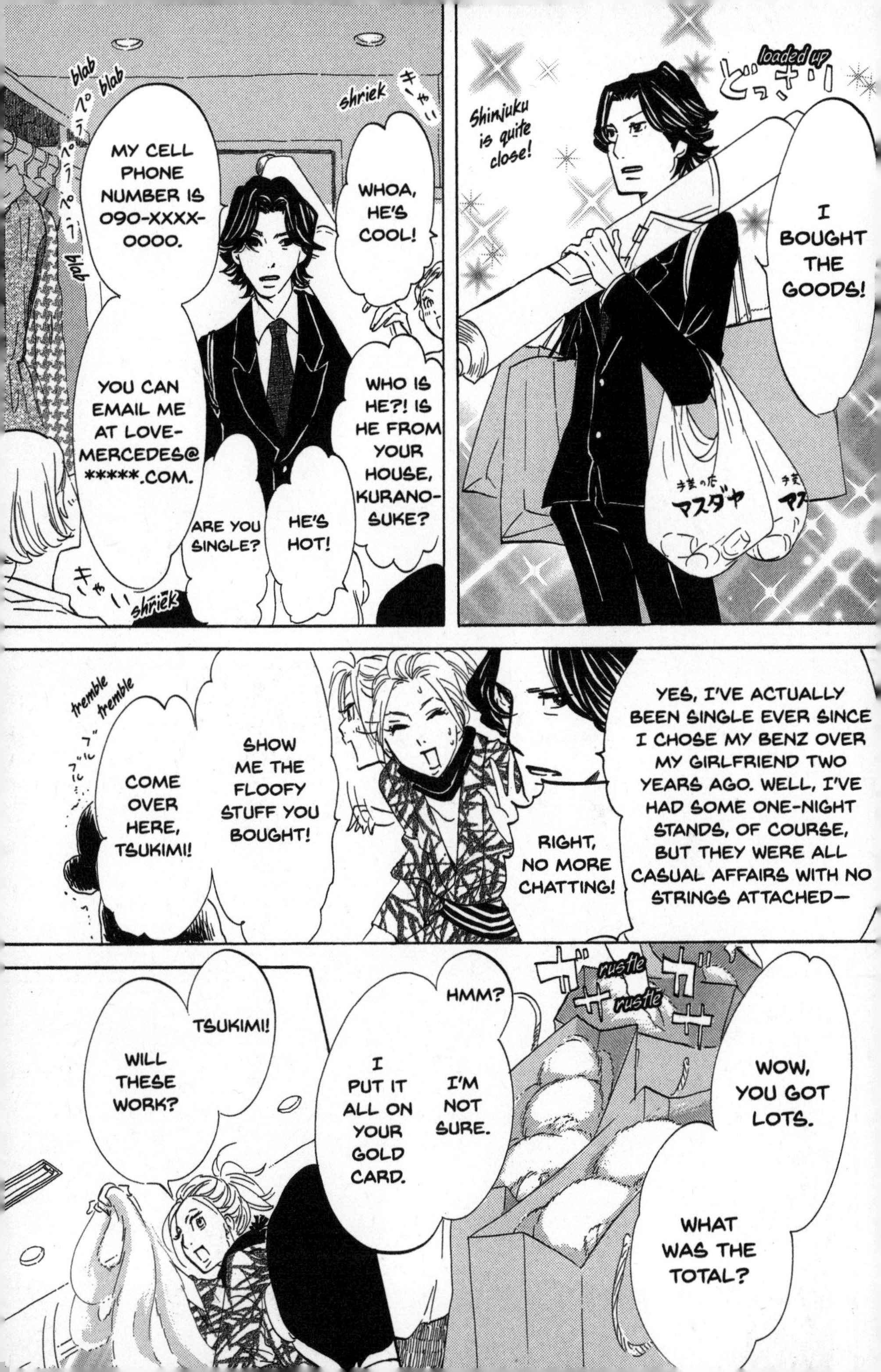
loaded up
I BOUGHT THE GOODS!
Shimjuku is quite close!
手芸の店 マスダヤ
WHOA, HE'S COOL!
shriek
MY CELL PHONE NUMBER IS 090-XXXX-0000.
blab blab
WHO IS HE?! IS HE FROM YOUR HOUSE, KURANOSUKE?
HE'S HOT!
ARE YOU SINGLE?
YOU CAN EMAIL ME AT LOVE-MERCEDES@*****.COM.
shriek
YES, I'VE ACTUALLY BEEN SINGLE EVER SINCE I CHOSE MY BENZ OVER MY GIRLFRIEND TWO YEARS AGO. WELL, I'VE HAD SOME ONE-NIGHT STANDS, OF COURSE, BUT THEY WERE ALL CASUAL AFFAIRS WITH NO STRINGS ATTACHED—
RIGHT, NO MORE CHATTING!
SHOW ME THE FLOOFY STUFF YOU BOUGHT!
COME OVER HERE, TSUKIMI!
tremble tremble
rustle rustle
WOW, YOU GOT LOTS.
WHAT WAS THE TOTAL?
HMM?
I'M NOT SURE.
I PUT IT ALL ON YOUR GOLD CARD.
TSUKIMI!
WILL THESE WORK?

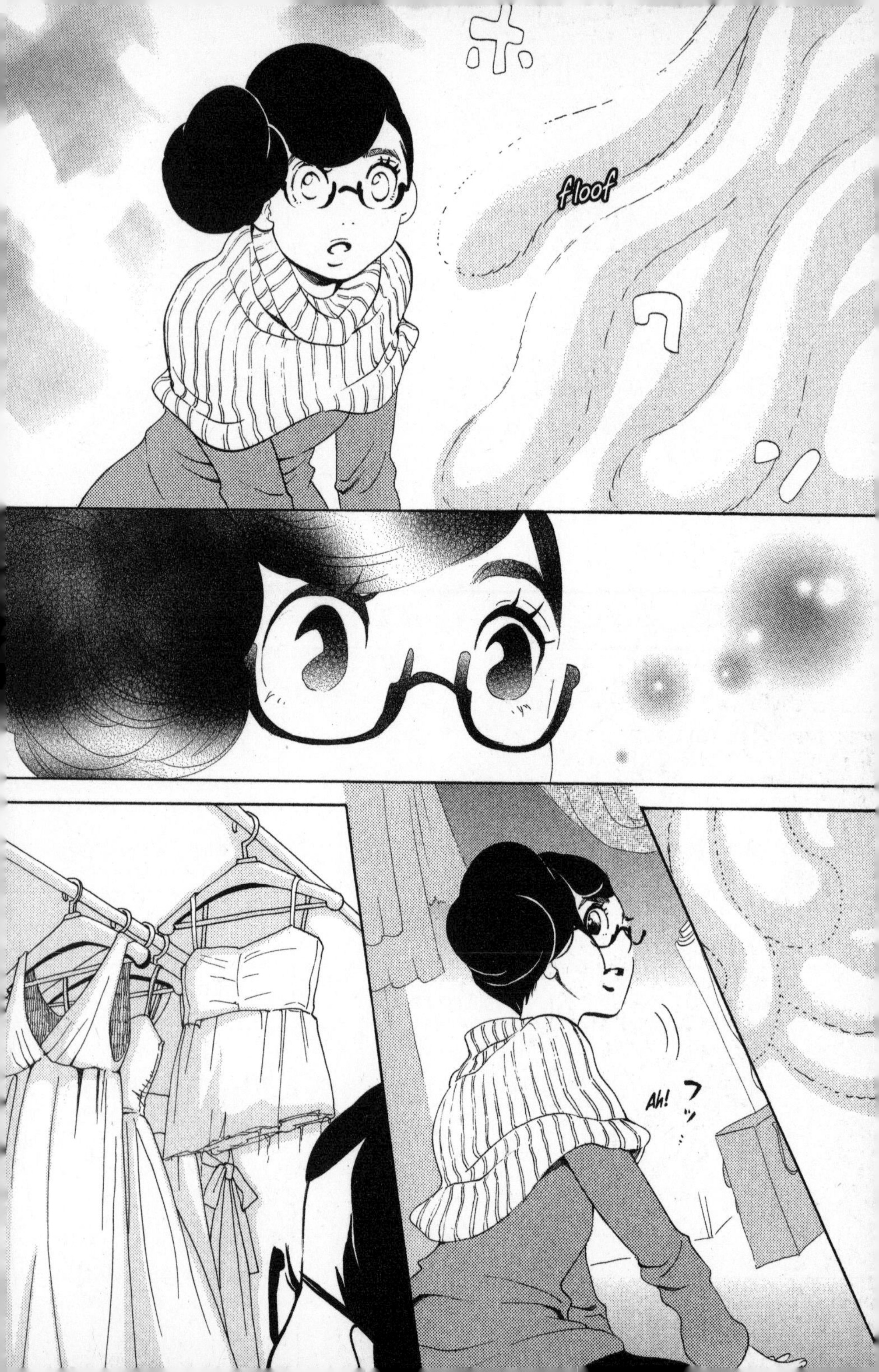
floof
Ah!

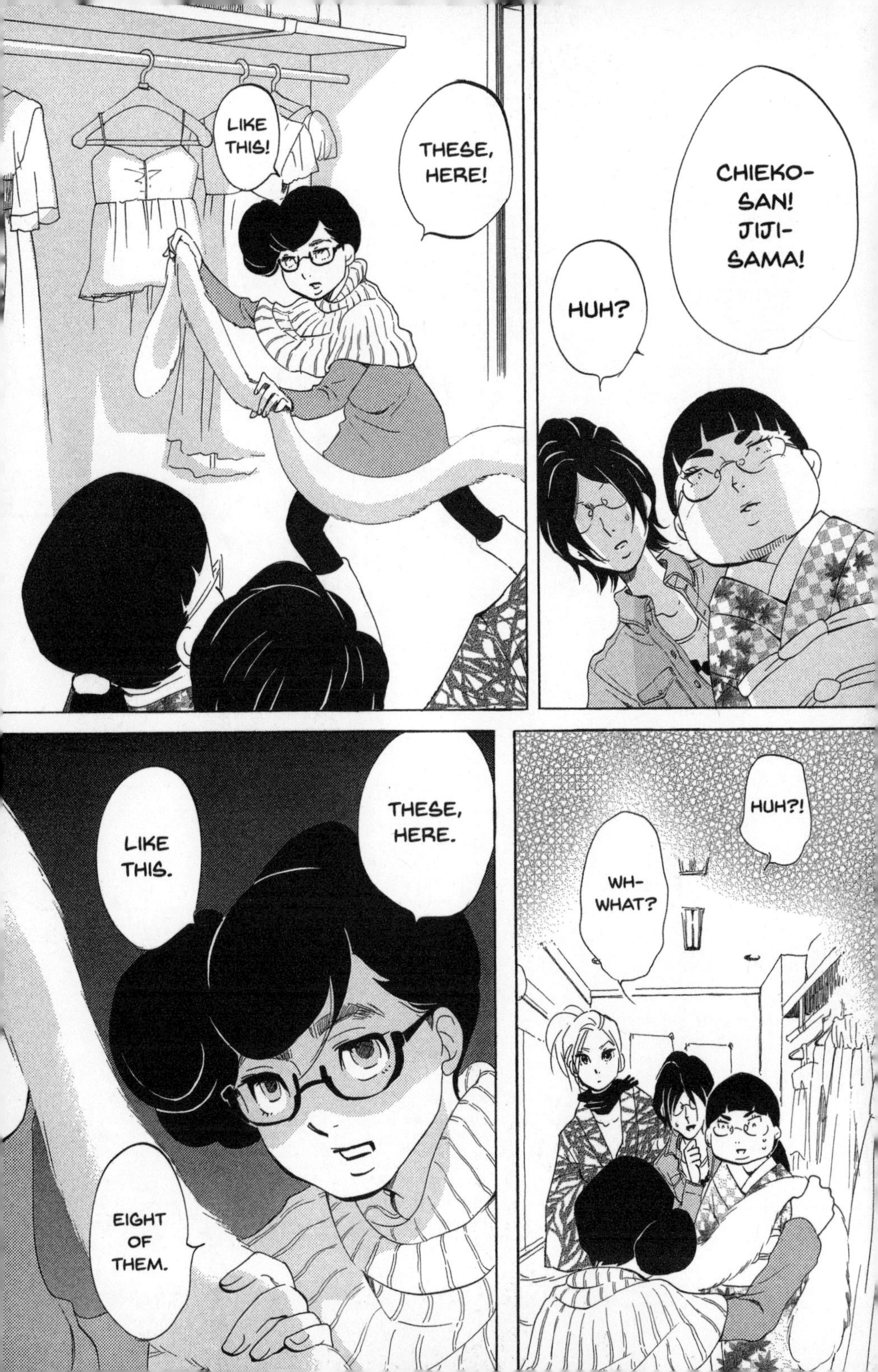
CHIEKO-SAN! JIJI-SAMA!
HUH?
THESE, HERE!
LIKE THIS!
HUH?!
WH-WHAT?
THESE, HERE.
LIKE THIS.
EIGHT OF THEM.

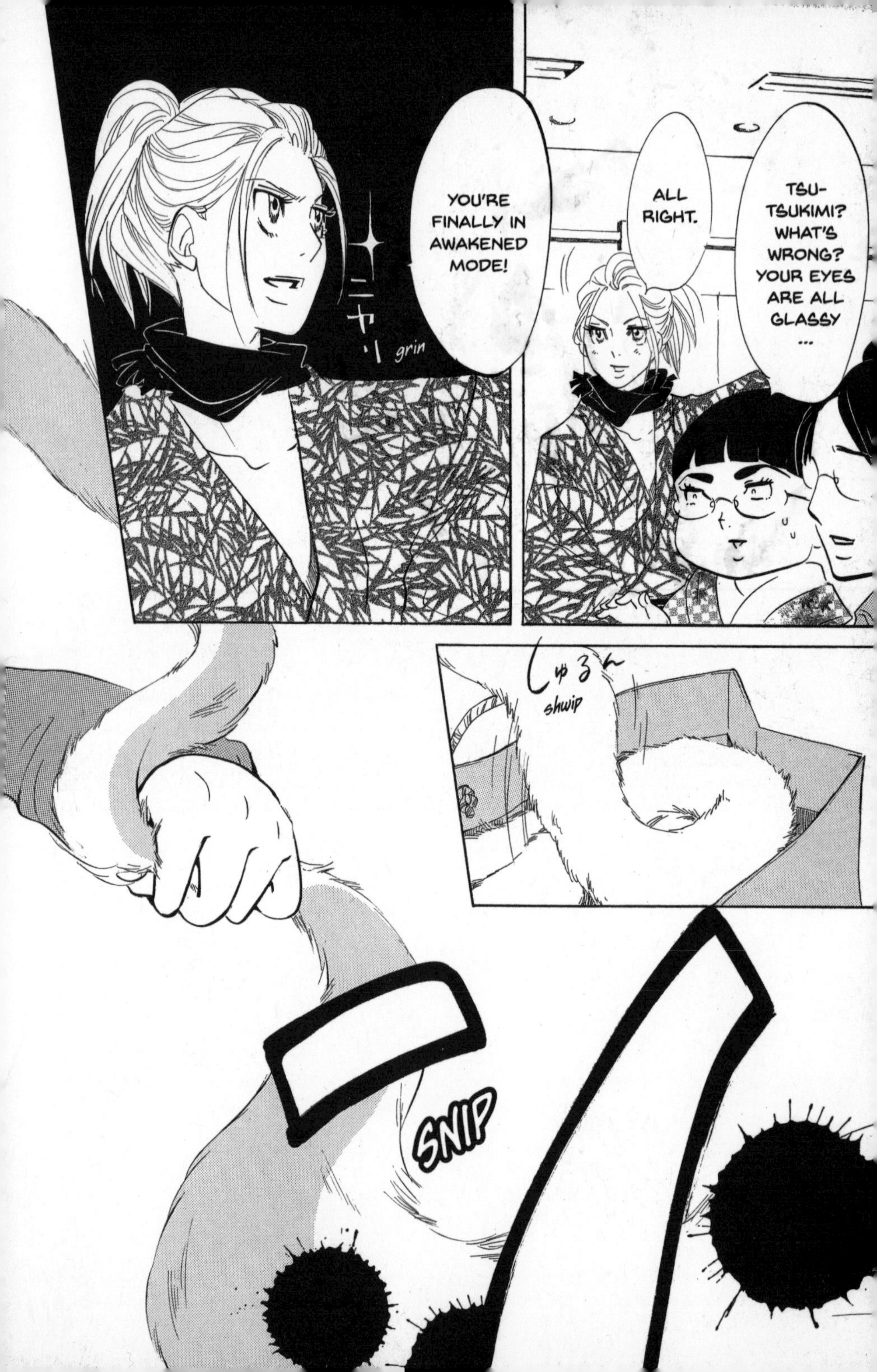
TSU-TSUKIMI? WHAT'S WRONG? YOUR EYES ARE ALL GLASSY ...
ALL RIGHT.
YOU'RE FINALLY IN AWAKENED MODE!
ニヤリ
grin
しゅるん
shwip
SNIP

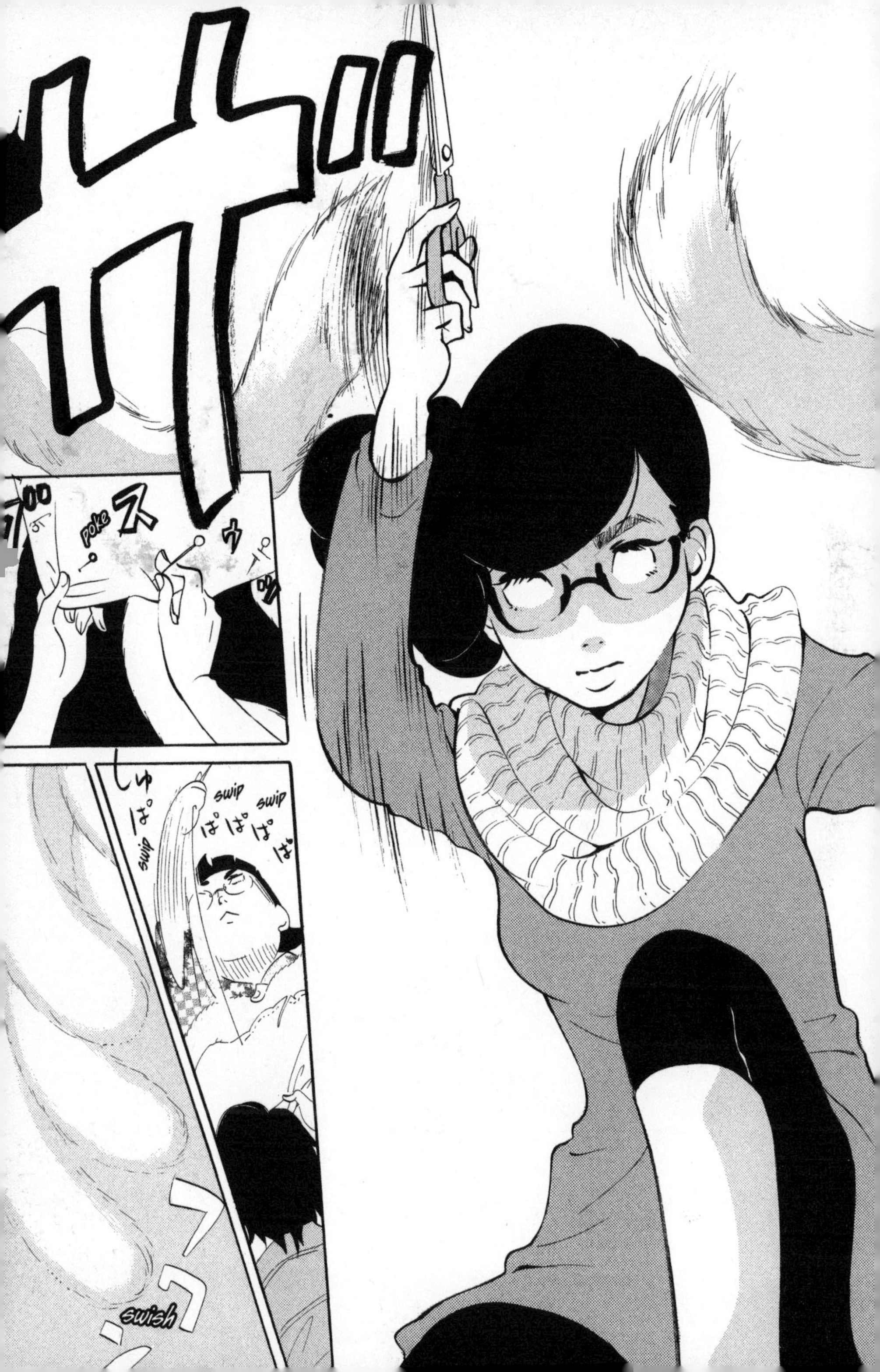
ザ
スゥ
poke
しゅぱぱぱぱ
swip
swip
swip
swish

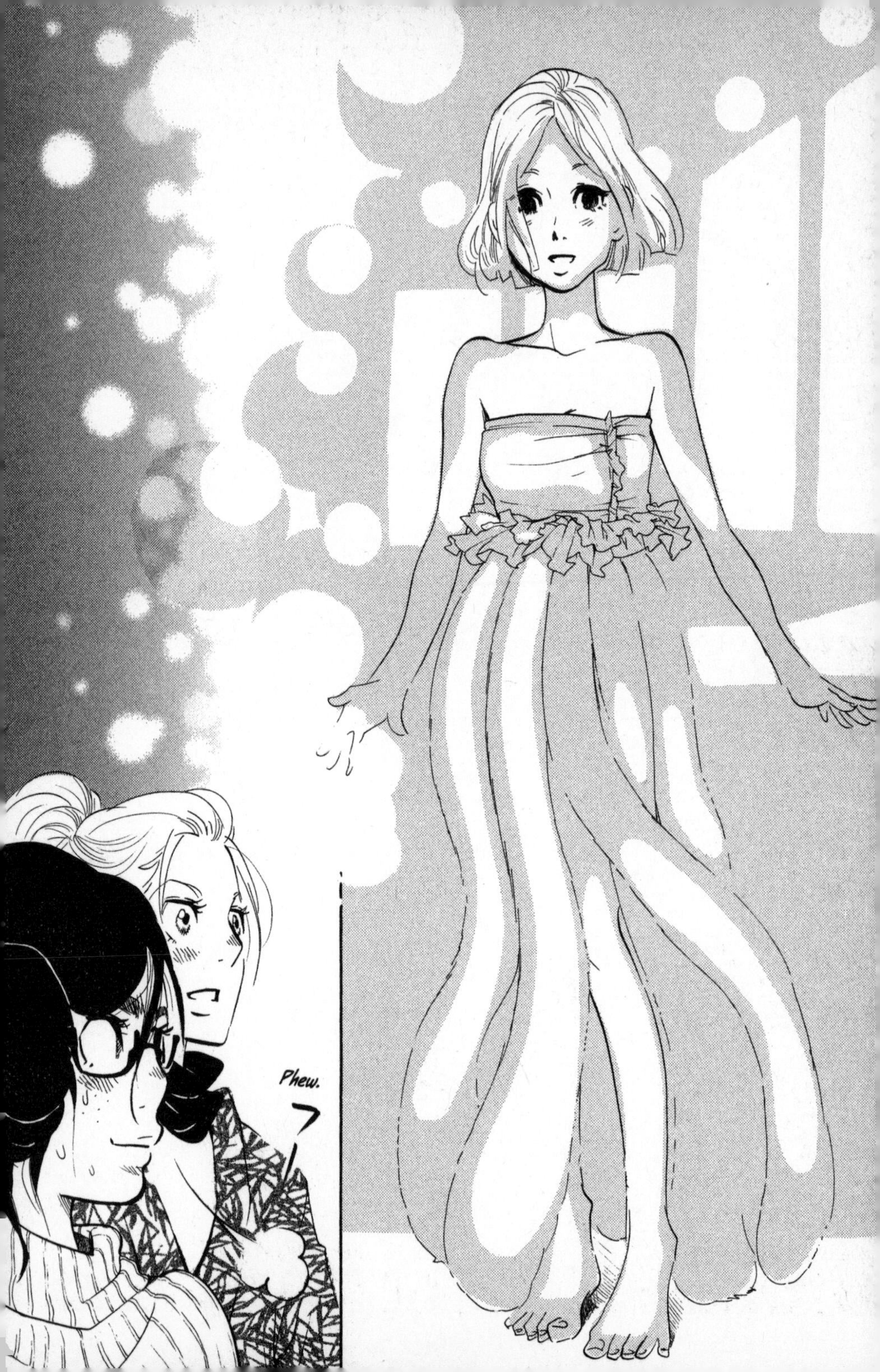
Phew.

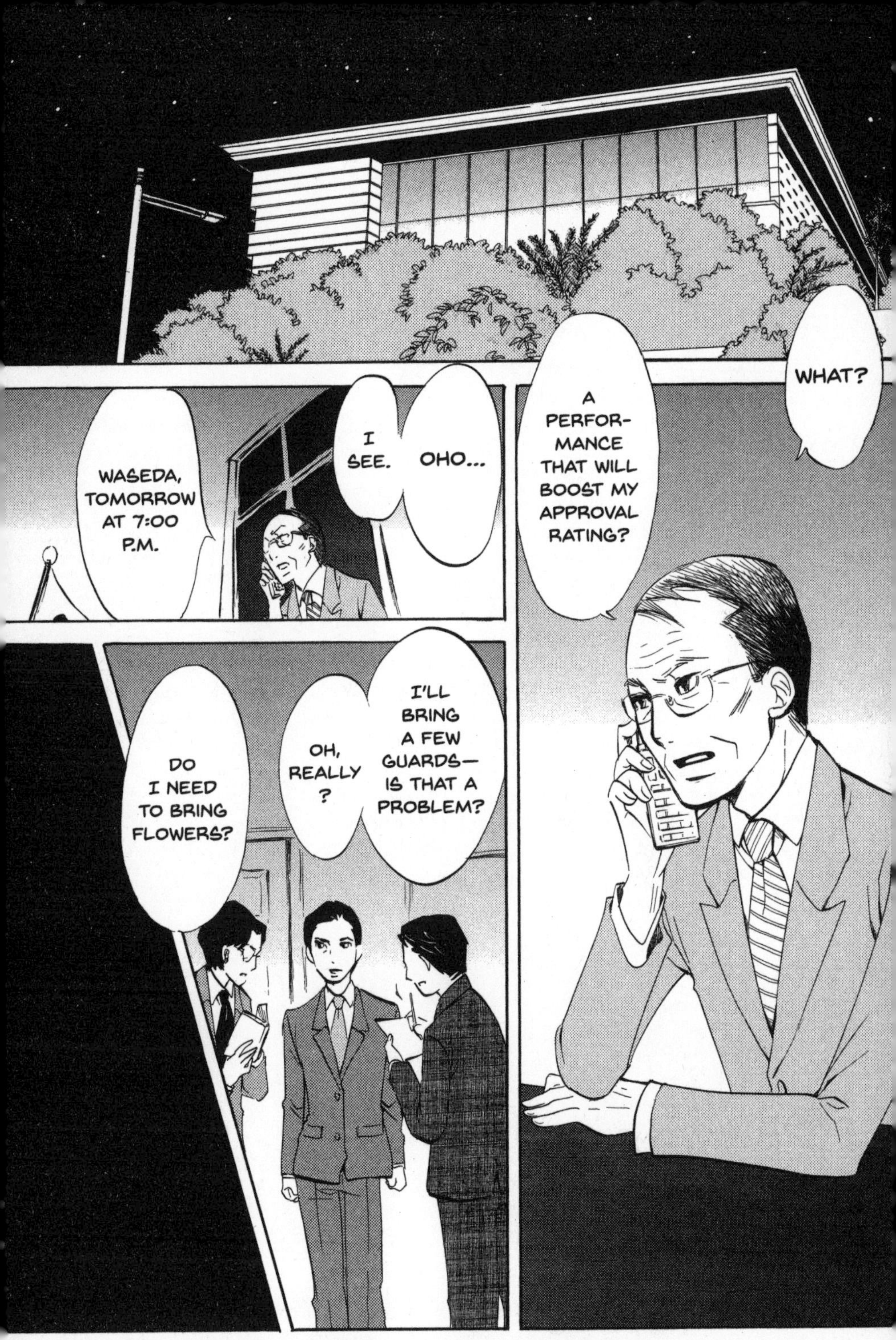
WHAT?
A PERFORMANCE THAT WILL BOOST MY APPROVAL RATING?
OHO...
I SEE.
WASEDA, TOMORROW AT 7:00 P.M.
I'LL BRING A FEW GUARDS— IS THAT A PROBLEM?
OH, REALLY?
DO I NEED TO BRING FLOWERS?

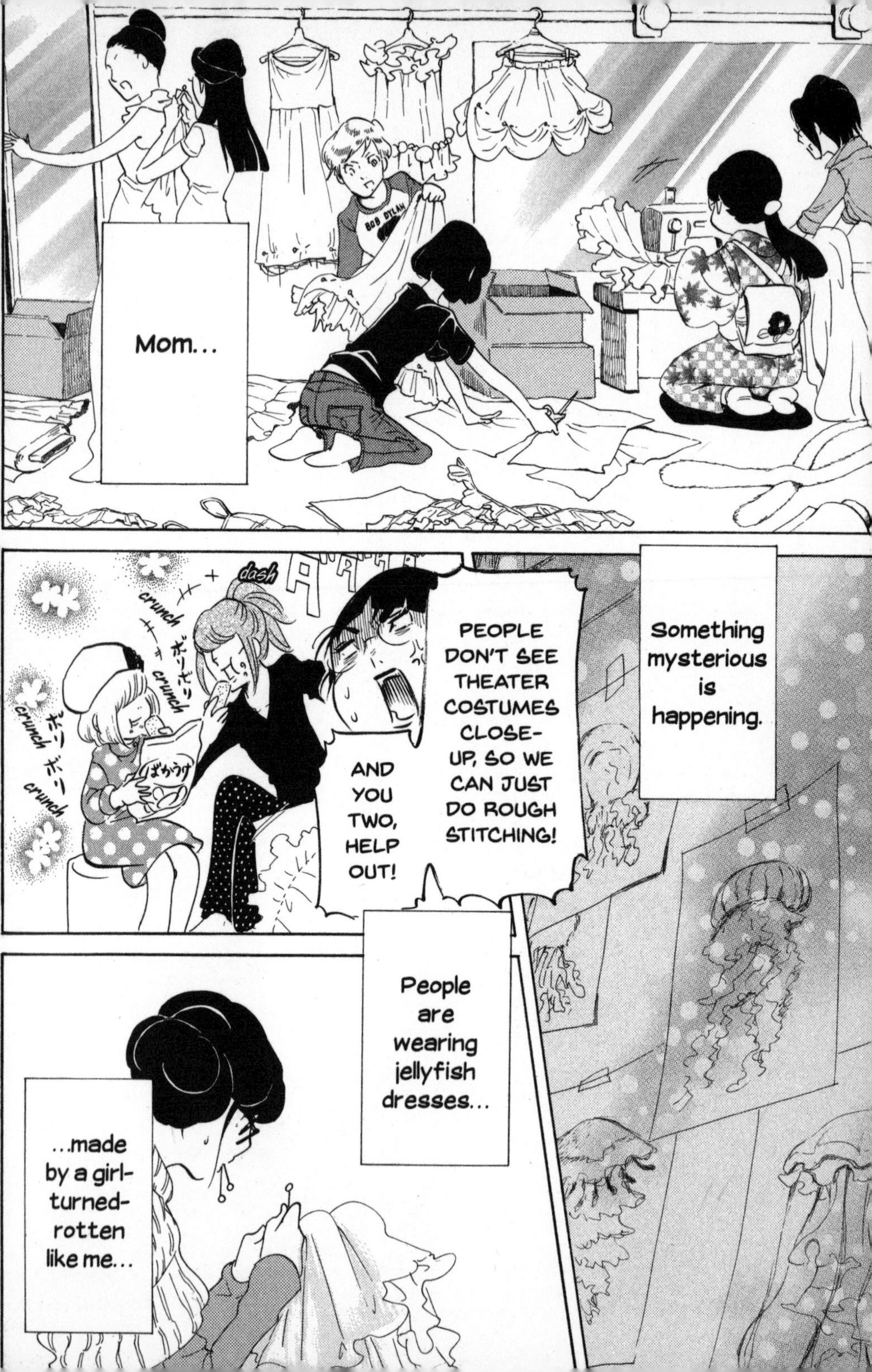
Mom...
Something mysterious is happening.
dash
PEOPLE DON'T SEE THEATER COSTUMES CLOSE-UP, SO WE CAN JUST DO ROUGH STITCHING!
AND YOU TWO, HELP OUT!
crunch
ボリボリ
crunch
ボリボリ
crunch
crunch
ばかうけ
People are wearing jellyfish dresses...
...made by a girl-turned-rotten like me...

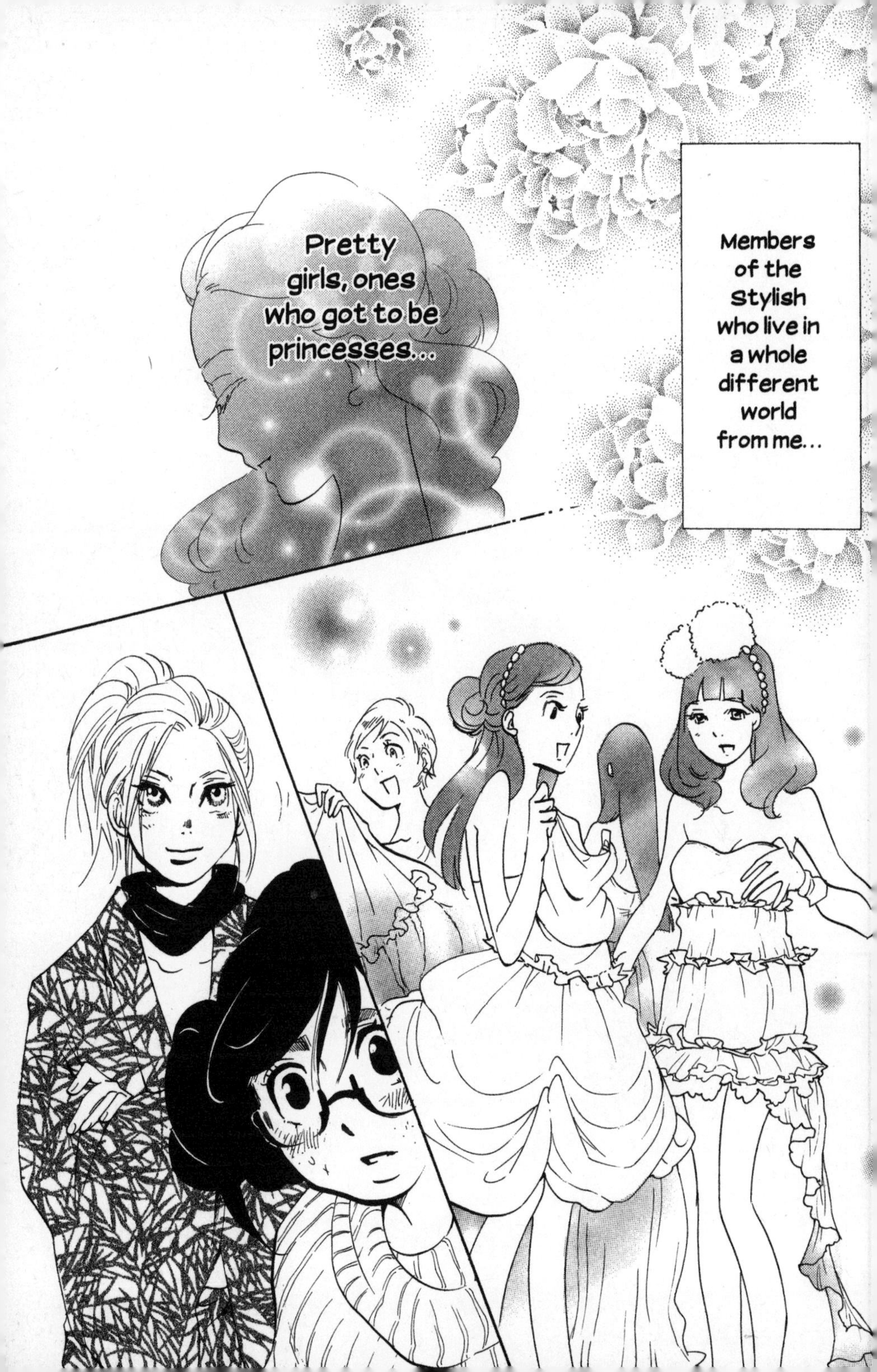
Members of the Stylish who live in a whole different world from me...
Pretty girls, ones who got to be princesses...

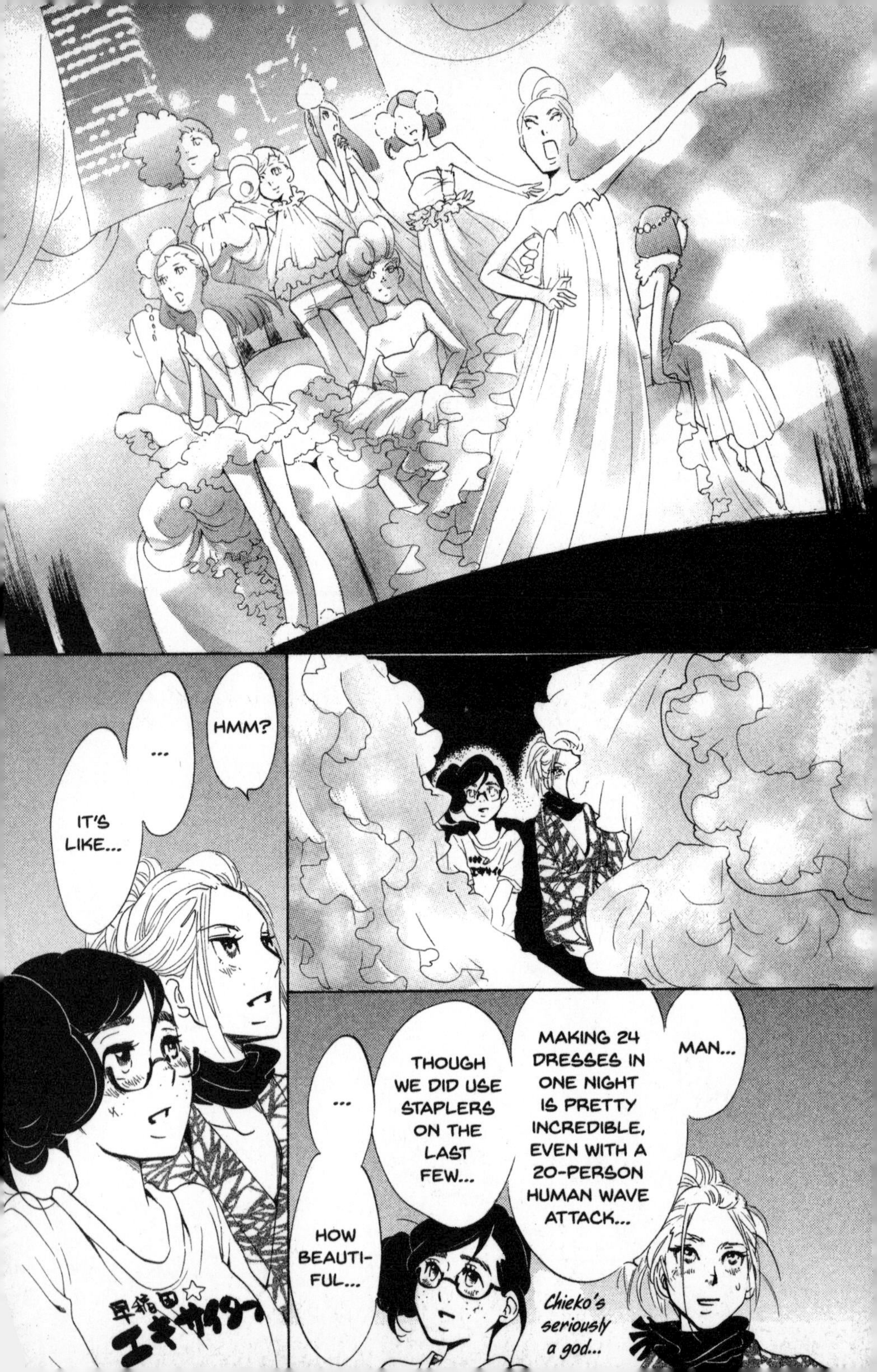
MAN...
MAKING 24 DRESSES IN ONE NIGHT IS PRETTY INCREDIBLE, EVEN WITH A 20-PERSON HUMAN WAVE ATTACK...
THOUGH WE DID USE STAPLERS ON THE LAST FEW...
...
Chieko's seriously a god...
HOW BEAUTI-FUL...
HMM?
...
IT'S LIKE...

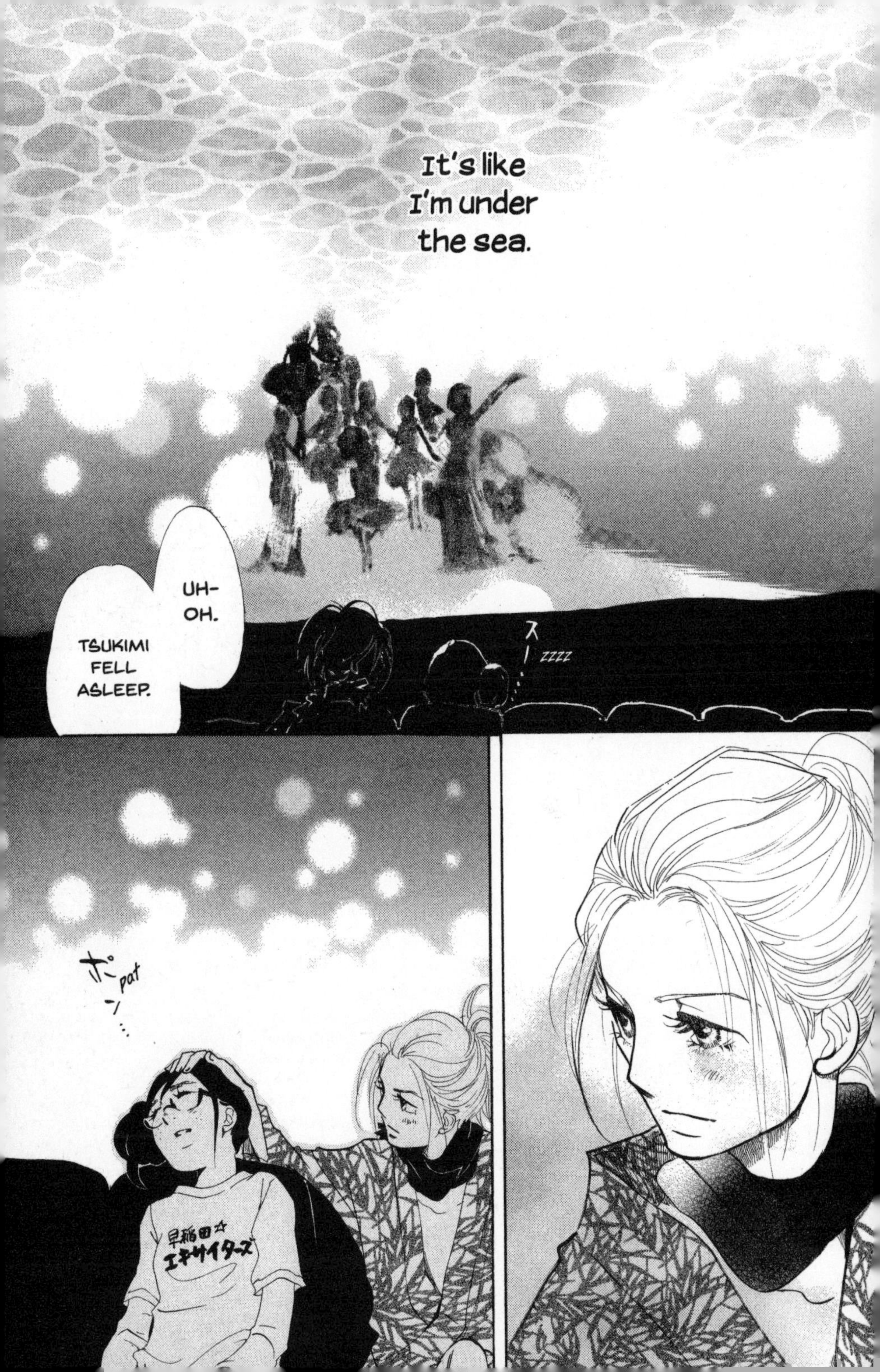
It's like I'm under the sea.
UH-OH.
TSUKIMI FELL ASLEEP.
スー zzzz
早稲田☆エキサイターズ
ポン… pat

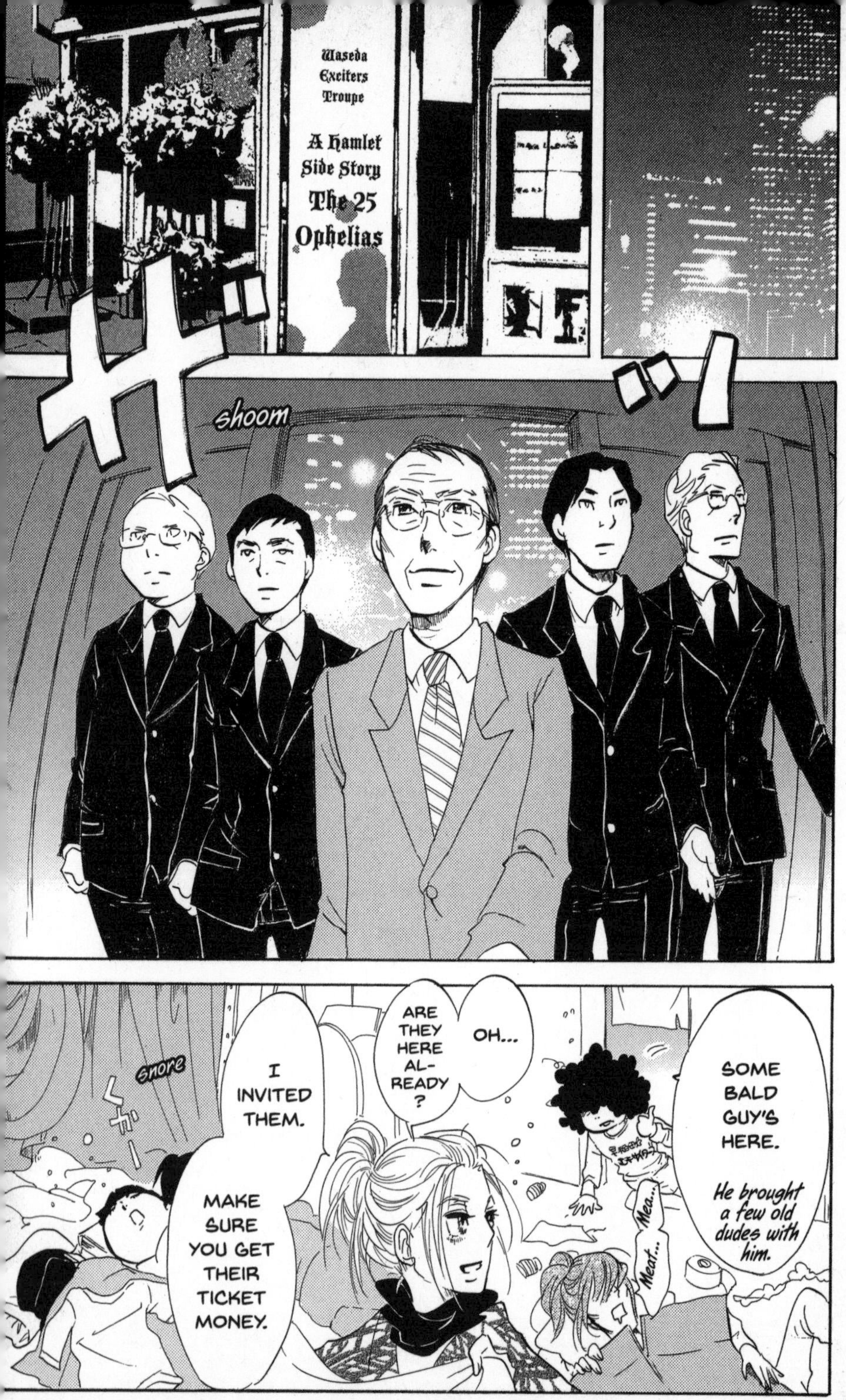
Waseda Exciters Troupe
A Hamlet Side Story The 25 Ophelias
shoom
SOME BALD GUY'S HERE.
He brought a few old dudes with him.
Meat... Meat...
OH...
ARE THEY HERE AL-READY?
I INVITED THEM.
MAKE SURE YOU GET THEIR TICKET MONEY.
snore

Episode 28
Jellydog Millionaire

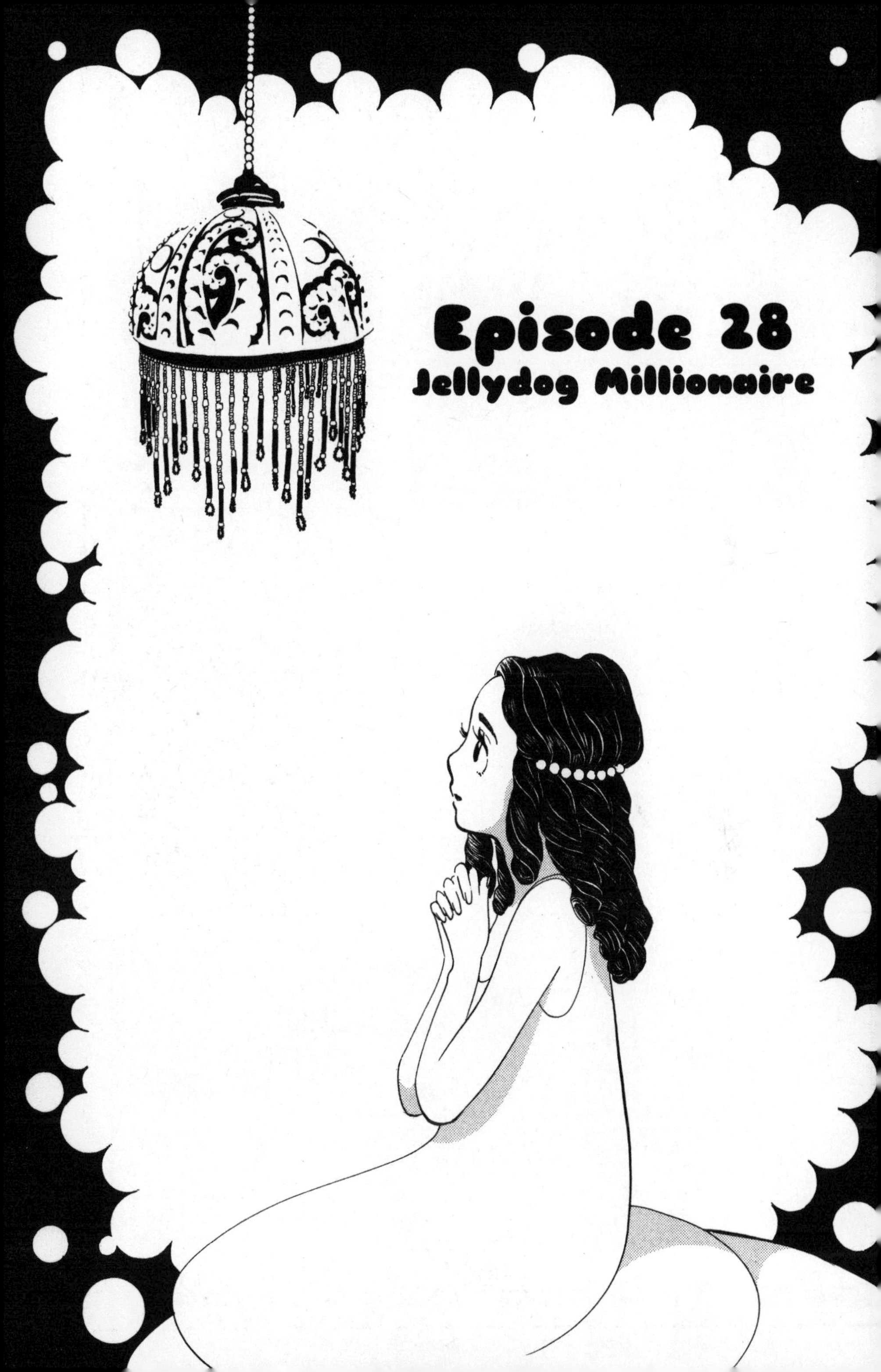

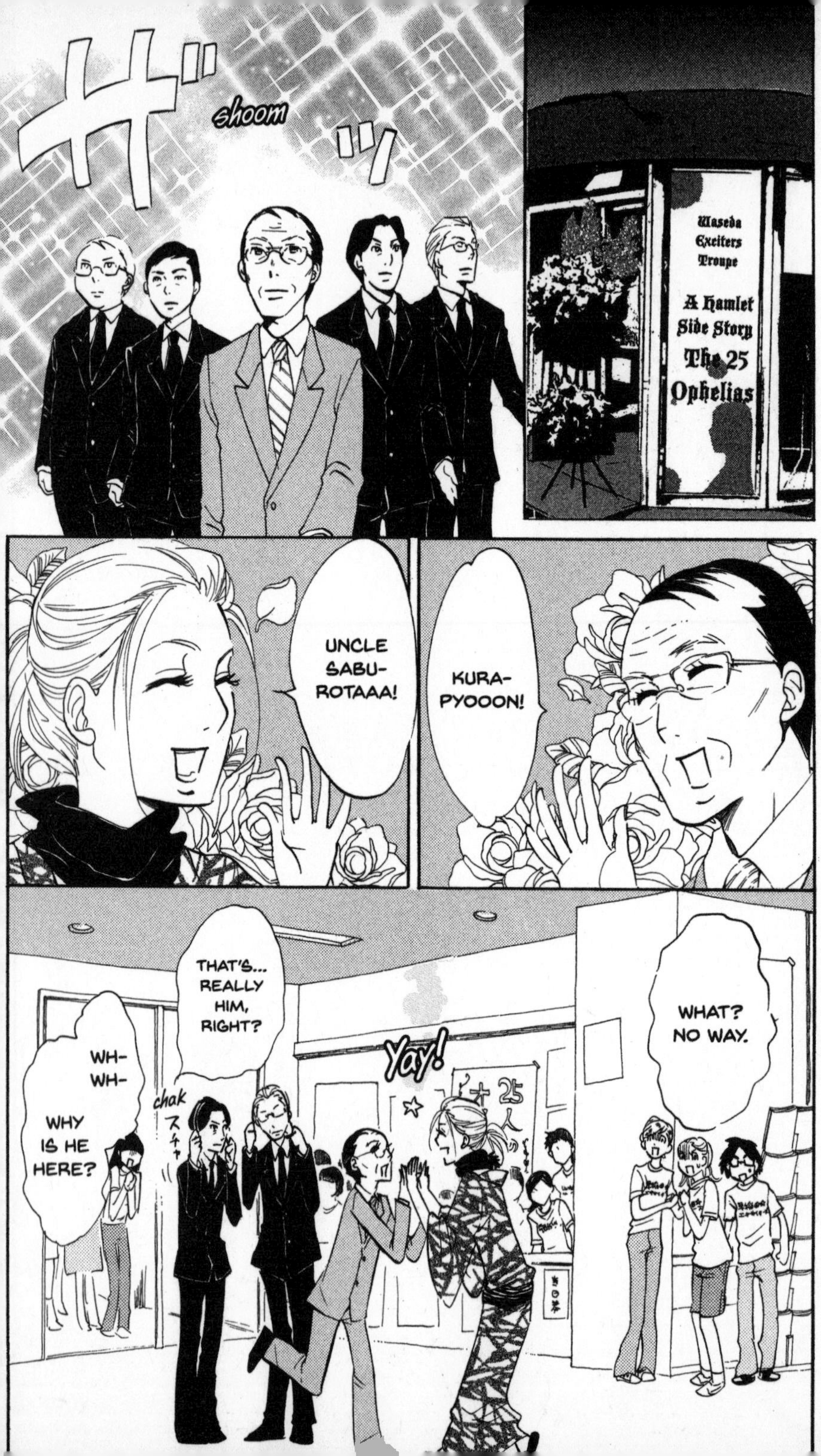
Waseda Exciters Troupe
A Hamlet Side Story The 25 Ophelias
shoom
KURA-PYOOON!
UNCLE SABU-ROTAAA!
WHAT? NO WAY.
Yay!
THAT'S... REALLY HIM, RIGHT?
chak
WH- WH-
WHY IS HE HERE?

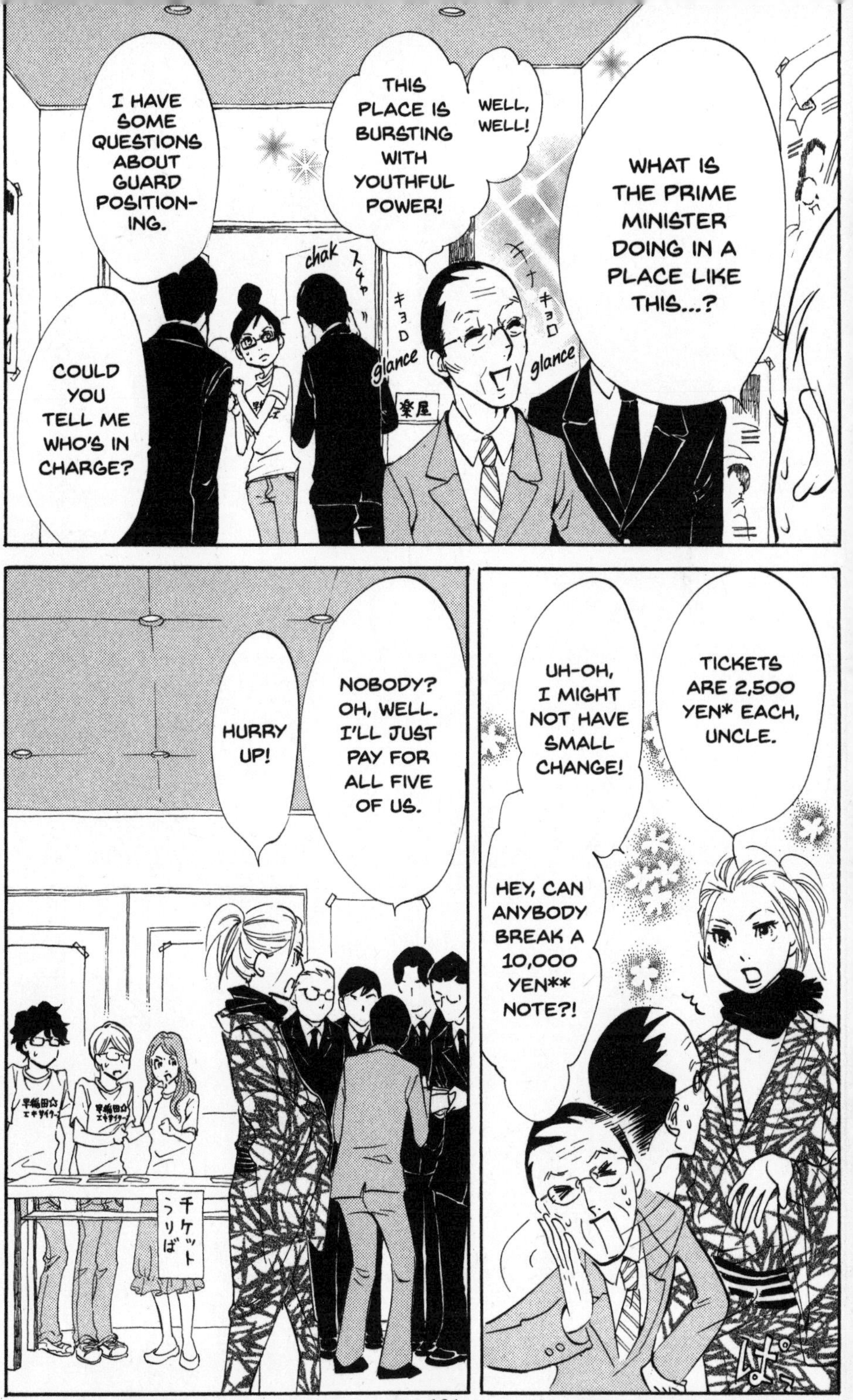
WHAT IS THE PRIME MINISTER DOING IN A PLACE LIKE THIS...?
WELL, WELL!
THIS PLACE IS BURSTING WITH YOUTHFUL POWER!
キョロ
glance
キョロ
glance
スチャ
chak
楽屋
I HAVE SOME QUESTIONS ABOUT GUARD POSITION-ING.
COULD YOU TELL ME WHO'S IN CHARGE?
TICKETS ARE 2,500 YEN* EACH, UNCLE.
UH-OH, I MIGHT NOT HAVE SMALL CHANGE!
HEY, CAN ANYBODY BREAK A 10,000 YEN** NOTE?!
ぱっ
NOBODY? OH, WELL. I'LL JUST PAY FOR ALL FIVE OF US.
HURRY UP!
チケットうりば

Sign: Tickets

*About $25 USD. **About $100 USD.

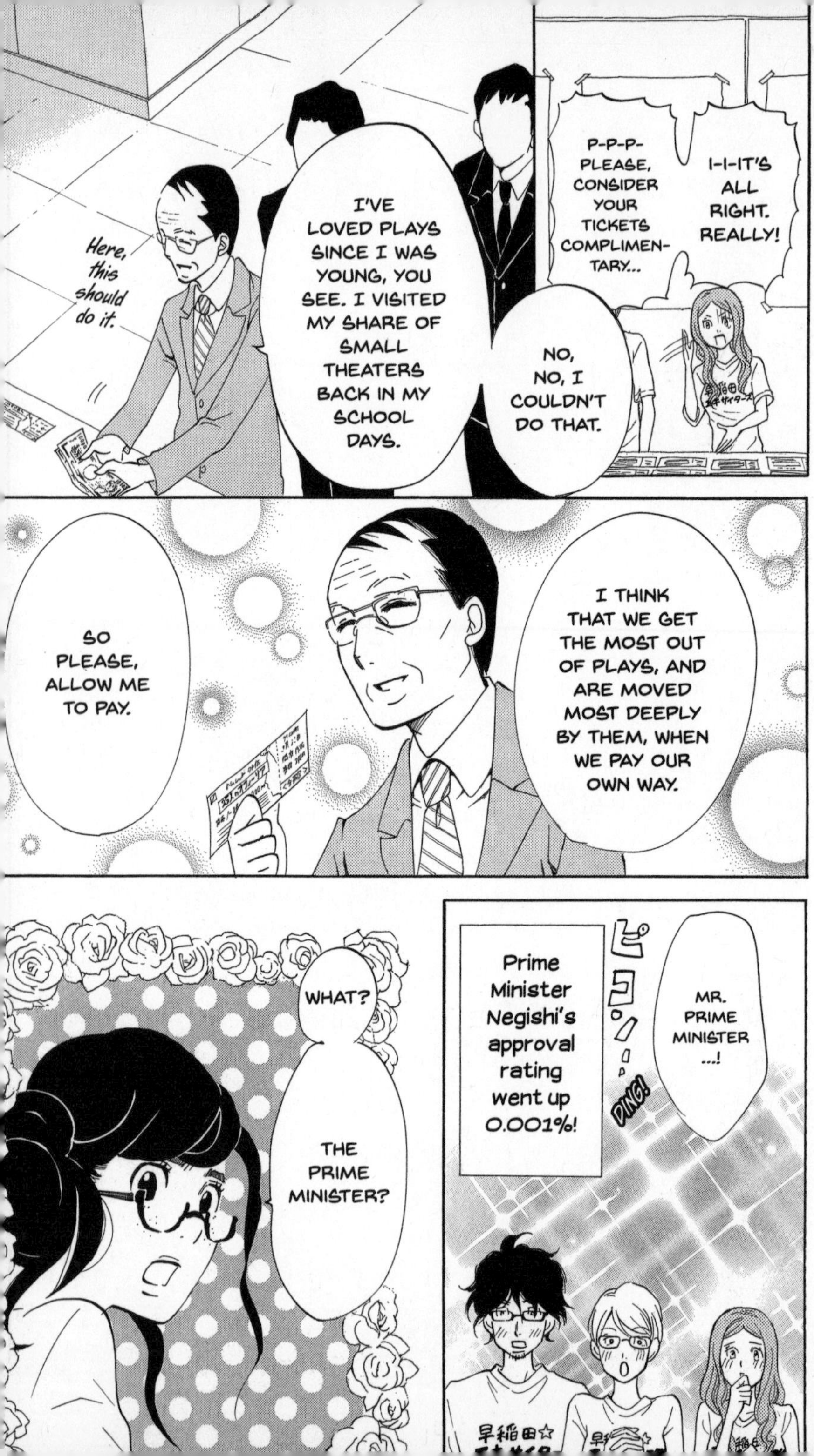
I-I-IT'S ALL RIGHT. REALLY!
P-P-P-PLEASE, CONSIDER YOUR TICKETS COMPLIMENTARY...
NO, NO, I COULDN'T DO THAT.
I'VE LOVED PLAYS SINCE I WAS YOUNG, YOU SEE. I VISITED MY SHARE OF SMALL THEATERS BACK IN MY SCHOOL DAYS.
Here, this should do it.
I THINK THAT WE GET THE MOST OUT OF PLAYS, AND ARE MOVED MOST DEEPLY BY THEM, WHEN WE PAY OUR OWN WAY.
SO PLEASE, ALLOW ME TO PAY.
MR. PRIME MINISTER ...!
ピコ
DING!
Prime Minister Negishi's approval rating went up 0.001%!
WHAT?
THE PRIME MINISTER?

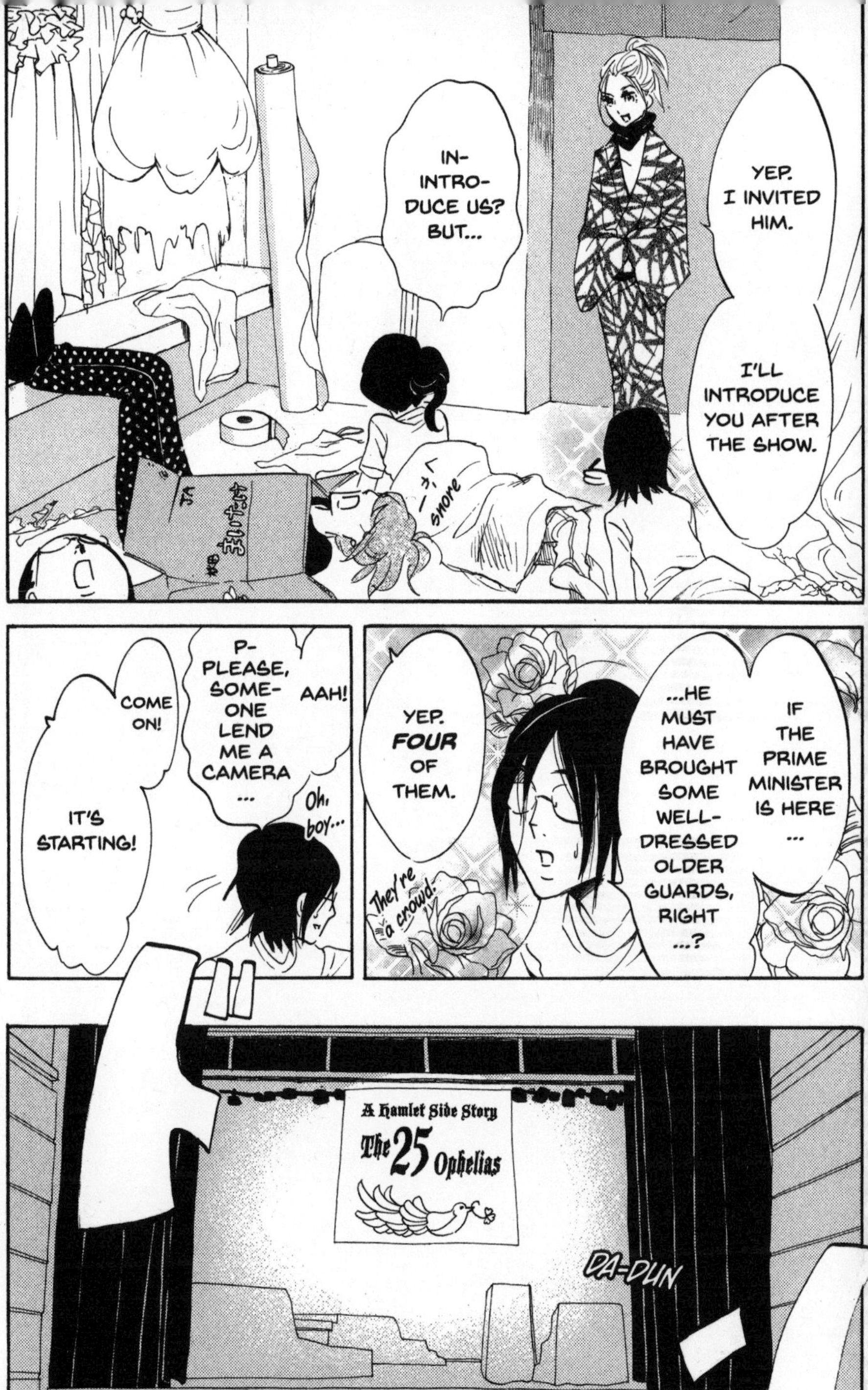
YEP. I INVITED HIM.
I'LL INTRODUCE YOU AFTER THE SHOW.
IN-INTRODUCE US? BUT...
snore
IF THE PRIME MINISTER IS HERE ...
...HE MUST HAVE BROUGHT SOME WELL-DRESSED OLDER GUARDS, RIGHT ...?
YEP. FOUR OF THEM.
They're a crowd.
AAH!
P-PLEASE, SOMEONE LEND ME A CAMERA ...
Oh, boy...
COME ON!
IT'S STARTING!
A Hamlet Side Story
The 25 Ophelias
DA-DUN

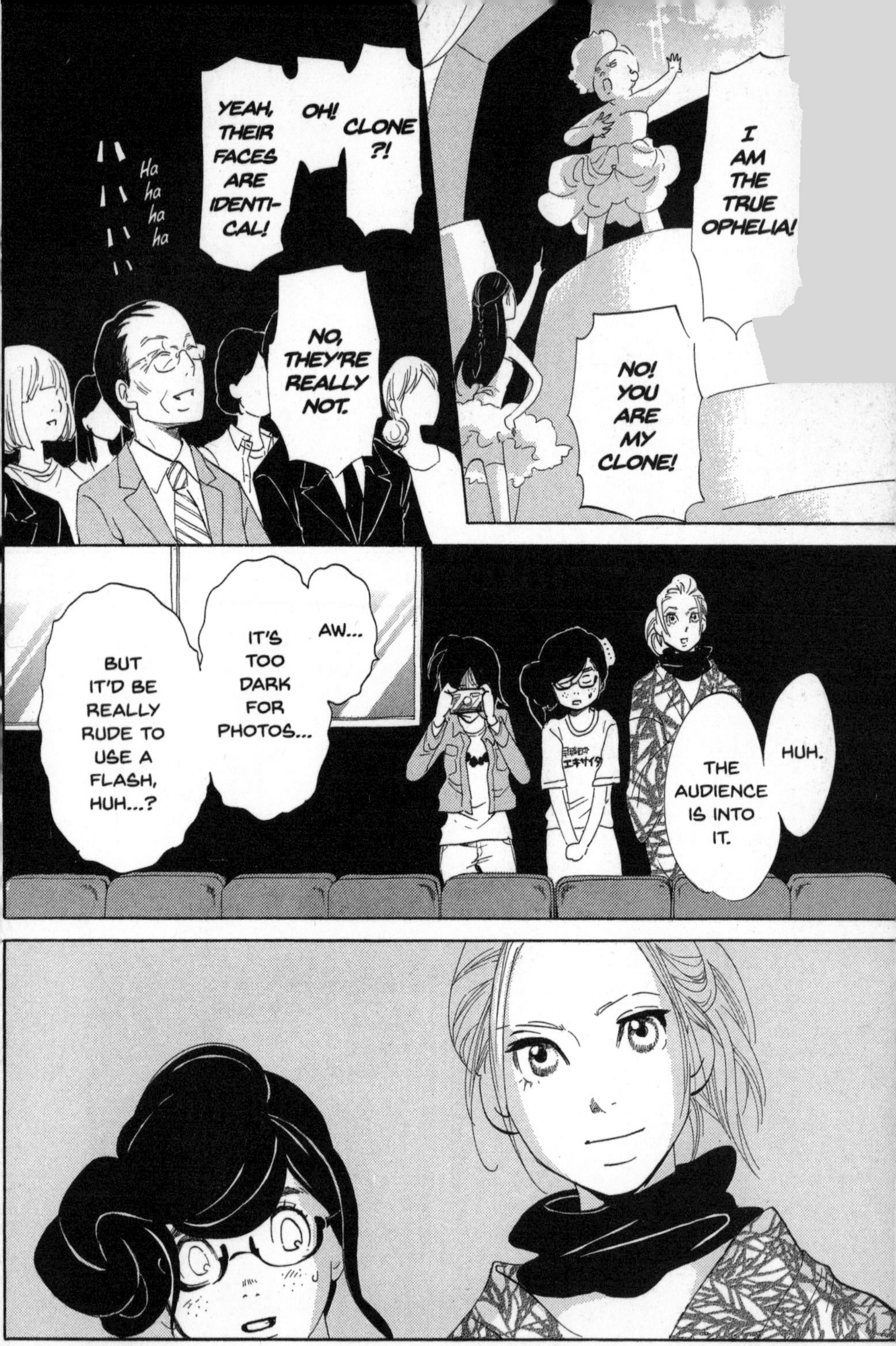

I AM THE TRUE OPHELIA!
NO! YOU ARE MY CLONE!
OH! CLONE ?!
YEAH, THEIR FACES ARE IDENTI-CAL!
Ha ha ha ha
NO, THEY'RE REALLY NOT.
HUH.
THE AUDIENCE IS INTO IT.
AW...
IT'S TOO DARK FOR PHOTOS...
BUT IT'D BE REALLY RUDE TO USE A FLASH, HUH...?

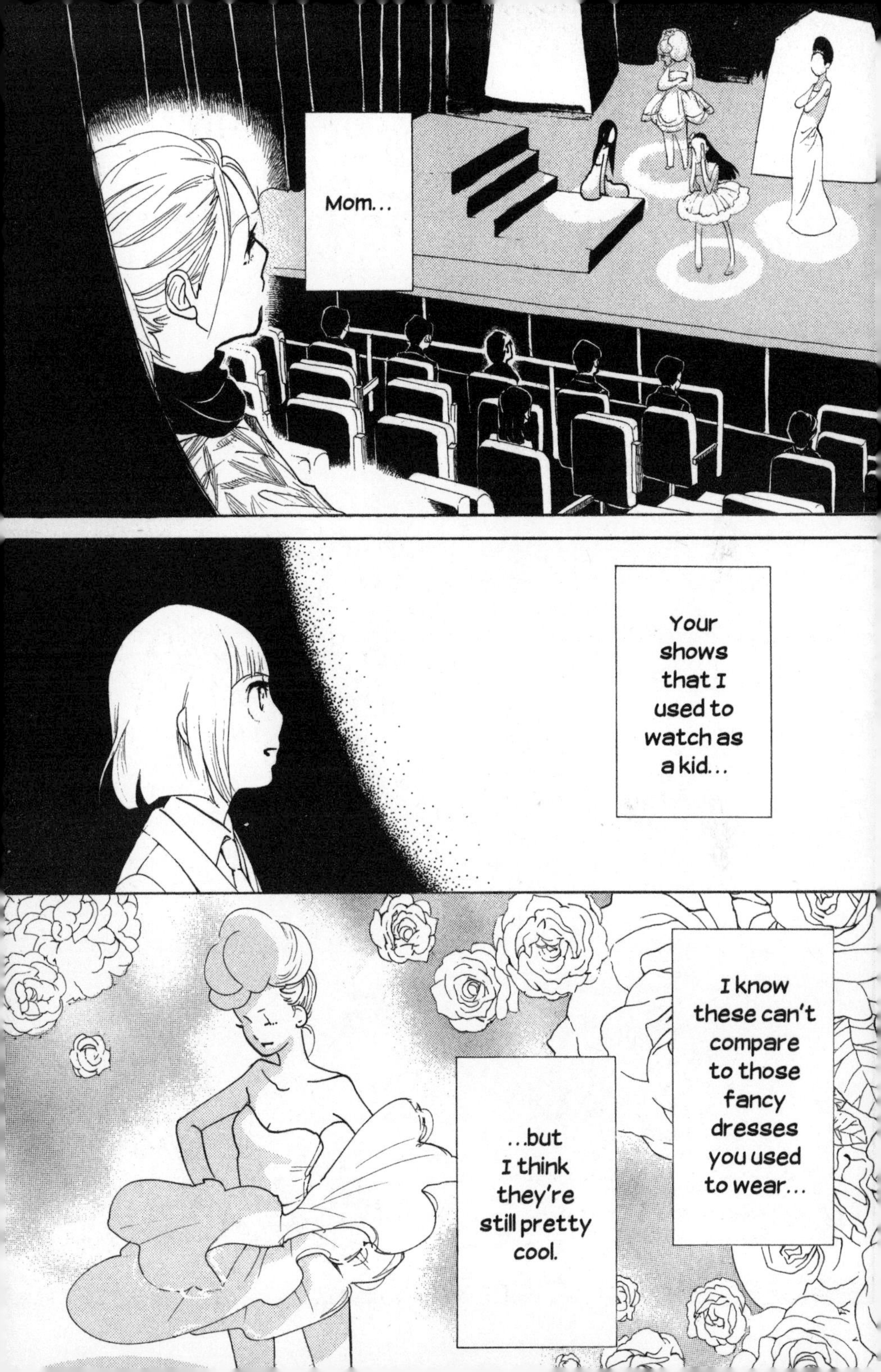
Mom...
Your shows that I used to watch as a kid...
I know these can't compare to those fancy dresses you used to wear...
...but I think they're still pretty cool.

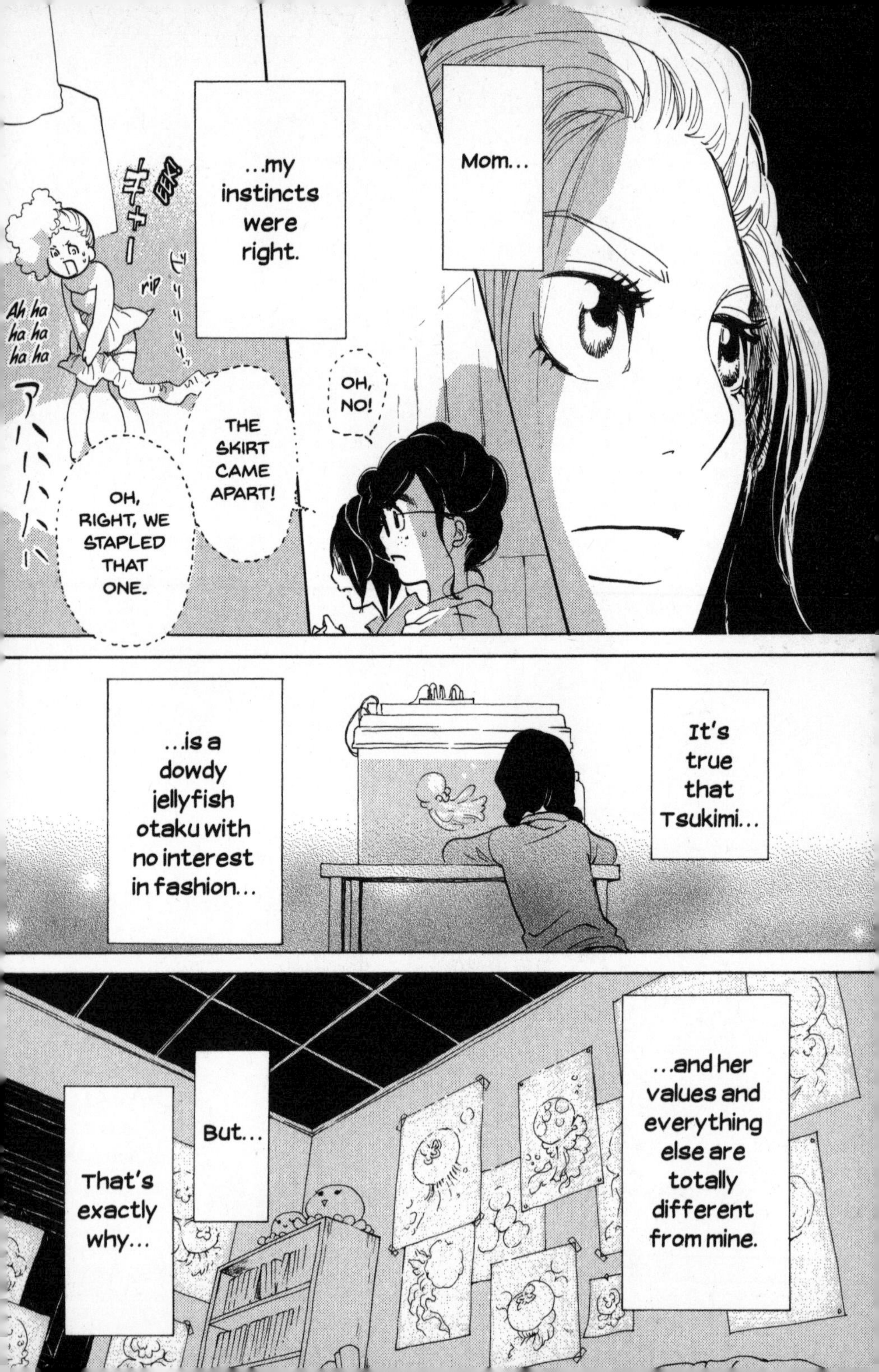

Mom...
...my instincts were right.
OH, NO!
THE SKIRT CAME APART!
EEK!
rip
Ah ha ha ha ha ha
OH, RIGHT, WE STAPLED THAT ONE.
It's true that Tsukimi...
...is a dowdy jellyfish otaku with no interest in fashion...
...and her values and everything else are totally different from mine.
But...
That's exactly why...

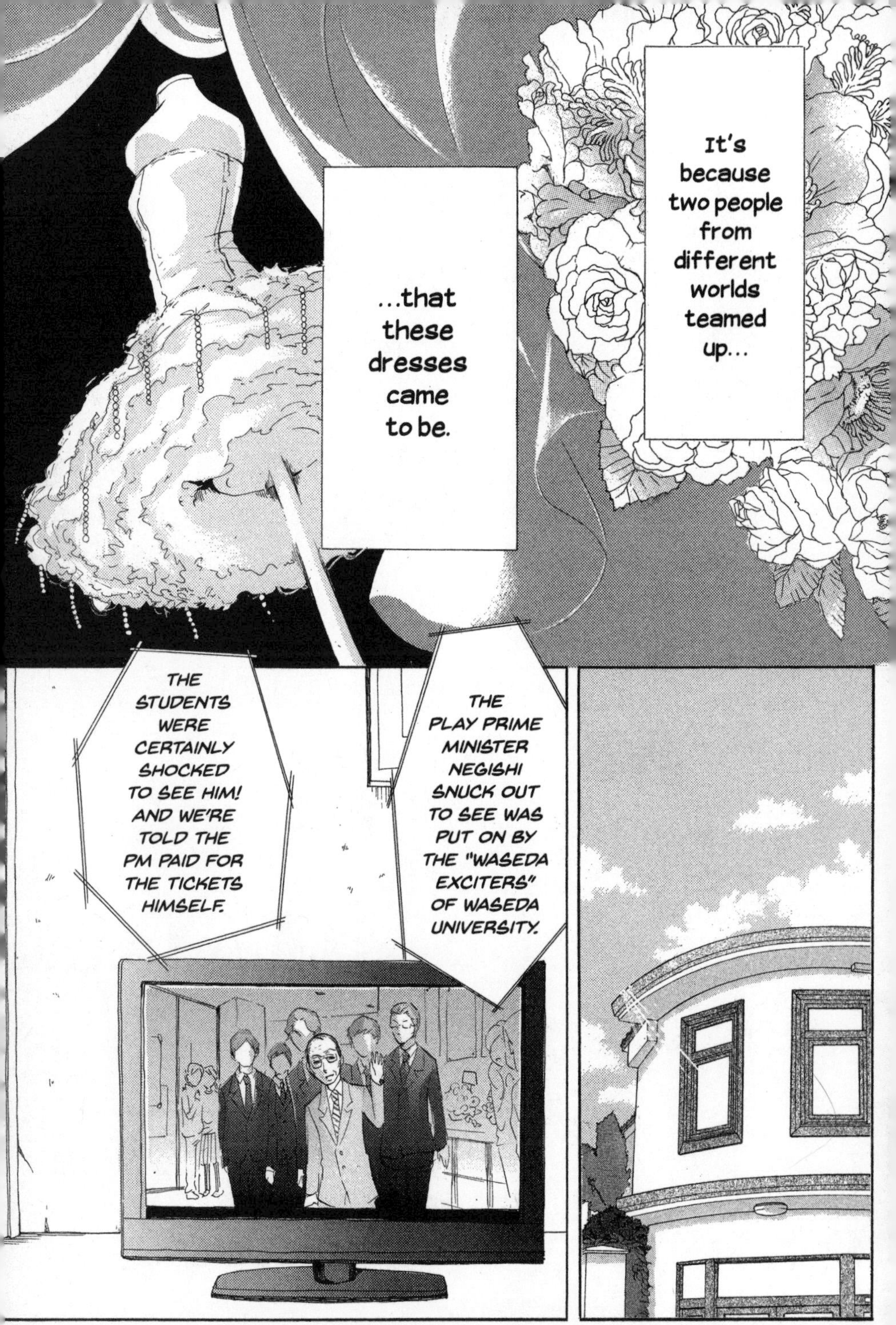
It's because two people from different worlds teamed up...
...that these dresses came to be.
THE PLAY PRIME MINISTER NEGISHI SNUCK OUT TO SEE WAS PUT ON BY THE "WASEDA EXCITERS" OF WASEDA UNIVERSITY.
THE STUDENTS WERE CERTAINLY SHOCKED TO SEE HIM! AND WE'RE TOLD THE PM PAID FOR THE TICKETS HIMSELF.

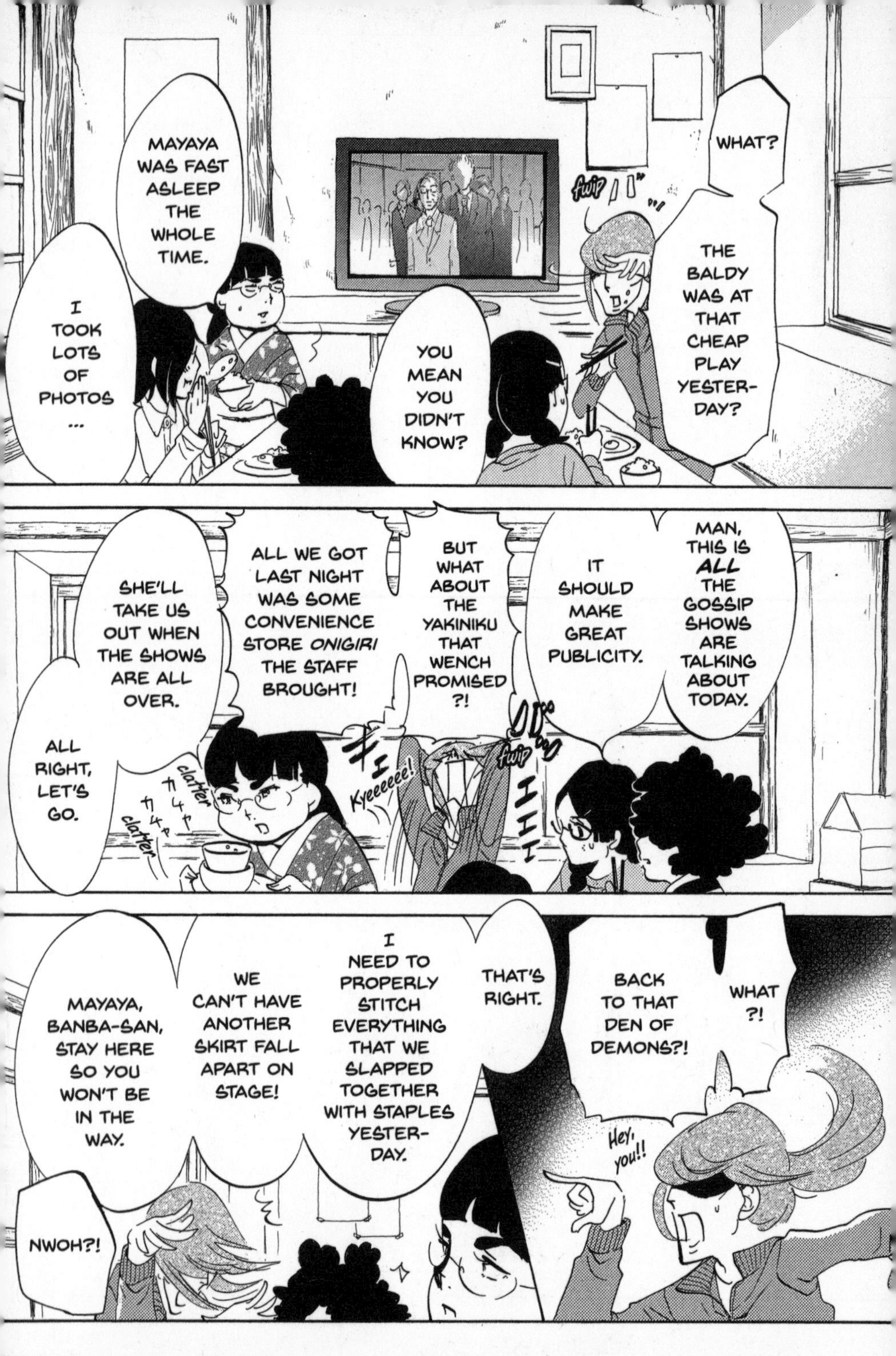
WHAT?
fwip
THE BALDY WAS AT THAT CHEAP PLAY YESTER-DAY?
YOU MEAN YOU DIDN'T KNOW?
MAYAYA WAS FAST ASLEEP THE WHOLE TIME.
I TOOK LOTS OF PHOTOS ...
MAN, THIS IS *ALL* THE GOSSIP SHOWS ARE TALKING ABOUT TODAY.
IT SHOULD MAKE GREAT PUBLICITY.
BUT WHAT ABOUT THE YAKINIKU THAT WENCH PROMISED?!
fwip
Kyeeeeee!
ALL WE GOT LAST NIGHT WAS SOME CONVENIENCE STORE *ONIGIRI* THE STAFF BROUGHT!
SHE'LL TAKE US OUT WHEN THE SHOWS ARE ALL OVER.
clatter
clatter
ALL RIGHT, LET'S GO.
WHAT?!
BACK TO THAT DEN OF DEMONS?!
Hey, you!!
THAT'S RIGHT.
I NEED TO PROPERLY STITCH EVERYTHING THAT WE SLAPPED TOGETHER WITH STAPLES YESTER-DAY.
WE CAN'T HAVE ANOTHER SKIRT FALL APART ON STAGE!
MAYAYA, BANBA-SAN, STAY HERE SO YOU WON'T BE IN THE WAY.
NWOH?!

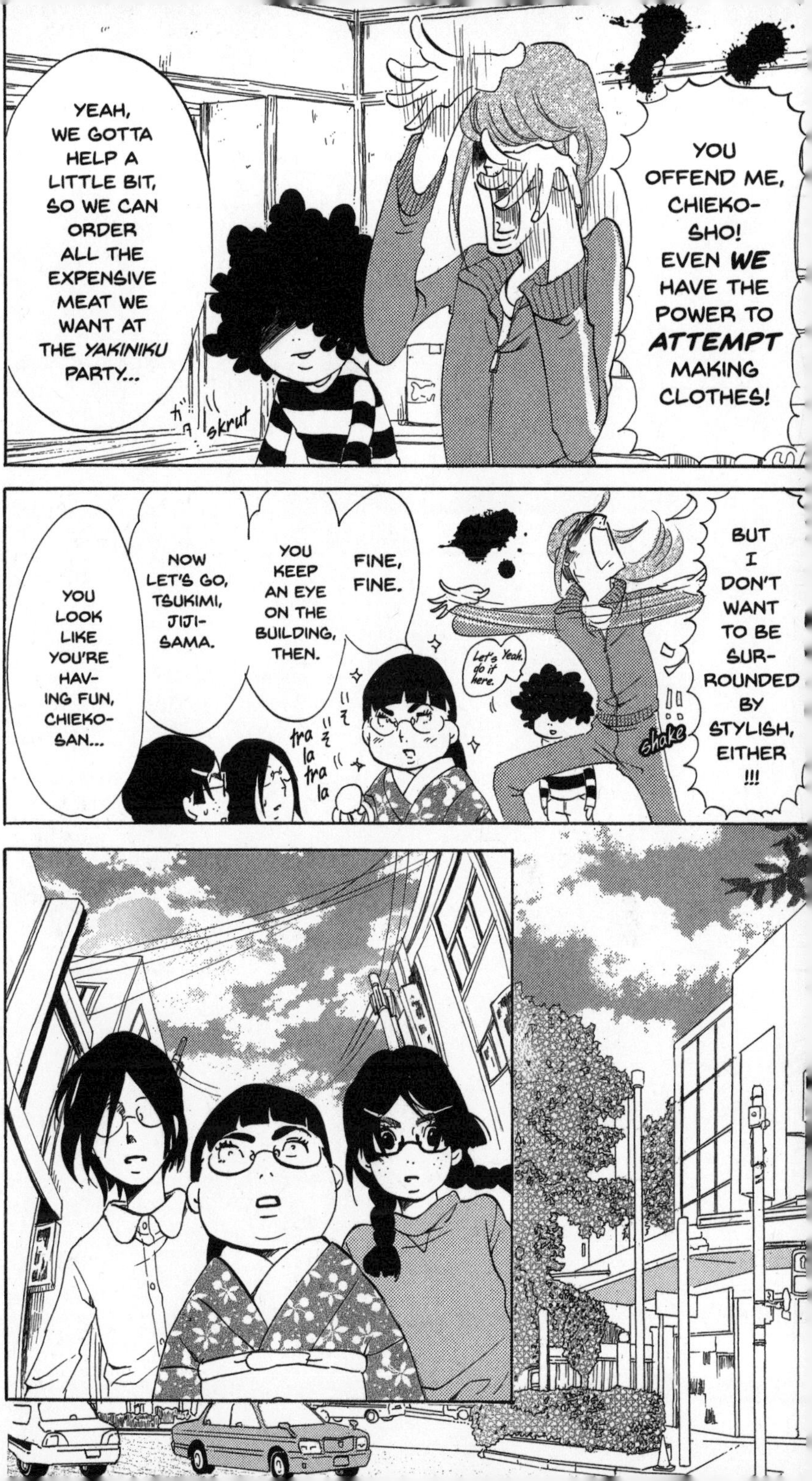
YOU OFFEND ME, CHIEKO-SHO! EVEN WE HAVE THE POWER TO ATTEMPT MAKING CLOTHES!
YEAH, WE GOTTA HELP A LITTLE BIT, SO WE CAN ORDER ALL THE EXPENSIVE MEAT WE WANT AT THE YAKINIKU PARTY...
skrut
BUT I DON'T WANT TO BE SUR-ROUNDED BY STYLISH, EITHER !!!
shake
Yeah.
Let's do it here.
FINE, FINE.
YOU KEEP AN EYE ON THE BUILDING, THEN.
NOW LET'S GO, TSUKIMI, JIJI-SAMA.
tra la tra la
YOU LOOK LIKE YOU'RE HAV-ING FUN, CHIEKO-SAN...

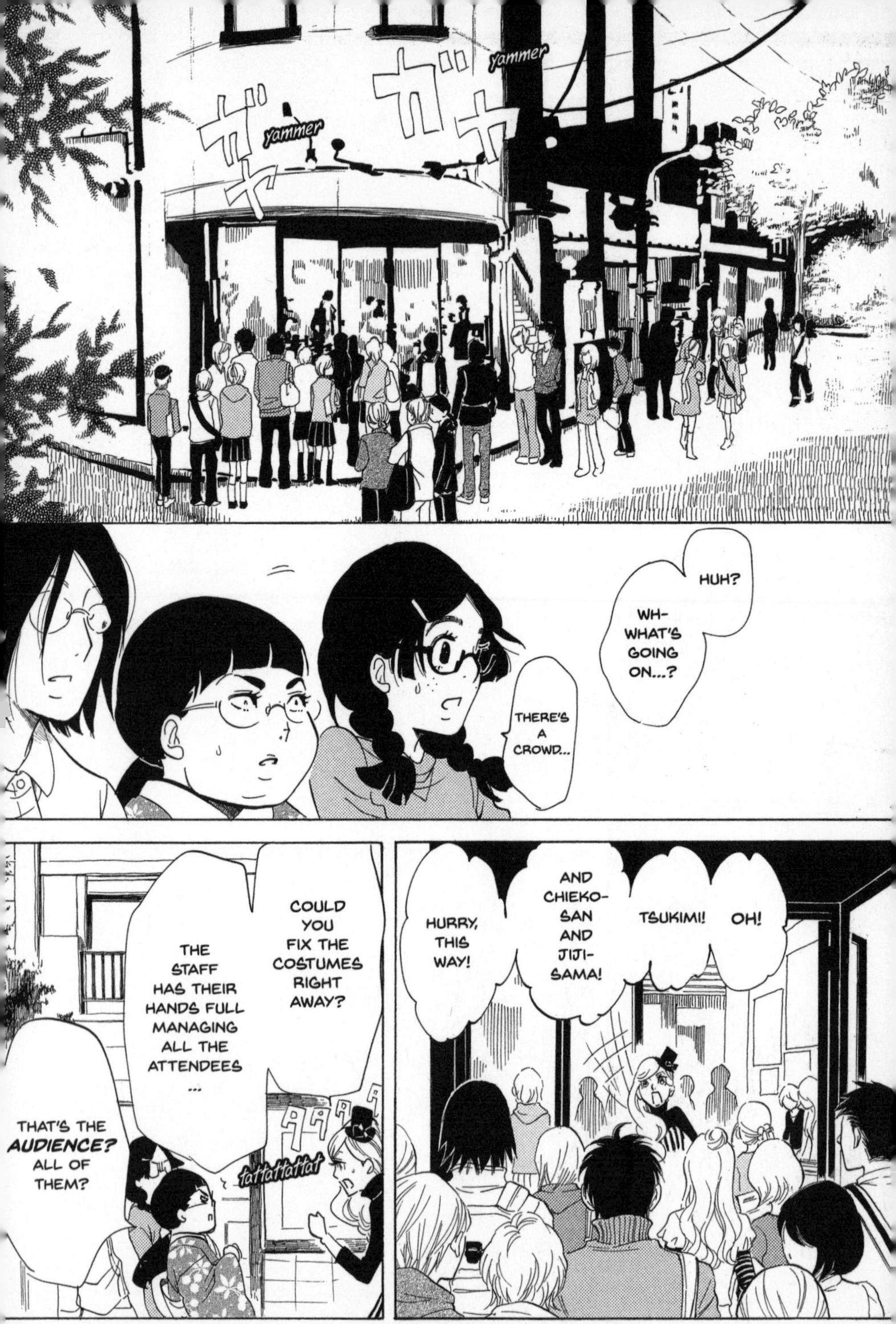
yammer
yammer
HUH?
WH- WHAT'S GOING ON...?
THERE'S A CROWD...
OH!
TSUKIMI!
AND CHIEKO-SAN AND JIJI-SAMA!
HURRY, THIS WAY!
COULD YOU FIX THE COSTUMES RIGHT AWAY?
THE STAFF HAS THEIR HANDS FULL MANAGING ALL THE ATTENDEES ...
tattattattat
THAT'S THE **AUDIENCE?** ALL OF THEM?

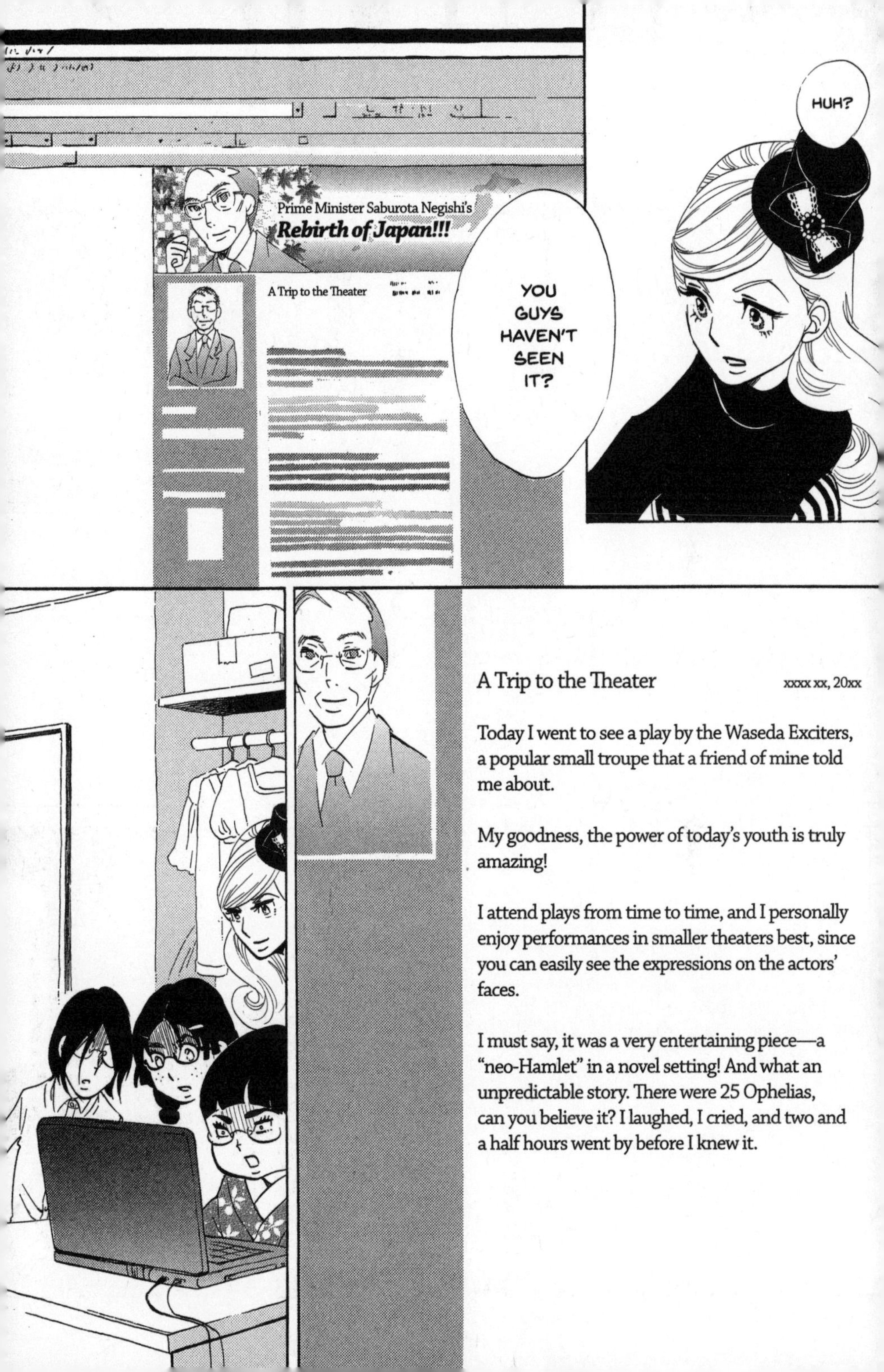
HUH?
YOU GUYS HAVEN'T SEEN IT?
Prime Minister Saburota Negishi's
Rebirth of Japan!!!
A Trip to the Theater
A Trip to the Theater
xxxx xx, 20xx
Today I went to see a play by the Waseda Exciters, a popular small troupe that a friend of mine told me about.
My goodness, the power of today's youth is truly amazing!
I attend plays from time to time, and I personally enjoy performances in smaller theaters best, since you can easily see the expressions on the actors' faces.
I must say, it was a very entertaining piece—a "neo-Hamlet" in a novel setting! And what an unpredictable story. There were 25 Ophelias, can you believe it? I laughed, I cried, and two and a half hours went by before I knew it.

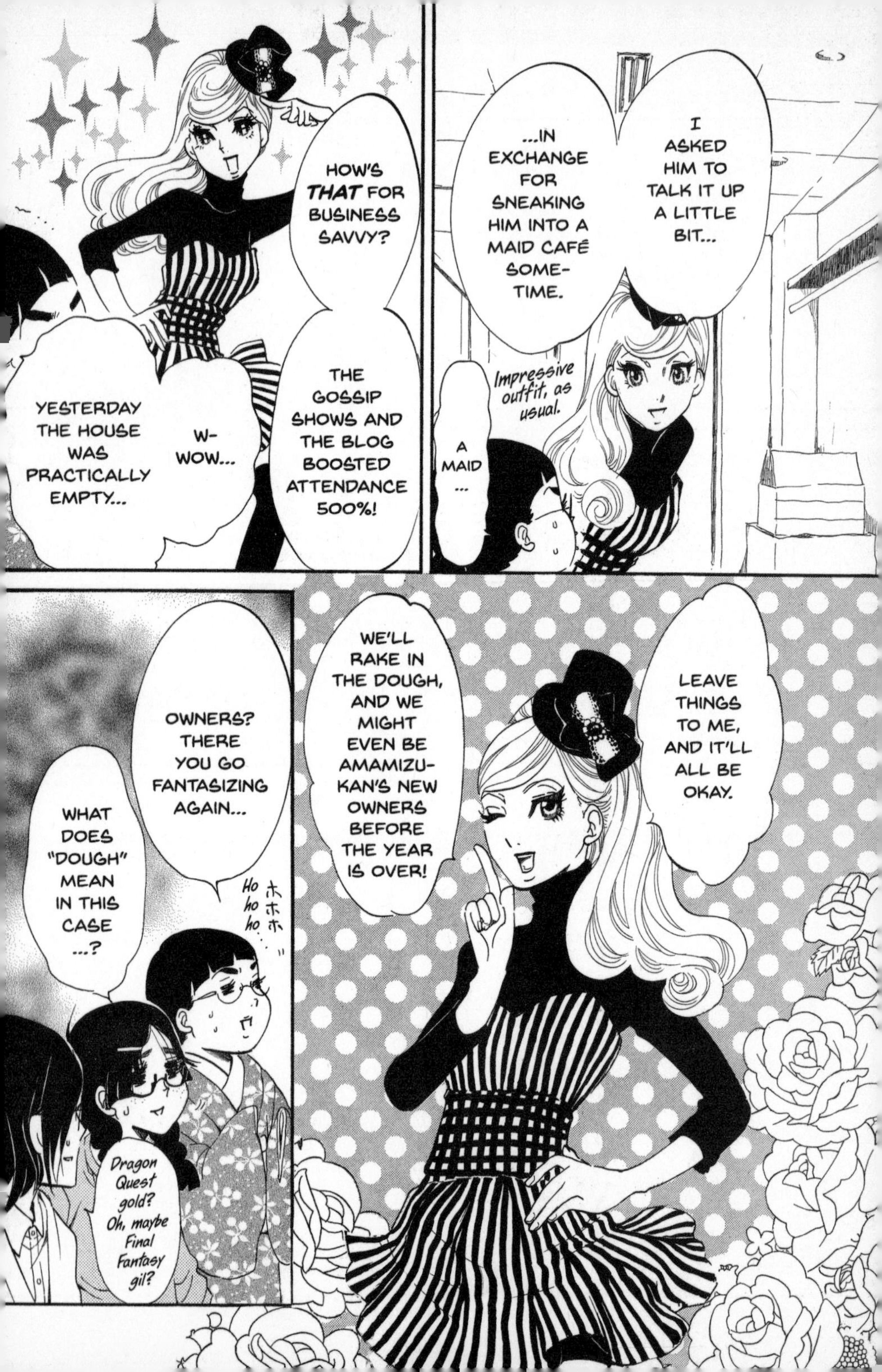
I ASKED HIM TO TALK IT UP A LITTLE BIT...
...IN EXCHANGE FOR SNEAKING HIM INTO A MAID CAFÉ SOMETIME.
Impressive outfit, as usual.
A MAID...
HOW'S **THAT** FOR BUSINESS SAVVY?
THE GOSSIP SHOWS AND THE BLOG BOOSTED ATTENDANCE 500%!
W-WOW...
YESTERDAY THE HOUSE WAS PRACTICALLY EMPTY...
LEAVE THINGS TO ME, AND IT'LL ALL BE OKAY.
WE'LL RAKE IN THE DOUGH, AND WE MIGHT EVEN BE AMAMIZUKAN'S NEW OWNERS BEFORE THE YEAR IS OVER!
OWNERS? THERE YOU GO FANTASIZING AGAIN...
Ho ho ho ホホホ
WHAT DOES "DOUGH" MEAN IN THIS CASE...?
Dragon Quest gold? Oh, maybe Final Fantasy gil?

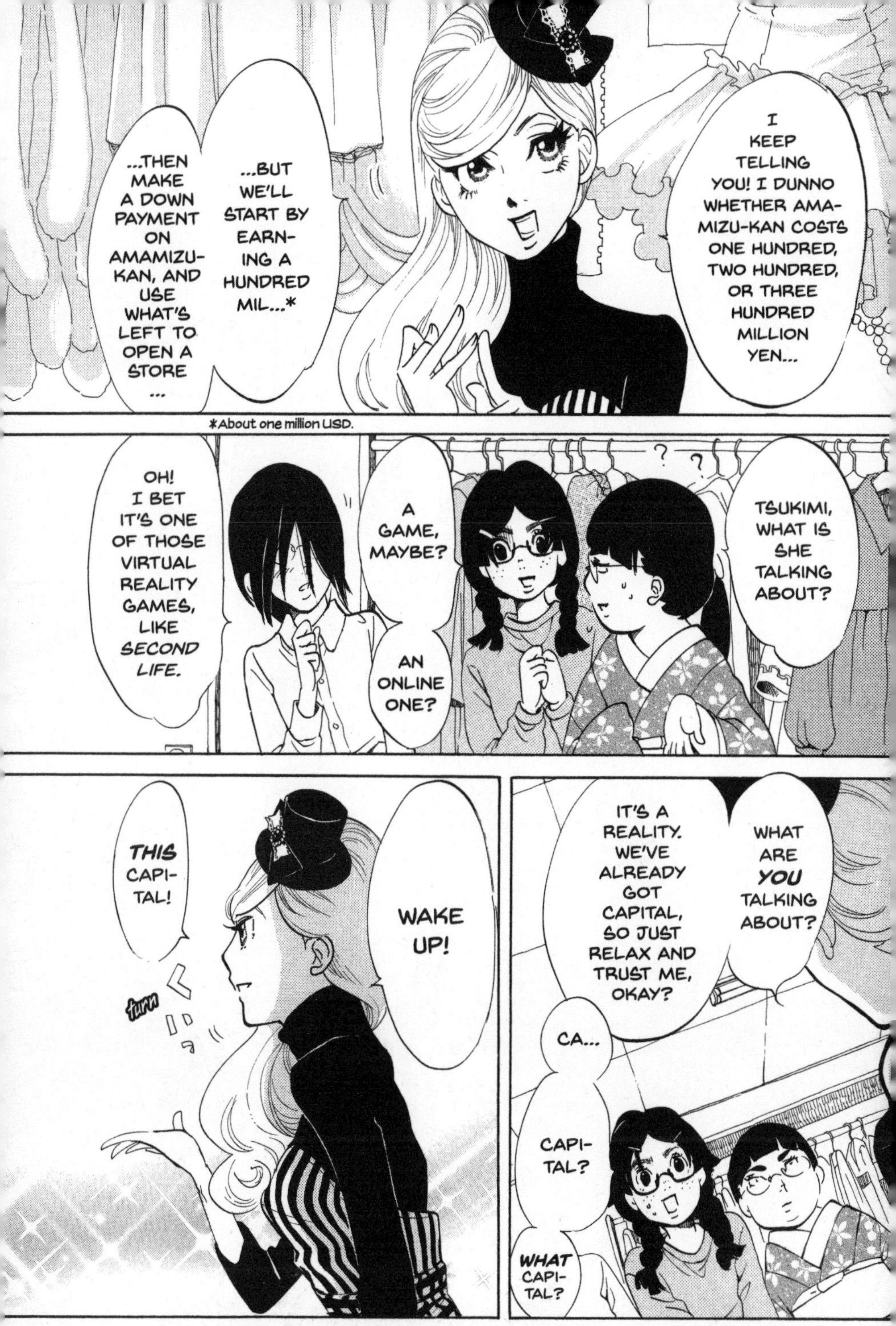
I KEEP TELLING YOU! I DUNNO WHETHER AMAMIZU-KAN COSTS ONE HUNDRED, TWO HUNDRED, OR THREE HUNDRED MILLION YEN...
...BUT WE'LL START BY EARNING A HUNDRED MIL...*
...THEN MAKE A DOWN PAYMENT ON AMAMIZU-KAN, AND USE WHAT'S LEFT TO OPEN A STORE...
TSUKIMI, WHAT IS SHE TALKING ABOUT?
A GAME, MAYBE?
AN ONLINE ONE?
OH! I BET IT'S ONE OF THOSE VIRTUAL REALITY GAMES, LIKE *SECOND LIFE*.
WHAT ARE *YOU* TALKING ABOUT?
IT'S A REALITY. WE'VE ALREADY GOT CAPITAL, SO JUST RELAX AND TRUST ME, OKAY?
CA...
CAPITAL?
WHAT CAPITAL?
WAKE UP!
THIS CAPITAL!
turn

*About one million USD.

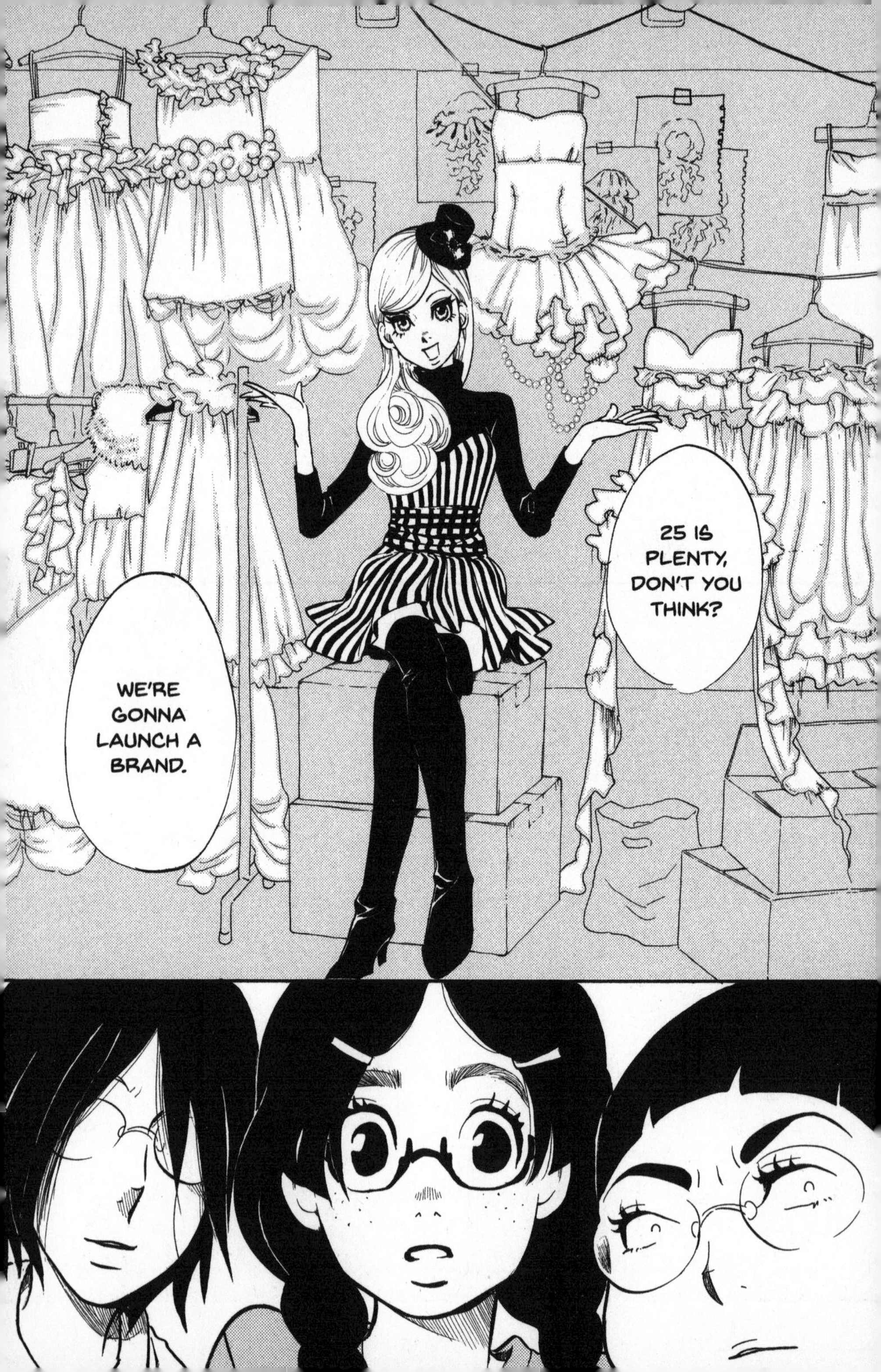
25 IS PLENTY, DON'T YOU THINK?
WE'RE GONNA LAUNCH A BRAND.

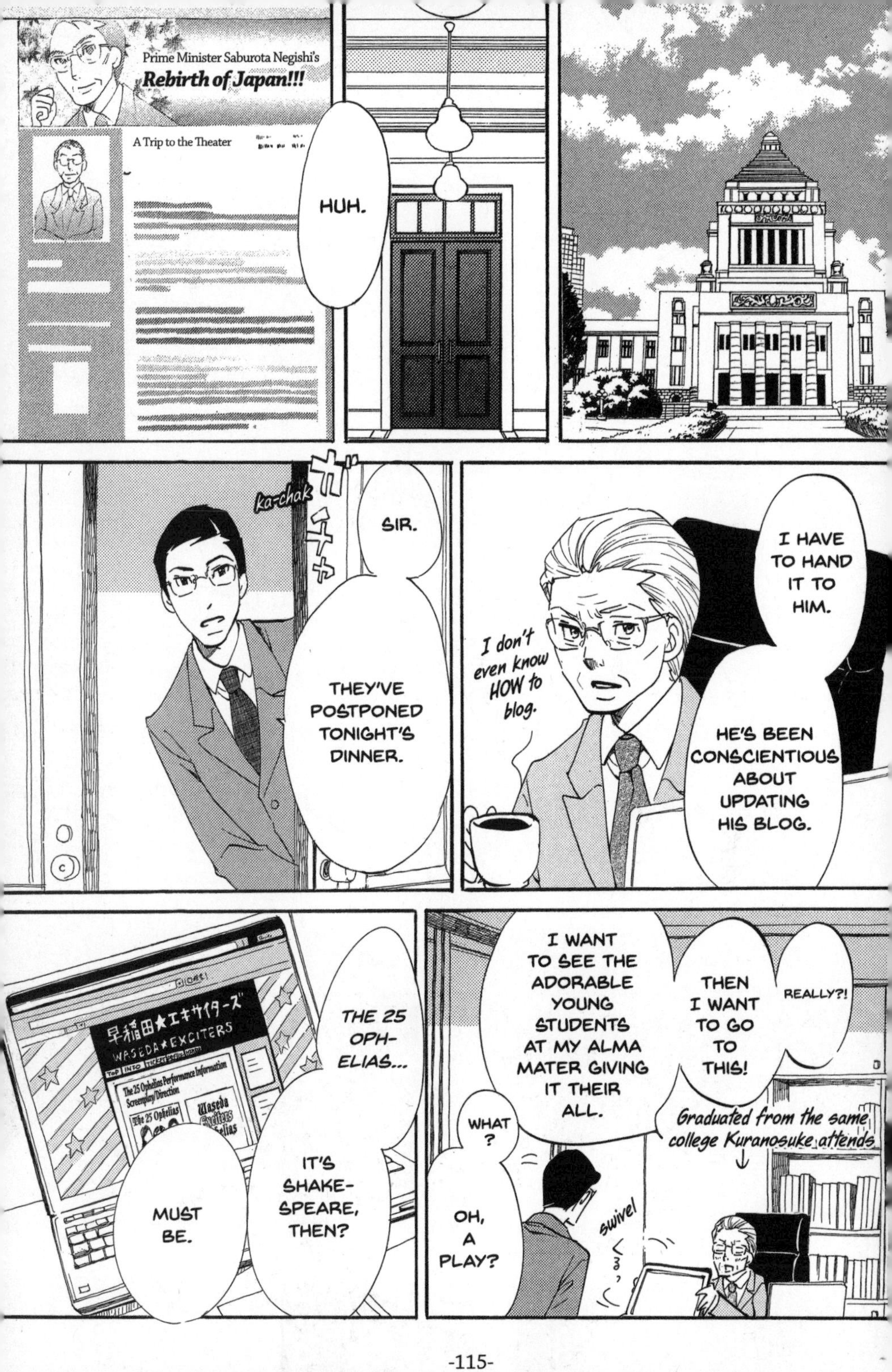
HUH.
Prime Minister Saburota Negishi's
Rebirth of Japan!!!
A Trip to the Theater
I HAVE TO HAND IT TO HIM.
HE'S BEEN CONSCIENTIOUS ABOUT UPDATING HIS BLOG.
I don't even know HOW to blog.
ka-chak
SIR.
THEY'VE POSTPONED TONIGHT'S DINNER.
REALLY?!
THEN I WANT TO GO TO THIS!
I WANT TO SEE THE ADORABLE YOUNG STUDENTS AT MY ALMA MATER GIVING IT THEIR ALL.
WHAT?
Graduated from the same college Kuranosuke attends
OH, A PLAY?
swivel
早稲田★エキサイターズ
WASEDA★EXCITERS
The 25 Ophelias Performance Information
Screenplay/Direction
The 25 Ophelias
Waseda Exciters
THE 25 OPH-ELIAS...
IT'S SHAKE-SPEARE, THEN?
MUST BE.

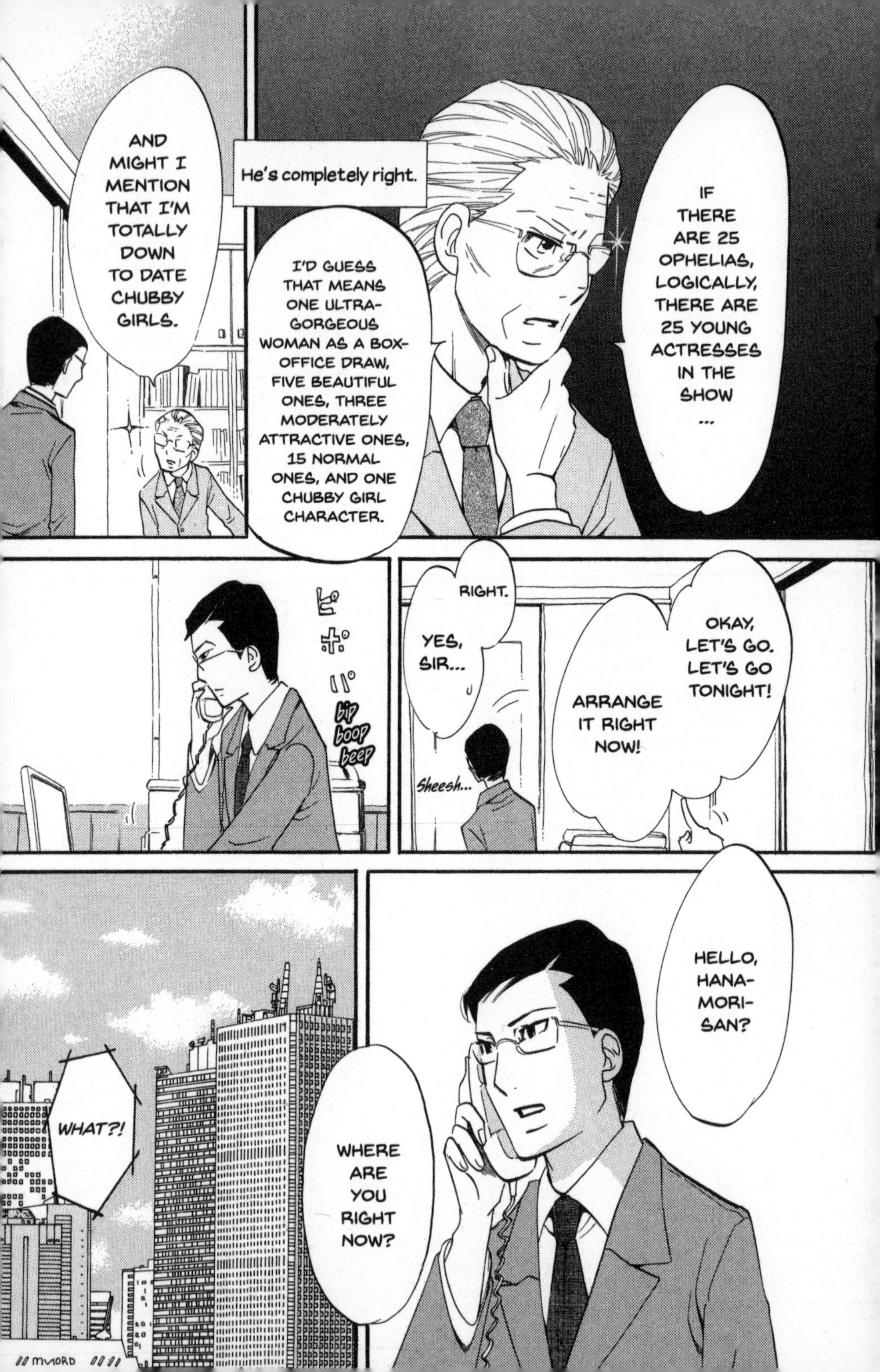
IF THERE ARE 25 OPHELIAS, LOGICALLY, THERE ARE 25 YOUNG ACTRESSES IN THE SHOW ...
I'D GUESS THAT MEANS ONE ULTRA-GORGEOUS WOMAN AS A BOX-OFFICE DRAW, FIVE BEAUTIFUL ONES, THREE MODERATELY ATTRACTIVE ONES, 15 NORMAL ONES, AND ONE CHUBBY GIRL CHARACTER.
He's completely right.
AND MIGHT I MENTION THAT I'M TOTALLY DOWN TO DATE CHUBBY GIRLS.
OKAY, LET'S GO. LET'S GO TONIGHT!
ARRANGE IT RIGHT NOW!
RIGHT.
YES, SIR...
Sheesh...
ピ ポ パ
bip boop beep
HELLO, HANA-MORI-SAN?
WHERE ARE YOU RIGHT NOW?
WHAT?!

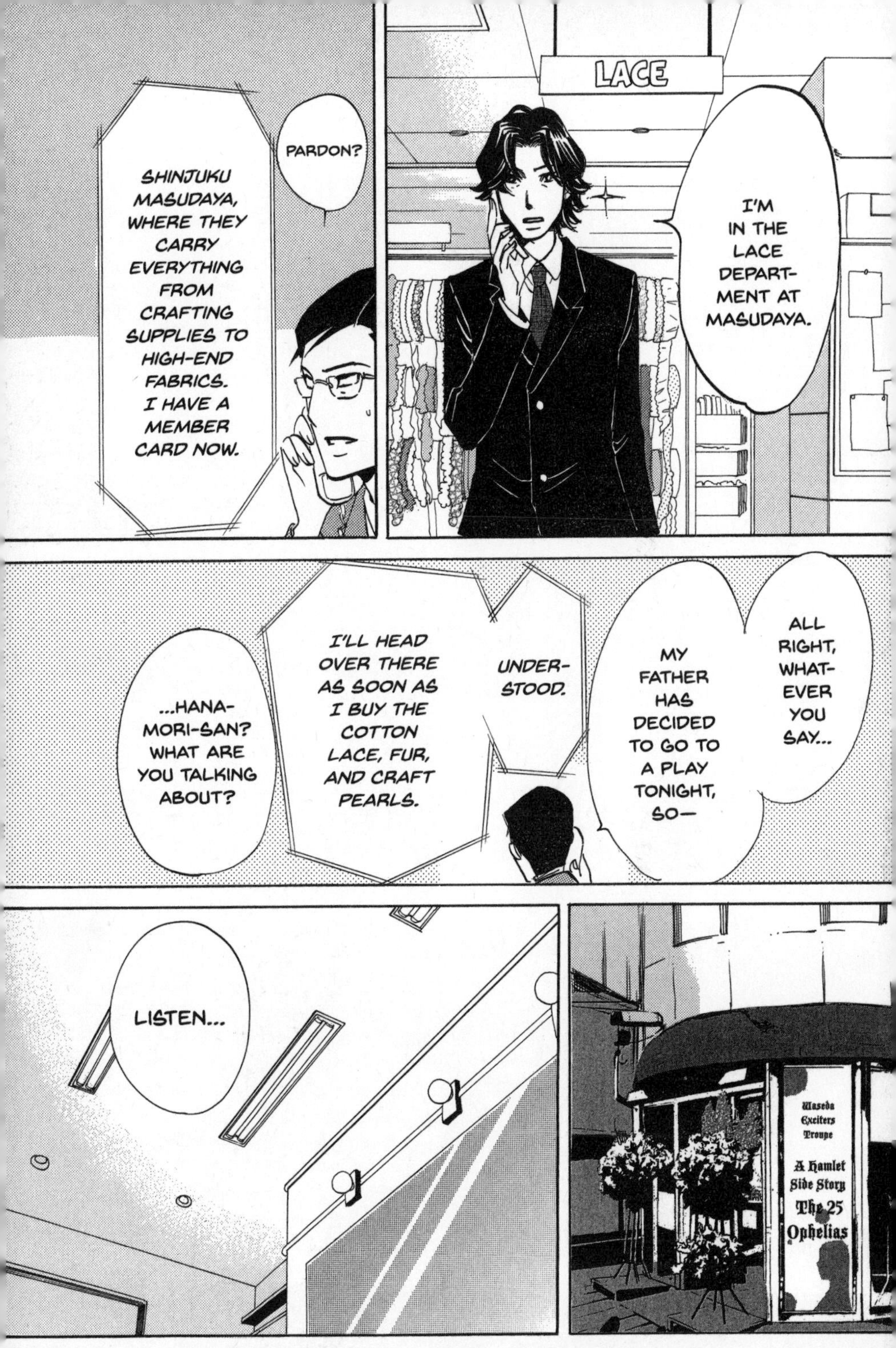
LACE
I'M IN THE LACE DEPARTMENT AT MASUDAYA.
PARDON?
SHINJUKU MASUDAYA, WHERE THEY CARRY EVERYTHING FROM CRAFTING SUPPLIES TO HIGH-END FABRICS. I HAVE A MEMBER CARD NOW.
ALL RIGHT, WHATEVER YOU SAY...
MY FATHER HAS DECIDED TO GO TO A PLAY TONIGHT, SO—
UNDERSTOOD.
I'LL HEAD OVER THERE AS SOON AS I BUY THE COTTON LACE, FUR, AND CRAFT PEARLS.
...HANAMORI-SAN? WHAT ARE YOU TALKING ABOUT?
Waseda Exciters Troupe
A Hamlet Side Story
The 25 Ophelias
LISTEN...

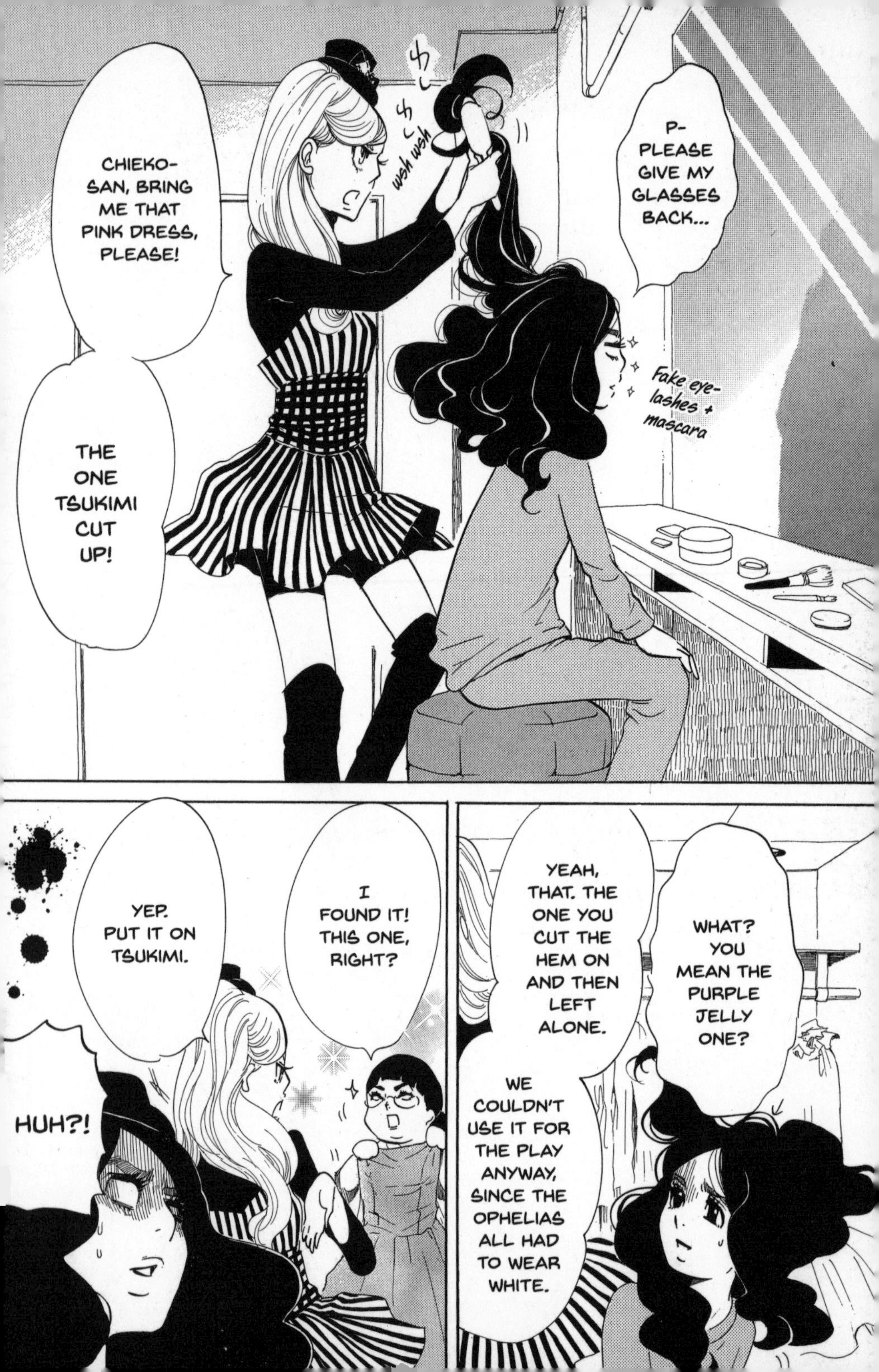
P- PLEASE GIVE MY GLASSES BACK...
Fake eye-lashes + mascara
wsh wsh
CHIEKO-SAN, BRING ME THAT PINK DRESS, PLEASE!
THE ONE TSUKIMI CUT UP!
WHAT? YOU MEAN THE PURPLE JELLY ONE?
YEAH, THAT. THE ONE YOU CUT THE HEM ON AND THEN LEFT ALONE.
WE COULDN'T USE IT FOR THE PLAY ANYWAY, SINCE THE OPHELIAS ALL HAD TO WEAR WHITE.
I FOUND IT! THIS ONE, RIGHT?
YEP. PUT IT ON TSUKIMI.
HUH?!

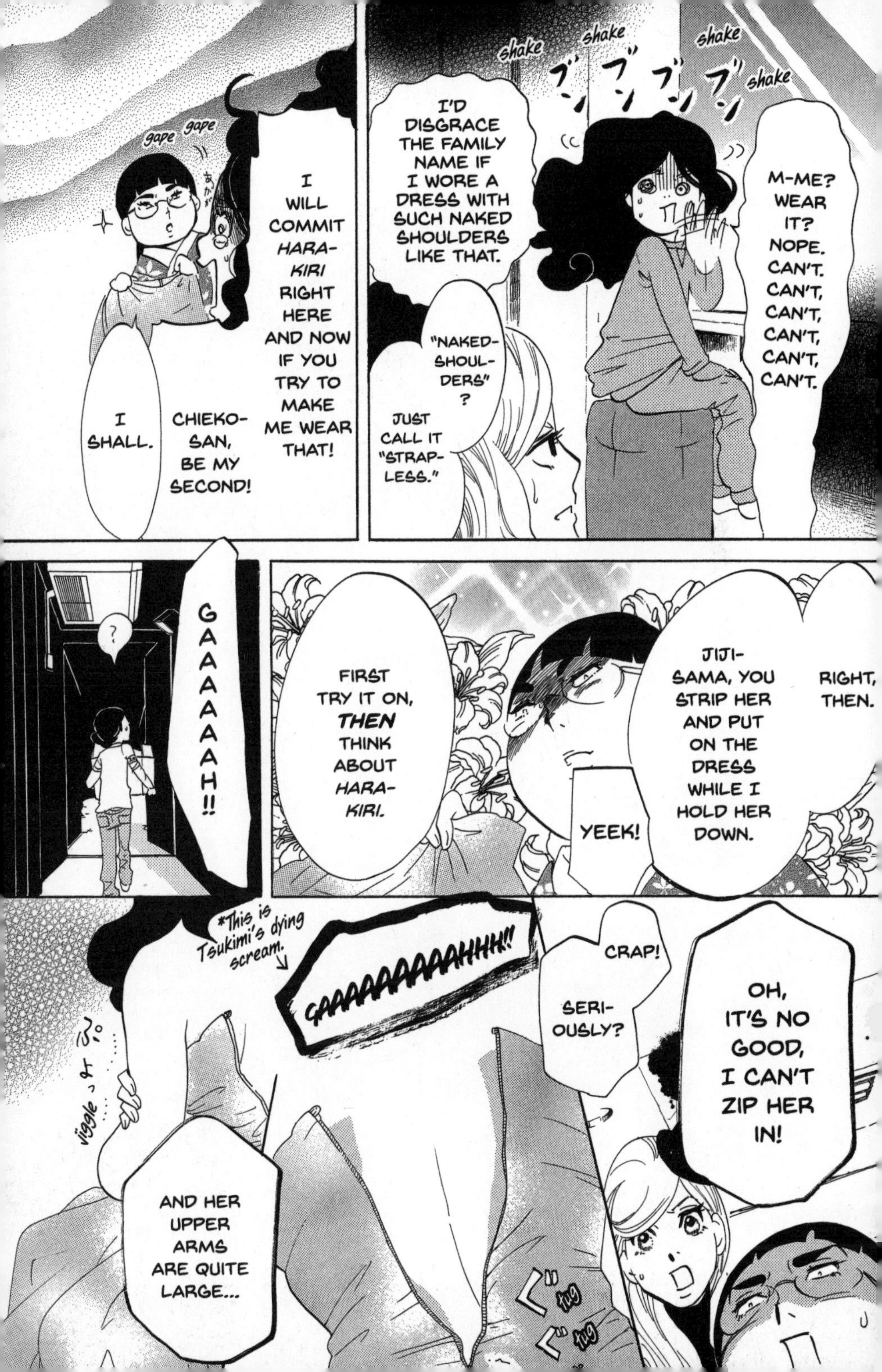
shake shake shake shake
M-ME? WEAR IT? NOPE. CAN'T. CAN'T, CAN'T, CAN'T, CAN'T, CAN'T.
I'D DISGRACE THE FAMILY NAME IF I WORE A DRESS WITH SUCH NAKED SHOULDERS LIKE THAT.
"NAKED-SHOULDERS"?
JUST CALL IT "STRAPLESS."
gape gape
I WILL COMMIT *HARA-KIRI* RIGHT HERE AND NOW IF YOU TRY TO MAKE ME WEAR THAT!
CHIEKO-SAN, BE MY SECOND!
I SHALL.
RIGHT, THEN.
JIJI-SAMA, YOU STRIP HER AND PUT ON THE DRESS WHILE I HOLD HER DOWN.
YEEK!
FIRST TRY IT ON, ***THEN*** THINK ABOUT *HARA-KIRI.*
GAAAAAAAH!!
?
OH, IT'S NO GOOD, I CAN'T ZIP HER IN!
CRAP!
SERIOUSLY?
GAAAAAAAAAHHH!!
*This is Tsukimi's dying scream.
AND HER UPPER ARMS ARE QUITE LARGE...
jiggle
tug
tug

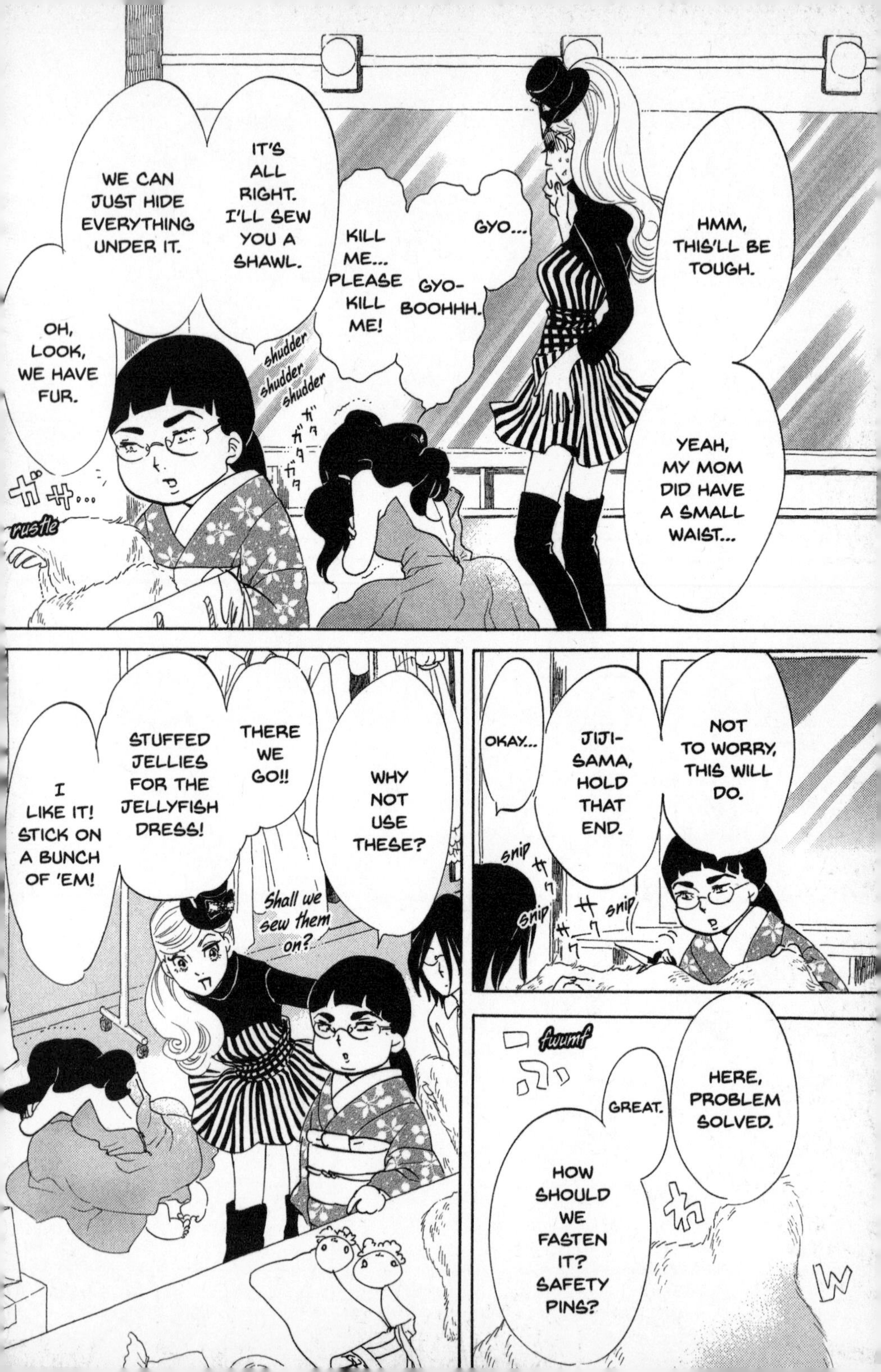
HMM, THIS'LL BE TOUGH.
YEAH, MY MOM DID HAVE A SMALL WAIST...
GYO... GYO-BOOHHH.
KILL ME... PLEASE KILL ME!
shudder shudder shudder
IT'S ALL RIGHT. I'LL SEW YOU A SHAWL.
WE CAN JUST HIDE EVERYTHING UNDER IT.
OH, LOOK, WE HAVE FUR.
rustle
NOT TO WORRY, THIS WILL DO.
JIJI-SAMA, HOLD THAT END.
OKAY...
snip
snip
snip
HERE, PROBLEM SOLVED.
GREAT.
fwumf
HOW SHOULD WE FASTEN IT? SAFETY PINS?
WHY NOT USE THESE?
THERE WE GO!!
STUFFED JELLIES FOR THE JELLYFISH DRESS!
I LIKE IT! STICK ON A BUNCH OF 'EM!
Shall we sew them on?

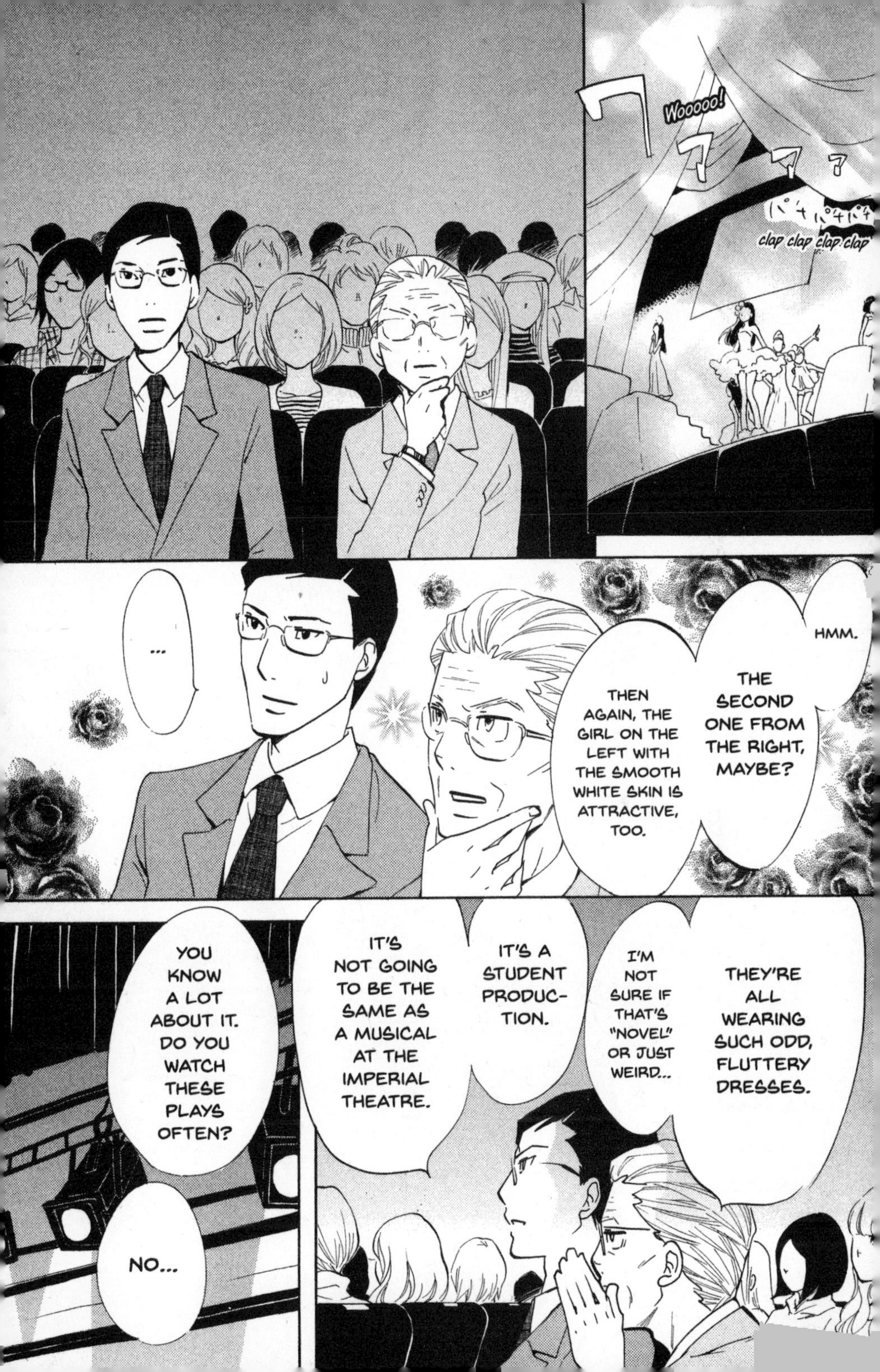
Wooooo!
clap clap clap clap
HMM.
THE SECOND ONE FROM THE RIGHT, MAYBE?
THEN AGAIN, THE GIRL ON THE LEFT WITH THE SMOOTH WHITE SKIN IS ATTRACTIVE, TOO.
...
THEY'RE ALL WEARING SUCH ODD, FLUTTERY DRESSES.
I'M NOT SURE IF THAT'S "NOVEL" OR JUST WEIRD...
IT'S A STUDENT PRODUC-TION.
IT'S NOT GOING TO BE THE SAME AS A MUSICAL AT THE IMPERIAL THEATRE.
YOU KNOW A LOT ABOUT IT. DO YOU WATCH THESE PLAYS OFTEN?
NO...

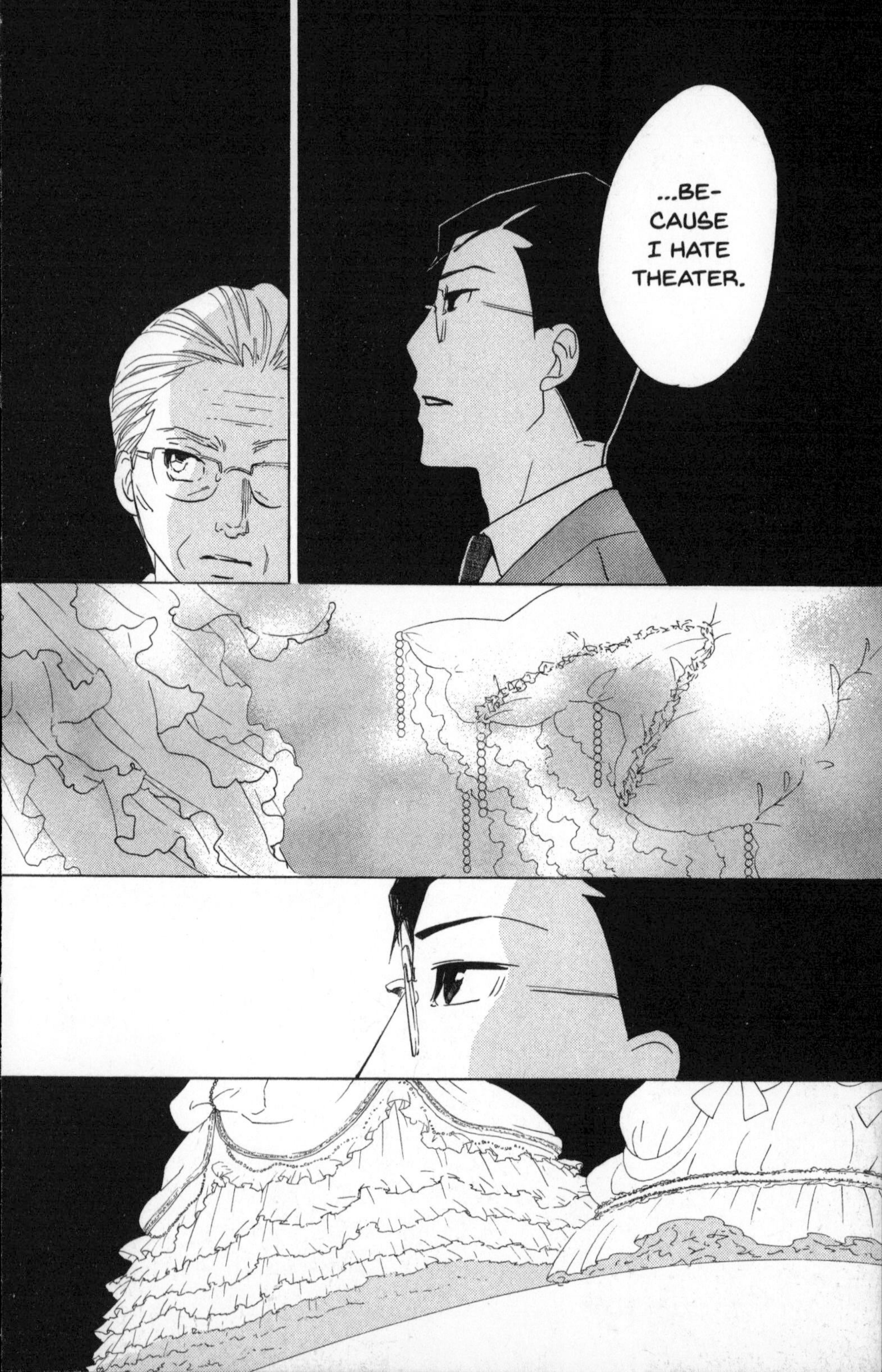
...BE-
CAUSE
I HATE
THEATER.

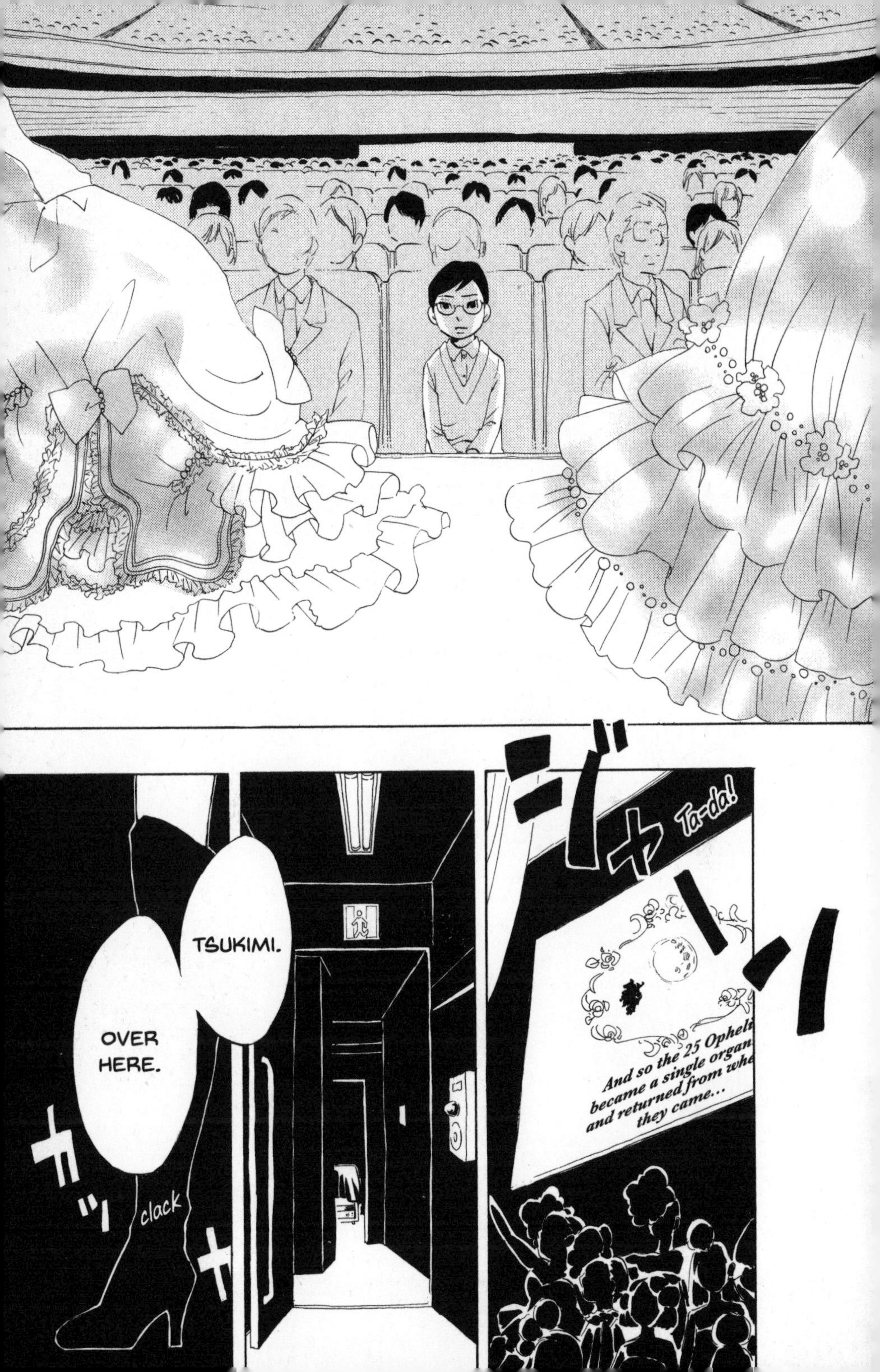
ジャーン
Ta-da!
And so the 25 Opheli
became a single organ
and returned from whe
they came...
TSUKIMI.
OVER HERE.
カッ
clack

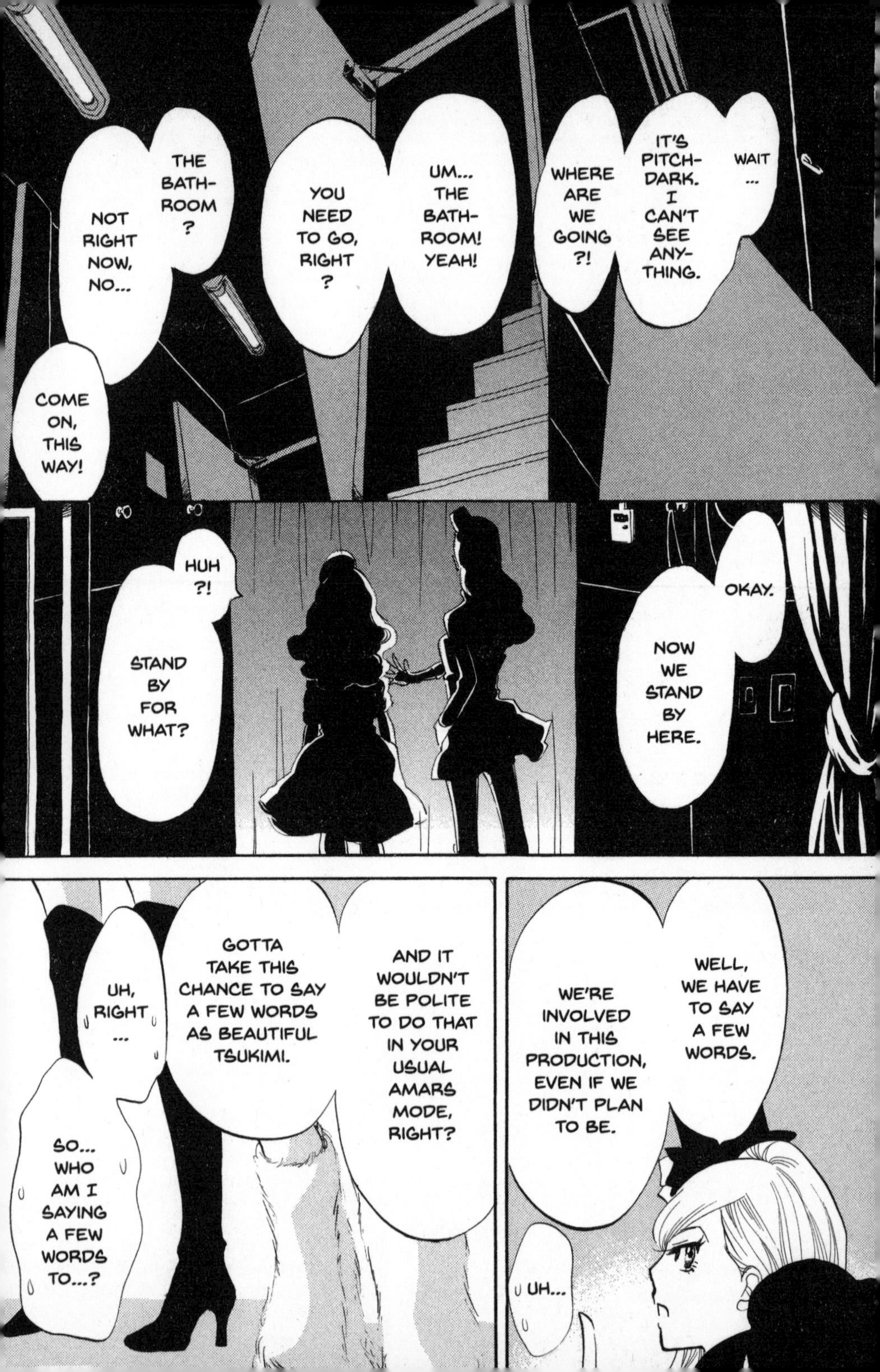
WAIT ...
IT'S PITCH-DARK. I CAN'T SEE ANYTHING.
WHERE ARE WE GOING?!
UM... THE BATHROOM! YEAH!
YOU NEED TO GO, RIGHT?
THE BATHROOM?
NOT RIGHT NOW, NO...
COME ON, THIS WAY!
OKAY.
NOW WE STAND BY HERE.
HUH?!
STAND BY FOR WHAT?
WELL, WE HAVE TO SAY A FEW WORDS.
WE'RE INVOLVED IN THIS PRODUCTION, EVEN IF WE DIDN'T PLAN TO BE.
UH...
AND IT WOULDN'T BE POLITE TO DO THAT IN YOUR USUAL AMARS MODE, RIGHT?
GOTTA TAKE THIS CHANCE TO SAY A FEW WORDS AS BEAUTIFUL TSUKIMI.
UH, RIGHT ...
SO... WHO AM I SAYING A FEW WORDS TO...?

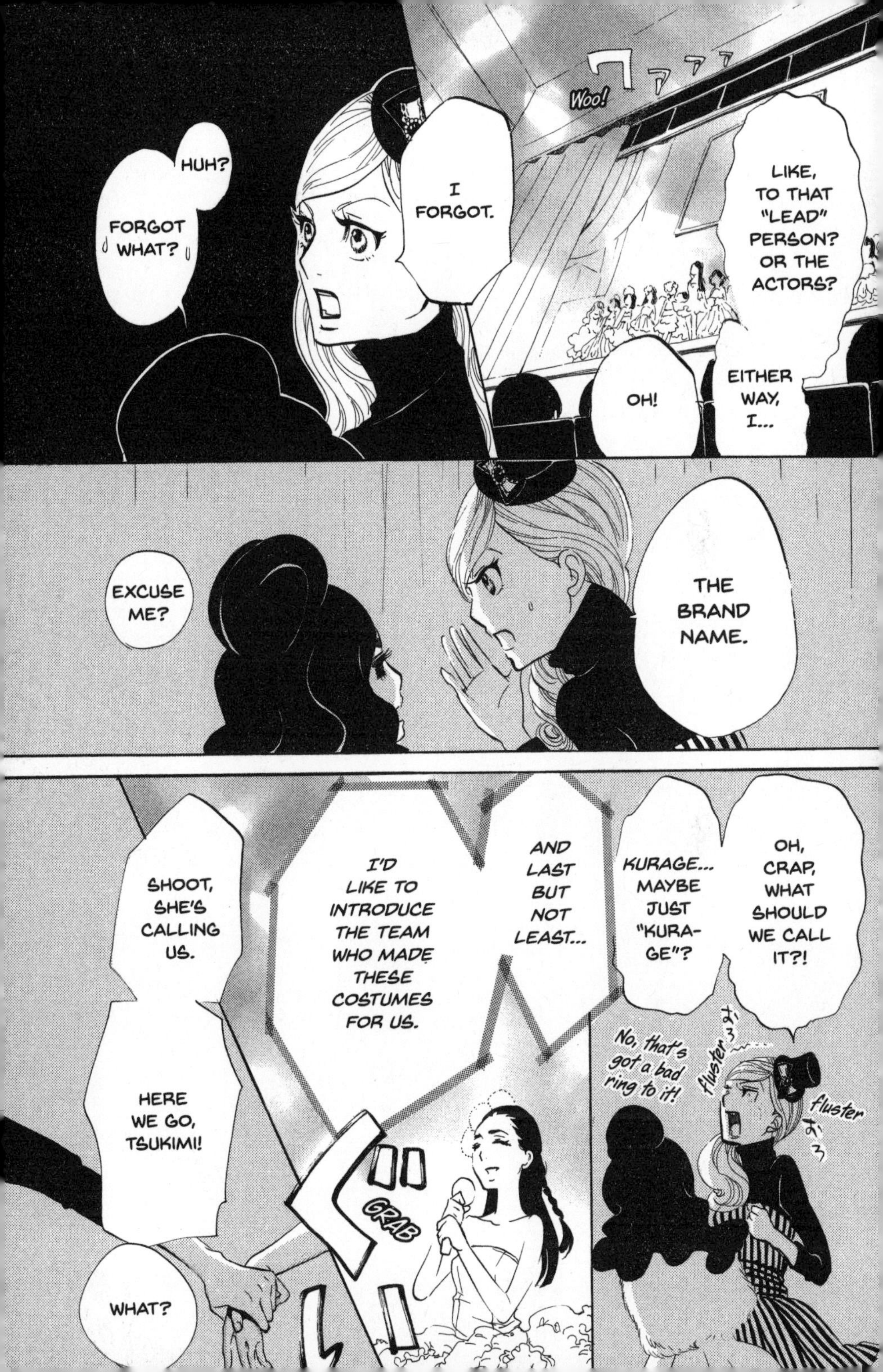
Woo!
LIKE, TO THAT "LEAD" PERSON? OR THE ACTORS?
EITHER WAY, I...
OH!
I FORGOT.
HUH?
FORGOT WHAT?
THE BRAND NAME.
EXCUSE ME?
OH, CRAP, WHAT SHOULD WE CALL IT?!
KURAGE... MAYBE JUST "KURA-GE"?
fluster
fluster
No, that's got a bad ring to it!
AND LAST BUT NOT LEAST...
I'D LIKE TO INTRODUCE THE TEAM WHO MADE THESE COSTUMES FOR US.
SHOOT, SHE'S CALLING US.
HERE WE GO, TSUKIMI!
GRAB
WHAT?

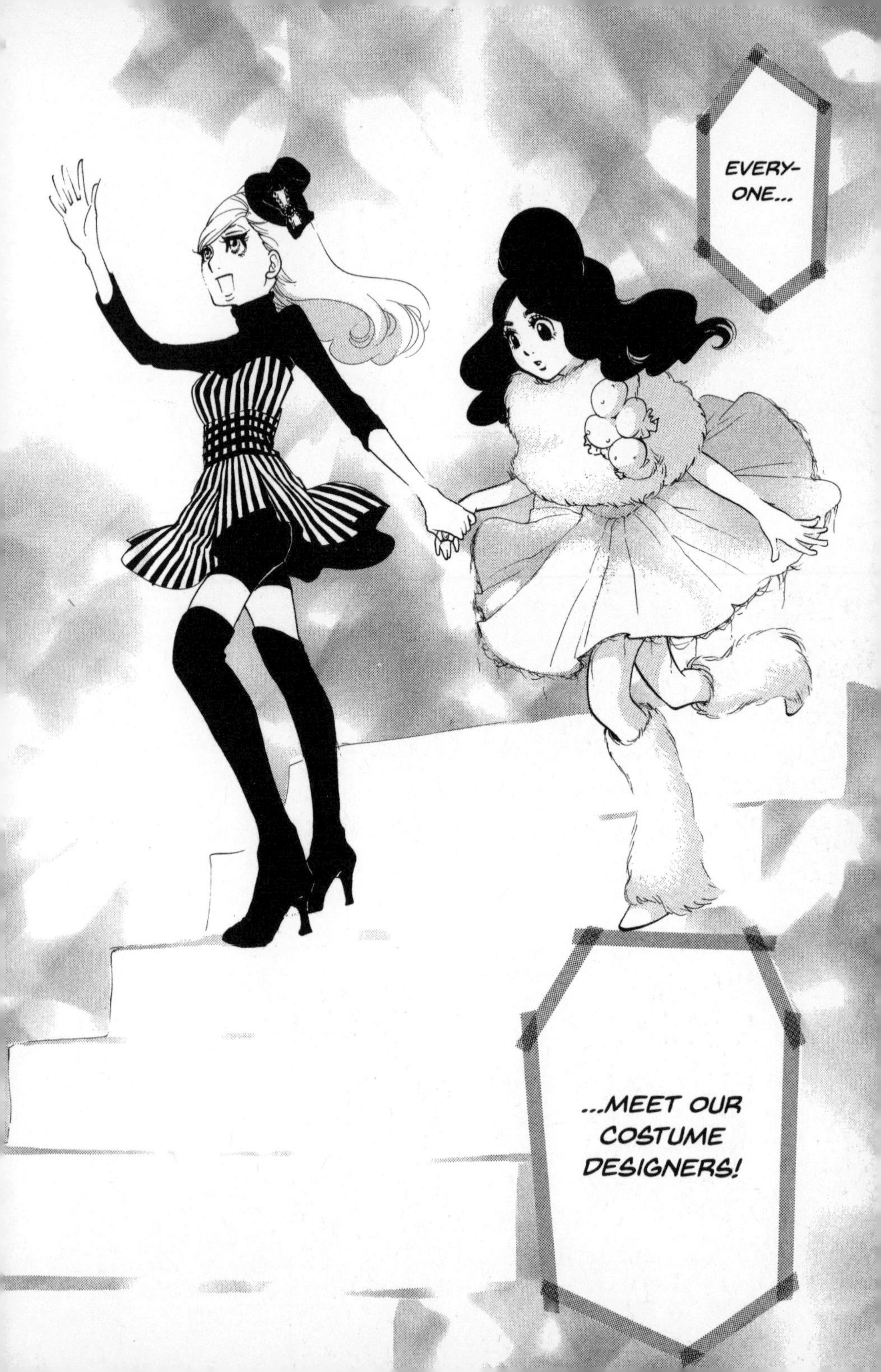
EVERY-ONE...
...MEET OUR COSTUME DESIGNERS!

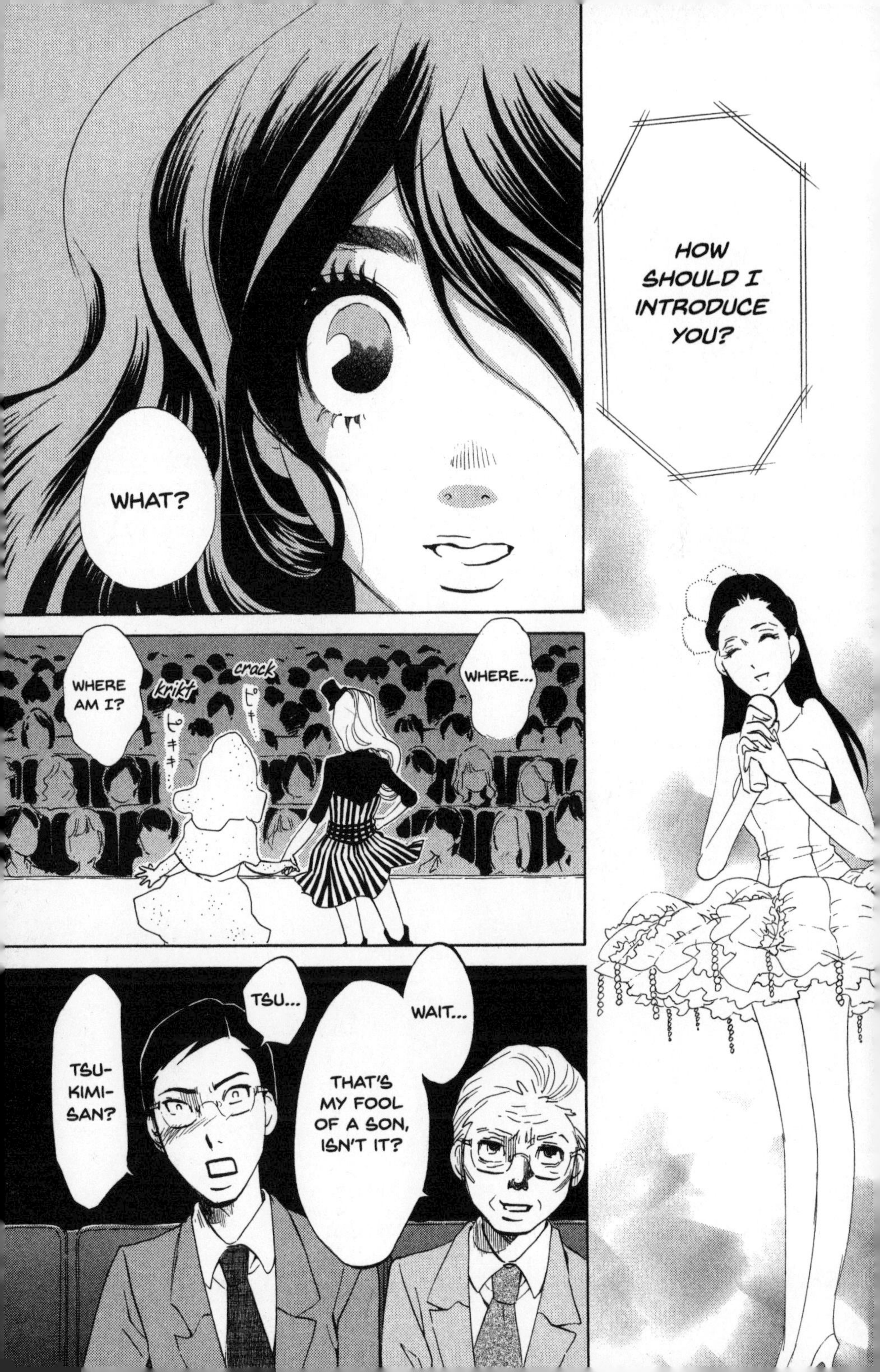
HOW SHOULD I INTRODUCE YOU?
WHAT?
WHERE...
crack
ピキ…
krikt
ピキキ…
WHERE AM I?
WAIT...
THAT'S MY FOOL OF A SON, ISN'T IT?
TSU...
TSU-KIMI-SAN?

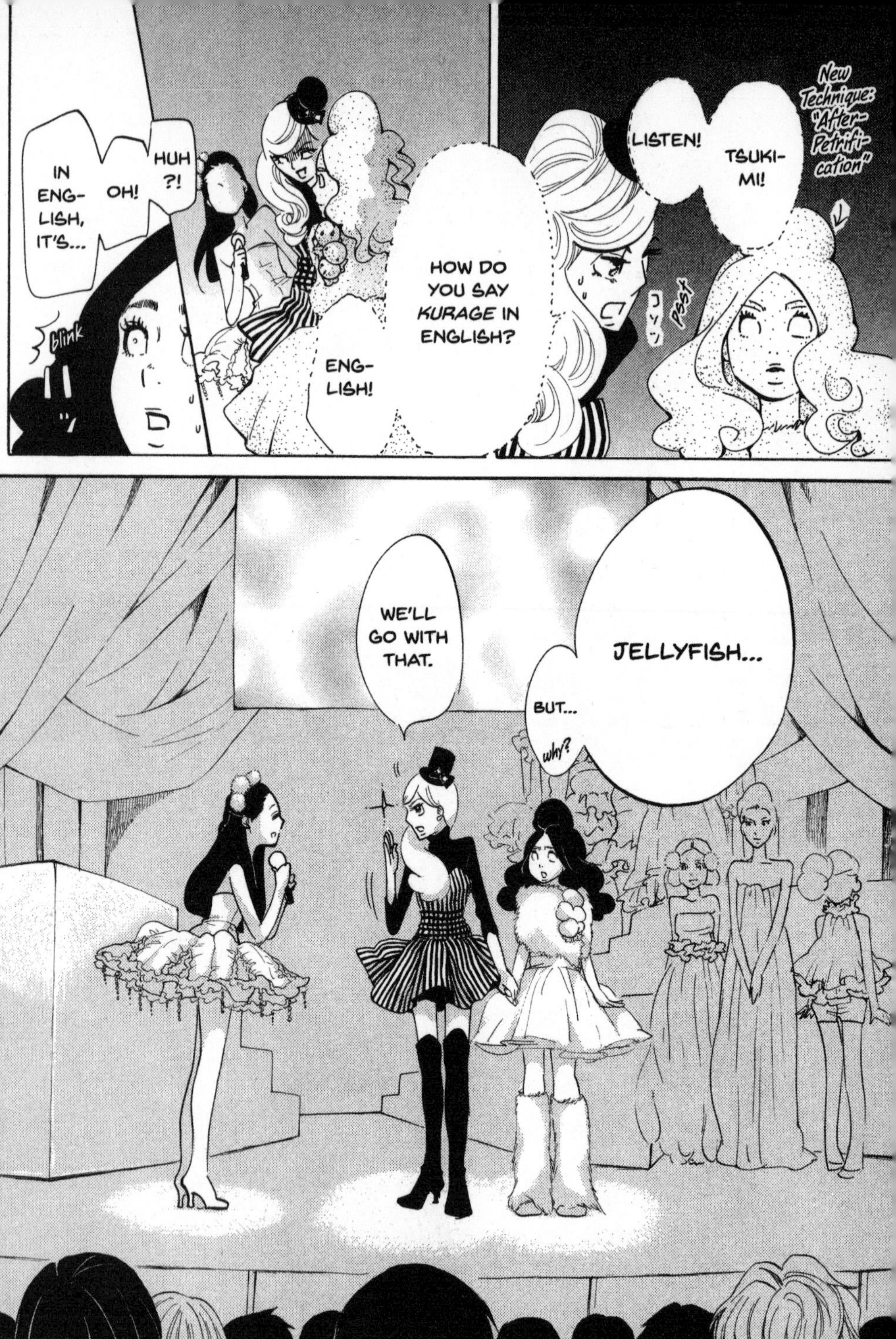
New Technique: "After-Petrification"
TSUKI-MI!
LISTEN!
psst
コソッ
HOW DO YOU SAY *KURAGE* IN ENGLISH?
ENG-LISH!
HUH?!
OH!
IN ENG-LISH, IT'S...
blink
JELLYFISH...
BUT...
why?
WE'LL GO WITH THAT.

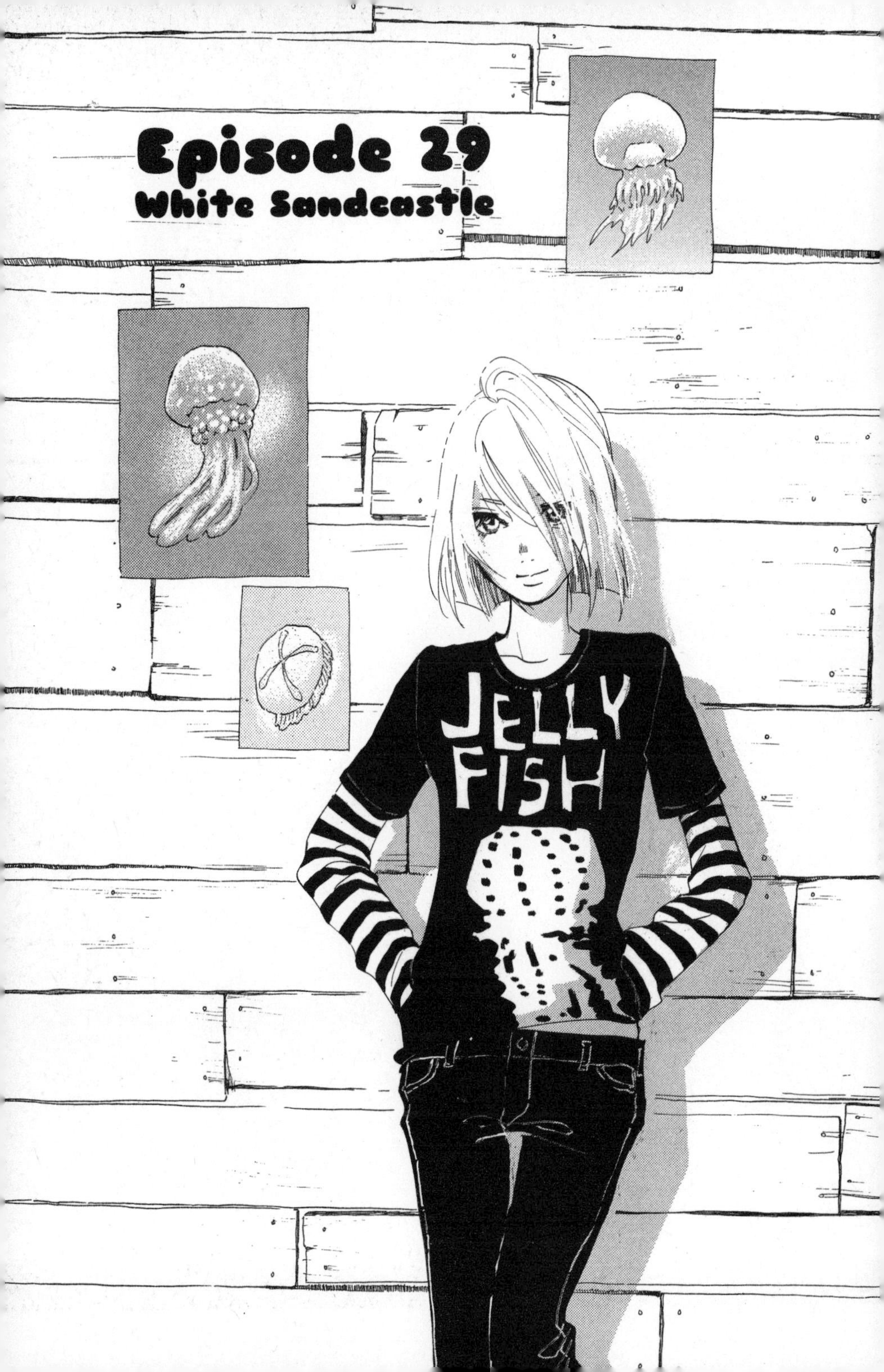
Episode 29
White Sandcastle
JELLY FISH

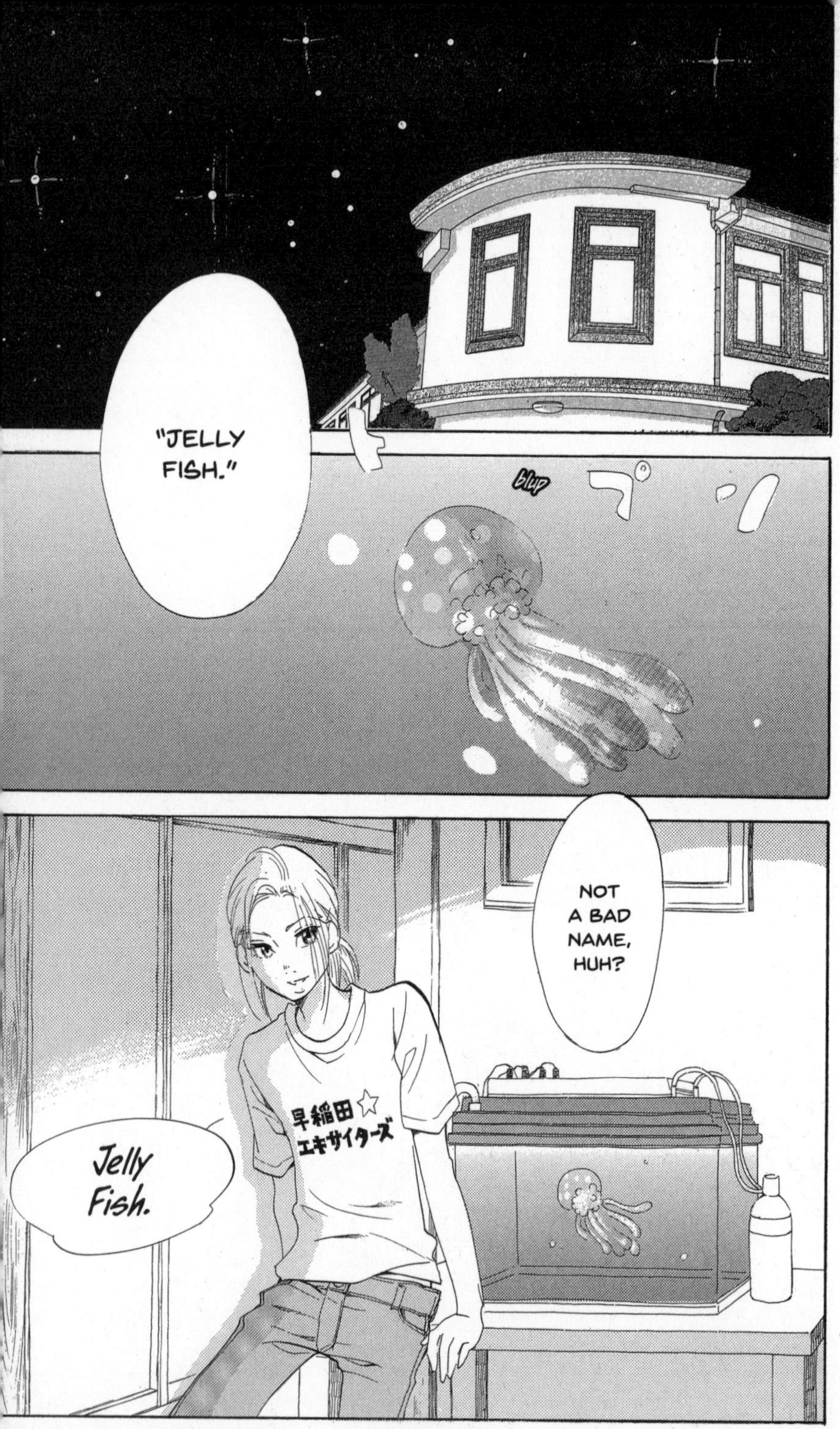
"JELLY FISH."
blup
NOT A BAD NAME, HUH?
早稲田☆エキサイターズ
Jelly Fish.

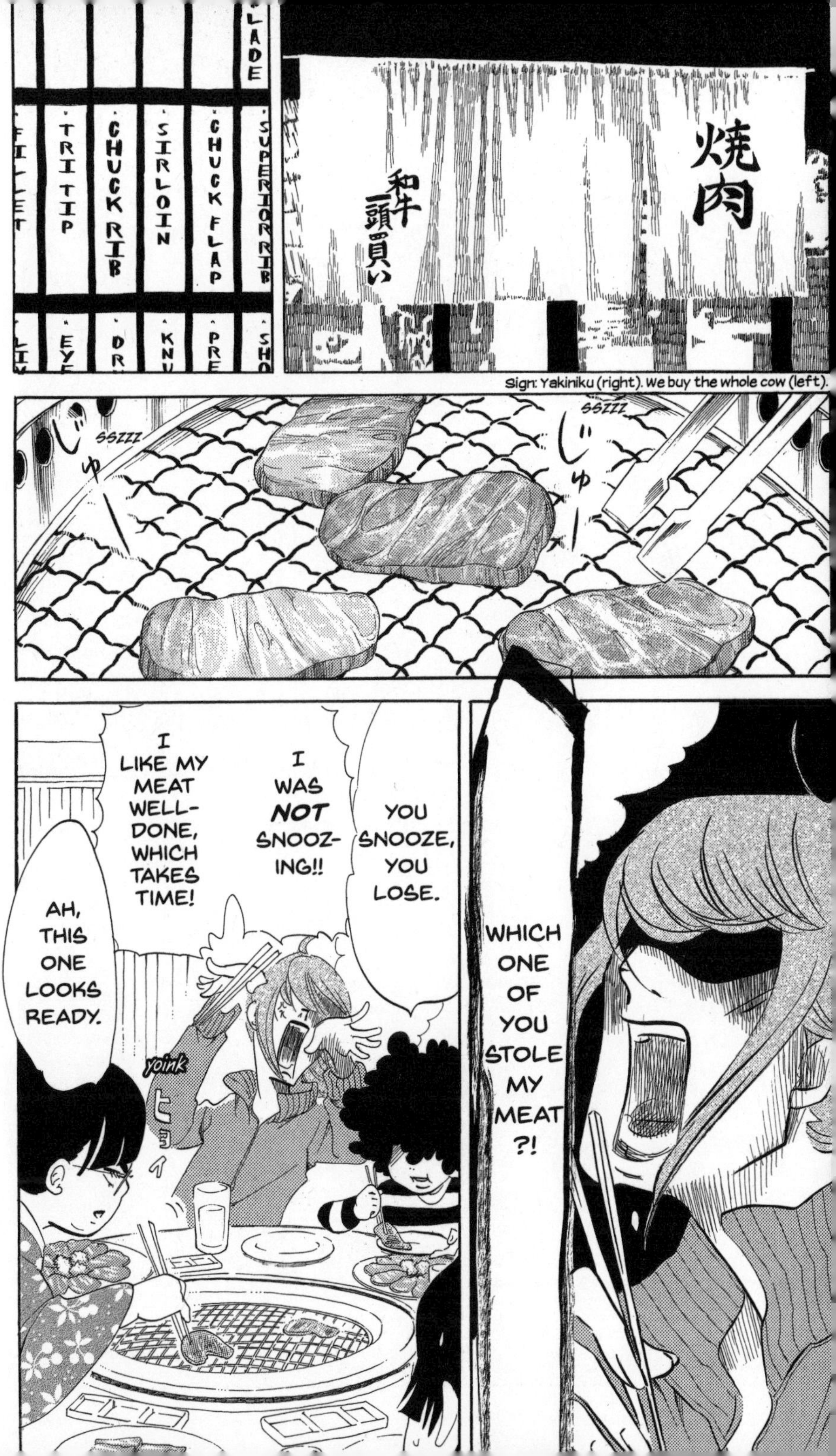
焼肉
和牛一頭買い
SUPERIOR RIB
CHUCK FLAP
SIRLOIN
CHUCK RIB
TRI TIP
FILLET
Sign: Yakiniku (right). We buy the whole cow (left).
SSZZZ じゅ〜
SSZZZ じゅ〜
WHICH ONE OF YOU STOLE MY MEAT?!
YOU SNOOZE, YOU LOSE.
I WAS NOT SNOOZING!!
I LIKE MY MEAT WELL-DONE, WHICH TAKES TIME!
AH, THIS ONE LOOKS READY.
yoink ヒョイ

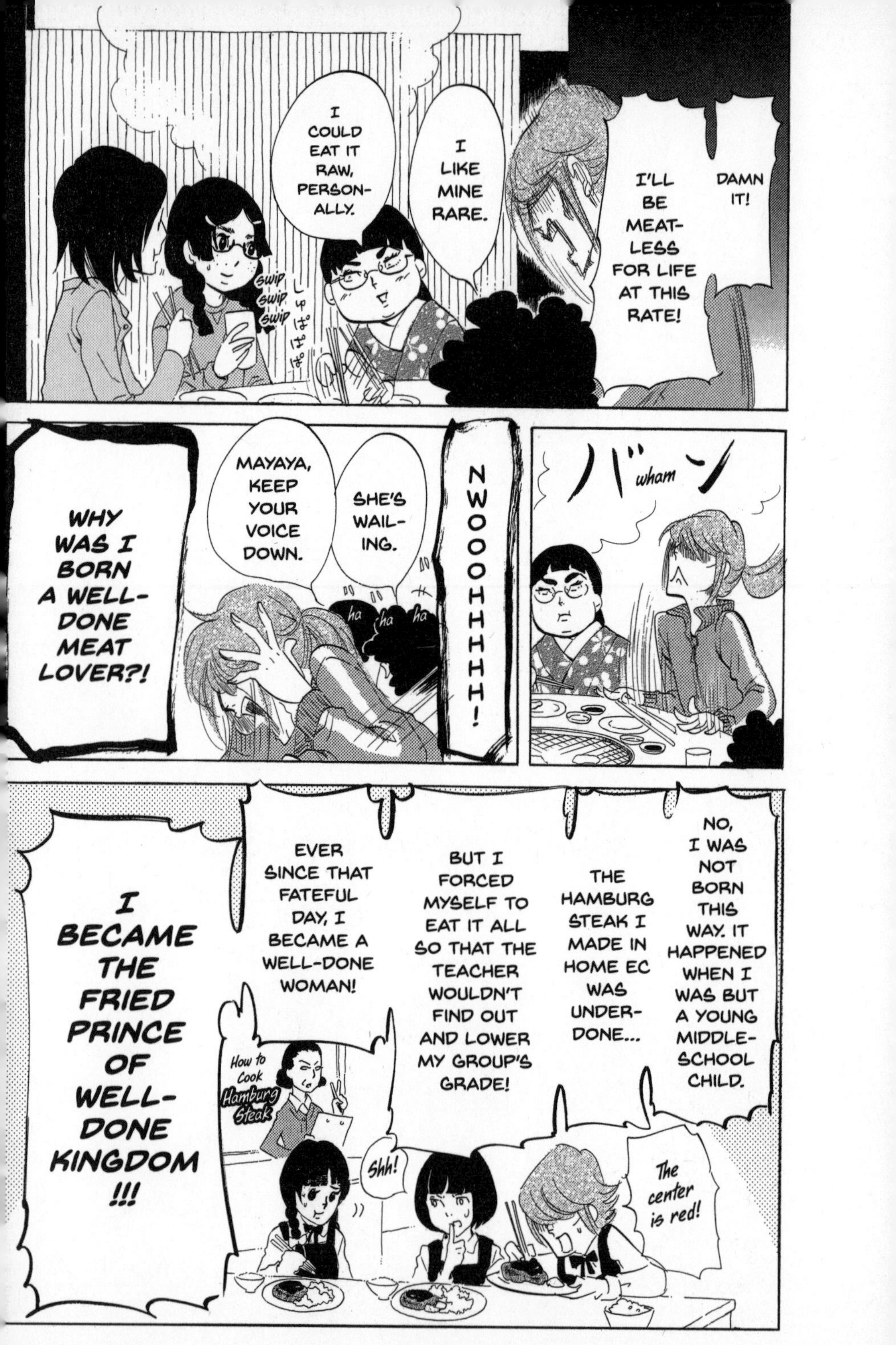
DAMN IT!
I'LL BE MEATLESS FOR LIFE AT THIS RATE!
I LIKE MINE RARE.
I COULD EAT IT RAW, PERSONALLY.
swip swip swip
しゅぱぱぱ
バーン
wham
NWOOOOHHHHHH!
SHE'S WAILING.
MAYAYA, KEEP YOUR VOICE DOWN.
ha ha ha
WHY WAS I BORN A WELL-DONE MEAT LOVER?!
NO, I WAS NOT BORN THIS WAY. IT HAPPENED WHEN I WAS BUT A YOUNG MIDDLE-SCHOOL CHILD.
THE HAMBURG STEAK I MADE IN HOME EC WAS UNDER-DONE...
BUT I FORCED MYSELF TO EAT IT ALL SO THAT THE TEACHER WOULDN'T FIND OUT AND LOWER MY GROUP'S GRADE!
EVER SINCE THAT FATEFUL DAY, I BECAME A WELL-DONE WOMAN!
I BECAME THE FRIED PRINCE OF WELL-DONE KINGDOM!!!
The center is red!
Shh!
How to Cook Hamburg Steak

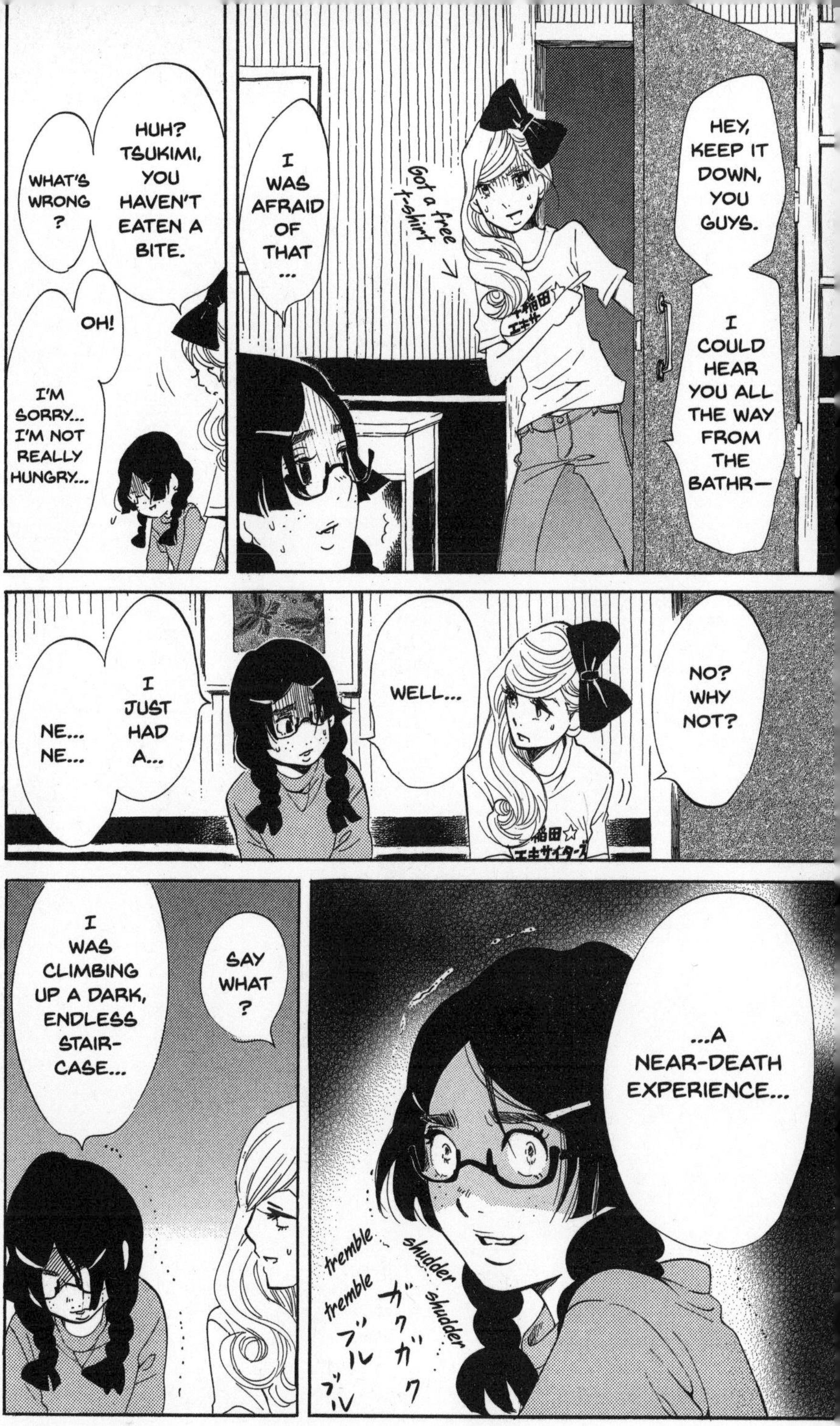
HEY, KEEP IT DOWN, YOU GUYS.
I COULD HEAR YOU ALL THE WAY FROM THE BATHR—
Got a free t-shirt
I WAS AFRAID OF THAT...
HUH? TSUKIMI, YOU HAVEN'T EATEN A BITE.
WHAT'S WRONG?
OH!
I'M SORRY... I'M NOT REALLY HUNGRY...
NO? WHY NOT?
WELL...
I JUST HAD A...
NE... NE...
...A NEAR-DEATH EXPERIENCE...
shudder shudder
tremble tremble
ガクガク
ブルブル
SAY WHAT?
I WAS CLIMBING UP A DARK, ENDLESS STAIR-CASE...

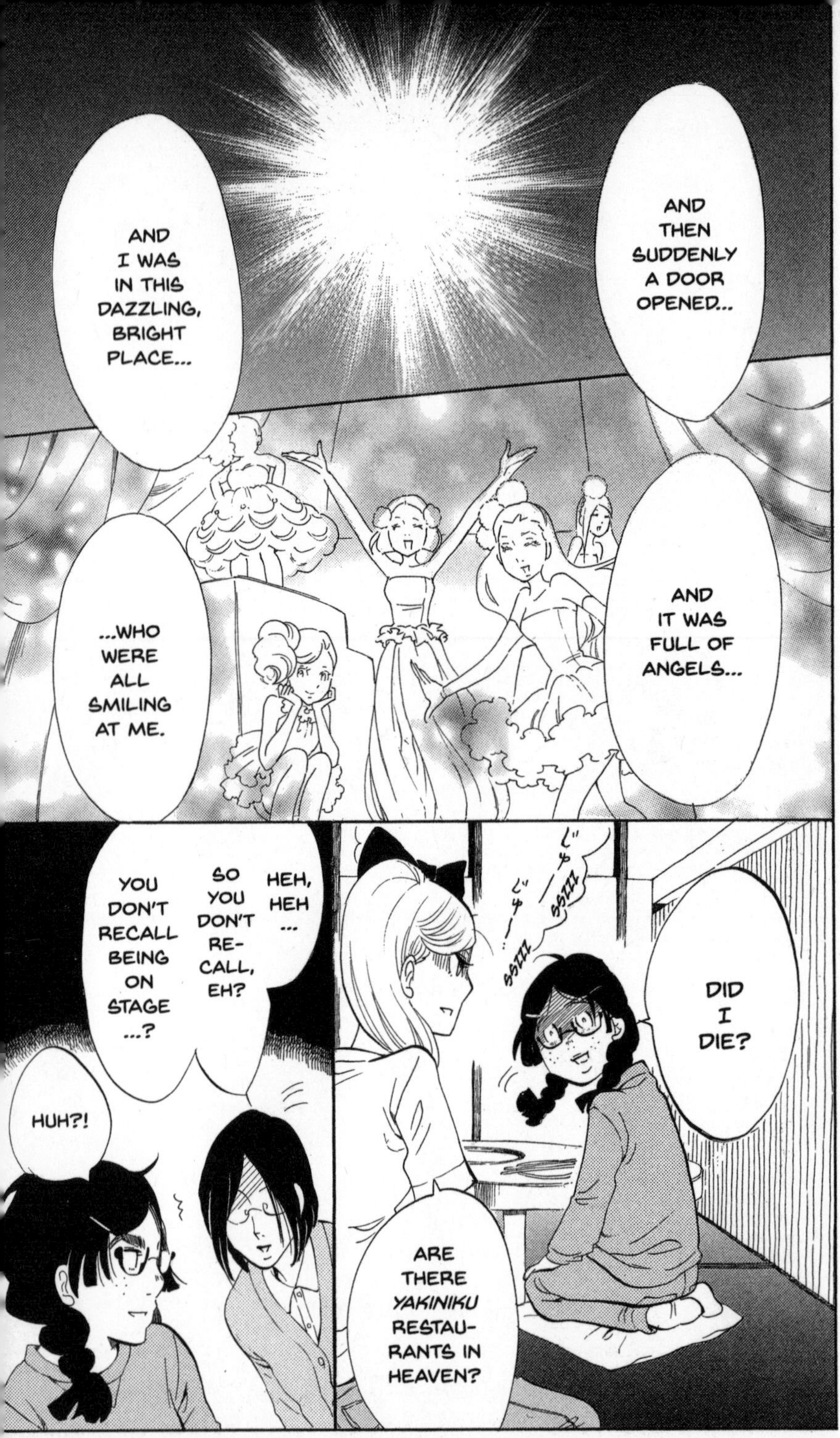
AND THEN SUDDENLY A DOOR OPENED...
AND I WAS IN THIS DAZZLING, BRIGHT PLACE...
AND IT WAS FULL OF ANGELS...
...WHO WERE ALL SMILING AT ME.
DID I DIE?
SSIZZZ
SSIZZZ
ARE THERE YAKINIKU RESTAURANTS IN HEAVEN?
HEH, HEH ...
SO YOU DON'T RE-CALL, EH?
YOU DON'T RECALL BEING ON STAGE ...?
HUH?!

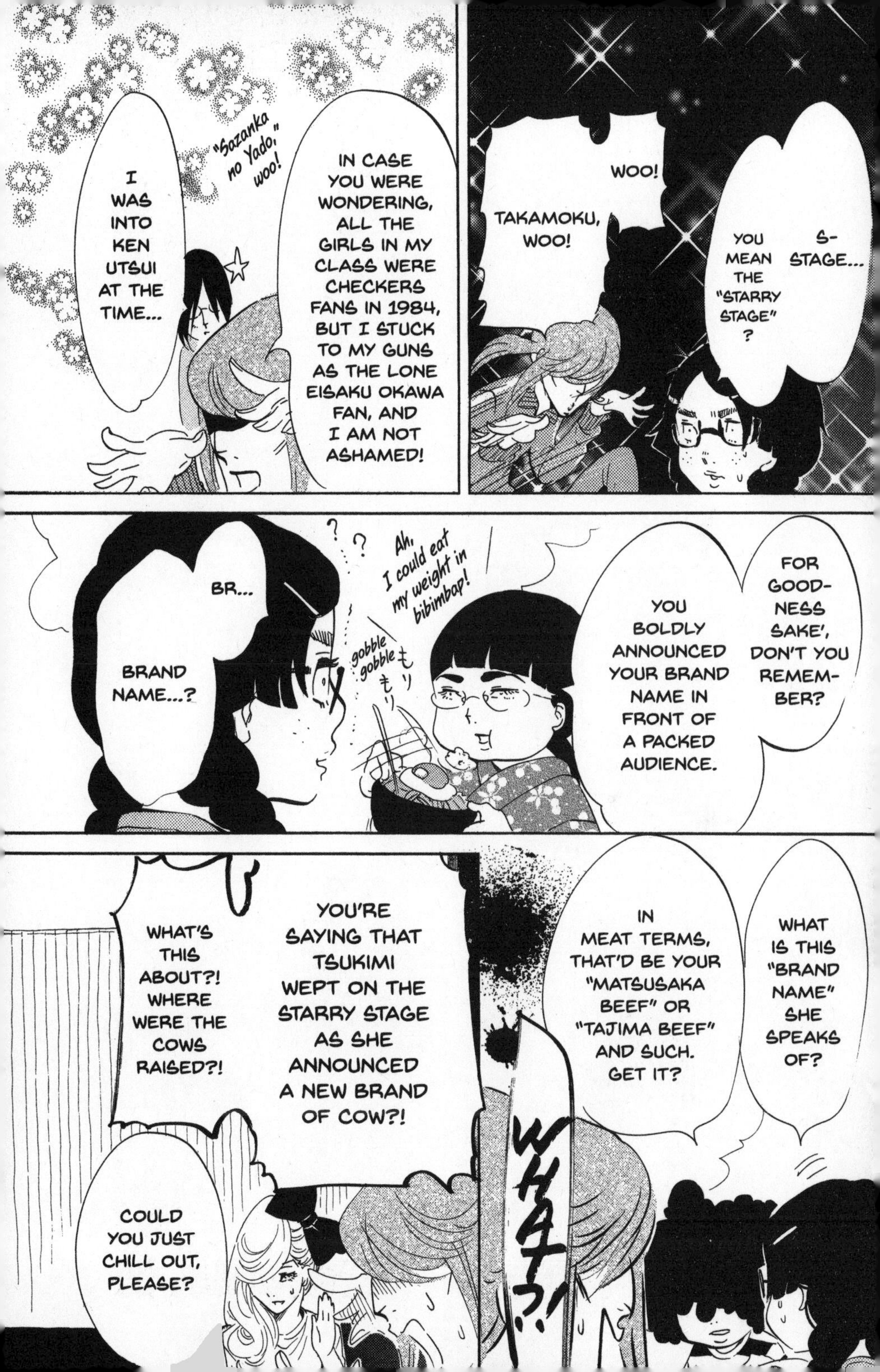
S-STAGE...
YOU MEAN THE "STARRY STAGE"?
WOO!
TAKAMOKU, WOO!
IN CASE YOU WERE WONDERING, ALL THE GIRLS IN MY CLASS WERE CHECKERS FANS IN 1984, BUT I STUCK TO MY GUNS AS THE LONE EISAKU OKAWA FAN, AND I AM NOT ASHAMED!
"Sazanka no Yado," woo!
I WAS INTO KEN UTSUI AT THE TIME...
FOR GOODNESS SAKE', DON'T YOU REMEMBER?
YOU BOLDLY ANNOUNCED YOUR BRAND NAME IN FRONT OF A PACKED AUDIENCE.
Ah, I could eat my weight in bibimbap!
gobble gobble
もり もり
BR...
BRAND NAME...?
WHAT IS THIS "BRAND NAME" SHE SPEAKS OF?
IN MEAT TERMS, THAT'D BE YOUR "MATSUSAKA BEEF" OR "TAJIMA BEEF" AND SUCH. GET IT?
WHAT?!
YOU'RE SAYING THAT TSUKIMI WEPT ON THE STARRY STAGE AS SHE ANNOUNCED A NEW BRAND OF COW?!
WHAT'S THIS ABOUT?! WHERE WERE THE COWS RAISED?!
COULD YOU JUST CHILL OUT, PLEASE?

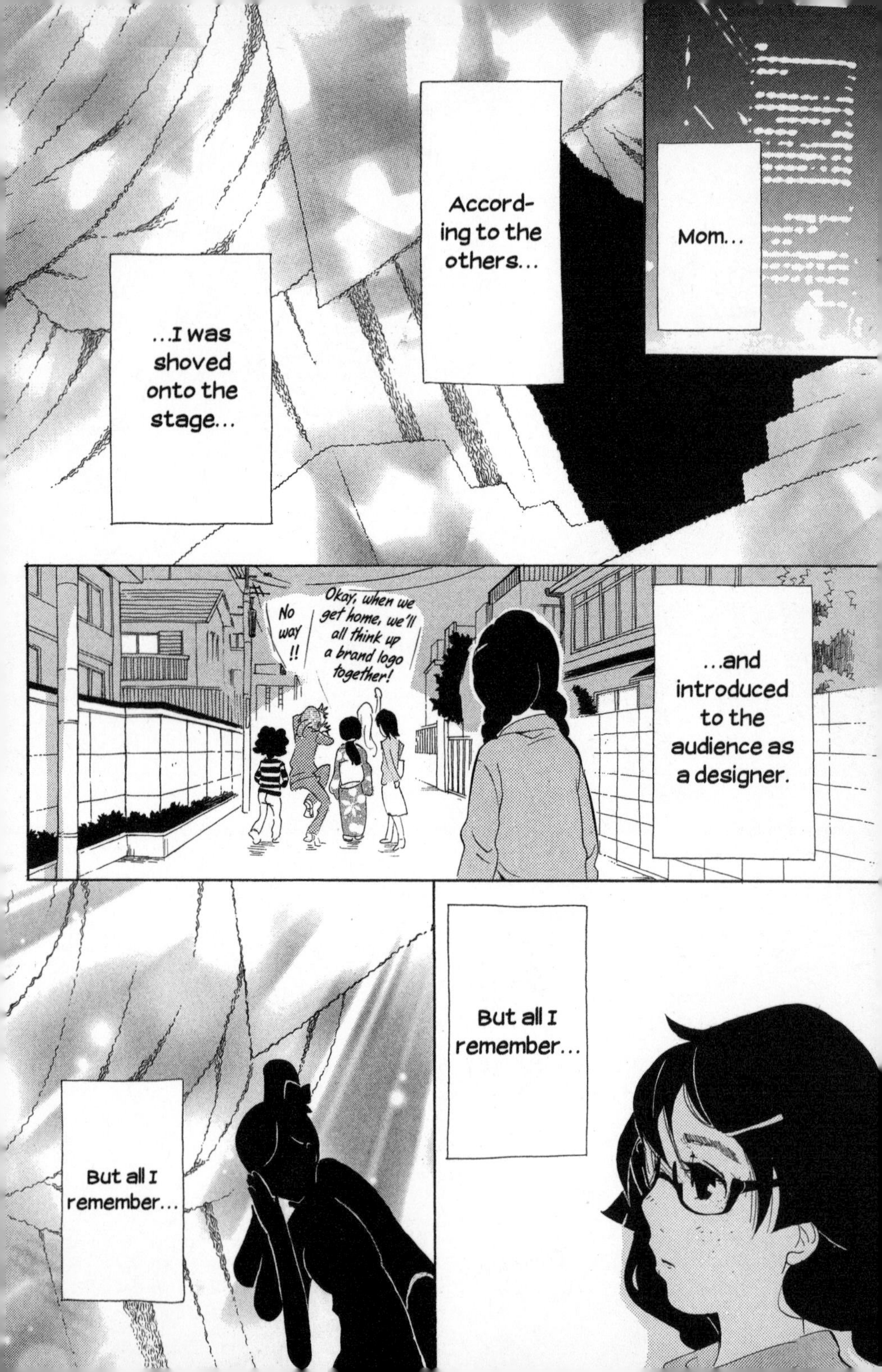
Mom...
According-ing to the others...
...I was shoved onto the stage...
...and introduced to the audience as a designer.
Okay, when we get home, we'll all think up a brand logo together!
No way!!
But all I remember...
But all I remember...

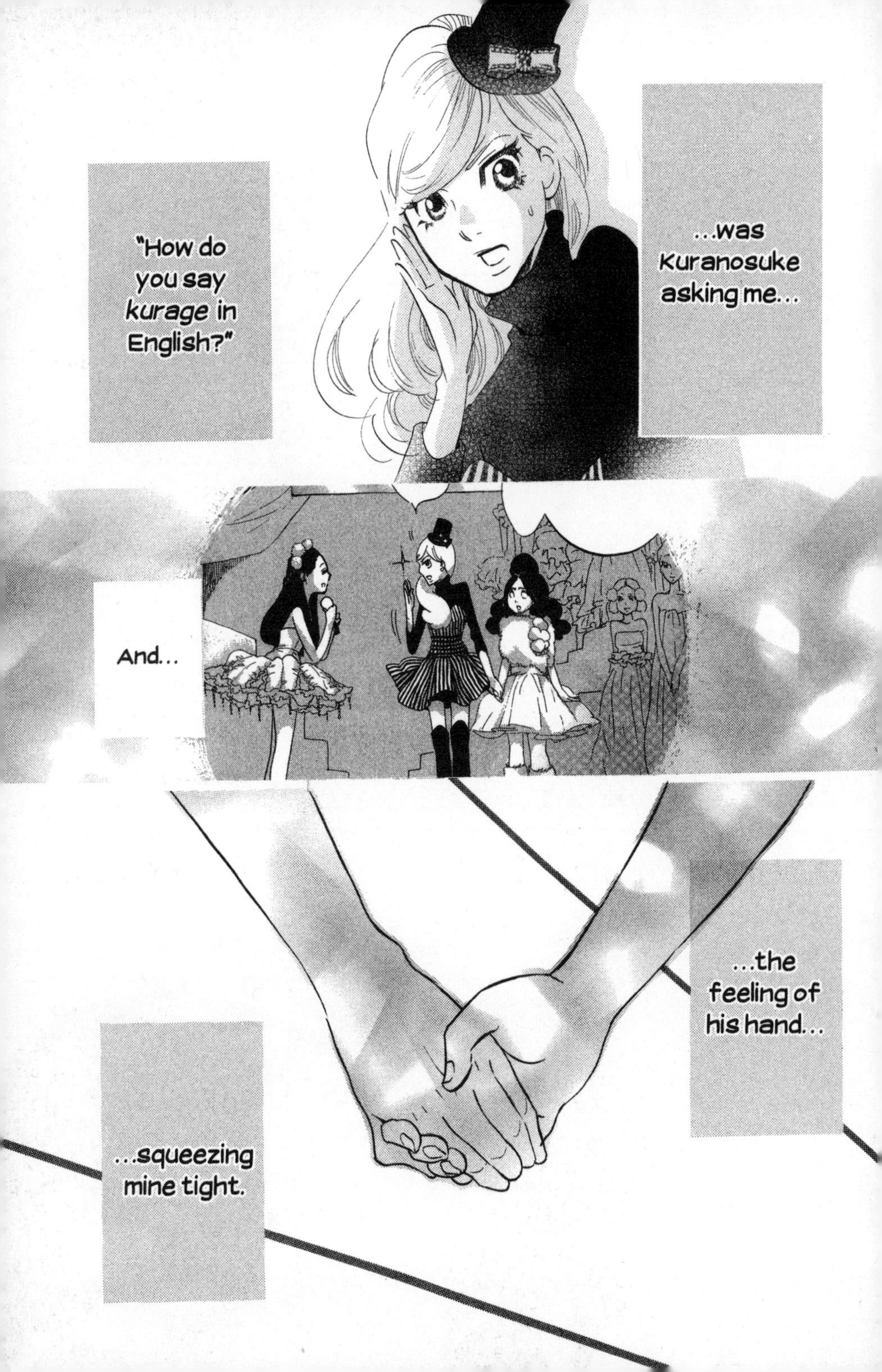
...was Kuranosuke asking me...
"How do you say *kurage* in English?"
And...
...the feeling of his hand...
...squeezing mine tight.

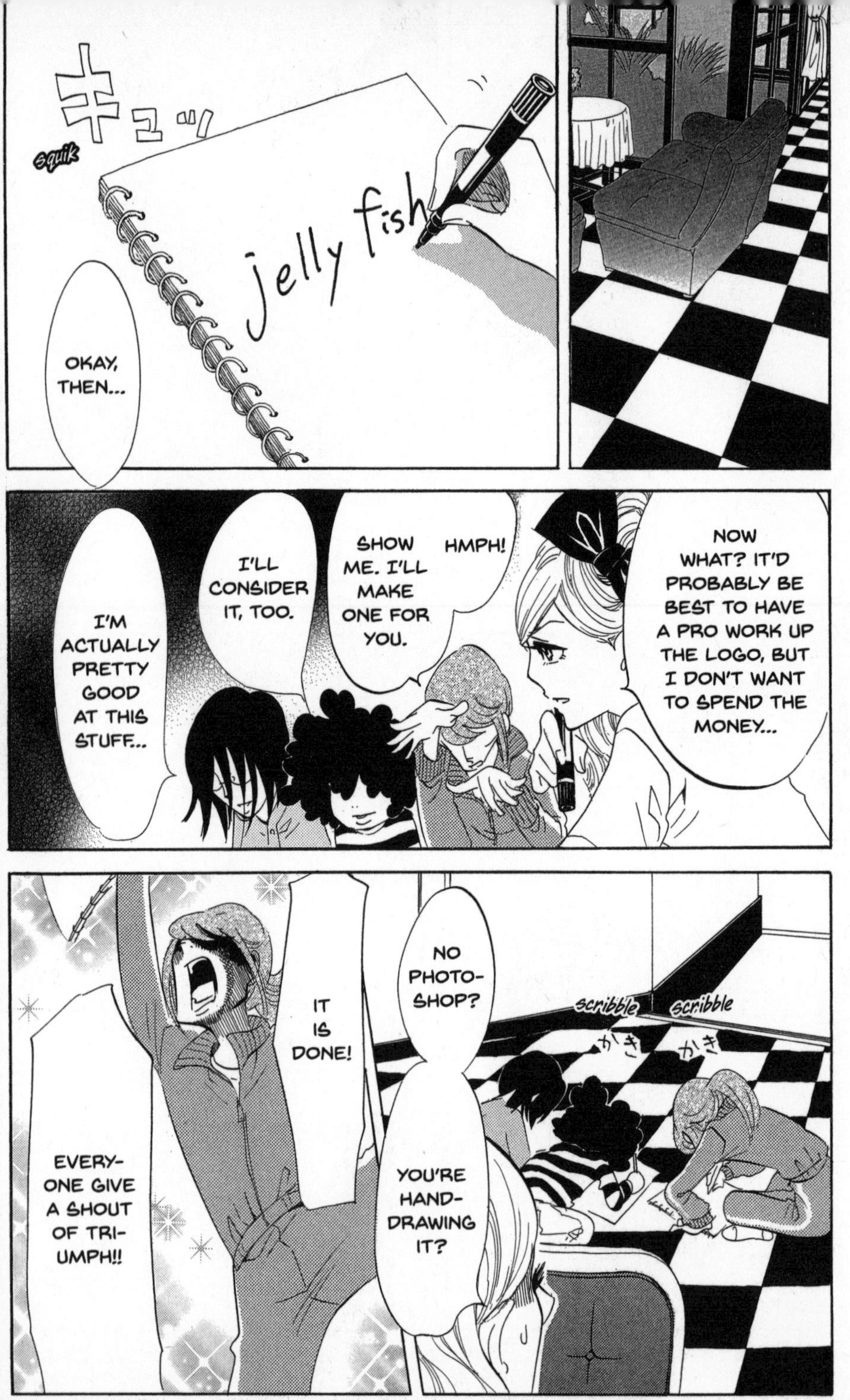
キュッ
squik
jelly fish
OKAY, THEN...
NOW WHAT? IT'D PROBABLY BE BEST TO HAVE A PRO WORK UP THE LOGO, BUT I DON'T WANT TO SPEND THE MONEY...
HMPH!
SHOW ME. I'LL MAKE ONE FOR YOU.
I'LL CONSIDER IT, TOO.
I'M ACTUALLY PRETTY GOOD AT THIS STUFF...
scribble
かき
scribble
かき
NO PHOTO-SHOP?
YOU'RE HAND-DRAWING IT?
IT IS DONE!
EVERY-ONE GIVE A SHOUT OF TRI-UMPH!!

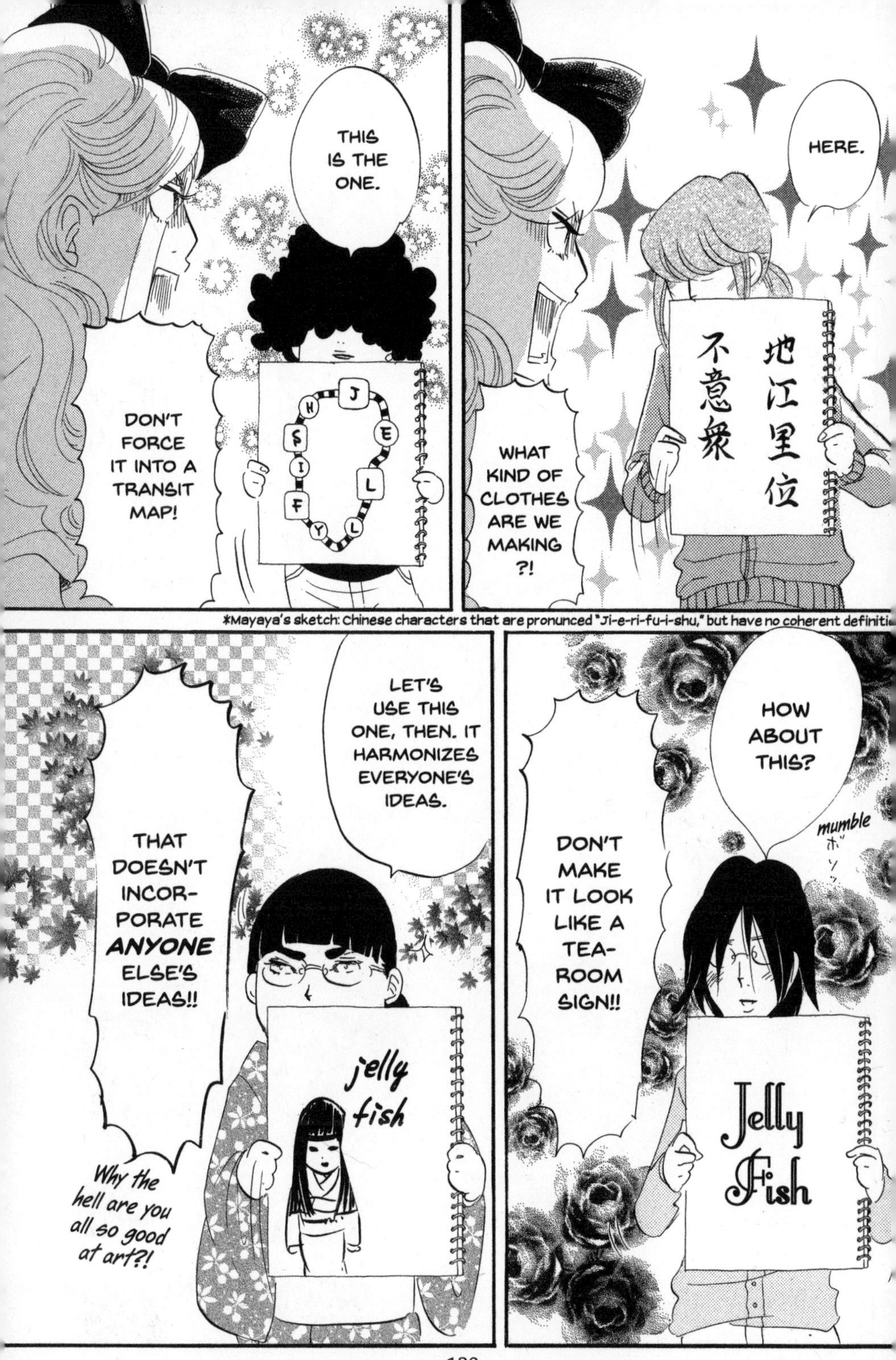
HERE.
WHAT KIND OF CLOTHES ARE WE MAKING?!
地江里位
不意衆
THIS IS THE ONE.
JELLYFISH
DON'T FORCE IT INTO A TRANSIT MAP!
*Mayaya's sketch: Chinese characters that are pronounced "Ji-e-ri-fu-i-shu," but have no coherent definiti
HOW ABOUT THIS?
mumble
ボソッ
Jelly Fish
DON'T MAKE IT LOOK LIKE A TEA-ROOM SIGN!!
LET'S USE THIS ONE, THEN. IT HARMONIZES EVERYONE'S IDEAS.
jelly fish
THAT DOESN'T INCORPORATE ANYONE ELSE'S IDEAS!!
Why the hell are you all so good at art?!

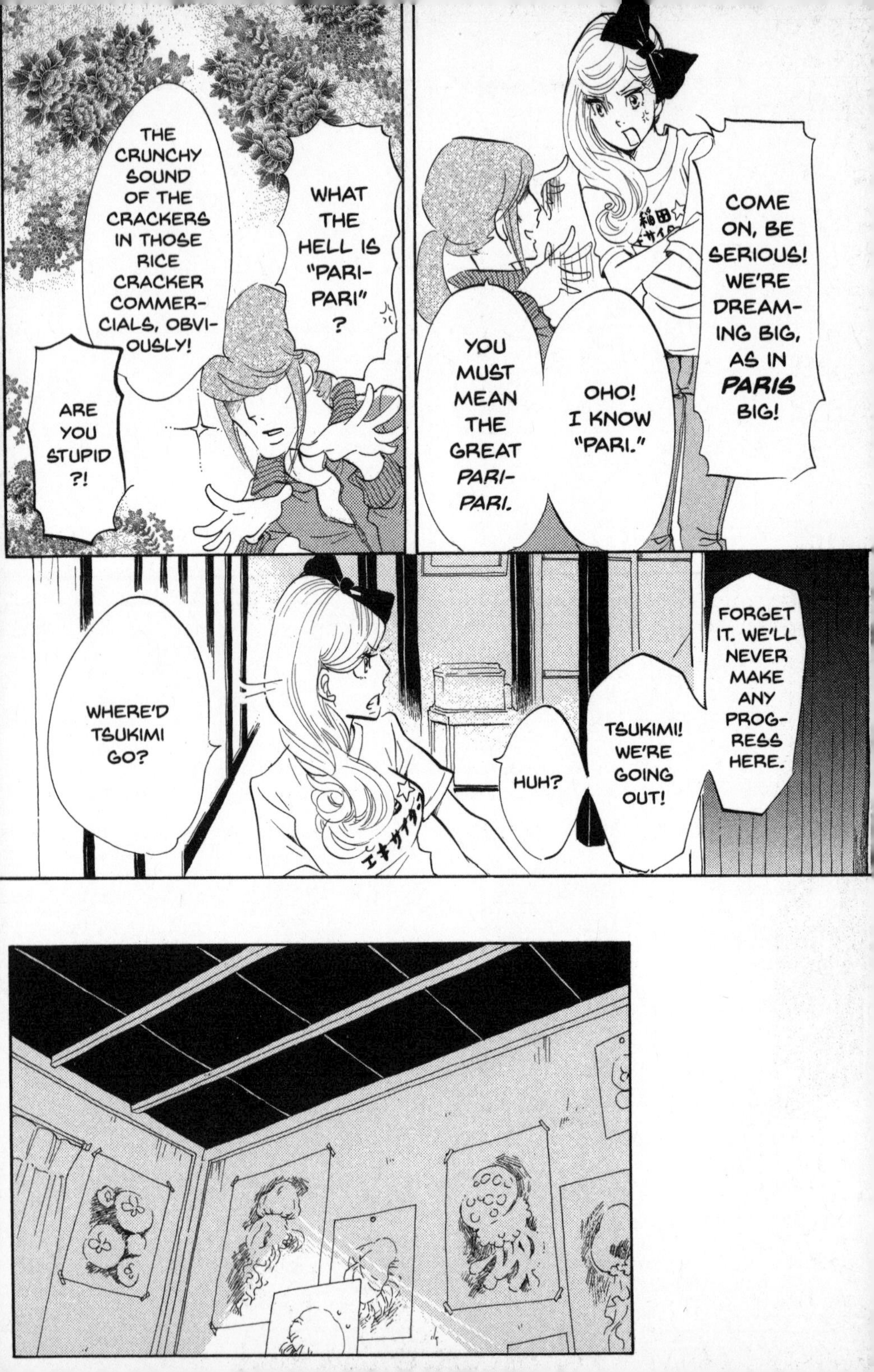
COME ON, BE SERIOUS! WE'RE DREAMING BIG, AS IN PARIS BIG!
OHO! I KNOW "PARI."
YOU MUST MEAN THE GREAT PARI-PARI.
WHAT THE HELL IS "PARI-PARI"?
THE CRUNCHY SOUND OF THE CRACKERS IN THOSE RICE CRACKER COMMERCIALS, OBVIOUSLY!
ARE YOU STUPID?!
FORGET IT. WE'LL NEVER MAKE ANY PROGRESS HERE.
TSUKIMI! WE'RE GOING OUT!
HUH?
WHERE'D TSUKIMI GO?

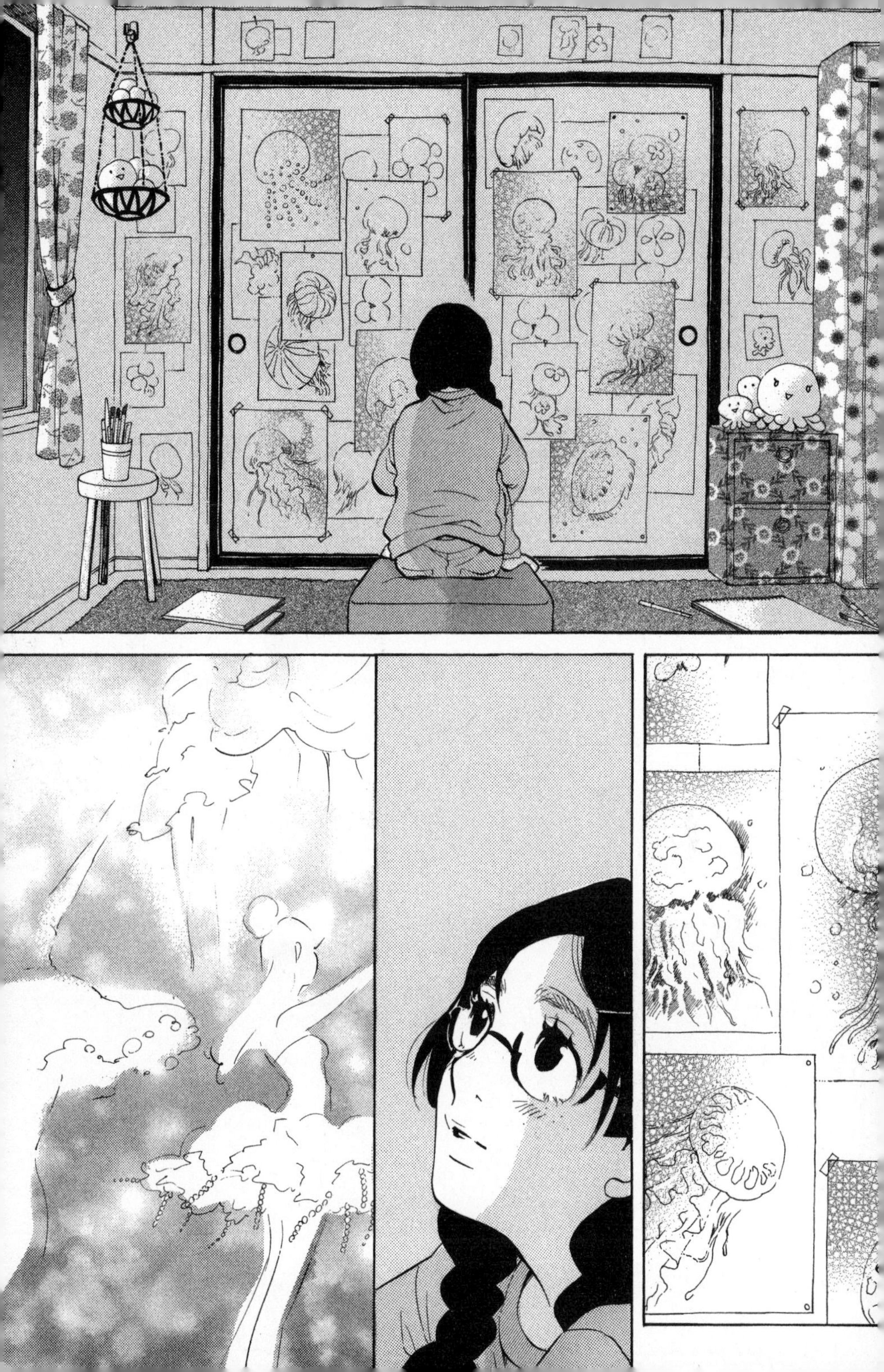

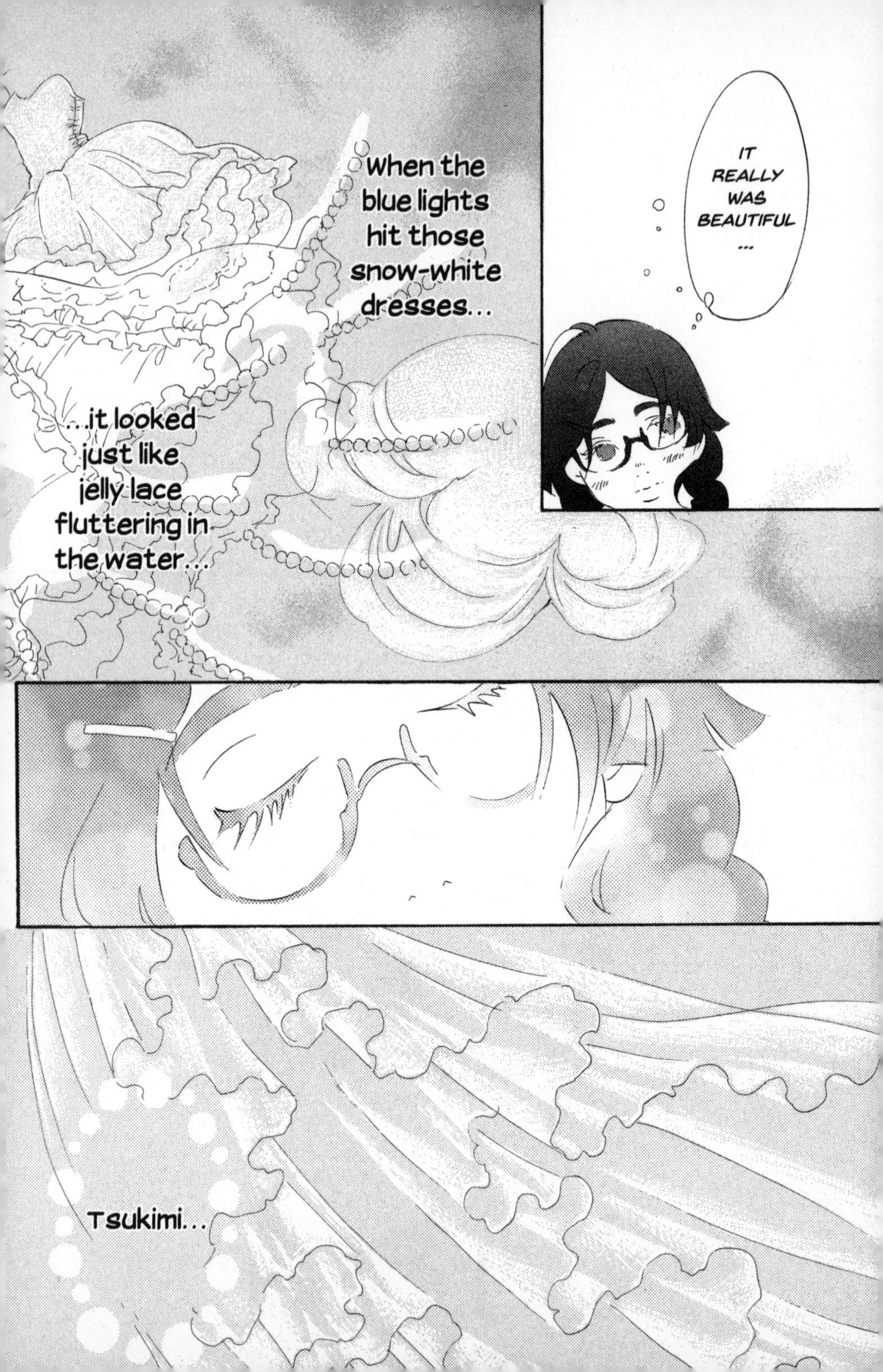
IT REALLY WAS BEAUTIFUL ...
When the blue lights hit those snow-white dresses...
...it looked just like jelly lace fluttering in the water...
Tsukimi...

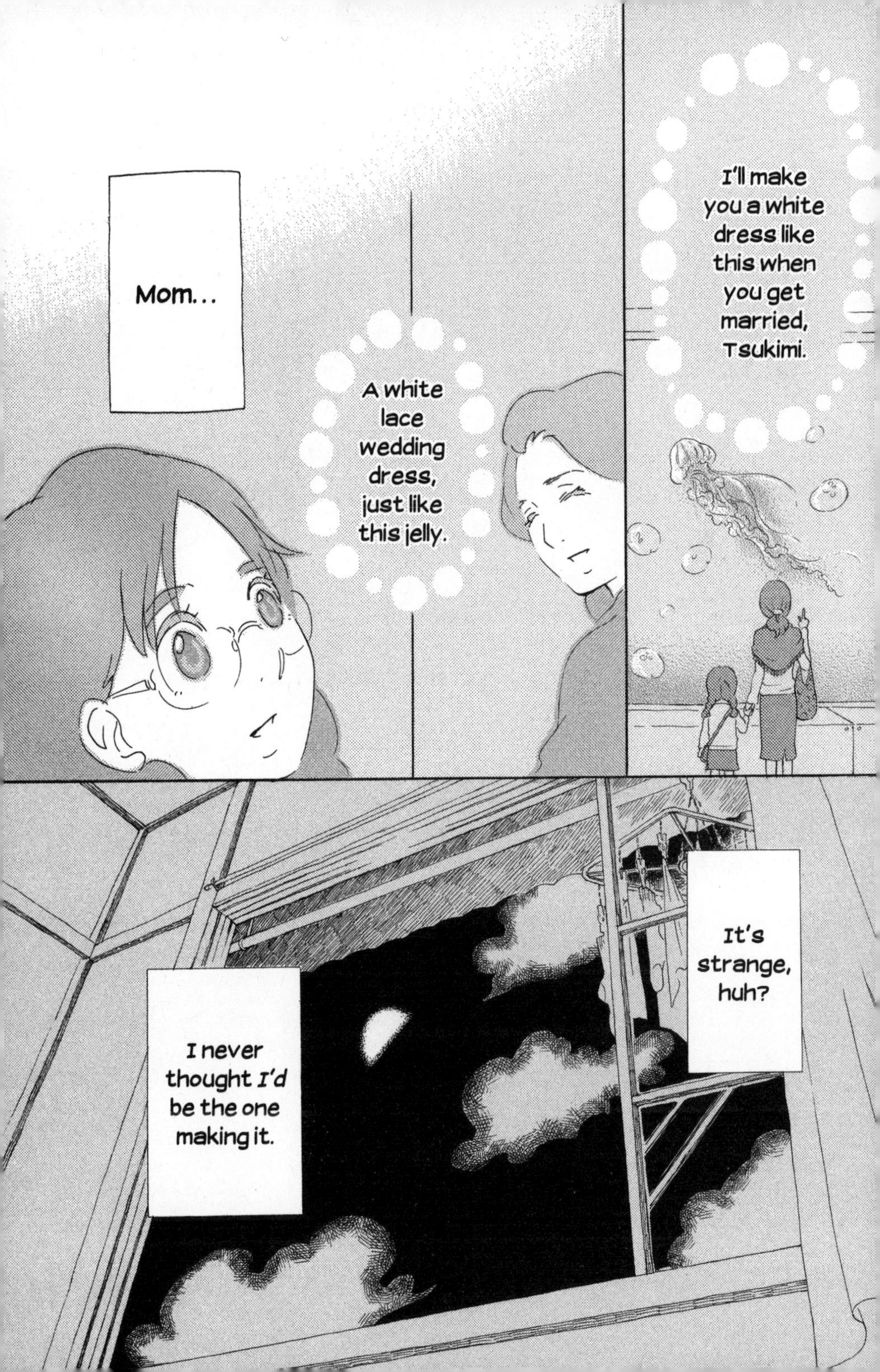
I'll make you a white dress like this when you get married, Tsukimi.
A white lace wedding dress, just like this jelly.
Mom...
It's strange, huh?
I never thought *I'd* be the one making it.

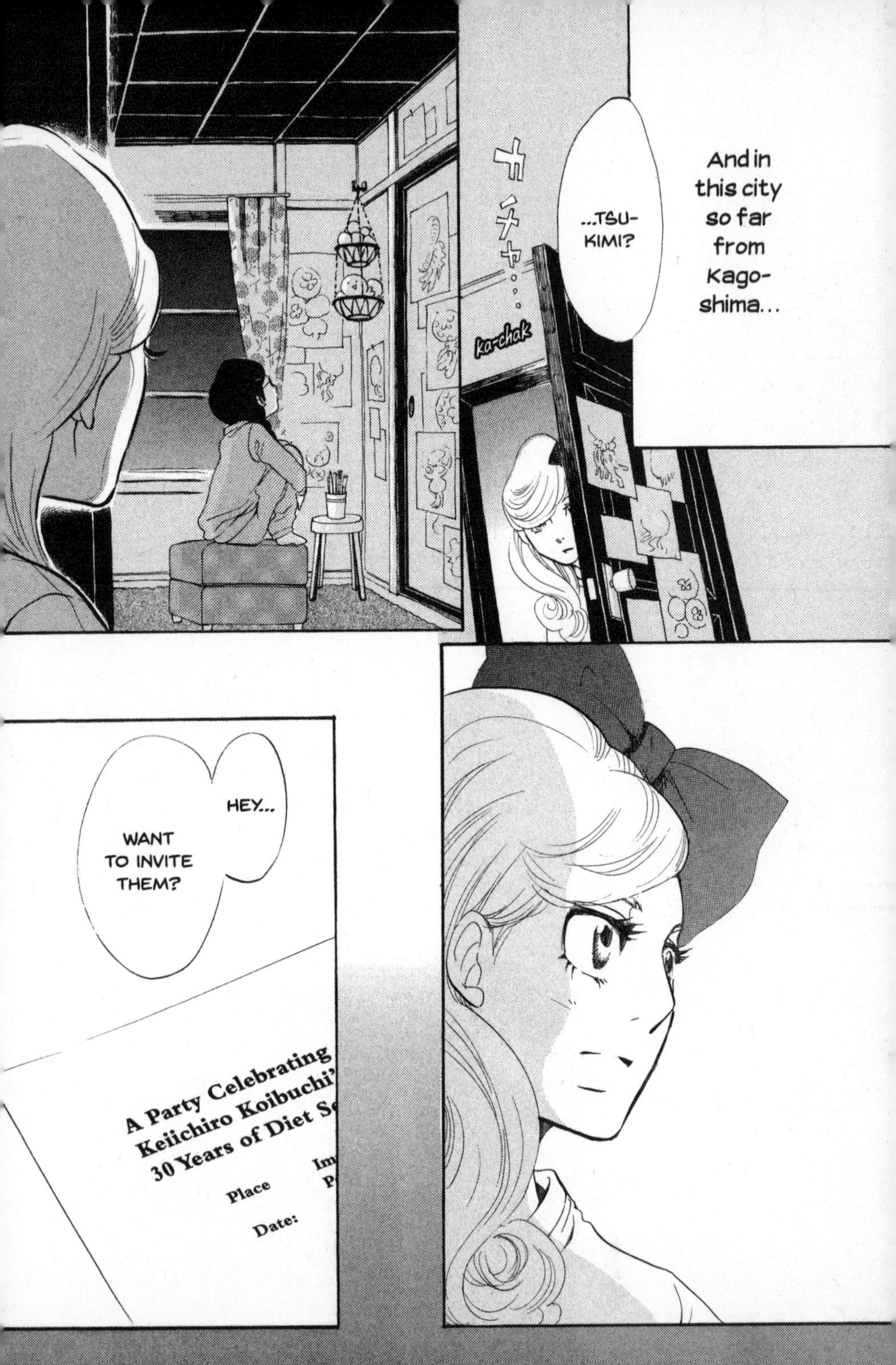
And in this city so far from Kago-shima…
...TSU-KIMI?
ka-chak
HEY...
WANT TO INVITE THEM?
A Party Celebrating
Keiichiro Koibuchi'
30 Years of Diet Se
Place
Date:

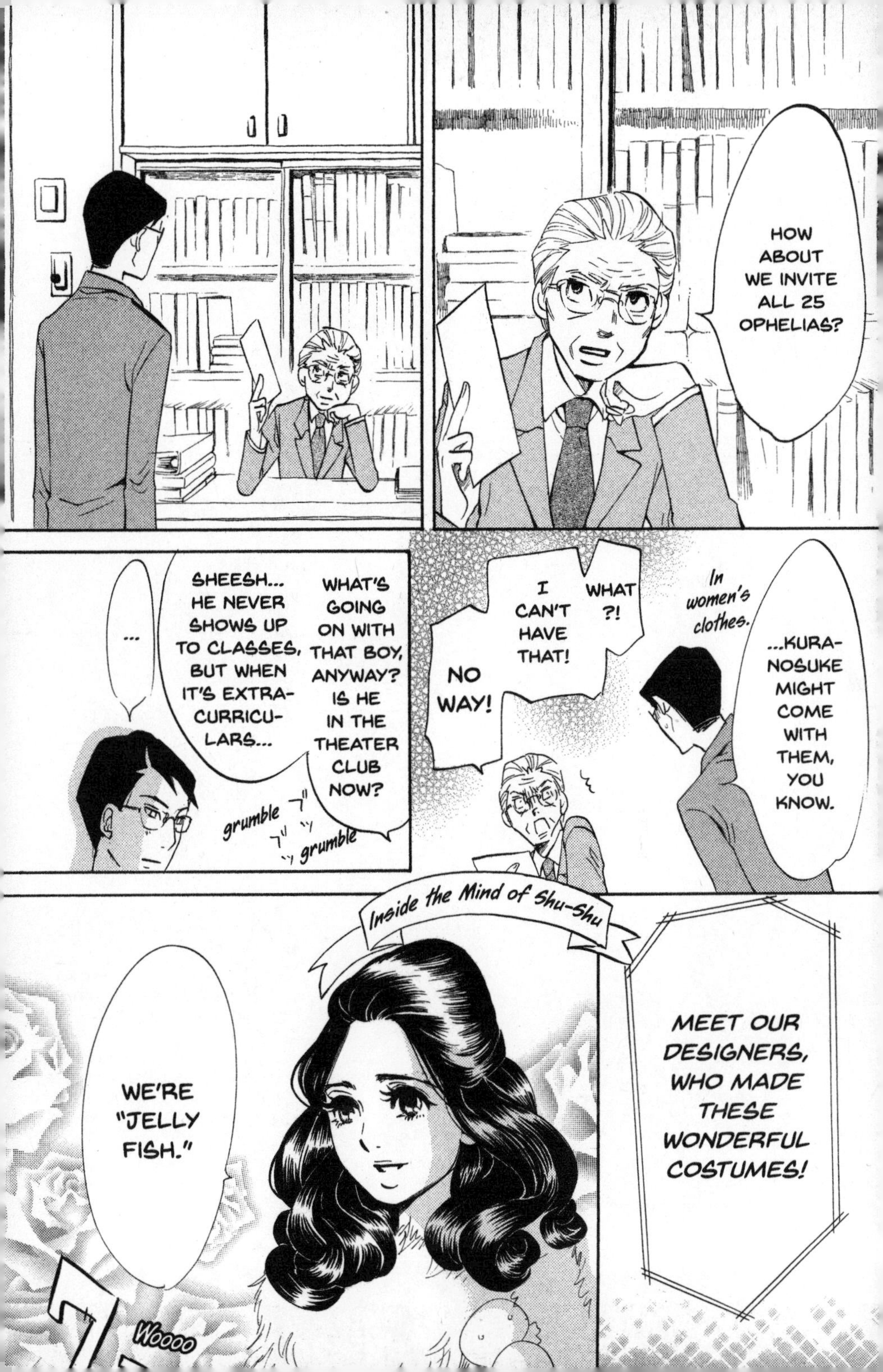
HOW ABOUT WE INVITE ALL 25 OPHELIAS?
In women's clothes.
...KURANOSUKE MIGHT COME WITH THEM, YOU KNOW.
WHAT?!
I CAN'T HAVE THAT!
NO WAY!
WHAT'S GOING ON WITH THAT BOY, ANYWAY? IS HE IN THE THEATER CLUB NOW?
SHEESH... HE NEVER SHOWS UP TO CLASSES, BUT WHEN IT'S EXTRA-CURRICULARS...
grumble grumble
...
Inside the Mind of Shu-Shu
MEET OUR DESIGNERS, WHO MADE THESE WONDERFUL COSTUMES!
WE'RE "JELLY FISH."
Woooo

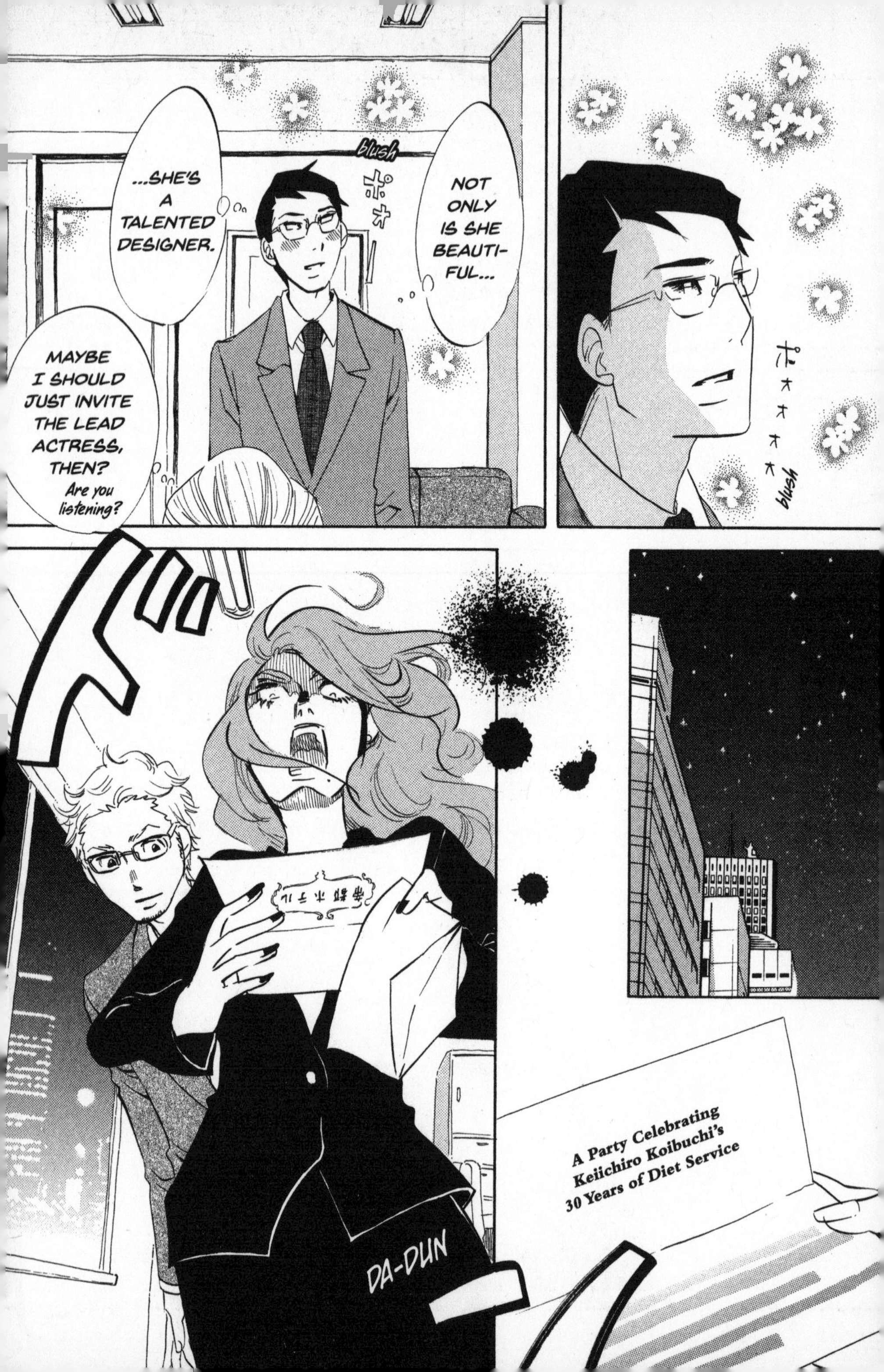
ポォォォォ
blush
NOT ONLY IS SHE BEAUTIFUL...
blush
ポォ
...SHE'S A TALENTED DESIGNER.
MAYBE I SHOULD JUST INVITE THE LEAD ACTRESS, THEN?
Are you listening?
A Party Celebrating Keiichiro Koibuchi's 30 Years of Diet Service
DA-DUN

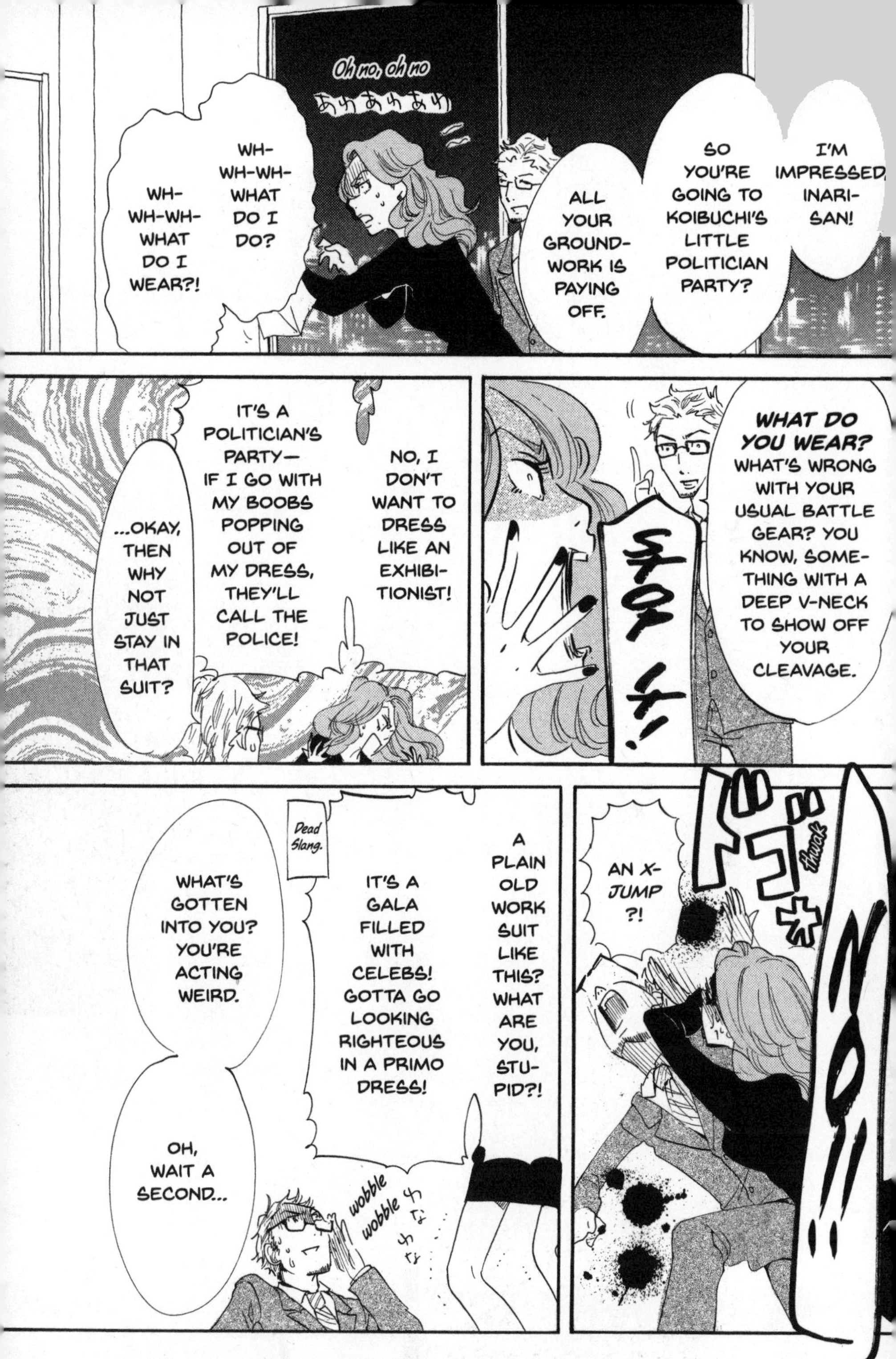
I'M IMPRESSED, INARI-SAN!
SO YOU'RE GOING TO KOIBUCHI'S LITTLE POLITICIAN PARTY?
ALL YOUR GROUND-WORK IS PAYING OFF.
Oh no, oh no
あわあわあわ
WH-WH-WH-WHAT DO I DO?
WH-WH-WH-WHAT DO I WEAR?!
WHAT DO YOU WEAR? WHAT'S WRONG WITH YOUR USUAL BATTLE GEAR? YOU KNOW, SOME-THING WITH A DEEP V-NECK TO SHOW OFF YOUR CLEAVAGE.
NO, I DON'T WANT TO DRESS LIKE AN EXHIBI-TIONIST!
IT'S A POLITICIAN'S PARTY— IF I GO WITH MY BOOBS POPPING OUT OF MY DRESS, THEY'LL CALL THE POLICE!
...OKAY, THEN WHY NOT JUST STAY IN THAT SUIT?
thwack
AN X-JUMP?!
A PLAIN OLD WORK SUIT LIKE THIS? WHAT ARE YOU, STU-PID?!
IT'S A GALA FILLED WITH CELEBS! GOTTA GO LOOKING RIGHTEOUS IN A PRIMO DRESS!
Dead Slang.
WHAT'S GOTTEN INTO YOU? YOU'RE ACTING WEIRD.
wobble wobble
OH, WAIT A SECOND...

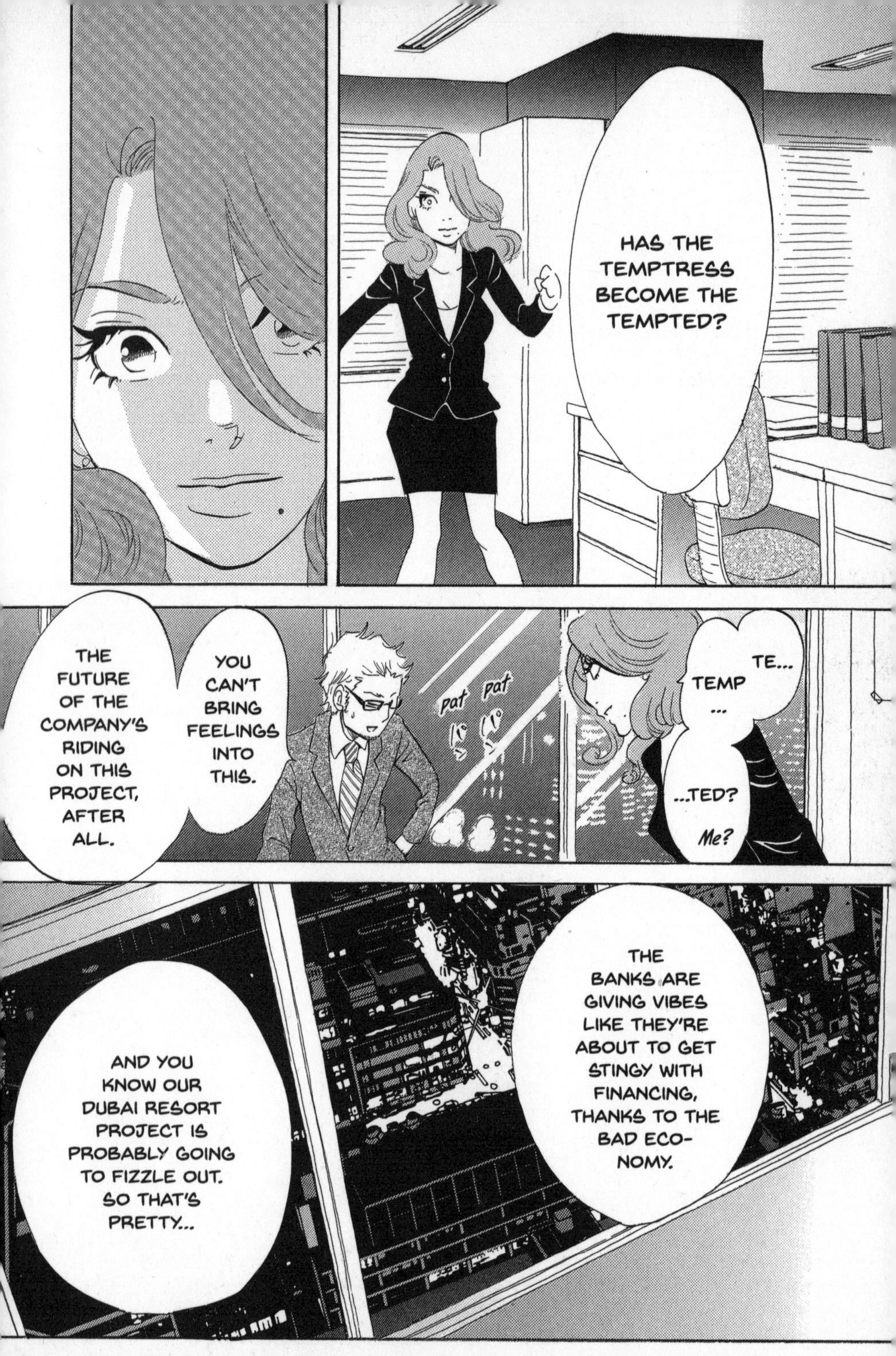
HAS THE TEMPTRESS BECOME THE TEMPTED?
TE... TEMP ...
...TED?
Me?
pat pat
YOU CAN'T BRING FEELINGS INTO THIS.
THE FUTURE OF THE COMPANY'S RIDING ON THIS PROJECT, AFTER ALL.
THE BANKS ARE GIVING VIBES LIKE THEY'RE ABOUT TO GET STINGY WITH FINANCING, THANKS TO THE BAD ECO-NOMY.
AND YOU KNOW OUR DUBAI RESORT PROJECT IS PROBABLY GOING TO FIZZLE OUT. SO THAT'S PRETTY...

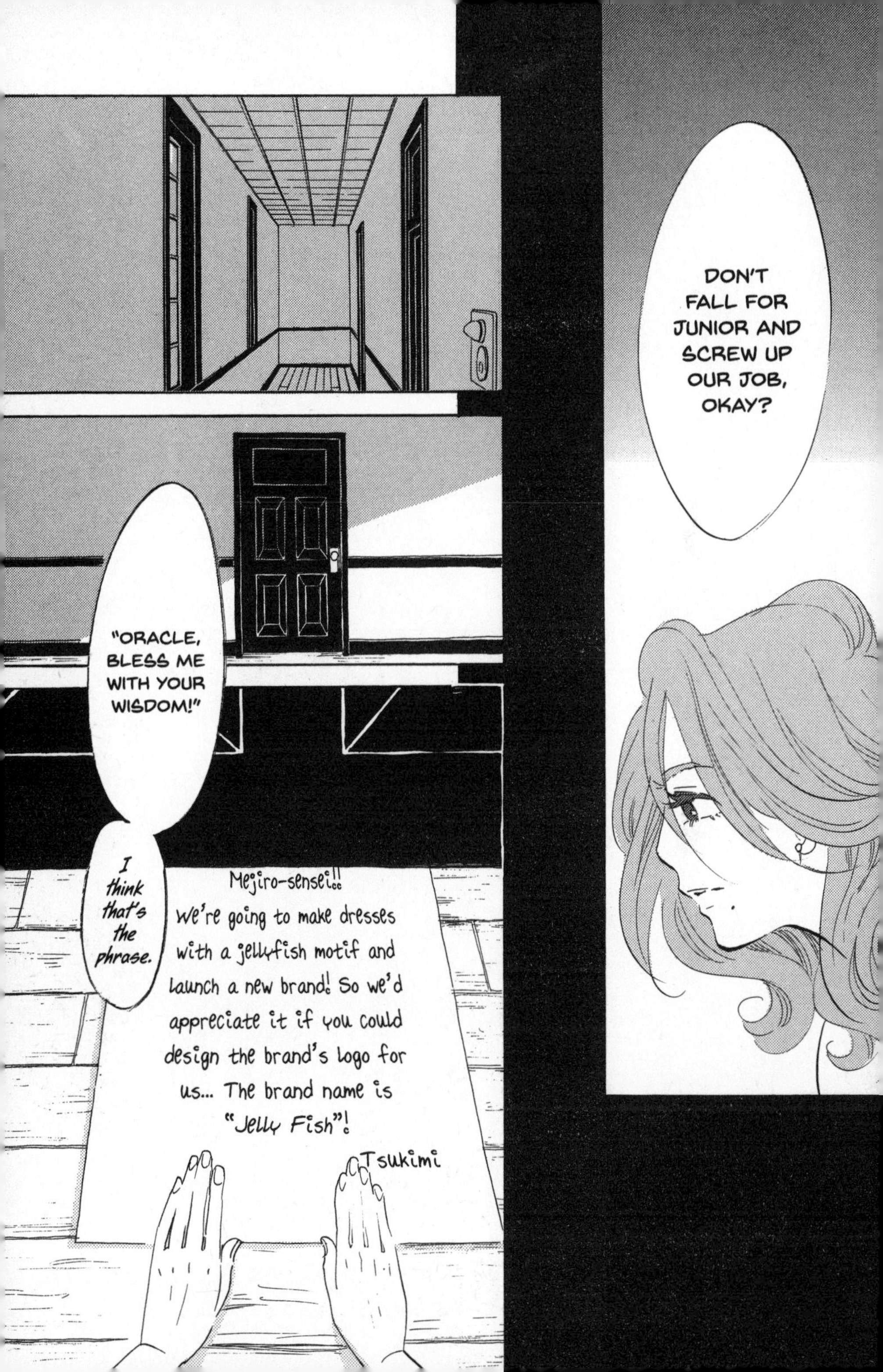
DON'T FALL FOR JUNIOR AND SCREW UP OUR JOB, OKAY?
"ORACLE, BLESS ME WITH YOUR WISDOM!"
I think that's the phrase.
Mejiro-sensei!! We're going to make dresses with a jellyfish motif and launch a new brand! So we'd appreciate it if you could design the brand's logo for us... The brand name is "Jelly Fish"!
Tsukimi

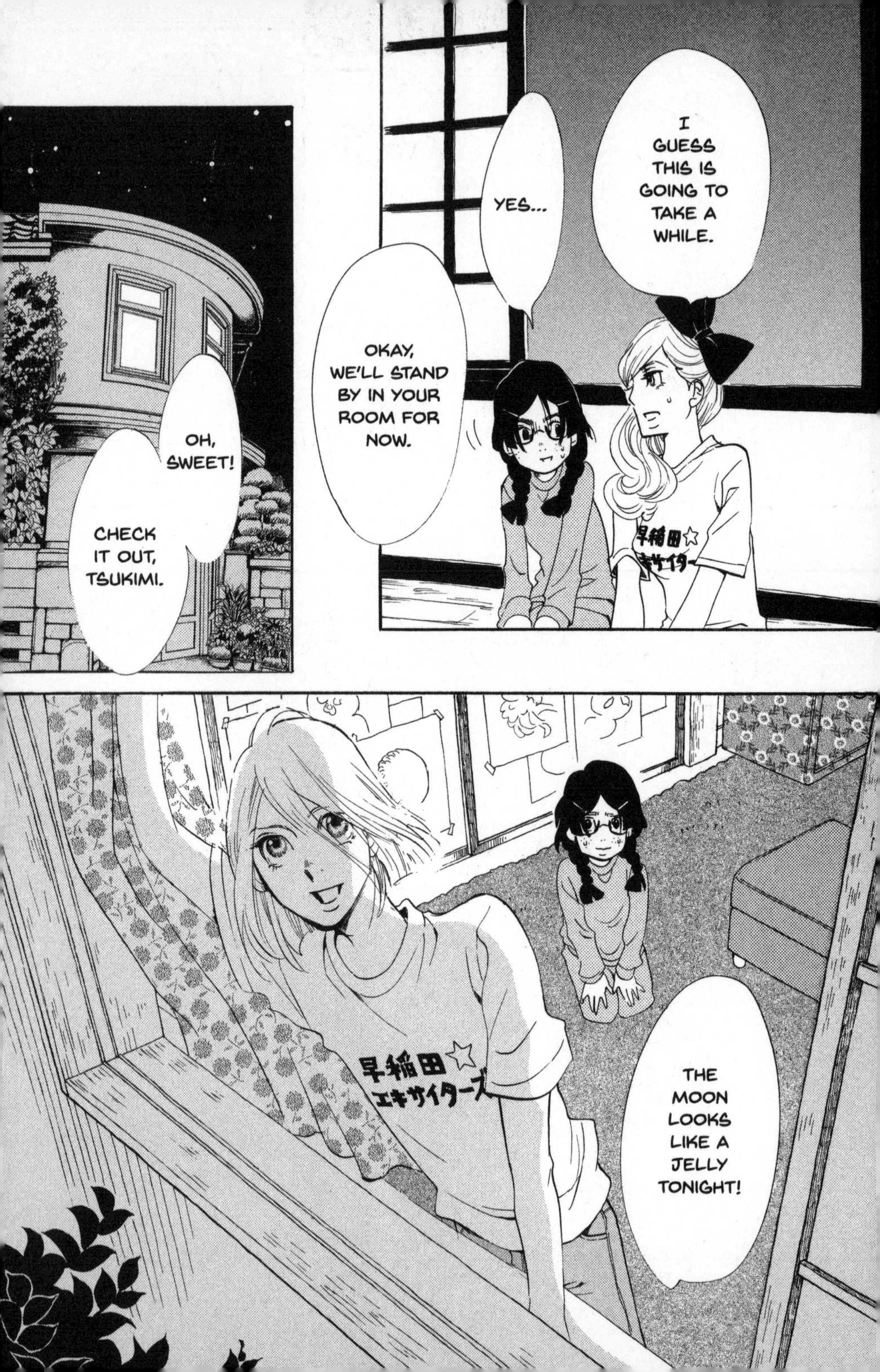
I GUESS THIS IS GOING TO TAKE A WHILE.
YES...
OKAY, WE'LL STAND BY IN YOUR ROOM FOR NOW.
OH, SWEET!
CHECK IT OUT, TSUKIMI.
早稲田☆エキサイターズ
THE MOON LOOKS LIKE A JELLY TONIGHT!

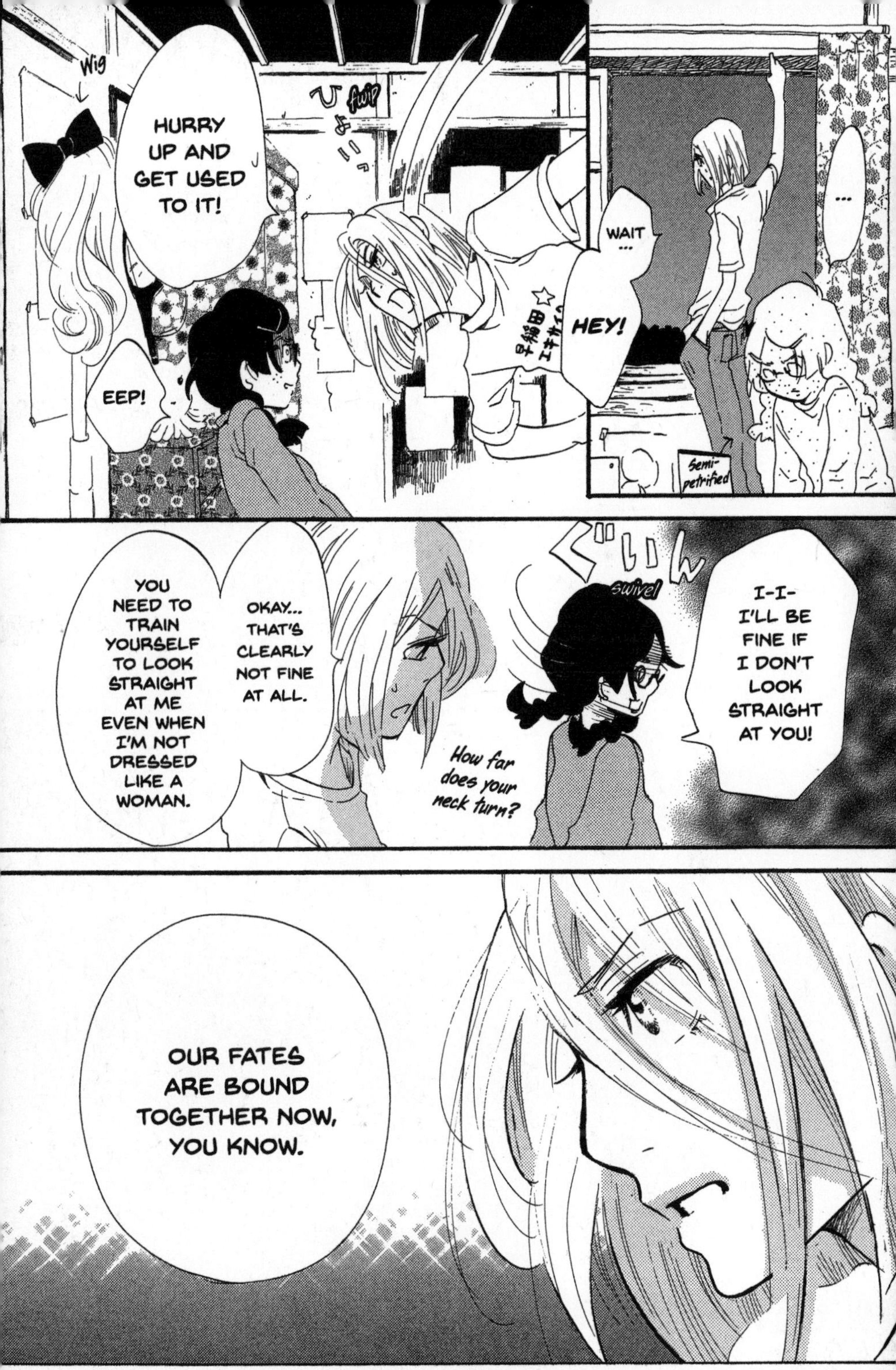
...
WAIT...
HEY!
Semi-petrified
fwip
HURRY UP AND GET USED TO IT!
Wig
EEP!
I-I- I'LL BE FINE IF I DON'T LOOK STRAIGHT AT YOU!
swivel
How far does your neck turn?
OKAY... THAT'S CLEARLY NOT FINE AT ALL.
YOU NEED TO TRAIN YOURSELF TO LOOK STRAIGHT AT ME EVEN WHEN I'M NOT DRESSED LIKE A WOMAN.
OUR FATES ARE BOUND TOGETHER NOW, YOU KNOW.

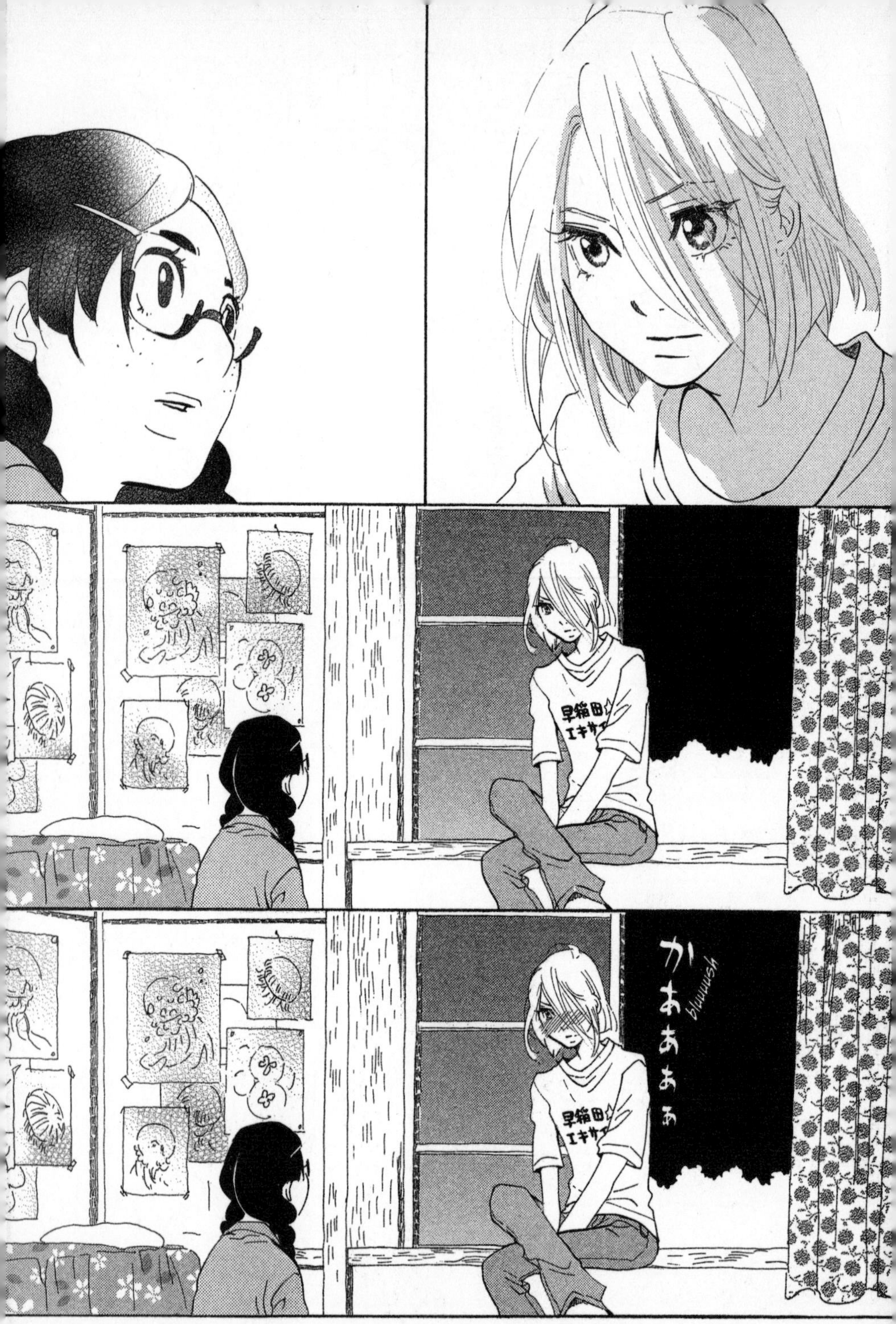
早稲田☆
かああああ
bluuuush

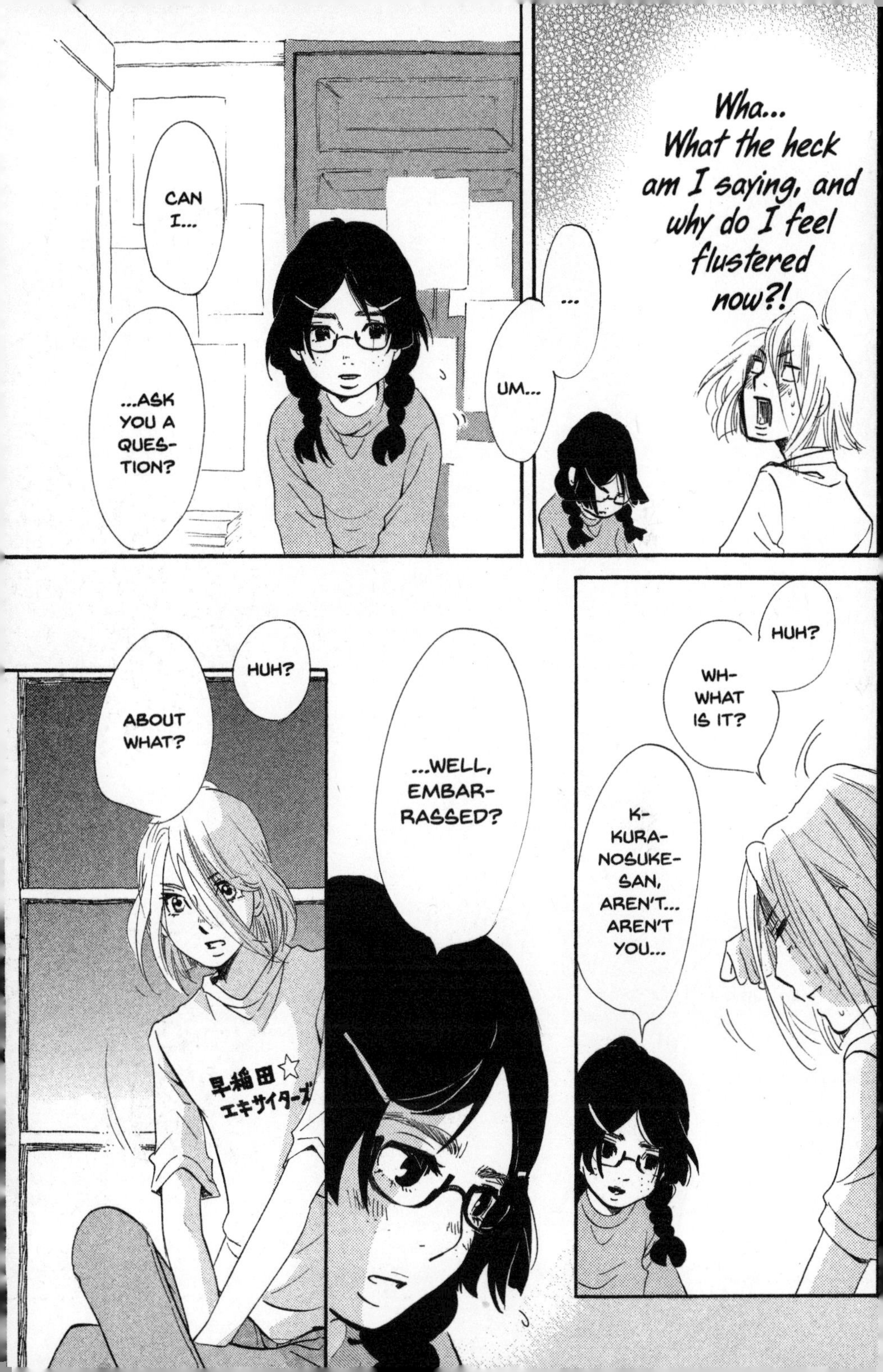
Wha... What the heck am I saying, and why do I feel flustered now?!
...
UM...
CAN I...
...ASK YOU A QUES-TION?
HUH?
WH- WHAT IS IT?
K- KURA-NOSUKE-SAN, AREN'T... AREN'T YOU...
...WELL, EMBAR-RASSED?
HUH?
ABOUT WHAT?
早稲田☆エキサイターズ

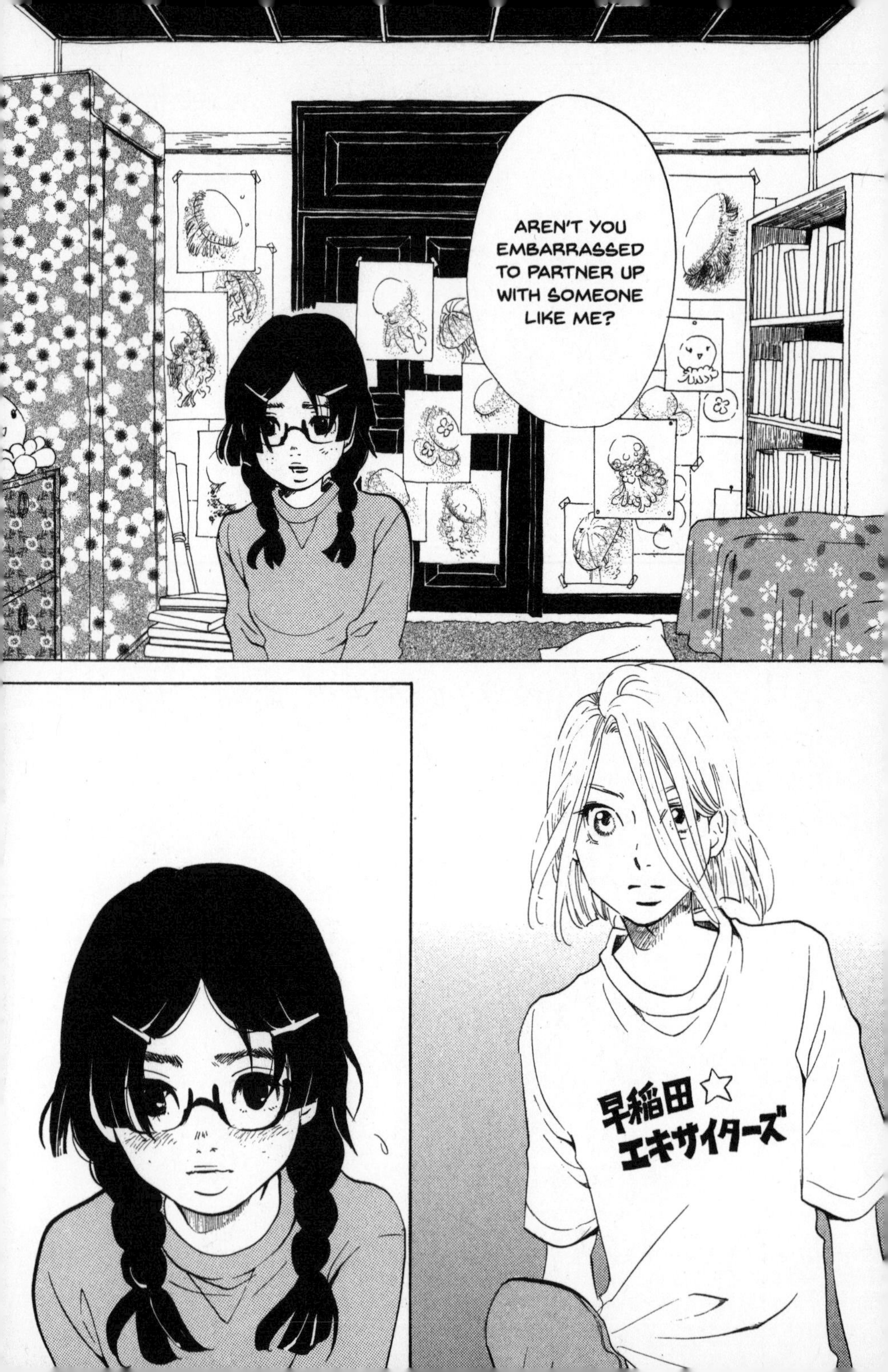
AREN'T YOU EMBARRASSED TO PARTNER UP WITH SOMEONE LIKE ME?
早稲田☆
エキサイターズ

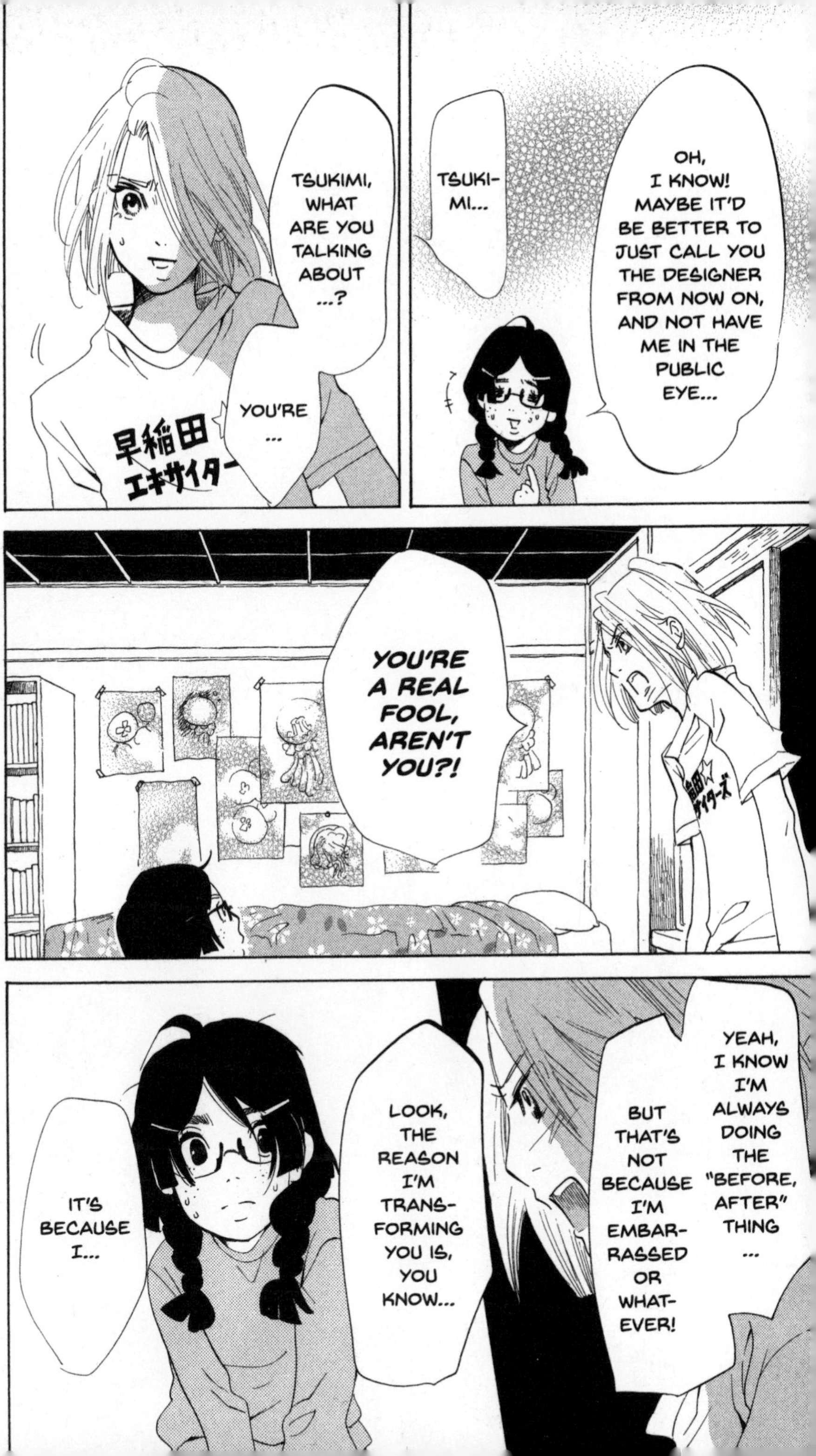
OH, I KNOW! MAYBE IT'D BE BETTER TO JUST CALL YOU THE DESIGNER FROM NOW ON, AND NOT HAVE ME IN THE PUBLIC EYE...
TSUKI-MI...
TSUKIMI, WHAT ARE YOU TALKING ABOUT ...?
YOU'RE ...
早稲田
エキサイター
YOU'RE A REAL FOOL, AREN'T YOU?!
YEAH, I KNOW I'M ALWAYS DOING THE "BEFORE, AFTER" THING ...
BUT THAT'S NOT BECAUSE I'M EMBARRASSED OR WHATEVER!
LOOK, THE REASON I'M TRANSFORMING YOU IS, YOU KNOW...
IT'S BECAUSE I...

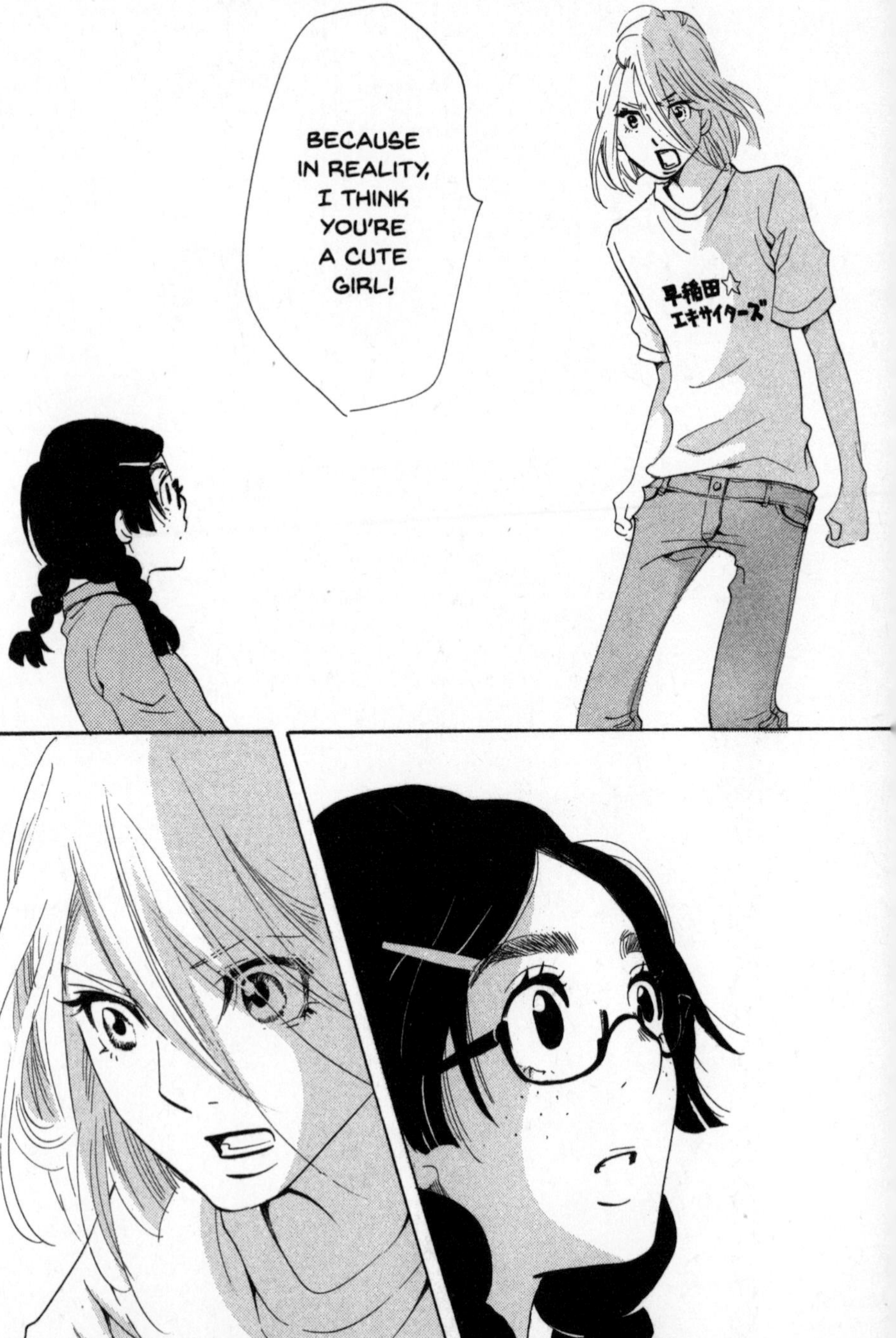
BECAUSE IN REALITY, I THINK YOU'RE A CUTE GIRL!
早稲田☆
エキサイターズ

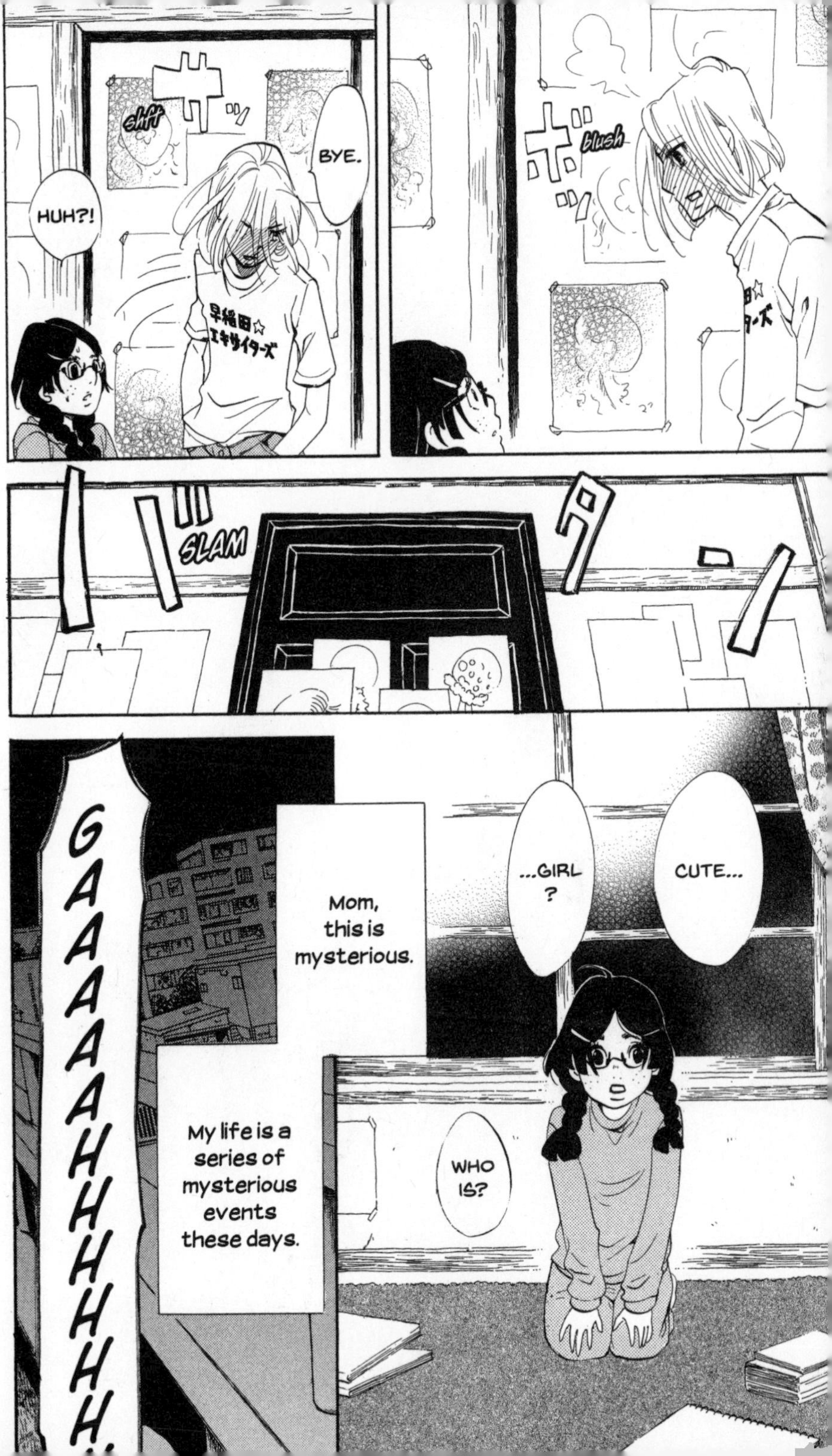
blush
BYE.
shfft
HUH?!
早稲田☆エキサイターズ
SLAM
CUTE...
...GIRL ?
Mom, this is mysterious.
WHO IS?
My life is a series of mysterious events these days.
GAAAAAAAHHHHHH!

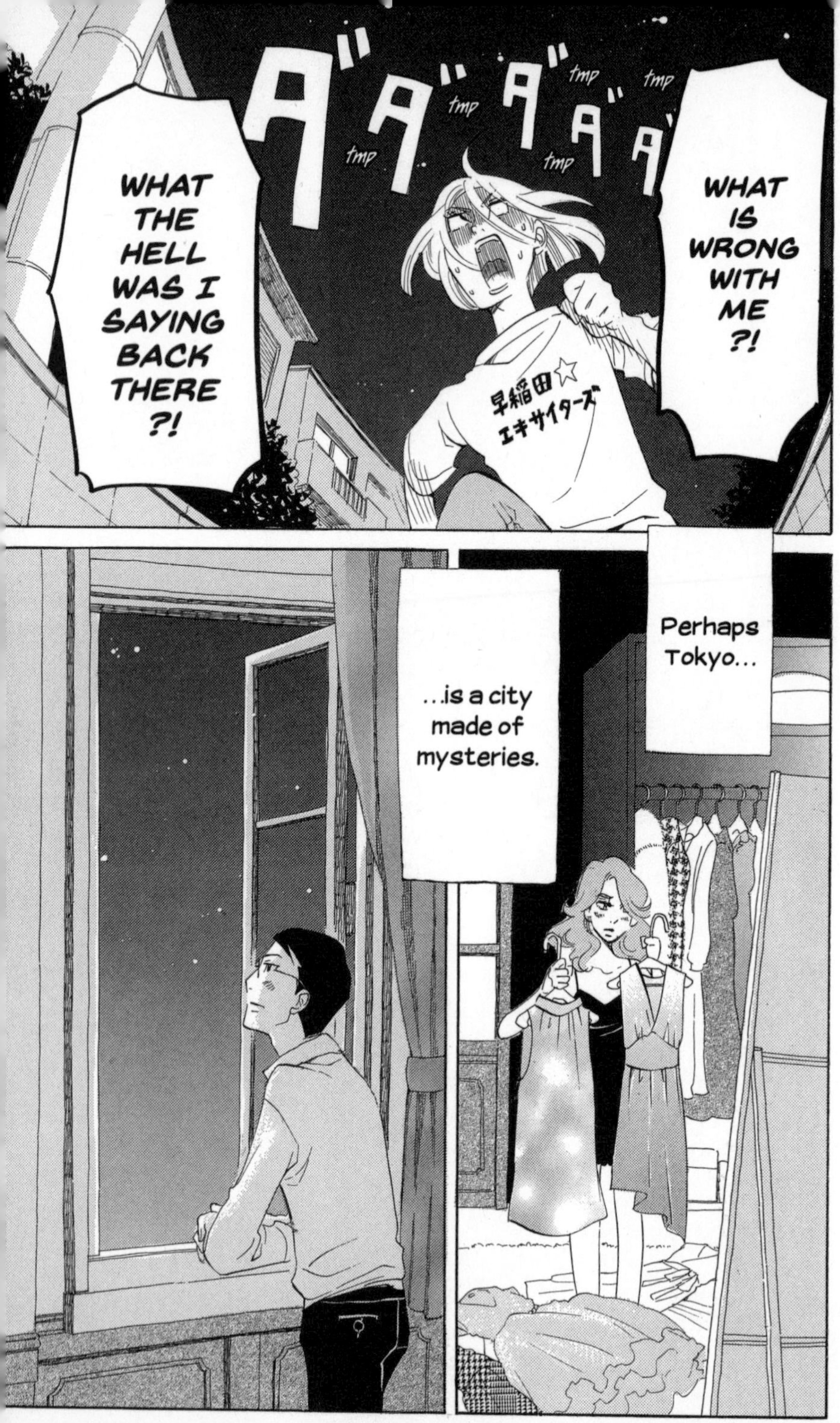
WHAT IS WRONG WITH ME ?!
ダダダダダダ
tmp tmp tmp tmp tmp
早稲田☆エキサイターズ
WHAT THE HELL WAS I SAYING BACK THERE ?!
Perhaps Tokyo...
...is a city made of mysteries.

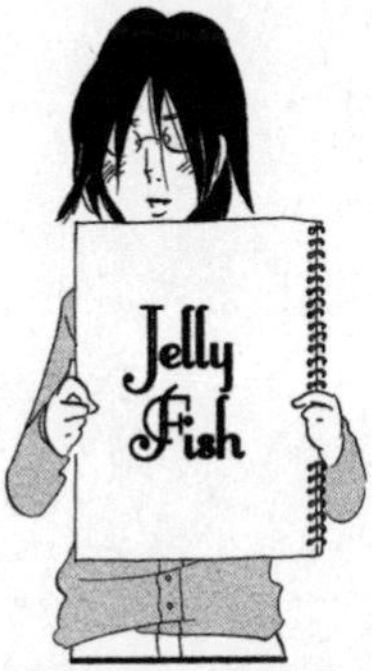
Jelly
Fish

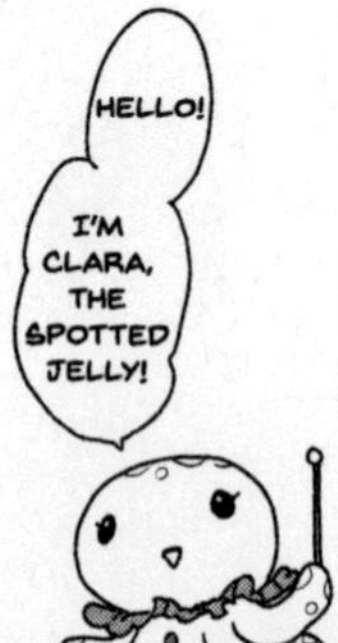
HELLO!
I'M CLARA, THE SPOTTED JELLY!

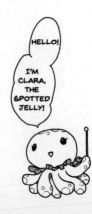

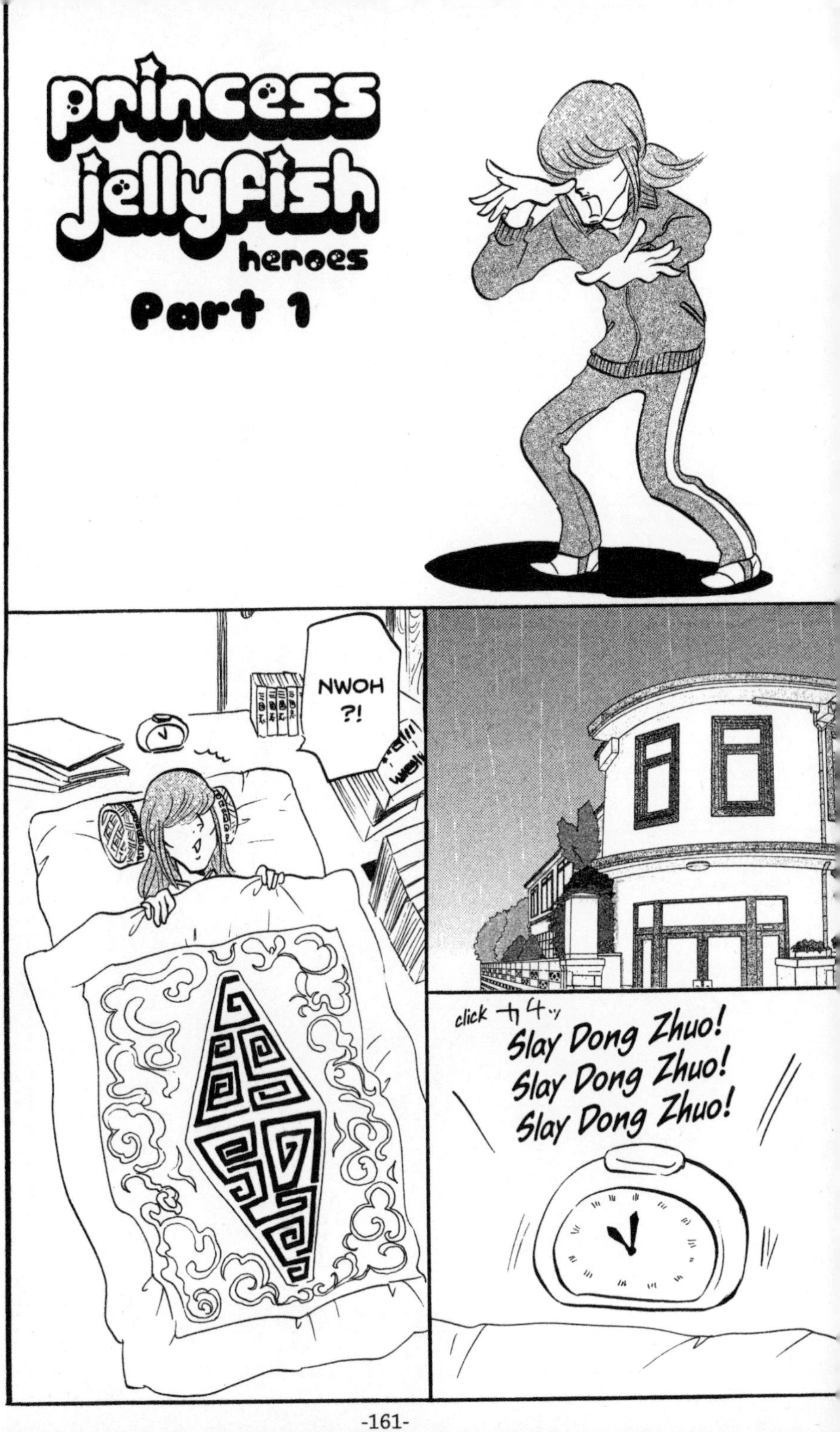
princess jellyfish heroes
Part 1
click カチッ
Slay Dong Zhuo!
Slay Dong Zhuo!
Slay Dong Zhuo!
NWOH ?!

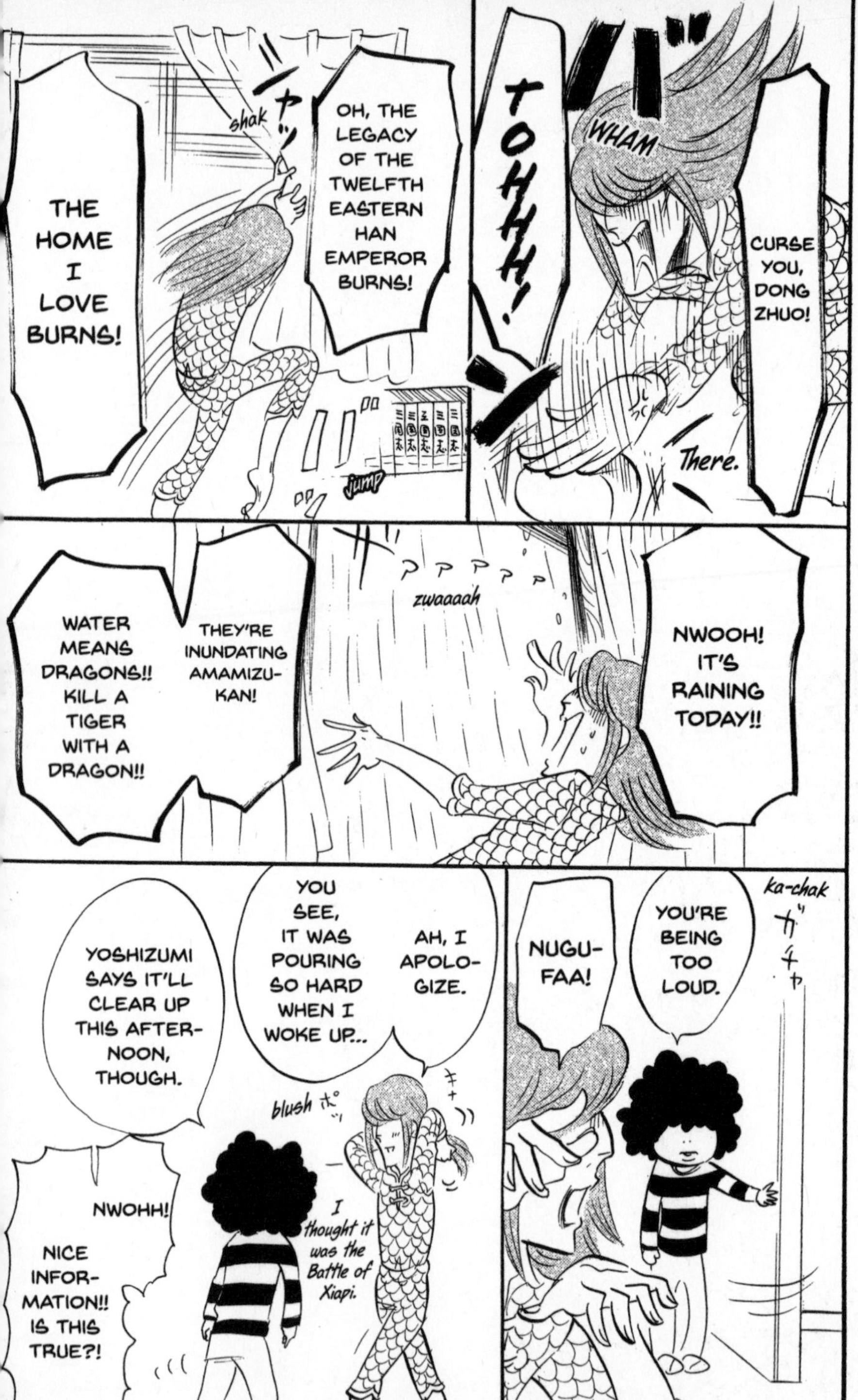
TOHHHH!
WHAM
CURSE YOU, DONG ZHUO!
There.
OH, THE LEGACY OF THE TWELFTH EASTERN HAN EMPEROR BURNS!
shak
THE HOME I LOVE BURNS!
jump
NWOOH! IT'S RAINING TODAY!!
zwaaaah
THEY'RE INUNDATING AMAMIZUKAN!
WATER MEANS DRAGONS!! KILL A TIGER WITH A DRAGON!!
ka-chak
YOU'RE BEING TOO LOUD.
NUGU-FAA!
AH, I APOLOGIZE.
YOU SEE, IT WAS POURING SO HARD WHEN I WOKE UP...
blush
YOSHIZUMI SAYS IT'LL CLEAR UP THIS AFTERNOON, THOUGH.
I thought it was the Battle of Xiapi.
NWOHH!
NICE INFORMATION!! IS THIS TRUE?!

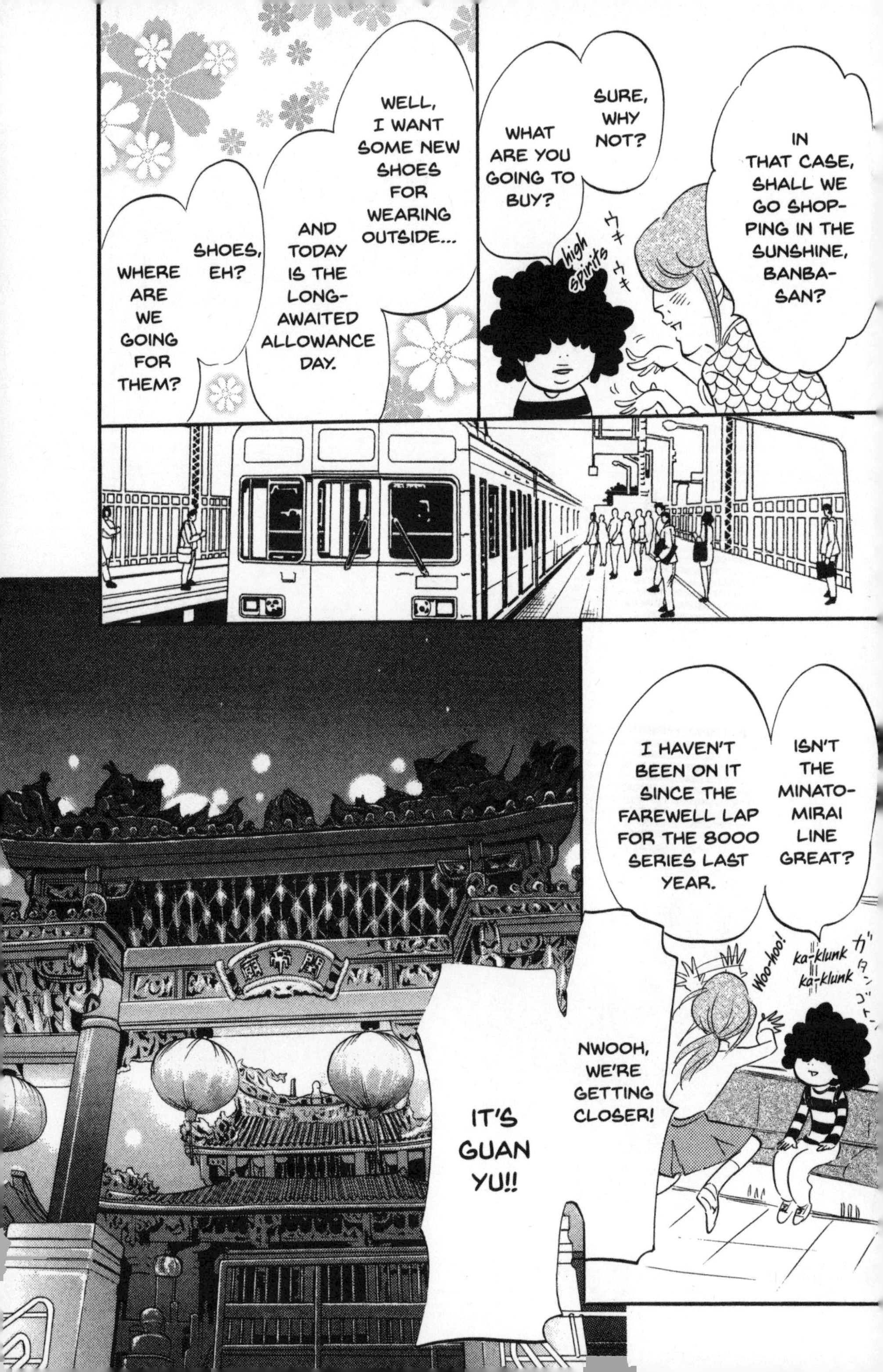
IN THAT CASE, SHALL WE GO SHOP-PING IN THE SUNSHINE, BANBA-SAN?
SURE, WHY NOT?
WHAT ARE YOU GOING TO BUY?
high spirits
ウキウキ
WELL, I WANT SOME NEW SHOES FOR WEARING OUTSIDE...
AND TODAY IS THE LONG-AWAITED ALLOWANCE DAY.
SHOES, EH?
WHERE ARE WE GOING FOR THEM?
ISN'T THE MINATO-MIRAI LINE GREAT?
I HAVEN'T BEEN ON IT SINCE THE FAREWELL LAP FOR THE 8000 SERIES LAST YEAR.
Woo-hoo!
ka-klunk ka-klunk
ガタンゴトン
NWOOH, WE'RE GETTING CLOSER!
IT'S GUAN YU!!

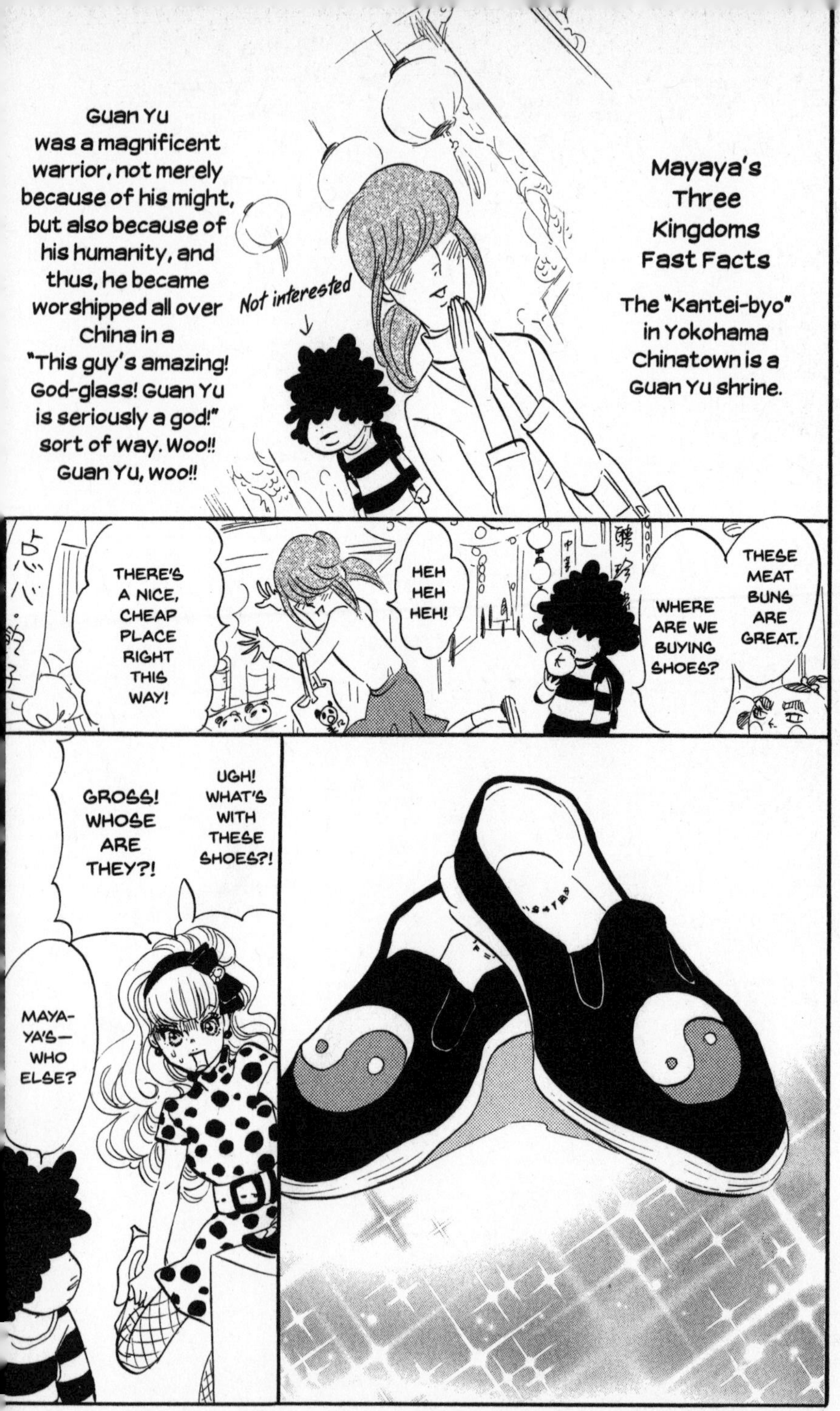
Mayaya's Three Kingdoms Fast Facts
The "Kantei-byo" in Yokohama Chinatown is a Guan Yu shrine.
Not interested
Guan Yu was a magnificent warrior, not merely because of his might, but also because of his humanity, and thus, he became worshipped all over China in a "This guy's amazing! God-glass! Guan Yu is seriously a god!" sort of way. Woo!! Guan Yu, woo!!
THESE MEAT BUNS ARE GREAT.
WHERE ARE WE BUYING SHOES?
HEH HEH HEH!
THERE'S A NICE, CHEAP PLACE RIGHT THIS WAY!
UGH! WHAT'S WITH THESE SHOES?!
GROSS! WHOSE ARE THEY?!
MAYA-YA'S— WHO ELSE?

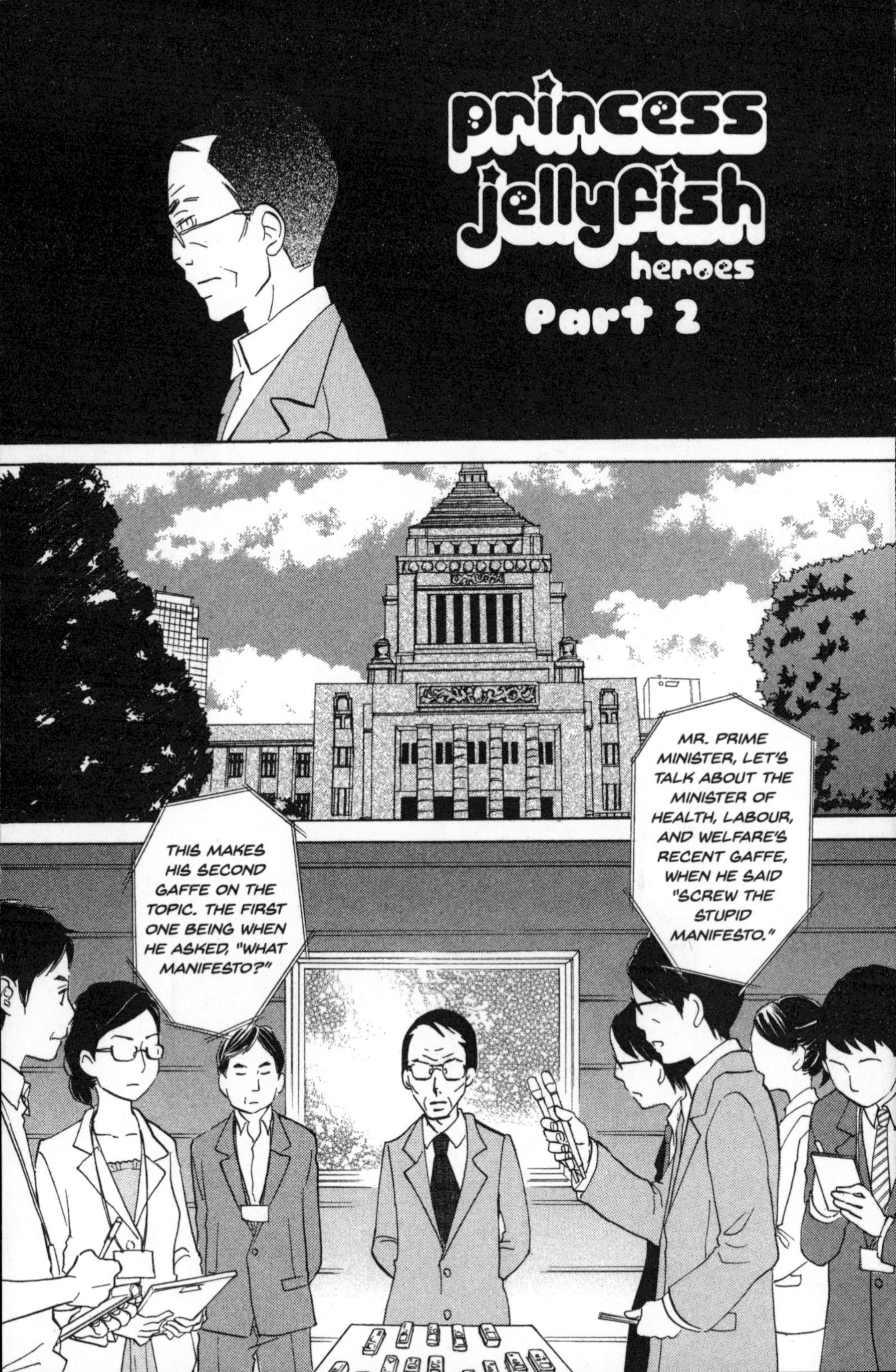
princess jellyfish
heroes
Part 2
MR. PRIME MINISTER, LET'S TALK ABOUT THE MINISTER OF HEALTH, LABOUR, AND WELFARE'S RECENT GAFFE, WHEN HE SAID "SCREW THE STUPID MANIFESTO."
THIS MAKES HIS SECOND GAFFE ON THE TOPIC. THE FIRST ONE BEING WHEN HE ASKED, "WHAT MANIFESTO?"

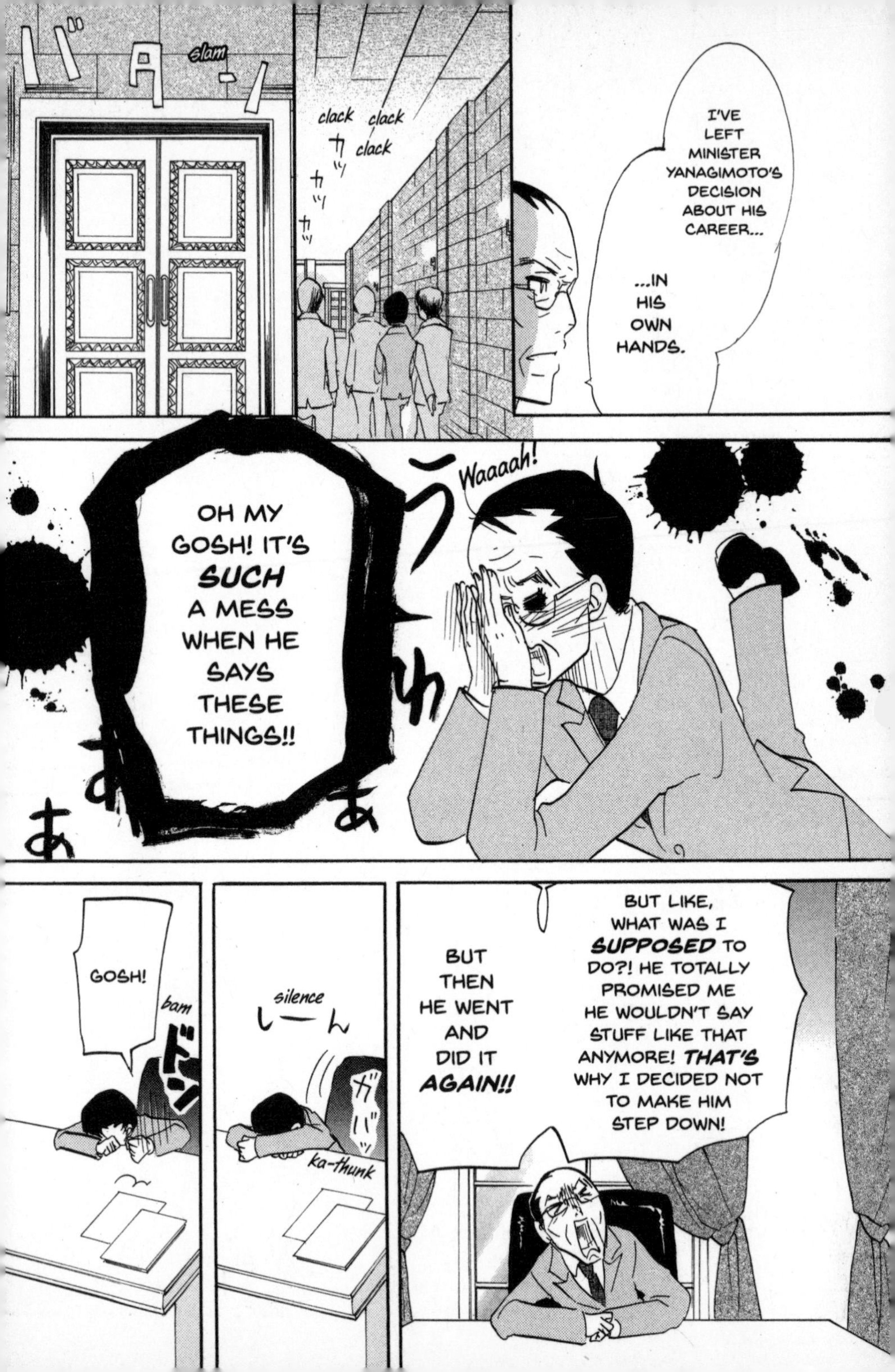
I'VE LEFT MINISTER YANAGIMOTO'S DECISION ABOUT HIS CAREER...
...IN HIS OWN HANDS.
clack clack clack
slam
Waaaah!
OH MY GOSH! IT'S **SUCH** A MESS WHEN HE SAYS THESE THINGS!!
BUT LIKE, WHAT WAS I **SUPPOSED** TO DO?! HE TOTALLY PROMISED ME HE WOULDN'T SAY STUFF LIKE THAT ANYMORE! **THAT'S** WHY I DECIDED NOT TO MAKE HIM STEP DOWN!
BUT THEN HE WENT AND DID IT **AGAIN!!**
silence
ka-thunk
GOSH!
bam

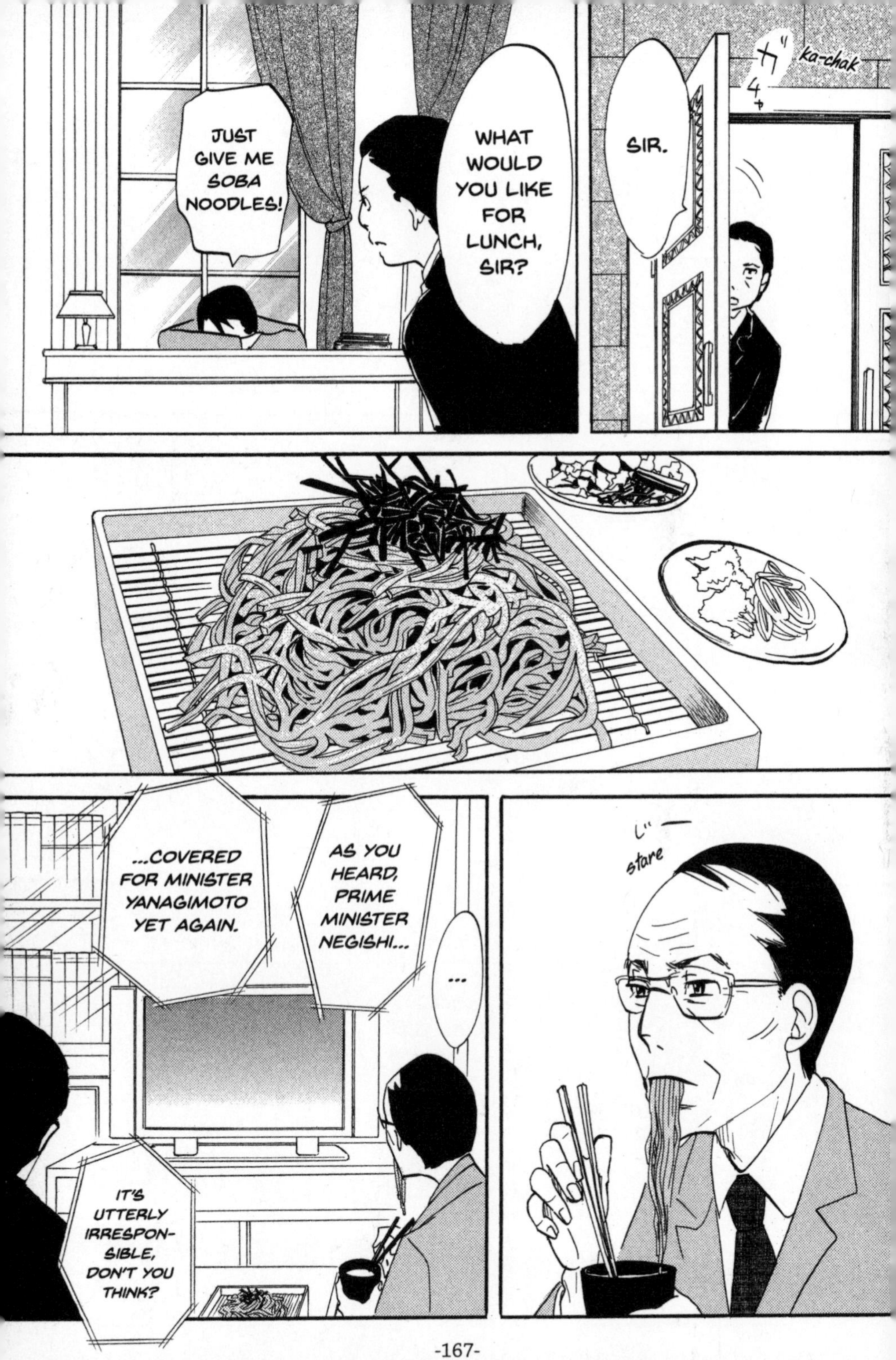
ガチャ
ka-chak
SIR.
WHAT WOULD YOU LIKE FOR LUNCH, SIR?
JUST GIVE ME SOBA NOODLES!
じー
stare
...
AS YOU HEARD, PRIME MINISTER NEGISHI...
...COVERED FOR MINISTER YANAGIMOTO YET AGAIN.
IT'S UTTERLY IRRESPONSIBLE, DON'T YOU THINK?

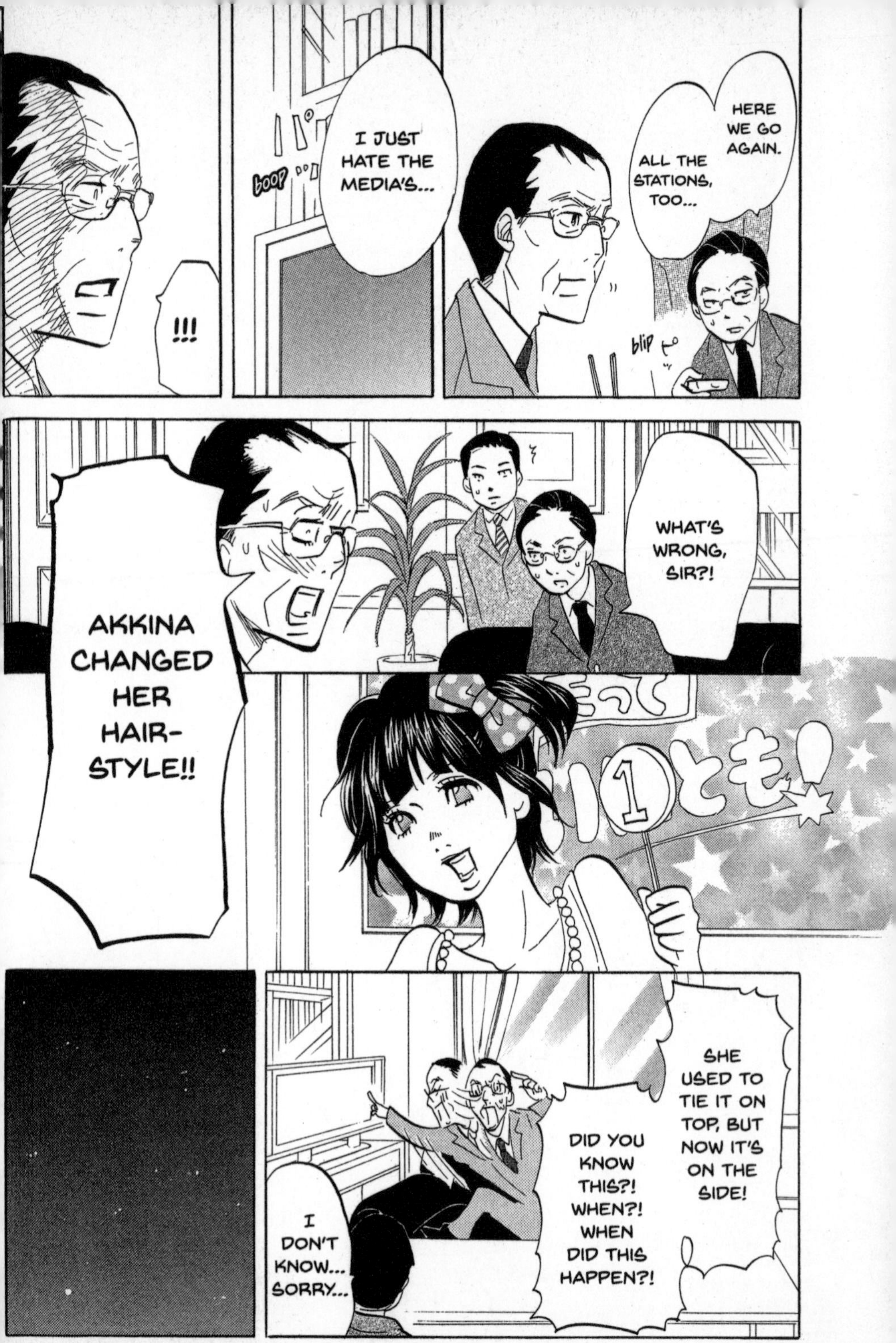
HERE WE GO AGAIN.
ALL THE STATIONS, TOO...
blip
I JUST HATE THE MEDIA'S...
boop
!!!
WHAT'S WRONG, SIR?!
AKKINA CHANGED HER HAIR-STYLE!!
SHE USED TO TIE IT ON TOP, BUT NOW IT'S ON THE SIDE!
DID YOU KNOW THIS?! WHEN?! WHEN DID THIS HAPPEN?!
I DON'T KNOW... SORRY...

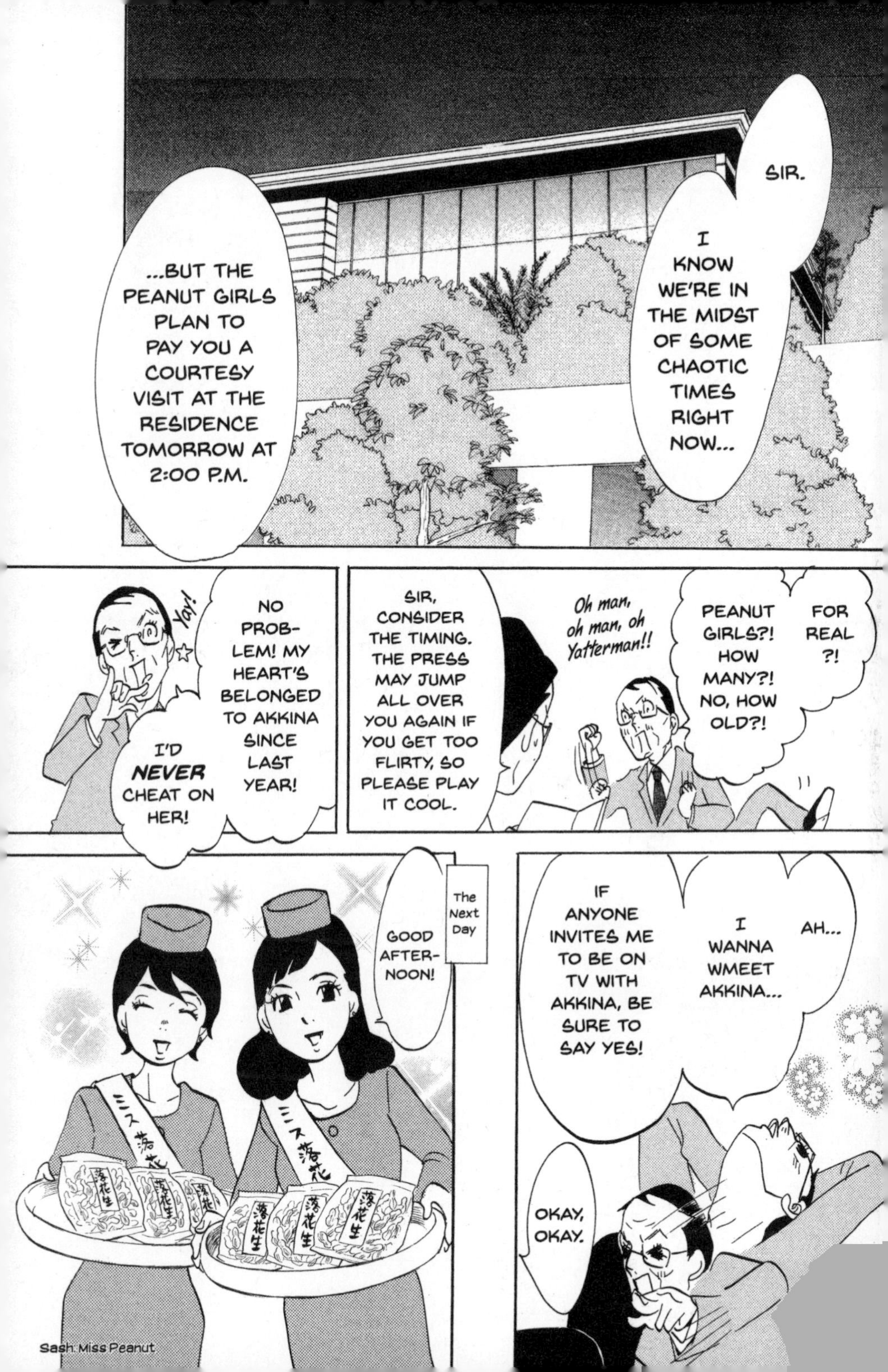
SIR.
I KNOW WE'RE IN THE MIDST OF SOME CHAOTIC TIMES RIGHT NOW...
...BUT THE PEANUT GIRLS PLAN TO PAY YOU A COURTESY VISIT AT THE RESIDENCE TOMORROW AT 2:00 P.M.
FOR REAL?!
PEANUT GIRLS?! HOW MANY?! NO, HOW OLD?!
Oh man, oh man, oh Yatterman!!
SIR, CONSIDER THE TIMING. THE PRESS MAY JUMP ALL OVER YOU AGAIN IF YOU GET TOO FLIRTY, SO PLEASE PLAY IT COOL.
Yay!
NO PROB-LEM! MY HEART'S BELONGED TO AKKINA SINCE LAST YEAR!
I'D **NEVER** CHEAT ON HER!
AH...
I WANNA WMEET AKKINA...
IF ANYONE INVITES ME TO BE ON TV WITH AKKINA, BE SURE TO SAY YES!
OKAY, OKAY.
The Next Day
GOOD AFTER-NOON!
ミス落花
ミス落花
落花生
落花生
落花生
落花生
落花生
Sash: Miss Peanut

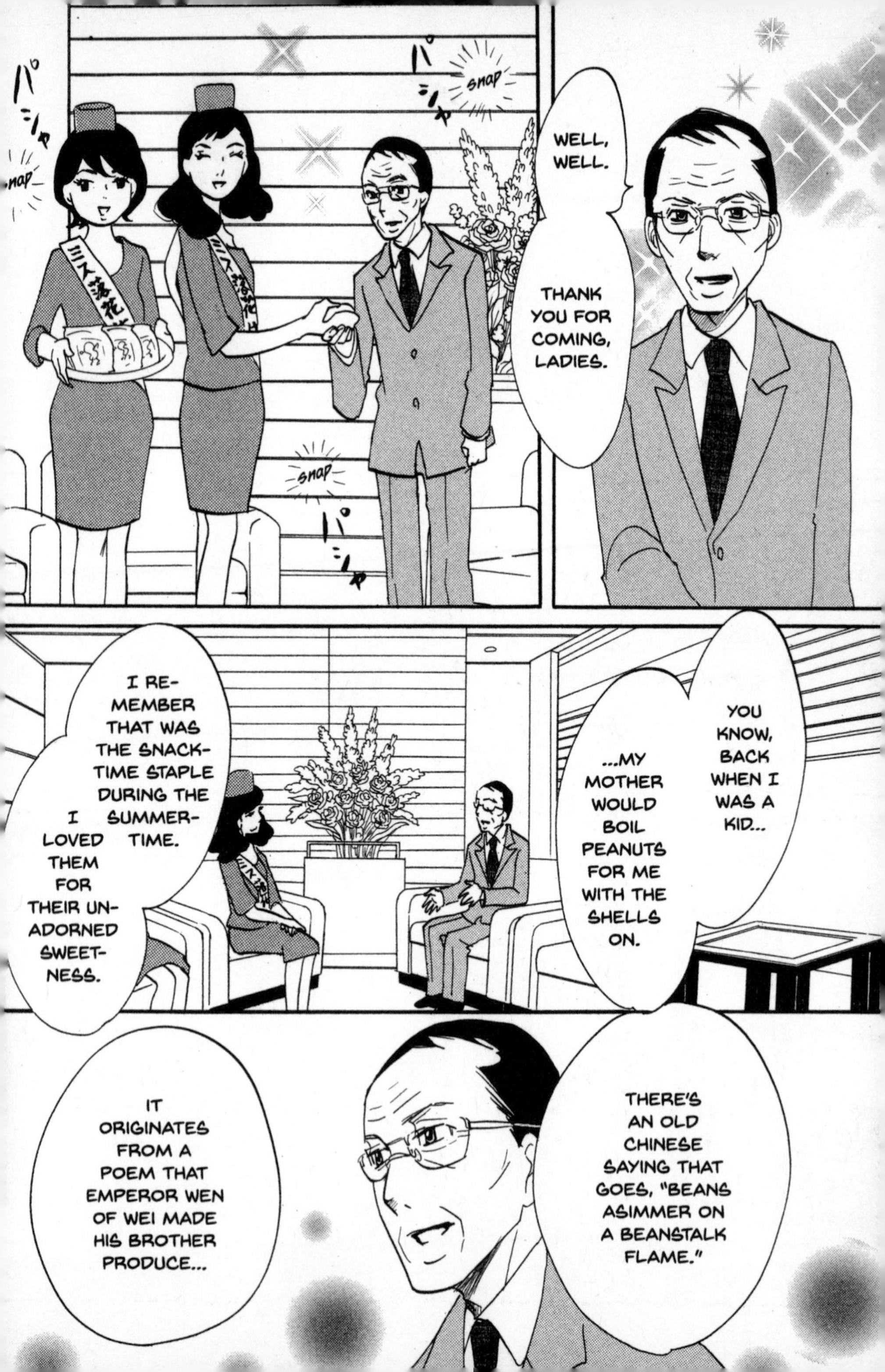
WELL, WELL.
THANK YOU FOR COMING, LADIES.
パシャ
snap
パシャ
snap
パシャ
snap
YOU KNOW, BACK WHEN I WAS A KID...
...MY MOTHER WOULD BOIL PEANUTS FOR ME WITH THE SHELLS ON.
I REMEMBER THAT WAS THE SNACK-TIME STAPLE DURING THE SUMMERTIME.
I LOVED THEM FOR THEIR UNADORNED SWEETNESS.
THERE'S AN OLD CHINESE SAYING THAT GOES, "BEANS ASIMMER ON A BEANSTALK FLAME."
IT ORIGINATES FROM A POEM THAT EMPEROR WEN OF WEI MADE HIS BROTHER PRODUCE...

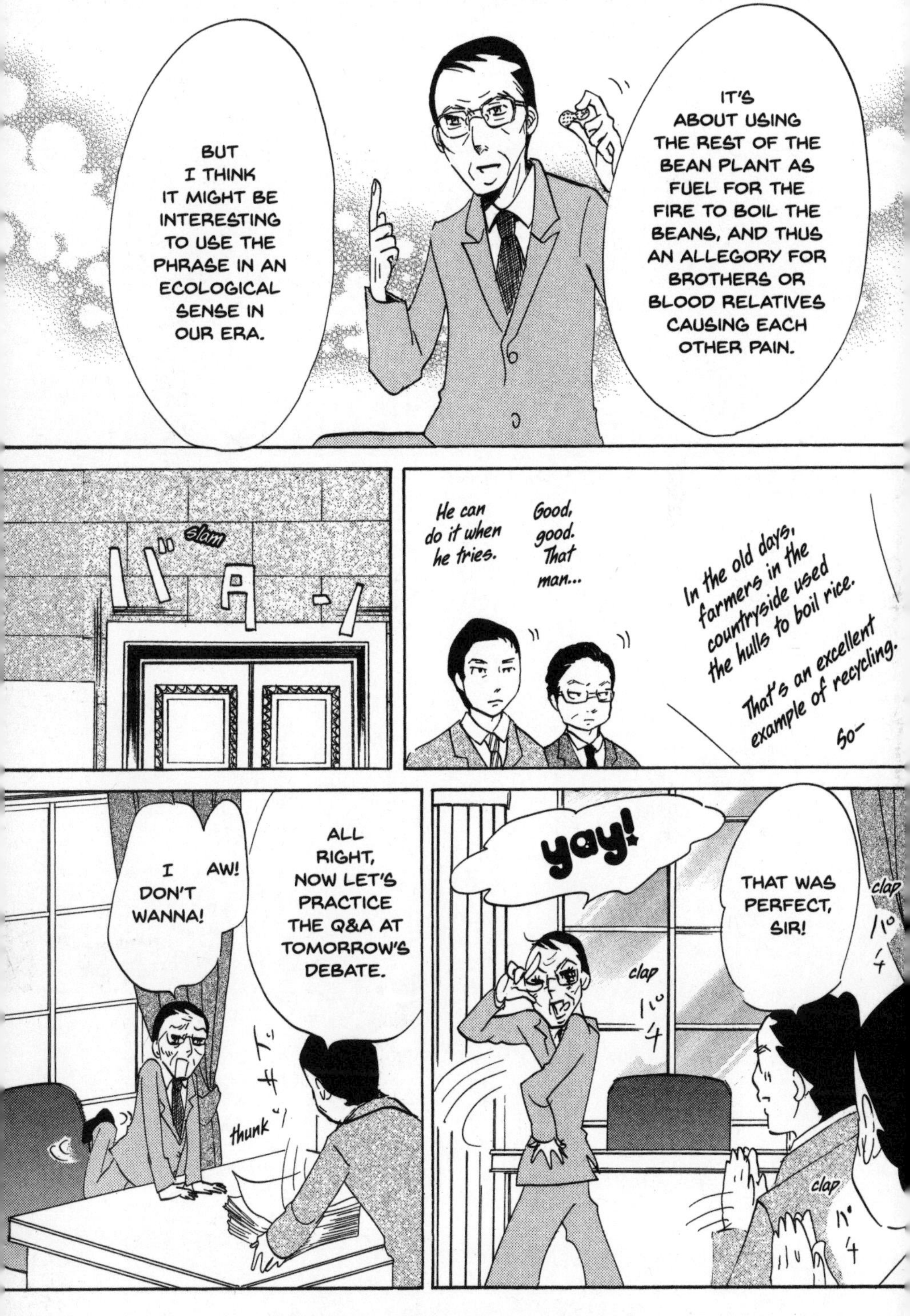
IT'S ABOUT USING THE REST OF THE BEAN PLANT AS FUEL FOR THE FIRE TO BOIL THE BEANS, AND THUS AN ALLEGORY FOR BROTHERS OR BLOOD RELATIVES CAUSING EACH OTHER PAIN.
BUT I THINK IT MIGHT BE INTERESTING TO USE THE PHRASE IN AN ECOLOGICAL SENSE IN OUR ERA.
In the old days, farmers in the countryside used the hulls to boil rice.
That's an excellent example of recycling.
So—
Good, good. That man...
He can do it when he tries.
slam
THAT WAS PERFECT, SIR!
clap
yay!
clap
clap
ALL RIGHT, NOW LET'S PRACTICE THE Q&A AT TOMORROW'S DEBATE.
AW! I DON'T WANNA!
thunk

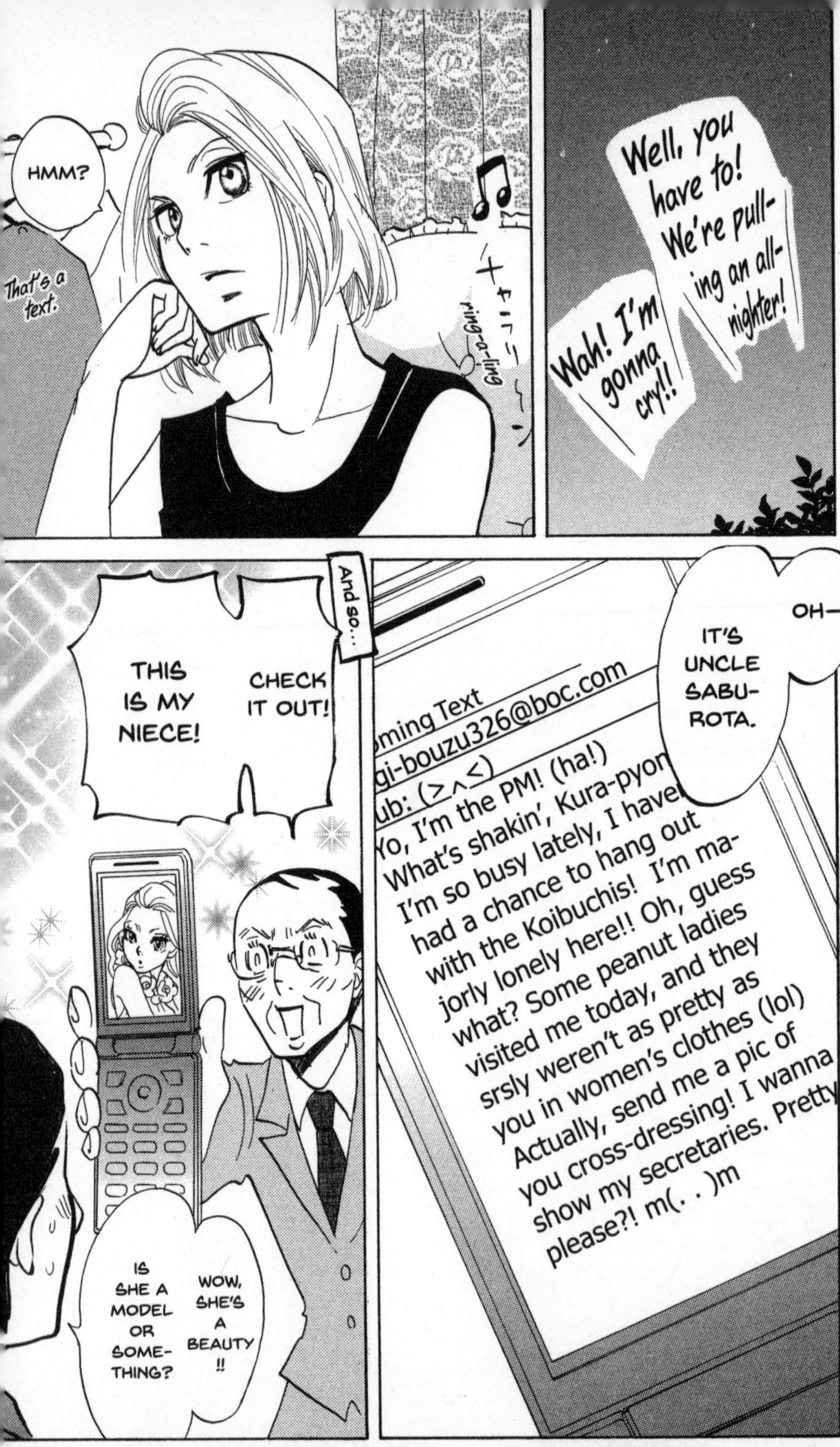
Well, you have to! We're pull-ing an all-nighter!
Wah! I'm gonna cry!!
ring-a-ling
HMM?
That's a text.
OH—
IT'S UNCLE SABU-ROTA.
oming Text
gi-bouzu326@boc.com
ub: (>^<)
Yo, I'm the PM! (ha!) What's shakin', Kura-pyon I'm so busy lately, I have had a chance to hang out with the Koibuchis! I'm ma-jorly lonely here!! Oh, guess what? Some peanut ladies visited me today, and they srsly weren't as pretty as you in women's clothes (lol) Actually, send me a pic of you cross-dressing! I wanna show my secretaries. Pretty please?! m(. .)m
And so...
CHECK IT OUT!
THIS IS MY NIECE!
WOW, SHE'S A BEAUTY !!
IS SHE A MODEL OR SOME-THING?

Princess Jellyfish Heroes Parts 1&2—End

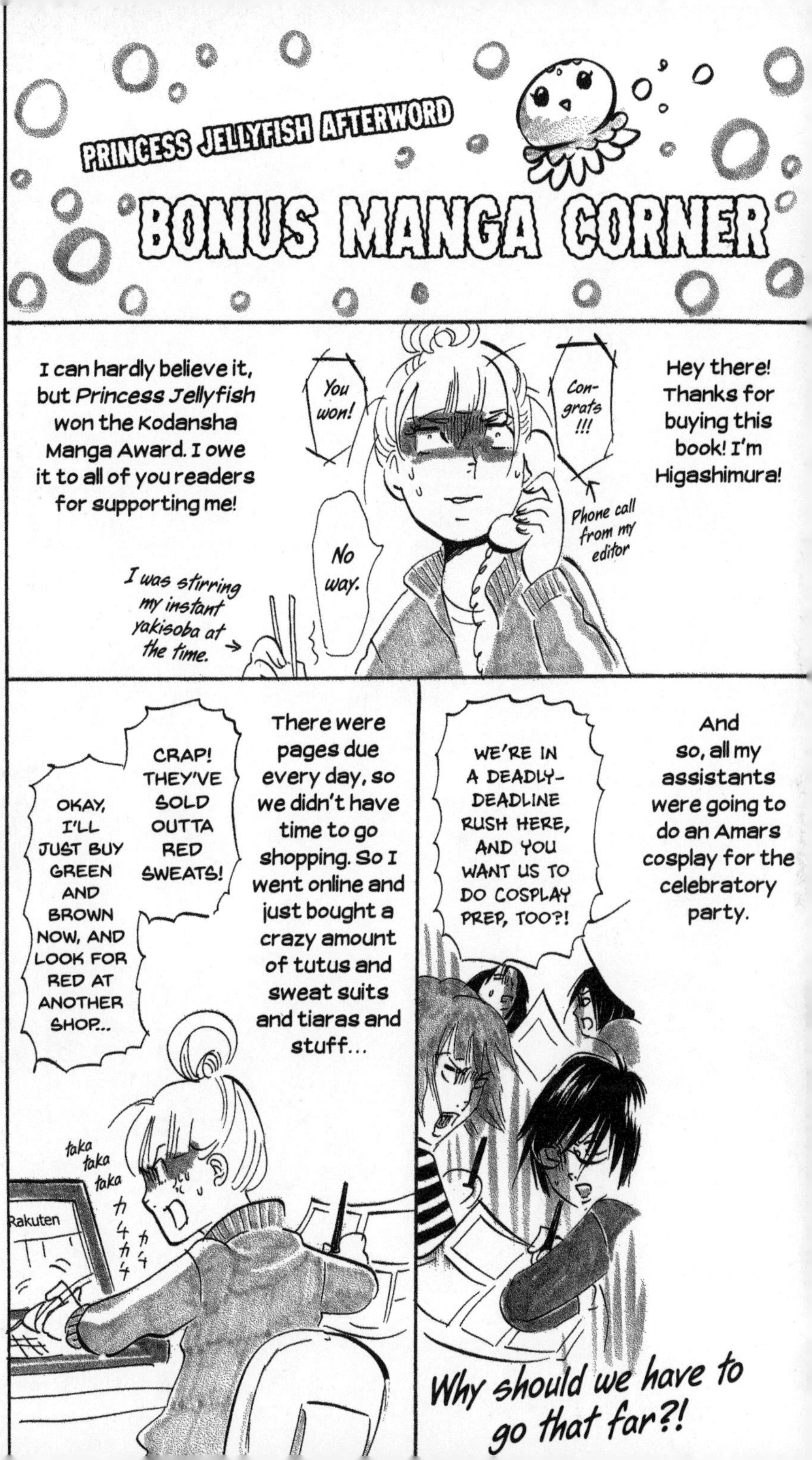
PRINCESS JELLYFISH AFTERWORD
BONUS MANGA CORNER
Hey there! Thanks for buying this book! I'm Higashimura!
Congrats!!!
Phone call from my editor
You won!
No way.
I can hardly believe it, but Princess Jellyfish won the Kodansha Manga Award. I owe it to all of you readers for supporting me!
I was stirring my instant yakisoba at the time.
And so, all my assistants were going to do an Amars cosplay for the celebratory party.
WE'RE IN A DEADLY-DEADLINE RUSH HERE, AND YOU WANT US TO DO COSPLAY PREP, TOO?!
Why should we have to go that far?!
There were pages due every day, so we didn't have time to go shopping. So I went online and just bought a crazy amount of tutus and sweat suits and tiaras and stuff...
CRAP! THEY'VE SOLD OUTTA RED SWEATS!
OKAY, I'LL JUST BUY GREEN AND BROWN NOW, AND LOOK FOR RED AT ANOTHER SHOP...
taka taka taka
Rakuten

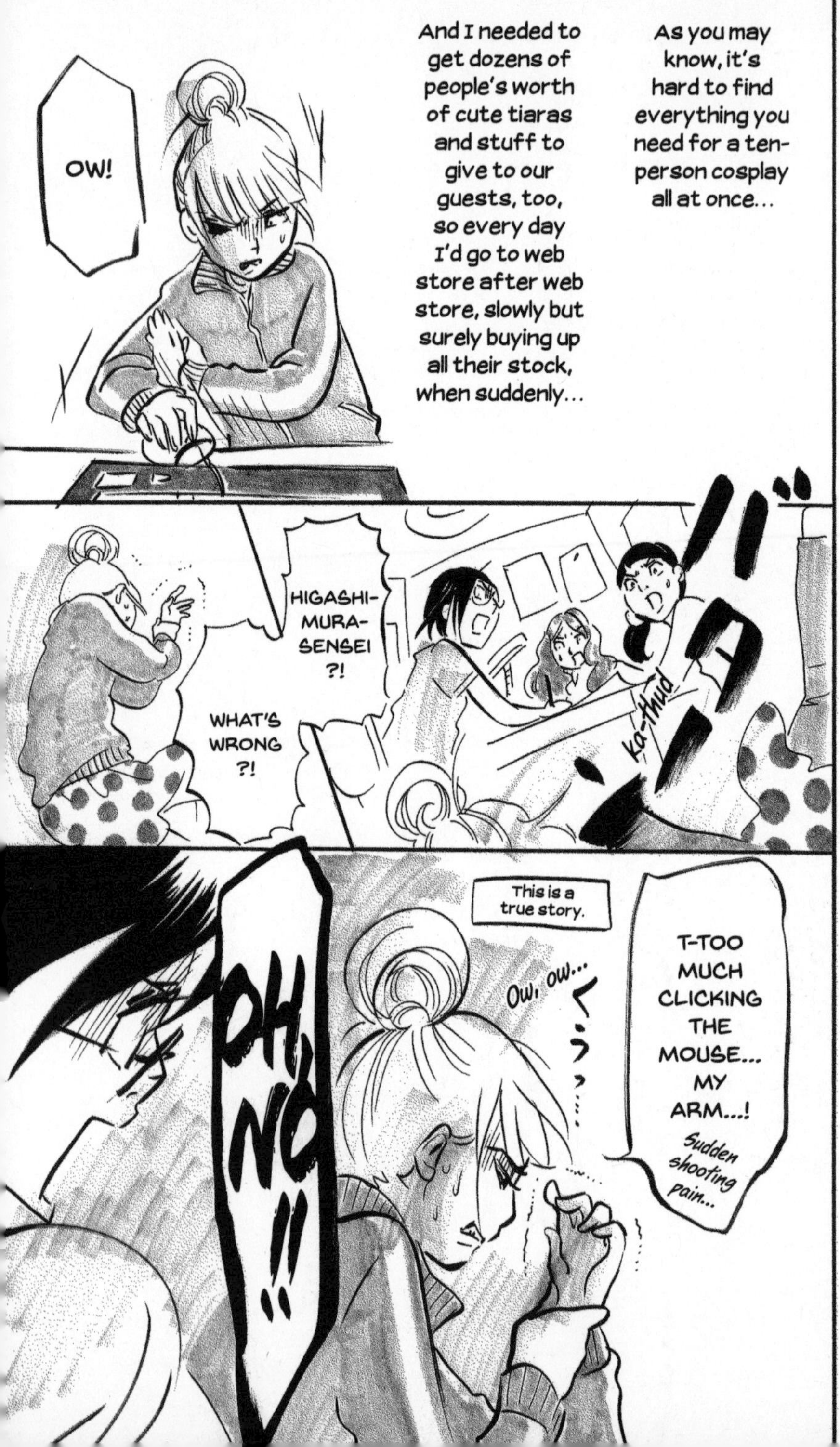
As you may know, it's hard to find everything you need for a ten-person cosplay all at once...
And I needed to get dozens of people's worth of cute tiaras and stuff to give to our guests, too, so every day I'd go to web store after web store, slowly but surely buying up all their stock, when suddenly...
OW!
ka-thud
HIGASHIMURA-SENSEI?!
WHAT'S WRONG?!
T-TOO MUCH CLICKING THE MOUSE... MY ARM...!
Sudden shooting pain...
This is a true story.
Ow, ow...
OH, NO!!

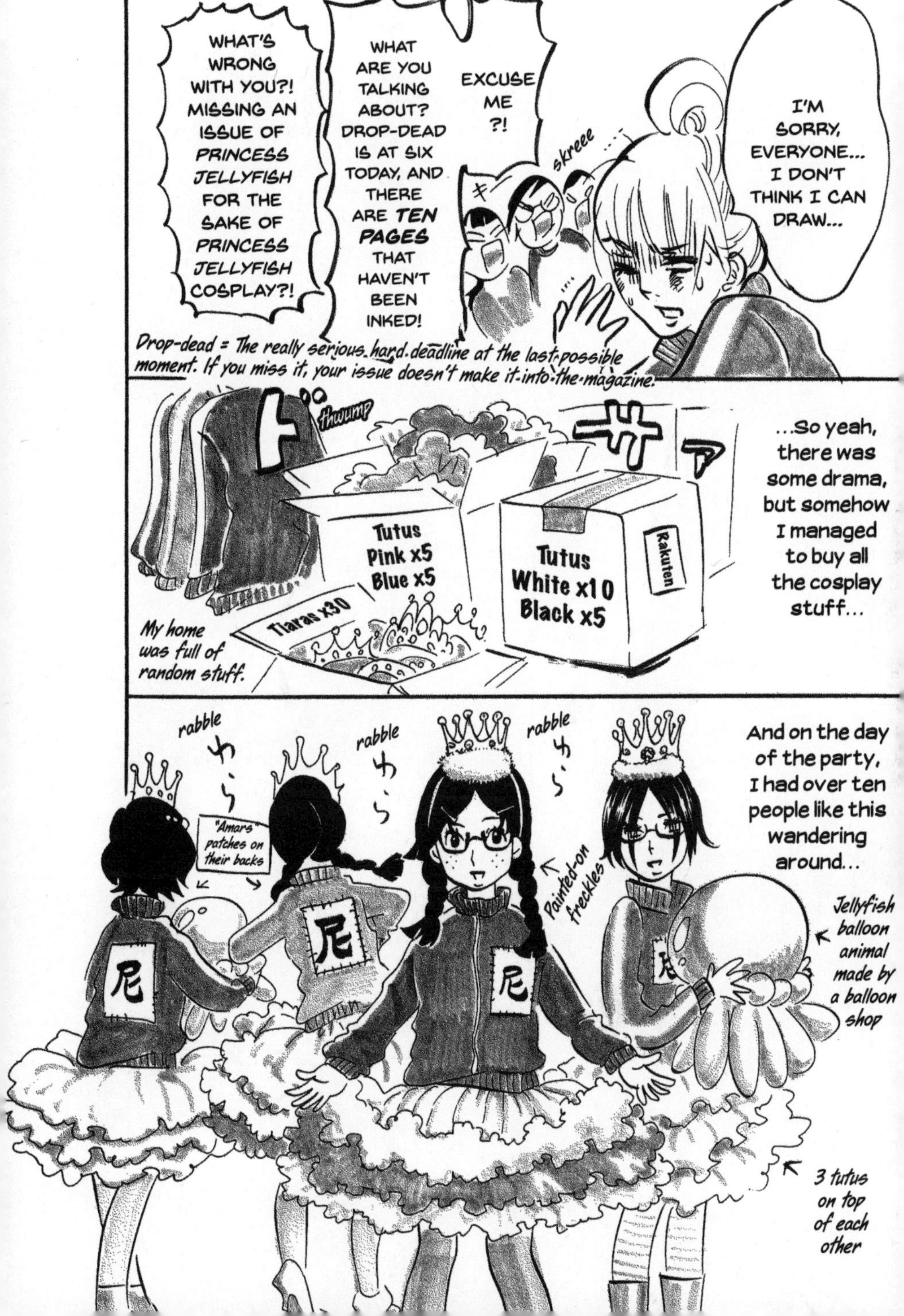
I'M SORRY, EVERYONE... I DON'T THINK I CAN DRAW...
skreee
EXCUSE ME ?!
WHAT ARE YOU TALKING ABOUT? DROP-DEAD IS AT SIX TODAY, AND THERE ARE TEN PAGES THAT HAVEN'T BEEN INKED!
WHAT'S WRONG WITH YOU?! MISSING AN ISSUE OF PRINCESS JELLYFISH FOR THE SAKE OF PRINCESS JELLYFISH COSPLAY?!
Drop-dead = The really serious hard deadline at the last possible moment. If you miss it, your issue doesn't make it into the magazine.
...So yeah, there was some drama, but somehow I managed to buy all the cosplay stuff...
Rakuten
Tutus White x10 Black x5
Tutus Pink x5 Blue x5
thwump
Tiaras x30
My home was full of random stuff.
And on the day of the party, I had over ten people like this wandering around...
rabble
rabble
rabble
Jellyfish balloon animal made by a balloon shop
Painted-on freckles
"Amars" patches on their backs
尼
尼
尼
3 tutus on top of each other

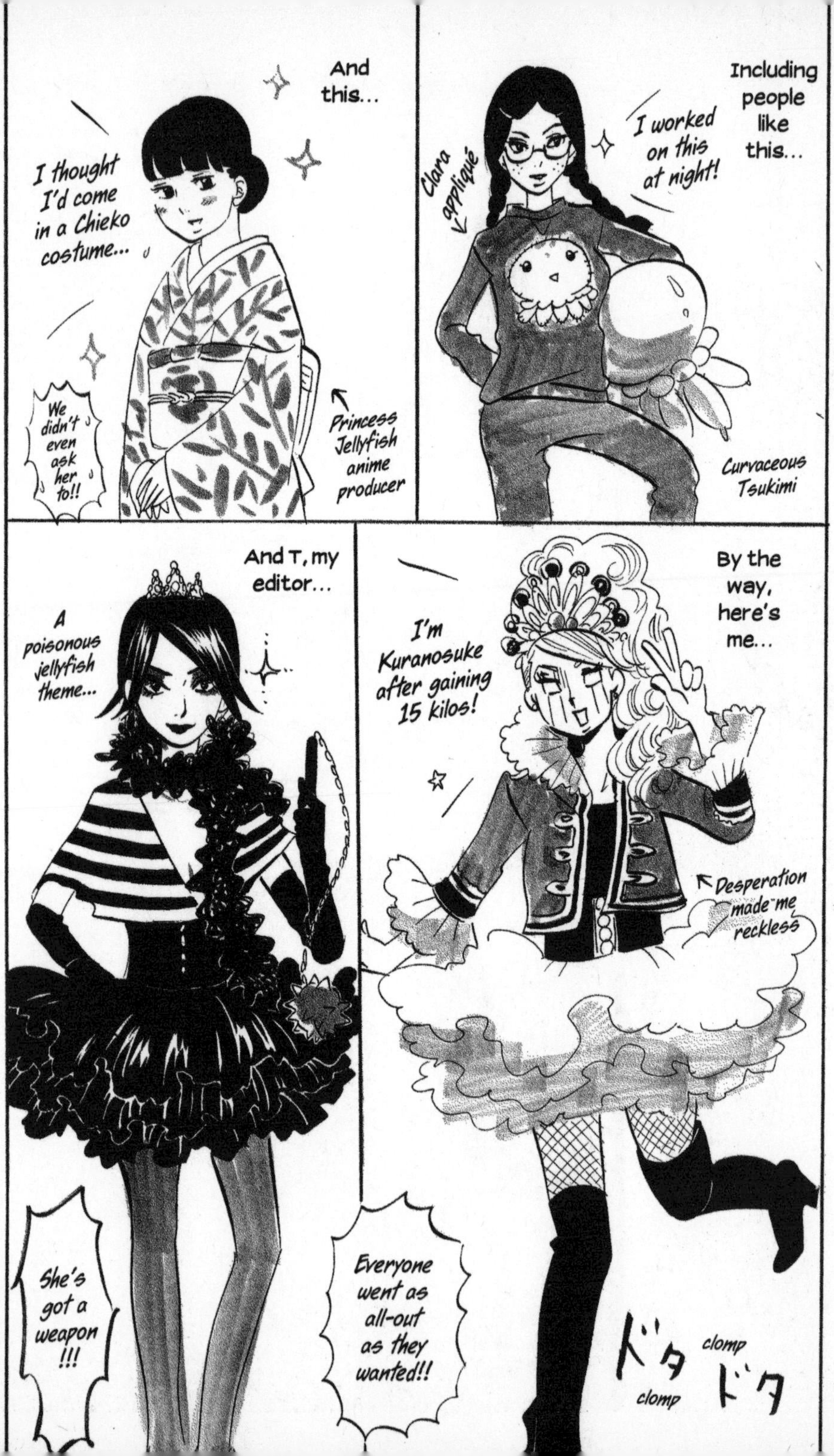
Including people like this...
I worked on this at night!
Clara appliqué
Curvaceous Tsukimi
And this...
I thought I'd come in a Chieko costume...
Princess Jellyfish anime producer
We didn't even ask her to!!
By the way, here's me...
I'm Kuranosuke after gaining 15 kilos!
Desperation made me reckless
ドタ clomp
ドタ clomp
Everyone went as all-out as they wanted!!
And T, my editor...
A poisonous jellyfish theme...
She's got a weapon!!!

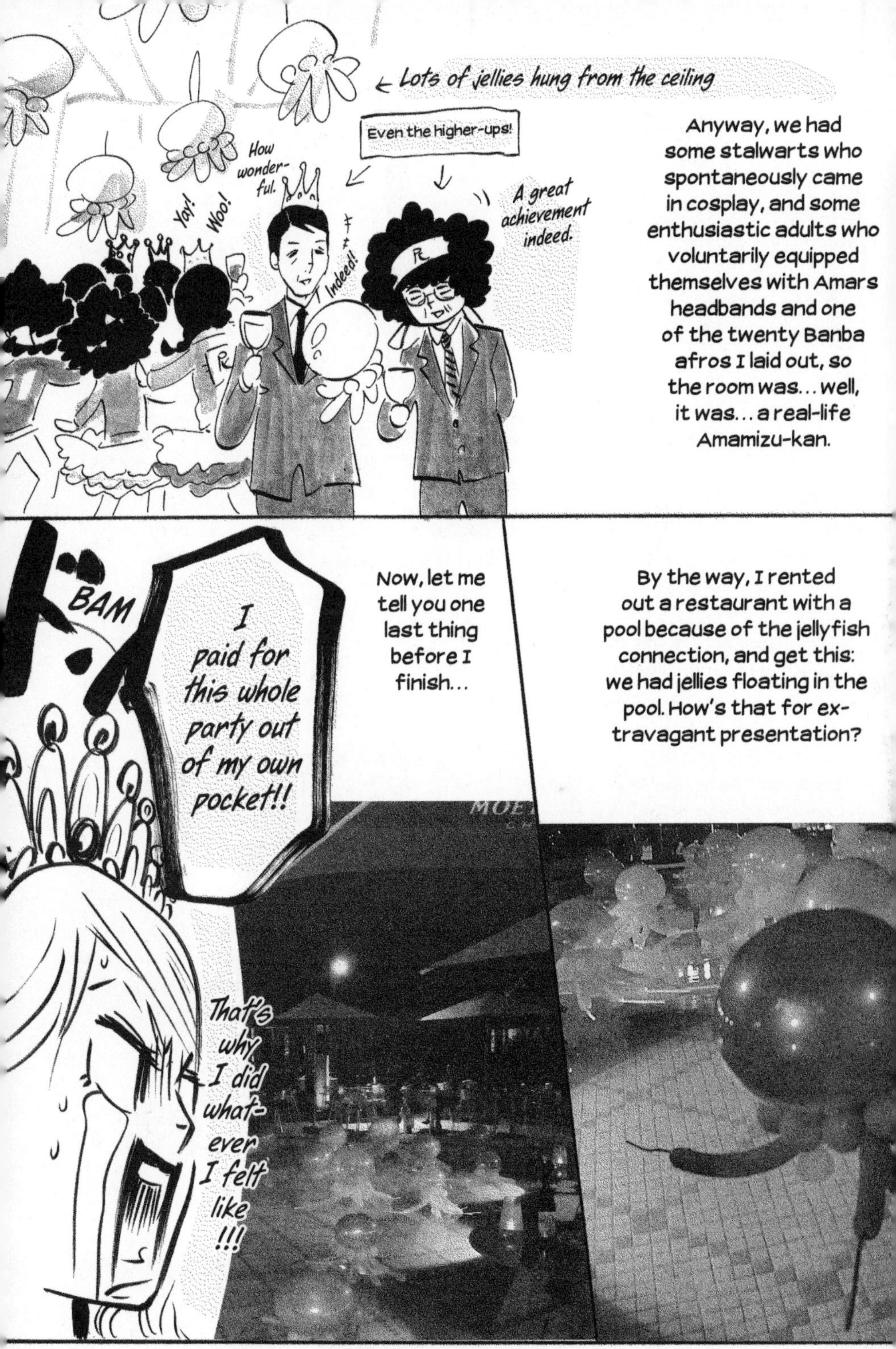

Lots of jellies hung from the ceiling
Anyway, we had some stalwarts who spontaneously came in cosplay, and some enthusiastic adults who voluntarily equipped themselves with Amars headbands and one of the twenty Banba afros I laid out, so the room was... well, it was... a real-life Amamizu-kan.
Even the higher-ups!
A great achievement indeed.
Indeed!
How wonderful.
Woo!
Yay!
By the way, I rented out a restaurant with a pool because of the jellyfish connection, and get this: we had jellies floating in the pool. How's that for extravagant presentation?
Now, let me tell you one last thing before I finish...
BAM
I paid for this whole party out of my own pocket!!
That's why I did whatever I felt like!!!

Translation Notes

Rock Me Hamlet!, page 35
Rock Me Hamlet is the Japanese release title of Andrew Fleming's 2008 film *Hamlet 2*.

Lotteria, page 45
Lotteria is a fast-food chain restaurant in Asia.

Wash your hands with Muse!!, page 45
Mayaya is looking for germ-killing power here, not inspiration—Muse is a brand of antibacterial soap in Japan.

Soseki-dono!!, page 74
Natsume Soseki (1867-1916), author of *Botchan* and *Kokoro*, was a prominent Japanese novelist. His portrait was on the 1,000-yen note from 1984 until 2004. The honorific *-dono* can mean "master" or "lord."

A girl turned rotten like me..., page 94
As referenced in the translation notes to volume 1, Tsukimi is identifying herself as a fujoshi, which, when literally translated means "rotten woman."

I will commit hara-kiri right here and now if you try to make me wear that! Chieko-san, be my second!, page 119
Hara-kiri, more commonly known as *seppuku* in Japanese, was the old warrior practice of ritually disemboweling oneself, either as a true suicide or as a death sentence that mandated suicide. It was considered the "honorable man's suicide," atoning for bad actions or cleansing oneself of shame, and being sentenced to death by *hara-kiri* was reserved for those considered worthy of an honorable death. The "second" at this type of suicide was responsible for beheading the person after self-disembowelment was performed. Depending on the era, this functioned as a merciful release from pain because if the person was beheaded right after the one committing *seppuku* made his first incision, he was spared the agony of a prolonged death.

White Sandcastle, page 129
[Spoiler Alert! Read me after you've finished the chapter!]
This title is a riff on the American movie, *White Palace*, starring Susan Sarandon. In Japanese, the wordplay with this title is directly related to Kuranosuke's declaration to Tsukimi at the end of the chapter. *White Palace* was released in Japan as *Boku no Utsukushii Hito dakara*, or "Because You're My Beautiful One." The Japanese title for this chapter of the manga is *"Boku no Kawaii Hito dakara,"* or "Because You're My Cute One."

Takamoku and the "Starry Stage," page 135
Yoshihiko Takamoku was a member of a now disbanded pop/rock group called the Checkers, whose single *"Hoshikuzu no Stage"* ("Starry Stage") was released in 1984. It featured a heartbroken man singing to the starry sky while imagining his dead sweetheart.

Eisaku Okawa and "Sazanka no Yado," page 135
Eisaku Okawa is an *enka* singer, and therefore not somebody the average schoolgirl is into. *Enka* is a traditional and older type of Japanese ballad. *"Sazanka no Yado"* is his biggest hit.

Ken Utsui, page 135
The late Ken Utsui was a Japanese actor who would have been in his fifties during the time period Jiji is referring to.

An X-jump?!, page 147
X Japan is a famous Japanese heavy metal band known for pioneering the *visual kei* genre in the 80s, which emphasizes elaborate makeup and costumes. Fans of X Japan would often do an "X-jump" at concerts, where they jumped up while crossing their forearms to make an "X."

Weather and Obsession, page 162
Mayaya and Banba even relate to the weather through their respective interests. Mayaya is afraid Amamizu-kan is facing the Battle of Xiapi because Cao Cao's forces flooded Lu Bu's stronghold during that battle in 198 CE. Banba is ready to reassure her with glad tidings of sunshine from her favorite weatherman, Yoshizumi Ishihara...who is also a train enthusiast!

Akkina changed her hairstyle!!, page 168
"Akkina" is a nickname for Akina Minami, whom you see on the television here. Prime Minister Negishi and his staff are watching *Waratte Iitomo!*, a variety show on which Akkina appeared regularly between 2008 and 2010, which is apparently what triggered Negishi's admiration for her. The show, long a Japanese TV staple, ended its more than 30-year run in 2014.

"Beans asimmer on a beanstalk flame.", page 170
If only Mayaya could hear these words, he might finally win her vote! This phrase is an excerpt from a poem by Cao Zhi, and is featured in Chapter 79 of *The Romance of Three Kingdoms*, wherein Cao Zhi's brother, the emperor, demands that he compose a poem within the time it takes to walk seven paces.

WHAT?

THE TYPE OF WOMEN I LIKE?

WELL, IF I WERE PRESSED TO RESPOND...

SOMEONE WHO LIKES BENZES AND UNDERSTANDS THE GREATNESS OF BENZES. IT'S PREFERABLE IF THEY WORK AT A BENZ DEALERSHIP AND ARE SERIOUS AND SINCERE. IN CAR TERMS, SOMEONE WHO'S JUST LIKE A MERCEDES-BENZ. EXCEPT AT TIMES, LIKE A HARLOT, TOO. AND FACE-WISE, I'D PICK KEIKO MATSUZAKA TYPES. IN REGARDS TO BODY TYPES, I'D SAY KEIKO MATSUZAKA AGAIN. IF A WOMAN LIKE KEIKO MATSUZAKA SUDDENLY APPEARED BEFORE ME, I'D INVITE HER ON A DRIVE IN A SECOND, PROBABLY.

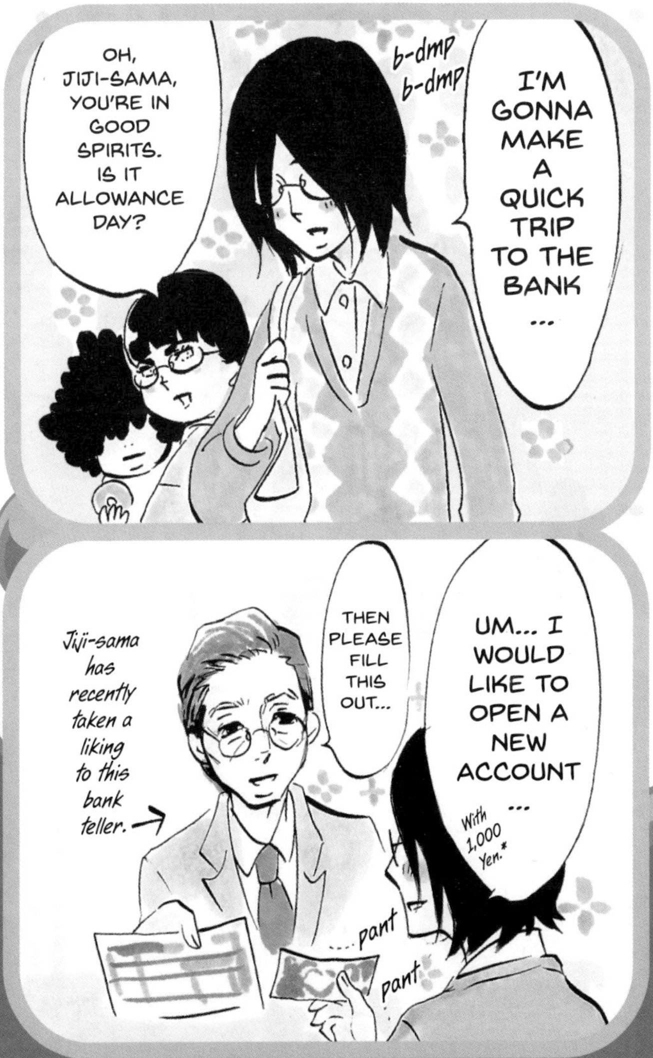
b-dmp b-dmp
I'M GONNA MAKE A QUICK TRIP TO THE BANK ...
OH, JIJI-SAMA, YOU'RE IN GOOD SPIRITS. IS IT ALLOWANCE DAY?
UM... I WOULD LIKE TO OPEN A NEW ACCOUNT ...
With 1,000 Yen.*
THEN PLEASE FILL THIS OUT...
Jiji-sama has recently taken a liking to this bank teller.
....pant
pant

*About $10 USD.

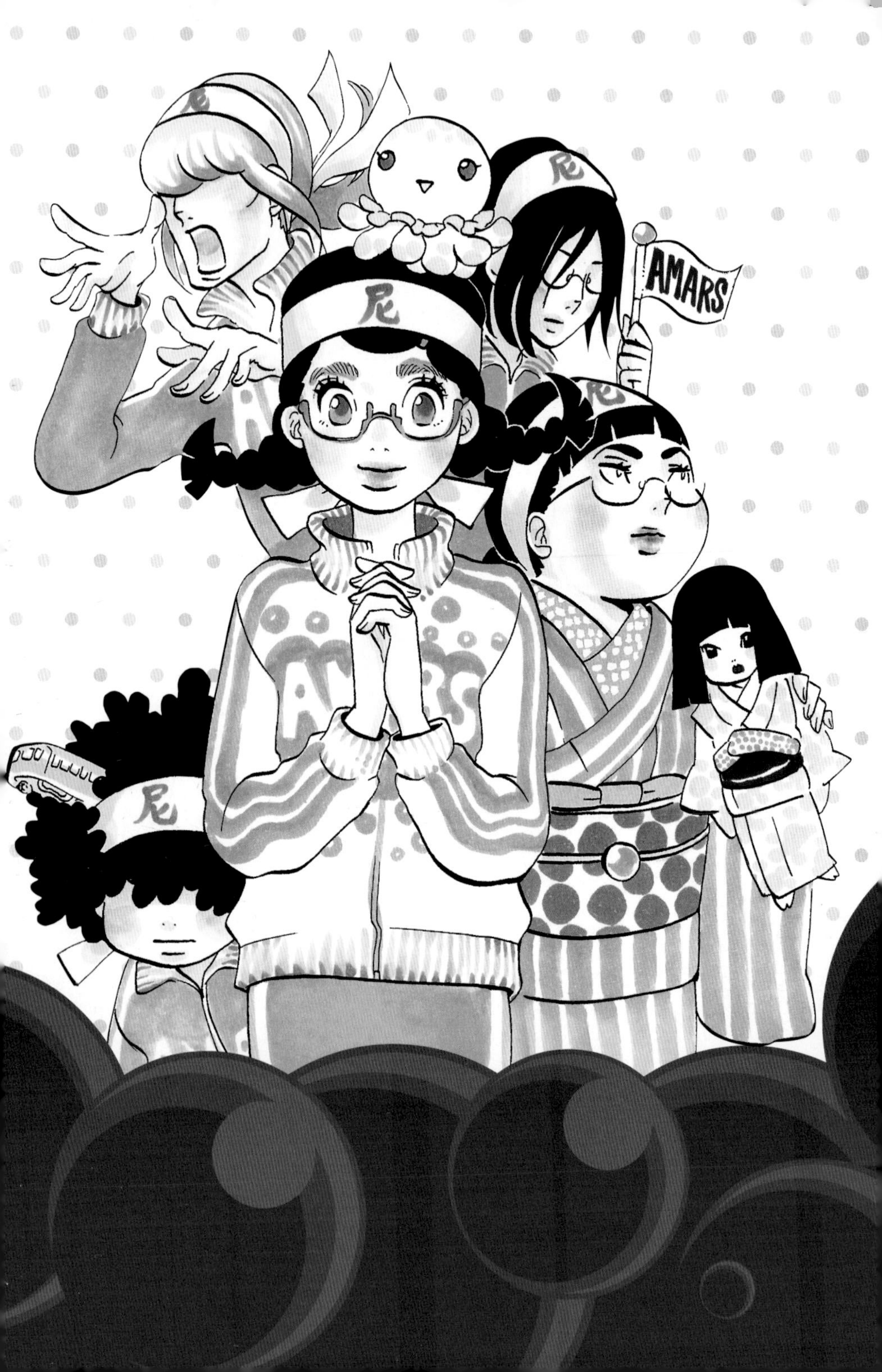
AMARS
AMARS

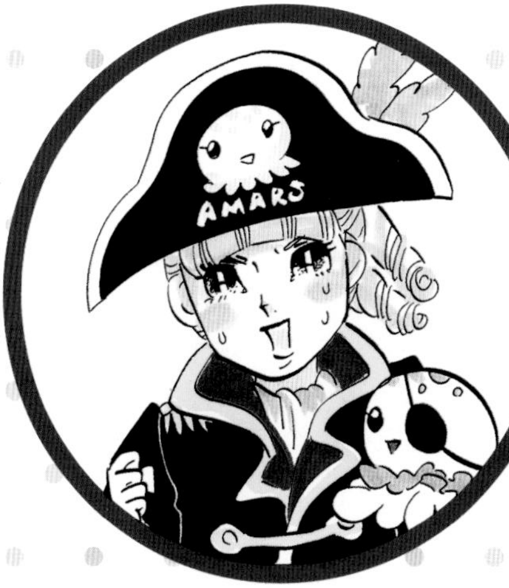
AMARS

DEAREST READERS!

HUGE NEWS!
PRINCESS JELLYFISH IS
GONNA BECOME AN ANIME!
EVERYONE IN AMARS IS MOVING
AND TALKING AND CAUSING ALL
SORTS OF TROUBLE!
I'M SO, SO, ***SO*** EXCITED
THAT I KEEP GETTING
DISTRACTED FROM WORK!
I NEED TO BUY A NEW TV!
I NEED TO BUY A NEW VCR!
HUH? BLU-RAY?
WHAT'S BLU-RAY?!
SOME NEW TYPE OF JELLYFISH?
AAH, THE WAVE OF TECHNOLOGY
HAS FINALLY HIT AMARS!
ANIME ADAPTATION *BANZAI!*

-AKIKO HIGASHIMURA

Episode 30
Deception

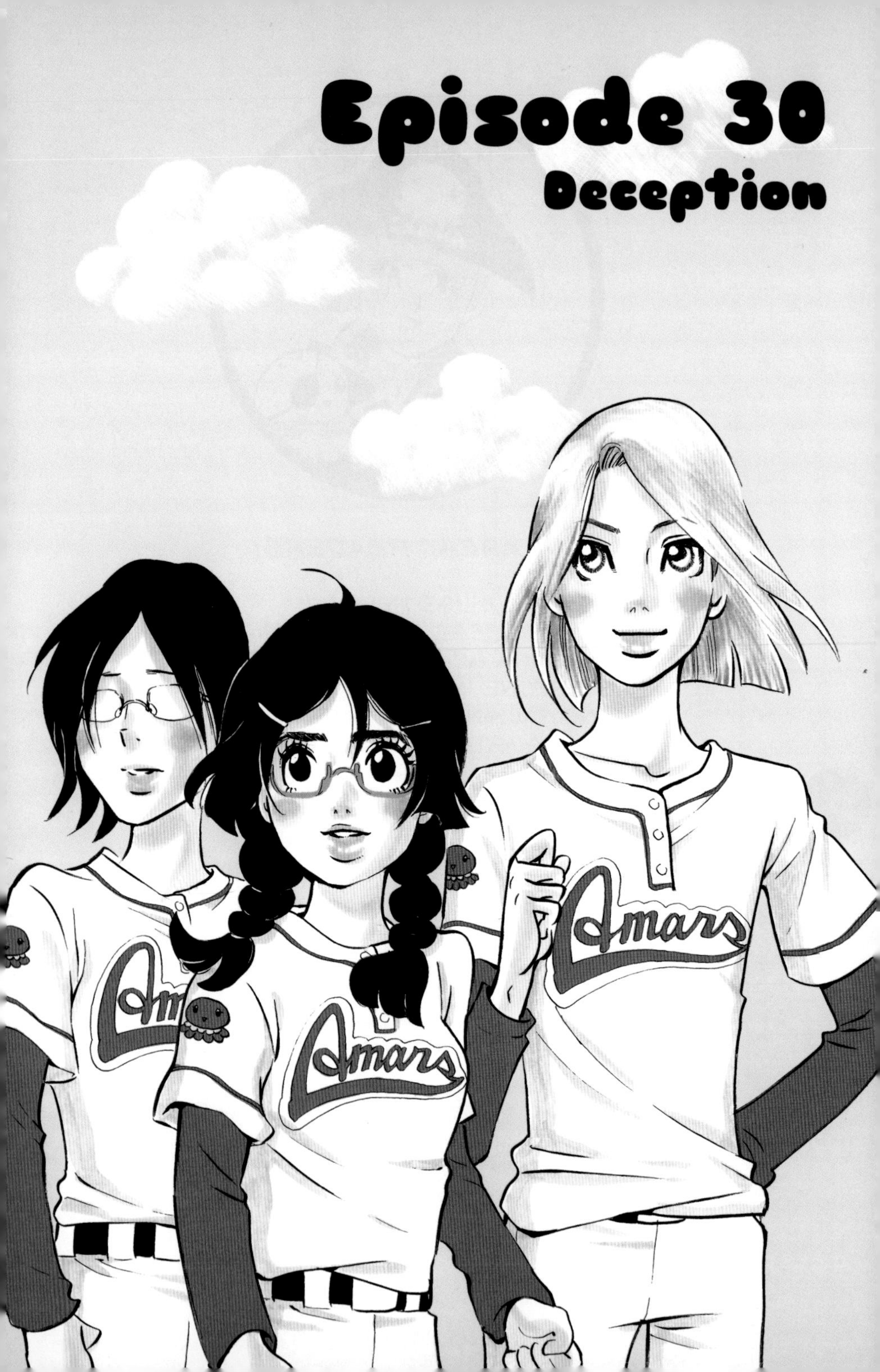
Amars
Amars
Amars

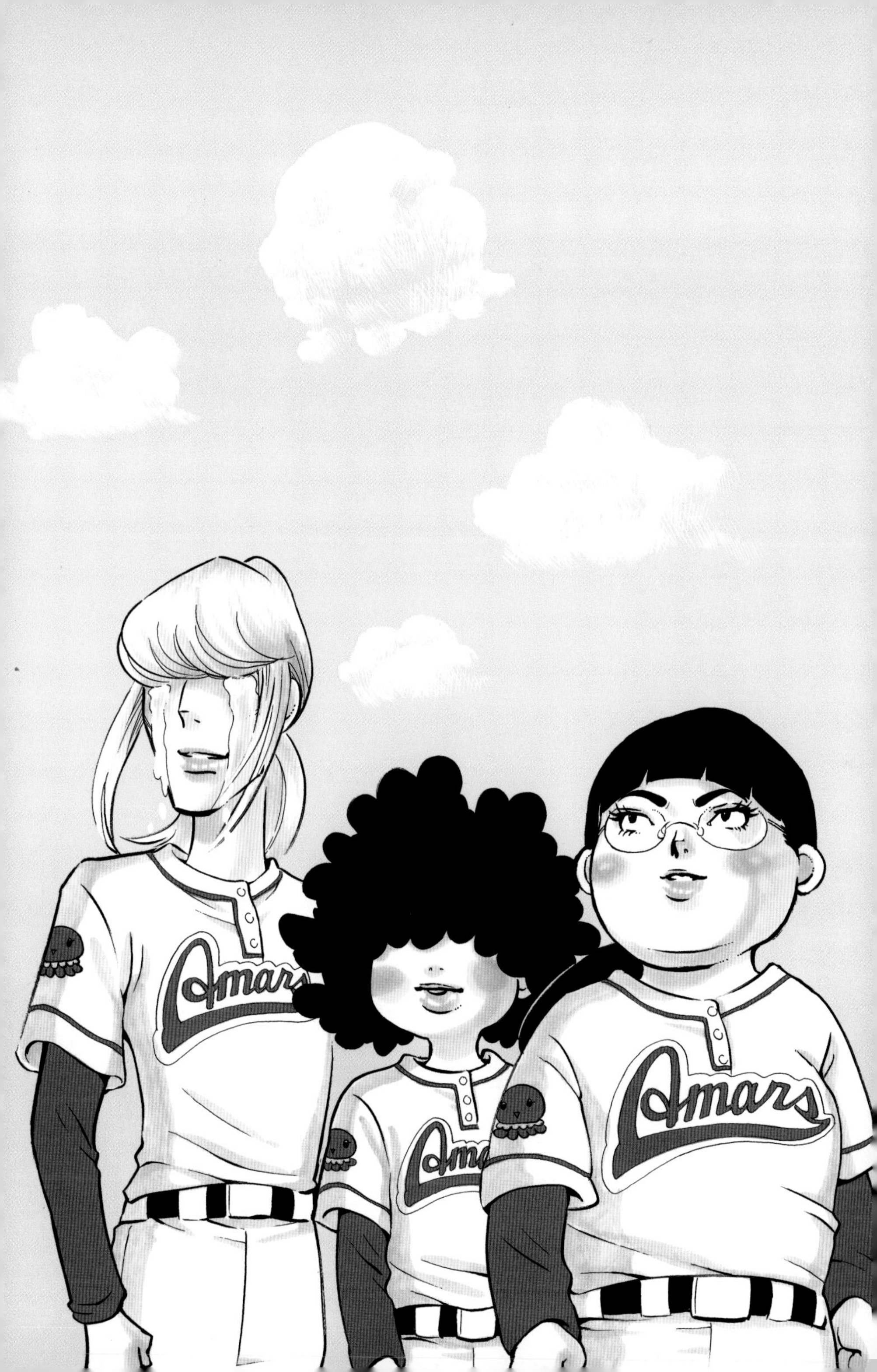
Amars
Amars

尼

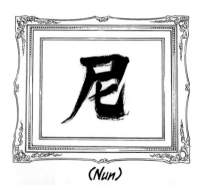

(Nun)

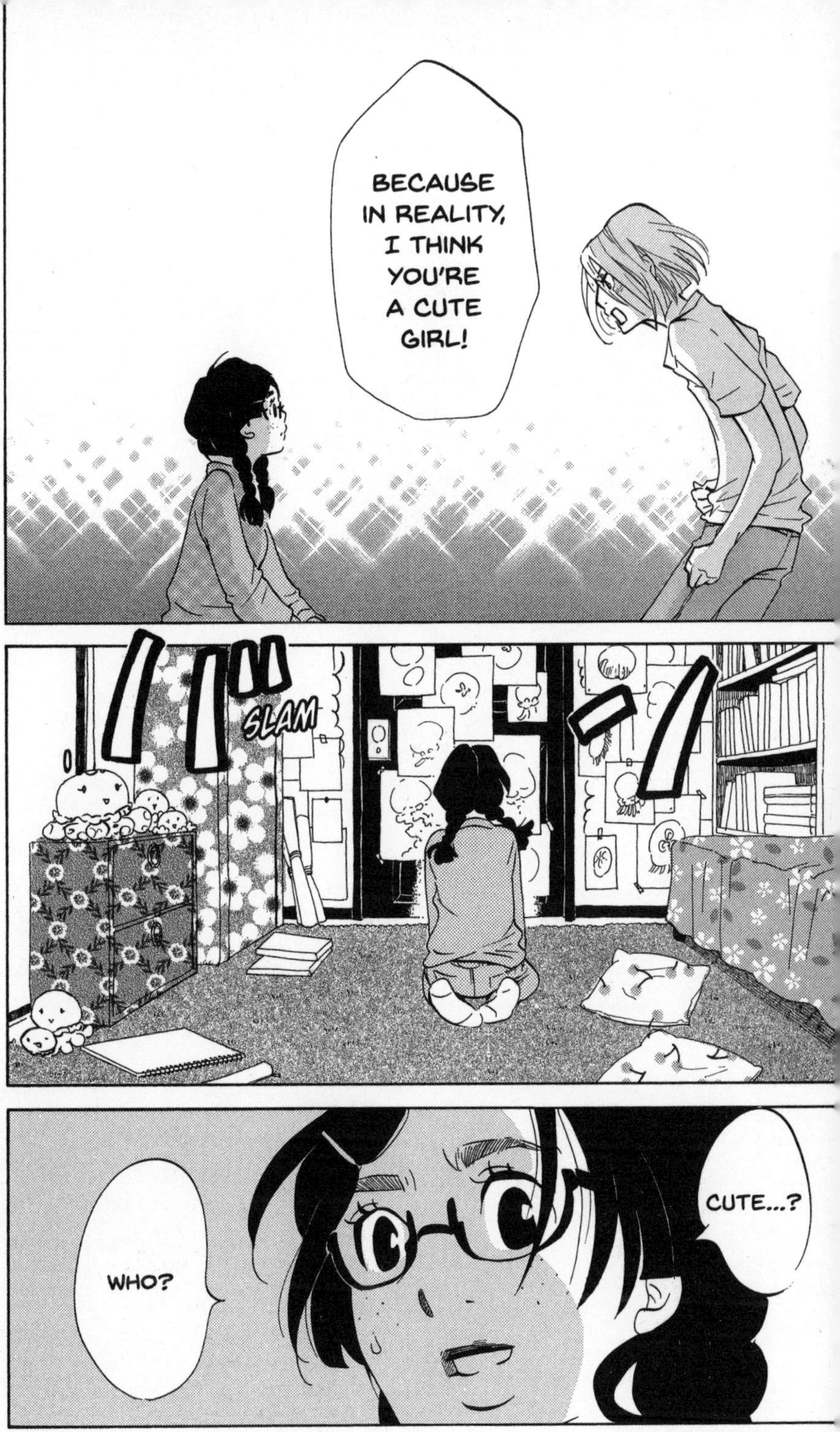
BECAUSE IN REALITY, I THINK YOU'RE A CUTE GIRL!
SLAM
CUTE...?
WHO?

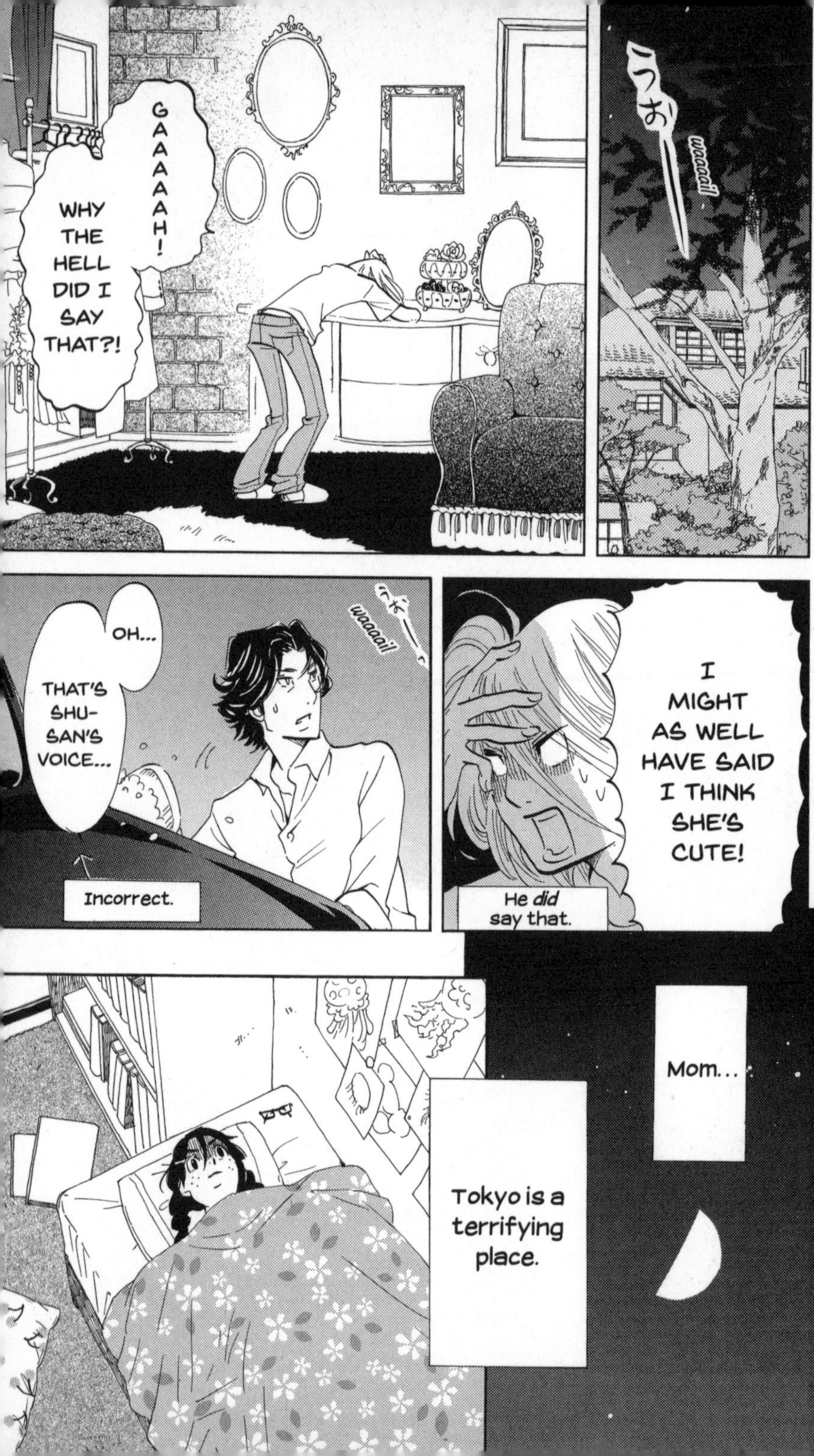
うお
waaaai!
GAAAAAH!
WHY THE HELL DID I SAY THAT?!
I MIGHT AS WELL HAVE SAID I THINK SHE'S CUTE!
He *did* say that.
うおー
waaaai!
OH...
THAT'S SHU-SAN'S VOICE...
Incorrect.
Mom...
Tokyo is a terrifying place.

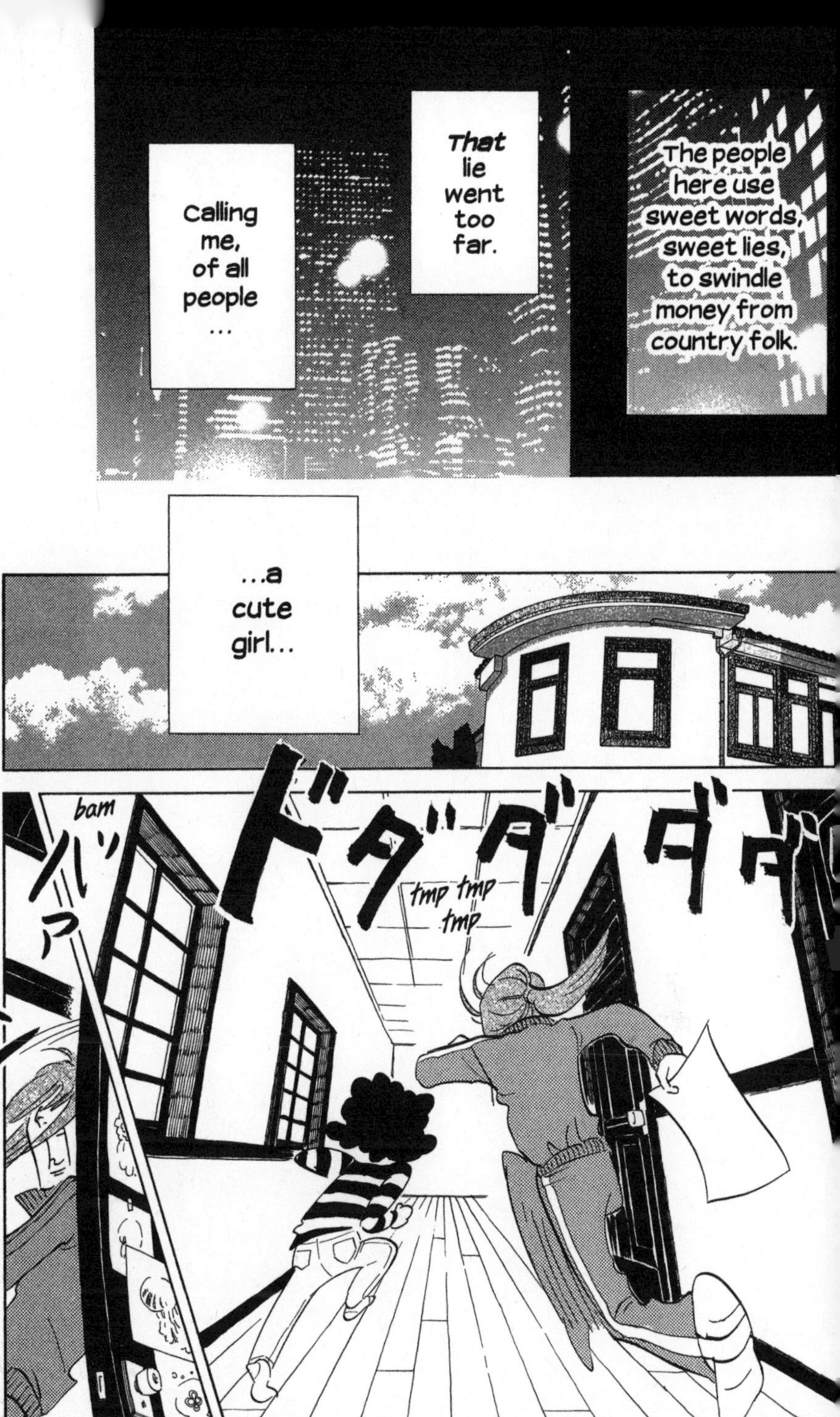
The people here use sweet words, sweet lies, to swindle money from country folk.
That lie went too far.
Calling me, of all people ...
...a cute girl...
ドダダ
tmp tmp tmp
bam

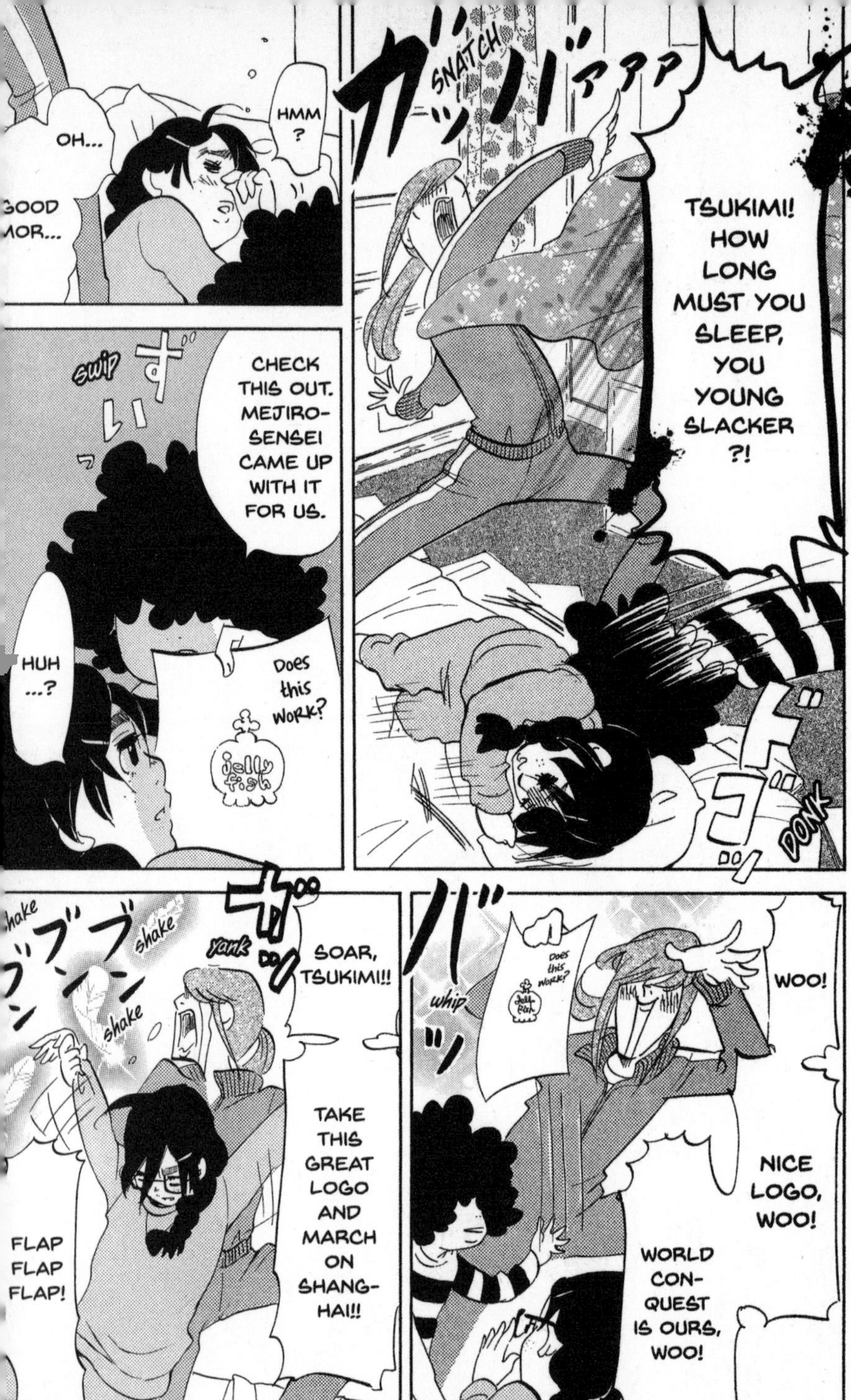
SNATCH
TSUKIMI! HOW LONG MUST YOU SLEEP, YOU YOUNG SLACKER?!
DONK
HMM?
OH...
GOOD MOR...
swip
CHECK THIS OUT. MEJIRO-SENSEI CAME UP WITH IT FOR US.
HUH...?
Does this work?
jelly fish
whip
Does this work?
WOO!
NICE LOGO, WOO!
WORLD CON-QUEST IS OURS, WOO!
shake
shake
shake
yank
SOAR, TSUKIMI!!
TAKE THIS GREAT LOGO AND MARCH ON SHANG-HAI!!
FLAP FLAP FLAP!

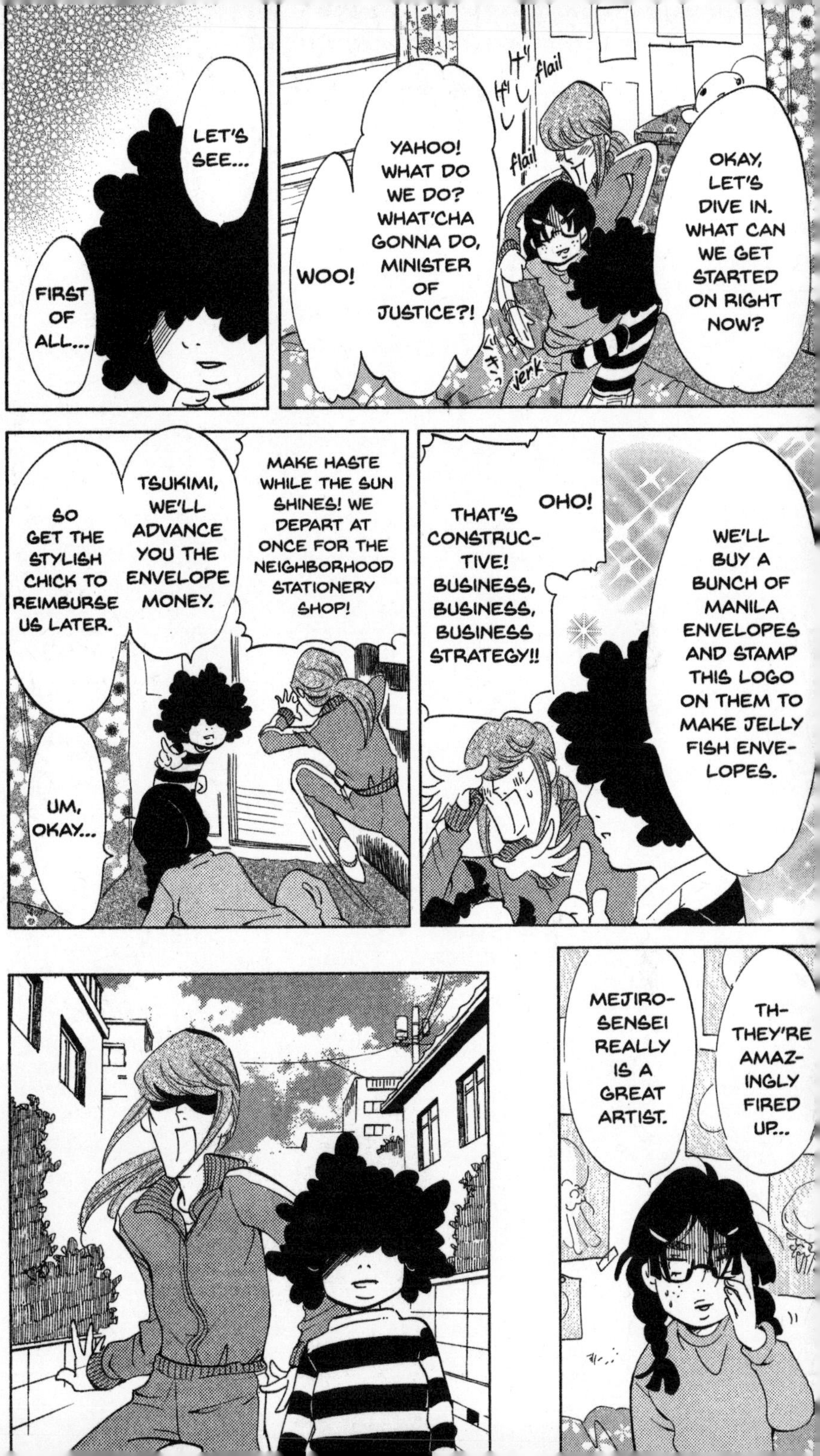
OKAY, LET'S DIVE IN. WHAT CAN WE GET STARTED ON RIGHT NOW?
flail
flail
YAHOO! WHAT DO WE DO? WHAT'CHA GONNA DO, MINISTER OF JUSTICE?!
WOO!
jerk
LET'S SEE...
FIRST OF ALL...
WE'LL BUY A BUNCH OF MANILA ENVELOPES AND STAMP THIS LOGO ON THEM TO MAKE JELLY FISH ENVELOPES.
OHO!
THAT'S CONSTRUCTIVE! BUSINESS, BUSINESS, BUSINESS STRATEGY!!
MAKE HASTE WHILE THE SUN SHINES! WE DEPART AT ONCE FOR THE NEIGHBORHOOD STATIONERY SHOP!
TSUKIMI, WE'LL ADVANCE YOU THE ENVELOPE MONEY.
SO GET THE STYLISH CHICK TO REIMBURSE US LATER.
UM, OKAY...
TH- THEY'RE AMAZINGLY FIRED UP...
MEJIRO-SENSEI REALLY IS A GREAT ARTIST.

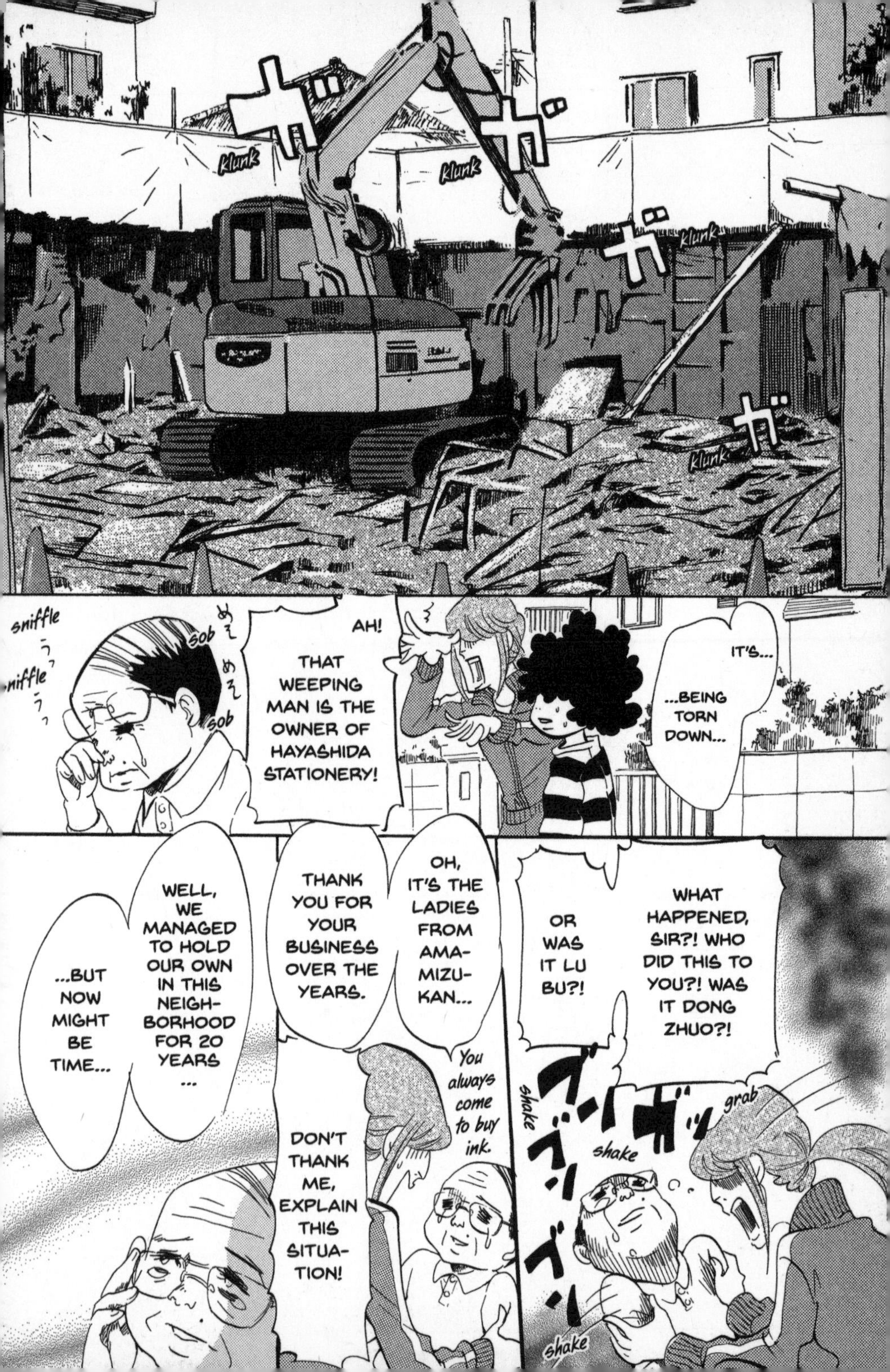
klunk
klunk
klunk
klunk
IT'S... ...BEING TORN DOWN...
AH! THAT WEEPING MAN IS THE OWNER OF HAYASHIDA STATIONERY!
sob
sob
sniffle
sniffle
WHAT HAPPENED, SIR?! WHO DID THIS TO YOU?! WAS IT DONG ZHUO?!
OR WAS IT LU BU?!
grab
shake
shake
shake
OH, IT'S THE LADIES FROM AMA-MIZU-KAN...
You always come to buy ink.
THANK YOU FOR YOUR BUSINESS OVER THE YEARS.
DON'T THANK ME, EXPLAIN THIS SITUATION!
WELL, WE MANAGED TO HOLD OUR OWN IN THIS NEIGHBORHOOD FOR 20 YEARS ...
...BUT NOW MIGHT BE TIME...

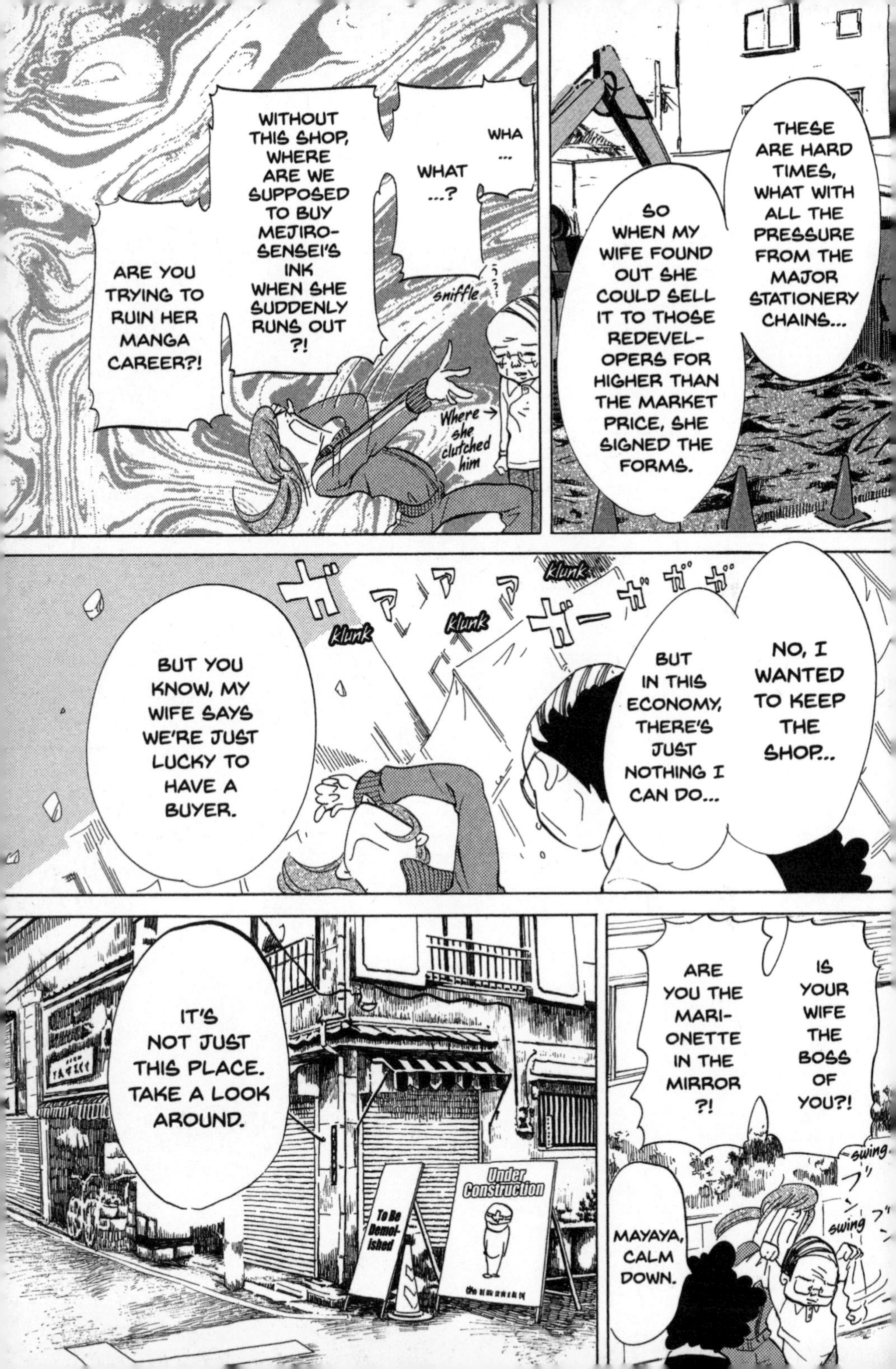
THESE ARE HARD TIMES, WHAT WITH ALL THE PRESSURE FROM THE MAJOR STATIONERY CHAINS...
SO WHEN MY WIFE FOUND OUT SHE COULD SELL IT TO THOSE REDEVELOPERS FOR HIGHER THAN THE MARKET PRICE, SHE SIGNED THE FORMS.
WHA...
WHAT...?
sniffle
WITHOUT THIS SHOP, WHERE ARE WE SUPPOSED TO BUY MEJIRO-SENSEI'S INK WHEN SHE SUDDENLY RUNS OUT?!
ARE YOU TRYING TO RUIN HER MANGA CAREER?!
Where she clutched him →
NO, I WANTED TO KEEP THE SHOP...
BUT IN THIS ECONOMY, THERE'S JUST NOTHING I CAN DO...
klunk
klunk
klunk
BUT YOU KNOW, MY WIFE SAYS WE'RE JUST LUCKY TO HAVE A BUYER.
IS YOUR WIFE THE BOSS OF YOU?!
ARE YOU THE MARIONETTE IN THE MIRROR?!
swing
swing
MAYAYA, CALM DOWN.
IT'S NOT JUST THIS PLACE. TAKE A LOOK AROUND.
Under Construction
To Be Demolished

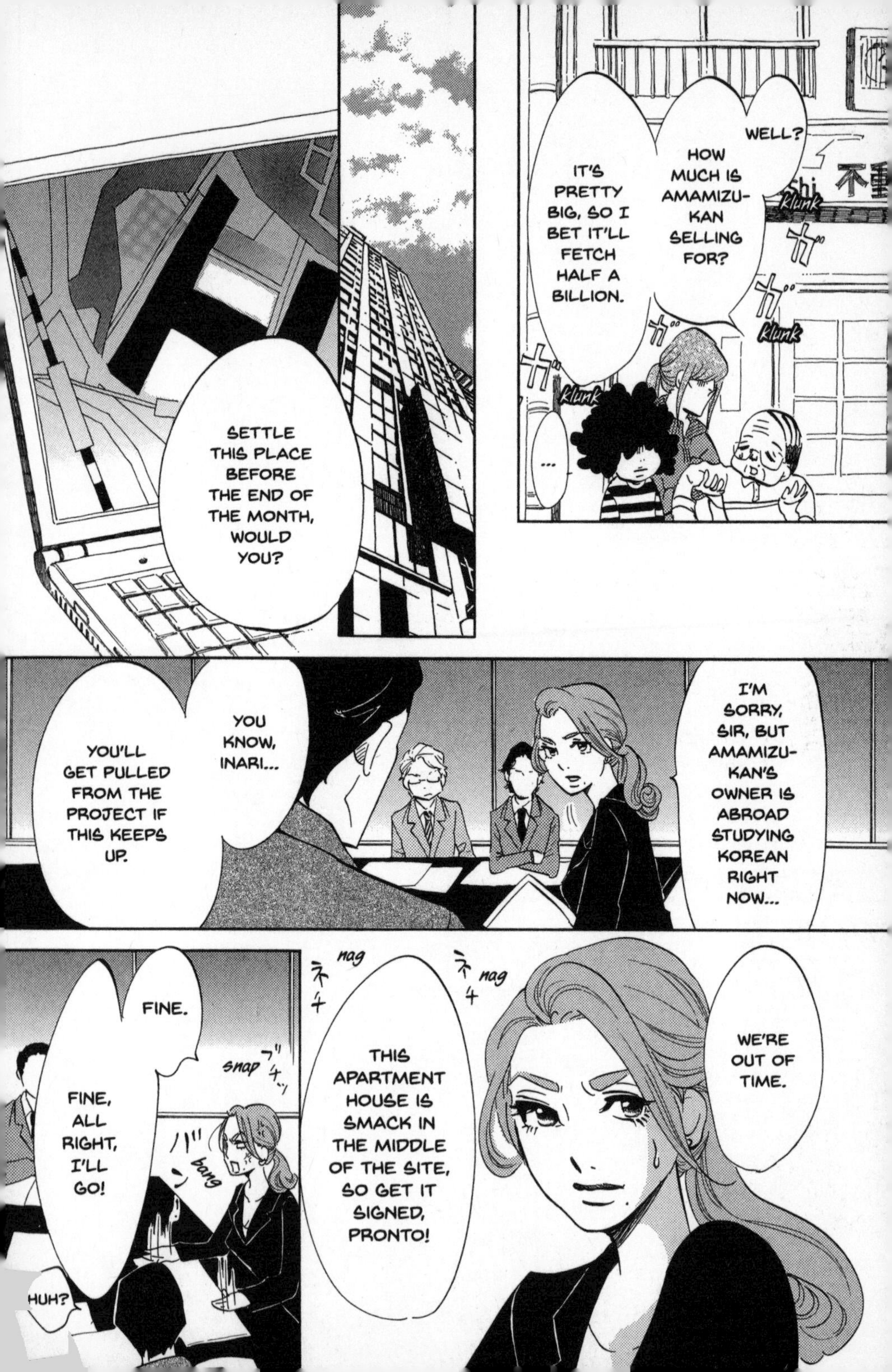
WELL?
HOW MUCH IS AMAMIZU-KAN SELLING FOR?
IT'S PRETTY BIG, SO I BET IT'LL FETCH HALF A BILLION.
ガ klunk
ガ klunk
ガ
ガ klunk
...
SETTLE THIS PLACE BEFORE THE END OF THE MONTH, WOULD YOU?
I'M SORRY, SIR, BUT AMAMIZU-KAN'S OWNER IS ABROAD STUDYING KOREAN RIGHT NOW...
YOU KNOW, INARI...
YOU'LL GET PULLED FROM THE PROJECT IF THIS KEEPS UP.
WE'RE OUT OF TIME.
ネチ nag
ネチ nag
THIS APARTMENT HOUSE IS SMACK IN THE MIDDLE OF THE SITE, SO GET IT SIGNED, PRONTO!
FINE.
ブチッ snap
FINE, ALL RIGHT, I'LL GO!
バン bang
HUH?

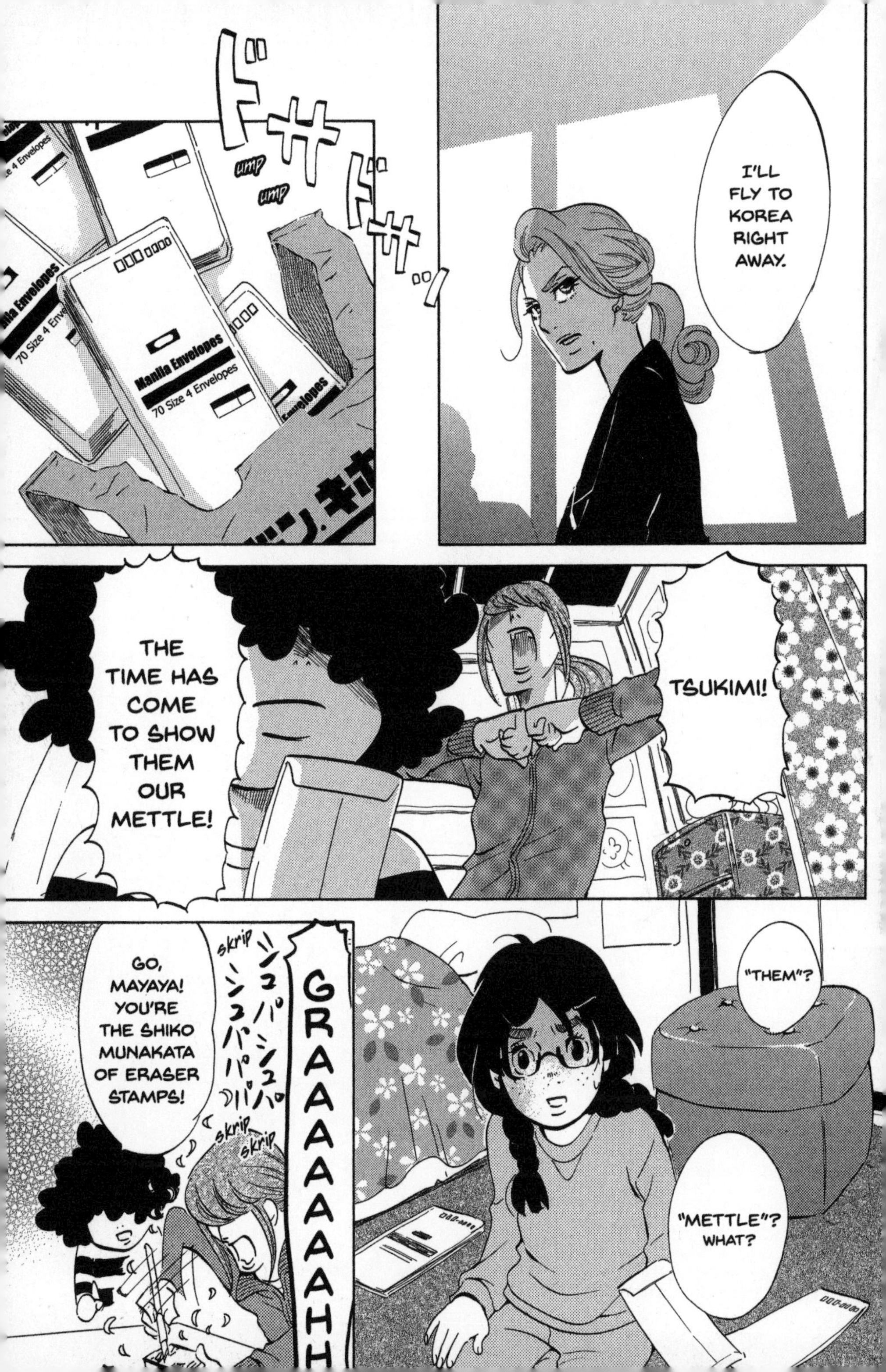

I'LL FLY TO KOREA RIGHT AWAY.
ump
ump
Manila Envelopes
70 Size 4 Envelopes
TSUKIMI!
THE TIME HAS COME TO SHOW THEM OUR METTLE!
"THEM"?
"METTLE"? WHAT?
GRAAAAAAAAAH
skrip
GO, MAYAYA! YOU'RE THE SHIKO MUNAKATA OF ERASER STAMPS!
skrip
skrip

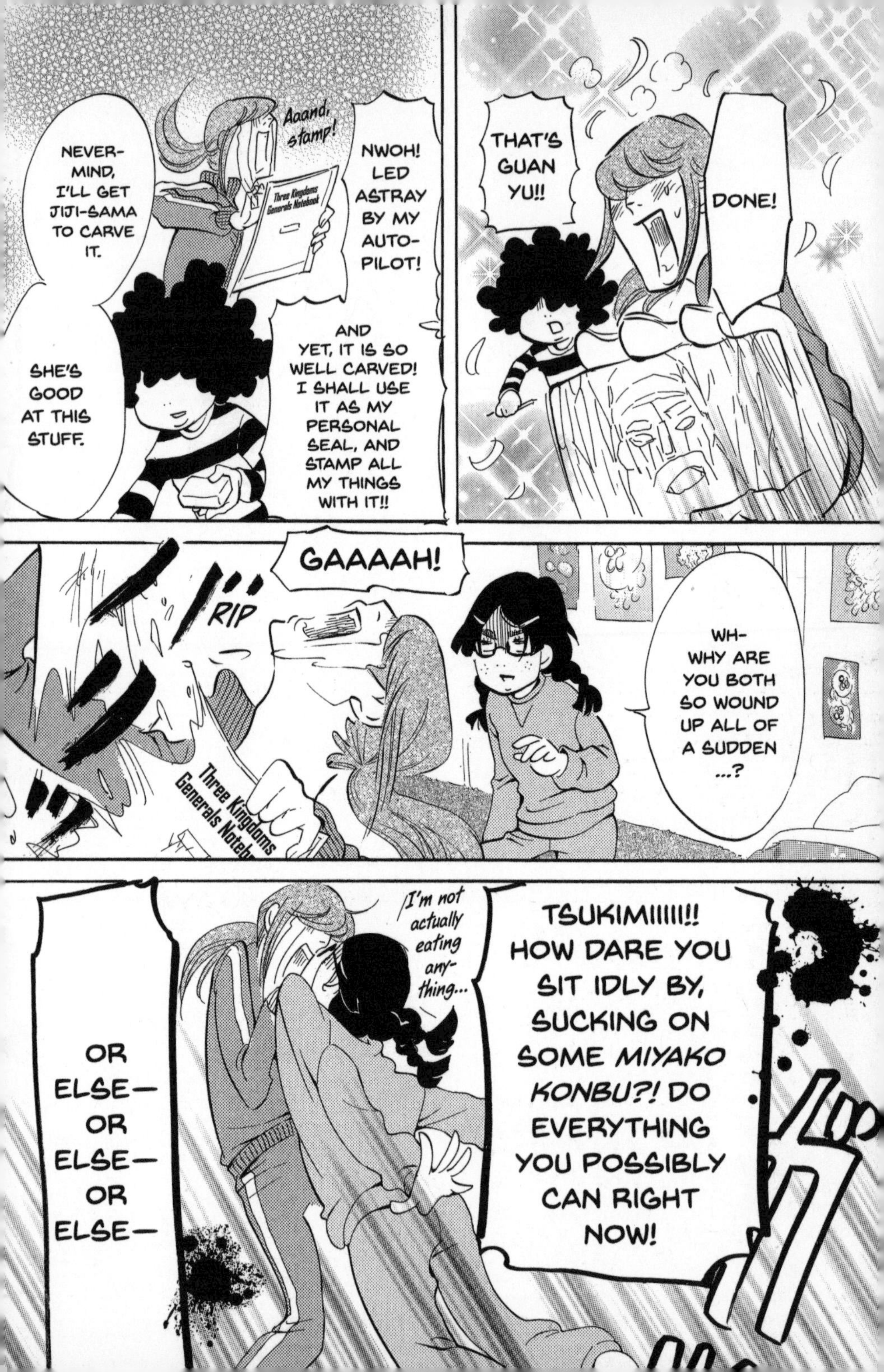
DONE!
THAT'S GUAN YU!!
NWOH! LED ASTRAY BY MY AUTO-PILOT!
Aaand, stamp!
Three Kingdoms Generals Notebook
NEVER-MIND, I'LL GET JIJI-SAMA TO CARVE IT.
AND YET, IT IS SO WELL CARVED! I SHALL USE IT AS MY PERSONAL SEAL, AND STAMP ALL MY THINGS WITH IT!!
SHE'S GOOD AT THIS STUFF.
WH- WHY ARE YOU BOTH SO WOUND UP ALL OF A SUDDEN ...?
GAAAAH!
RIP
TSUKIMIIIIII!! HOW DARE YOU SIT IDLY BY, SUCKING ON SOME *MIYAKO KONBU*?! DO EVERYTHING YOU POSSIBLY CAN RIGHT NOW!
I'm not actually eating anything...
OR ELSE— OR ELSE— OR ELSE—

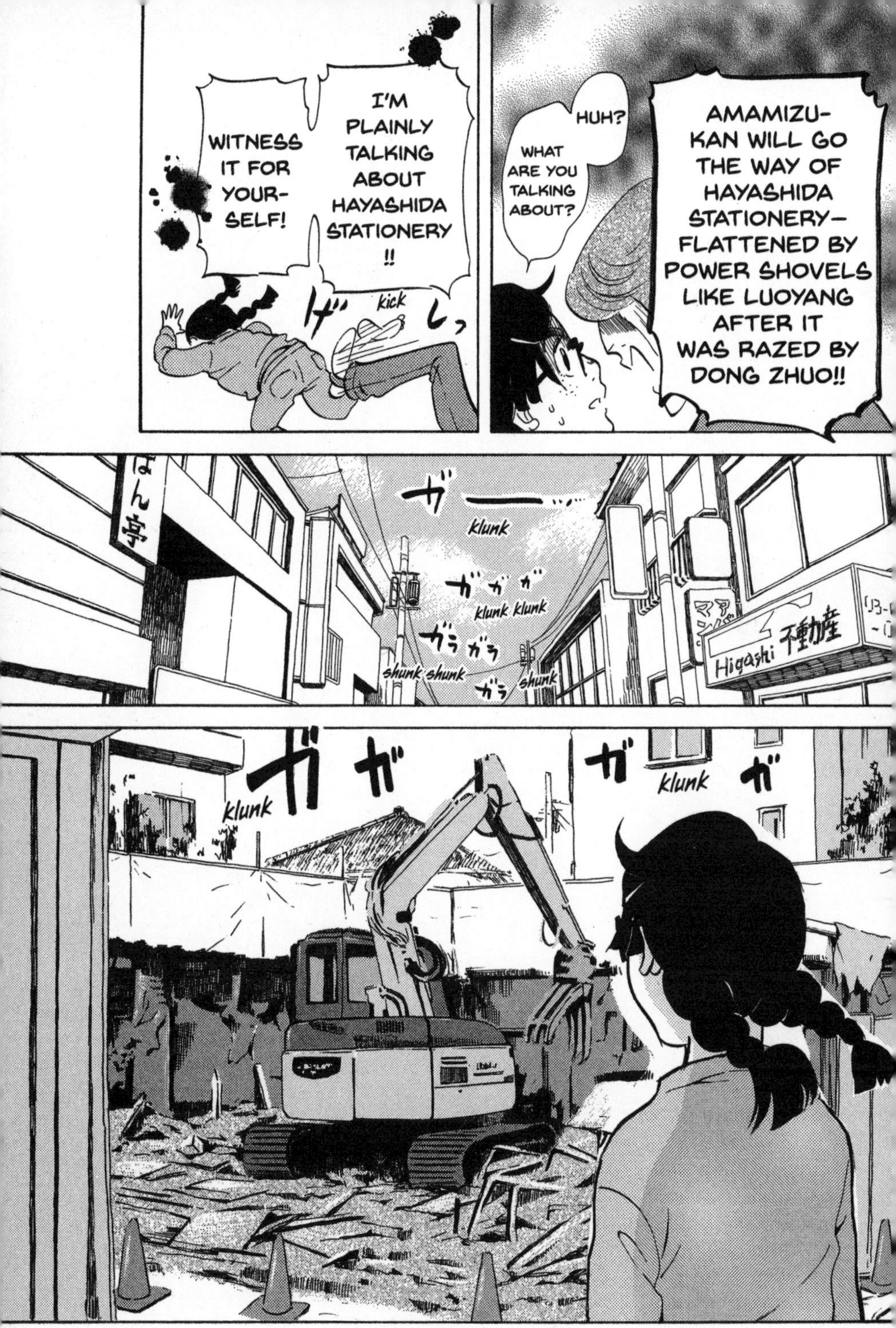
AMAMIZU-KAN WILL GO THE WAY OF HAYASHIDA STATIONERY— FLATTENED BY POWER SHOVELS LIKE LUOYANG AFTER IT WAS RAZED BY DONG ZHUO!!
HUH?
WHAT ARE YOU TALKING ABOUT?
I'M PLAINLY TALKING ABOUT HAYASHIDA STATIONERY !!
WITNESS IT FOR YOUR-SELF!
kick
klunk
klunk klunk
shunk shunk
shunk
Higashi 不動産
klunk
klunk

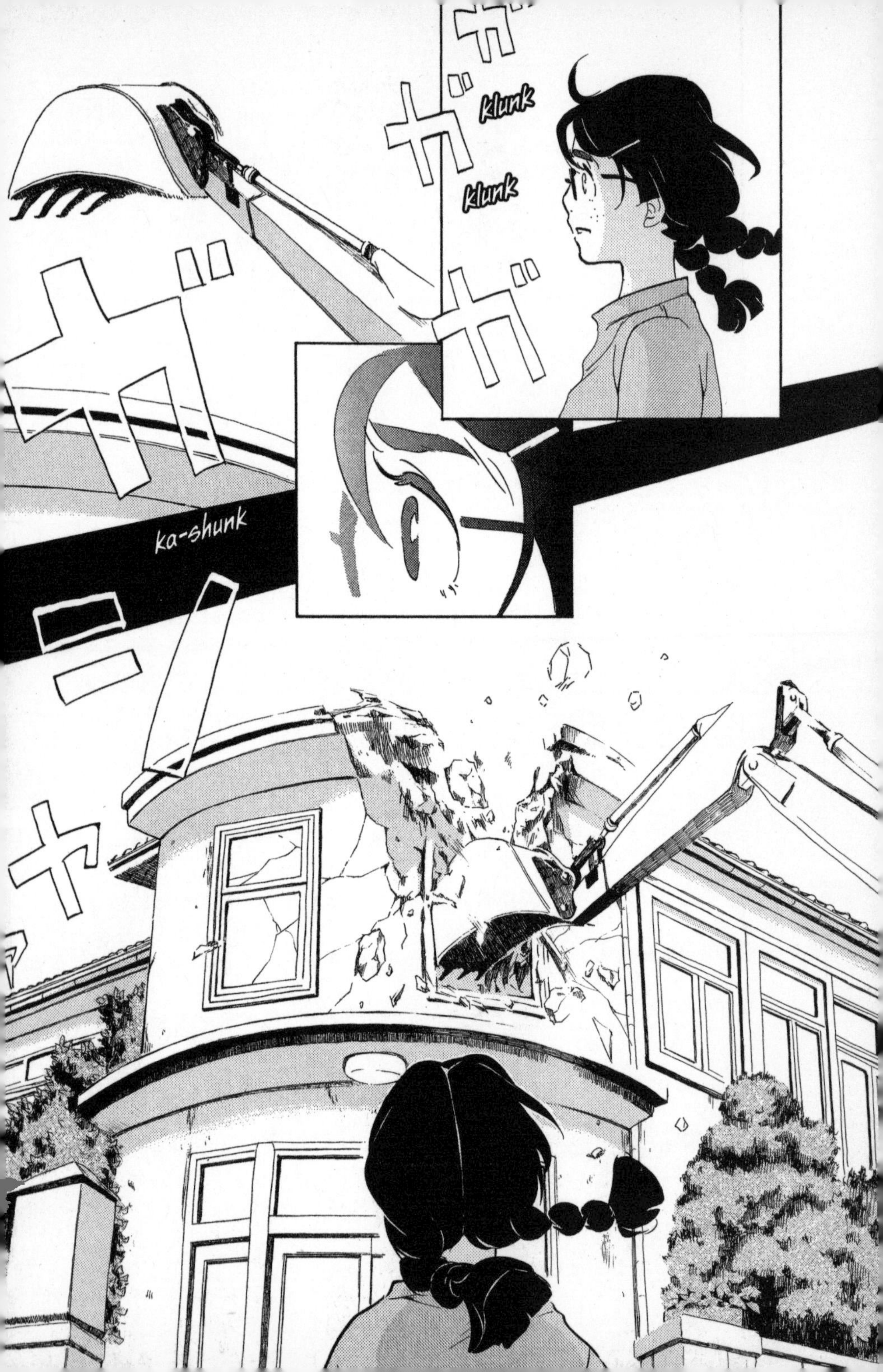
klunk
klunk
ka-shunk

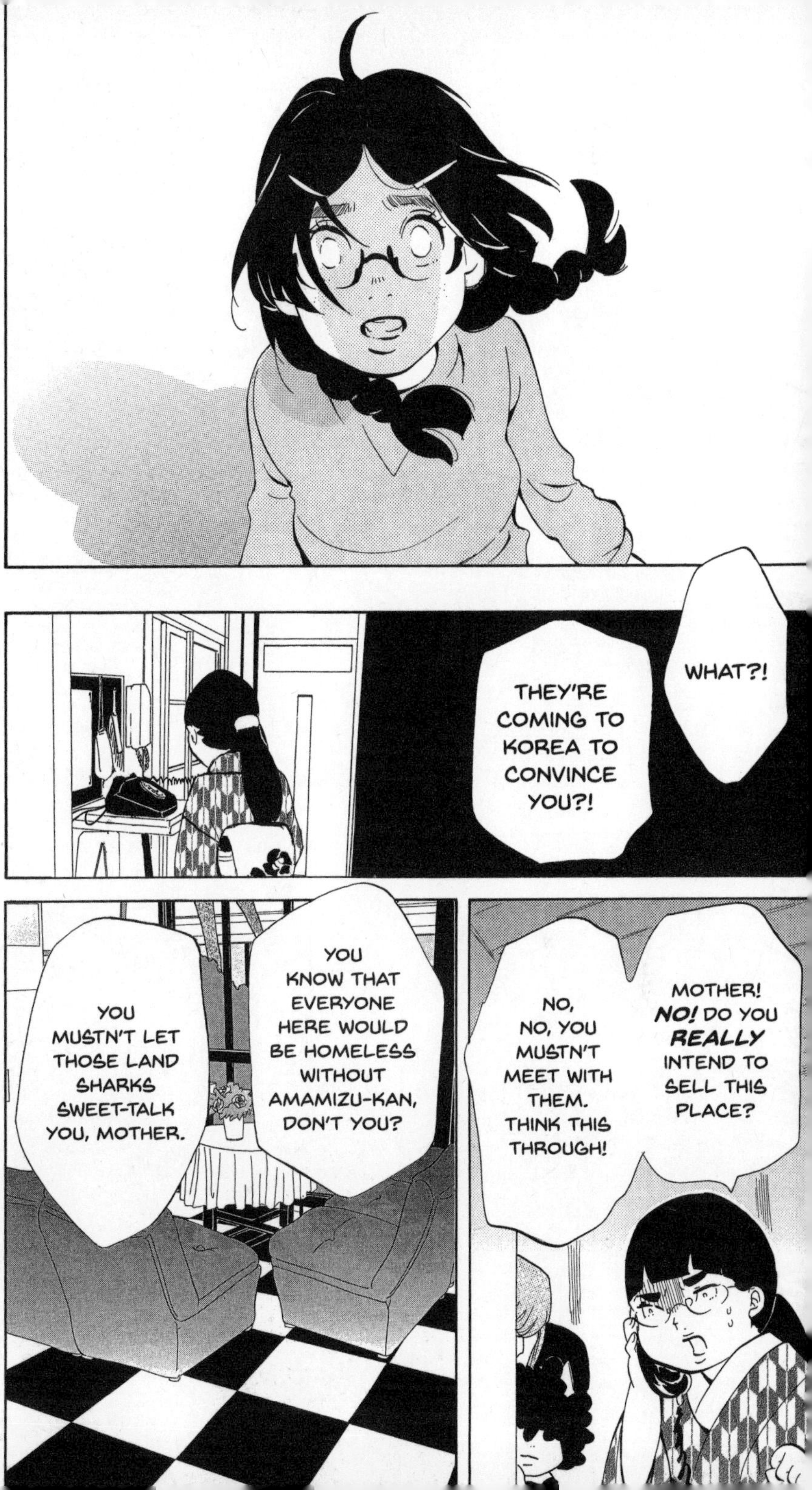
WHAT?!
THEY'RE COMING TO KOREA TO CONVINCE YOU?!
MOTHER! NO! DO YOU REALLY INTEND TO SELL THIS PLACE?
NO, NO, YOU MUSTN'T MEET WITH THEM. THINK THIS THROUGH!
YOU KNOW THAT EVERYONE HERE WOULD BE HOMELESS WITHOUT AMAMIZU-KAN, DON'T YOU?
YOU MUSTN'T LET THOSE LAND SHARKS SWEET-TALK YOU, MOTHER.

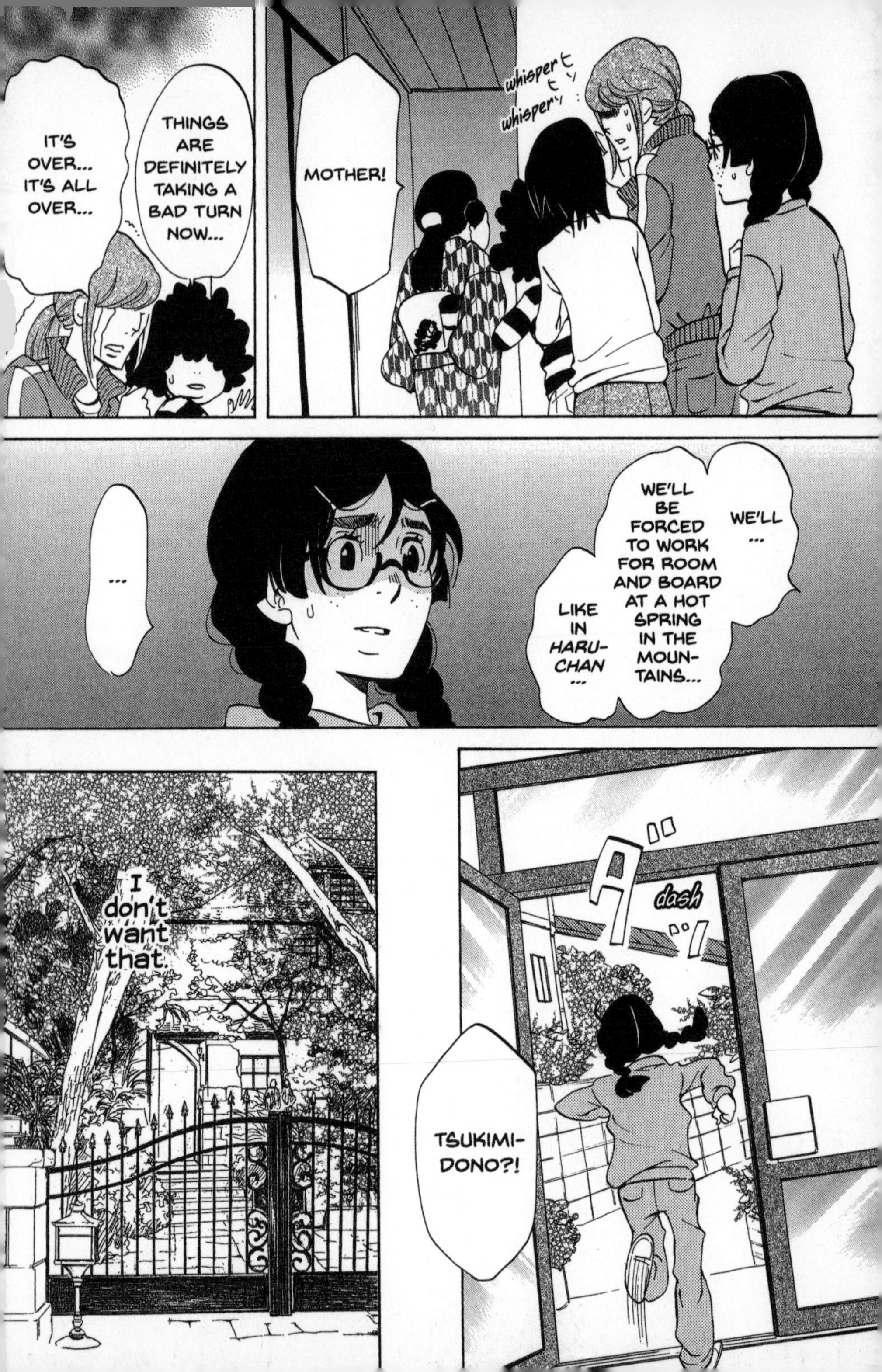
whisper
ヒソ
whisper
ヒソ
MOTHER!
THINGS ARE DEFINITELY TAKING A BAD TURN NOW...
IT'S OVER... IT'S ALL OVER...
WE'LL ...
WE'LL BE FORCED TO WORK FOR ROOM AND BOARD AT A HOT SPRING IN THE MOUNTAINS...
LIKE IN HARU-CHAN ...
...
dash
TSUKIMI-DONO?!
I don't want that.

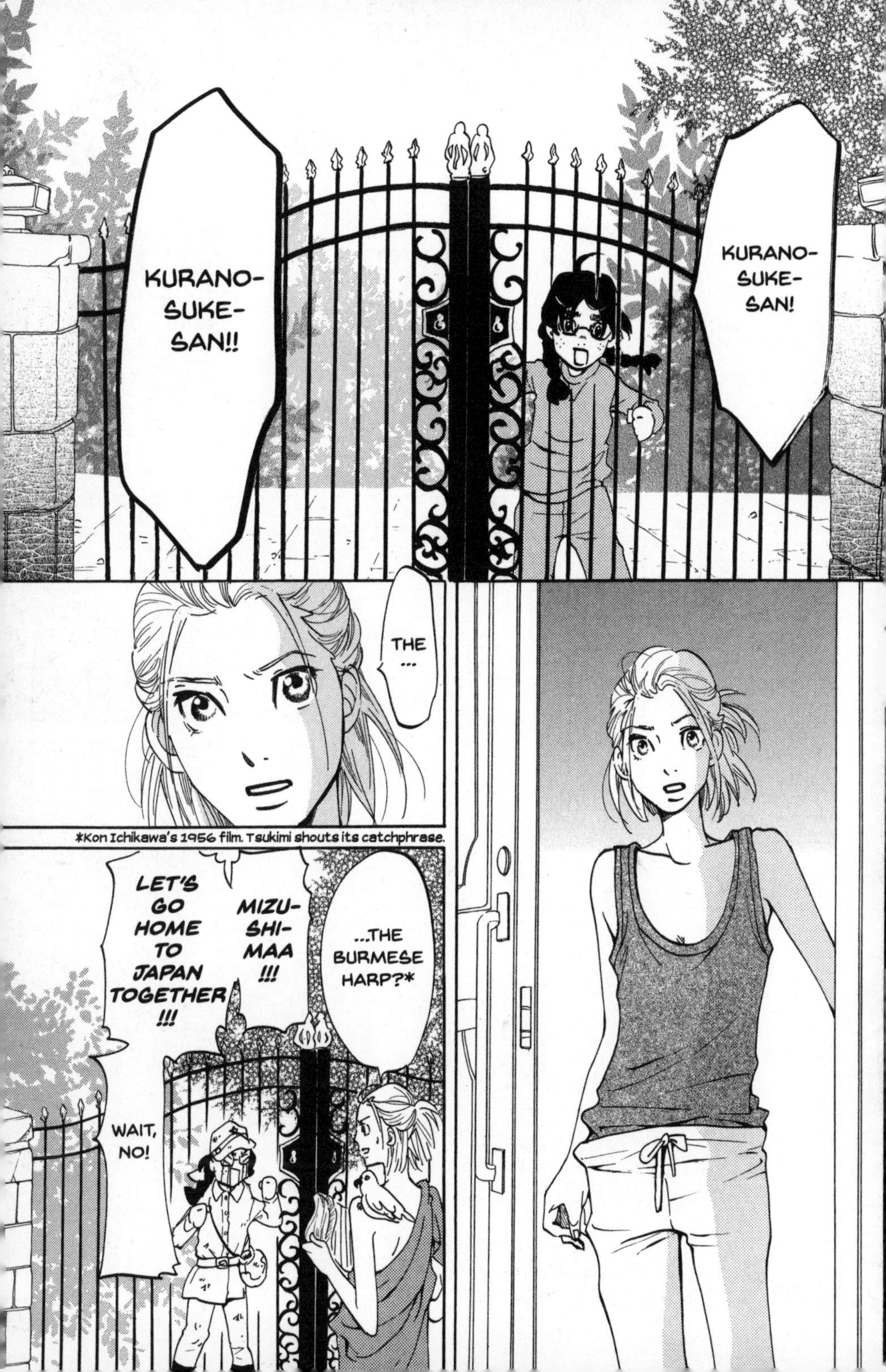
KURANO-SUKE-SAN!
KURANO-SUKE-SAN!!
THE ...
...THE BURMESE HARP?*
MIZU-SHI-MAA !!!
LET'S GO HOME TO JAPAN TOGETHER !!!
WAIT, NO!

*Kon Ichikawa's 1956 film. Tsukimi shouts its catchphrase.

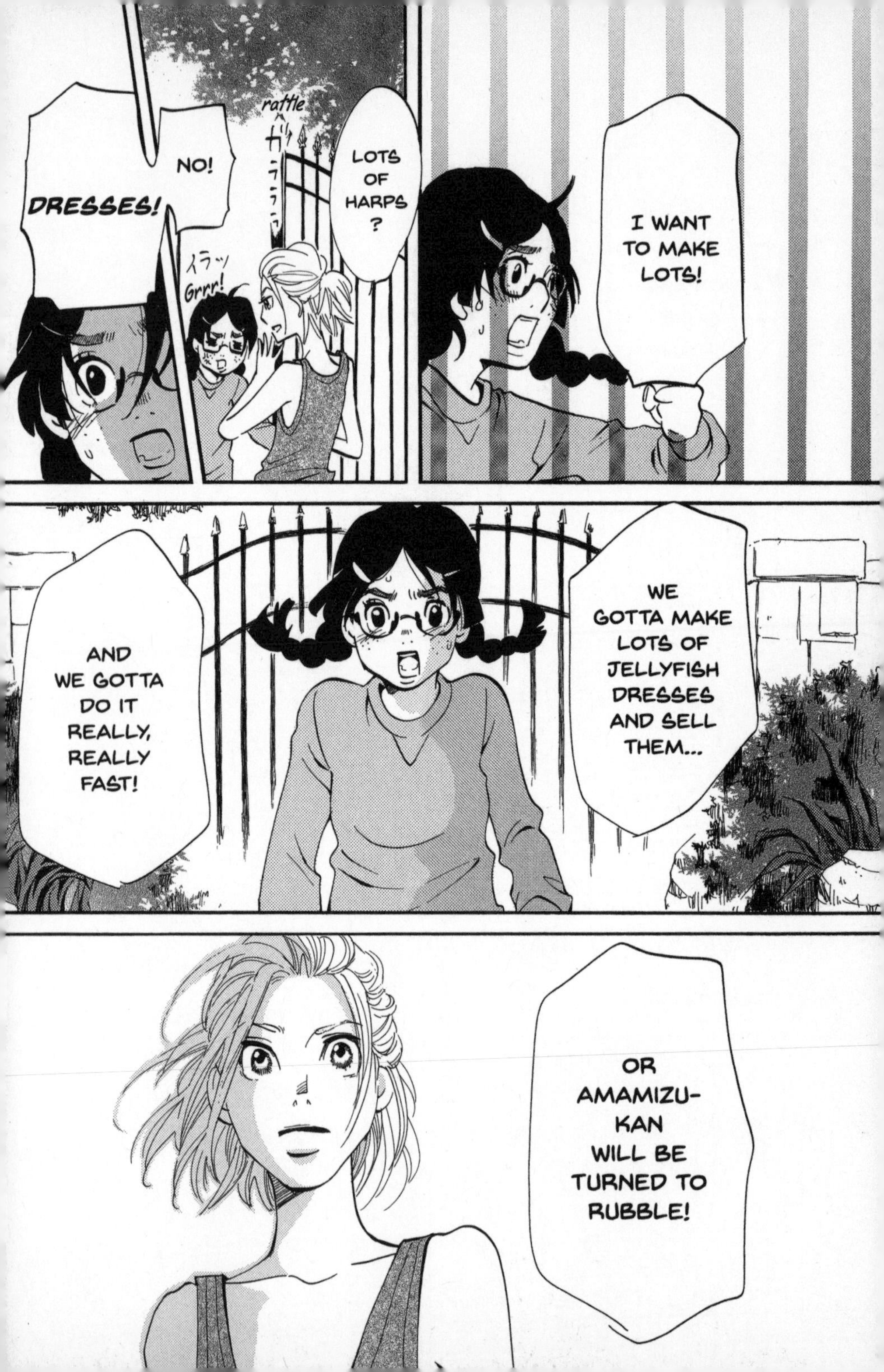
I WANT TO MAKE LOTS!
LOTS OF HARPS?
rattle
ガラララ
NO!
DRESSES!
イラッ
Grrr!
WE GOTTA MAKE LOTS OF JELLYFISH DRESSES AND SELL THEM...
AND WE GOTTA DO IT REALLY, REALLY FAST!
OR AMAMIZU-KAN WILL BE TURNED TO RUBBLE!

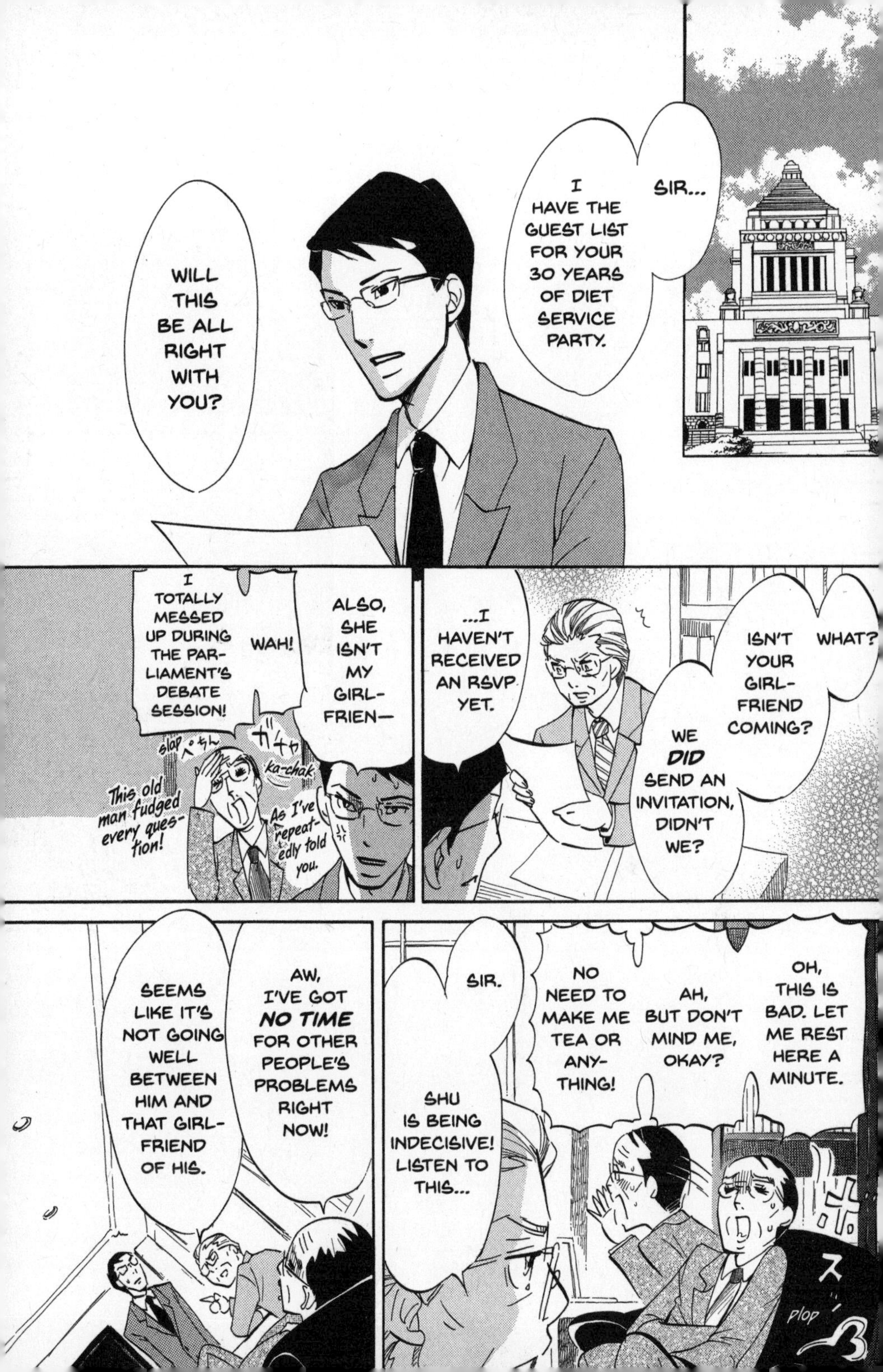
SIR...
I HAVE THE GUEST LIST FOR YOUR 30 YEARS OF DIET SERVICE PARTY.
WILL THIS BE ALL RIGHT WITH YOU?
WHAT?
ISN'T YOUR GIRL-FRIEND COMING?
WE *DID* SEND AN INVITATION, DIDN'T WE?
...I HAVEN'T RECEIVED AN RSVP YET.
ALSO, SHE ISN'T MY GIRL-FRIEN—
As I've repeat-edly told you.
ka-chak
WAH!
I TOTALLY MESSED UP DURING THE PAR-LIAMENT'S DEBATE SESSION!
slap
This old man fudged every ques-tion!
OH, THIS IS BAD. LET ME REST HERE A MINUTE.
AH, BUT DON'T MIND ME, OKAY?
NO NEED TO MAKE ME TEA OR ANY-THING!
plop
SIR.
SHU IS BEING INDECISIVE! LISTEN TO THIS...
AW, I'VE GOT *NO TIME* FOR OTHER PEOPLE'S PROBLEMS RIGHT NOW!
SEEMS LIKE IT'S NOT GOING WELL BETWEEN HIM AND THAT GIRL-FRIEND OF HIS.

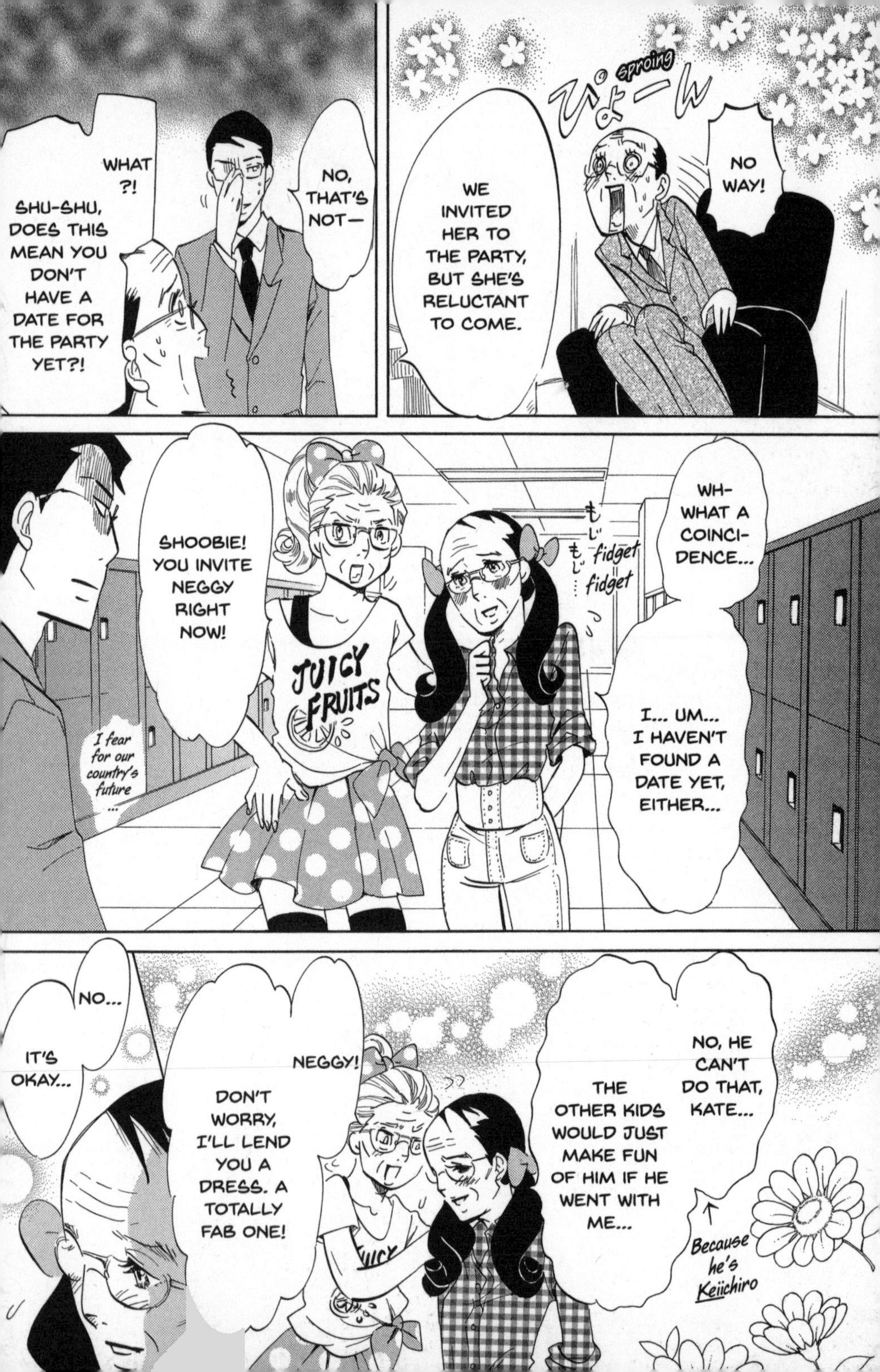
ぴょーん sproing
NO WAY!
WE INVITED HER TO THE PARTY, BUT SHE'S RELUCTANT TO COME.
NO, THAT'S NOT—
WHAT?!
SHU-SHU, DOES THIS MEAN YOU DON'T HAVE A DATE FOR THE PARTY YET?!
WH-WHAT A COINCIDENCE...
I... UM... I HAVEN'T FOUND A DATE YET, EITHER...
もじもじ…
fidget fidget
SHOOBIE! YOU INVITE NEGGY RIGHT NOW!
JUICY FRUITS
I fear for our country's future...
NO, HE CAN'T DO THAT, KATE...
THE OTHER KIDS WOULD JUST MAKE FUN OF HIM IF HE WENT WITH ME...
Because he's Keiichiro
NEGGY!
DON'T WORRY, I'LL LEND YOU A DRESS. A TOTALLY FAB ONE!
NO...
IT'S OKAY...

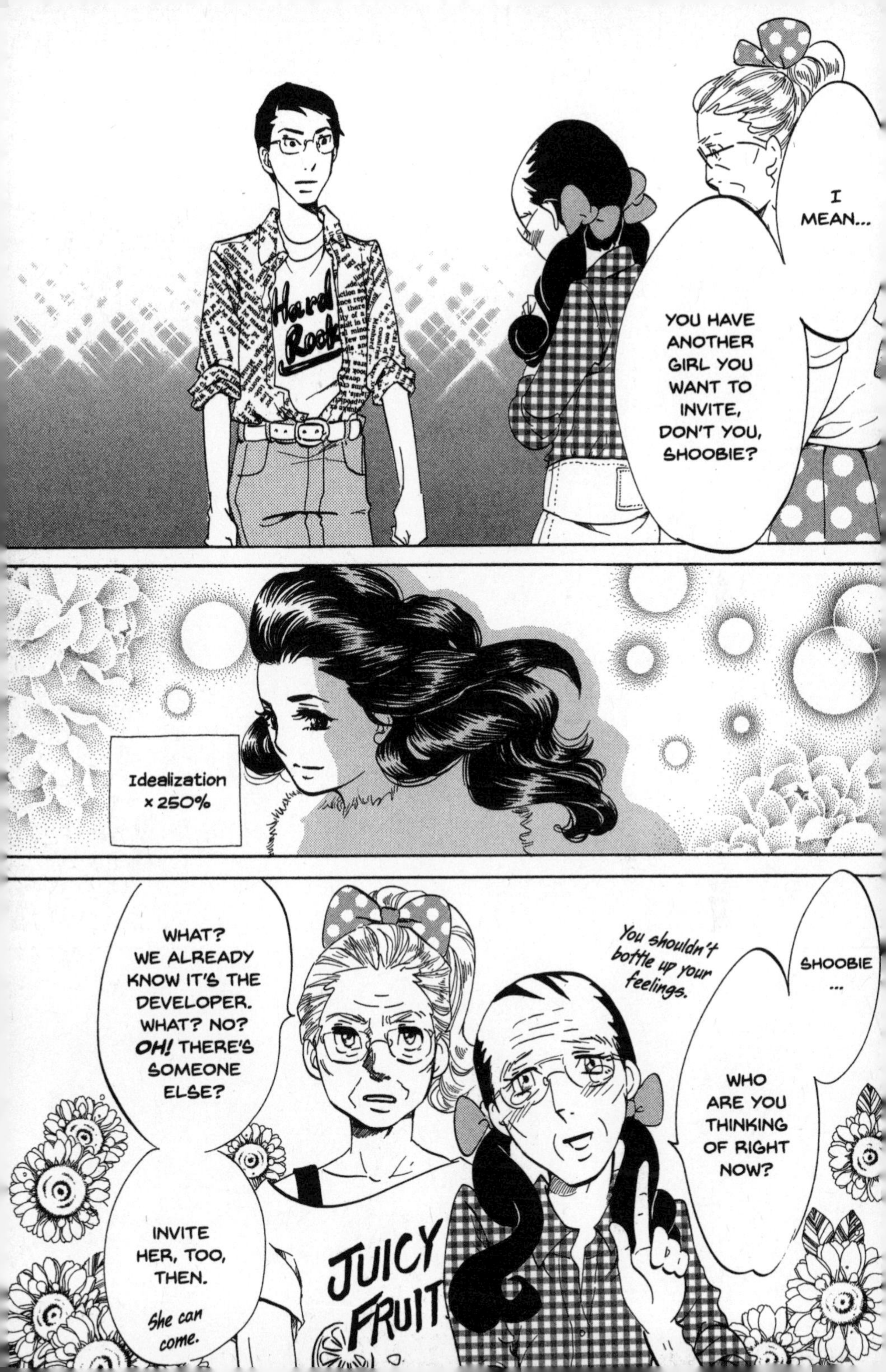

I MEAN...
YOU HAVE ANOTHER GIRL YOU WANT TO INVITE, DON'T YOU, SHOOBIE?
Idealization × 250%
SHOOBIE ...
WHO ARE YOU THINKING OF RIGHT NOW?
You shouldn't bottle up your feelings.
WHAT? WE ALREADY KNOW IT'S THE DEVELOPER. WHAT? NO? OH! THERE'S SOMEONE ELSE?
INVITE HER, TOO, THEN.
She can come.
JUICY FRUIT

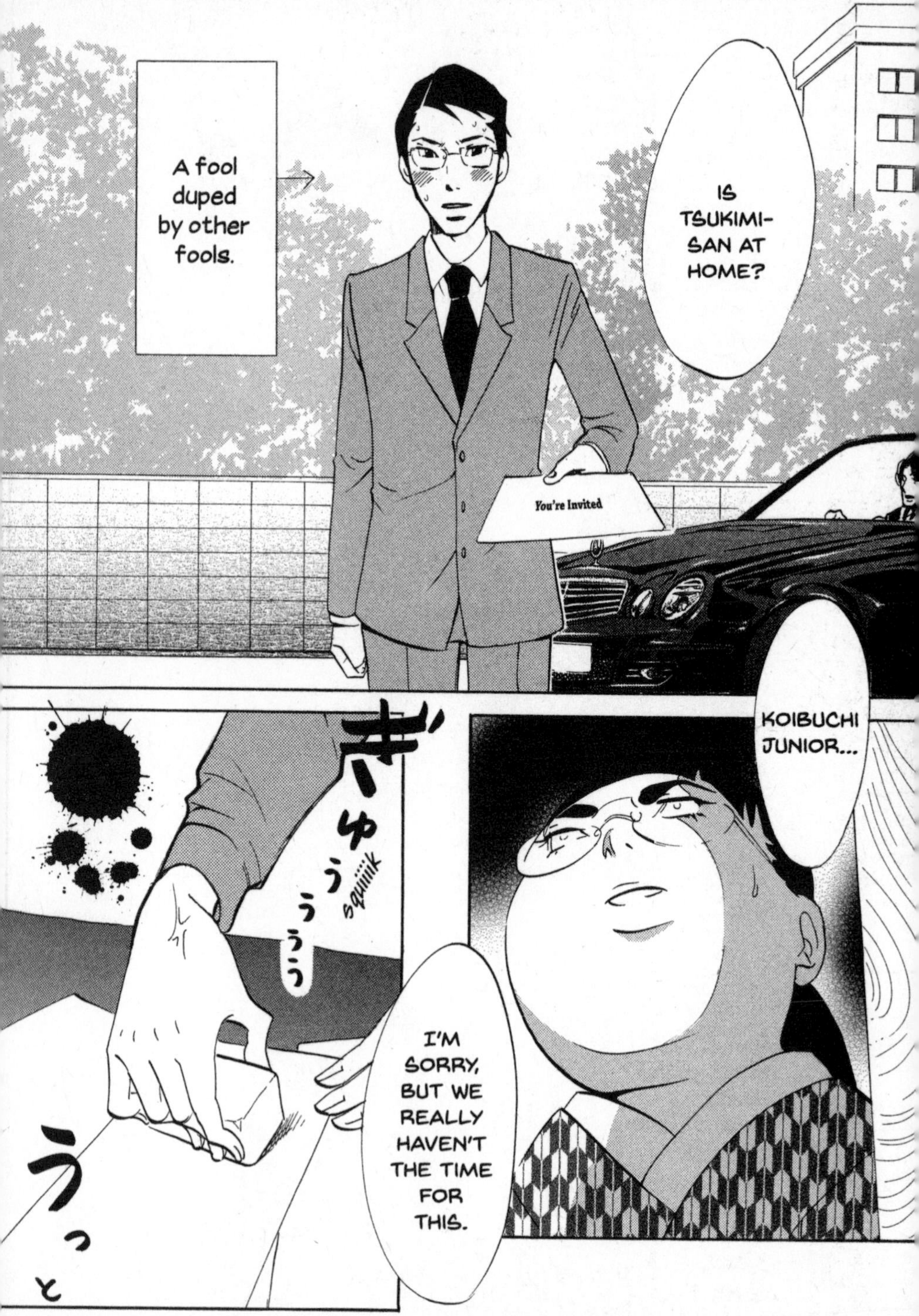
IS TSUKIMI-SAN AT HOME?
A fool duped by other fools.
You're Invited
KOIBUCHI JUNIOR...
I'M SORRY, BUT WE REALLY HAVEN'T THE TIME FOR THIS.
ぎゅううう
squiiiik
うっと

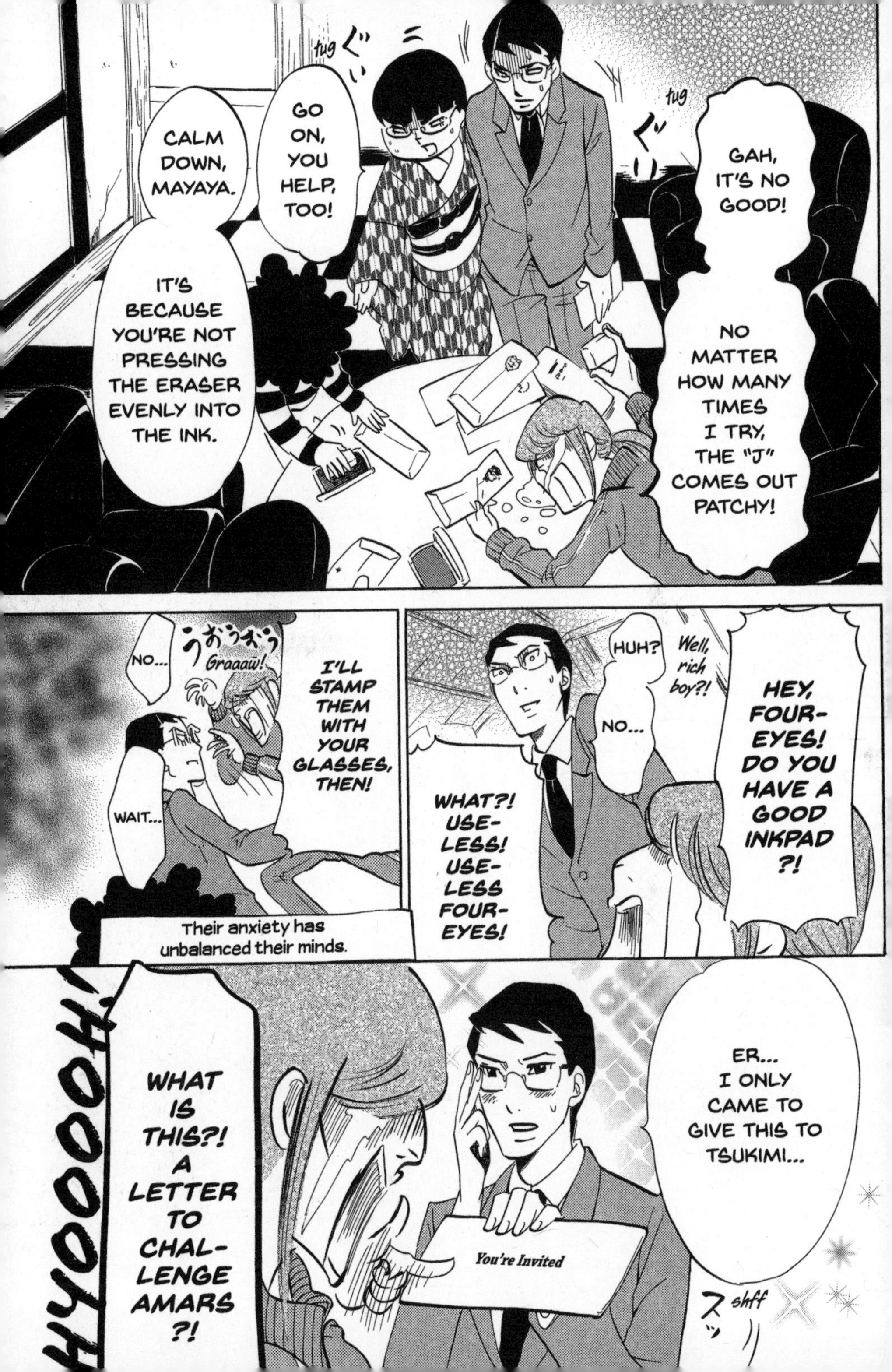
ぐい tug
GAH, IT'S NO GOOD!
NO MATTER HOW MANY TIMES I TRY, THE "J" COMES OUT PATCHY!
ぐい tug
GO ON, YOU HELP, TOO!
CALM DOWN, MAYAYA.
IT'S BECAUSE YOU'RE NOT PRESSING THE ERASER EVENLY INTO THE INK.
HEY, FOUR-EYES! DO YOU HAVE A GOOD INKPAD?!
Well, rich boy?!
HUH?
NO...
WHAT?! USE-LESS! USE-LESS FOUR-EYES!
I'LL STAMP THEM WITH YOUR GLASSES, THEN!
うおうおう Graaaw!
NO...
WAIT...
Their anxiety has unbalanced their minds.
ER... I ONLY CAME TO GIVE THIS TO TSUKIMI...
You're Invited
スッ shff
WHAT IS THIS?! A LETTER TO CHAL-LENGE AMARS?!
HYOOOOH!

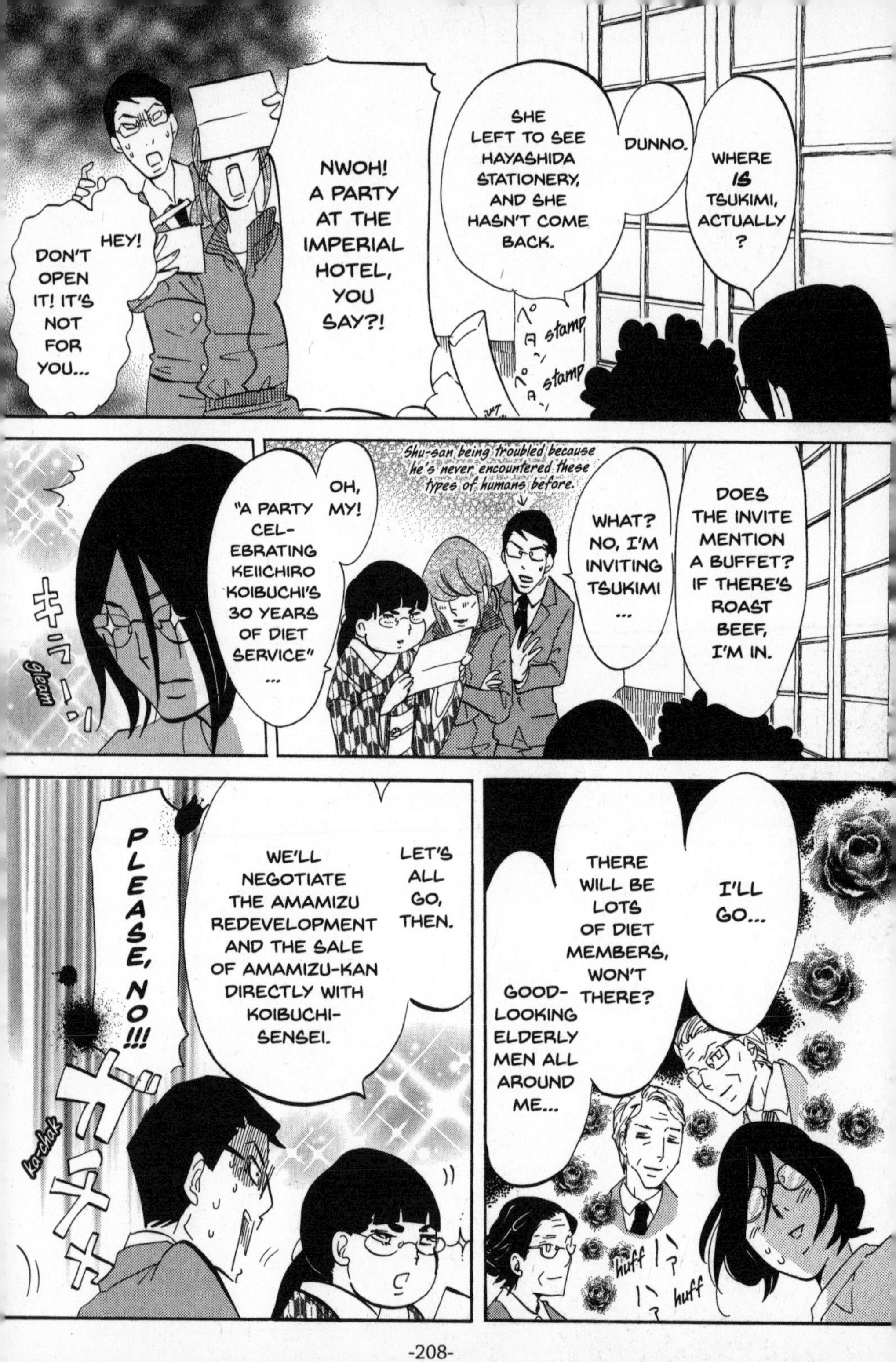
WHERE IS TSUKIMI, ACTUALLY?
DUNNO.
SHE LEFT TO SEE HAYASHIDA STATIONERY, AND SHE HASN'T COME BACK.
stamp
stamp
NWOH! A PARTY AT THE IMPERIAL HOTEL, YOU SAY?!
HEY! DON'T OPEN IT! IT'S NOT FOR YOU...
DOES THE INVITE MENTION A BUFFET? IF THERE'S ROAST BEEF, I'M IN.
WHAT? NO, I'M INVITING TSUKIMI...
Shu-san being troubled because he's never encountered these types of humans before.
OH, MY!
"A PARTY CEL-EBRATING KEIICHIRO KOIBUCHI'S 30 YEARS OF DIET SERVICE"...
gleam
I'LL GO...
THERE WILL BE LOTS OF DIET MEMBERS, WON'T THERE?
GOOD-LOOKING ELDERLY MEN ALL AROUND ME...
huff
huff
LET'S ALL GO, THEN.
WE'LL NEGOTIATE THE AMAMIZU REDEVELOPMENT AND THE SALE OF AMAMIZU-KAN DIRECTLY WITH KOIBUCHI-SENSEI.
PLEASE, NO!!!
ka-chak

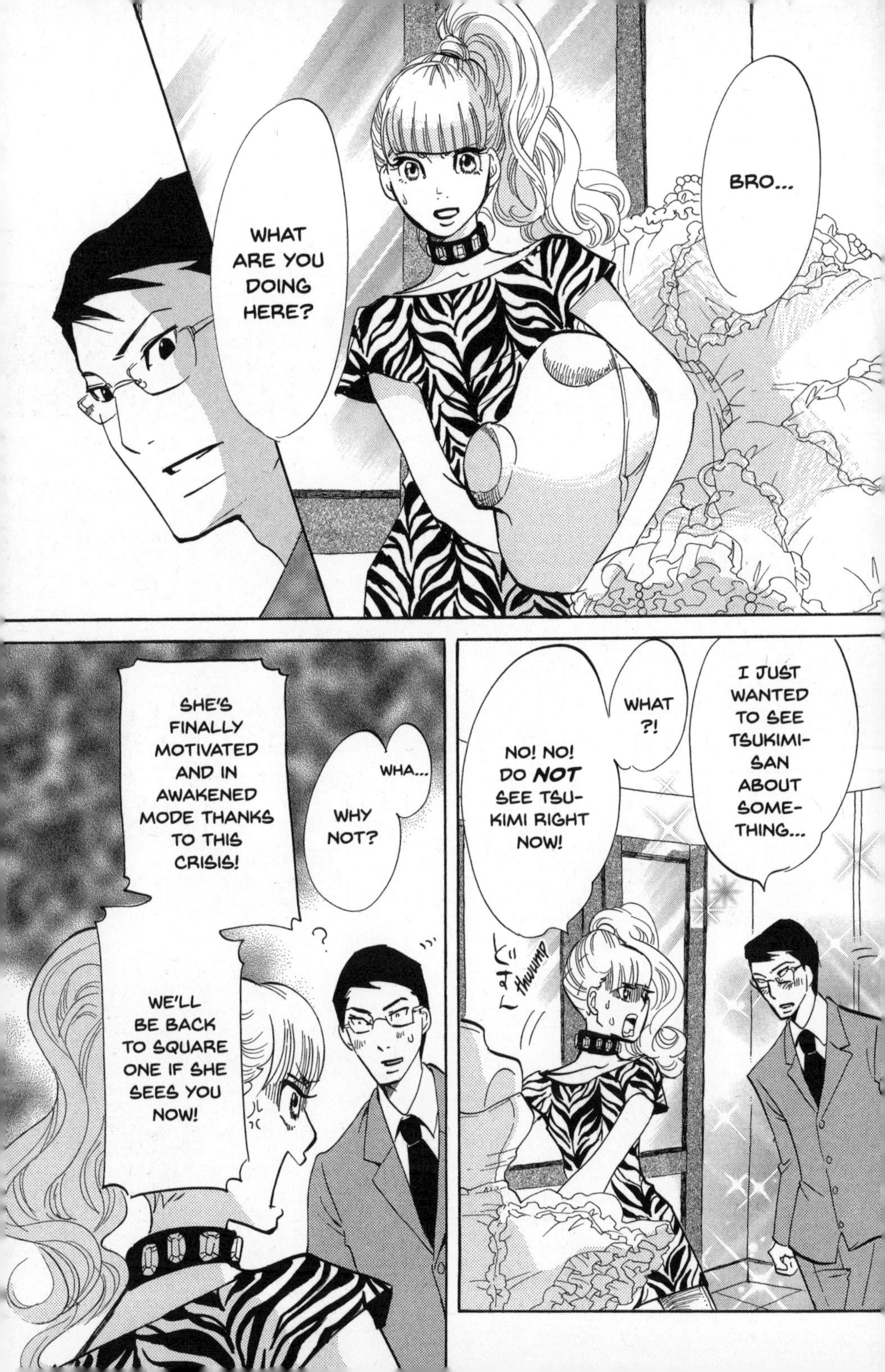
BRO...
WHAT ARE YOU DOING HERE?
I JUST WANTED TO SEE TSUKIMI-SAN ABOUT SOMETHING...
WHAT ?!
NO! NO! DO NOT SEE TSUKIMI RIGHT NOW!
どすん
THWUMP
WHA...
WHY NOT?
SHE'S FINALLY MOTIVATED AND IN AWAKENED MODE THANKS TO THIS CRISIS!
WE'LL BE BACK TO SQUARE ONE IF SHE SEES YOU NOW!

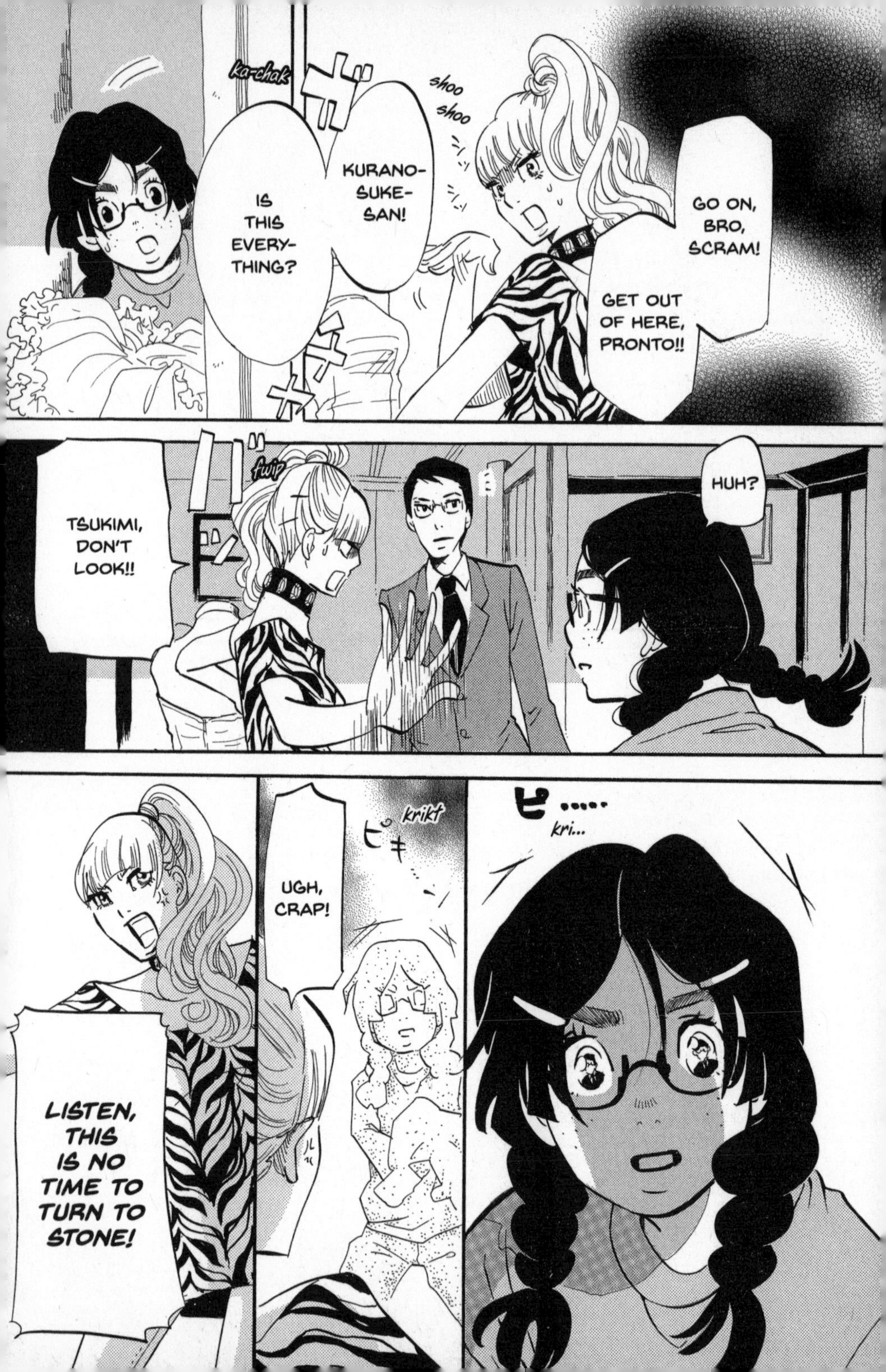
GO ON, BRO, SCRAM!
GET OUT OF HERE, PRONTO!!
shoo shoo
KURANO-SUKE-SAN!
ka-chak
IS THIS EVERY-THING?
HUH?
fwip
TSUKIMI, DON'T LOOK!!
kri...
krikt
UGH, CRAP!
LISTEN, THIS IS NO TIME TO TURN TO STONE!

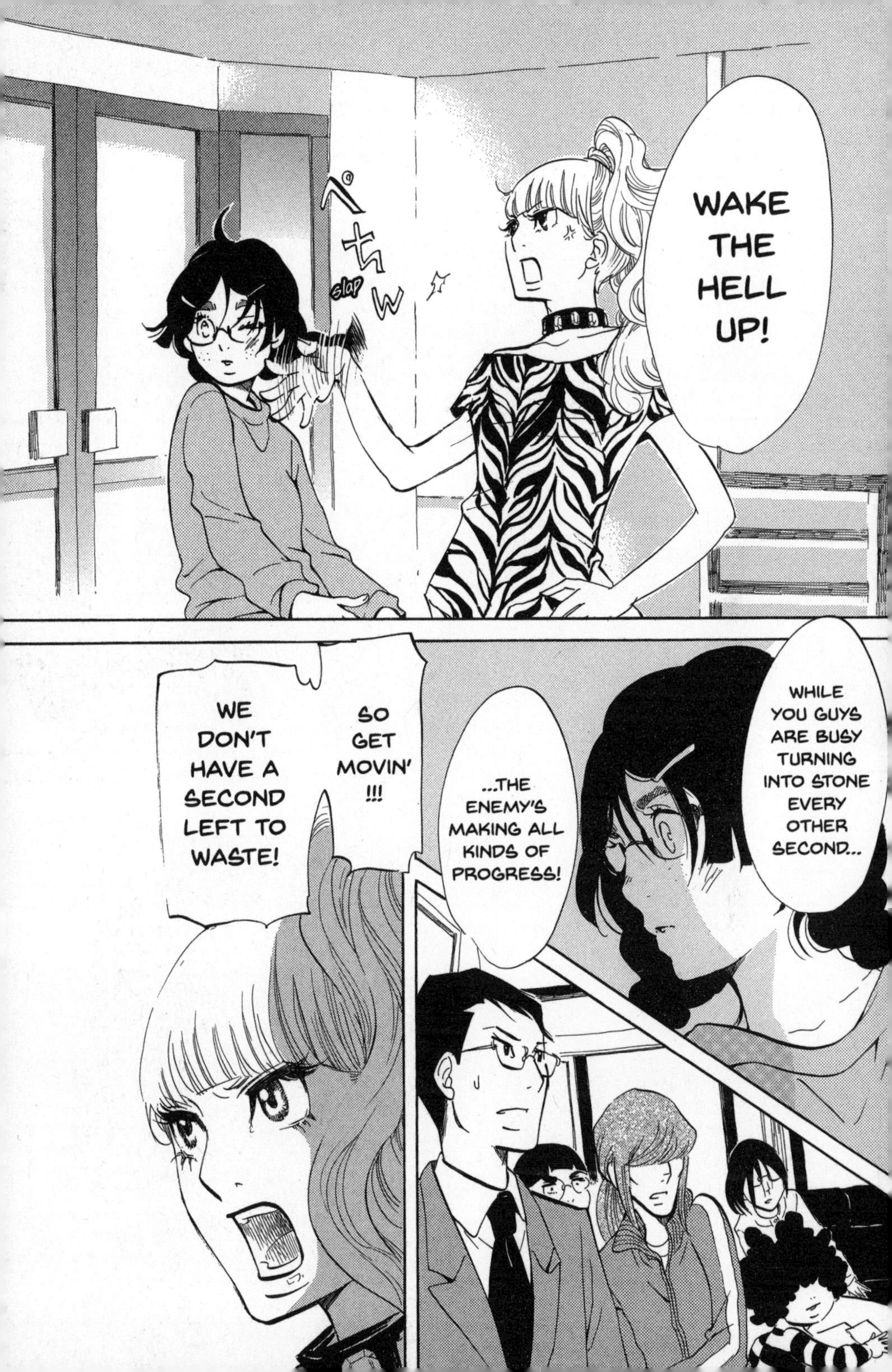
ぺちw
slap
WAKE THE HELL UP!
WHILE YOU GUYS ARE BUSY TURNING INTO STONE EVERY OTHER SECOND...
...THE ENEMY'S MAKING ALL KINDS OF PROGRESS!
WE DON'T HAVE A SECOND LEFT TO WASTE!
SO GET MOVIN' !!!

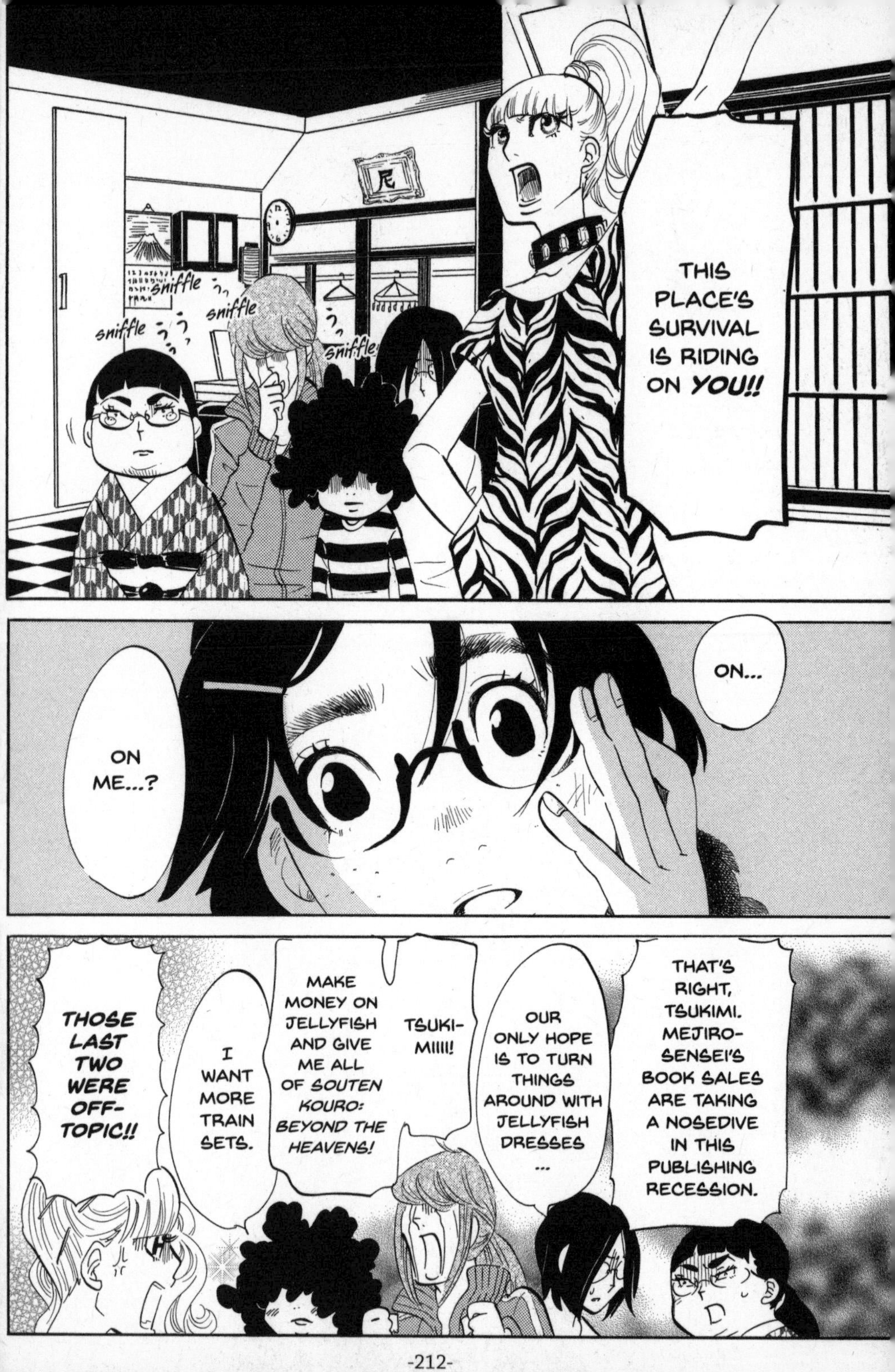
THIS PLACE'S SURVIVAL IS RIDING ON *YOU!!*
sniffle
sniffle
sniffle
sniffle
ON...
ON ME...?
THAT'S RIGHT, TSUKIMI. MEJIRO-SENSEI'S BOOK SALES ARE TAKING A NOSEDIVE IN THIS PUBLISHING RECESSION.
OUR ONLY HOPE IS TO TURN THINGS AROUND WITH JELLYFISH DRESSES ...
TSUKI-MIIII!
MAKE MONEY ON JELLYFISH AND GIVE ME ALL OF *SOUTEN KOURO: BEYOND THE HEAVENS!*
I WANT MORE TRAIN SETS.
THOSE LAST TWO WERE OFF-TOPIC!!

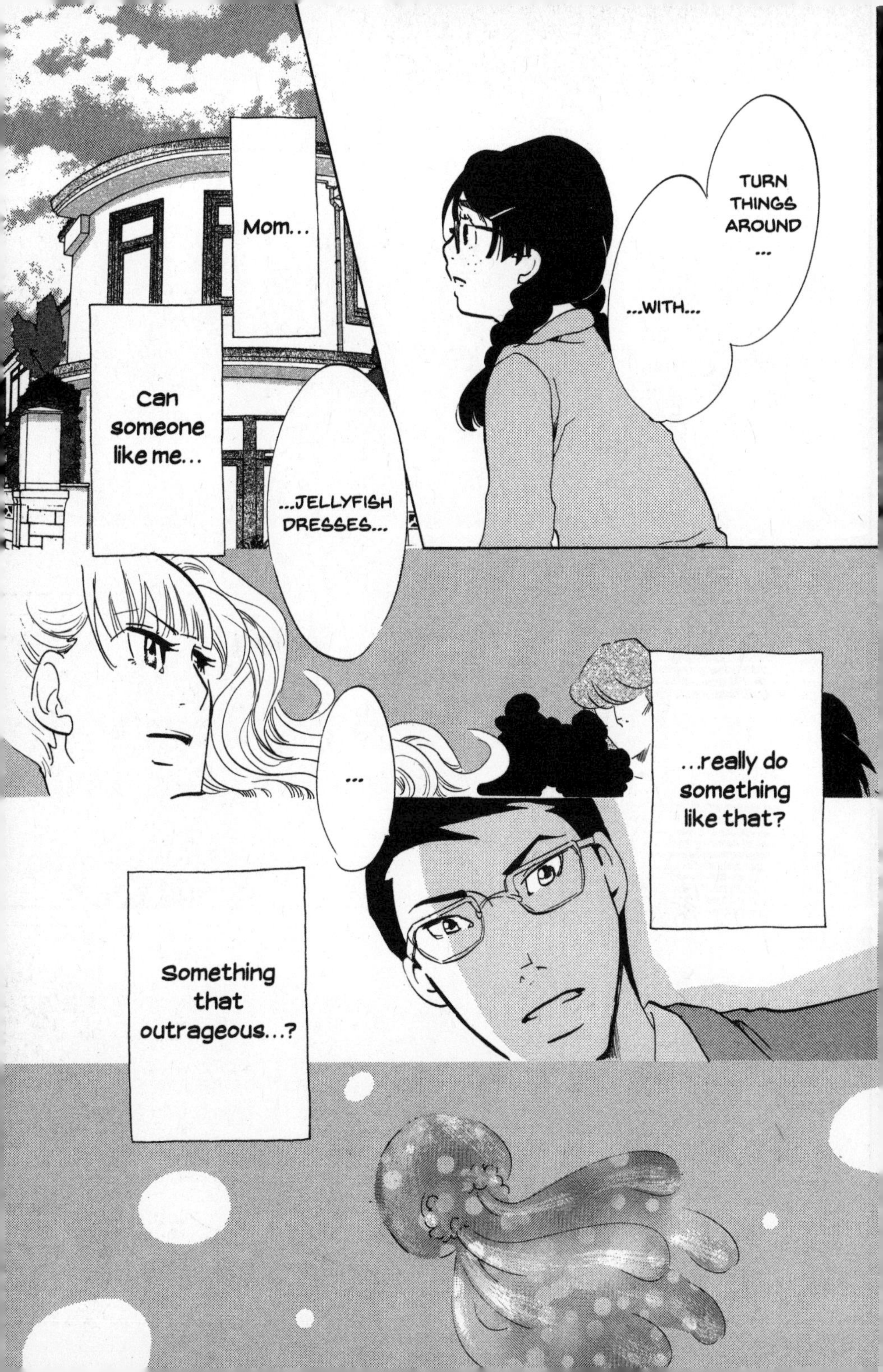
TURN THINGS AROUND ...
...WITH...
Mom...
Can someone like me...
...JELLYFISH DRESSES...
...really do something like that?
...
Something that outrageous...?

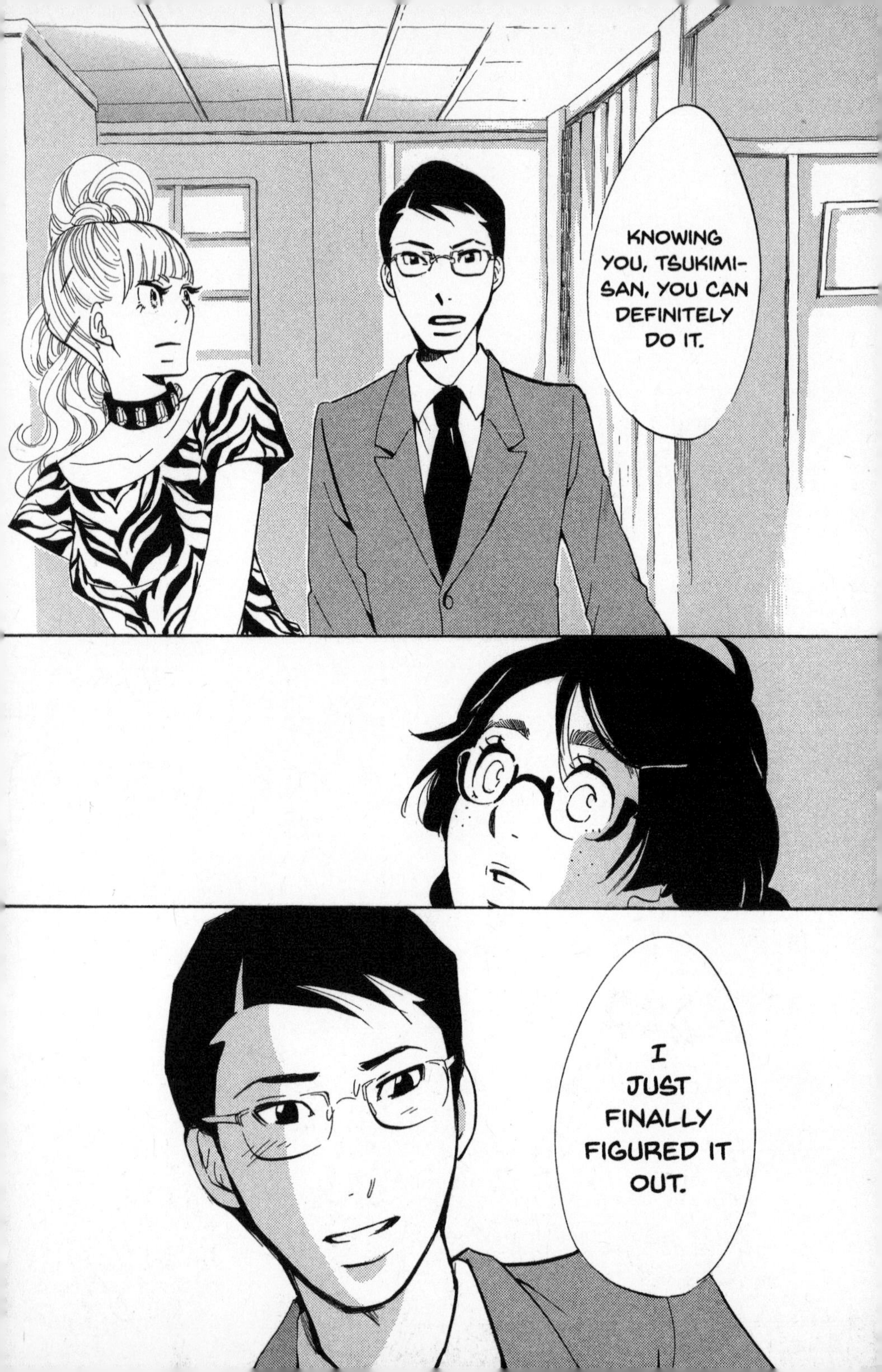
KNOWING YOU, TSUKIMI-SAN, YOU CAN DEFINITELY DO IT.
I JUST FINALLY FIGURED IT OUT.

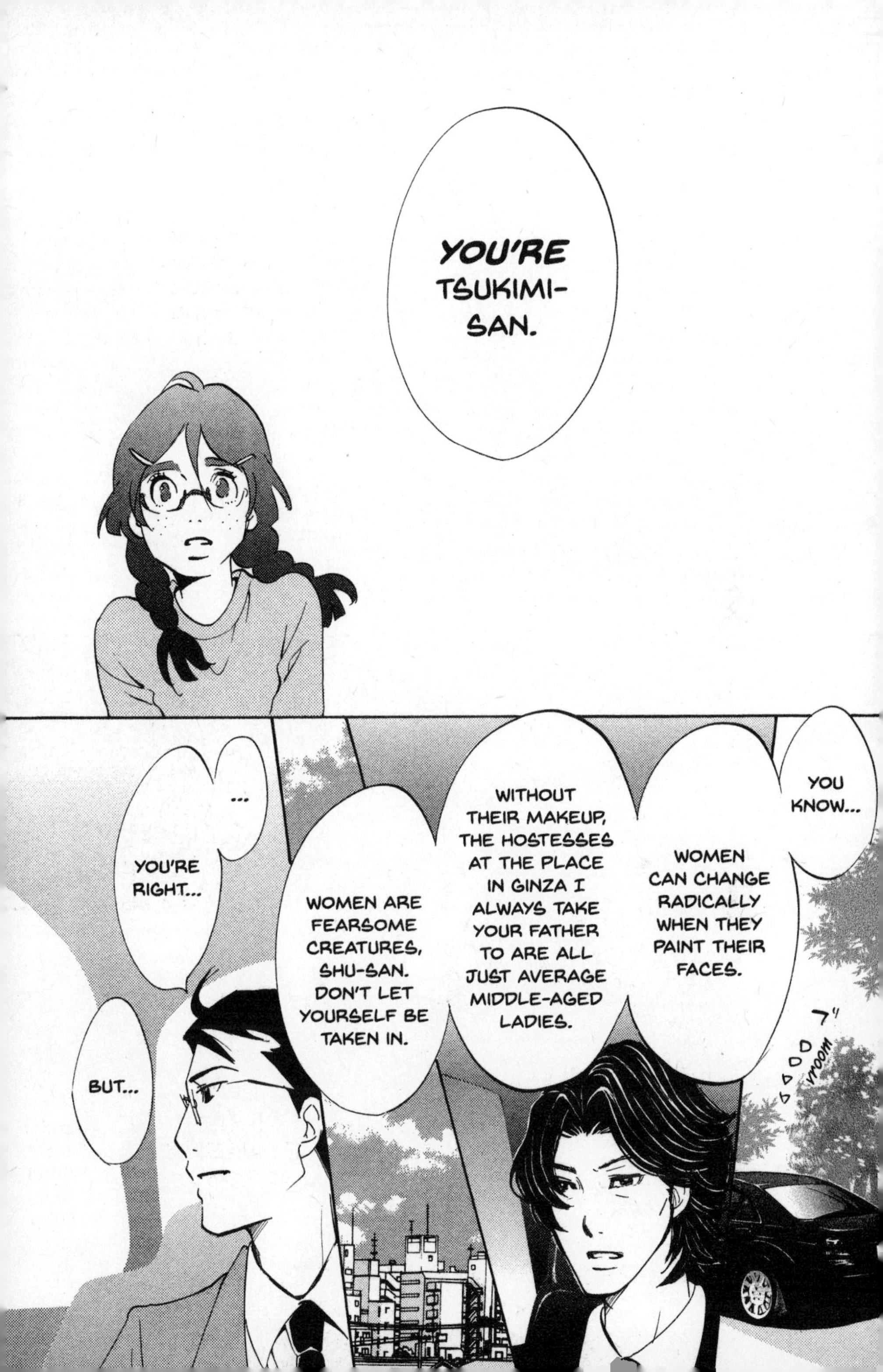
YOU'RE TSUKIMI-SAN.
YOU KNOW...
WOMEN CAN CHANGE RADICALLY WHEN THEY PAINT THEIR FACES.
vroom
WITHOUT THEIR MAKEUP, THE HOSTESSES AT THE PLACE IN GINZA I ALWAYS TAKE YOUR FATHER TO ARE ALL JUST AVERAGE MIDDLE-AGED LADIES.
WOMEN ARE FEARSOME CREATURES, SHU-SAN. DON'T LET YOURSELF BE TAKEN IN.
...
YOU'RE RIGHT...
BUT...

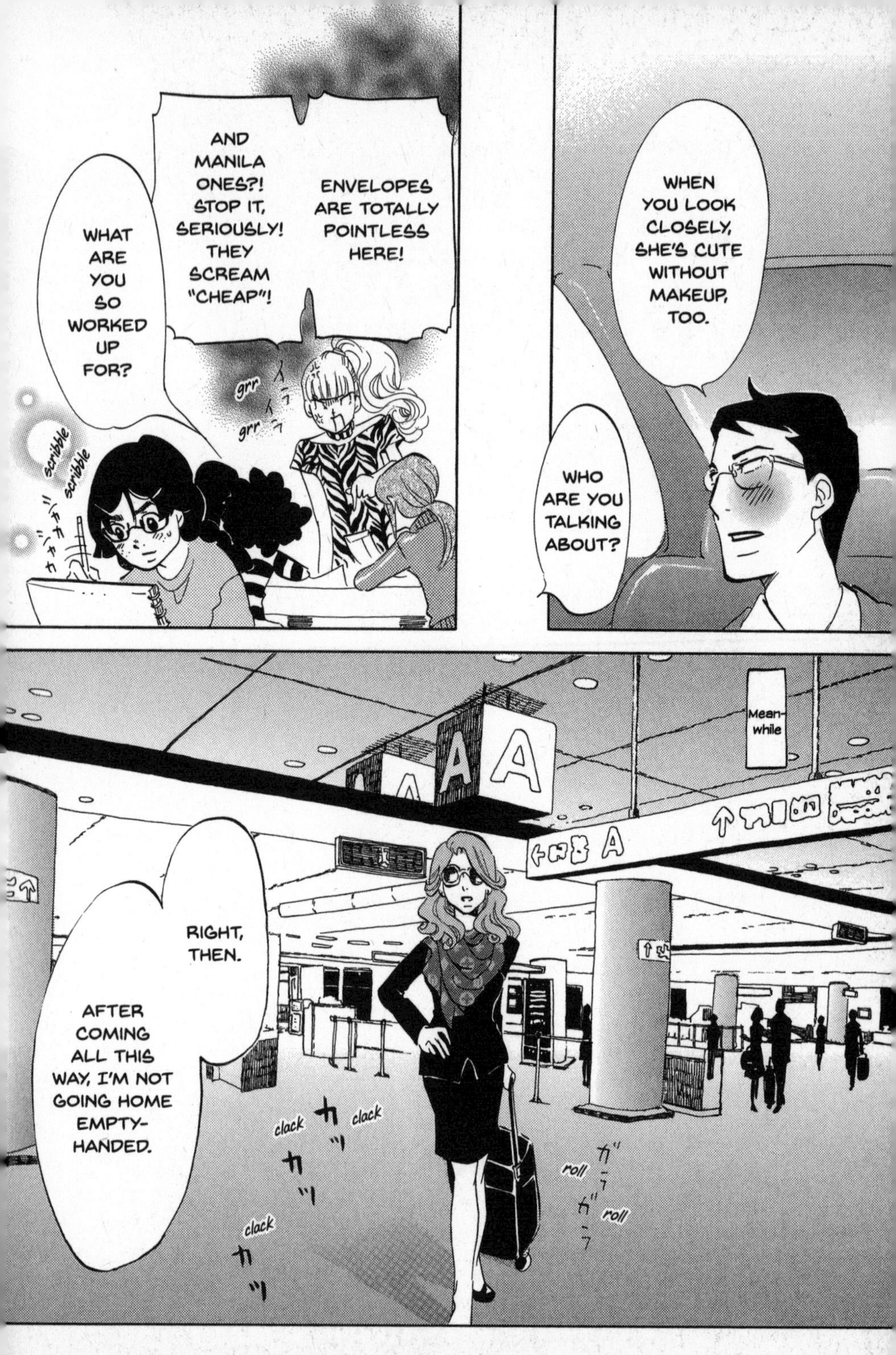
WHEN YOU LOOK CLOSELY, SHE'S CUTE WITHOUT MAKEUP, TOO.
WHO ARE YOU TALKING ABOUT?
ENVELOPES ARE TOTALLY POINTLESS HERE!
AND MANILA ONES?! STOP IT, SERIOUSLY! THEY SCREAM "CHEAP"!
WHAT ARE YOU SO WORKED UP FOR?
grr
grr
scribble
scribble
Mean-while
RIGHT, THEN.
AFTER COMING ALL THIS WAY, I'M NOT GOING HOME EMPTY-HANDED.
clack
clack
roll
roll
clack

Episode 31

Dolly Girls

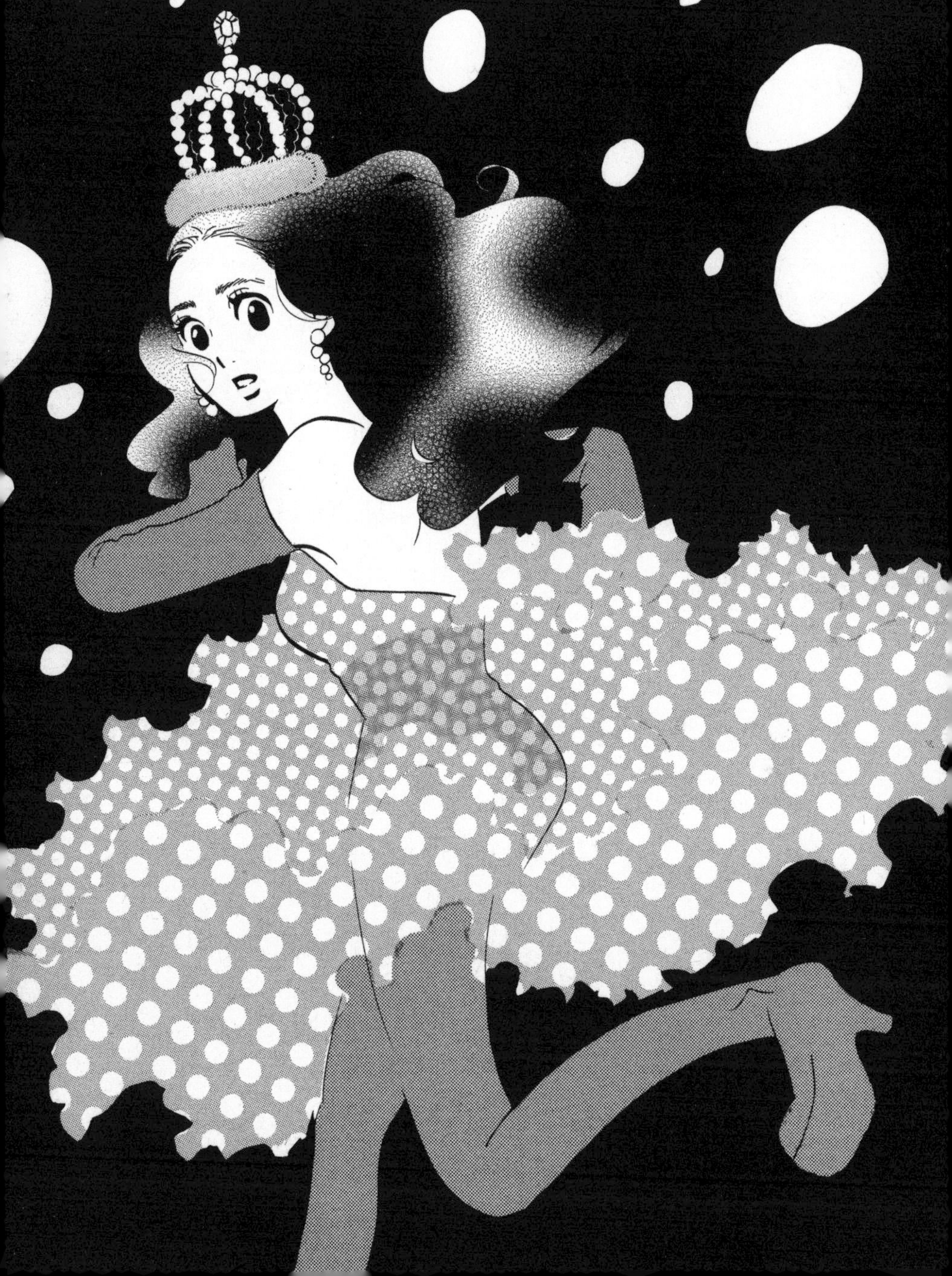

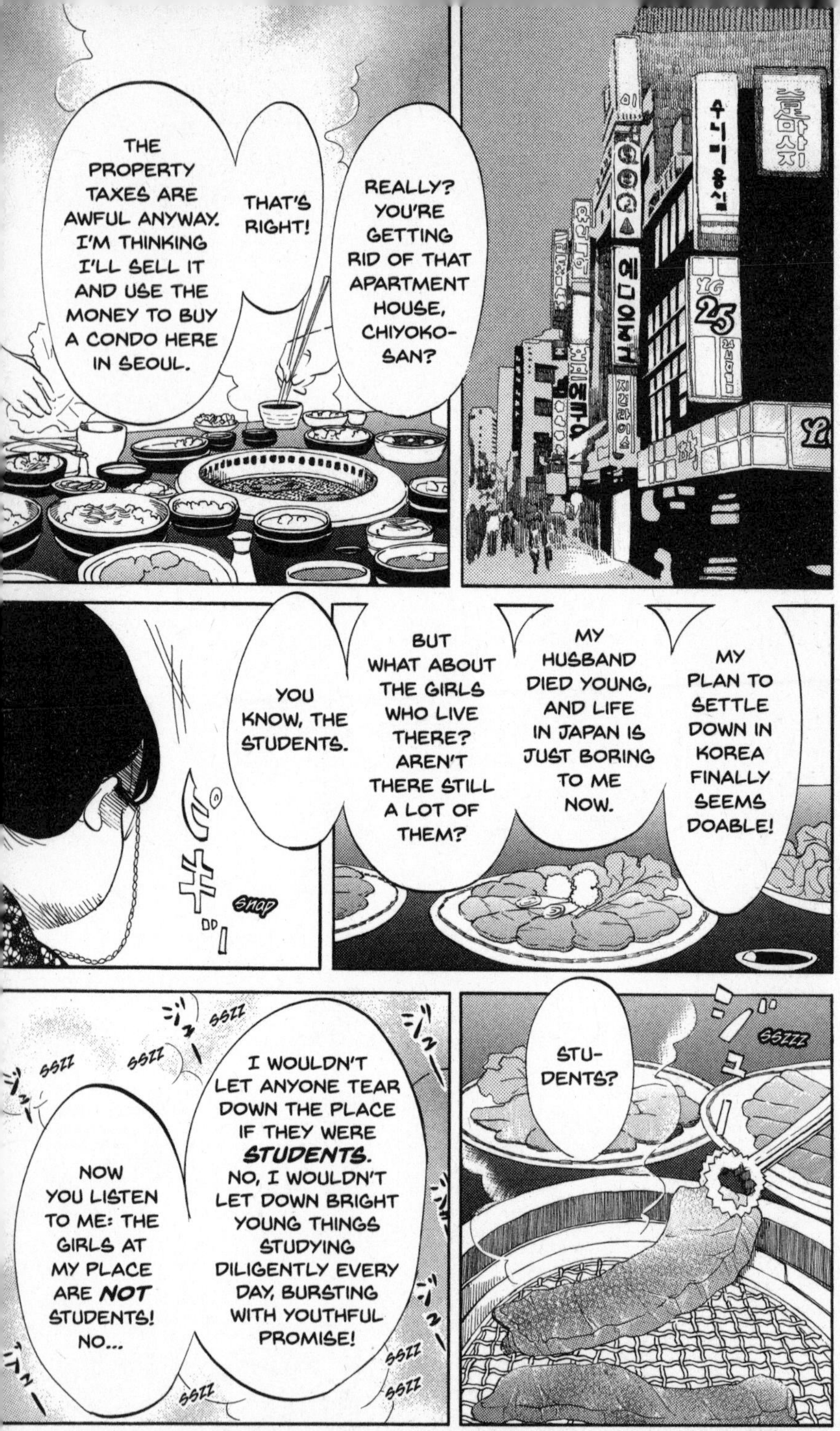
REALLY? YOU'RE GETTING RID OF THAT APARTMENT HOUSE, CHIYOKO-SAN?
THAT'S RIGHT!
THE PROPERTY TAXES ARE AWFUL ANYWAY. I'M THINKING I'LL SELL IT AND USE THE MONEY TO BUY A CONDO HERE IN SEOUL.
MY PLAN TO SETTLE DOWN IN KOREA FINALLY SEEMS DOABLE!
MY HUSBAND DIED YOUNG, AND LIFE IN JAPAN IS JUST BORING TO ME NOW.
BUT WHAT ABOUT THE GIRLS WHO LIVE THERE? AREN'T THERE STILL A LOT OF THEM?
YOU KNOW, THE STUDENTS.
Snap
SSZZZ
STU-DENTS?
I WOULDN'T LET ANYONE TEAR DOWN THE PLACE IF THEY WERE *STUDENTS.* NO, I WOULDN'T LET DOWN BRIGHT YOUNG THINGS STUDYING DILIGENTLY EVERY DAY, BURSTING WITH YOUTHFUL PROMISE!
NOW YOU LISTEN TO ME: THE GIRLS AT MY PLACE ARE *NOT* STUDENTS! NO...
SSZZ

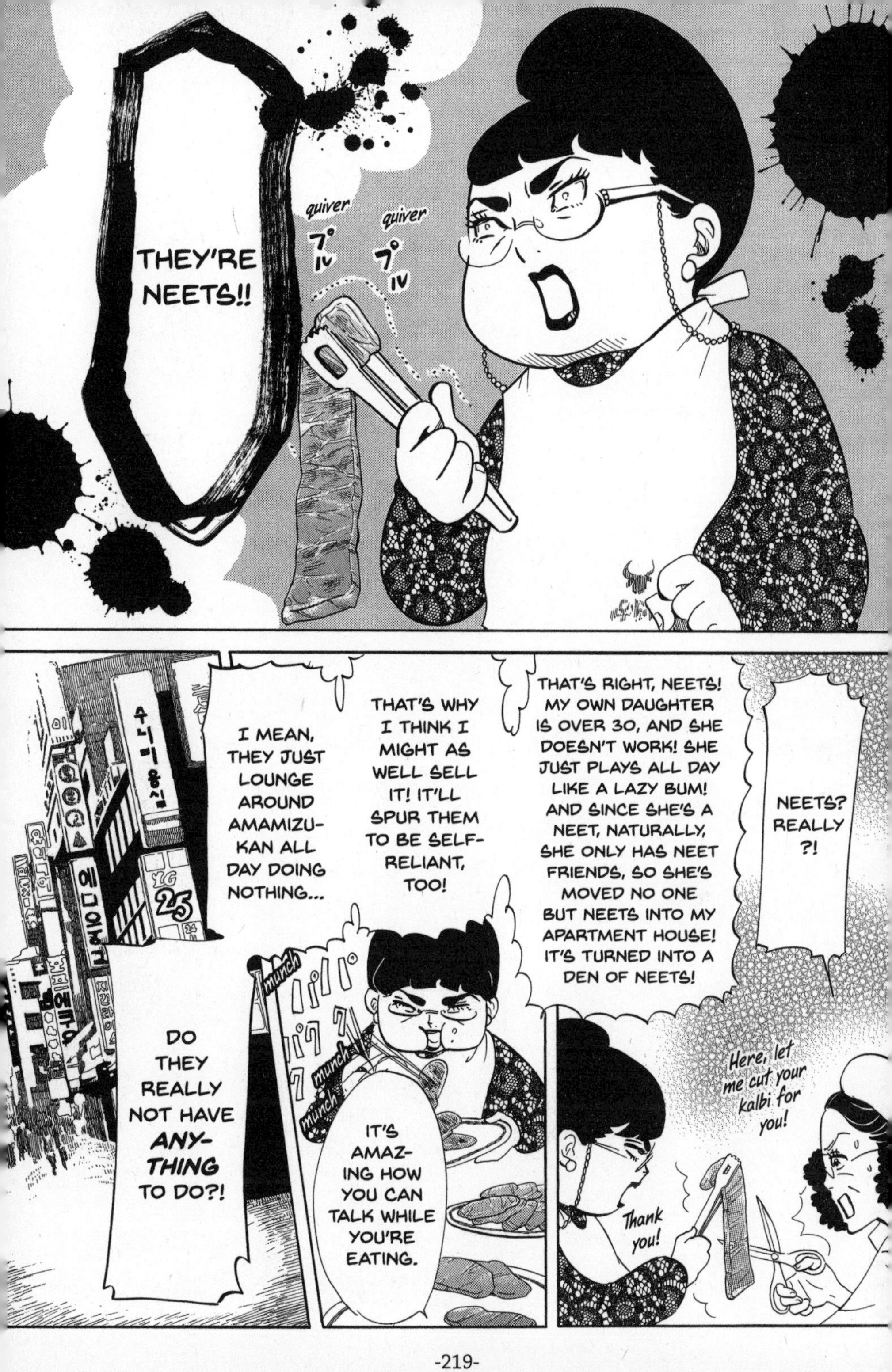

quiver
quiver
THEY'RE NEETS!!
NEETS? REALLY ?!
THAT'S RIGHT, NEETS! MY OWN DAUGHTER IS OVER 30, AND SHE DOESN'T WORK! SHE JUST PLAYS ALL DAY LIKE A LAZY BUM! AND SINCE SHE'S A NEET, NATURALLY, SHE ONLY HAS NEET FRIENDS, SO SHE'S MOVED NO ONE BUT NEETS INTO MY APARTMENT HOUSE! IT'S TURNED INTO A DEN OF NEETS!
Here, let me cut your kalbi for you!
Thank you!
THAT'S WHY I THINK I MIGHT AS WELL SELL IT! IT'LL SPUR THEM TO BE SELF-RELIANT, TOO!
munch
munch
munch
IT'S AMAZING HOW YOU CAN TALK WHILE YOU'RE EATING.
I MEAN, THEY JUST LOUNGE AROUND AMAMIZUKAN ALL DAY DOING NOTHING...
DO THEY REALLY NOT HAVE ANYTHING TO DO?!

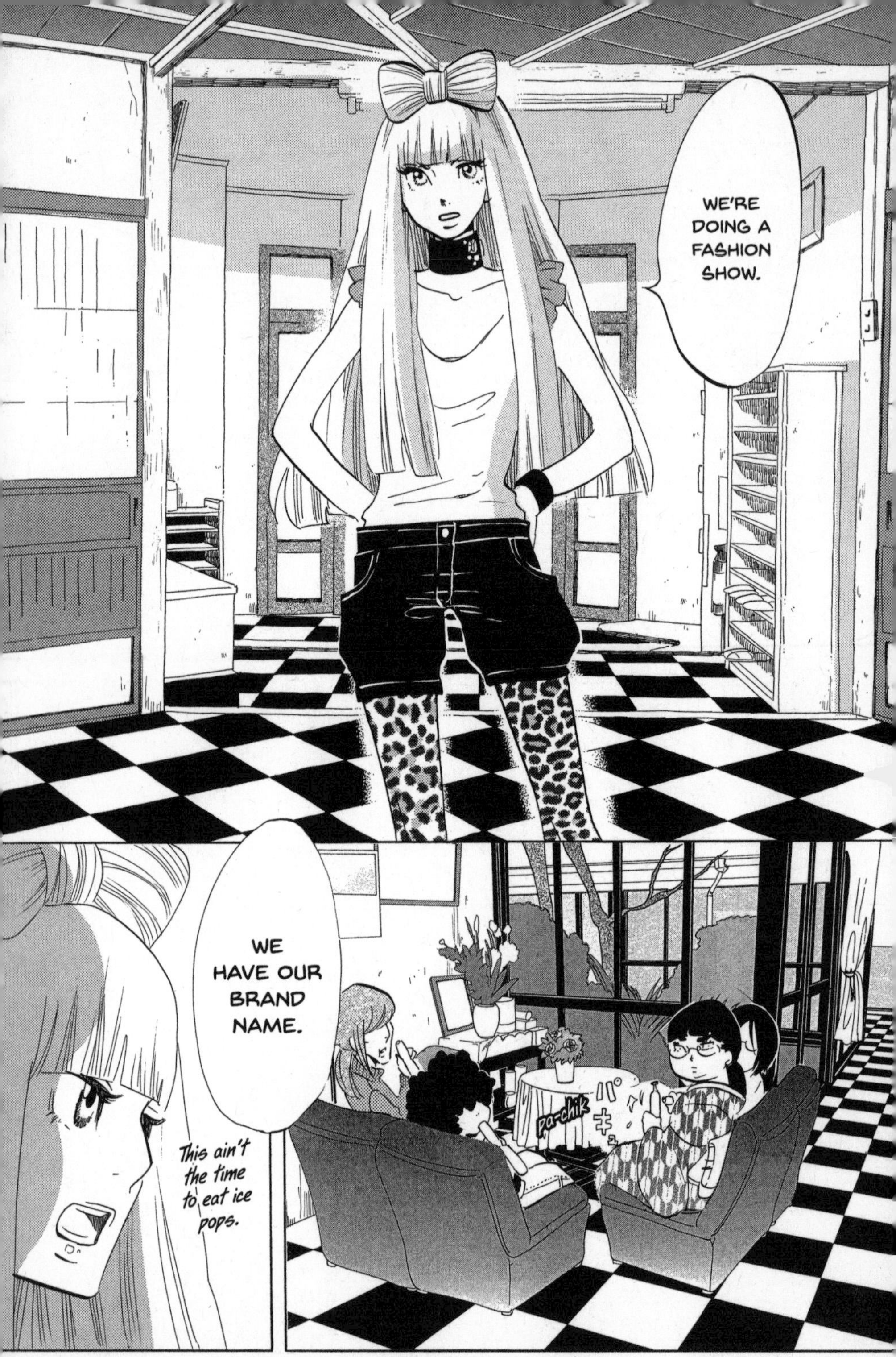
WE'RE DOING A FASHION SHOW.
pa-chik
WE HAVE OUR BRAND NAME.
This ain't the time to eat ice pops.

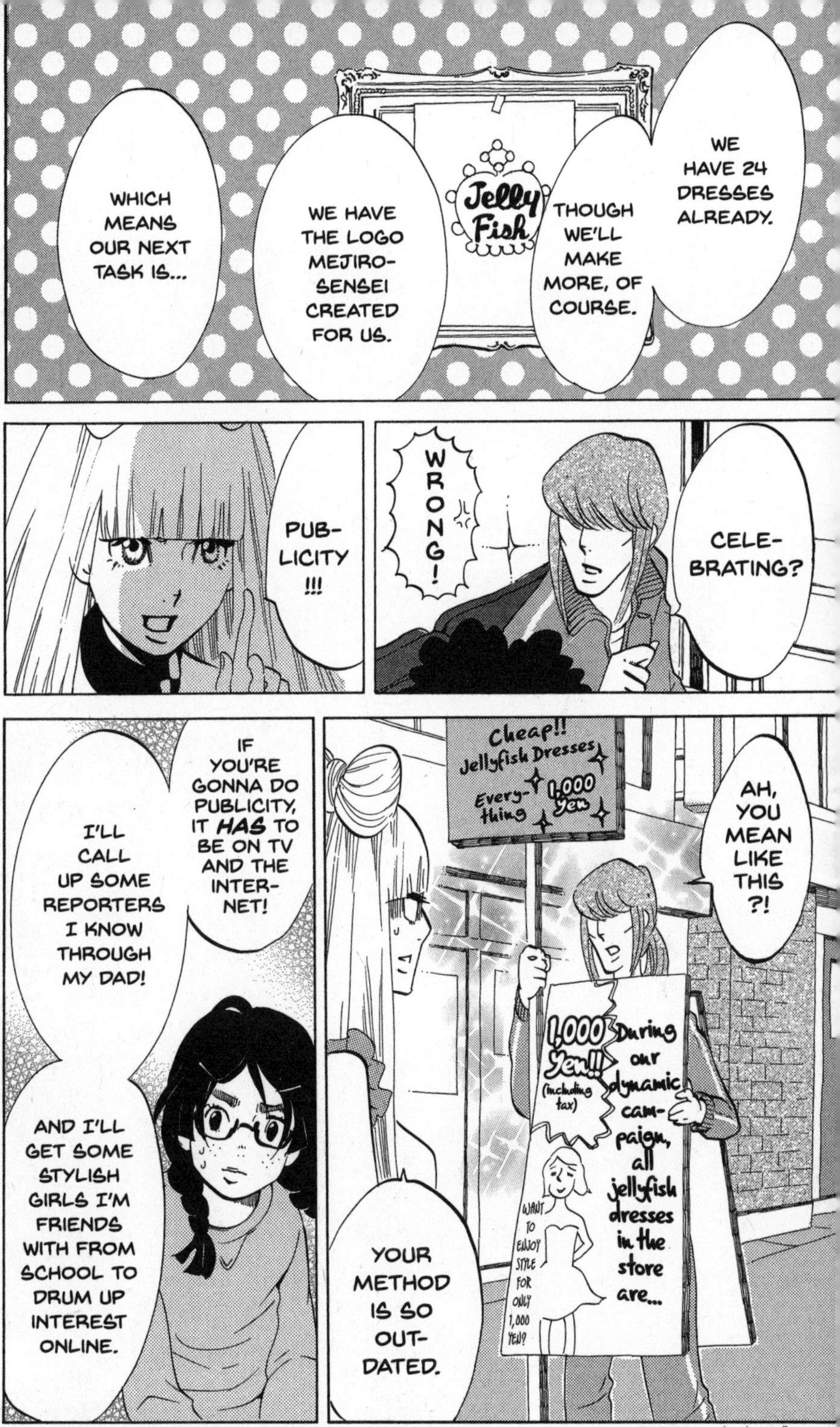
WE HAVE 24 DRESSES ALREADY.
THOUGH WE'LL MAKE MORE, OF COURSE.
Jelly Fish
WE HAVE THE LOGO MEJIRO-SENSEI CREATED FOR US.
WHICH MEANS OUR NEXT TASK IS...
CELEBRATING?
WRONG!
PUBLICITY!!!
AH, YOU MEAN LIKE THIS?!
Cheap!! Jellyfish Dresses Every-thing 1,000 Yen
1,000 Yen!! (including tax)
During our dynamic campaign, all jellyfish dresses in the store are...
WANT TO ENJOY STYLE FOR ONLY 1,000 YEN?
YOUR METHOD IS SO OUT-DATED.
IF YOU'RE GONNA DO PUBLICITY, IT *HAS* TO BE ON TV AND THE INTER-NET!
I'LL CALL UP SOME REPORTERS I KNOW THROUGH MY DAD!
AND I'LL GET SOME STYLISH GIRLS I'M FRIENDS WITH FROM SCHOOL TO DRUM UP INTEREST ONLINE.

*1,000 Yen is about $10 US!

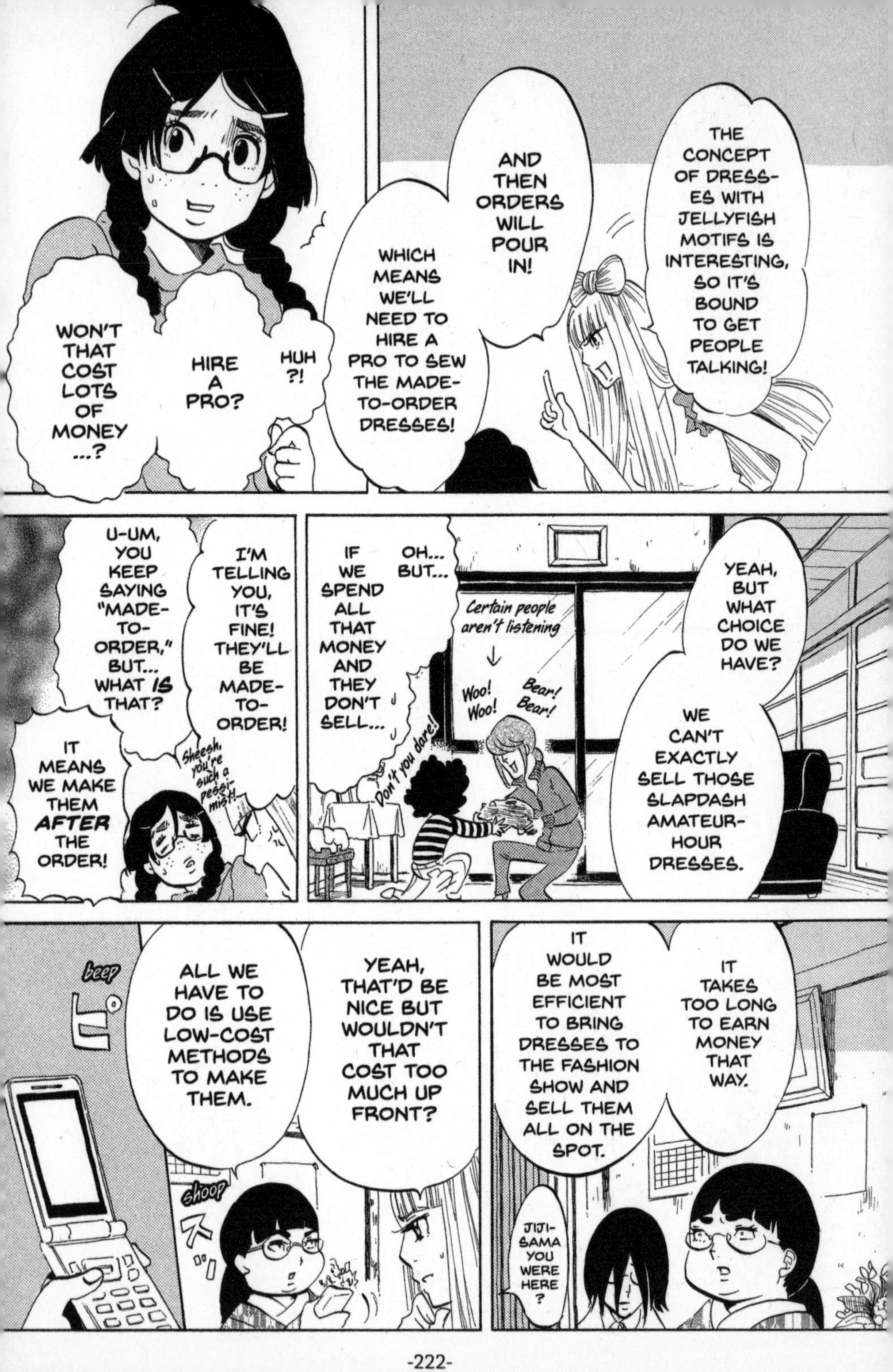
THE CONCEPT OF DRESSES WITH JELLYFISH MOTIFS IS INTERESTING, SO IT'S BOUND TO GET PEOPLE TALKING!
AND THEN ORDERS WILL POUR IN!
WHICH MEANS WE'LL NEED TO HIRE A PRO TO SEW THE MADE-TO-ORDER DRESSES!
HUH?!
HIRE A PRO?
WON'T THAT COST LOTS OF MONEY ...?
YEAH, BUT WHAT CHOICE DO WE HAVE?
WE CAN'T EXACTLY SELL THOSE SLAPDASH AMATEUR-HOUR DRESSES.
OH... BUT...
IF WE SPEND ALL THAT MONEY AND THEY DON'T SELL...
Certain people aren't listening
Bear! Bear!
Woo! Woo!
Don't you dare!
I'M TELLING YOU, IT'S FINE! THEY'LL BE MADE-TO-ORDER!
U-UM, YOU KEEP SAYING "MADE-TO-ORDER," BUT... WHAT *IS* THAT?
Sheesh, you're such a pessimist!
IT MEANS WE MAKE THEM **AFTER** THE ORDER!
IT TAKES TOO LONG TO EARN MONEY THAT WAY.
IT WOULD BE MOST EFFICIENT TO BRING DRESSES TO THE FASHION SHOW AND SELL THEM ALL ON THE SPOT.
JIJI-SAMA YOU WERE HERE?
YEAH, THAT'D BE NICE BUT WOULDN'T THAT COST TOO MUCH UP FRONT?
ALL WE HAVE TO DO IS USE LOW-COST METHODS TO MAKE THEM.
beep
shoop

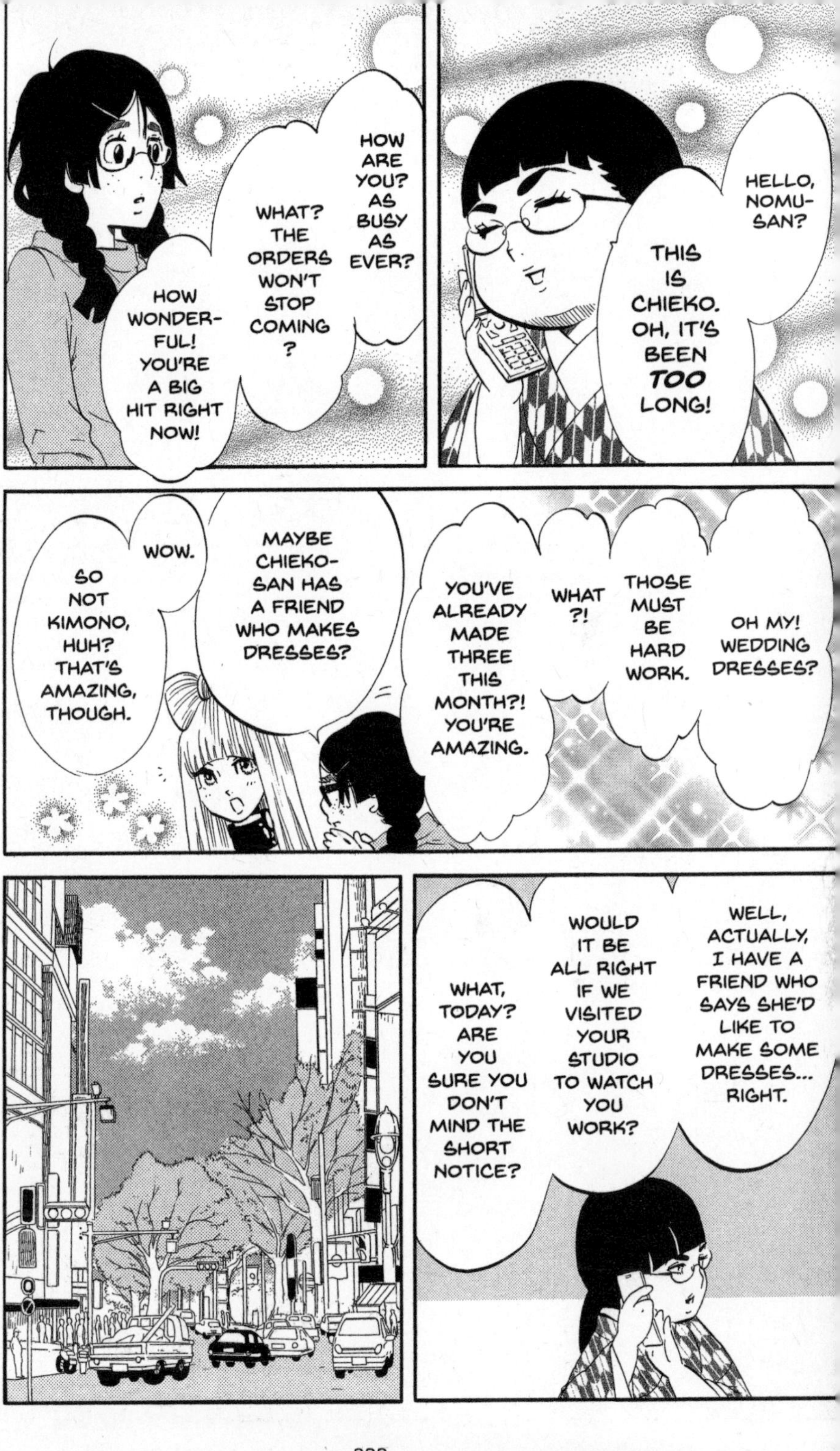
HELLO, NOMU-SAN?
THIS IS CHIEKO. OH, IT'S BEEN *TOO* LONG!
HOW ARE YOU? AS BUSY AS EVER?
WHAT? THE ORDERS WON'T STOP COMING?
HOW WONDERFUL! YOU'RE A BIG HIT RIGHT NOW!
OH MY! WEDDING DRESSES?
THOSE MUST BE HARD WORK.
WHAT?!
YOU'VE ALREADY MADE THREE THIS MONTH?! YOU'RE AMAZING.
MAYBE CHIEKO-SAN HAS A FRIEND WHO MAKES DRESSES?
WOW.
SO NOT KIMONO, HUH? THAT'S AMAZING, THOUGH.
WELL, ACTUALLY, I HAVE A FRIEND WHO SAYS SHE'D LIKE TO MAKE SOME DRESSES... RIGHT.
WOULD IT BE ALL RIGHT IF WE VISITED YOUR STUDIO TO WATCH YOU WORK?
WHAT, TODAY? ARE YOU SURE YOU DON'T MIND THE SHORT NOTICE?

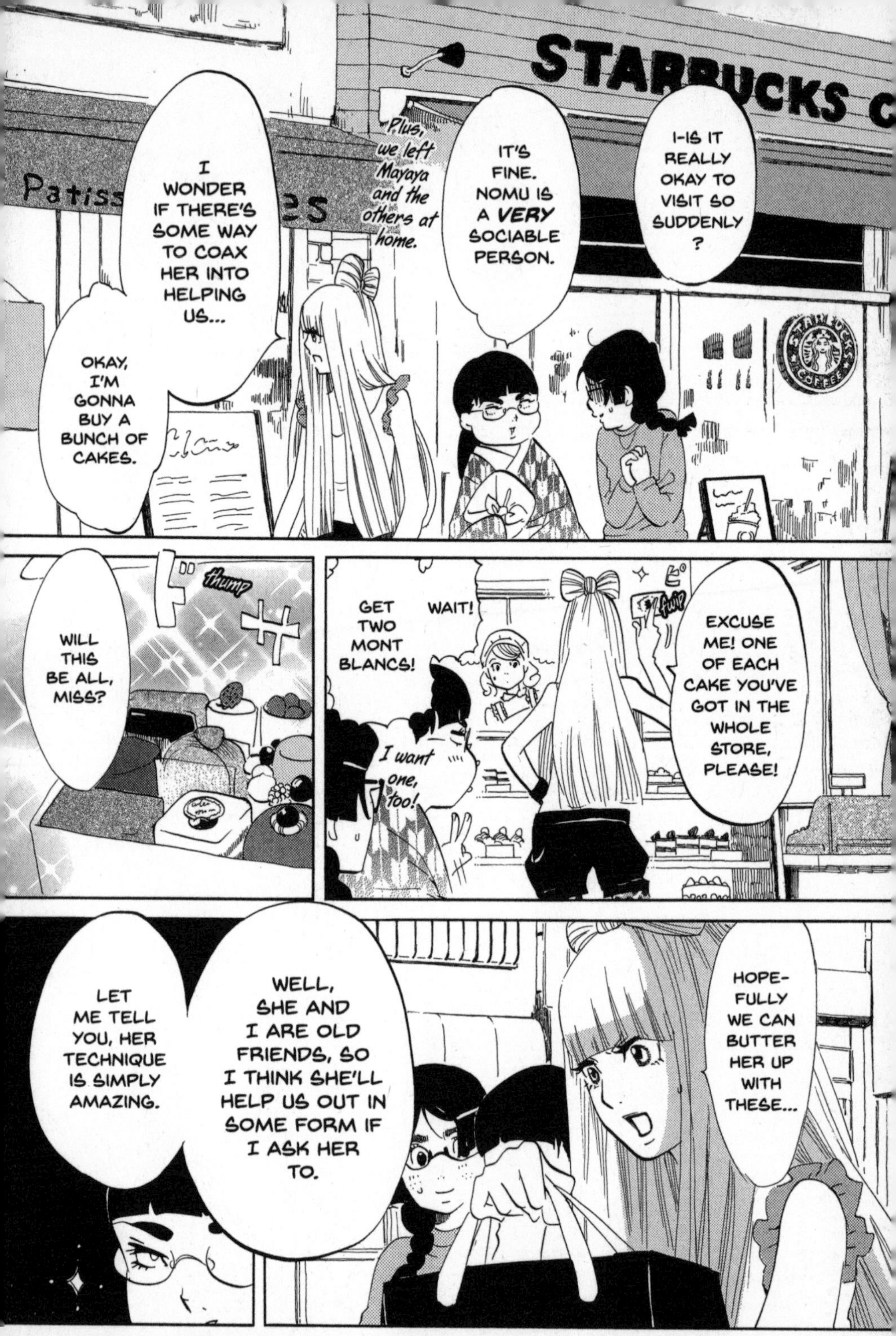
I-IS IT REALLY OKAY TO VISIT SO SUDDENLY?
IT'S FINE. NOMU IS A *VERY* SOCIABLE PERSON.
Plus, we left Mayaya and the others at home.
I WONDER IF THERE'S SOME WAY TO COAX HER INTO HELPING US...
OKAY, I'M GONNA BUY A BUNCH OF CAKES.
EXCUSE ME! ONE OF EACH CAKE YOU'VE GOT IN THE WHOLE STORE, PLEASE!
flip
WAIT!
GET TWO MONT BLANCS!
I want one, too!
thump
WILL THIS BE ALL, MISS?
HOPEFULLY WE CAN BUTTER HER UP WITH THESE...
WELL, SHE AND I ARE OLD FRIENDS, SO I THINK SHE'LL HELP US OUT IN SOME FORM IF I ASK HER TO.
LET ME TELL YOU, HER TECHNIQUE IS SIMPLY AMAZING.

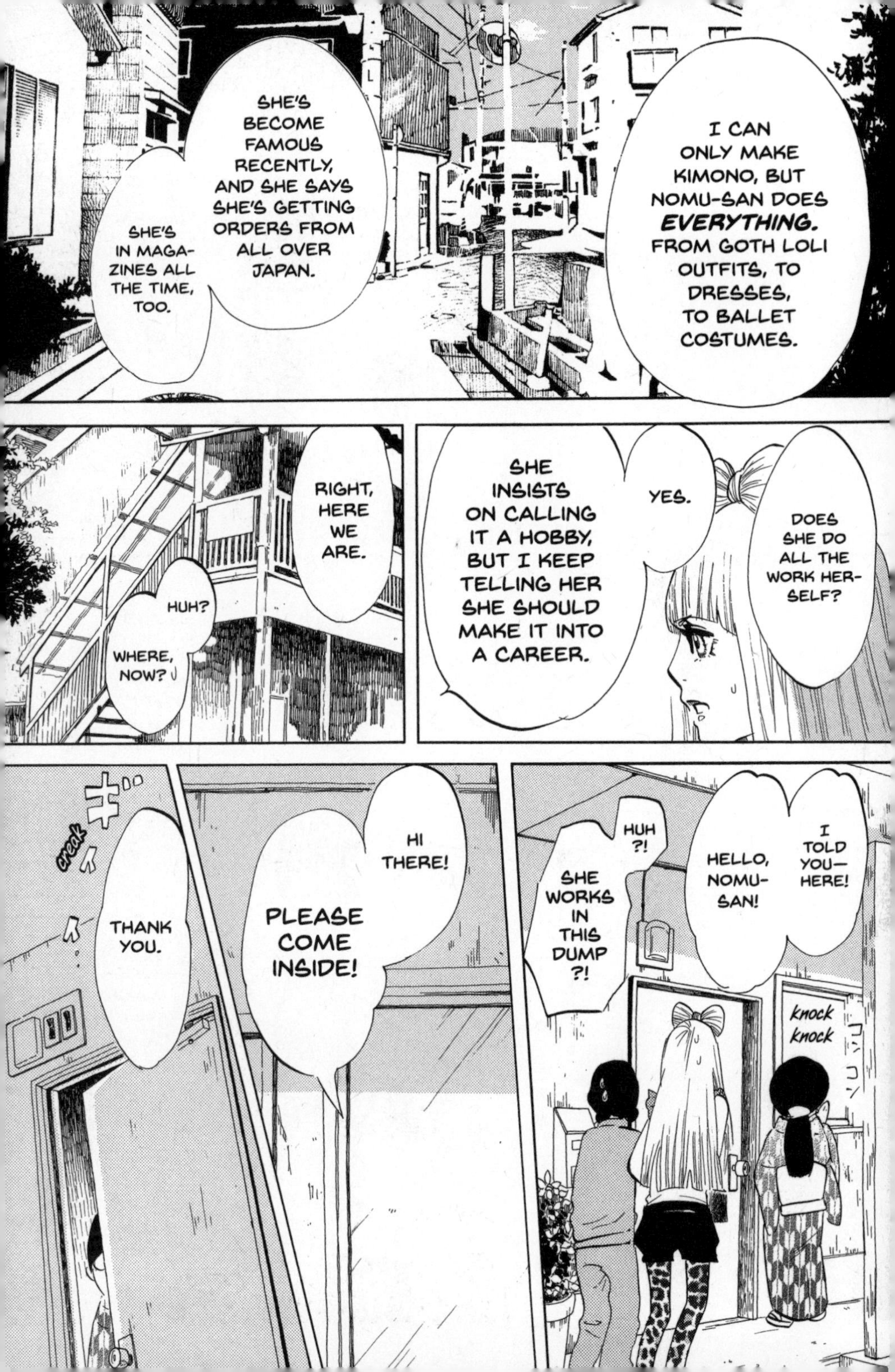
I CAN ONLY MAKE KIMONO, BUT NOMU-SAN DOES **EVERYTHING.** FROM GOTH LOLI OUTFITS, TO DRESSES, TO BALLET COSTUMES.
SHE'S BECOME FAMOUS RECENTLY, AND SHE SAYS SHE'S GETTING ORDERS FROM ALL OVER JAPAN.
SHE'S IN MAGAZINES ALL THE TIME, TOO.
DOES SHE DO ALL THE WORK HERSELF?
YES.
SHE INSISTS ON CALLING IT A HOBBY, BUT I KEEP TELLING HER SHE SHOULD MAKE IT INTO A CAREER.
RIGHT, HERE WE ARE.
HUH?
WHERE, NOW?
I TOLD YOU— HERE!
HELLO, NOMU-SAN!
knock knock
HUH ?!
SHE WORKS IN THIS DUMP ?!
HI THERE!
PLEASE COME INSIDE!
creak
THANK YOU.

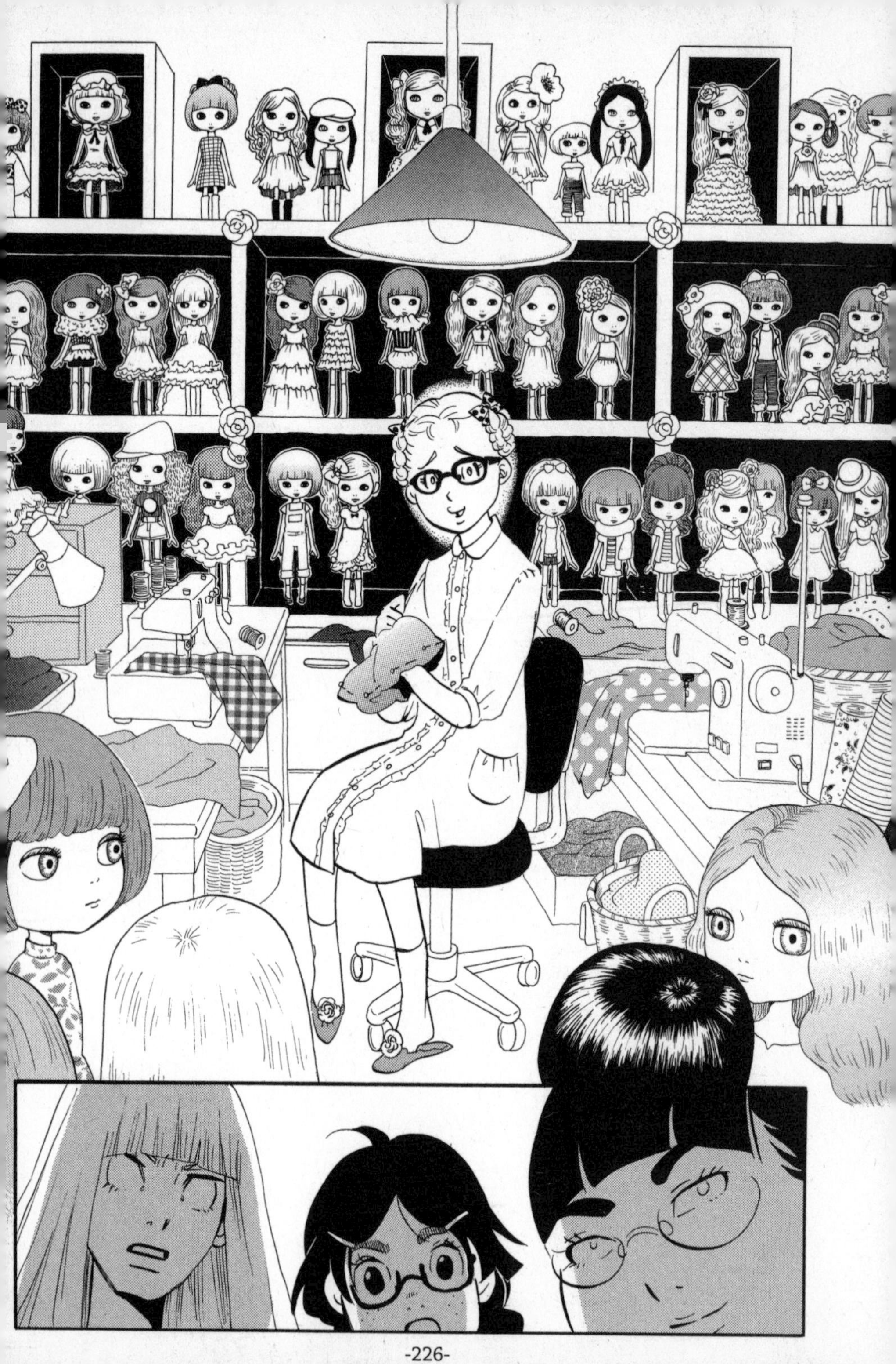

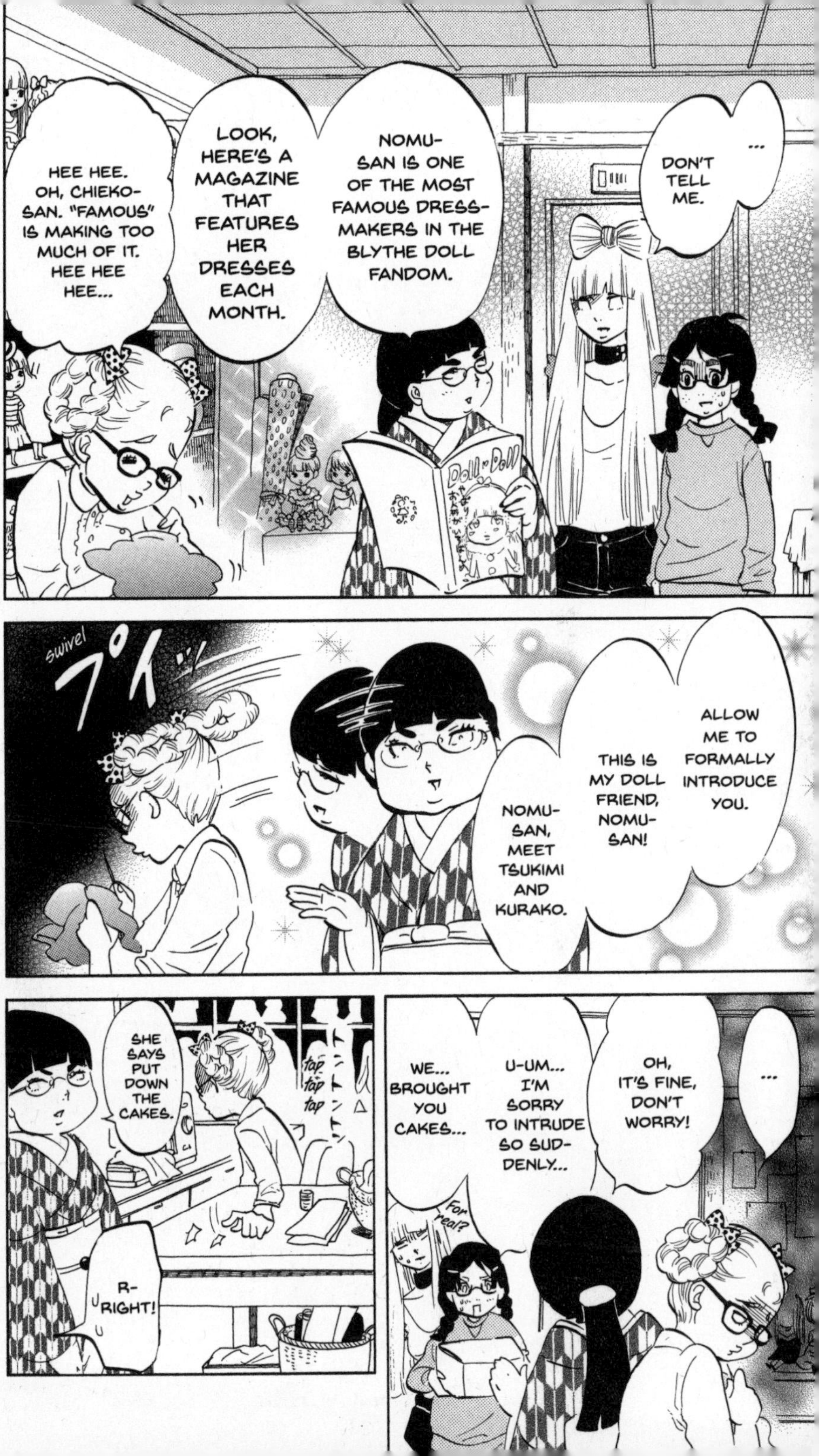
...
DON'T TELL ME.
NOMU-SAN IS ONE OF THE MOST FAMOUS DRESS-MAKERS IN THE BLYTHE DOLL FANDOM.
LOOK, HERE'S A MAGAZINE THAT FEATURES HER DRESSES EACH MONTH.
HEE HEE. OH, CHIEKO-SAN. "FAMOUS" IS MAKING TOO MUCH OF IT. HEE HEE HEE...
Doll Doll
swivel
ALLOW ME TO FORMALLY INTRODUCE YOU.
THIS IS MY DOLL FRIEND, NOMU-SAN!
NOMU-SAN, MEET TSUKIMI AND KURAKO.
...
OH, IT'S FINE, DON'T WORRY!
U-UM... I'M SORRY TO INTRUDE SO SUD-DENLY...
WE... BROUGHT YOU CAKES...
For real?
SHE SAYS PUT DOWN THE CAKES.
tap tap tap
R-RIGHT!

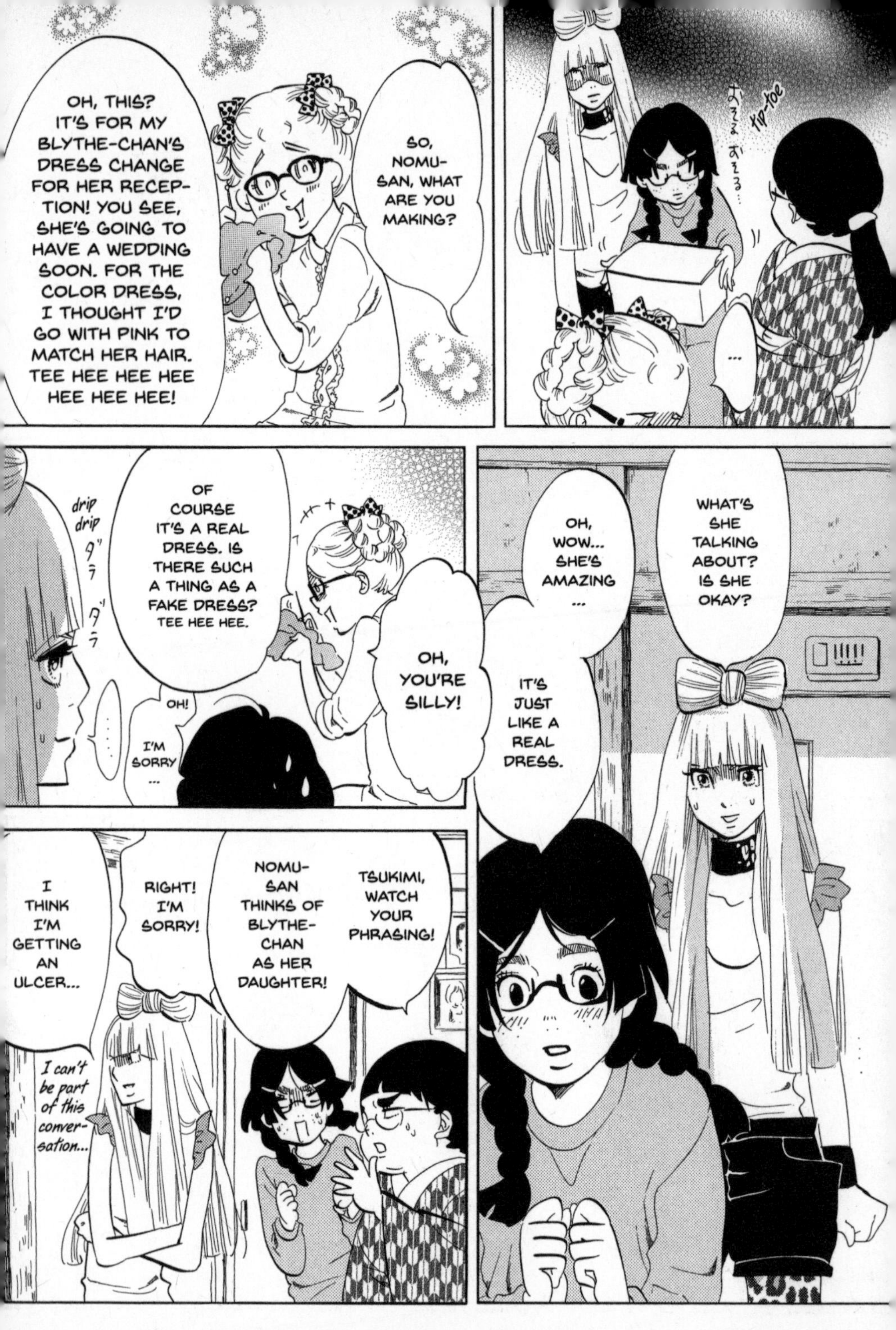
tip-toe
おそるおそる…
…
SO, NOMU-SAN, WHAT ARE YOU MAKING?
OH, THIS? IT'S FOR MY BLYTHE-CHAN'S DRESS CHANGE FOR HER RECEPTION! YOU SEE, SHE'S GOING TO HAVE A WEDDING SOON. FOR THE COLOR DRESS, I THOUGHT I'D GO WITH PINK TO MATCH HER HAIR. TEE HEE HEE HEE HEE HEE HEE!
WHAT'S SHE TALKING ABOUT? IS SHE OKAY?
OH, WOW... SHE'S AMAZING ...
IT'S JUST LIKE A REAL DRESS.
…
OF COURSE IT'S A REAL DRESS. IS THERE SUCH A THING AS A FAKE DRESS? TEE HEE HEE.
OH, YOU'RE SILLY!
OH! I'M SORRY ...
drip drip
ダラダラ
......
TSUKIMI, WATCH YOUR PHRASING!
NOMU-SAN THINKS OF BLYTHE-CHAN AS HER DAUGHTER!
RIGHT! I'M SORRY!
I THINK I'M GETTING AN ULCER...
I can't be part of this conversation...

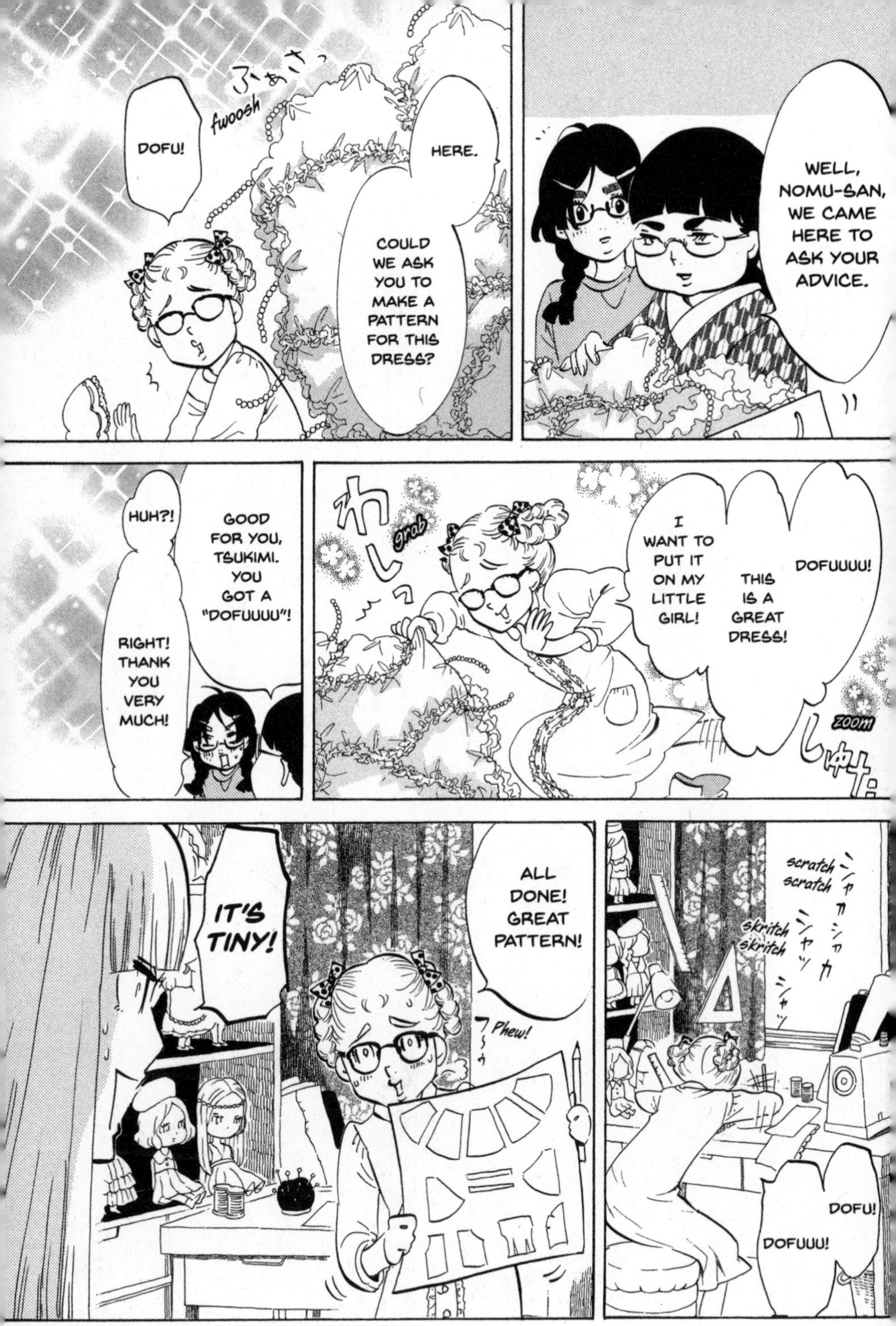
WELL, NOMU-SAN, WE CAME HERE TO ASK YOUR ADVICE.
HERE.
COULD WE ASK YOU TO MAKE A PATTERN FOR THIS DRESS?
fwoosh
DOFU!
DOFUUUU!
THIS IS A GREAT DRESS!
I WANT TO PUT IT ON MY LITTLE GIRL!
grab
zoom
GOOD FOR YOU, TSUKIMI. YOU GOT A "DOFUUUU"!
HUH?!
RIGHT! THANK YOU VERY MUCH!
scratch scratch
skritch skritch
DOFU!
DOFUUU!
ALL DONE! GREAT PATTERN!
Phew!
IT'S TINY!

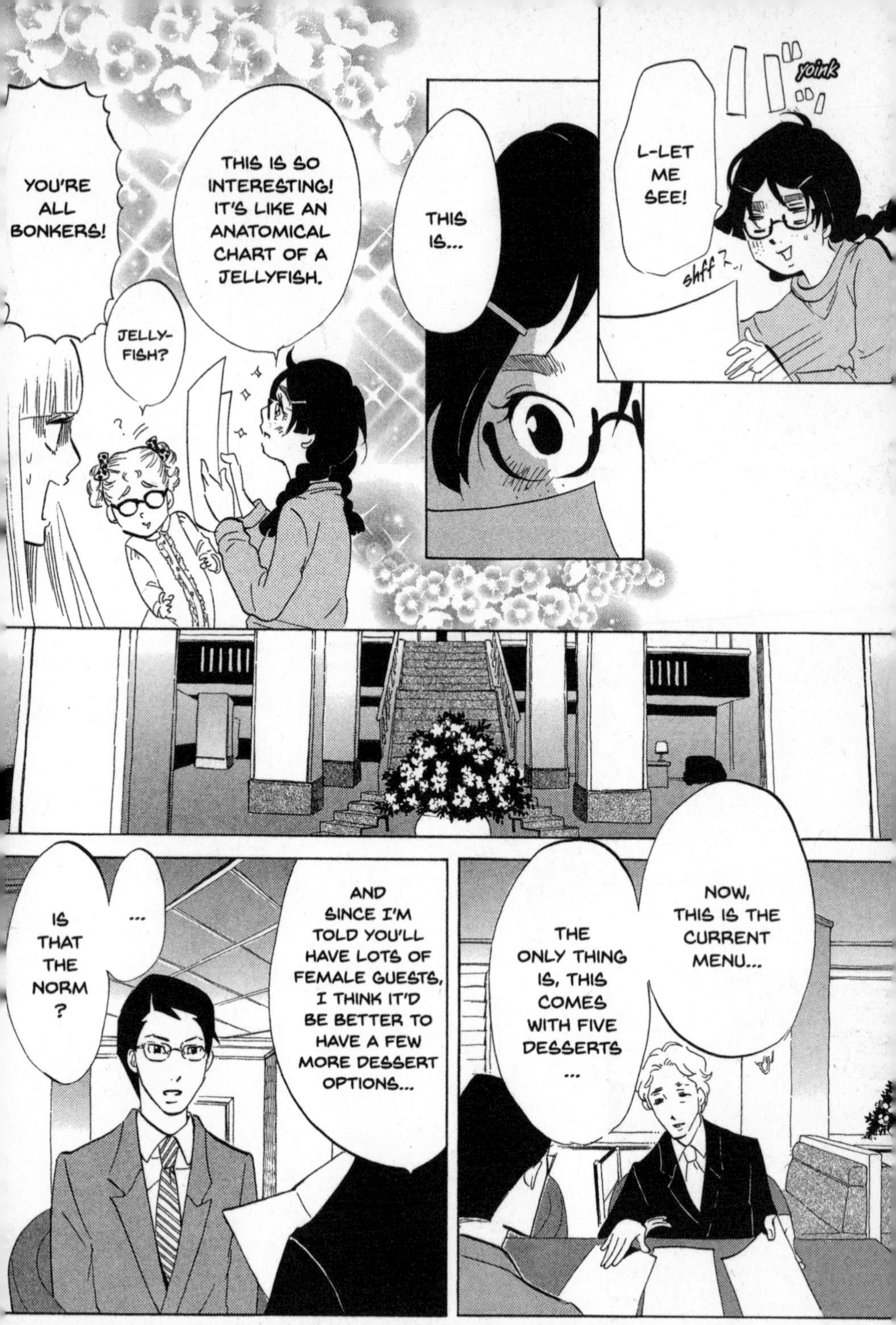
yoink
L-LET ME SEE!
shff
THIS IS...
THIS IS SO INTERESTING! IT'S LIKE AN ANATOMICAL CHART OF A JELLYFISH.
JELLY-FISH?
YOU'RE ALL BONKERS!
NOW, THIS IS THE CURRENT MENU...
THE ONLY THING IS, THIS COMES WITH FIVE DESSERTS...
AND SINCE I'M TOLD YOU'LL HAVE LOTS OF FEMALE GUESTS, I THINK IT'D BE BETTER TO HAVE A FEW MORE DESSERT OPTIONS...
...
IS THAT THE NORM?

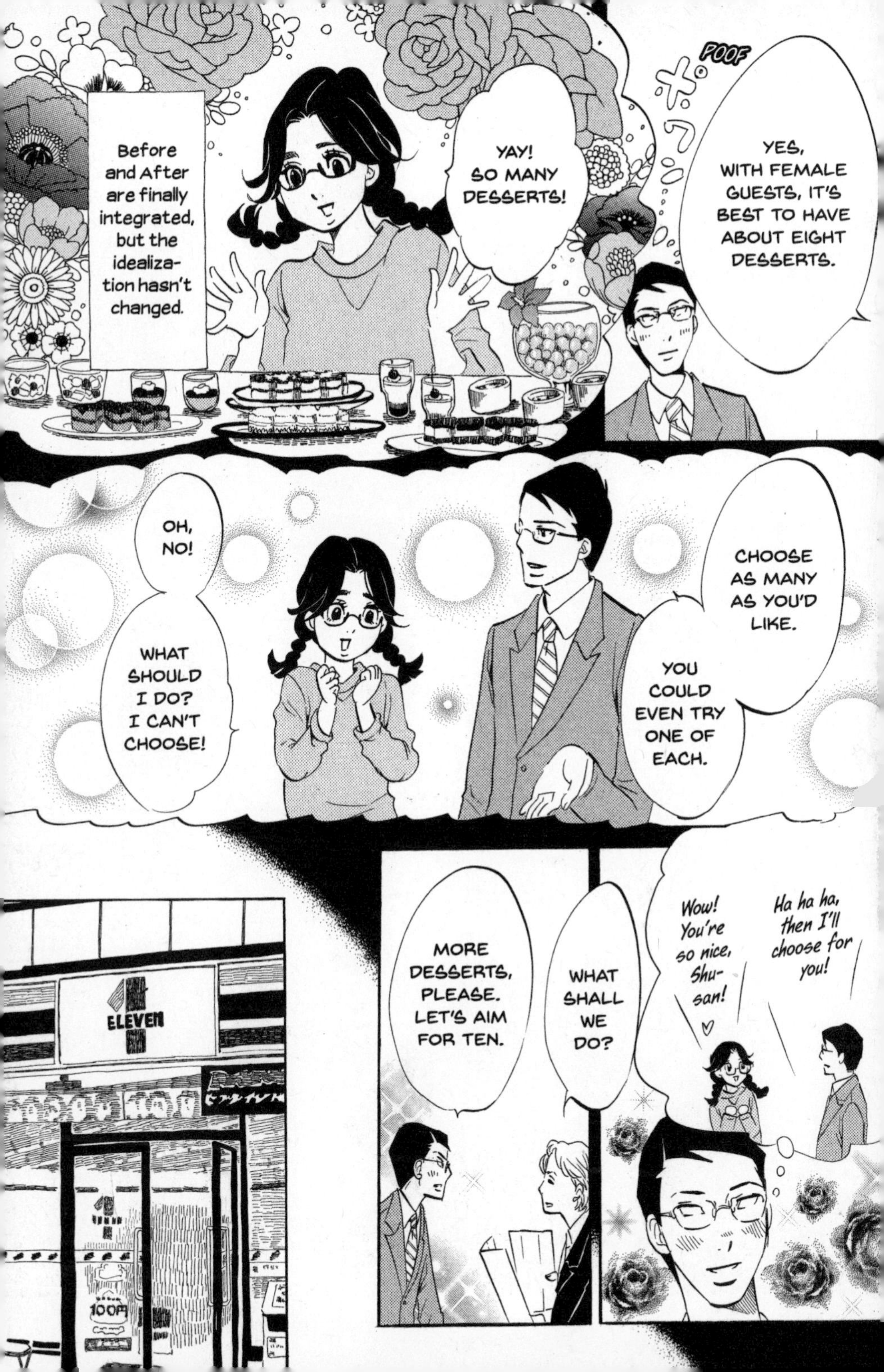
POOF
YES, WITH FEMALE GUESTS, IT'S BEST TO HAVE ABOUT EIGHT DESSERTS.
YAY! SO MANY DESSERTS!
Before and After are finally integrated, but the idealization hasn't changed.
CHOOSE AS MANY AS YOU'D LIKE.
YOU COULD EVEN TRY ONE OF EACH.
OH, NO!
WHAT SHOULD I DO? I CAN'T CHOOSE!
Ha ha ha, then I'll choose for you!
Wow! You're so nice, Shu-san!
WHAT SHALL WE DO?
MORE DESSERTS, PLEASE. LET'S AIM FOR TEN.
ELEVEN
100円

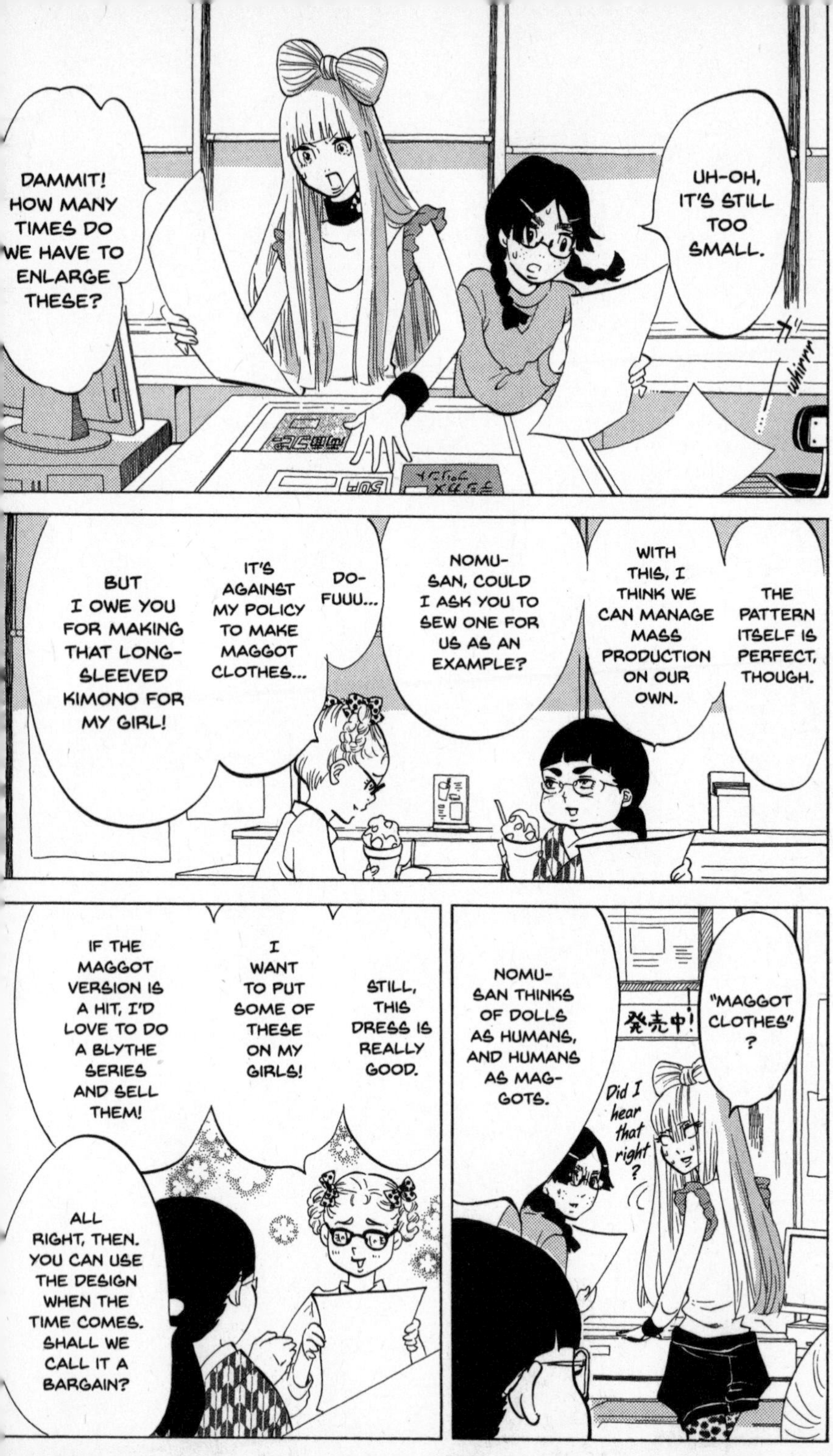
UH-OH, IT'S STILL TOO SMALL.
whirrr
DAMMIT! HOW MANY TIMES DO WE HAVE TO ENLARGE THESE?
THE PATTERN ITSELF IS PERFECT, THOUGH.
WITH THIS, I THINK WE CAN MANAGE MASS PRODUCTION ON OUR OWN.
NOMU-SAN, COULD I ASK YOU TO SEW ONE FOR US AS AN EXAMPLE?
DO-FUUU...
IT'S AGAINST MY POLICY TO MAKE MAGGOT CLOTHES...
BUT I OWE YOU FOR MAKING THAT LONG-SLEEVED KIMONO FOR MY GIRL!
"MAGGOT CLOTHES"?
発売中!
NOMU-SAN THINKS OF DOLLS AS HUMANS, AND HUMANS AS MAG-GOTS.
Did I hear that right?
STILL, THIS DRESS IS REALLY GOOD.
I WANT TO PUT SOME OF THESE ON MY GIRLS!
IF THE MAGGOT VERSION IS A HIT, I'D LOVE TO DO A BLYTHE SERIES AND SELL THEM!
ALL RIGHT, THEN. YOU CAN USE THE DESIGN WHEN THE TIME COMES. SHALL WE CALL IT A BARGAIN?

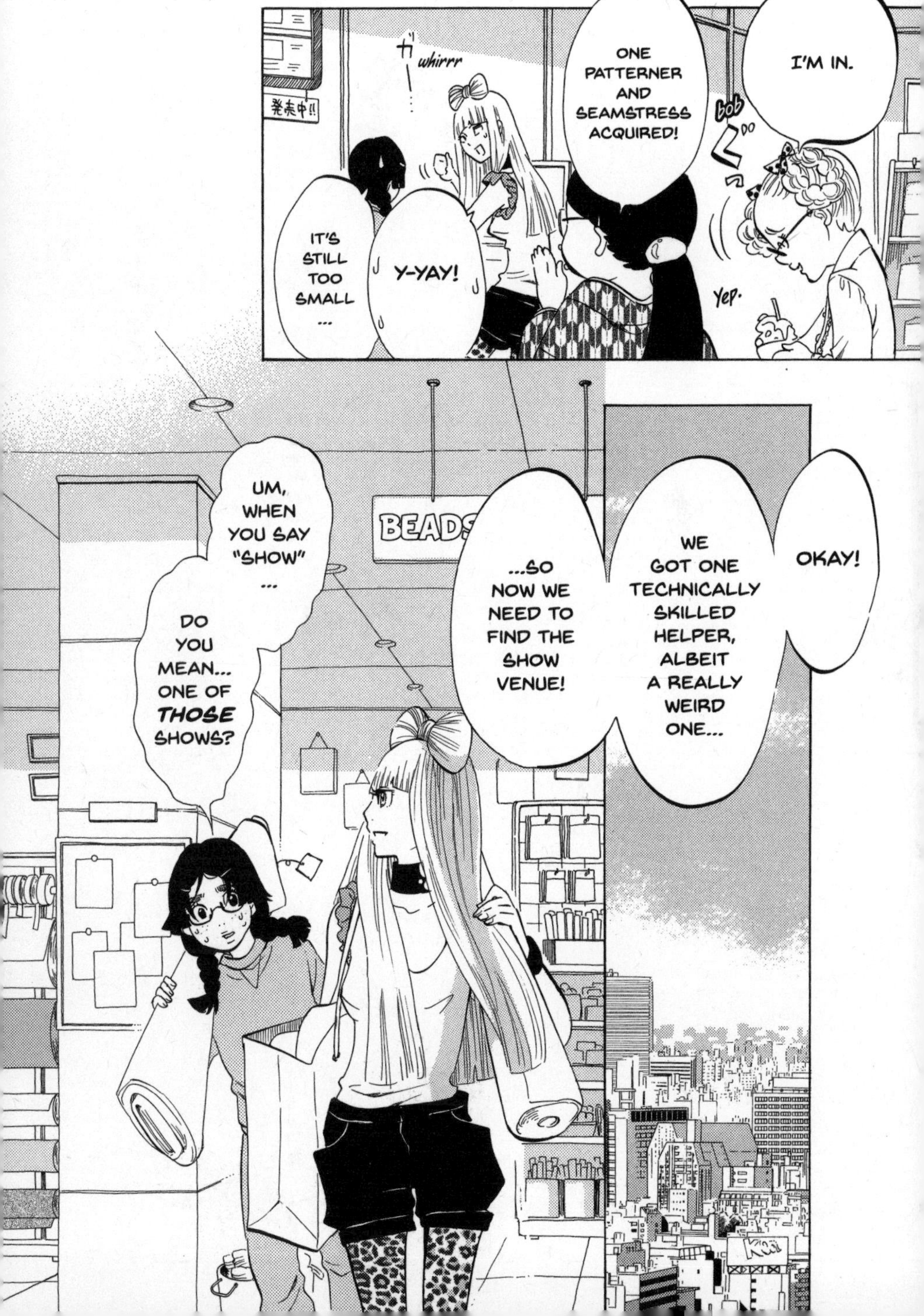
I'M IN.
bob
Yep.
ONE PATTERNER AND SEAMSTRESS ACQUIRED!
ガ whirrr
発表中!!
Y-YAY!
IT'S STILL TOO SMALL...
OKAY!
WE GOT ONE TECHNICALLY SKILLED HELPER, ALBEIT A REALLY WEIRD ONE...
...SO NOW WE NEED TO FIND THE SHOW VENUE!
BEADS
UM, WHEN YOU SAY "SHOW"...
DO YOU MEAN... ONE OF *THOSE* SHOWS?

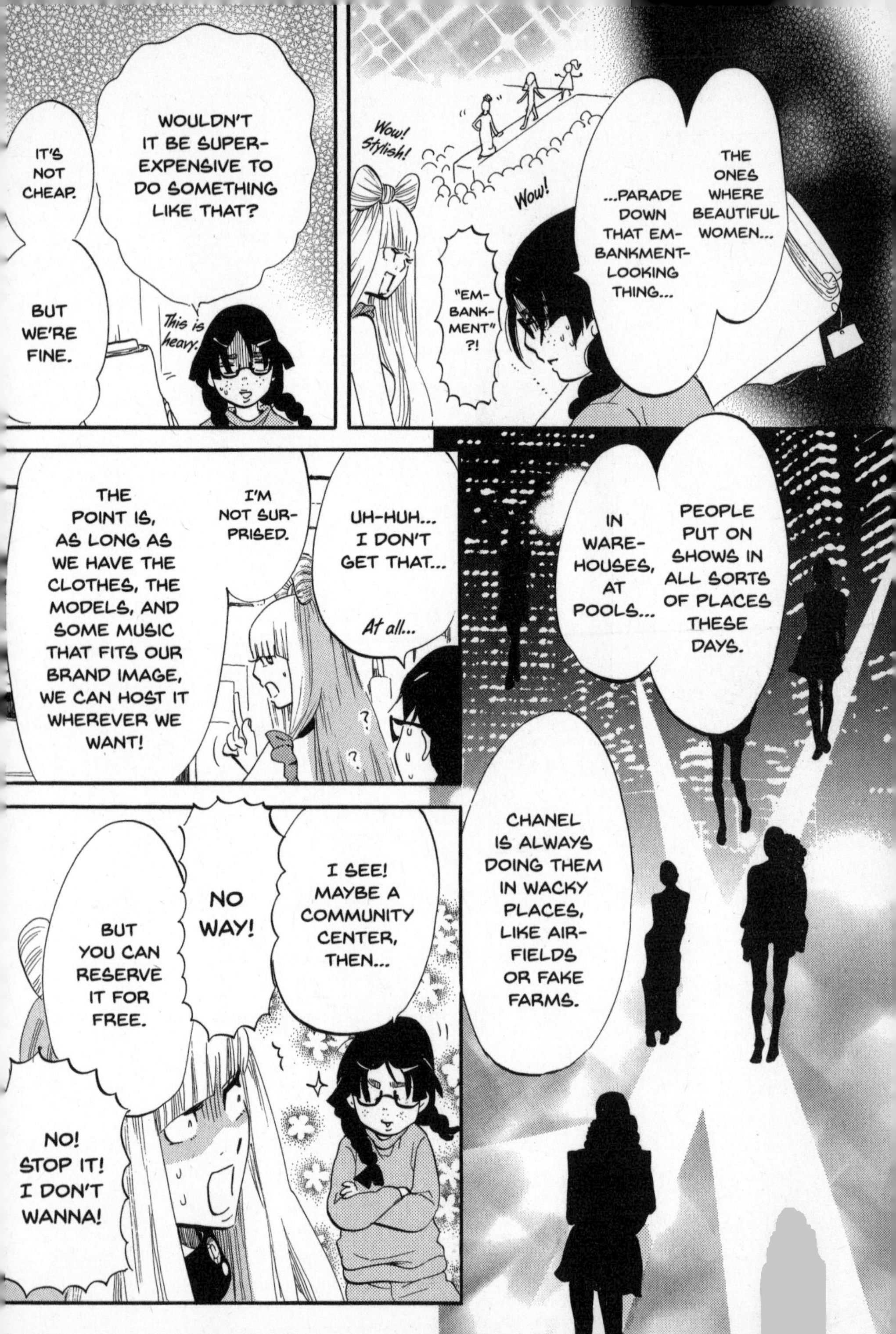
THE ONES WHERE BEAUTIFUL WOMEN...
...PARADE DOWN THAT EM-BANKMENT-LOOKING THING...
Wow!
Wow! Stylish!
"EM-BANKMENT"?!
WOULDN'T IT BE SUPER-EXPENSIVE TO DO SOMETHING LIKE THAT?
IT'S NOT CHEAP.
This is heavy.
BUT WE'RE FINE.
PEOPLE PUT ON SHOWS IN ALL SORTS OF PLACES THESE DAYS.
IN WARE-HOUSES, AT POOLS...
CHANEL IS ALWAYS DOING THEM IN WACKY PLACES, LIKE AIR-FIELDS OR FAKE FARMS.
UH-HUH... I DON'T GET THAT...
At all...
I'M NOT SUR-PRISED.
THE POINT IS, AS LONG AS WE HAVE THE CLOTHES, THE MODELS, AND SOME MUSIC THAT FITS OUR BRAND IMAGE, WE CAN HOST IT WHEREVER WE WANT!
I SEE! MAYBE A COMMUNITY CENTER, THEN...
NO WAY!
BUT YOU CAN RESERVE IT FOR FREE.
NO! STOP IT! I DON'T WANNA!

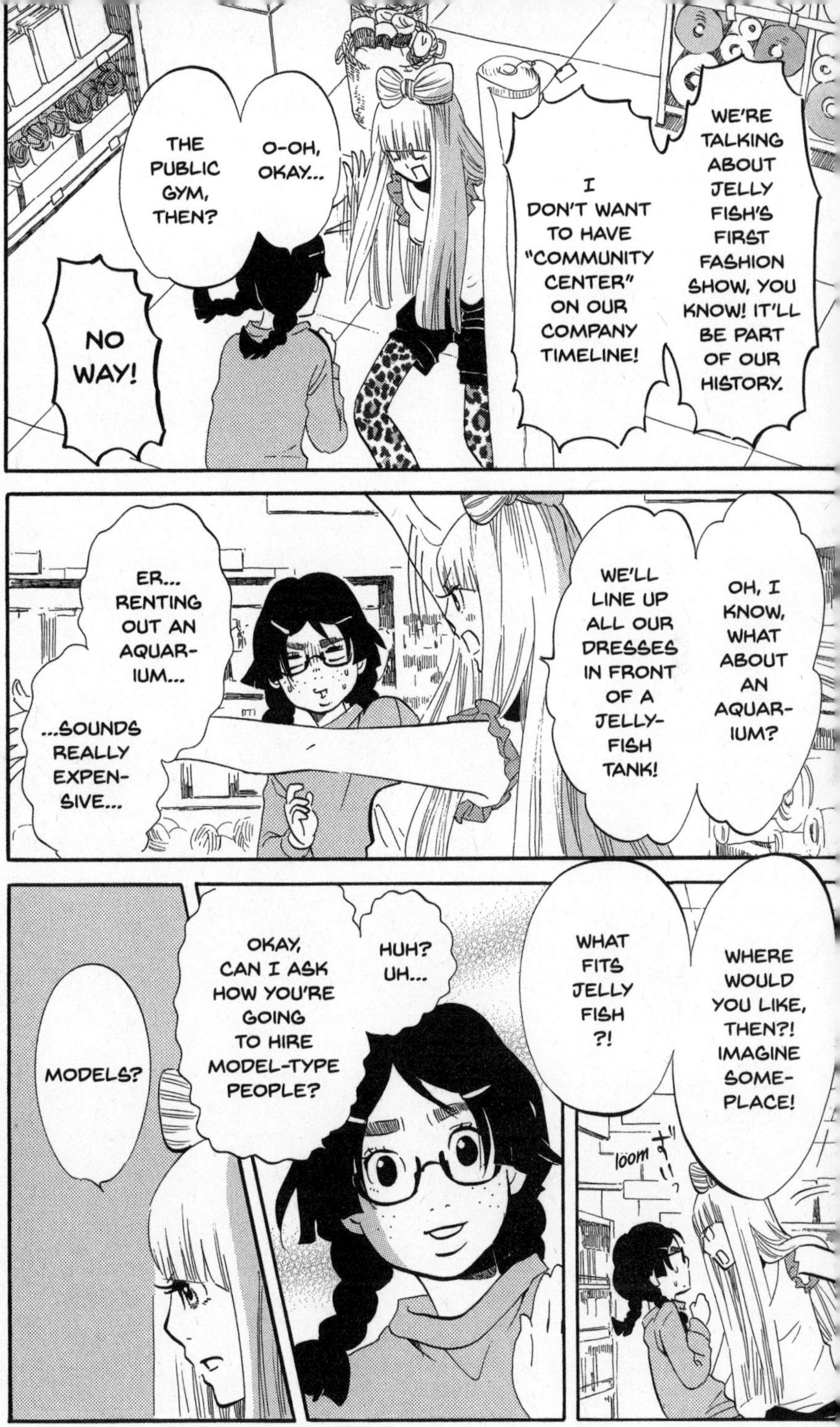
WE'RE TALKING ABOUT JELLY FISH'S FIRST FASHION SHOW, YOU KNOW! IT'LL BE PART OF OUR HISTORY.
I DON'T WANT TO HAVE "COMMUNITY CENTER" ON OUR COMPANY TIMELINE!
O-OH, OKAY...
THE PUBLIC GYM, THEN?
NO WAY!
OH, I KNOW, WHAT ABOUT AN AQUARIUM?
WE'LL LINE UP ALL OUR DRESSES IN FRONT OF A JELLYFISH TANK!
ER... RENTING OUT AN AQUARIUM...
...SOUNDS REALLY EXPENSIVE...
WHERE WOULD YOU LIKE, THEN?! IMAGINE SOMEPLACE!
WHAT FITS JELLY FISH?!
loom
HUH? UH...
OKAY, CAN I ASK HOW YOU'RE GOING TO HIRE MODEL-TYPE PEOPLE?
MODELS?

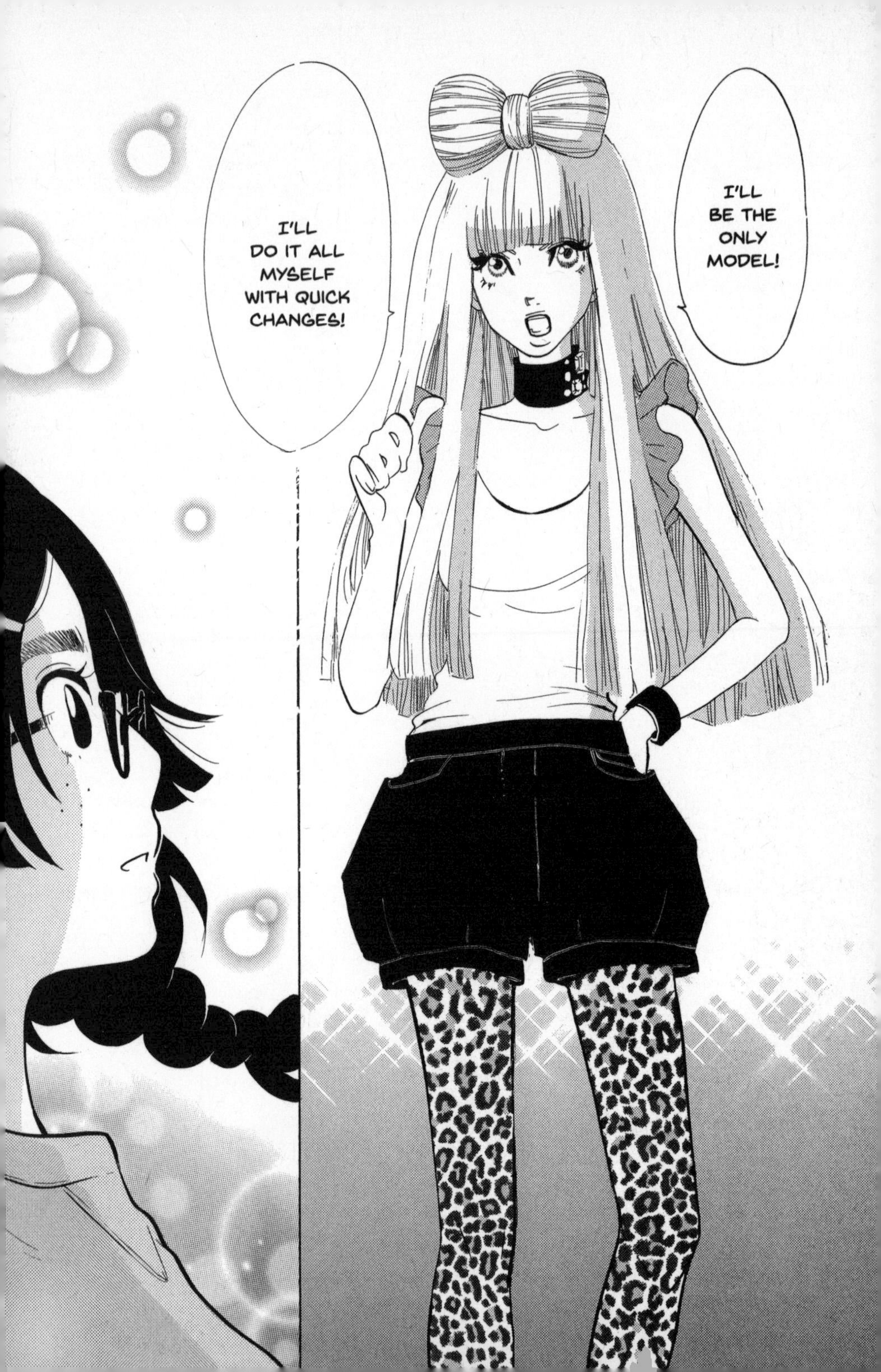
I'LL BE THE ONLY MODEL!
I'LL DO IT ALL MYSELF WITH QUICK CHANGES!

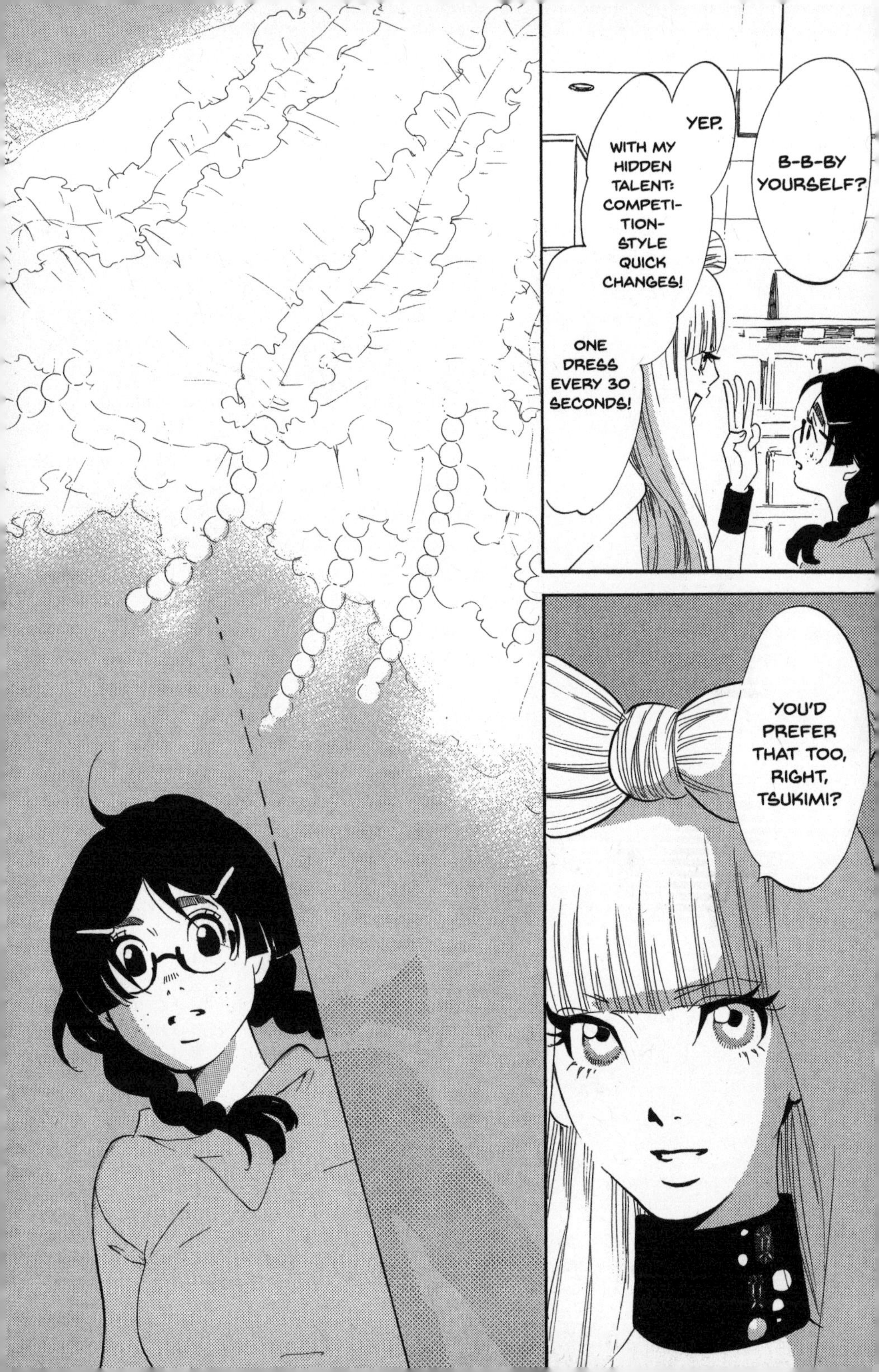
B-B-BY YOURSELF?
YEP.
WITH MY HIDDEN TALENT: COMPETITION-STYLE QUICK CHANGES!
ONE DRESS EVERY 30 SECONDS!
YOU'D PREFER THAT TOO, RIGHT, TSUKIMI?

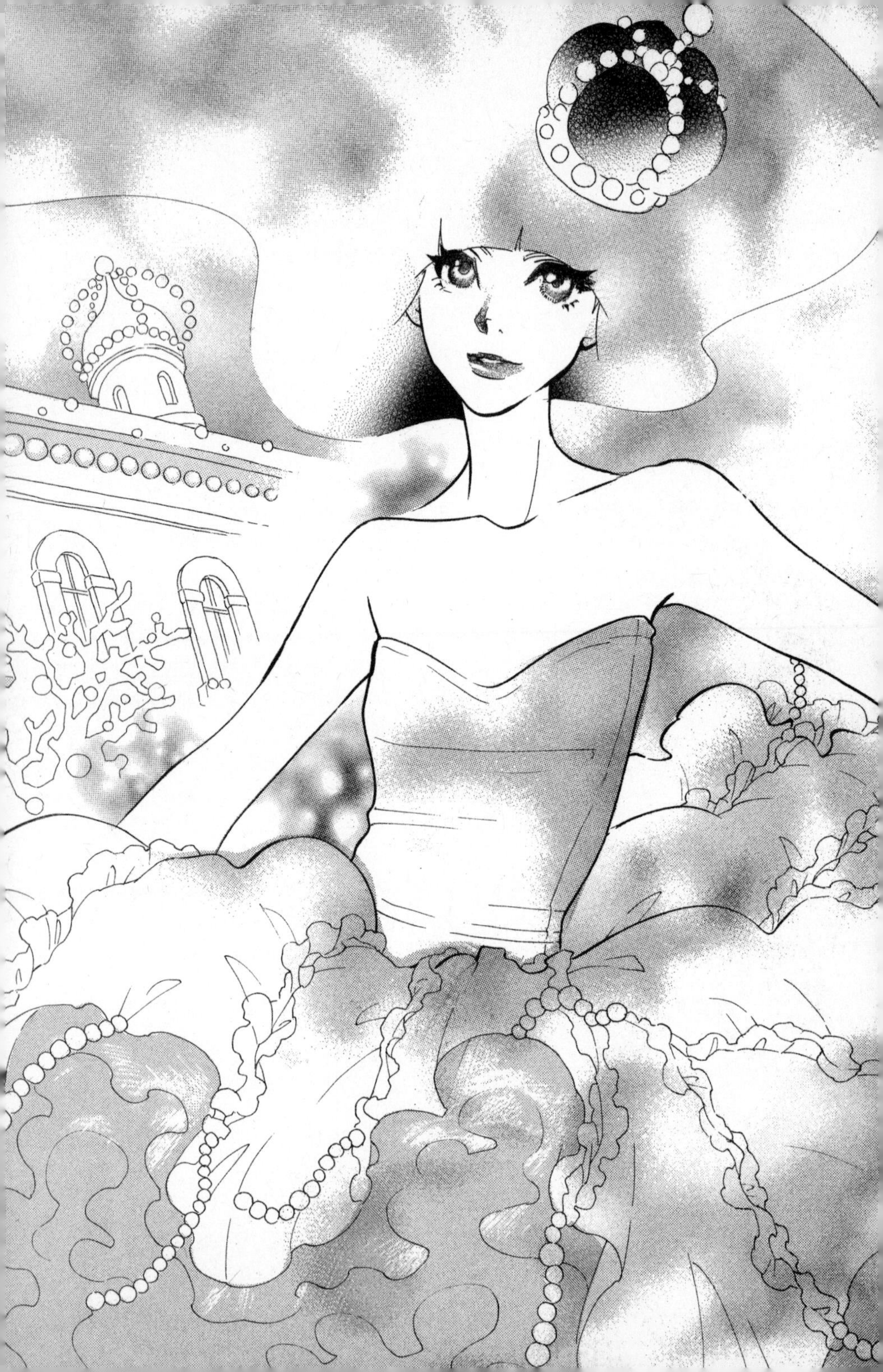

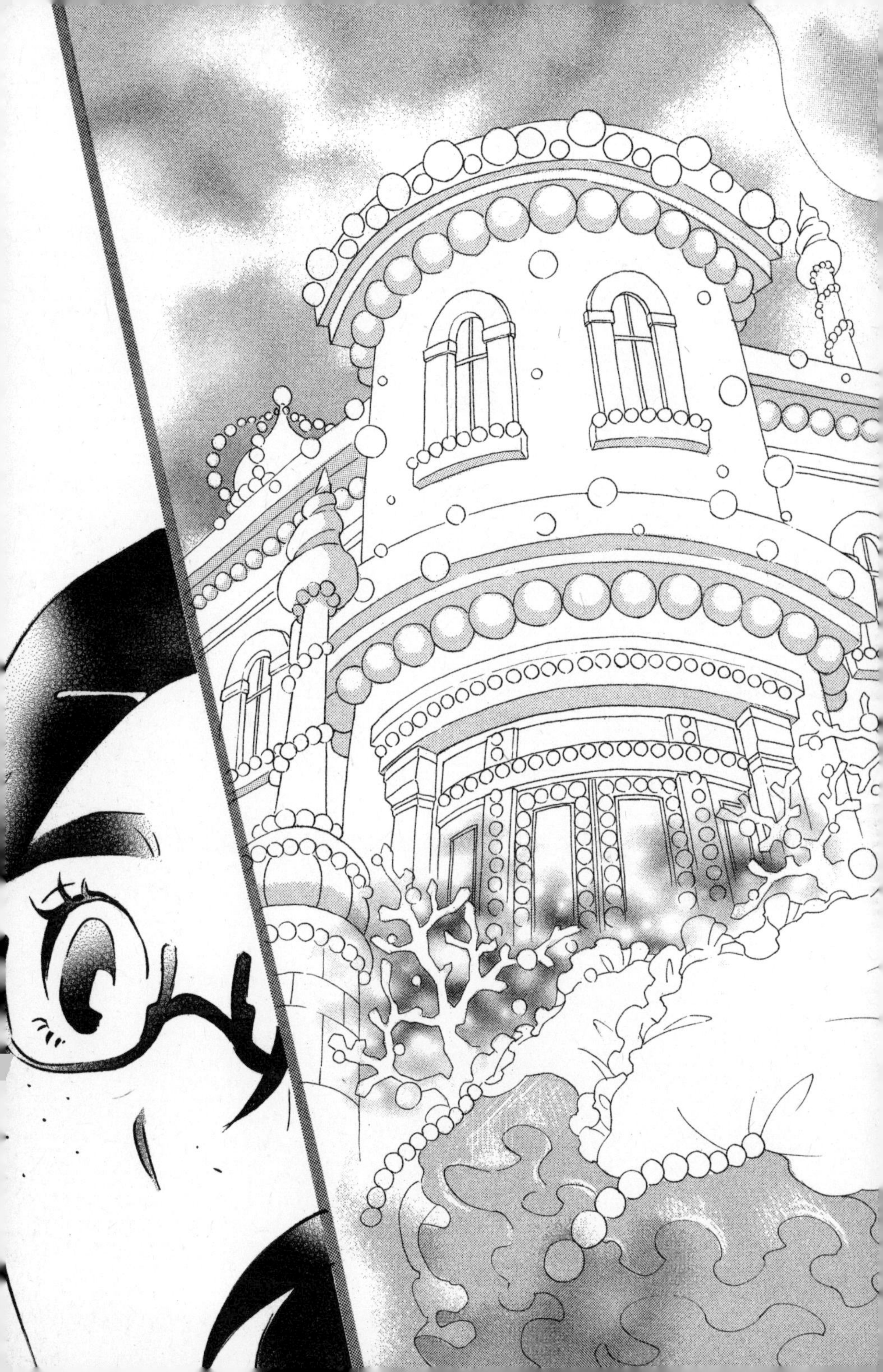

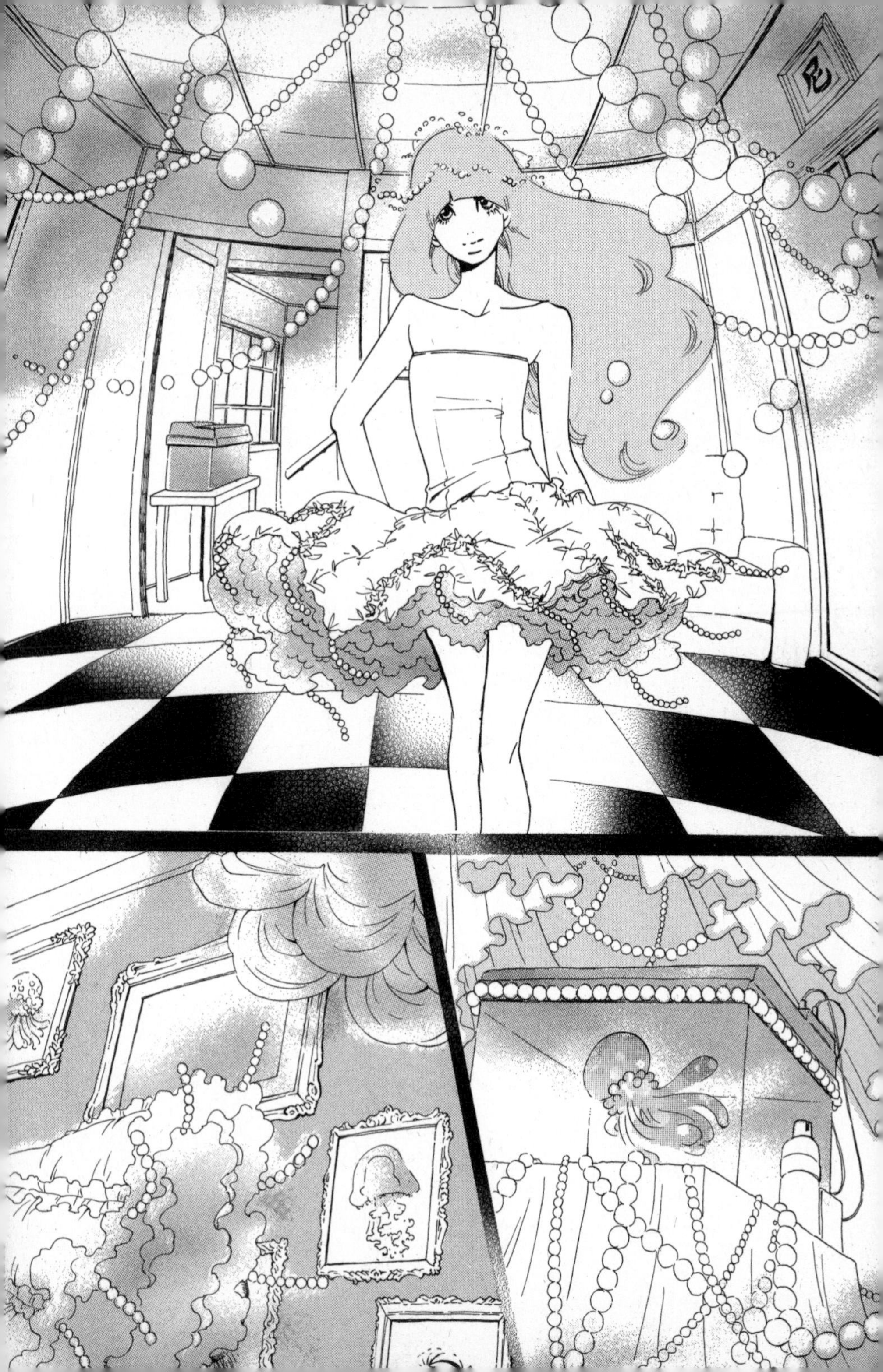
尼

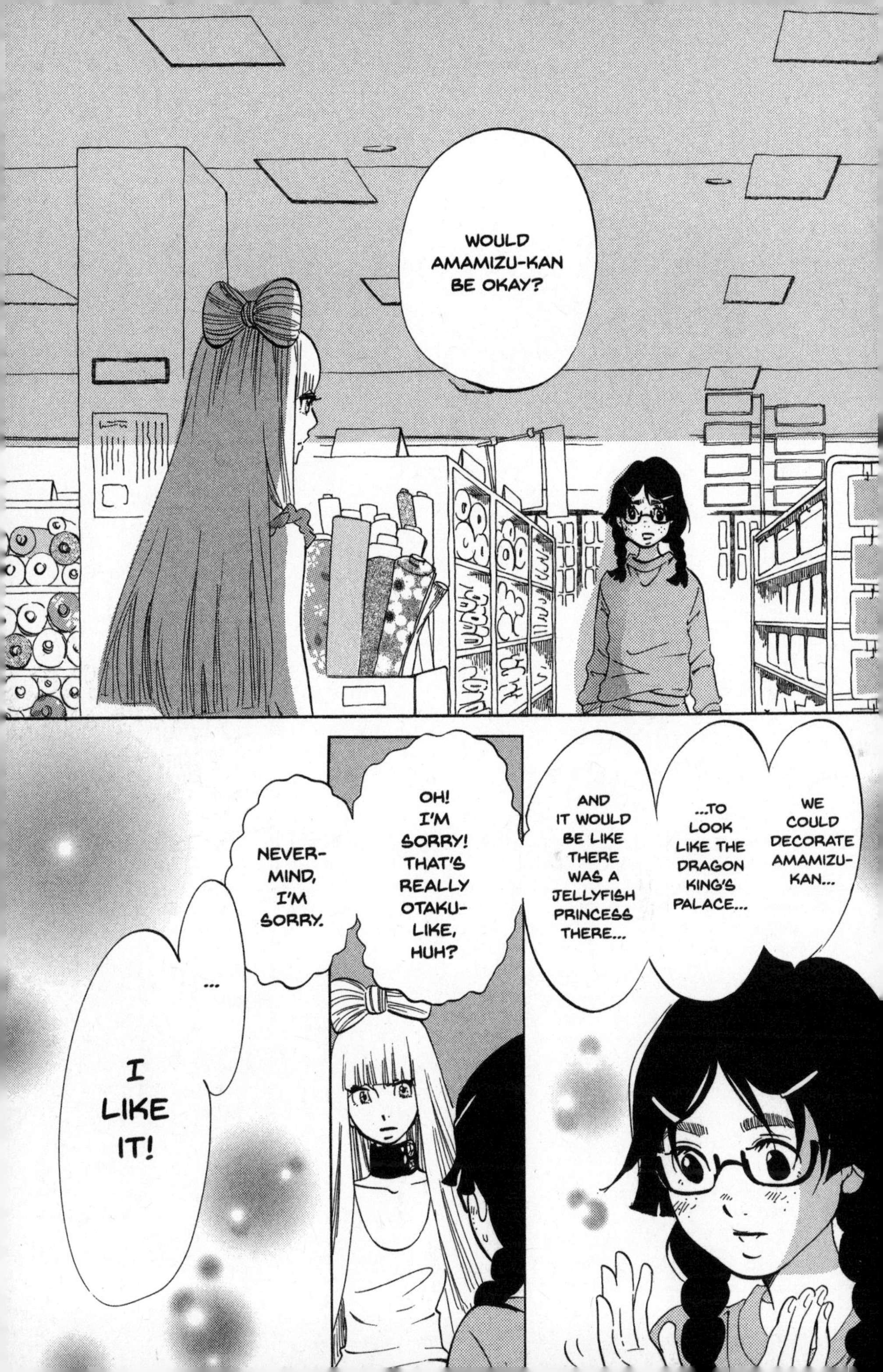
WOULD AMAMIZU-KAN BE OKAY?
WE COULD DECORATE AMAMIZU-KAN...
...TO LOOK LIKE THE DRAGON KING'S PALACE...
AND IT WOULD BE LIKE THERE WAS A JELLYFISH PRINCESS THERE...
OH! I'M SORRY! THAT'S REALLY OTAKU-LIKE, HUH?
NEVER-MIND, I'M SORRY.
...
I LIKE IT!

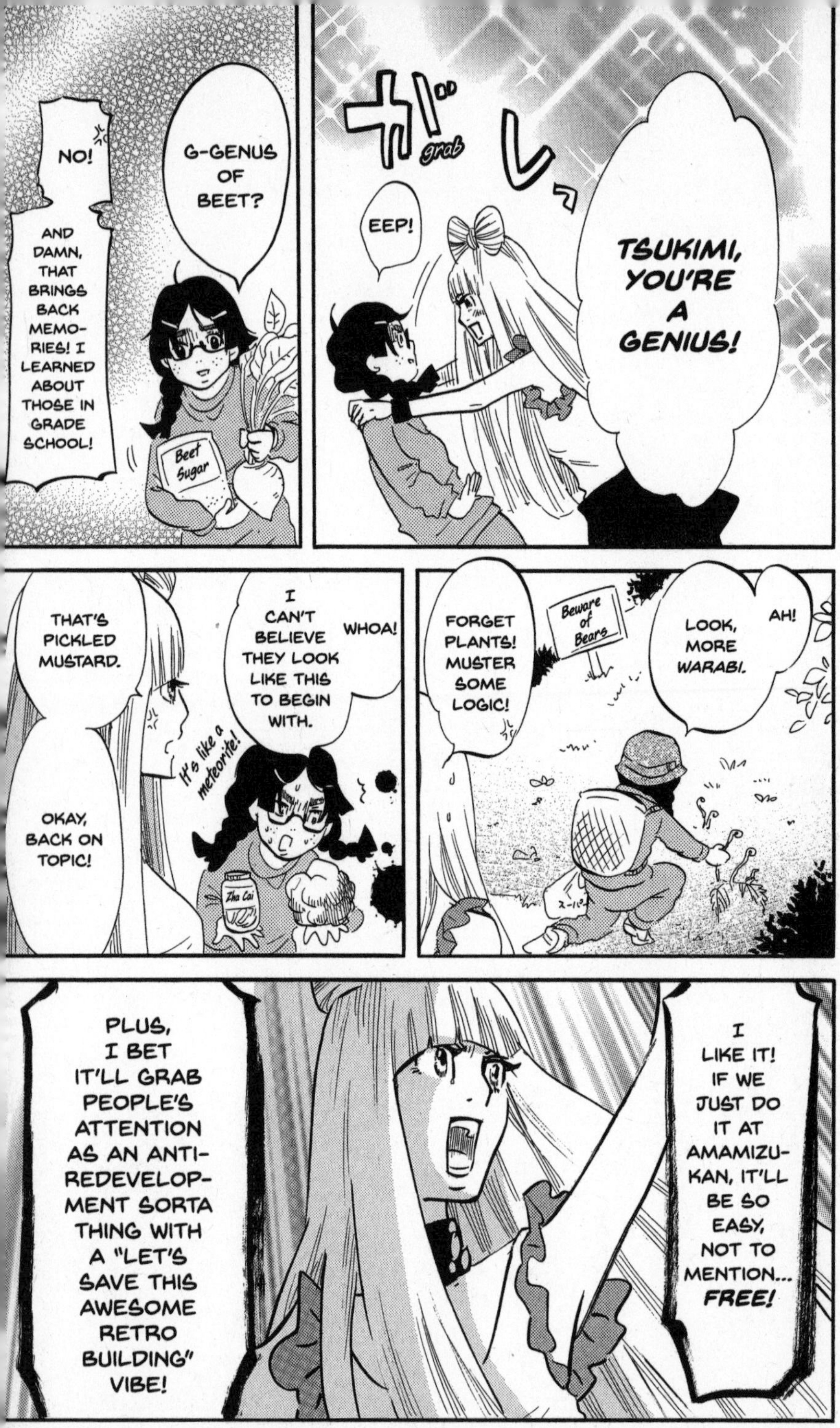
TSUKIMI, YOU'RE A GENIUS!
grab
EEP!
G-GENUS OF BEET?
NO!
AND DAMN, THAT BRINGS BACK MEMO-RIES! I LEARNED ABOUT THOSE IN GRADE SCHOOL!
Beet Sugar
AH!
LOOK, MORE WARABI.
Beware of Bears
FORGET PLANTS! MUSTER SOME LOGIC!
WHOA!
I CAN'T BELIEVE THEY LOOK LIKE THIS TO BEGIN WITH.
It's like a meteorite!
THAT'S PICKLED MUSTARD.
OKAY, BACK ON TOPIC!
Zha Cai
I LIKE IT! IF WE JUST DO IT AT AMAMIZU-KAN, IT'LL BE SO EASY, NOT TO MENTION... FREE!
PLUS, I BET IT'LL GRAB PEOPLE'S ATTENTION AS AN ANTI-REDEVELOP-MENT SORTA THING WITH A "LET'S SAVE THIS AWESOME RETRO BUILDING" VIBE!

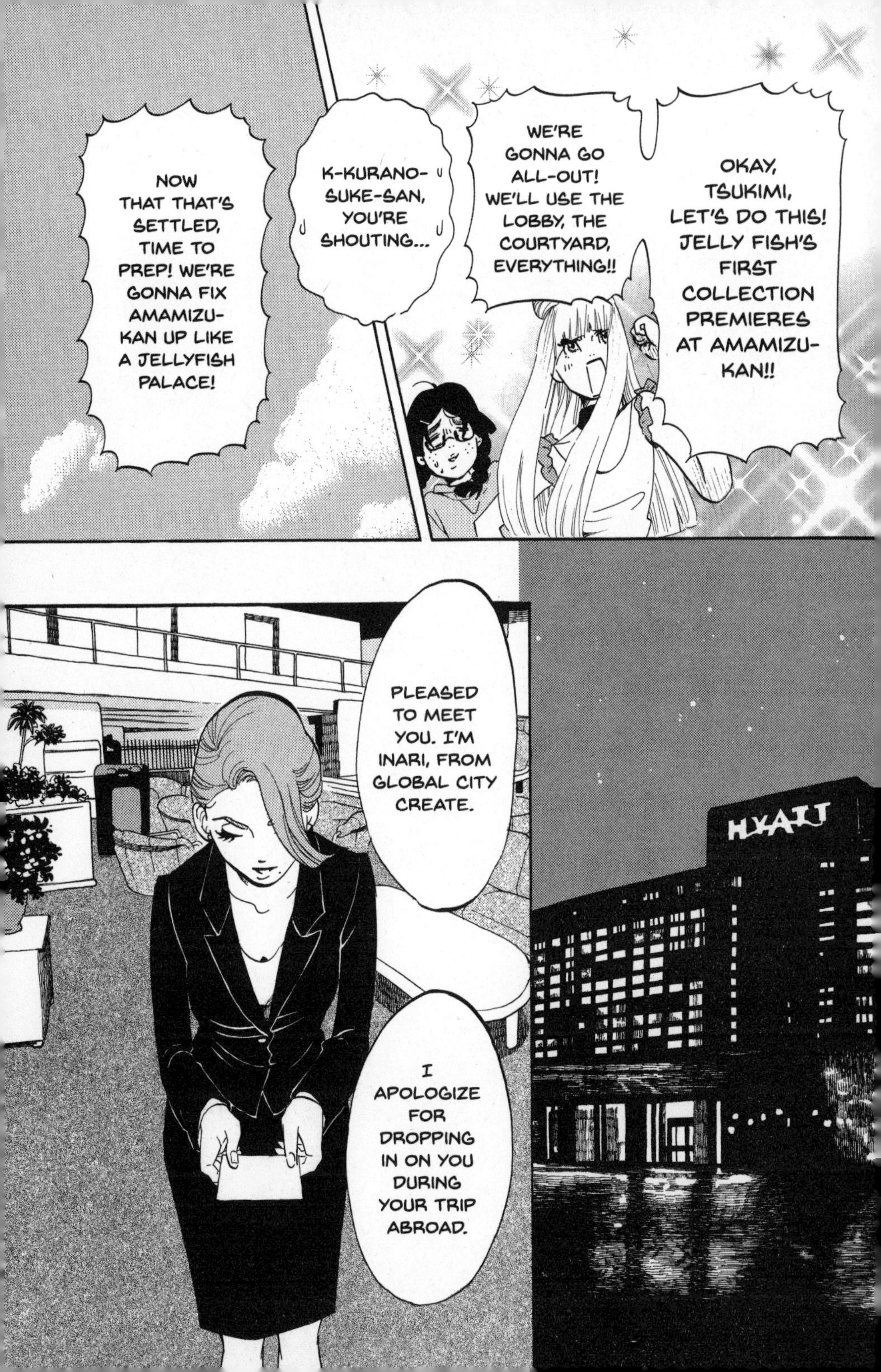
OKAY, TSUKIMI, LET'S DO THIS! JELLY FISH'S FIRST COLLECTION PREMIERES AT AMAMIZU-KAN!!
WE'RE GONNA GO ALL-OUT! WE'LL USE THE LOBBY, THE COURTYARD, EVERYTHING!!
K-KURANO-SUKE-SAN, YOU'RE SHOUTING...
NOW THAT THAT'S SETTLED, TIME TO PREP! WE'RE GONNA FIX AMAMIZU-KAN UP LIKE A JELLYFISH PALACE!
HYATT
PLEASED TO MEET YOU. I'M INARI, FROM GLOBAL CITY CREATE.
I APOLOGIZE FOR DROPPING IN ON YOU DURING YOUR TRIP ABROAD.

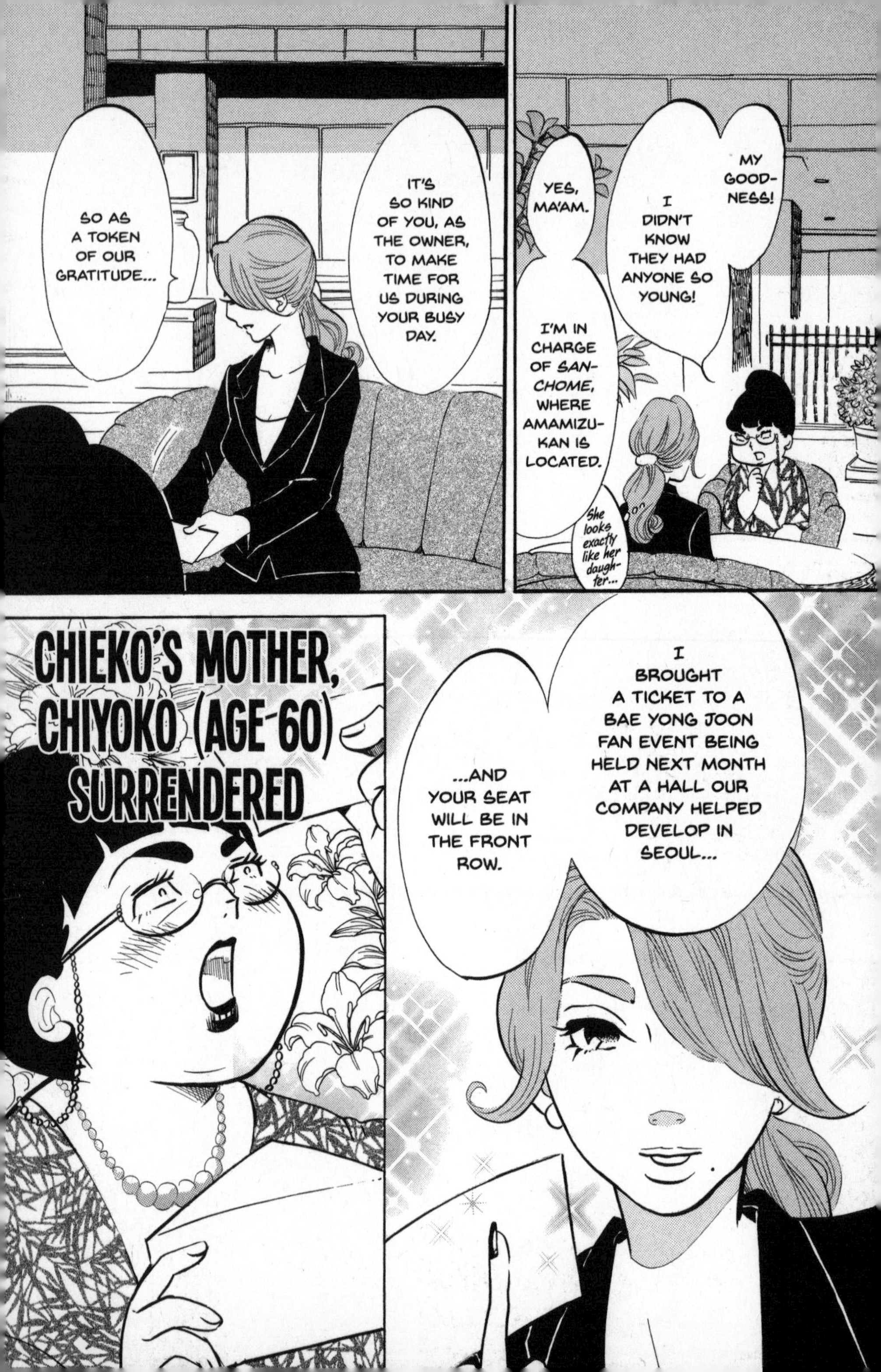

MY GOODNESS! I DIDN'T KNOW THEY HAD ANYONE SO YOUNG!
YES, MA'AM.
I'M IN CHARGE OF SAN-CHOME, WHERE AMAMIZU-KAN IS LOCATED.
She looks exactly like her daugh-ter...
IT'S SO KIND OF YOU, AS THE OWNER, TO MAKE TIME FOR US DURING YOUR BUSY DAY.
SO AS A TOKEN OF OUR GRATITUDE...
I BROUGHT A TICKET TO A BAE YONG JOON FAN EVENT BEING HELD NEXT MONTH AT A HALL OUR COMPANY HELPED DEVELOP IN SEOUL...
...AND YOUR SEAT WILL BE IN THE FRONT ROW.
CHIEKO'S MOTHER, CHIYOKO (AGE 60) SURRENDERED

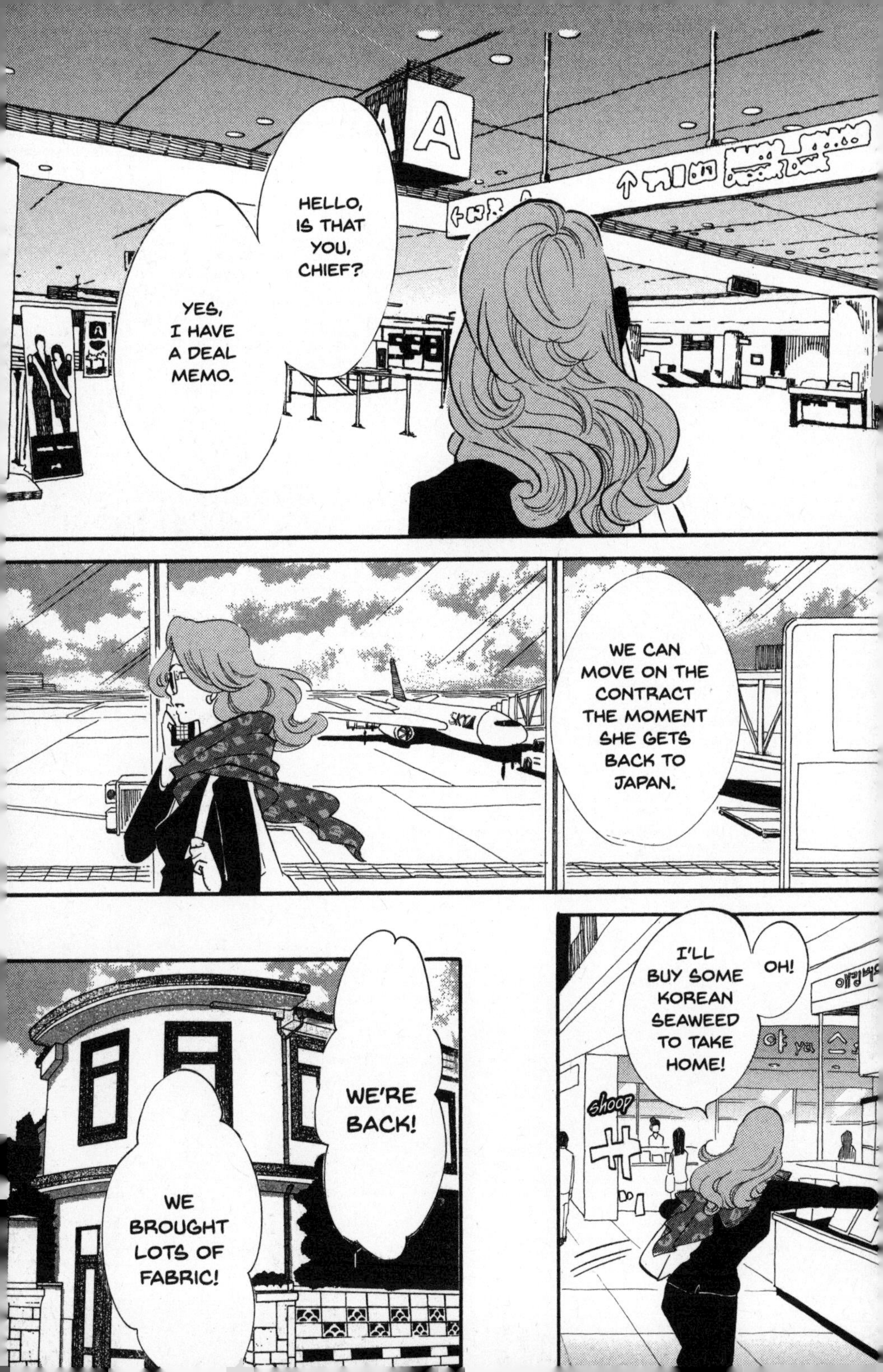
HELLO, IS THAT YOU, CHIEF?
YES, I HAVE A DEAL MEMO.
WE CAN MOVE ON THE CONTRACT THE MOMENT SHE GETS BACK TO JAPAN.
OH!
I'LL BUY SOME KOREAN SEAWEED TO TAKE HOME!
shoop
WE'RE BACK!
WE BROUGHT LOTS OF FABRIC!

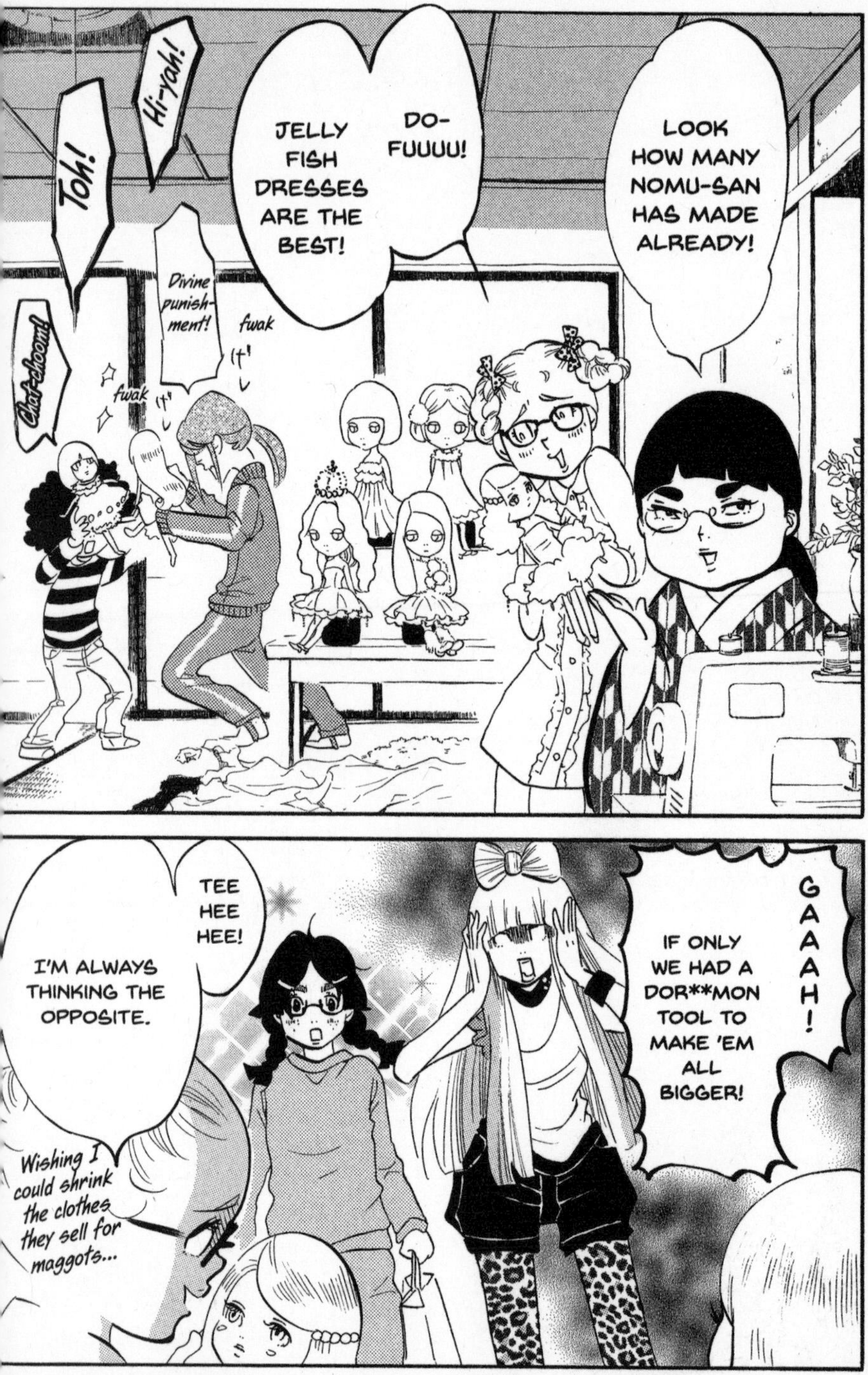
LOOK HOW MANY NOMU-SAN HAS MADE ALREADY!
DO-FUUUU!
JELLY FISH DRESSES ARE THE BEST!
Hi-yah!
Toh!
Divine punishment!
fwak
fwak
Chat-choom!
GAAAH!
IF ONLY WE HAD A DOR**MON TOOL TO MAKE 'EM ALL BIGGER!
TEE HEE HEE!
I'M ALWAYS THINKING THE OPPOSITE.
Wishing I could shrink the clothes they sell for maggots...

もじ fidget
もじ fidget
もじ……ン

Episode 32

Amars: Countdown to Destruction

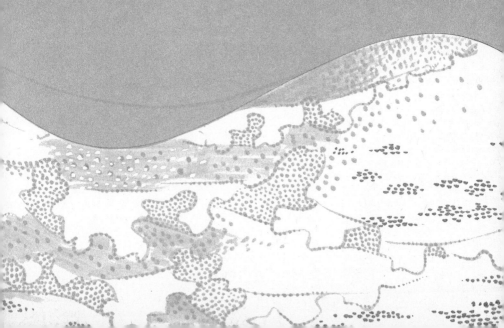

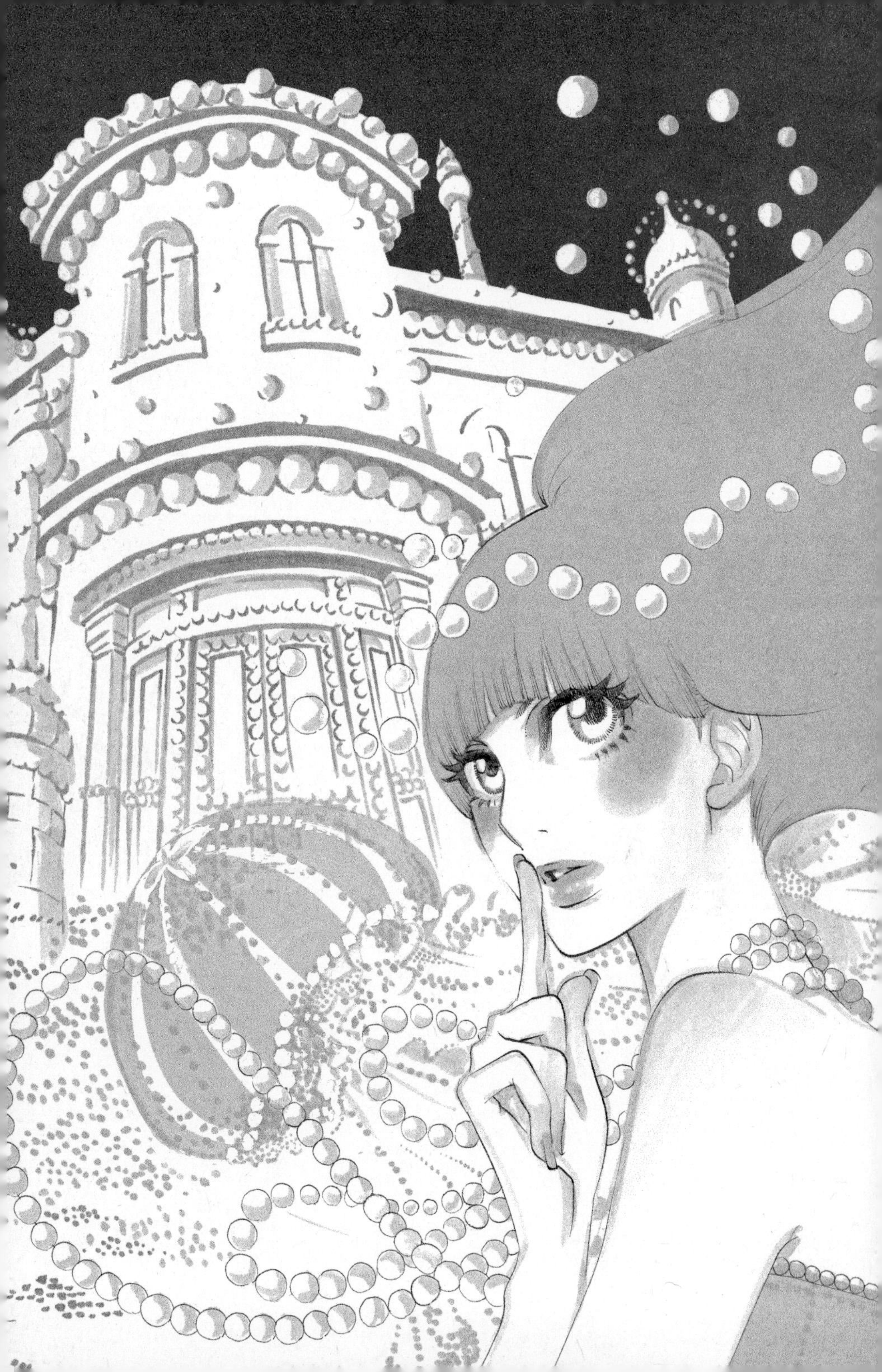

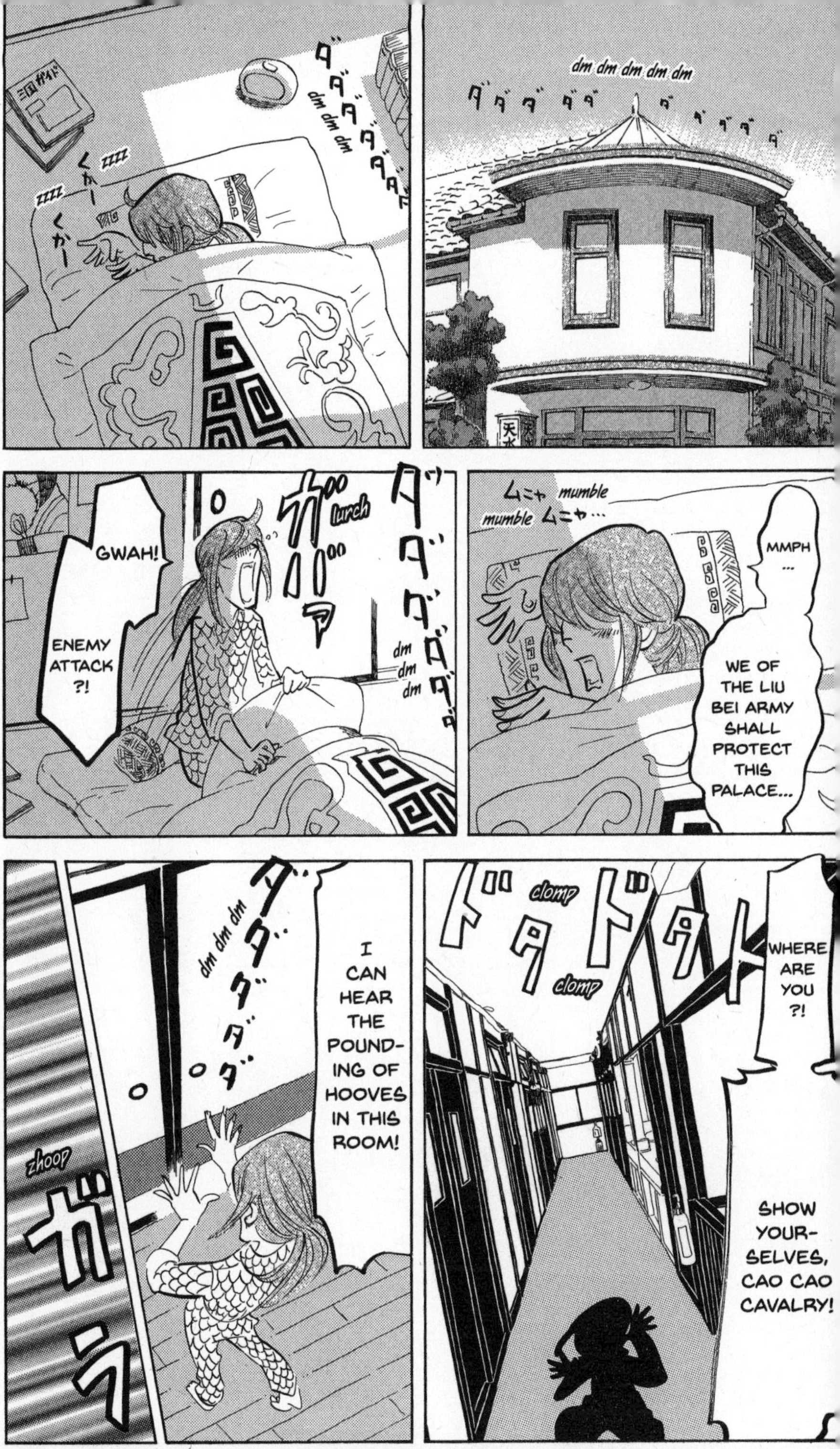

dm dm dm dm dm
dm dm dm
zzzz
zzzz
mumble
mumble
MMPH...
WE OF THE LIU BEI ARMY SHALL PROTECT THIS PALACE...
lurch
GWAH!
ENEMY ATTACK?!
dm dm dm
clomp
clomp
WHERE ARE YOU?!
SHOW YOURSELVES, CAO CAO CAVALRY!
dm dm dm
I CAN HEAR THE POUNDING OF HOOVES IN THIS ROOM!
zhoop

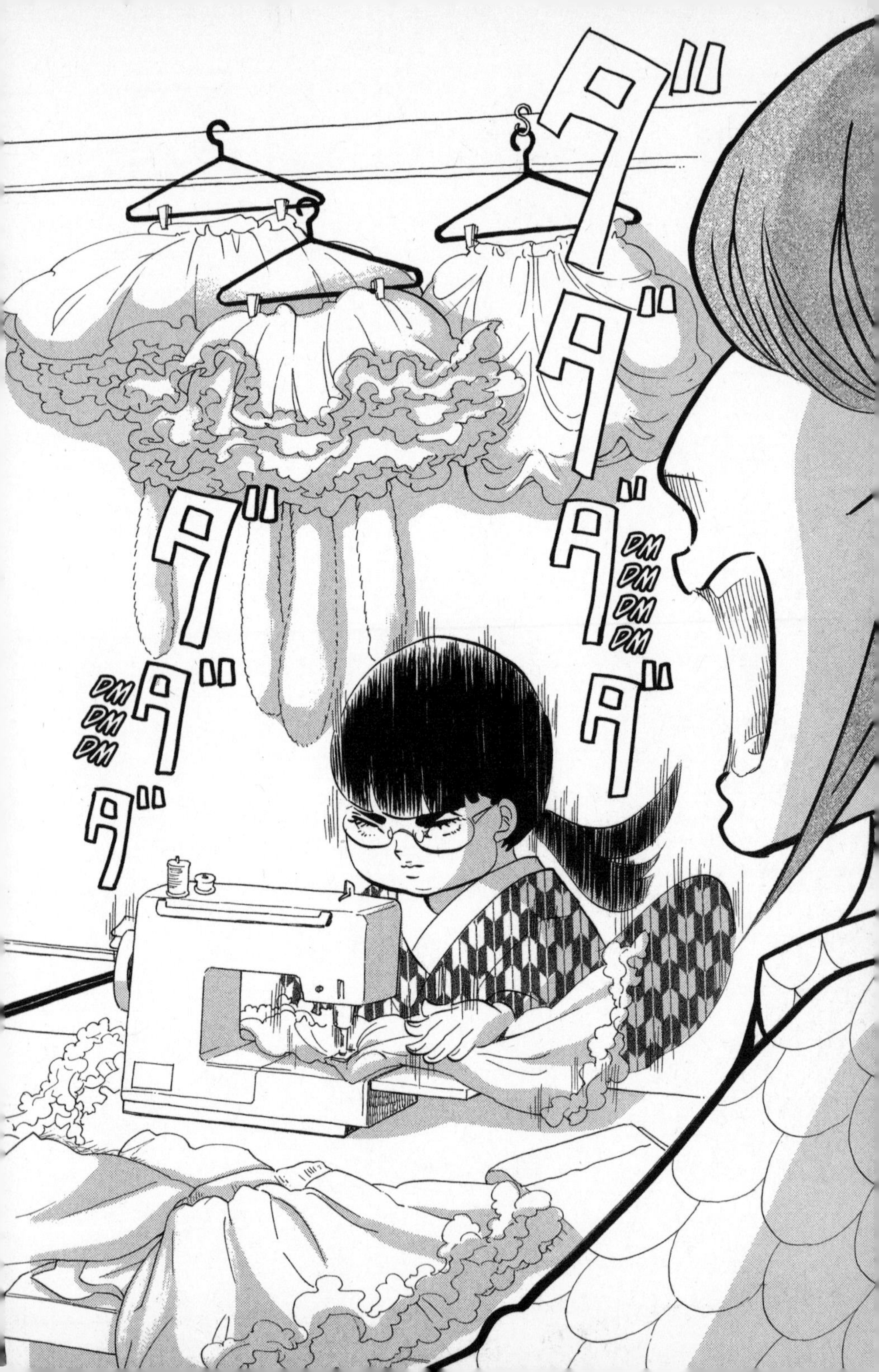
ダダダダ
DM
DM
DM
DM
ダダダ
DM
DM
DM

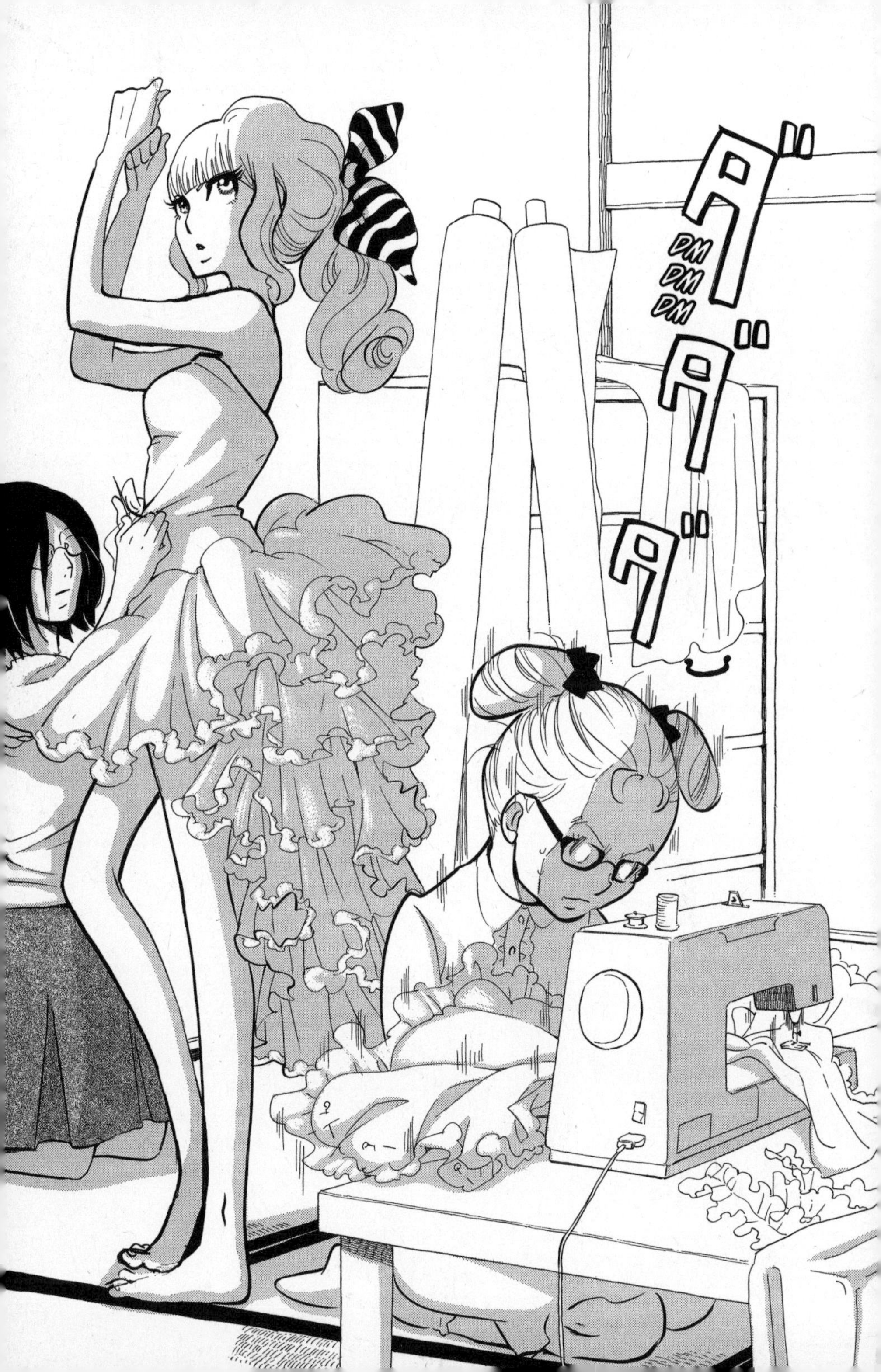
ダダダ
DM
DM
DM

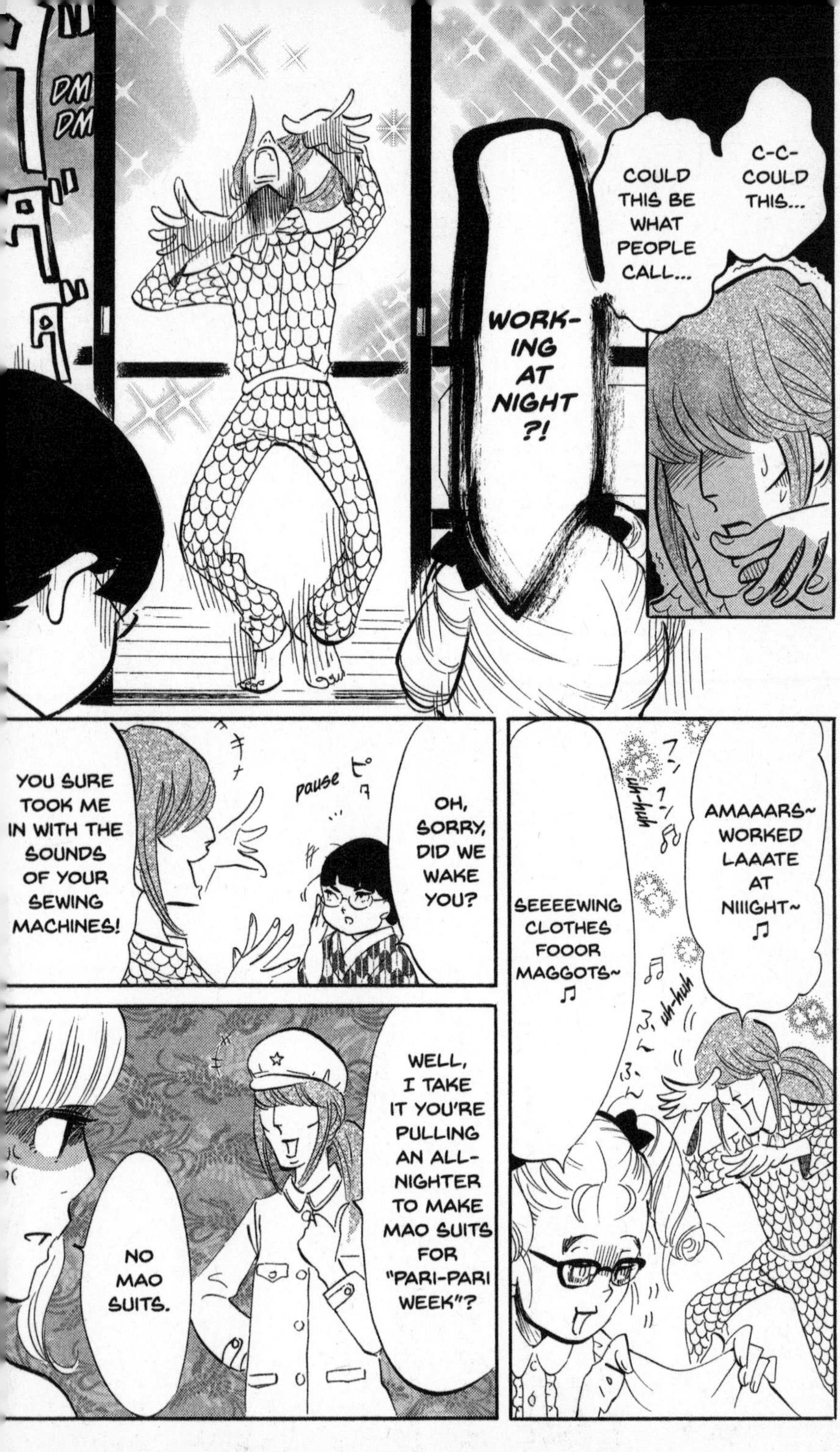
C-C-COULD THIS...
COULD THIS BE WHAT PEOPLE CALL...
WORKING AT NIGHT?!
DM DM
AMAAARS~ WORKED LAAATE AT NIIIGHT~ ♫
uh-huh
SEEEEWING CLOTHES FOOOR MAGGOTS~ ♫
uh-huh
OH, SORRY, DID WE WAKE YOU?
pause
YOU SURE TOOK ME IN WITH THE SOUNDS OF YOUR SEWING MACHINES!
WELL, I TAKE IT YOU'RE PULLING AN ALL-NIGHTER TO MAKE MAO SUITS FOR "PARI-PARI WEEK"?
NO MAO SUITS.

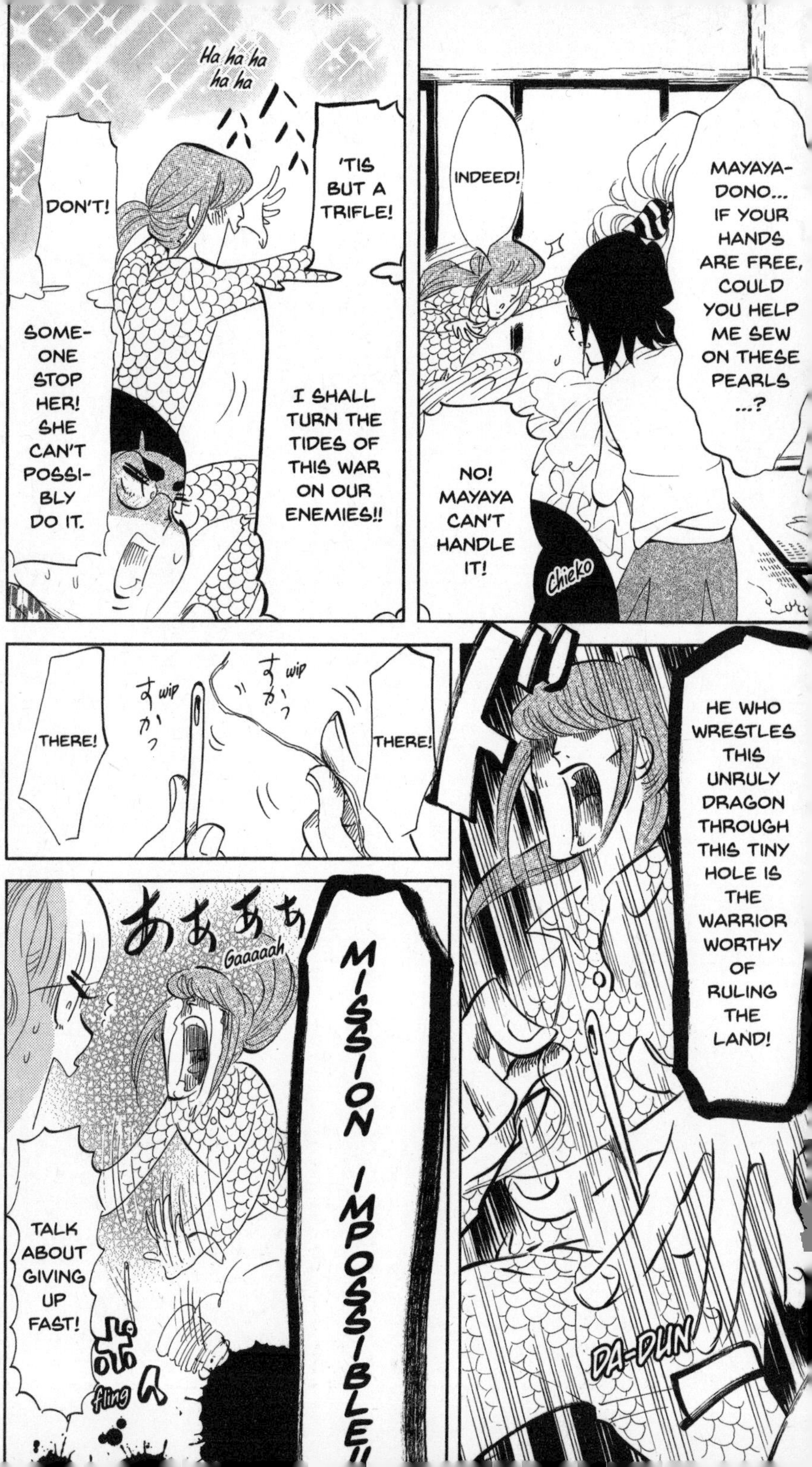
MAYAYA-DONO... IF YOUR HANDS ARE FREE, COULD YOU HELP ME SEW ON THESE PEARLS ...?
INDEED!
NO! MAYAYA CAN'T HANDLE IT!
Chieko
Ha ha ha ha ha
'TIS BUT A TRIFLE!
DON'T!
I SHALL TURN THE TIDES OF THIS WAR ON OUR ENEMIES!!
SOME-ONE STOP HER! SHE CAN'T POSSI-BLY DO IT.
HE WHO WRESTLES THIS UNRULY DRAGON THROUGH THIS TINY HOLE IS THE WARRIOR WORTHY OF RULING THE LAND!
DA-DUN
THERE!
wip
wip
THERE!
MISSION IMPOSSIBLE!!
Gaaaaah
TALK ABOUT GIVING UP FAST!
fling

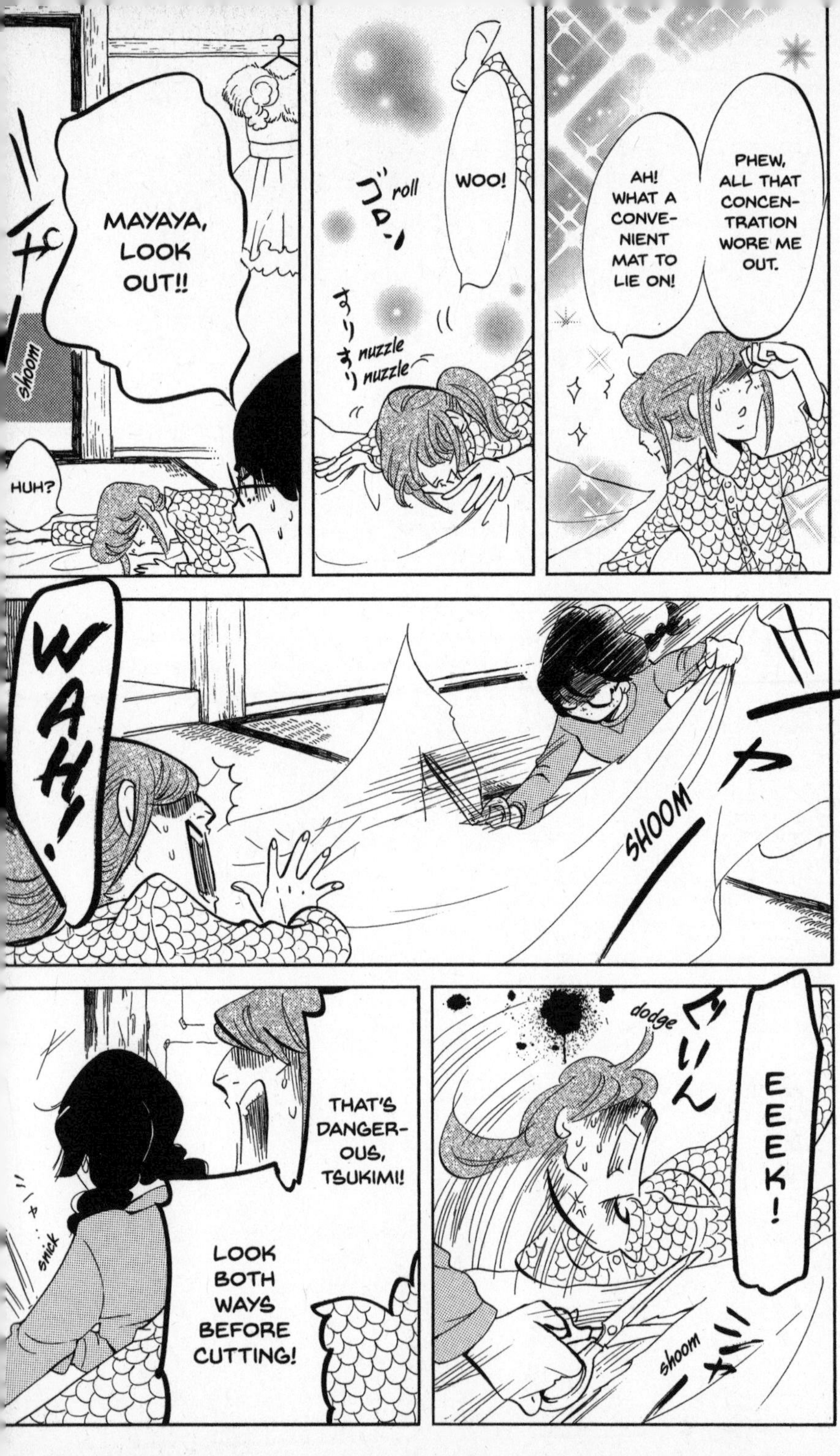
PHEW, ALL THAT CONCEN-TRATION WORE ME OUT.
AH! WHAT A CONVE-NIENT MAT TO LIE ON!
WOO!
ゴロン roll
すりすり nuzzle nuzzle
MAYAYA, LOOK OUT!!
shoom
HUH?
SHOOM
WAH!
EEEK!
dodge
shoom
THAT'S DANGER-OUS, TSUKIMI!
LOOK BOTH WAYS BEFORE CUTTING!
snick

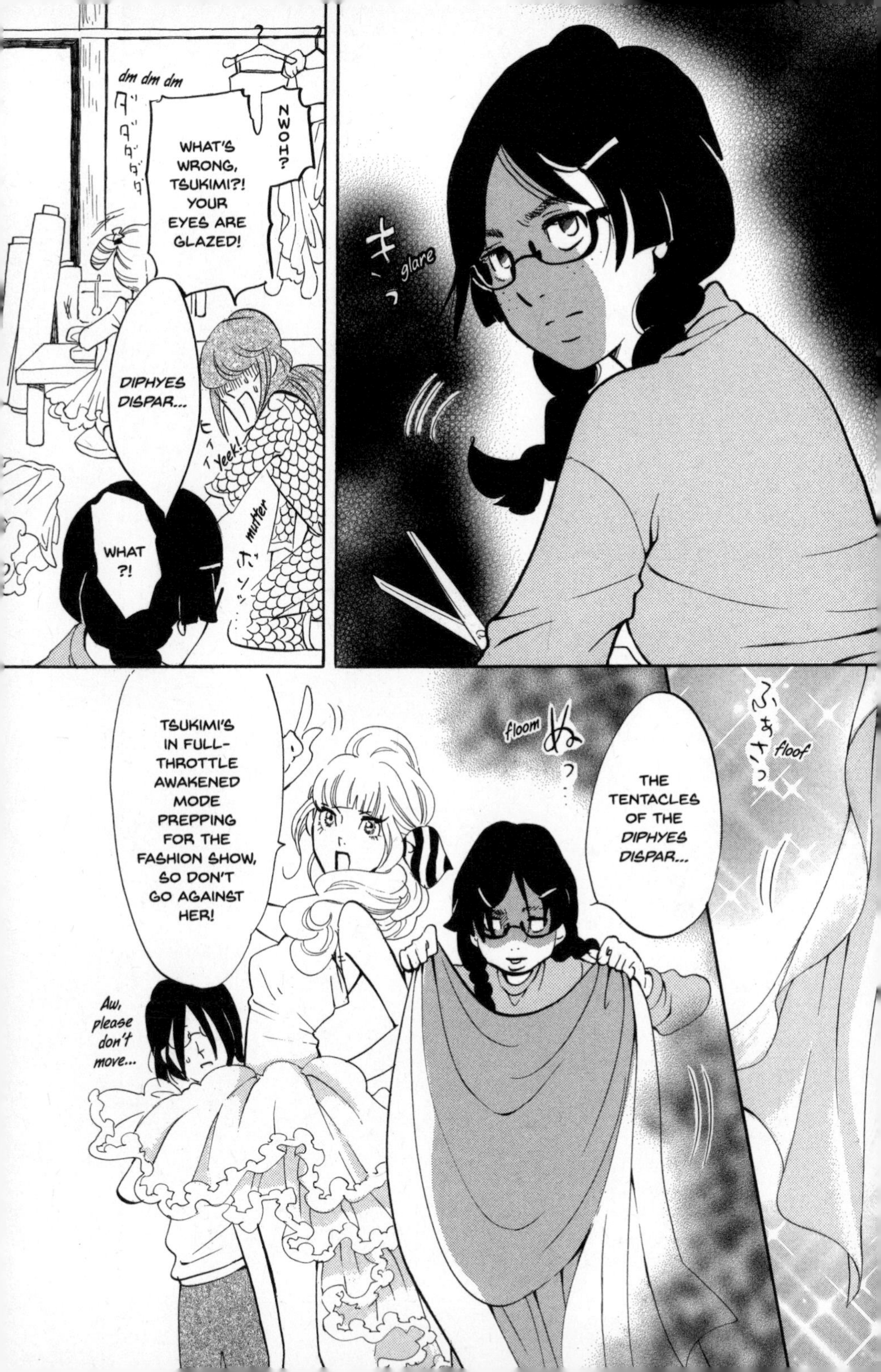
glare
NWOH?
dm dm dm
WHAT'S WRONG, TSUKIMI?! YOUR EYES ARE GLAZED!
DIPHYES DISPAR...
Yeek!
mutter
WHAT?!
floof
THE TENTACLES OF THE DIPHYES DISPAR...
floom
TSUKIMI'S IN FULL-THROTTLE AWAKENED MODE PREPPING FOR THE FASHION SHOW, SO DON'T GO AGAINST HER!
Aw, please don't move...

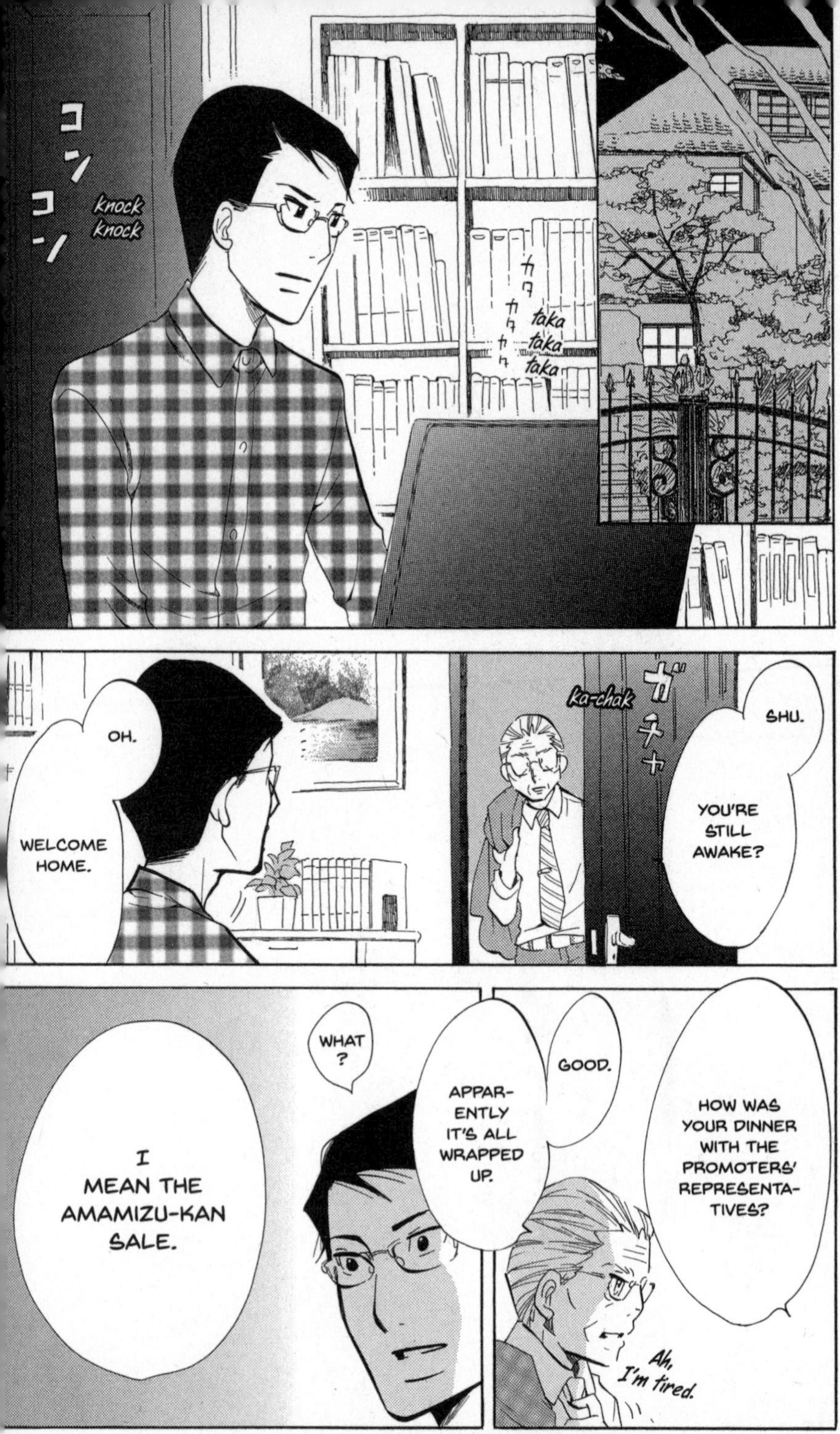
カタカタカタ
taka taka taka
コンコン
knock knock
ガチャ
ka-chak
SHU.
YOU'RE STILL AWAKE?
OH.
WELCOME HOME.
HOW WAS YOUR DINNER WITH THE PROMOTERS' REPRESENTA-TIVES?
GOOD.
Ah, I'm tired.
APPAR-ENTLY IT'S ALL WRAPPED UP.
WHAT?
I MEAN THE AMAMIZU-KAN SALE.

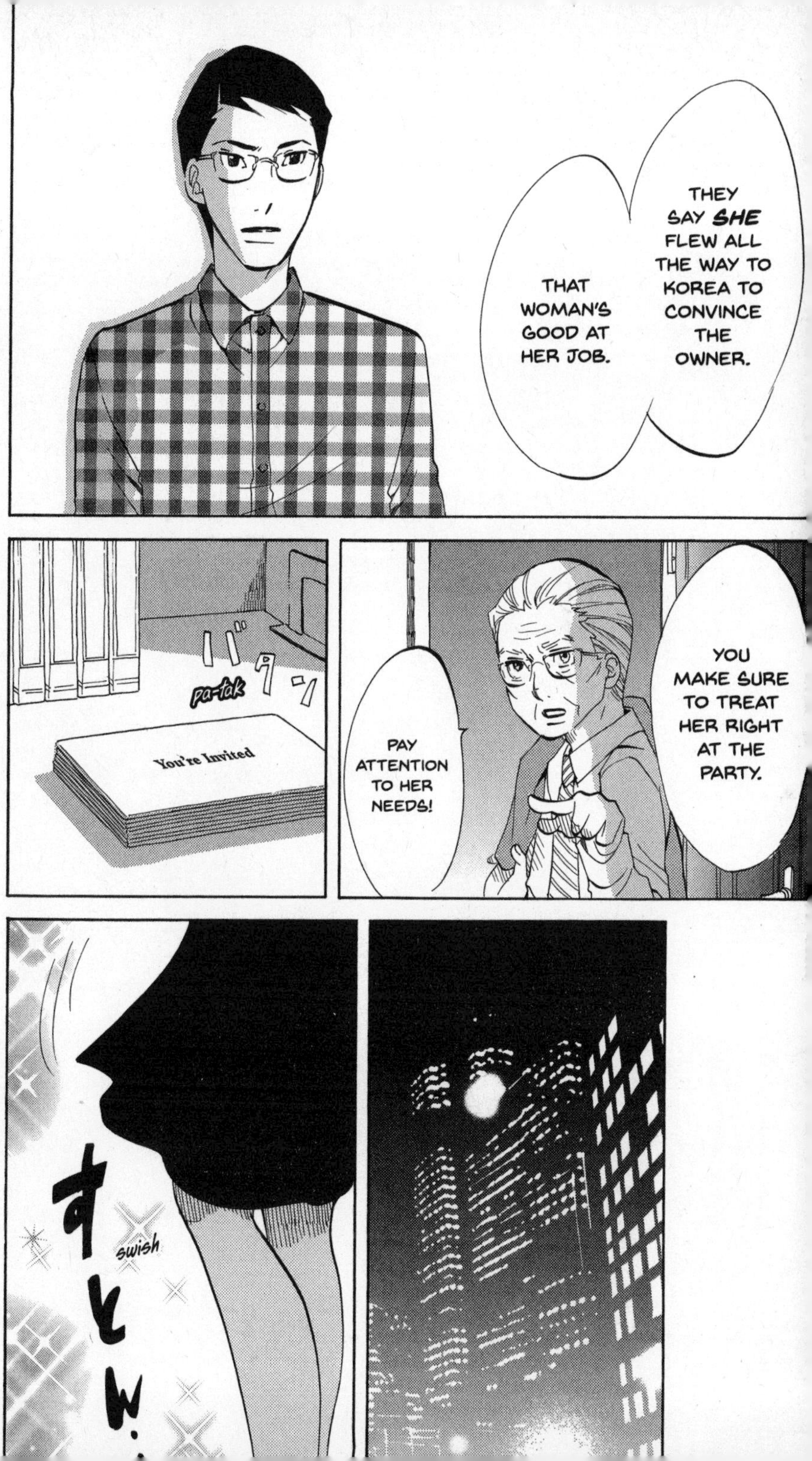
THEY SAY **SHE** FLEW ALL THE WAY TO KOREA TO CONVINCE THE OWNER.
THAT WOMAN'S GOOD AT HER JOB.
YOU MAKE SURE TO TREAT HER RIGHT AT THE PARTY.
PAY ATTENTION TO HER NEEDS!
pa-tak
You're Invited
swish

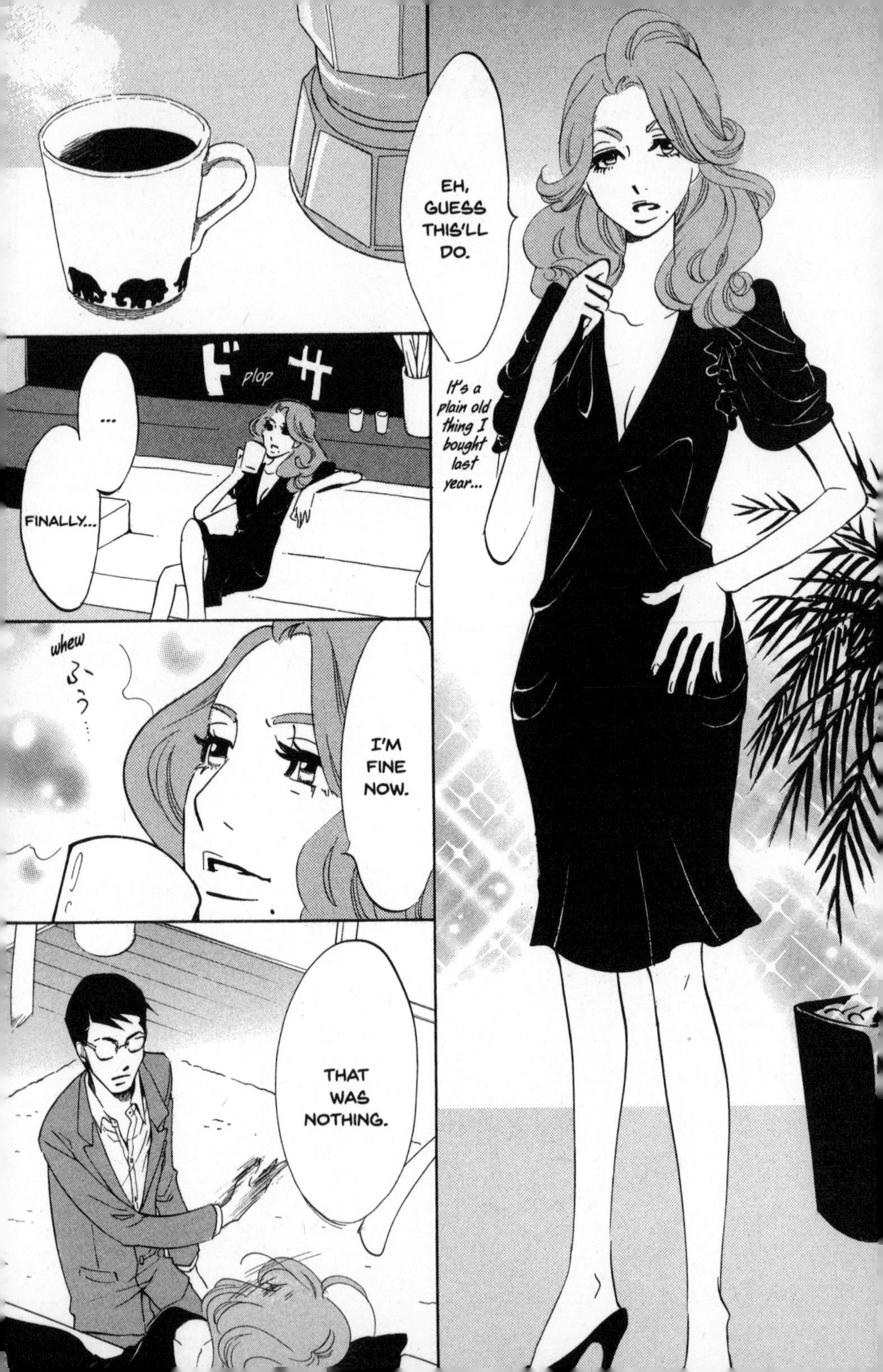
EH, GUESS THIS'LL DO.
It's a plain old thing I bought last year...
ドサ
plop
...
FINALLY...
whew
ふぅ…
I'M FINE NOW.
THAT WAS NOTHING.

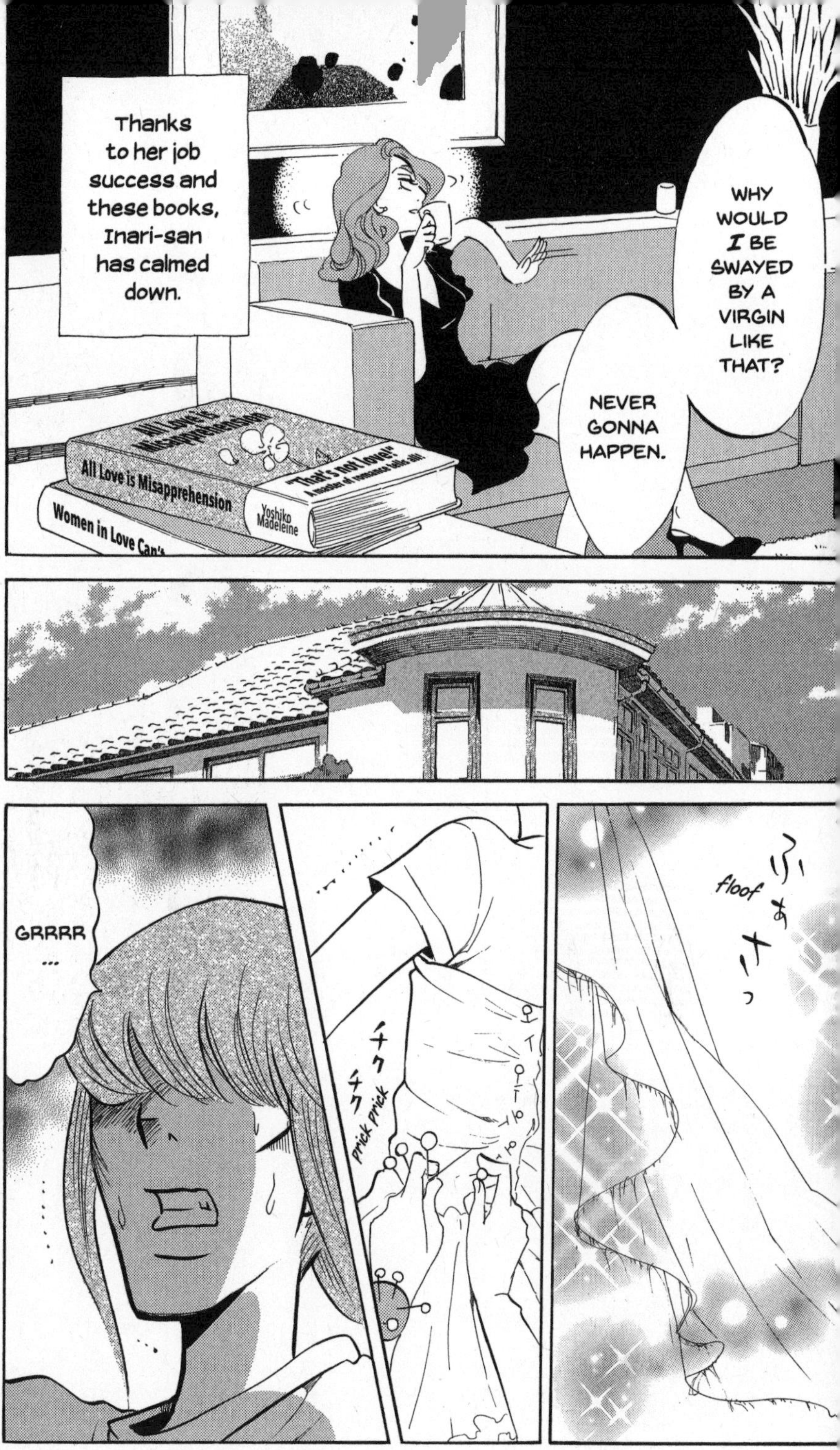
WHY WOULD I BE SWAYED BY A VIRGIN LIKE THAT?
NEVER GONNA HAPPEN.
Thanks to her job success and these books, Inari-san has calmed down.
All Love is Misapprehension
"That's not love!" A master of romance tells all!
Yoshiko Madeleine
Women in Love Can't
ふぁさっ
floof
チクチク
prick prick
GRRRR ...

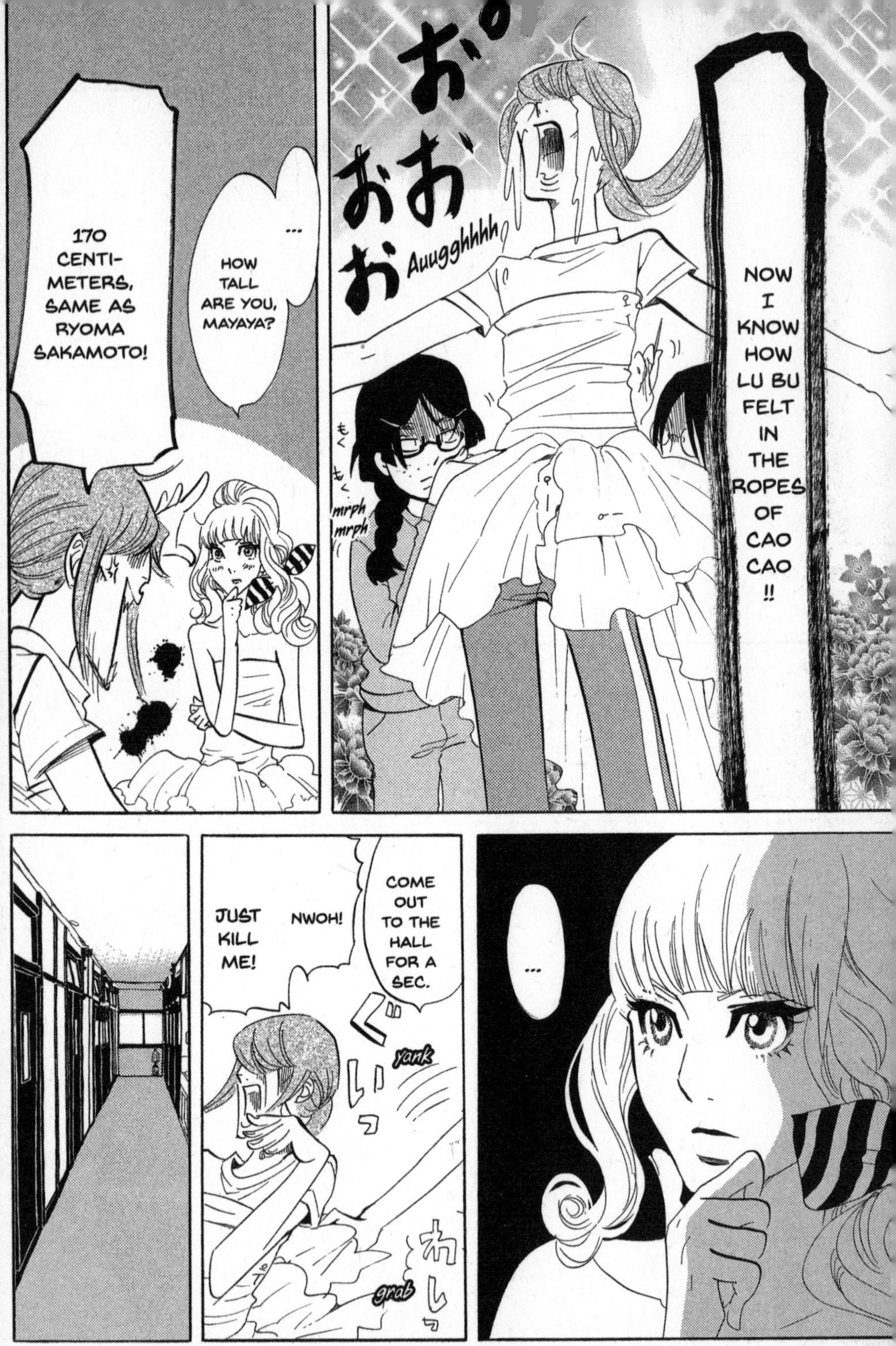
おおおお
Auugghhhh
NOW I KNOW HOW LU BU FELT IN THE ROPES OF CAO CAO !!
もくもく
mrph mrph
...
HOW TALL ARE YOU, MAYAYA?
170 CENTIMETERS, SAME AS RYOMA SAKAMOTO!
...
COME OUT TO THE HALL FOR A SEC.
NWOH!
JUST KILL ME!
ぐいっ
yank
わしっ
grab

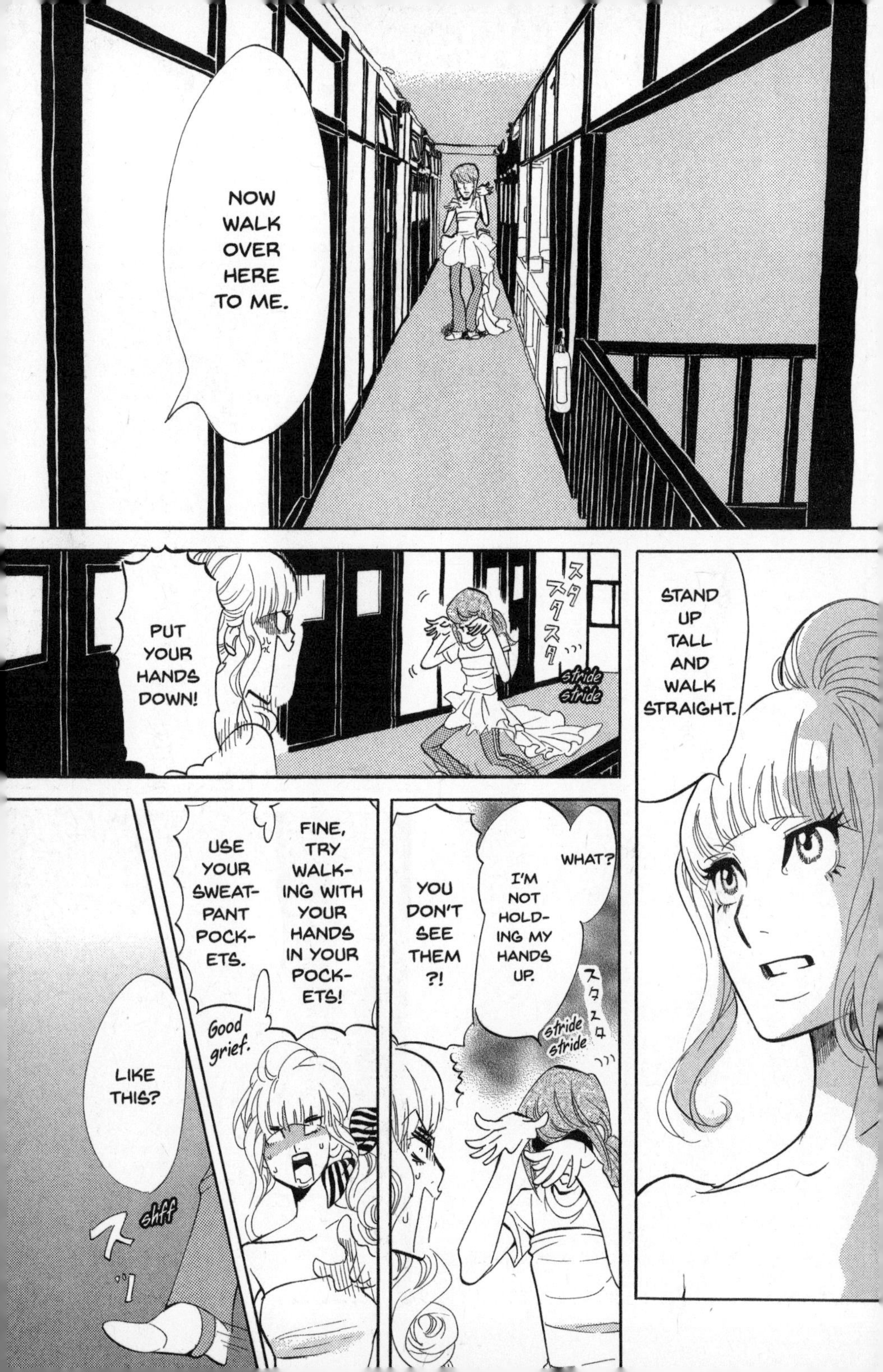
NOW WALK OVER HERE TO ME.
STAND UP TALL AND WALK STRAIGHT.
スタスタ
stride stride
PUT YOUR HANDS DOWN!
WHAT?
I'M NOT HOLDING MY HANDS UP.
スタスタ
stride stride
YOU DON'T SEE THEM?!
FINE, TRY WALKING WITH YOUR HANDS IN YOUR POCKETS!
Good grief.
USE YOUR SWEAT-PANT POCKETS.
LIKE THIS?
スッ
shff

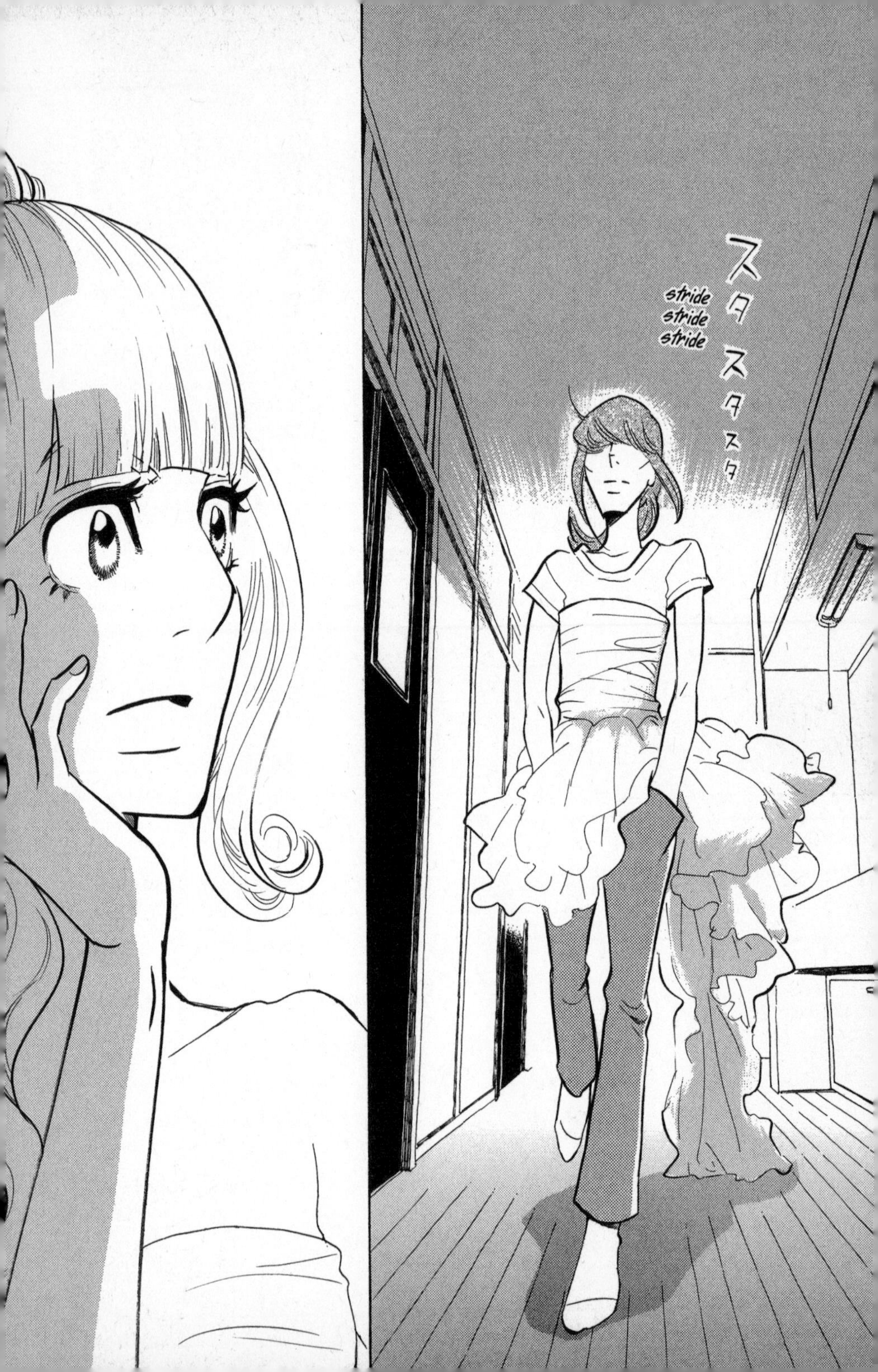
スタスタスタスタ
stride
stride
stride

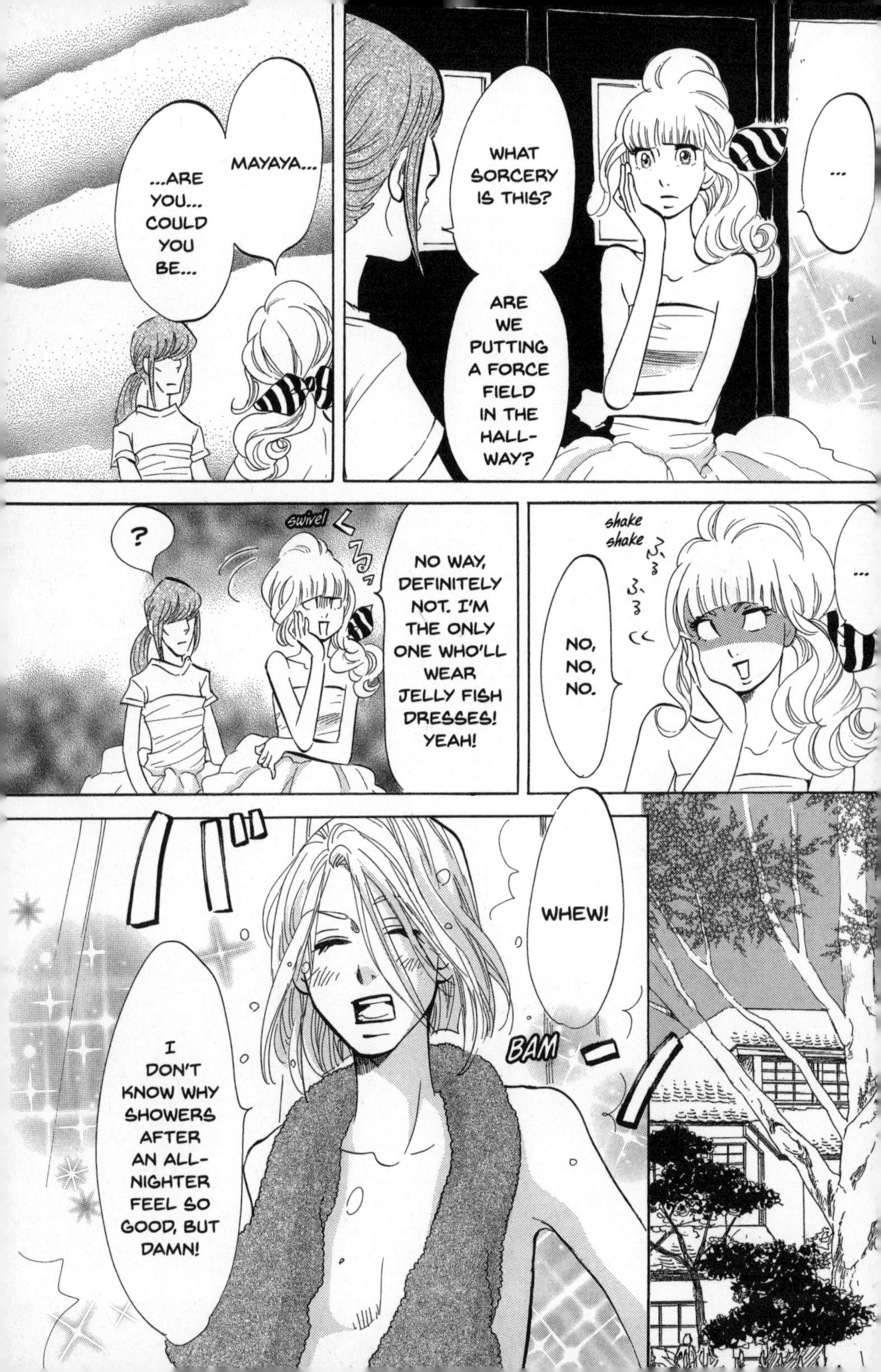
...
WHAT SORCERY IS THIS?
ARE WE PUTTING A FORCE FIELD IN THE HALL-WAY?
MAYAYA...
...ARE YOU... COULD YOU BE...
...
shake shake
NO, NO, NO.
swivel
NO WAY, DEFINITELY NOT. I'M THE ONLY ONE WHO'LL WEAR JELLY FISH DRESSES! YEAH!
?
BAM
WHEW!
I DON'T KNOW WHY SHOWERS AFTER AN ALL-NIGHTER FEEL SO GOOD, BUT DAMN!

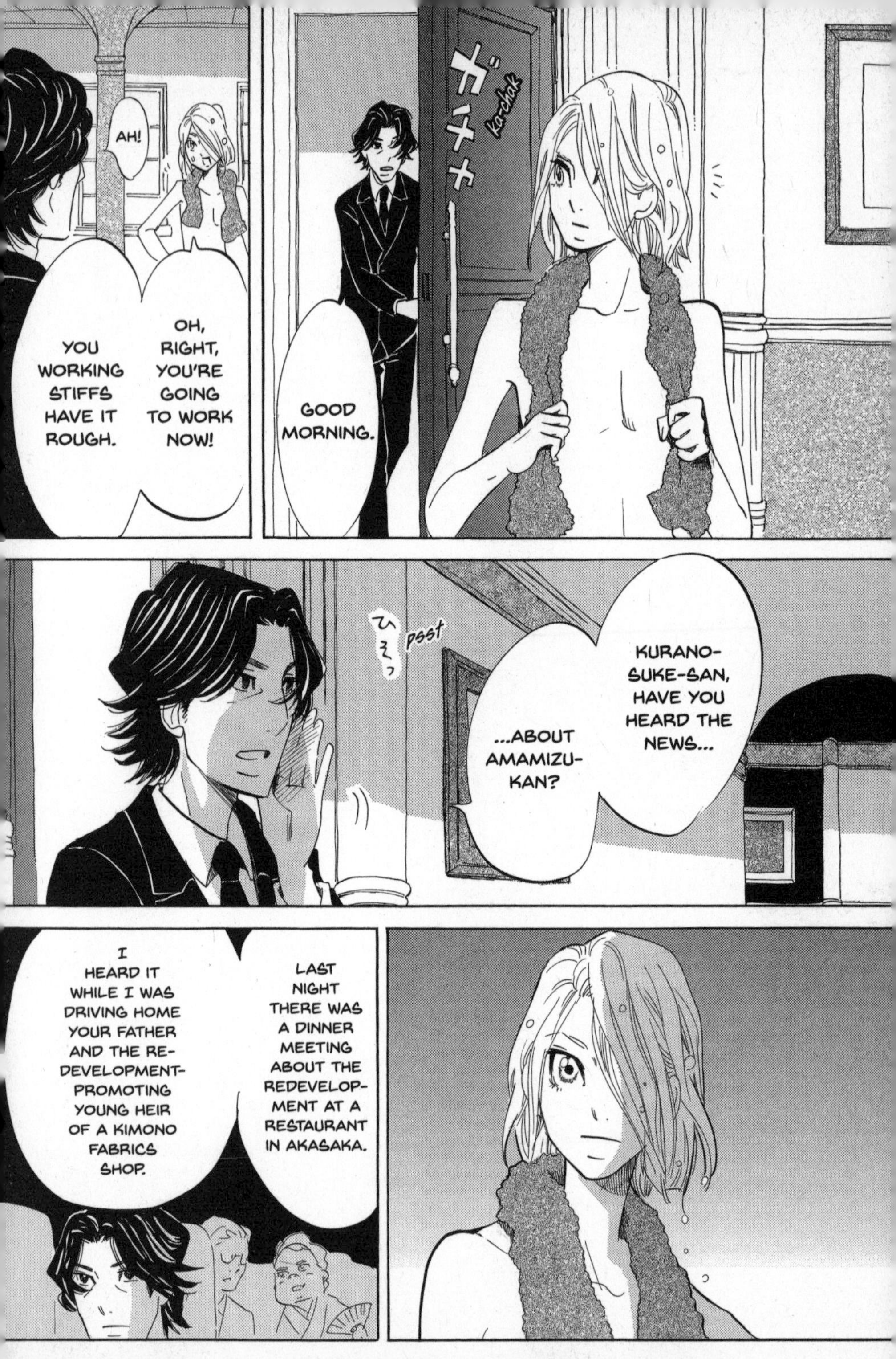
ka-chak
GOOD MORNING.
AH!
OH, RIGHT, YOU'RE GOING TO WORK NOW!
YOU WORKING STIFFS HAVE IT ROUGH.
psst
KURANO-SUKE-SAN, HAVE YOU HEARD THE NEWS...
...ABOUT AMAMIZU-KAN?
LAST NIGHT THERE WAS A DINNER MEETING ABOUT THE REDEVELOP-MENT AT A RESTAURANT IN AKASAKA.
I HEARD IT WHILE I WAS DRIVING HOME YOUR FATHER AND THE RE-DEVELOPMENT-PROMOTING YOUNG HEIR OF A KIMONO FABRICS SHOP.

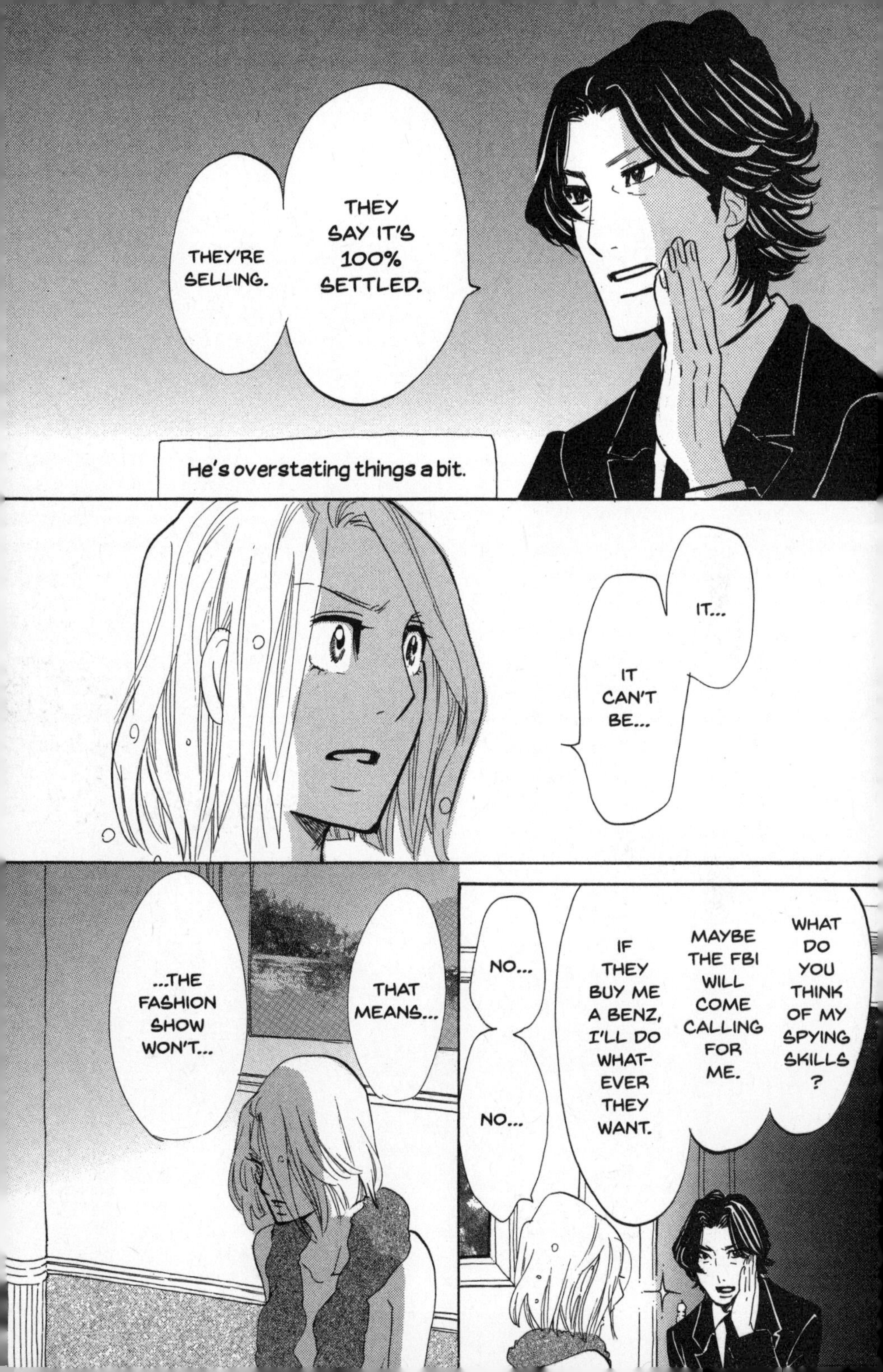
THEY SAY IT'S 100% SETTLED.
THEY'RE SELLING.
He's overstating things a bit.
IT...
IT CAN'T BE...
WHAT DO YOU THINK OF MY SPYING SKILLS?
MAYBE THE FBI WILL COME CALLING FOR ME.
IF THEY BUY ME A BENZ, I'LL DO WHAT-EVER THEY WANT.
NO...
NO...
THAT MEANS...
...THE FASHION SHOW WON'T...

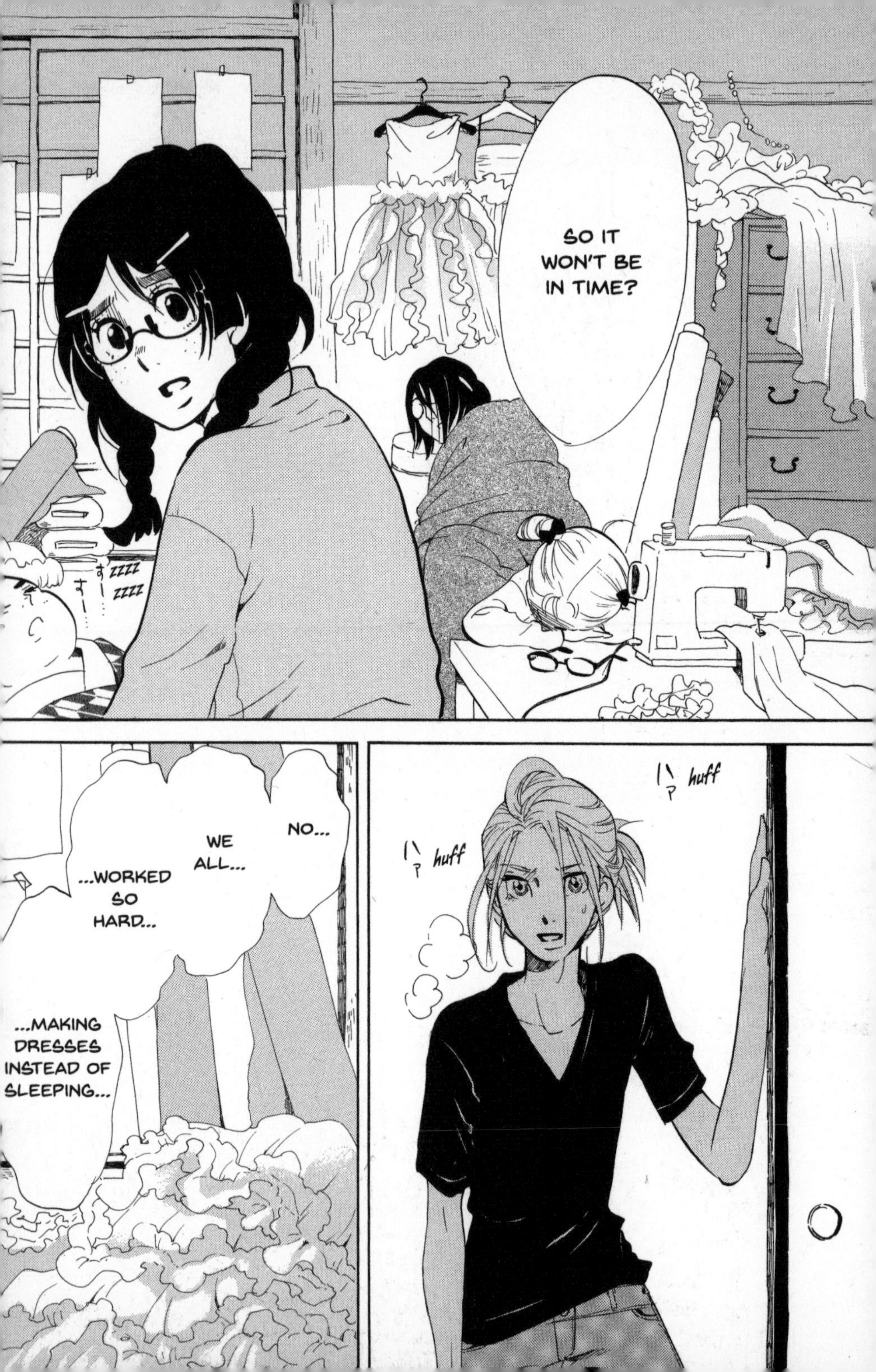
SO IT WON'T BE IN TIME?
zzzz
zzzz
huff
huff
NO...
WE ALL...
...WORKED SO HARD...
...MAKING DRESSES INSTEAD OF SLEEPING...

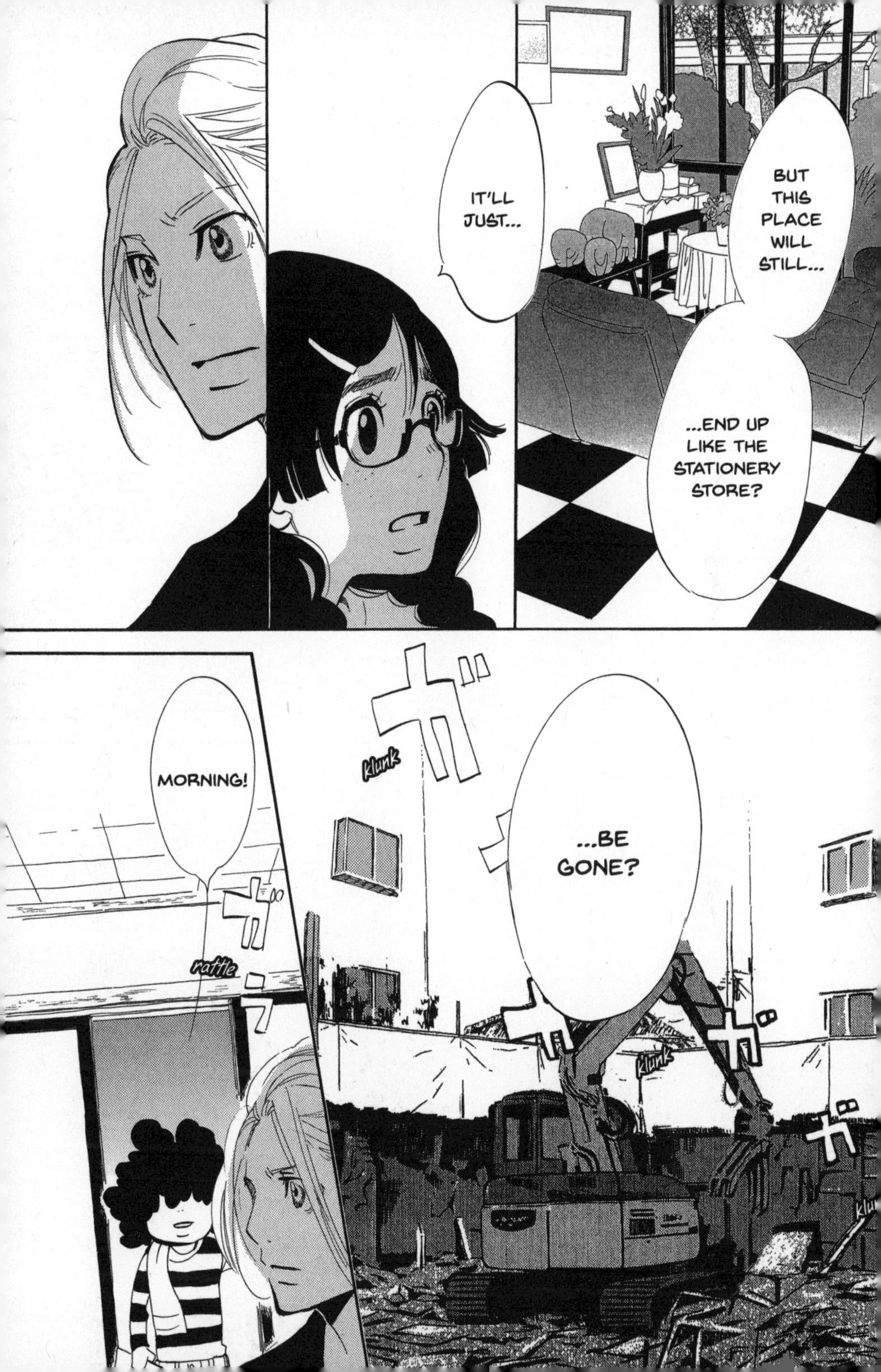
BUT THIS PLACE WILL STILL...
...END UP LIKE THE STATIONERY STORE?
IT'LL JUST...
...BE GONE?
klunk
klunk
MORNING!
rattle

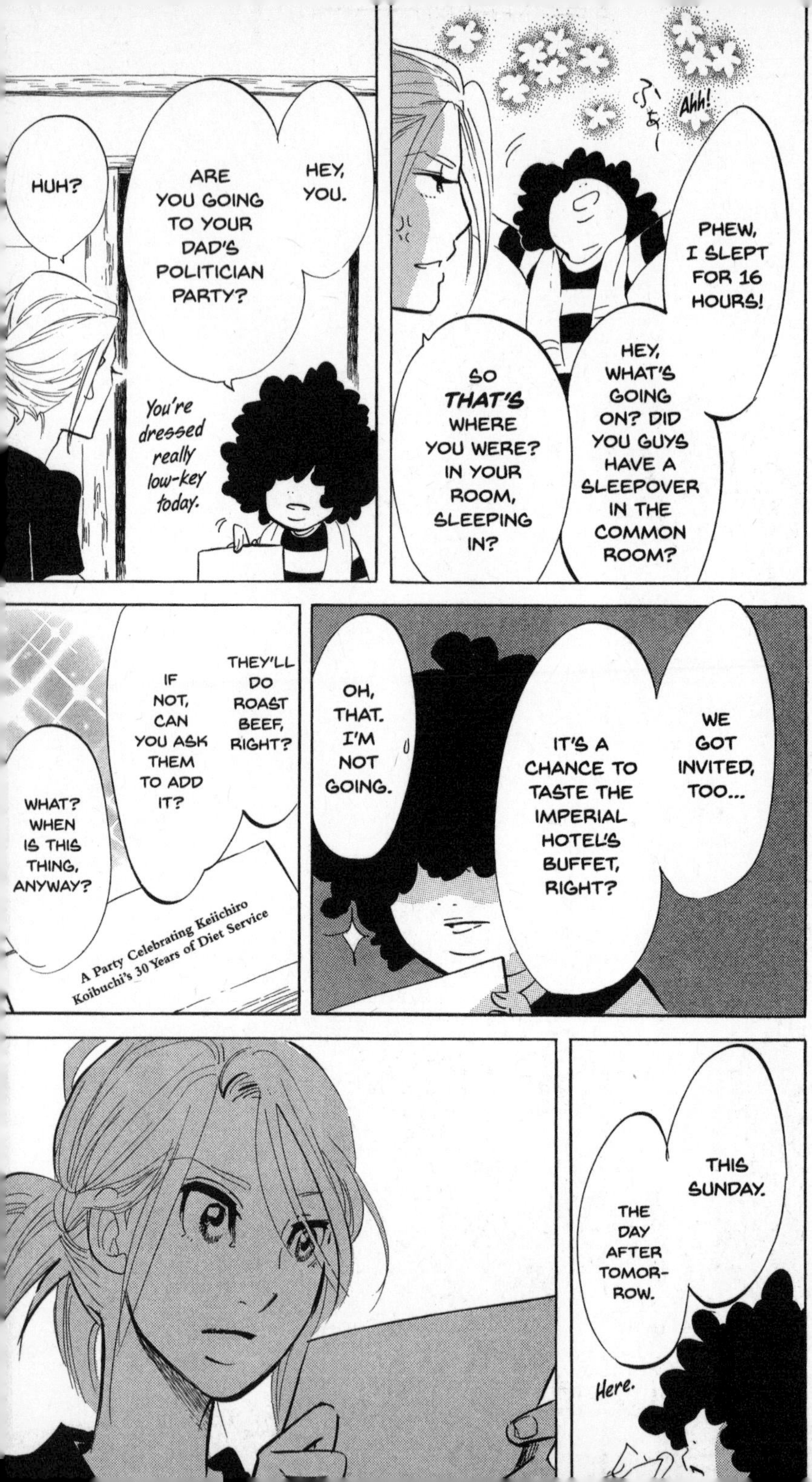
Ahh!
PHEW, I SLEPT FOR 16 HOURS!
HEY, WHAT'S GOING ON? DID YOU GUYS HAVE A SLEEPOVER IN THE COMMON ROOM?
SO *THAT'S* WHERE YOU WERE? IN YOUR ROOM, SLEEPING IN?
HEY, YOU.
ARE YOU GOING TO YOUR DAD'S POLITICIAN PARTY?
HUH?
You're dressed really low-key today.
WE GOT INVITED, TOO...
IT'S A CHANCE TO TASTE THE IMPERIAL HOTEL'S BUFFET, RIGHT?
OH, THAT. I'M NOT GOING.
THEY'LL DO ROAST BEEF, RIGHT?
IF NOT, CAN YOU ASK THEM TO ADD IT?
WHAT? WHEN IS THIS THING, ANYWAY?
A Party Celebrating Keiichiro Koibuchi's 30 Years of Diet Service
THIS SUNDAY.
THE DAY AFTER TOMORROW.
Here.

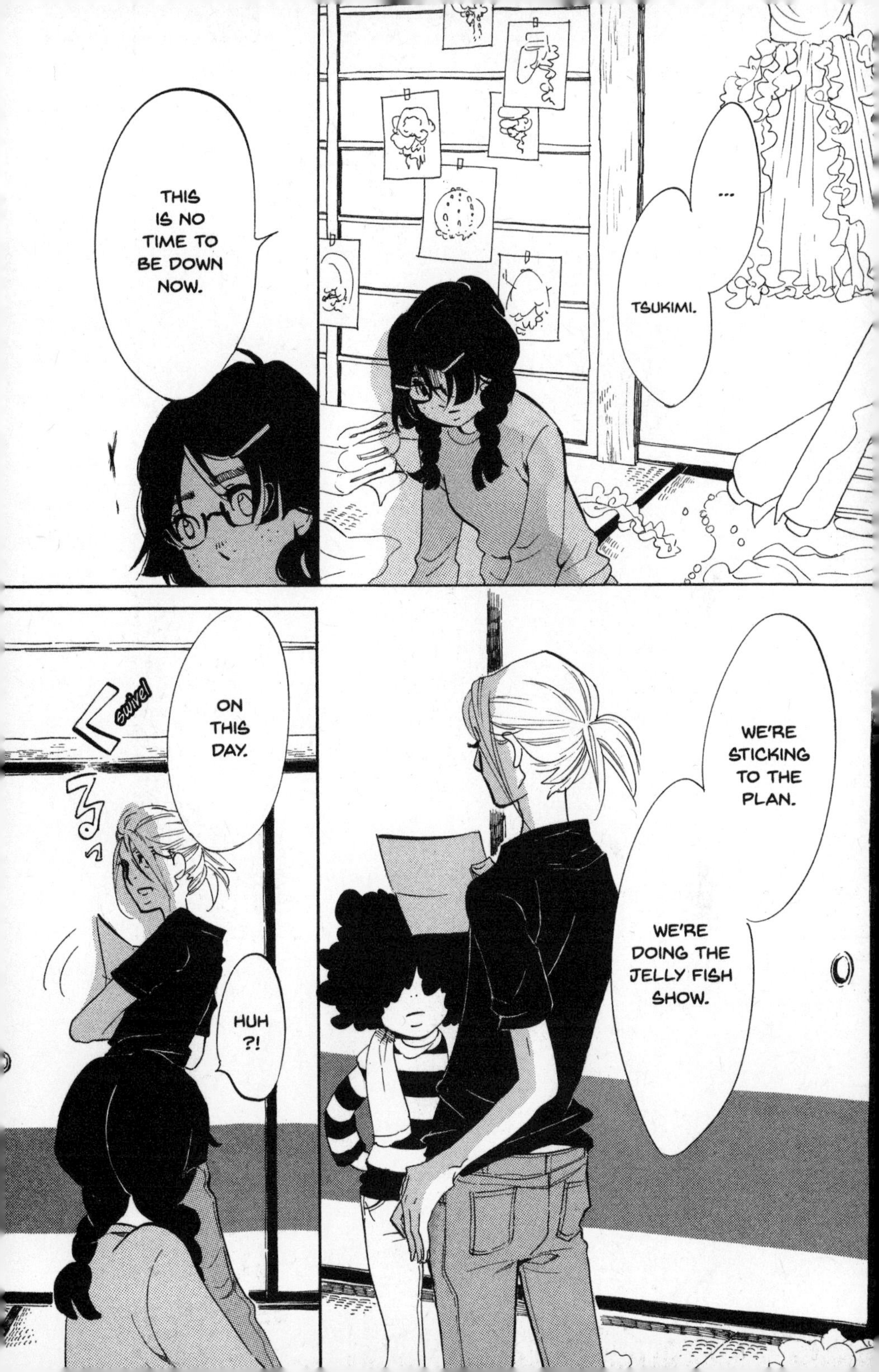
...
TSUKIMI.
THIS IS NO TIME TO BE DOWN NOW.
WE'RE STICKING TO THE PLAN.
WE'RE DOING THE JELLY FISH SHOW.
ON THIS DAY.
swivel
HUH?!

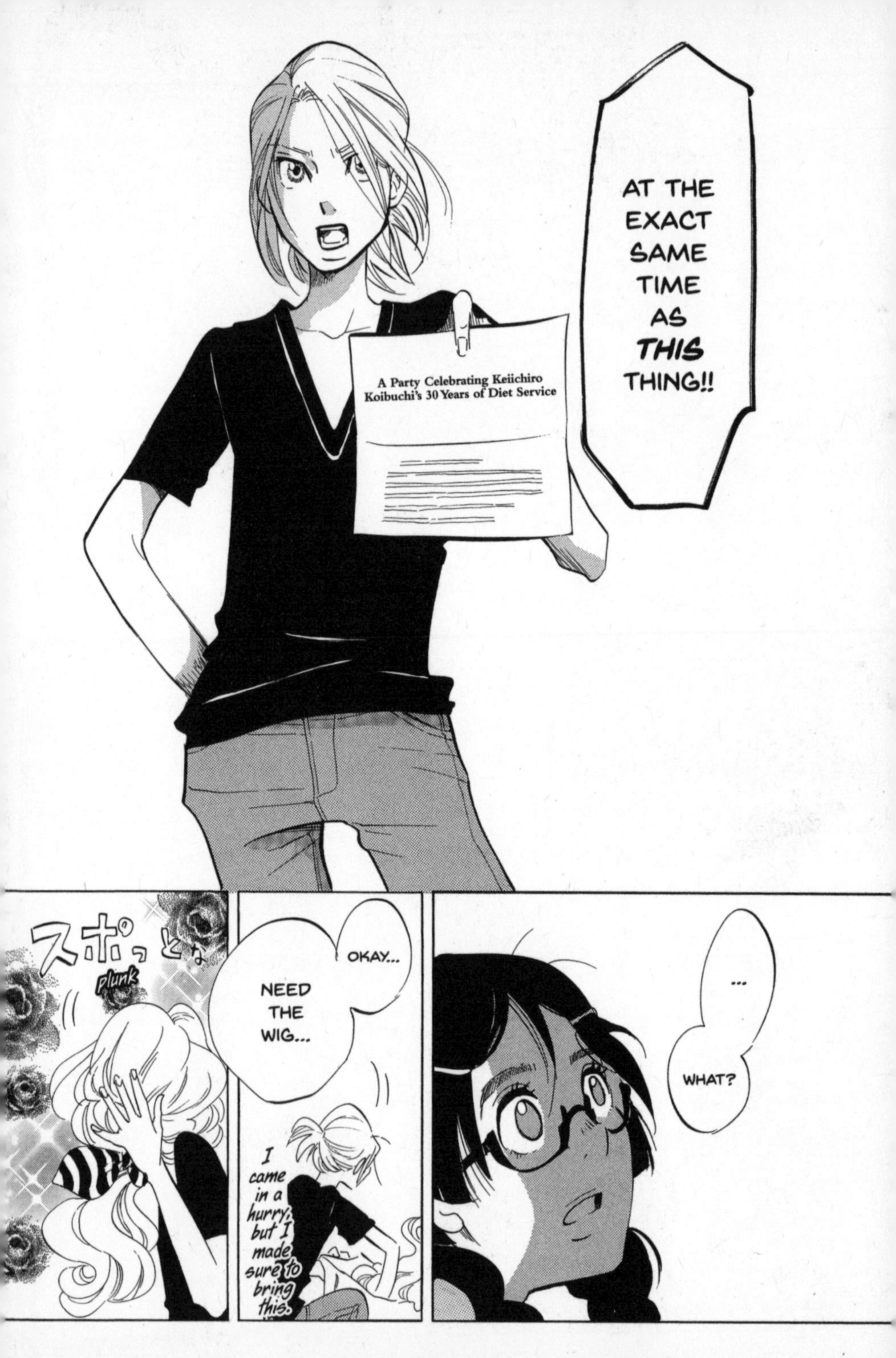
AT THE EXACT SAME TIME AS **THIS** THING!!
A Party Celebrating Keiichiro Koibuchi's 30 Years of Diet Service
...
WHAT?
OKAY... NEED THE WIG...
I came in a hurry, but I made sure to bring this.
スポっとな
plunk

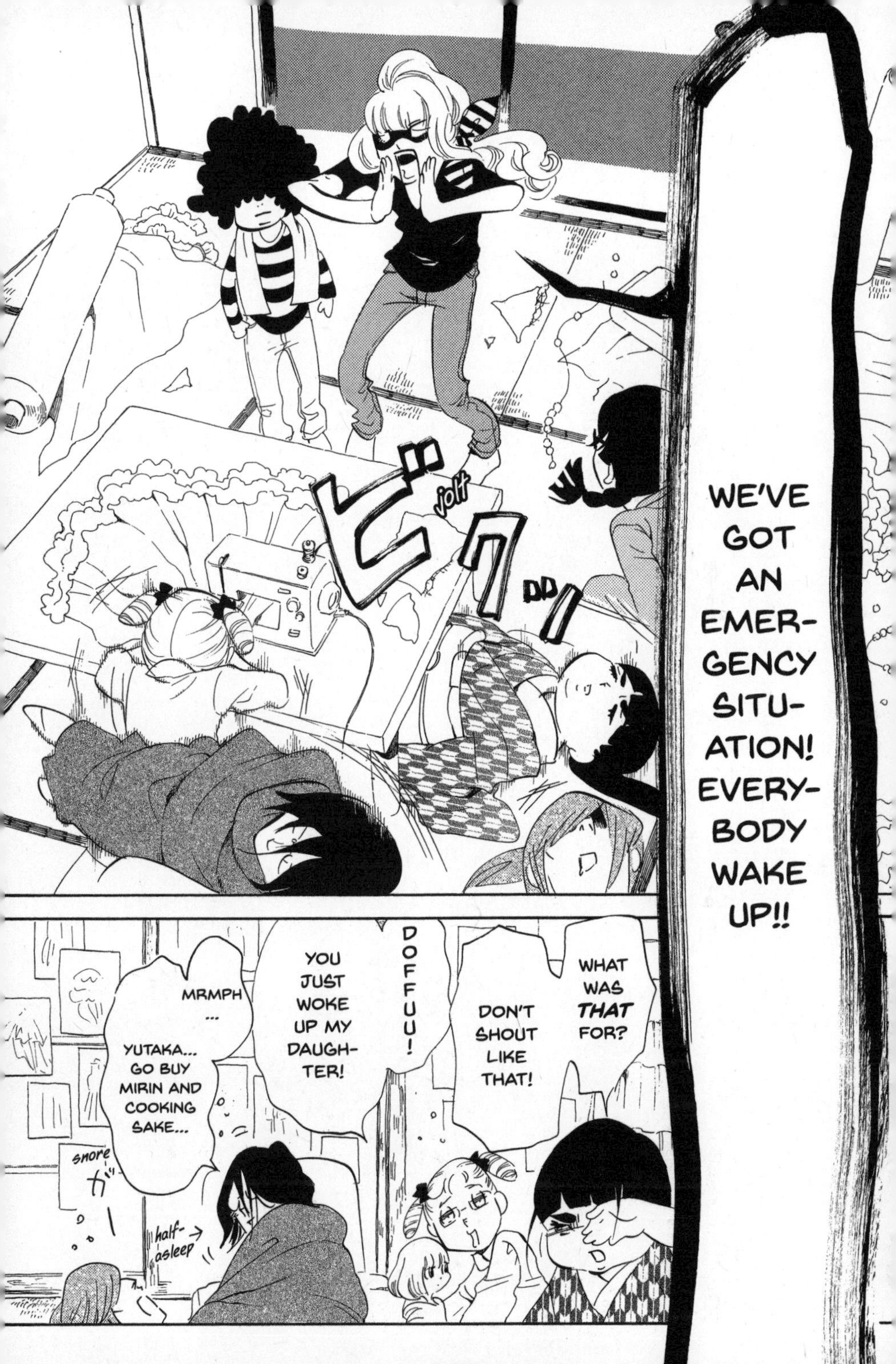
WE'VE GOT AN EMER-GENCY SITU-ATION! EVERY-BODY WAKE UP!!
jolt
WHAT WAS THAT FOR?
DON'T SHOUT LIKE THAT!
DOFFUU!
YOU JUST WOKE UP MY DAUGH-TER!
MRMPH ...
YUTAKA... GO BUY MIRIN AND COOKING SAKE...
snore
half-asleep

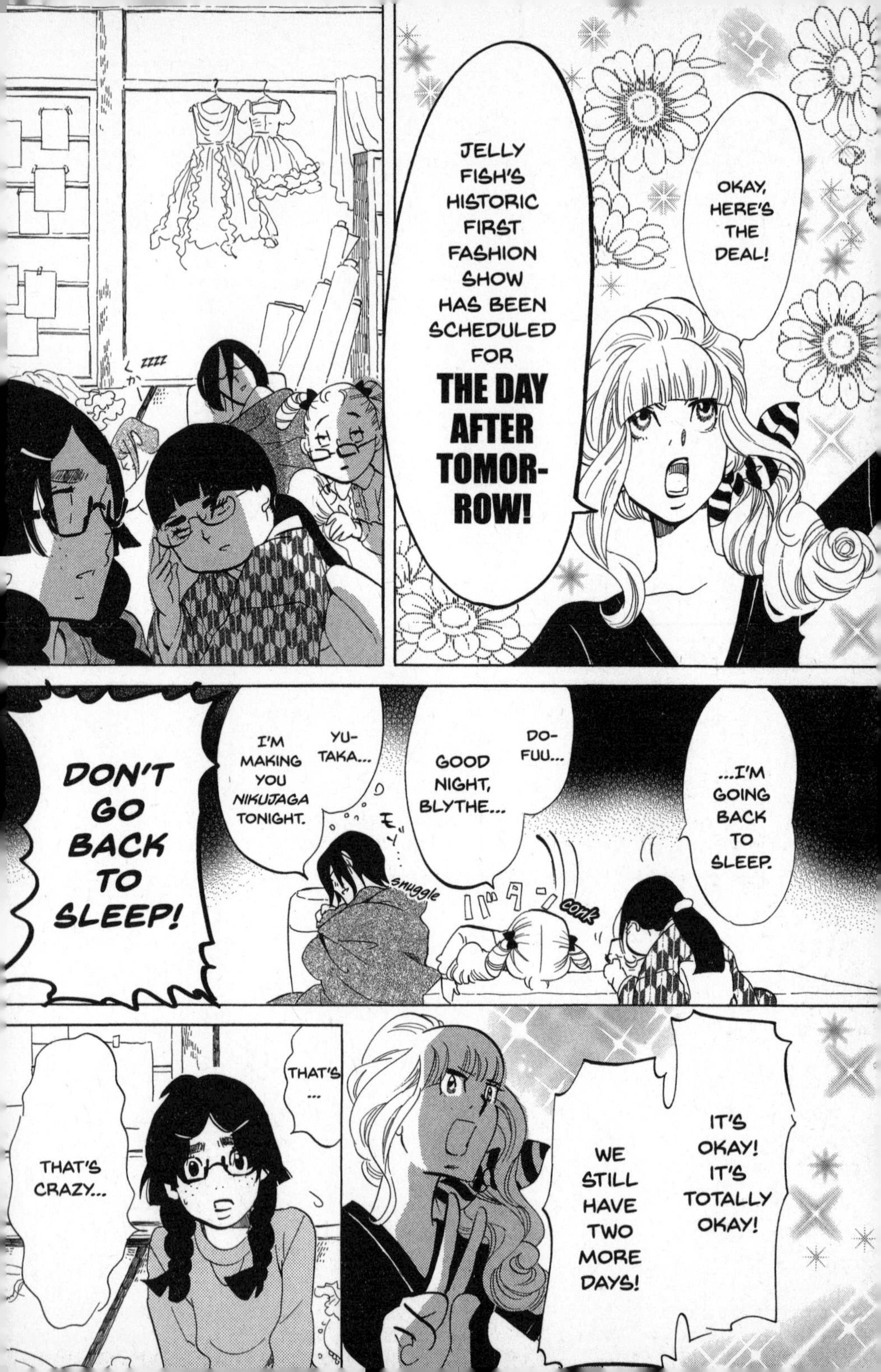
OKAY, HERE'S THE DEAL!
JELLY FISH'S HISTORIC FIRST FASHION SHOW HAS BEEN SCHEDULED FOR THE DAY AFTER TOMORROW!
ZZZZ
...I'M GOING BACK TO SLEEP.
cork
DO-FUU...
GOOD NIGHT, BLYTHE...
snuggle
YU-TAKA...
I'M MAKING YOU NIKUJAGA TONIGHT.
DON'T GO BACK TO SLEEP!
IT'S OKAY! IT'S TOTALLY OKAY!
WE STILL HAVE TWO MORE DAYS!
THAT'S...
THAT'S CRAZY...

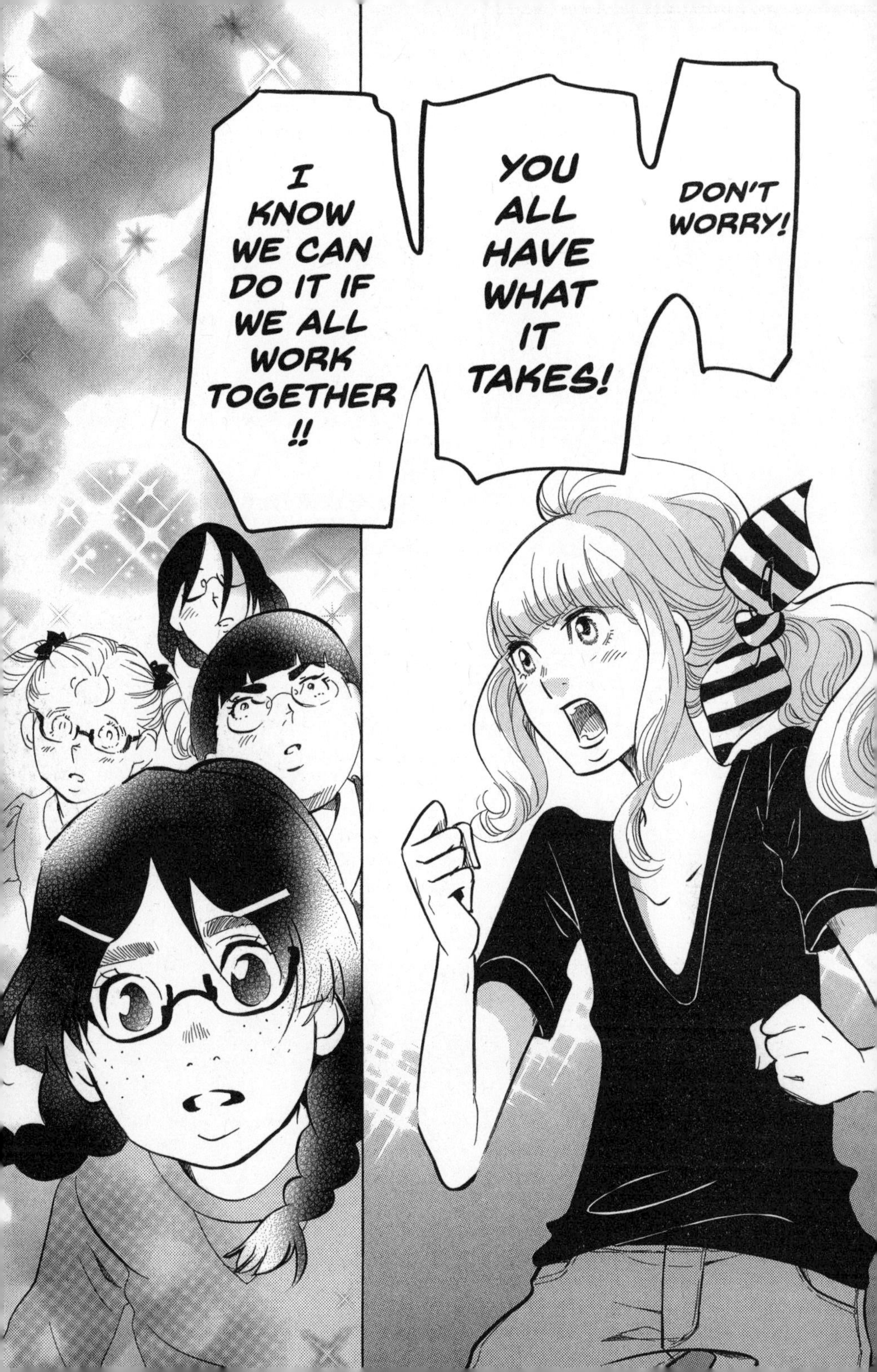
DON'T WORRY!
YOU ALL HAVE WHAT IT TAKES!
I KNOW WE CAN DO IT IF WE ALL WORK TOGETHER!!

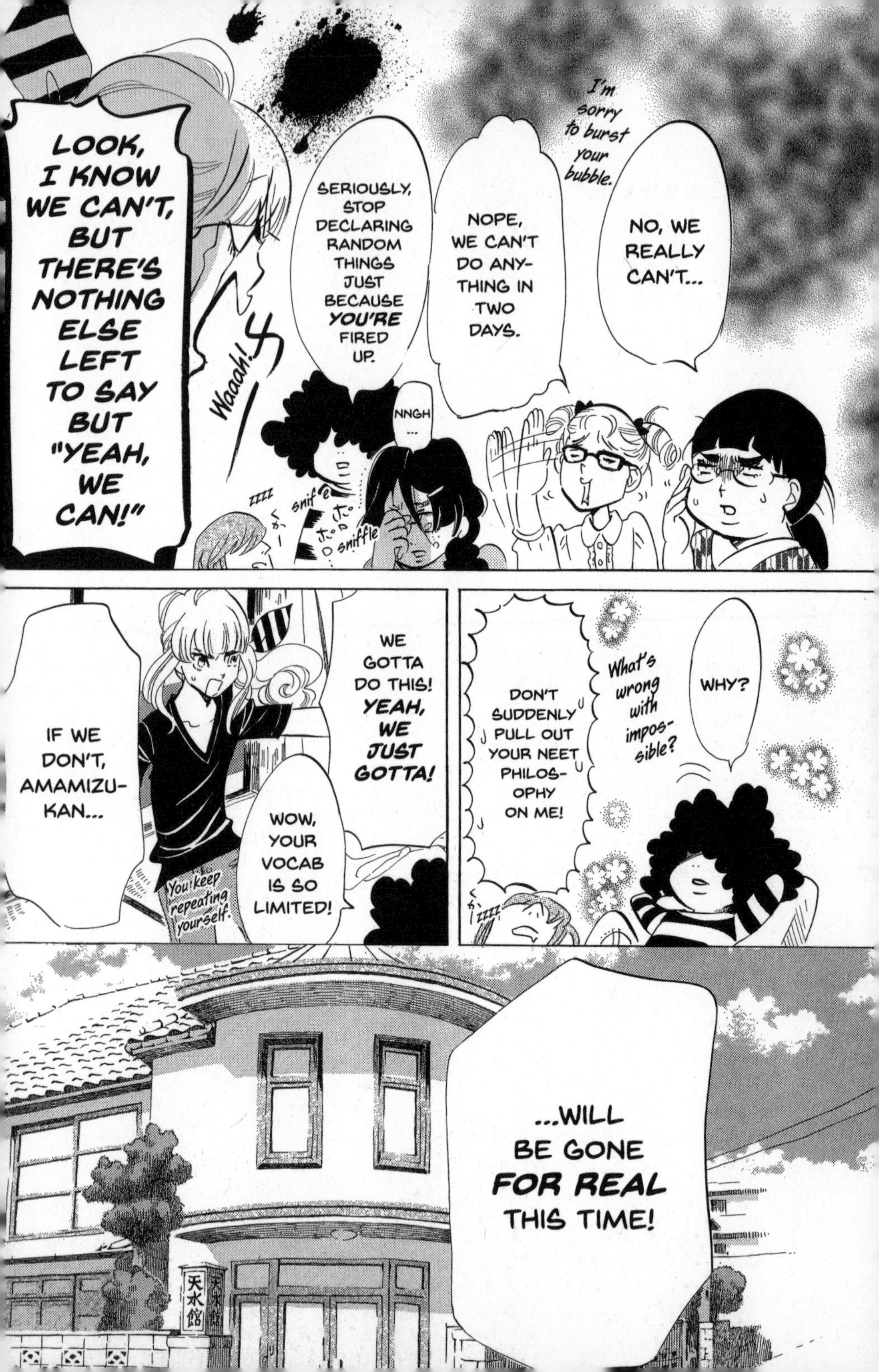
I'm sorry to burst your bubble.
NO, WE REALLY CAN'T...
NOPE, WE CAN'T DO ANYTHING IN TWO DAYS.
SERIOUSLY, STOP DECLARING RANDOM THINGS JUST BECAUSE YOU'RE FIRED UP.
NNGH...
sniff
sniffle
zzzz
LOOK, I KNOW WE CAN'T, BUT THERE'S NOTHING ELSE LEFT TO SAY BUT "YEAH, WE CAN!"
Waaah!
WHY?
What's wrong with impossible?
DON'T SUDDENLY PULL OUT YOUR NEET PHILOSOPHY ON ME!
zzzz
WE GOTTA DO THIS! YEAH, WE JUST GOTTA!
WOW, YOUR VOCAB IS SO LIMITED!
You keep repeating yourself.
IF WE DON'T, AMAMIZU-KAN...
天水館
...WILL BE GONE FOR REAL THIS TIME!

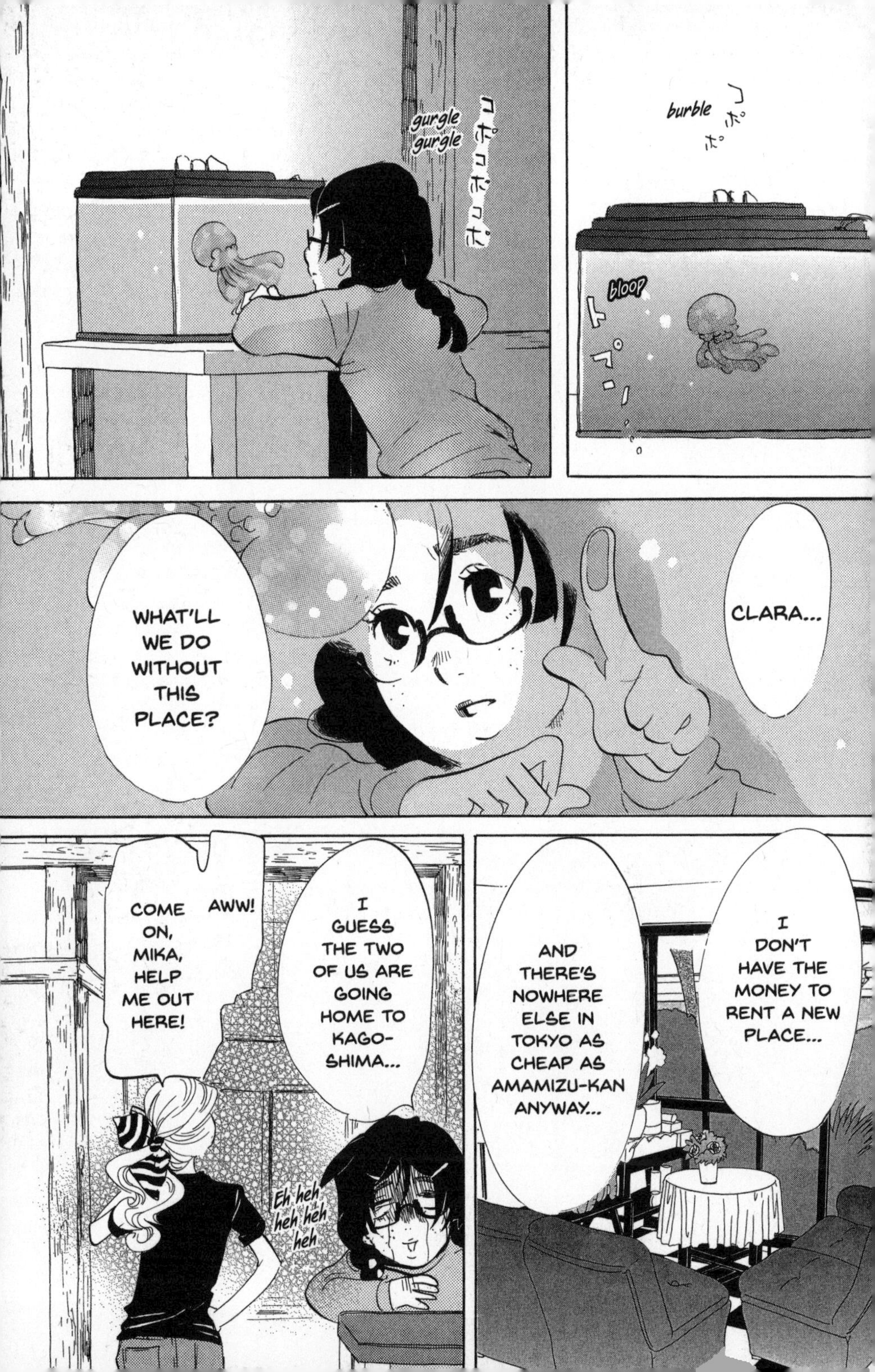
burble
コポポ
bloop
gurgle gurgle
コポコポコポ
CLARA...
WHAT'LL WE DO WITHOUT THIS PLACE?
I DON'T HAVE THE MONEY TO RENT A NEW PLACE...
AND THERE'S NOWHERE ELSE IN TOKYO AS CHEAP AS AMAMIZU-KAN ANYWAY...
I GUESS THE TWO OF US ARE GOING HOME TO KAGO-SHIMA...
Eh heh heh heh heh heh
AWW!
COME ON, MIKA, HELP ME OUT HERE!

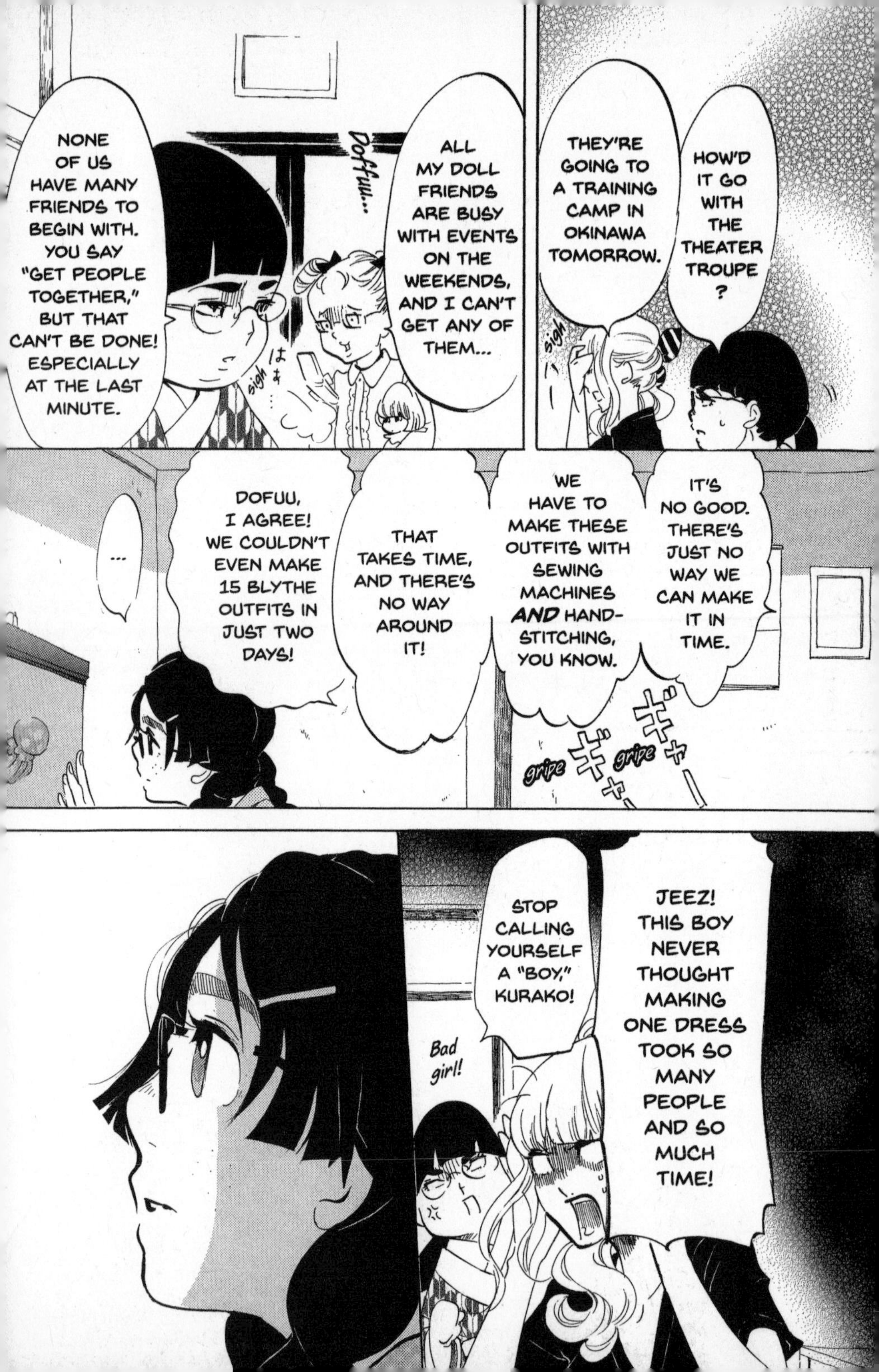
HOW'D IT GO WITH THE THEATER TROUPE?
THEY'RE GOING TO A TRAINING CAMP IN OKINAWA TOMORROW.
sigh
ALL MY DOLL FRIENDS ARE BUSY WITH EVENTS ON THE WEEKENDS, AND I CAN'T GET ANY OF THEM...
Dofuu...
sigh
NONE OF US HAVE MANY FRIENDS TO BEGIN WITH. YOU SAY "GET PEOPLE TOGETHER," BUT THAT CAN'T BE DONE! ESPECIALLY AT THE LAST MINUTE.
IT'S NO GOOD. THERE'S JUST NO WAY WE CAN MAKE IT IN TIME.
WE HAVE TO MAKE THESE OUTFITS WITH SEWING MACHINES ***AND*** HAND-STITCHING, YOU KNOW.
gripe gripe
THAT TAKES TIME, AND THERE'S NO WAY AROUND IT!
DOFUU, I AGREE! WE COULDN'T EVEN MAKE 15 BLYTHE OUTFITS IN JUST TWO DAYS!
...
JEEZ! THIS BOY NEVER THOUGHT MAKING ONE DRESS TOOK SO MANY PEOPLE AND SO MUCH TIME!
STOP CALLING YOURSELF A "BOY," KURAKO!
Bad girl!

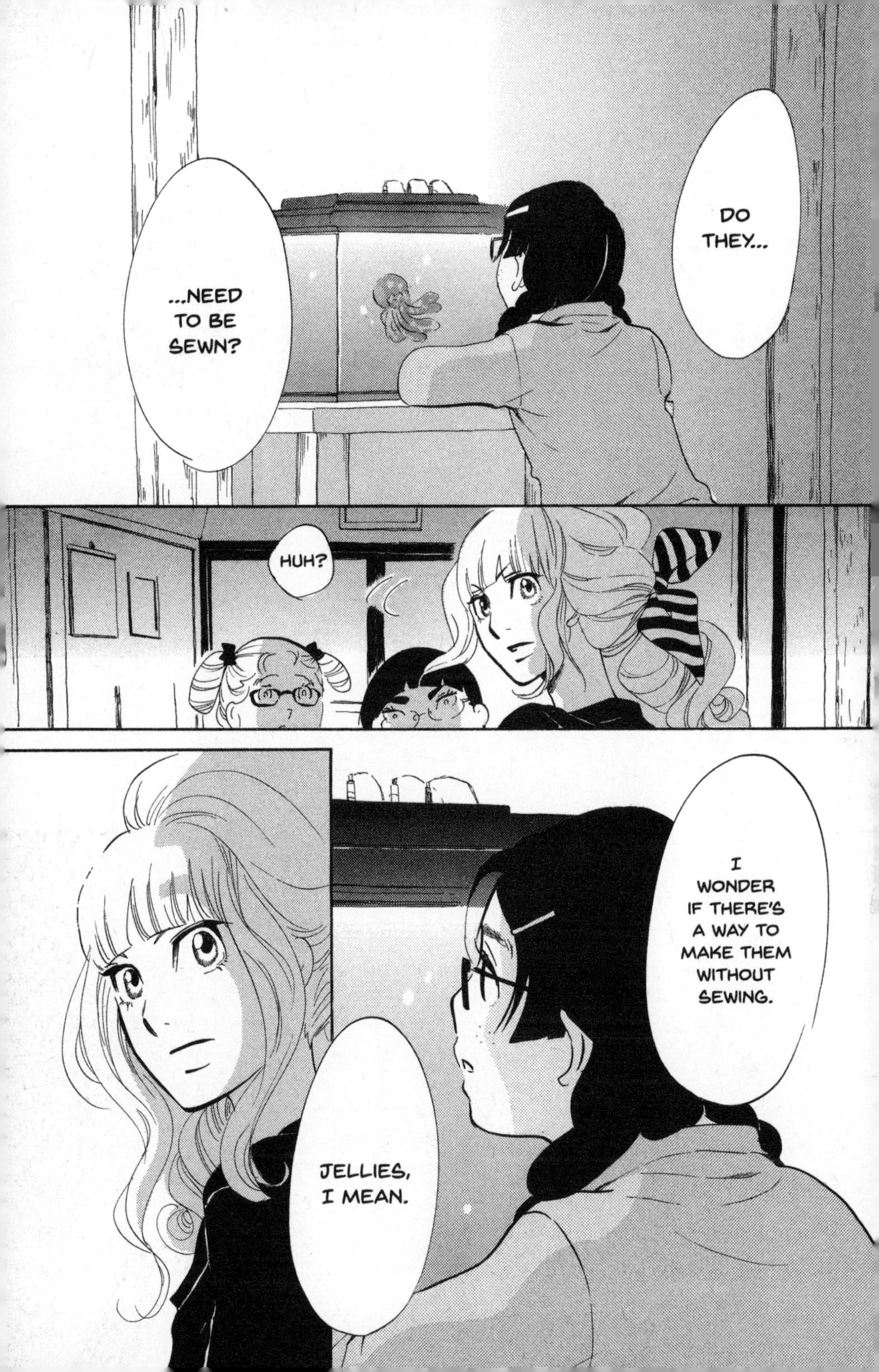
DO THEY...
...NEED TO BE SEWN?
HUH?
I WONDER IF THERE'S A WAY TO MAKE THEM WITHOUT SEWING.
JELLIES, I MEAN.

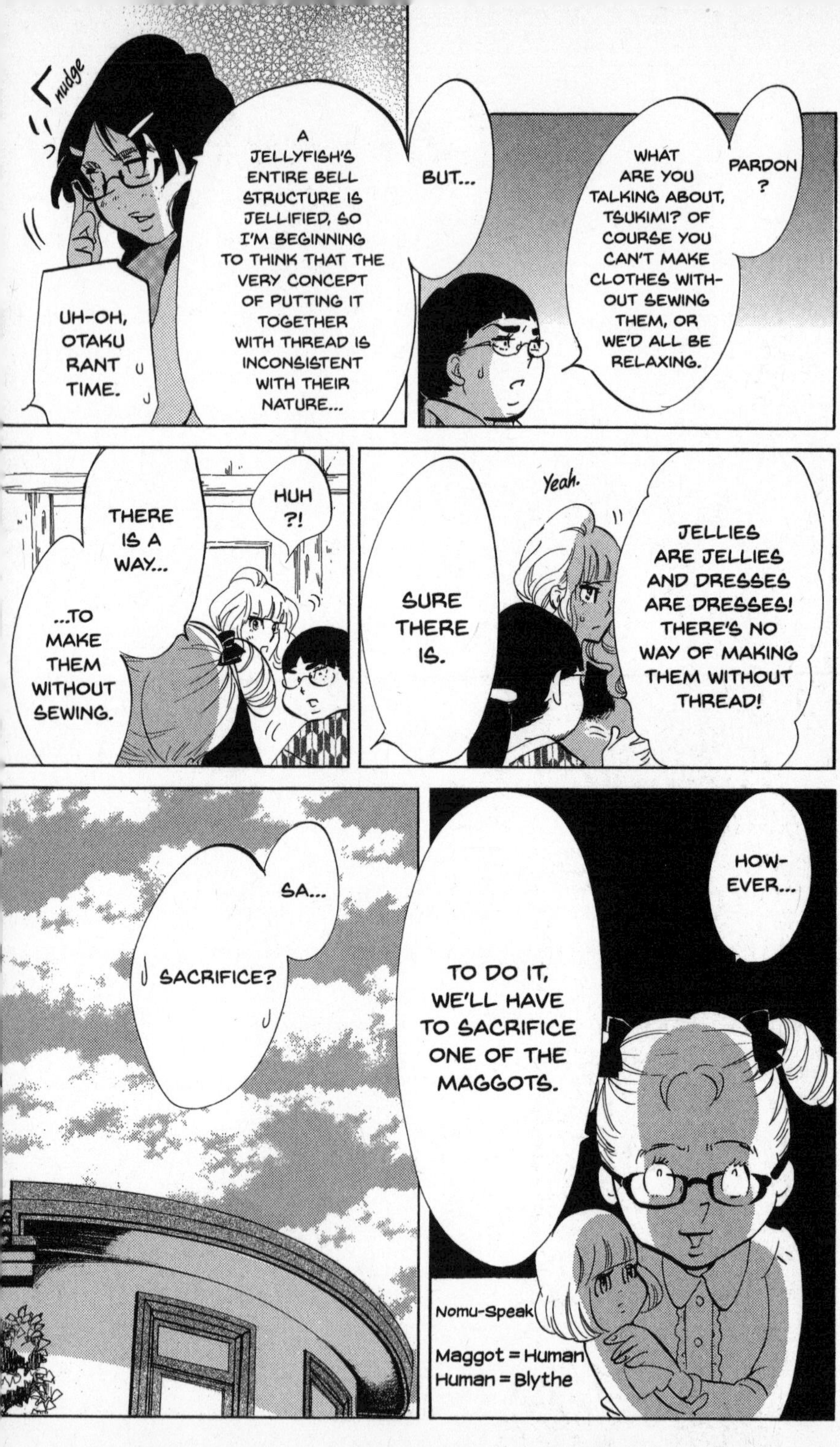
PARDON?
WHAT ARE YOU TALKING ABOUT, TSUKIMI? OF COURSE YOU CAN'T MAKE CLOTHES WITH-OUT SEWING THEM, OR WE'D ALL BE RELAXING.
BUT...
A JELLYFISH'S ENTIRE BELL STRUCTURE IS JELLIFIED, SO I'M BEGINNING TO THINK THAT THE VERY CONCEPT OF PUTTING IT TOGETHER WITH THREAD IS INCONSISTENT WITH THEIR NATURE...
nudge
UH-OH, OTAKU RANT TIME.
JELLIES ARE JELLIES AND DRESSES ARE DRESSES! THERE'S NO WAY OF MAKING THEM WITHOUT THREAD!
Yeah.
SURE THERE IS.
HUH?!
THERE IS A WAY...
...TO MAKE THEM WITHOUT SEWING.
HOW-EVER...
TO DO IT, WE'LL HAVE TO SACRIFICE ONE OF THE MAGGOTS.
Nomu-Speak
Maggot = Human
Human = Blythe
SA...
SACRIFICE?

Episode 33

007: From Amamizu-kan with Love

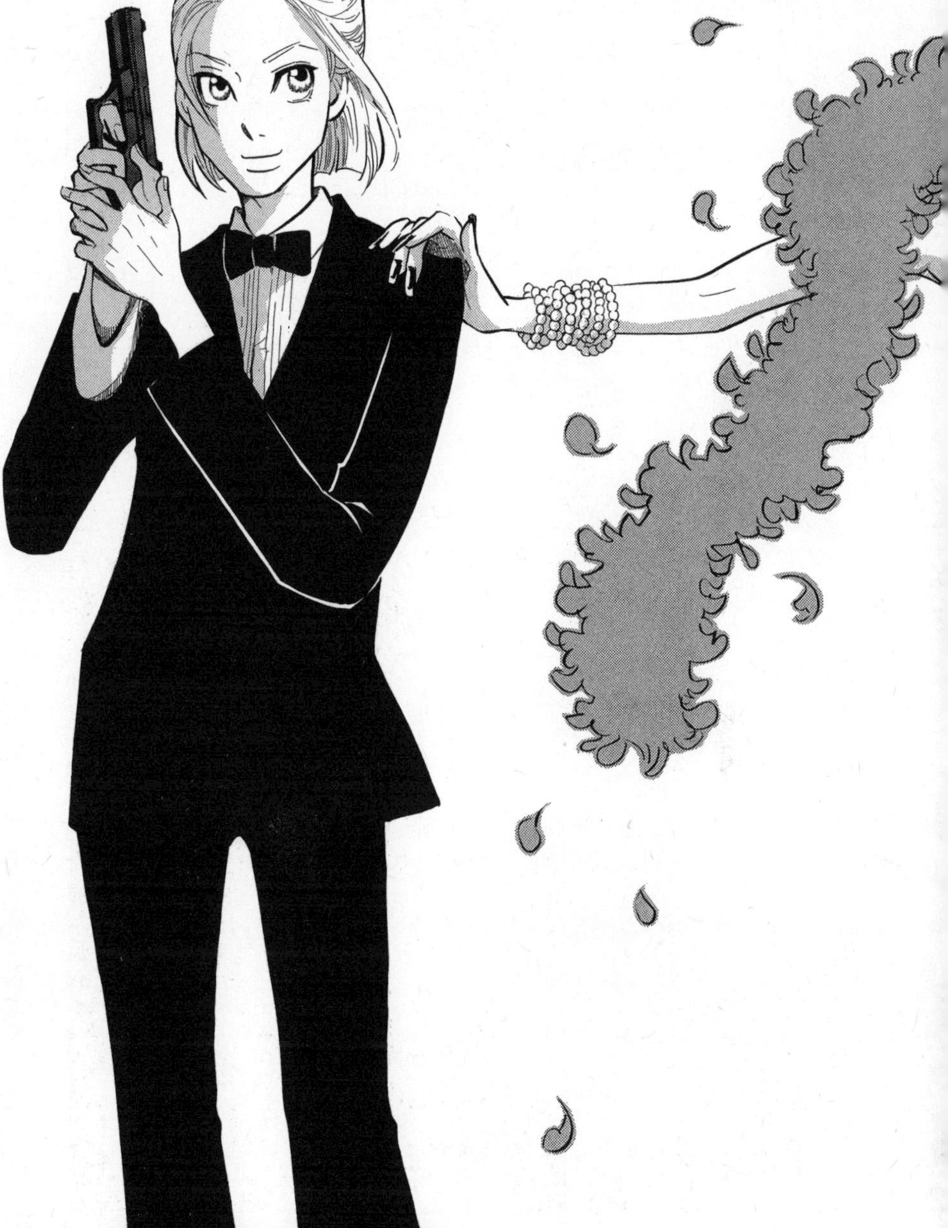

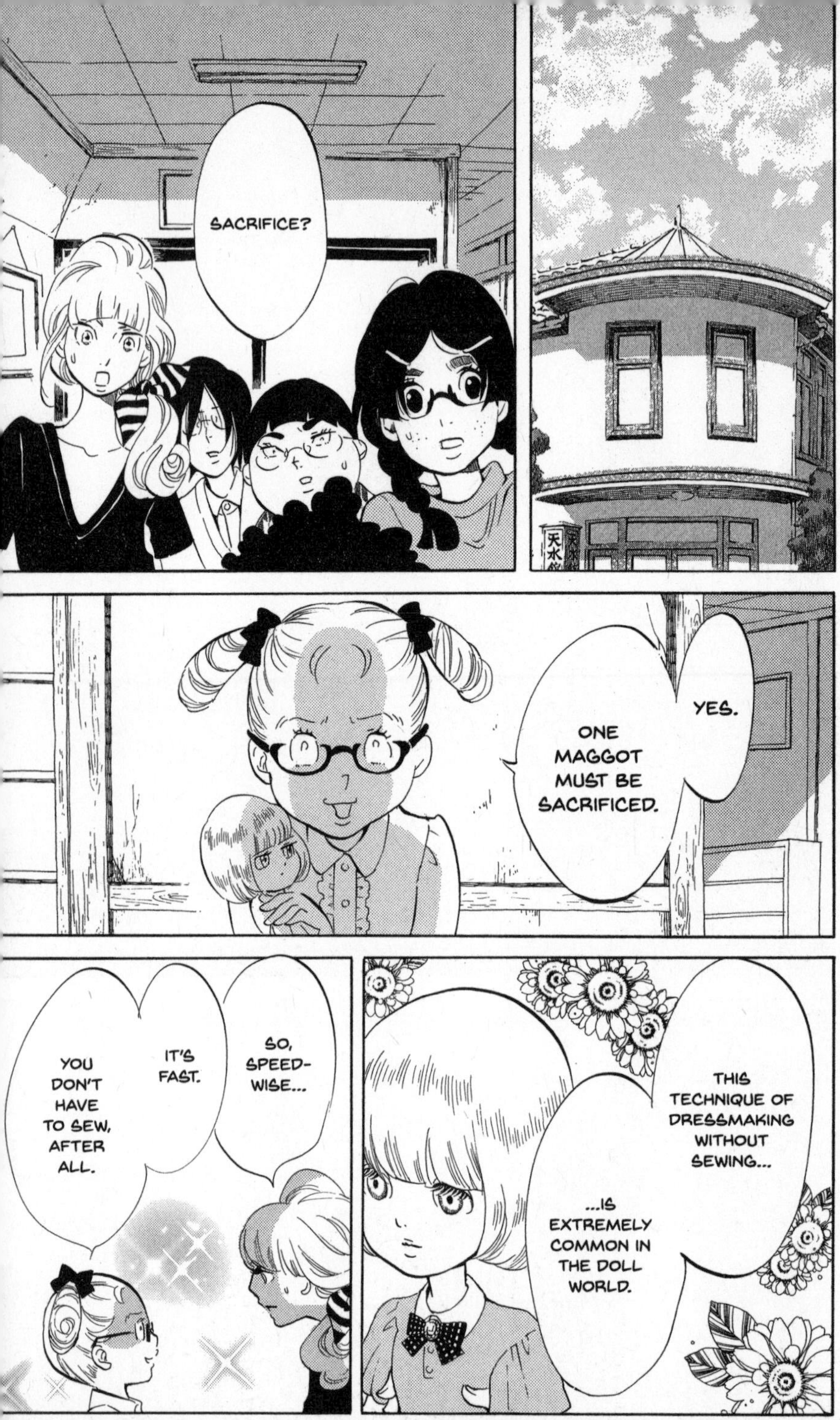
SACRIFICE?
YES.
ONE MAGGOT MUST BE SACRIFICED.
THIS TECHNIQUE OF DRESSMAKING WITHOUT SEWING...
...IS EXTREMELY COMMON IN THE DOLL WORLD.
SO, SPEED-WISE...
IT'S FAST.
YOU DON'T HAVE TO SEW, AFTER ALL.

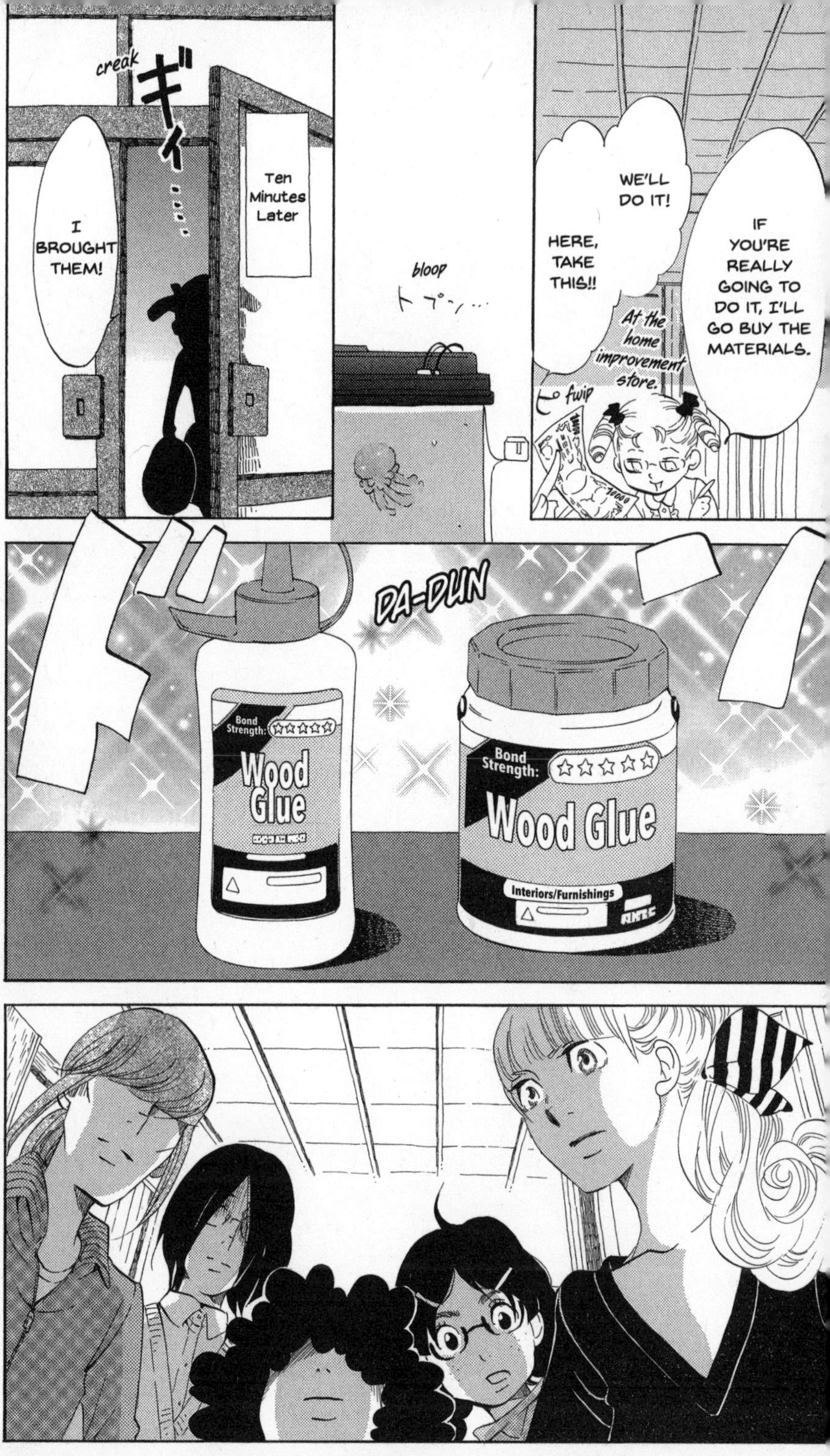
IF YOU'RE REALLY GOING TO DO IT, I'LL GO BUY THE MATERIALS.
At the home improvement store.
WE'LL DO IT!
HERE, TAKE THIS!!
fwip
bloop
creak
Ten Minutes Later
I BROUGHT THEM!
DA-DUN
Bond Strength:
Wood Glue
Bond Strength:
Wood Glue
Interiors/Furnishings

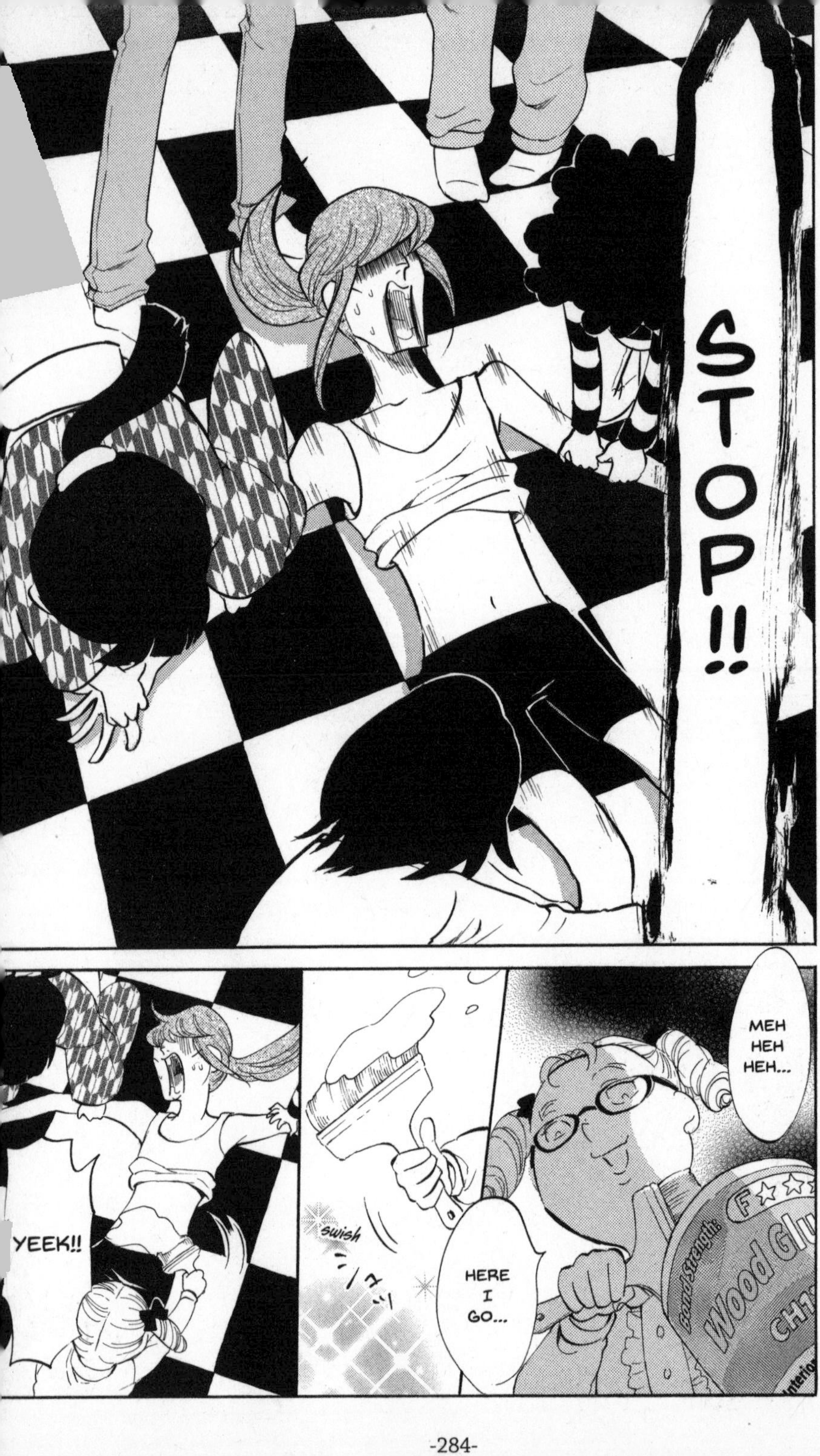
STOP!!
MEH HEH HEH...
HERE I GO...
swish
YEEK!!

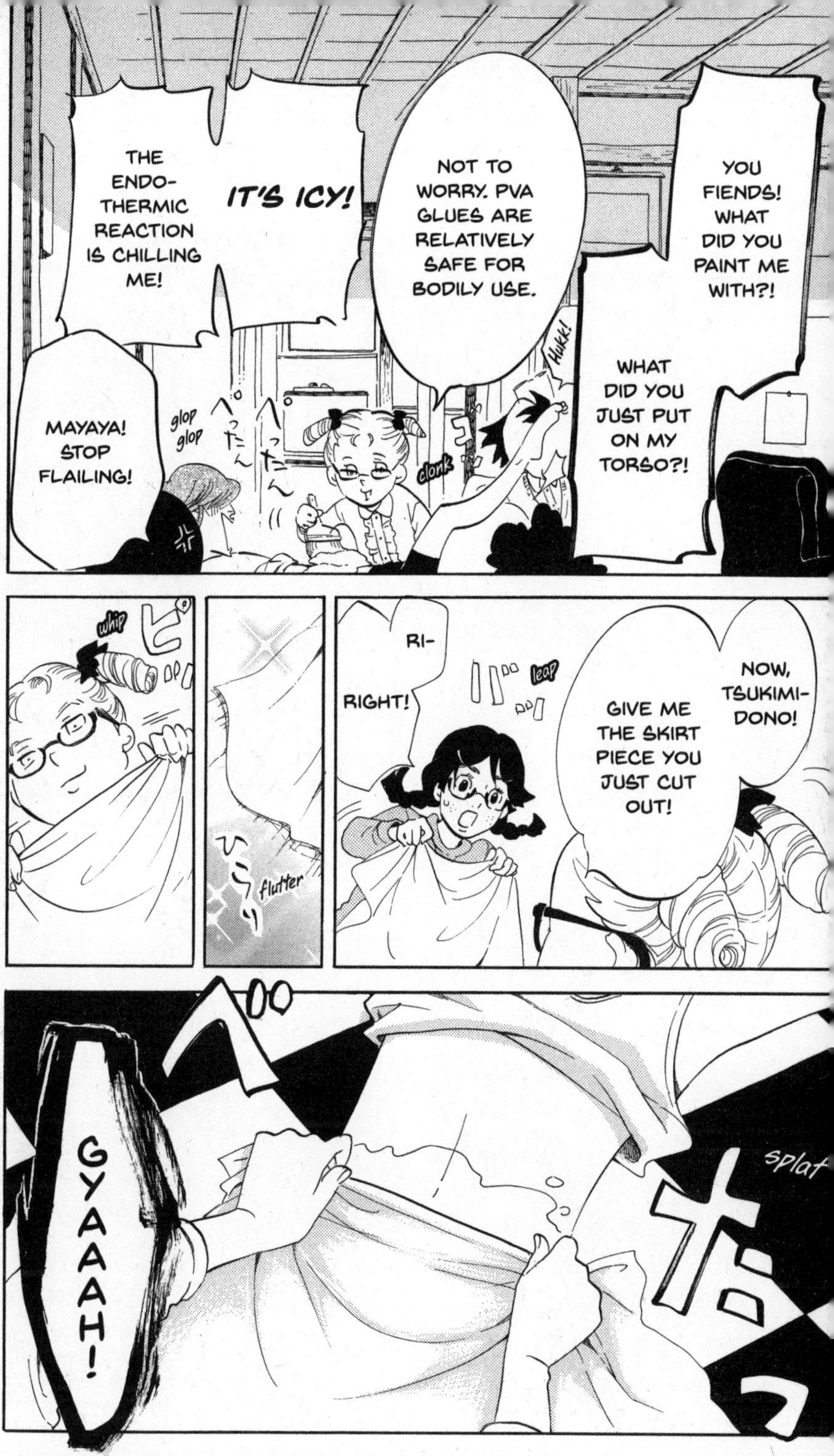
YOU FIENDS! WHAT DID YOU PAINT ME WITH?!
Hukk!
WHAT DID YOU JUST PUT ON MY TORSO?!
NOT TO WORRY. PVA GLUES ARE RELATIVELY SAFE FOR BODILY USE.
clonk
IT'S ICY!
THE ENDO-THERMIC REACTION IS CHILLING ME!
MAYAYA! STOP FLAILING!
glop glop
NOW, TSUKIMI-DONO!
GIVE ME THE SKIRT PIECE YOU JUST CUT OUT!
leap
RI-
RIGHT!
flutter
whip
splat
GYAAAH!

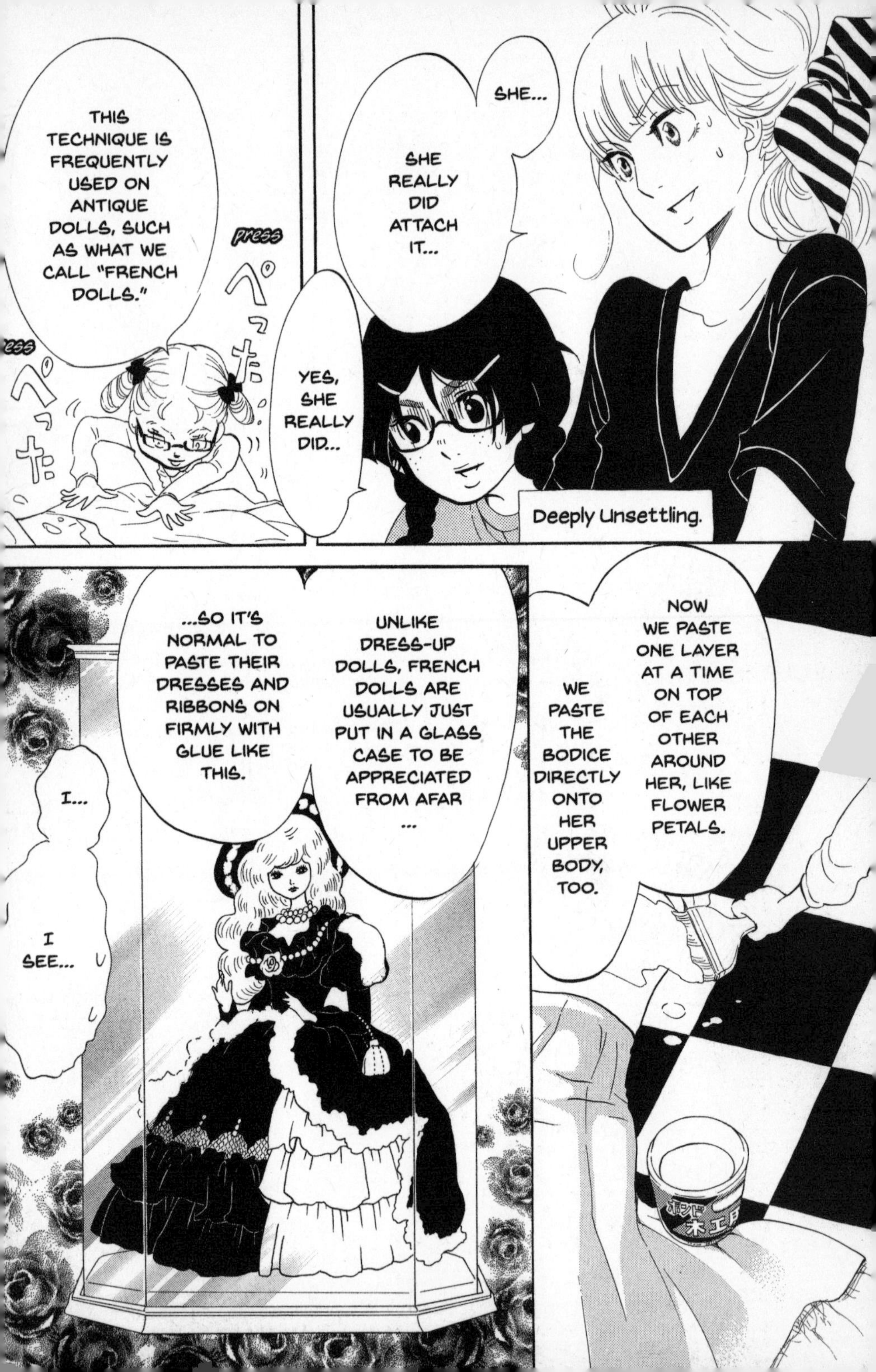
SHE...
SHE REALLY DID ATTACH IT...
YES, SHE REALLY DID...
Deeply Unsettling.
THIS TECHNIQUE IS FREQUENTLY USED ON ANTIQUE DOLLS, SUCH AS WHAT WE CALL "FRENCH DOLLS."
press
NOW WE PASTE ONE LAYER AT A TIME ON TOP OF EACH OTHER AROUND HER, LIKE FLOWER PETALS.
WE PASTE THE BODICE DIRECTLY ONTO HER UPPER BODY, TOO.
UNLIKE DRESS-UP DOLLS, FRENCH DOLLS ARE USUALLY JUST PUT IN A GLASS CASE TO BE APPRECIATED FROM AFAR ...
...SO IT'S NORMAL TO PASTE THEIR DRESSES AND RIBBONS ON FIRMLY WITH GLUE LIKE THIS.
I...
I SEE...

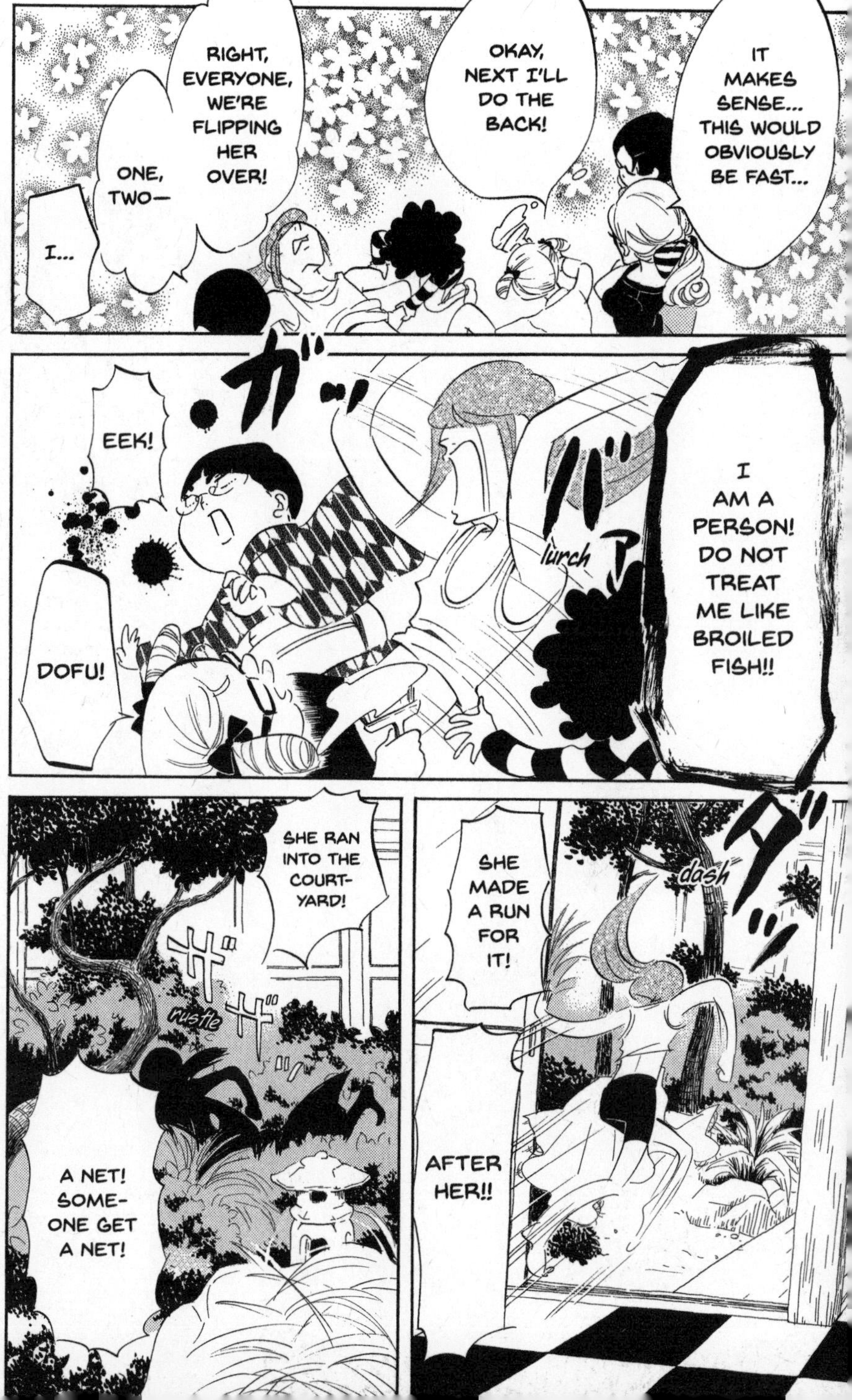
IT MAKES SENSE... THIS WOULD OBVIOUSLY BE FAST...
OKAY, NEXT I'LL DO THE BACK!
RIGHT, EVERYONE, WE'RE FLIPPING HER OVER!
ONE, TWO—
I...
I AM A PERSON! DO NOT TREAT ME LIKE BROILED FISH!!
lurch
EEK!
DOFU!
dash
SHE MADE A RUN FOR IT!
AFTER HER!!
SHE RAN INTO THE COURT-YARD!
rustle
A NET! SOME-ONE GET A NET!

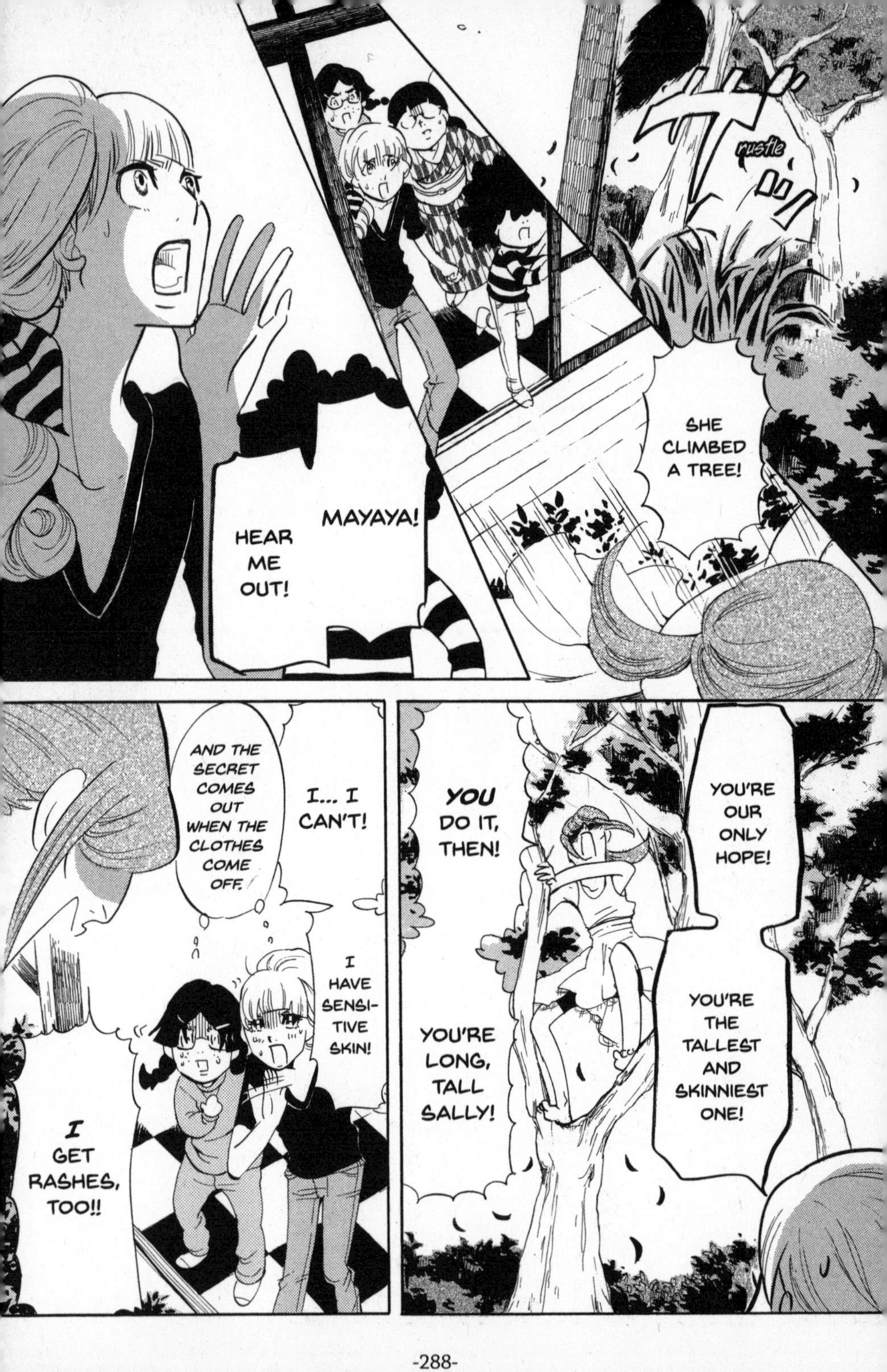
rustle
SHE CLIMBED A TREE!
MAYAYA!
HEAR ME OUT!
YOU'RE OUR ONLY HOPE!
YOU'RE THE TALLEST AND SKINNIEST ONE!
YOU DO IT, THEN!
YOU'RE LONG, TALL SALLY!
I... I CAN'T!
AND THE SECRET COMES OUT WHEN THE CLOTHES COME OFF.
I HAVE SENSITIVE SKIN!
I GET RASHES, TOO!!

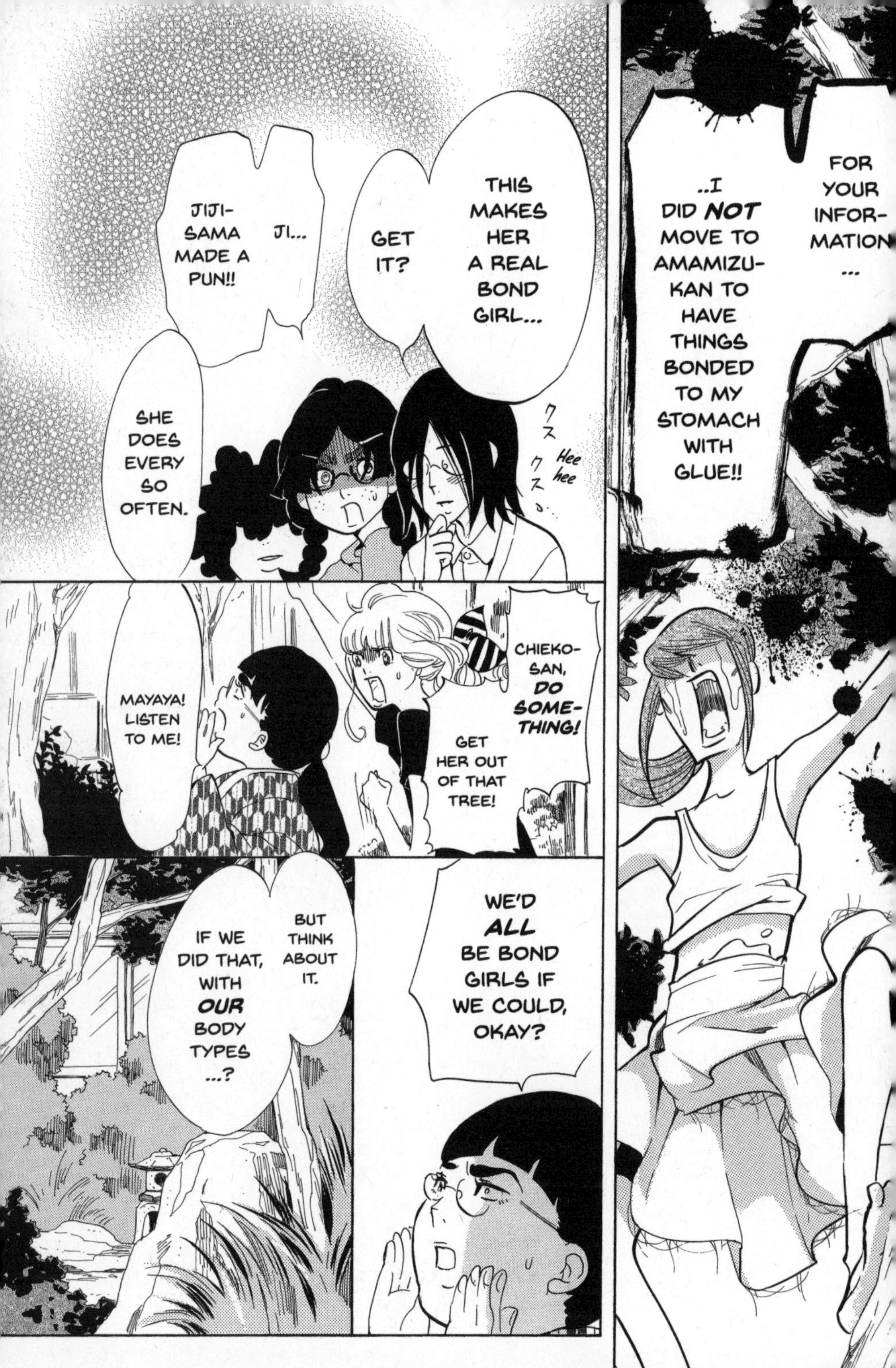
FOR YOUR INFORMATION...
..I DID NOT MOVE TO AMAMIZUKAN TO HAVE THINGS BONDED TO MY STOMACH WITH GLUE!!
THIS MAKES HER A REAL BOND GIRL...
GET IT?
JI...
JIJI-SAMA MADE A PUN!!
クス クス
Hee hee
SHE DOES EVERY SO OFTEN.
CHIEKO-SAN, DO SOMETHING!
GET HER OUT OF THAT TREE!
MAYAYA! LISTEN TO ME!
WE'D ALL BE BOND GIRLS IF WE COULD, OKAY?
BUT THINK ABOUT IT.
IF WE DID THAT, WITH OUR BODY TYPES ...?

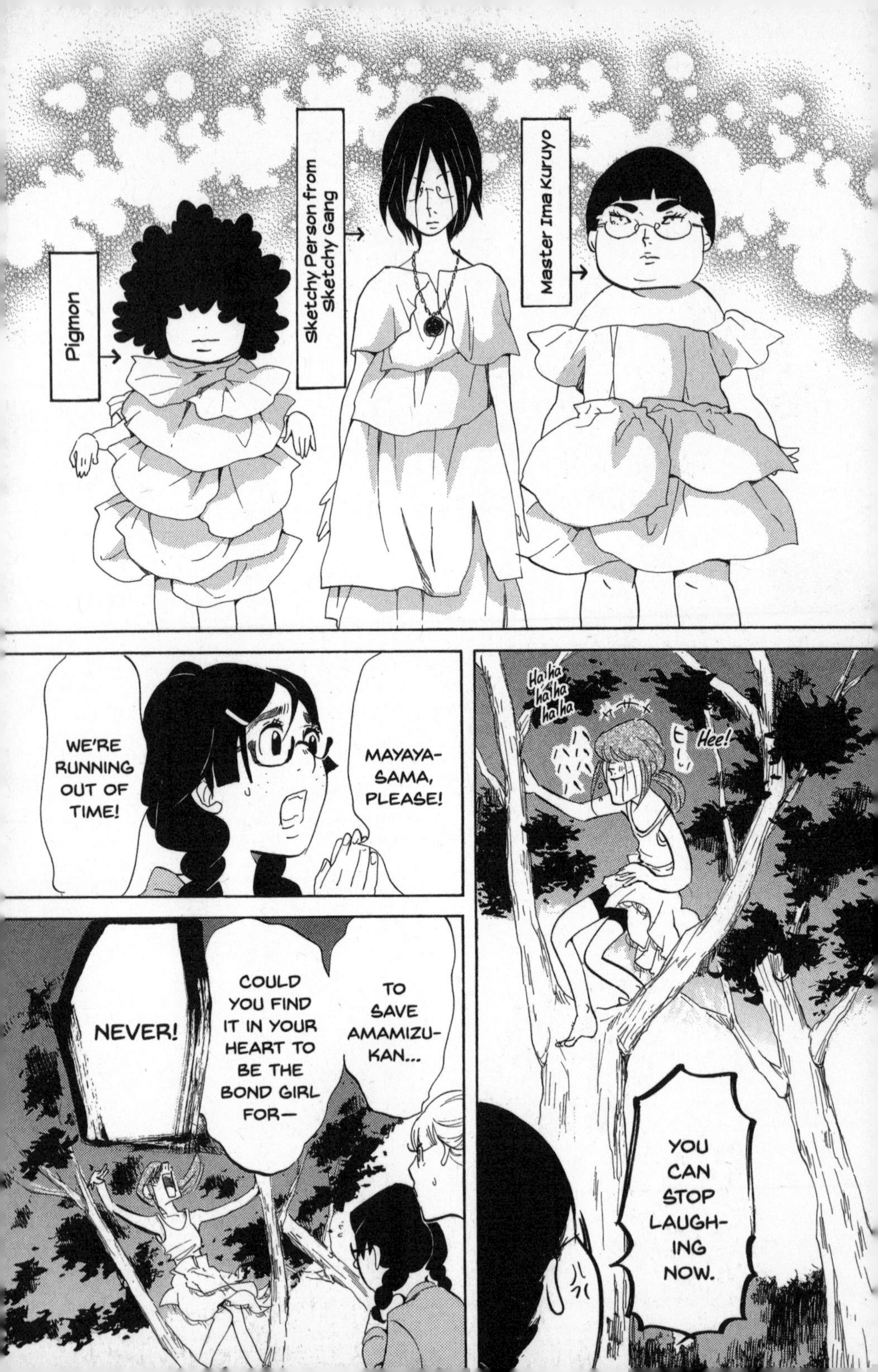
Master Ima Kuruyo
Sketchy Person from Sketchy Gang
Pigmon
Ha ha ha ha ha ha
Hee!
YOU CAN STOP LAUGHING NOW.
MAYAYA-SAMA, PLEASE!
WE'RE RUNNING OUT OF TIME!
TO SAVE AMAMIZUKAN...
COULD YOU FIND IT IN YOUR HEART TO BE THE BOND GIRL FOR—
NEVER!

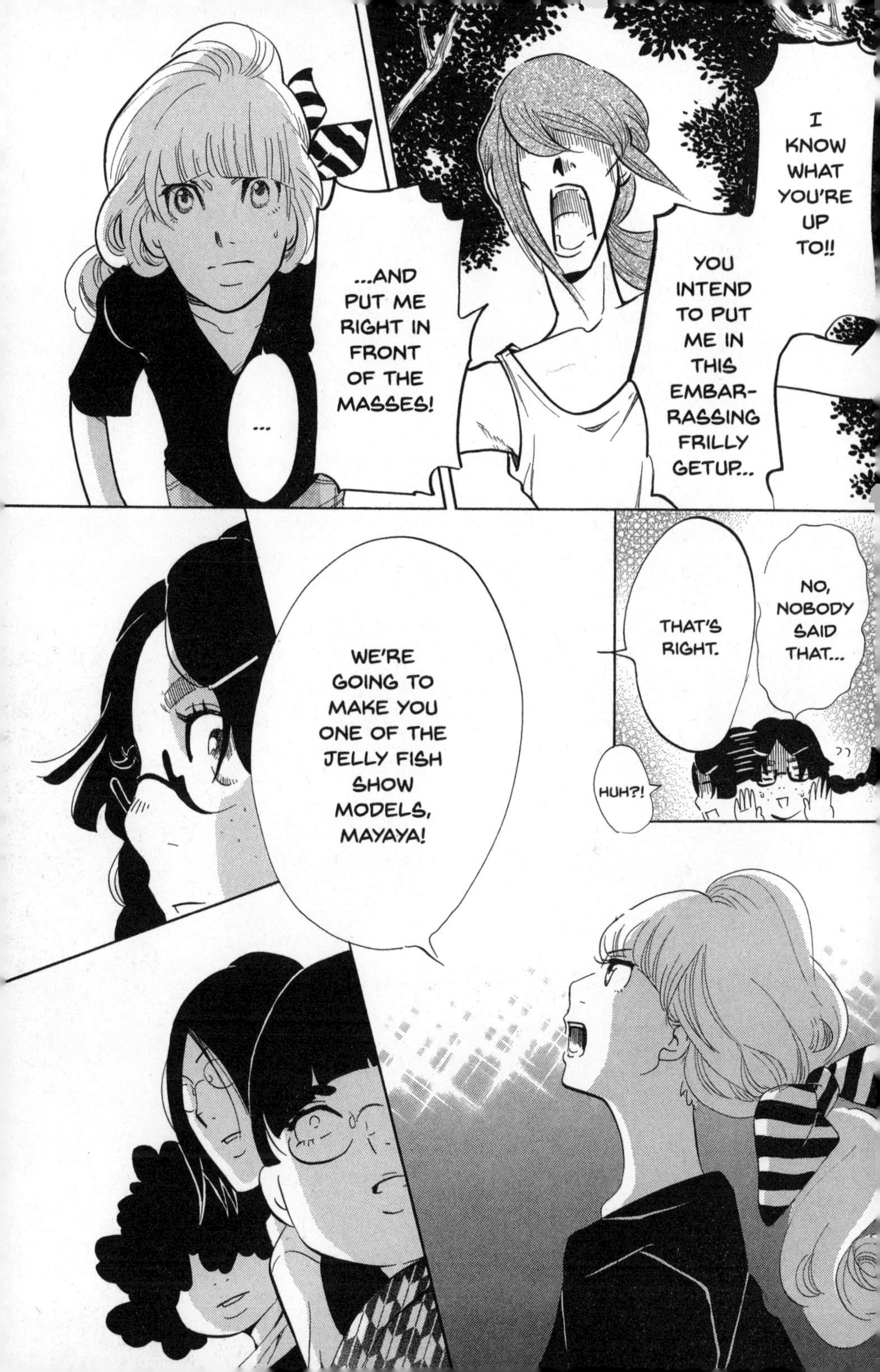
I KNOW WHAT YOU'RE UP TO!!
YOU INTEND TO PUT ME IN THIS EMBARRASSING FRILLY GETUP...
...AND PUT ME RIGHT IN FRONT OF THE MASSES!
...
NO, NOBODY SAID THAT...
THAT'S RIGHT.
HUH?!
WE'RE GOING TO MAKE YOU ONE OF THE JELLY FISH SHOW MODELS, MAYAYA!

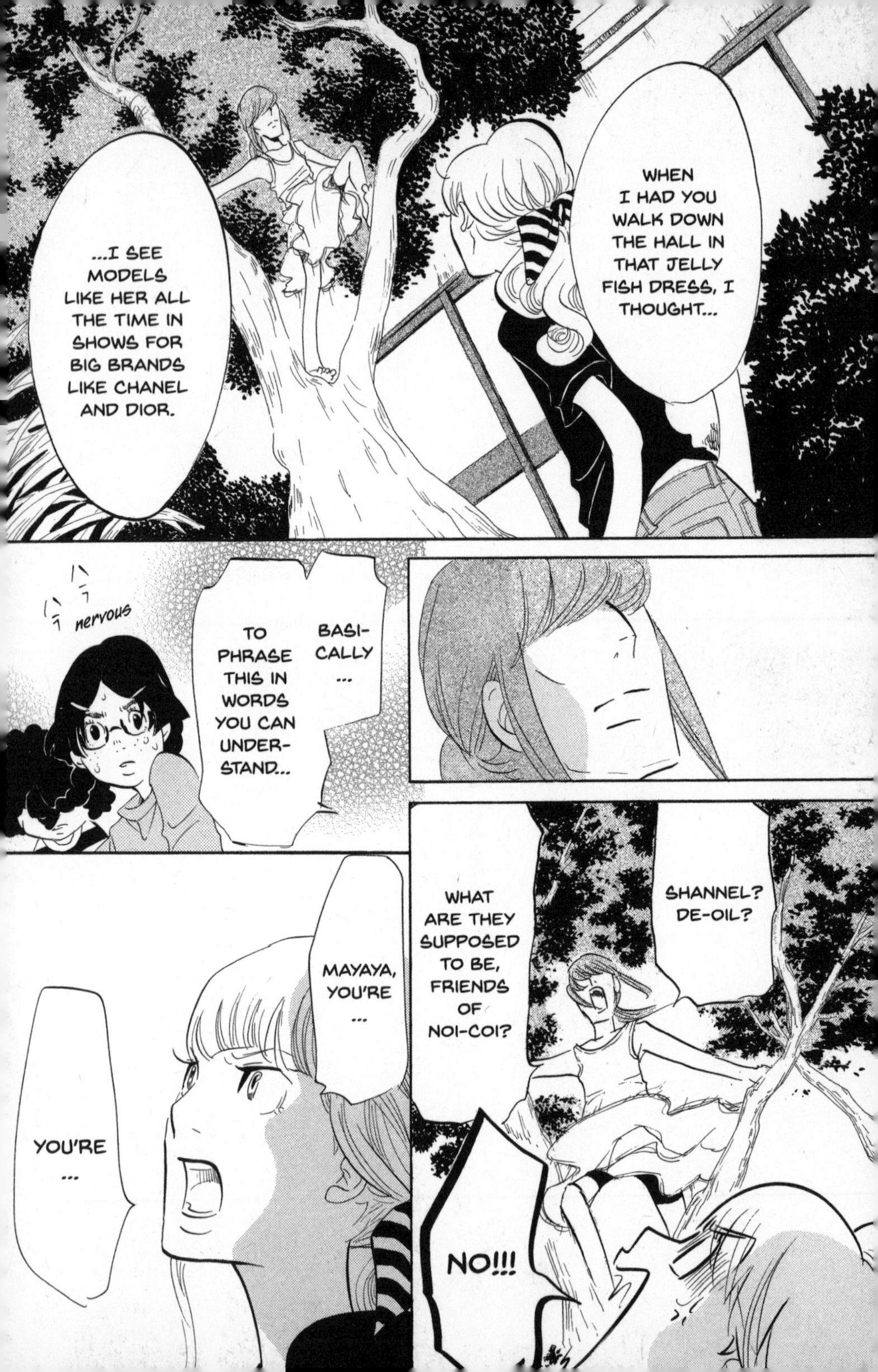
WHEN I HAD YOU WALK DOWN THE HALL IN THAT JELLY FISH DRESS, I THOUGHT...
...I SEE MODELS LIKE HER ALL THE TIME IN SHOWS FOR BIG BRANDS LIKE CHANEL AND DIOR.
BASI-CALLY ...
TO PHRASE THIS IN WORDS YOU CAN UNDER-STAND...
nervous
SHANNEL? DE-OIL?
WHAT ARE THEY SUPPOSED TO BE, FRIENDS OF NOI-COI?
NO!!!
MAYAYA, YOU'RE ...
YOU'RE ...

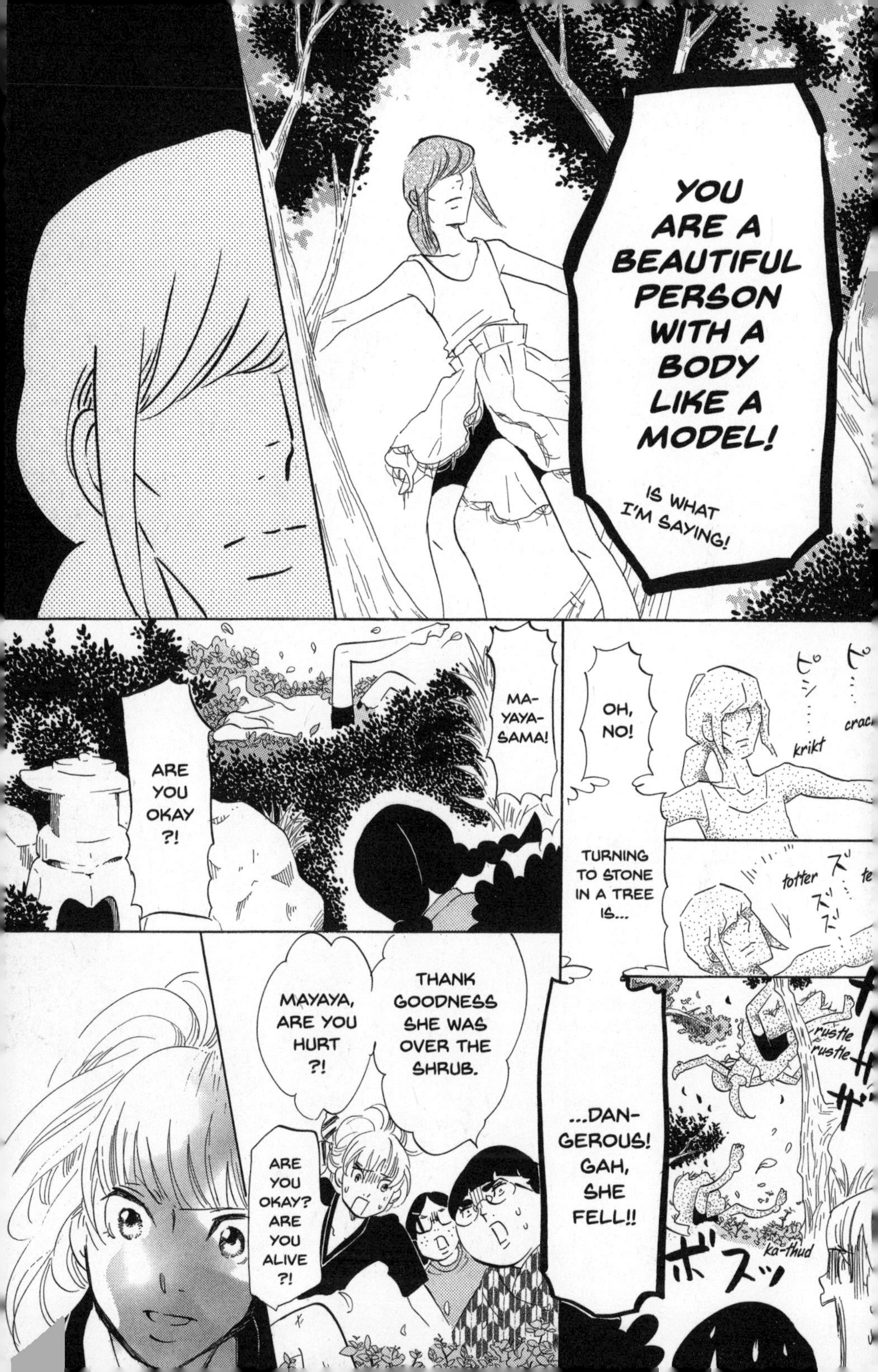
YOU ARE A BEAUTIFUL PERSON WITH A BODY LIKE A MODEL!
IS WHAT I'M SAYING!
crack
krikt
OH, NO!
totter
TURNING TO STONE IN A TREE IS...
MA-YAYA-SAMA!
ARE YOU OKAY?!
rustle rustle
ボスッ
ka-thud
...DAN-GEROUS! GAH, SHE FELL!!
THANK GOODNESS SHE WAS OVER THE SHRUB.
MAYAYA, ARE YOU HURT?!
ARE YOU OKAY? ARE YOU ALIVE?!

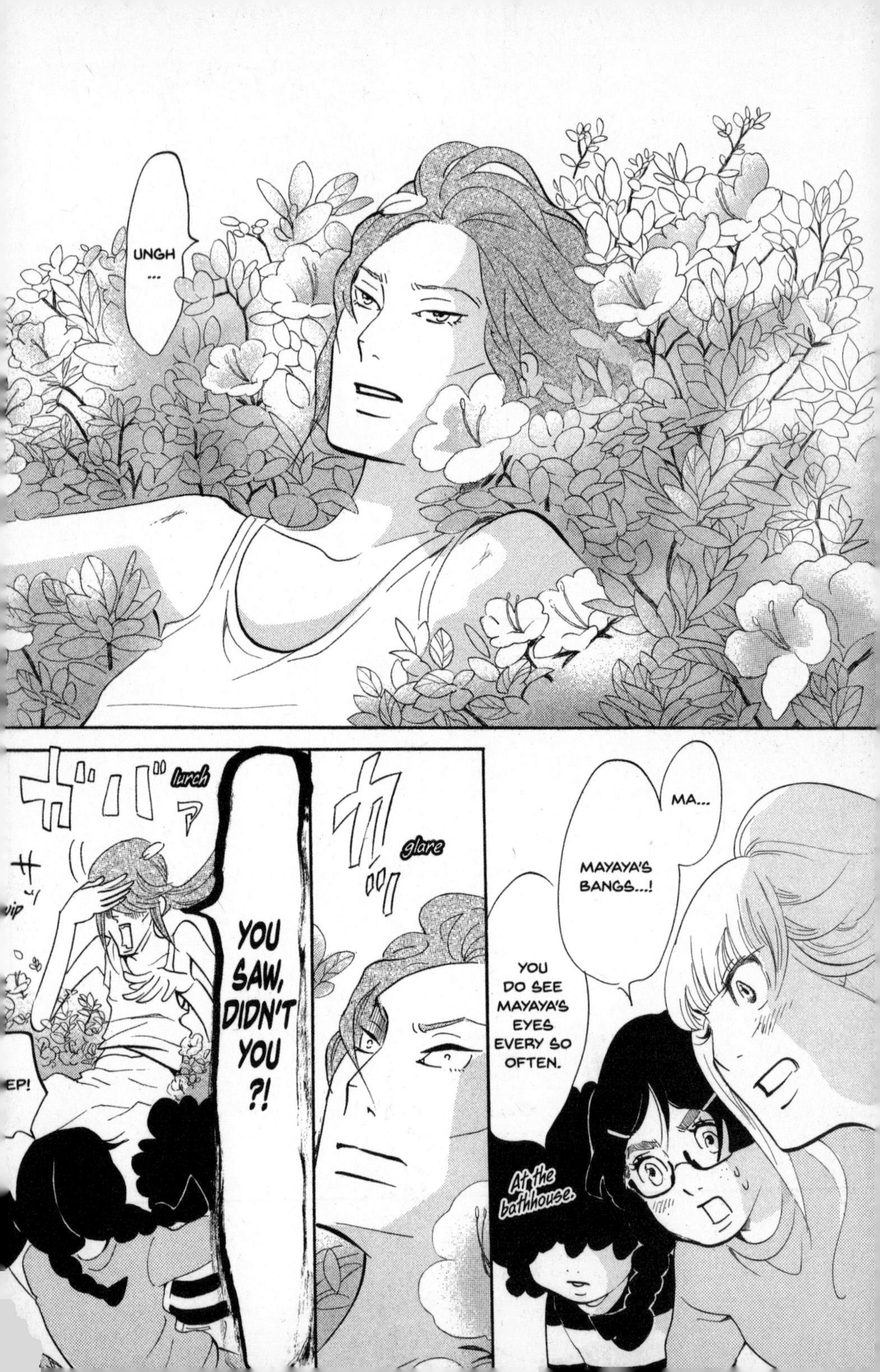
UNGH ...
MA...
MAYAYA'S BANGS...!
YOU DO SEE MAYAYA'S EYES EVERY SO OFTEN.
At the bathhouse.
glare
YOU SAW, DIDN'T YOU ?!
lurch
EP!

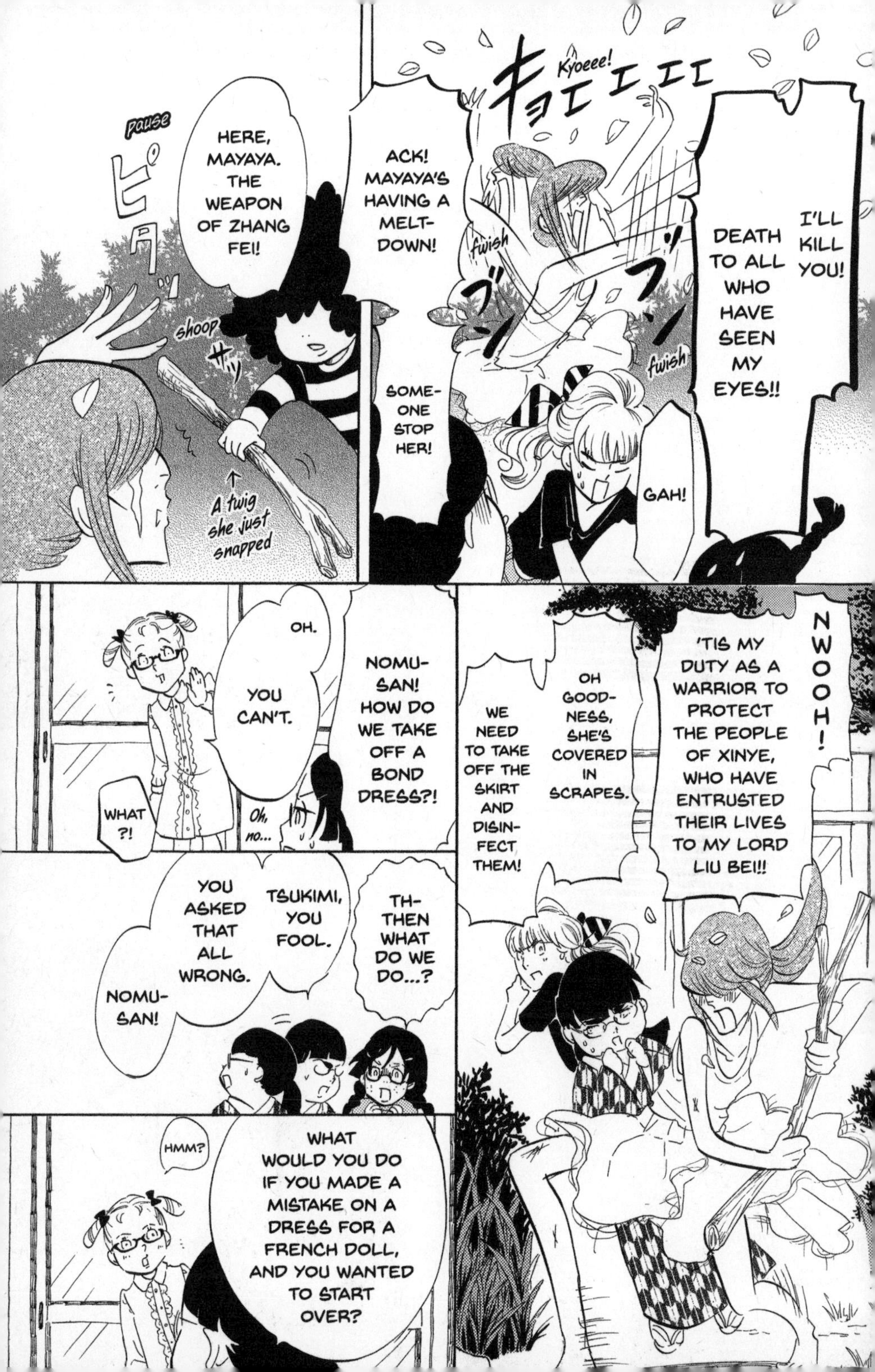
Kyoeee!
I'LL KILL YOU!
DEATH TO ALL WHO HAVE SEEN MY EYES!!
fwish
fwish
GAH!
ACK! MAYAYA'S HAVING A MELT-DOWN!
SOME-ONE STOP HER!
HERE, MAYAYA. THE WEAPON OF ZHANG FEI!
pause
shoop
A twig she just snapped
NWOOOH!
'TIS MY DUTY AS A WARRIOR TO PROTECT THE PEOPLE OF XINYE, WHO HAVE ENTRUSTED THEIR LIVES TO MY LORD LIU BEI!!
OH GOOD-NESS, SHE'S COVERED IN SCRAPES.
WE NEED TO TAKE OFF THE SKIRT AND DISIN-FECT THEM!
NOMU-SAN! HOW DO WE TAKE OFF A BOND DRESS?!
OH.
YOU CAN'T.
Oh, no...
WHAT?!
TH-THEN WHAT DO WE DO...?
TSUKIMI, YOU FOOL.
YOU ASKED THAT ALL WRONG.
NOMU-SAN!
WHAT WOULD YOU DO IF YOU MADE A MISTAKE ON A DRESS FOR A FRENCH DOLL, AND YOU WANTED TO START OVER?
HMM?

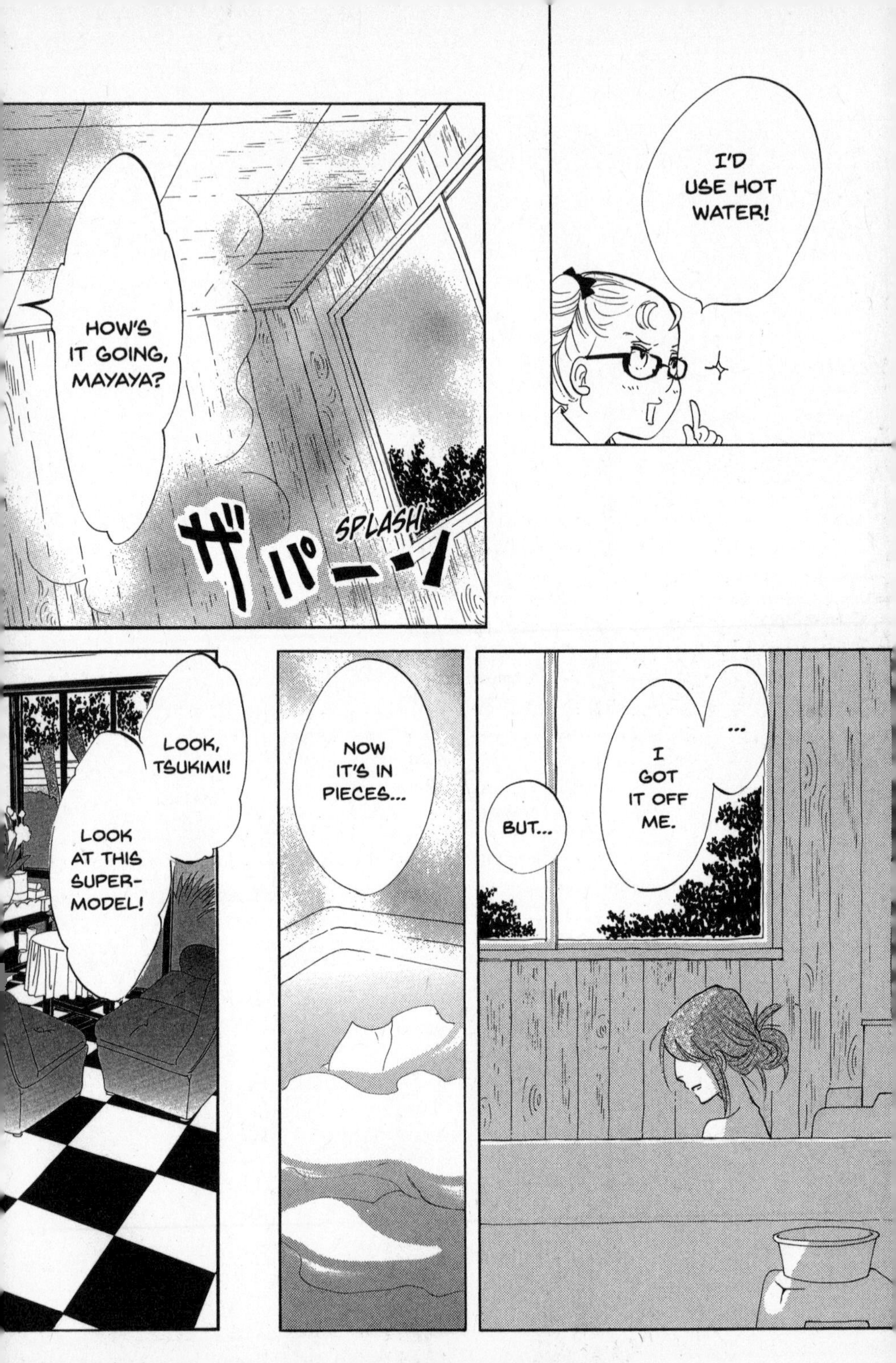
I'D USE HOT WATER!
HOW'S IT GOING, MAYAYA?
ザパーン
SPLASH
...
I GOT IT OFF ME.
BUT...
NOW IT'S IN PIECES...
LOOK, TSUKIMI!
LOOK AT THIS SUPER-MODEL!

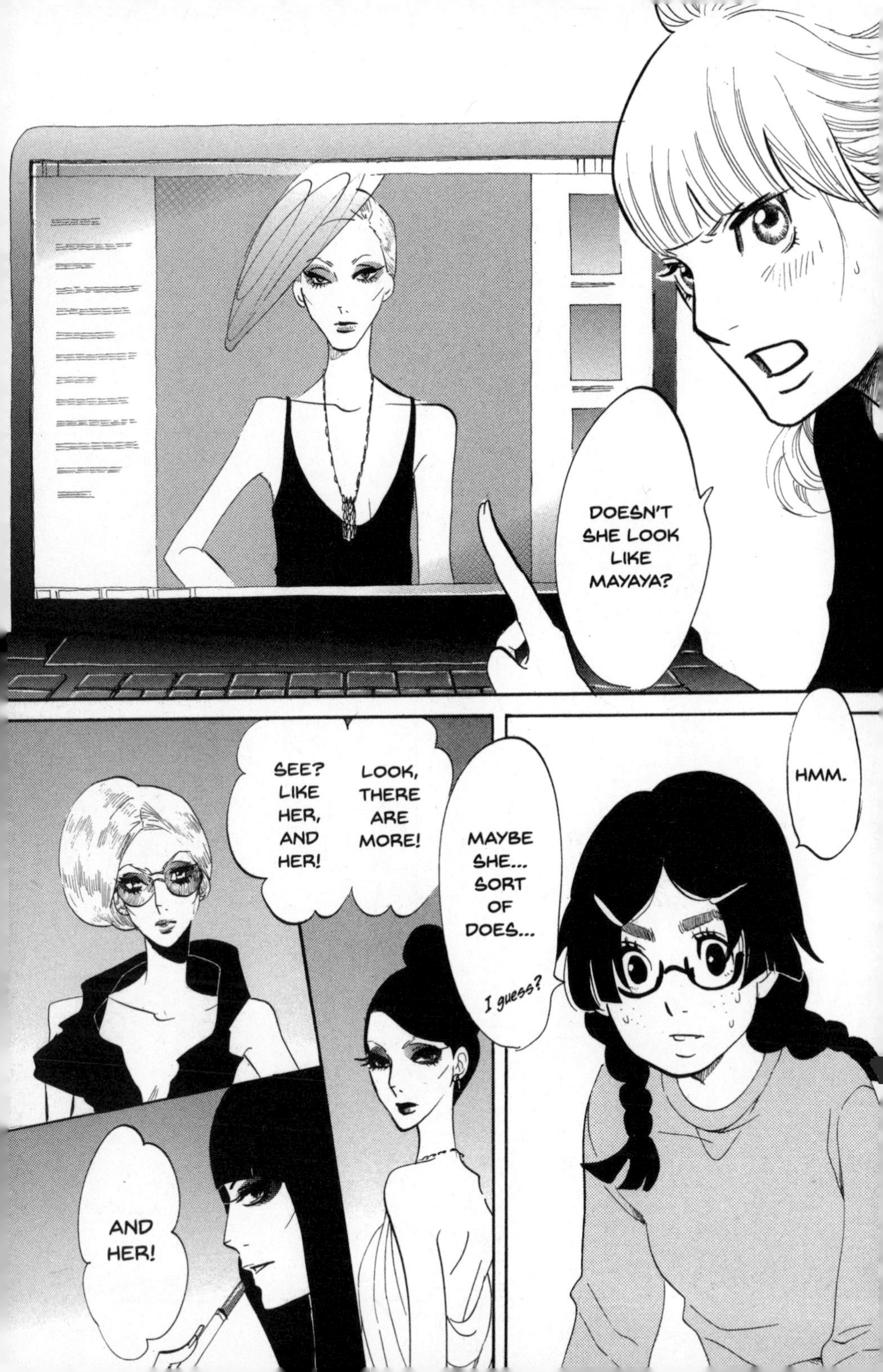
DOESN'T SHE LOOK LIKE MAYAYA?
HMM.
MAYBE SHE... SORT OF DOES...
I guess?
LOOK, THERE ARE MORE!
SEE? LIKE HER, AND HER!
AND HER!

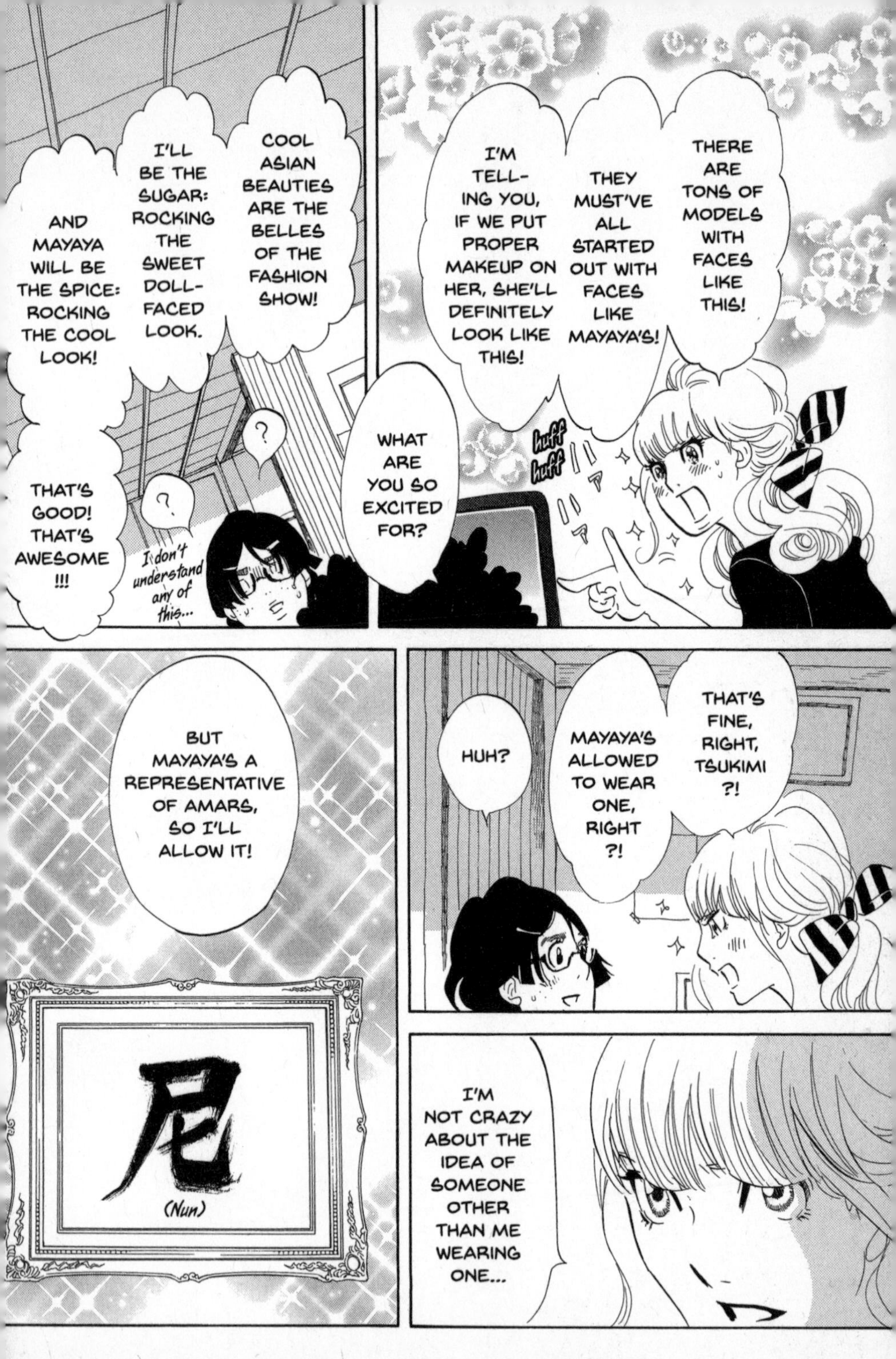
THERE ARE TONS OF MODELS WITH FACES LIKE THIS!
THEY MUST'VE ALL STARTED OUT WITH FACES LIKE MAYAYA'S!
I'M TELL-ING YOU, IF WE PUT PROPER MAKEUP ON HER, SHE'LL DEFINITELY LOOK LIKE THIS!
huff huff
WHAT ARE YOU SO EXCITED FOR?
COOL ASIAN BEAUTIES ARE THE BELLES OF THE FASHION SHOW!
I'LL BE THE SUGAR: ROCKING THE SWEET DOLL-FACED LOOK.
AND MAYAYA WILL BE THE SPICE: ROCKING THE COOL LOOK!
?
?
THAT'S GOOD! THAT'S AWESOME!!!
I don't understand any of this...
THAT'S FINE, RIGHT, TSUKIMI?!
MAYAYA'S ALLOWED TO WEAR ONE, RIGHT?!
HUH?
I'M NOT CRAZY ABOUT THE IDEA OF SOMEONE OTHER THAN ME WEARING ONE...
BUT MAYAYA'S A REPRESENTATIVE OF AMARS, SO I'LL ALLOW IT!
尼
(Nun)

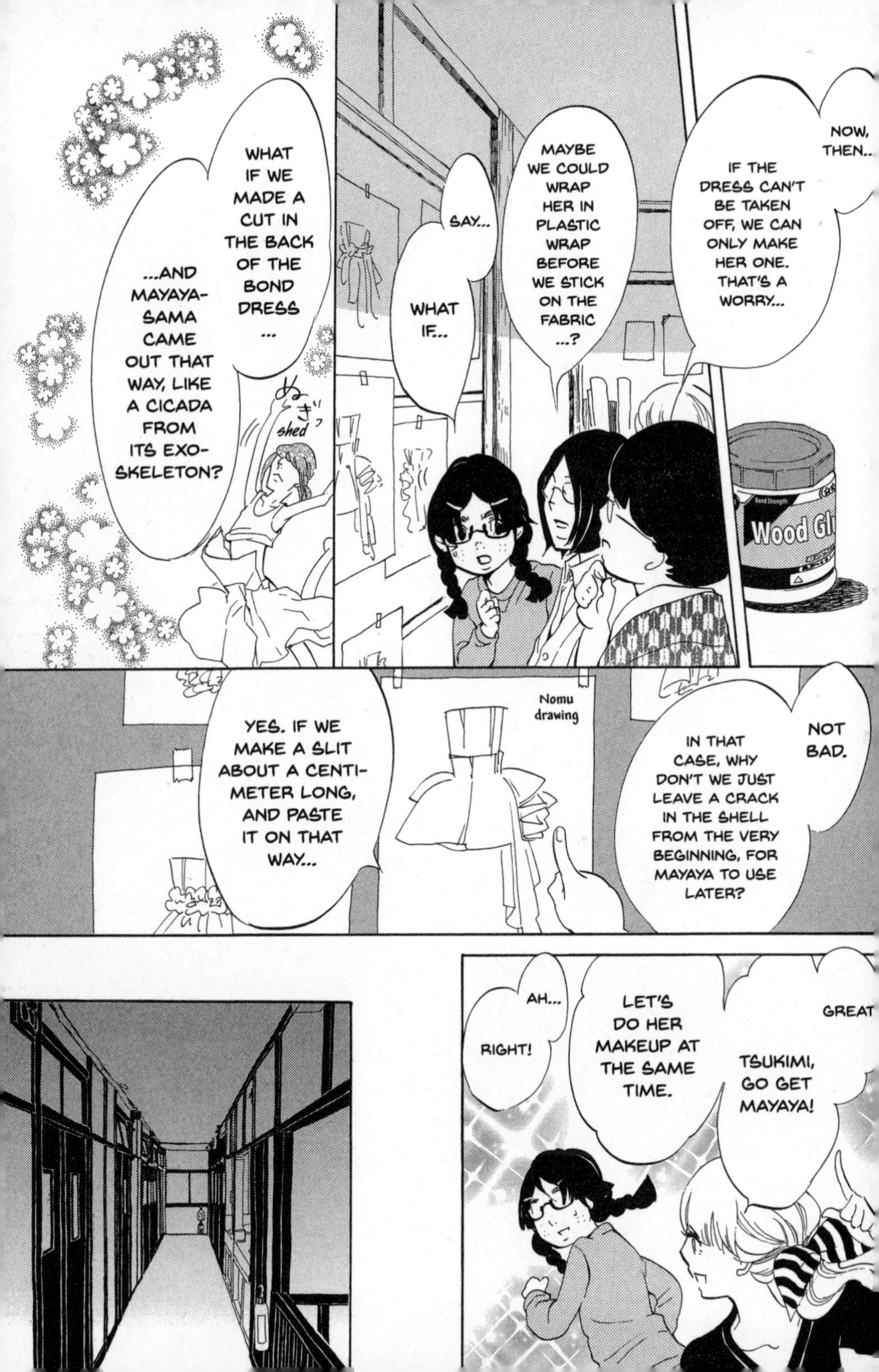
NOW, THEN...
IF THE DRESS CAN'T BE TAKEN OFF, WE CAN ONLY MAKE HER ONE. THAT'S A WORRY...
MAYBE WE COULD WRAP HER IN PLASTIC WRAP BEFORE WE STICK ON THE FABRIC ...?
SAY... WHAT IF...
WHAT IF WE MADE A CUT IN THE BACK OF THE BOND DRESS ...
...AND MAYAYA-SAMA CAME OUT THAT WAY, LIKE A CICADA FROM ITS EXO-SKELETON?
ぬぎっ
shed
NOT BAD.
IN THAT CASE, WHY DON'T WE JUST LEAVE A CRACK IN THE SHELL FROM THE VERY BEGINNING, FOR MAYAYA TO USE LATER?
Nomu drawing
YES. IF WE MAKE A SLIT ABOUT A CENTI-METER LONG, AND PASTE IT ON THAT WAY...
Wood Gl
GREAT
TSUKIMI, GO GET MAYAYA!
LET'S DO HER MAKEUP AT THE SAME TIME.
AH... RIGHT!

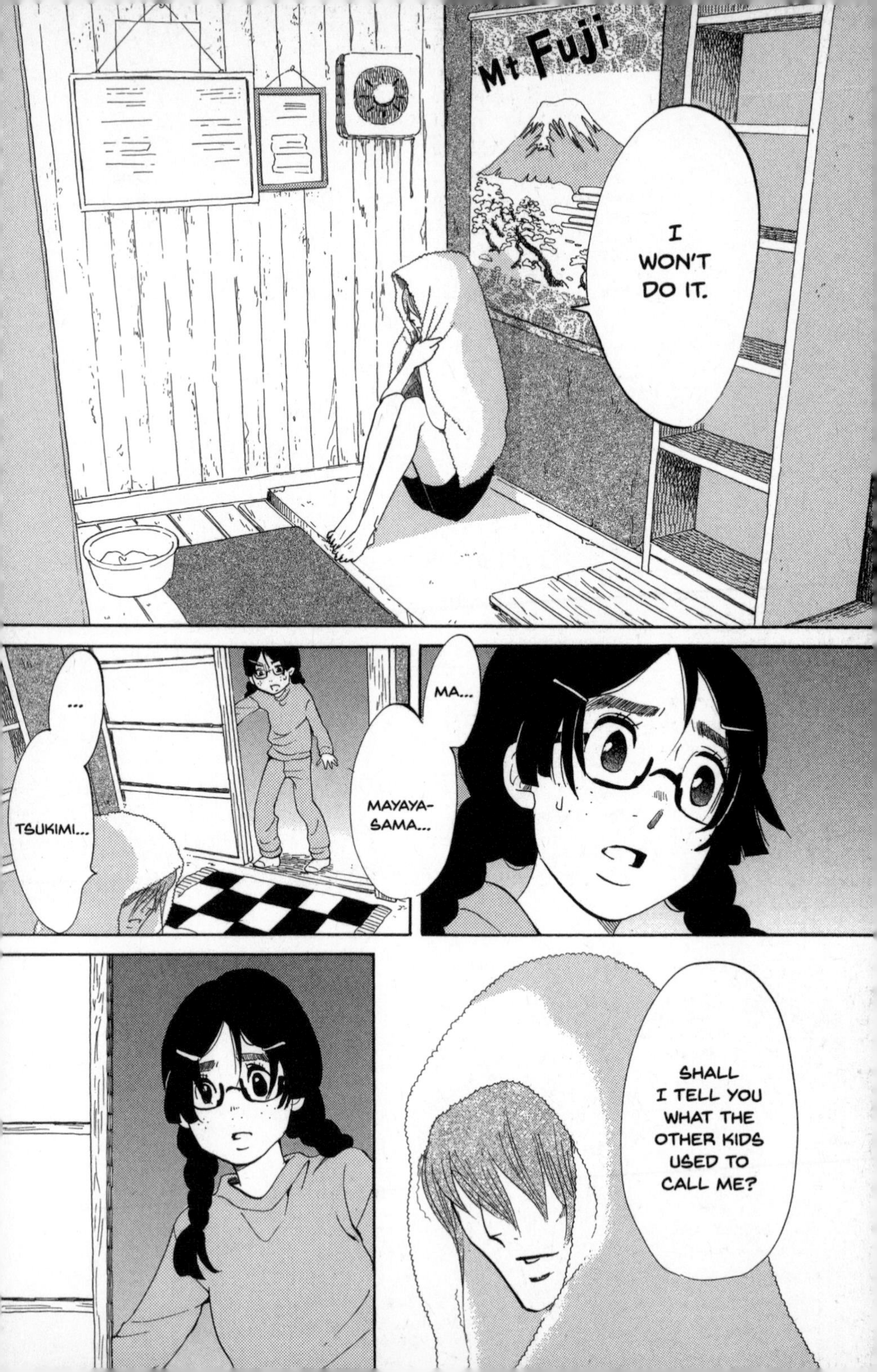
Mt Fuji
I WON'T DO IT.
MA...
MAYAYA-SAMA...
...
TSUKIMI...
SHALL I TELL YOU WHAT THE OTHER KIDS USED TO CALL ME?

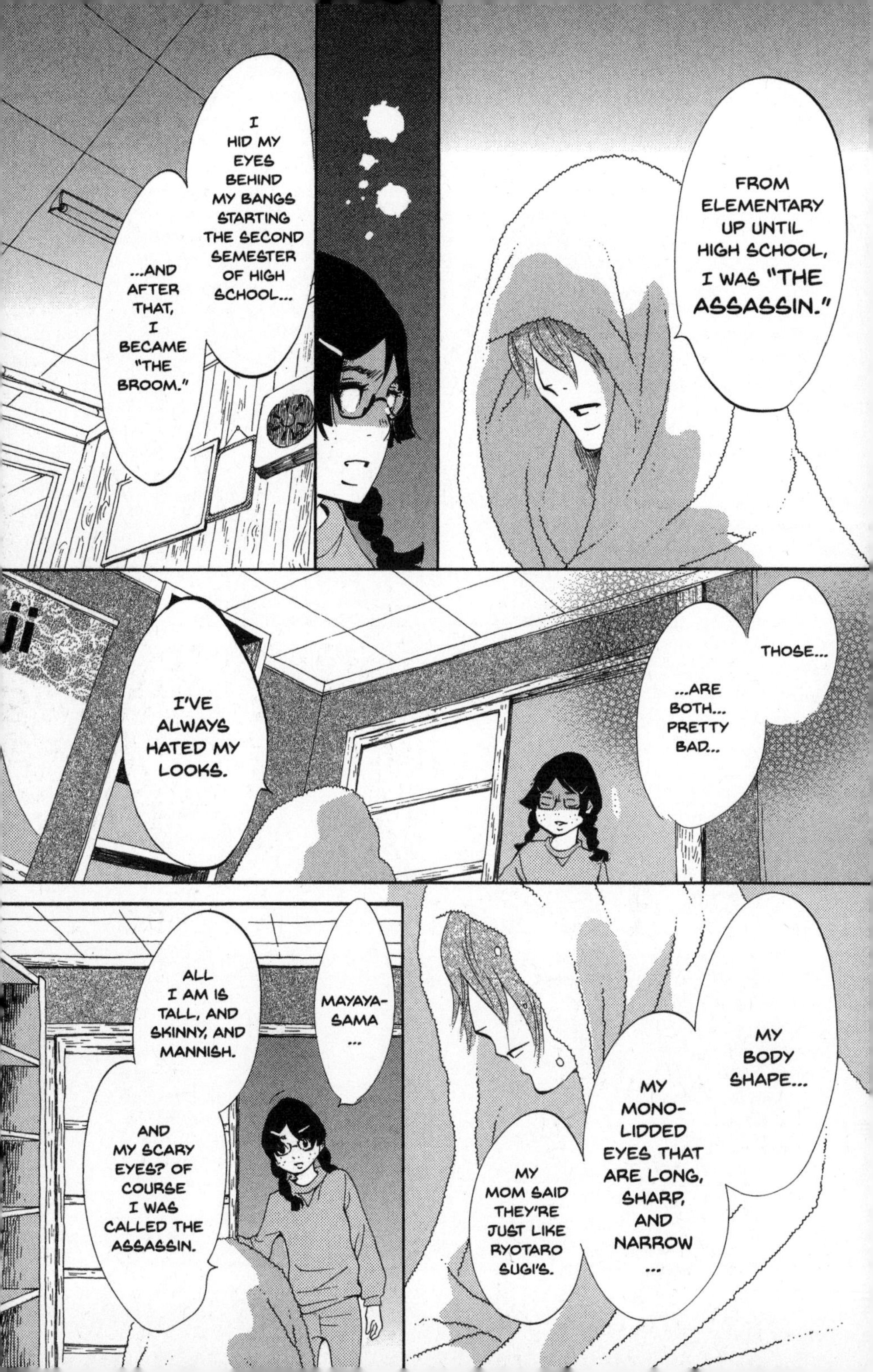
FROM ELEMENTARY UP UNTIL HIGH SCHOOL, I WAS "THE ASSASSIN."
I HID MY EYES BEHIND MY BANGS STARTING THE SECOND SEMESTER OF HIGH SCHOOL...
...AND AFTER THAT, I BECAME "THE BROOM."
THOSE...
...ARE BOTH... PRETTY BAD...
I'VE ALWAYS HATED MY LOOKS.
MY BODY SHAPE...
MY MONO-LIDDED EYES THAT ARE LONG, SHARP, AND NARROW ...
MY MOM SAID THEY'RE JUST LIKE RYOTARO SUGI'S.
MAYAYA-SAMA ...
ALL I AM IS TALL, AND SKINNY, AND MANNISH.
AND MY SCARY EYES? OF COURSE I WAS CALLED THE ASSASSIN.

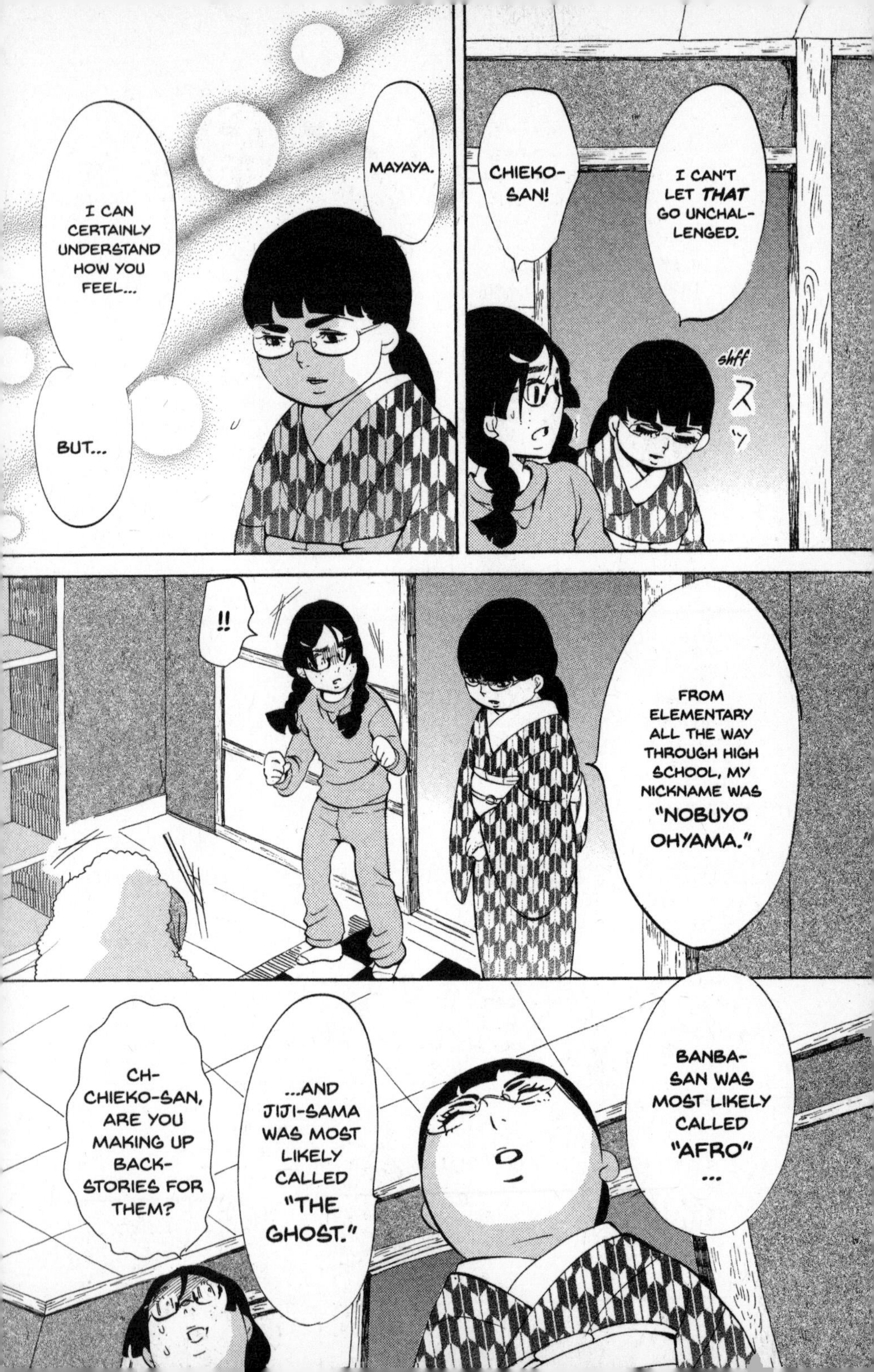

I CAN'T LET **THAT** GO UNCHALLENGED.
CHIEKO-SAN!
shff
スッ
MAYAYA.
I CAN CERTAINLY UNDERSTAND HOW YOU FEEL...
BUT...
FROM ELEMENTARY ALL THE WAY THROUGH HIGH SCHOOL, MY NICKNAME WAS "NOBUYO OHYAMA."
!!
BANBA-SAN WAS MOST LIKELY CALLED "AFRO" ...
...AND JIJI-SAMA WAS MOST LIKELY CALLED "THE GHOST."
CH-CHIEKO-SAN, ARE YOU MAKING UP BACK-STORIES FOR THEM?

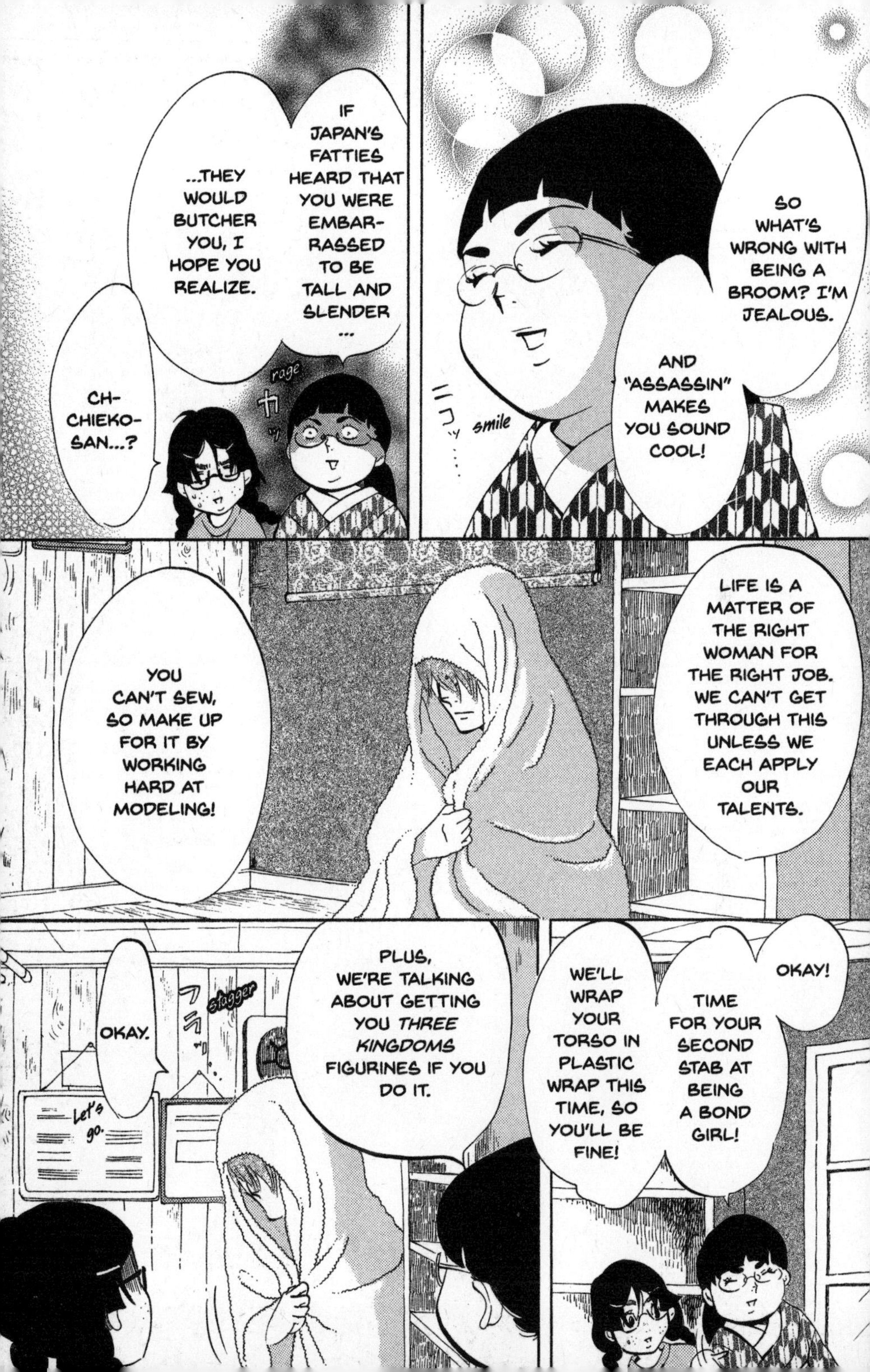
SO WHAT'S WRONG WITH BEING A BROOM? I'M JEALOUS.
AND "ASSASSIN" MAKES YOU SOUND COOL!
smile
IF JAPAN'S FATTIES HEARD THAT YOU WERE EMBAR-RASSED TO BE TALL AND SLENDER...
...THEY WOULD BUTCHER YOU, I HOPE YOU REALIZE.
rage
CH-CHIEKO-SAN...?
LIFE IS A MATTER OF THE RIGHT WOMAN FOR THE RIGHT JOB. WE CAN'T GET THROUGH THIS UNLESS WE EACH APPLY OUR TALENTS.
YOU CAN'T SEW, SO MAKE UP FOR IT BY WORKING HARD AT MODELING!
OKAY!
TIME FOR YOUR SECOND STAB AT BEING A BOND GIRL!
WE'LL WRAP YOUR TORSO IN PLASTIC WRAP THIS TIME, SO YOU'LL BE FINE!
PLUS, WE'RE TALKING ABOUT GETTING YOU *THREE KINGDOMS* FIGURINES IF YOU DO IT.
stagger
OKAY.
Let's go.

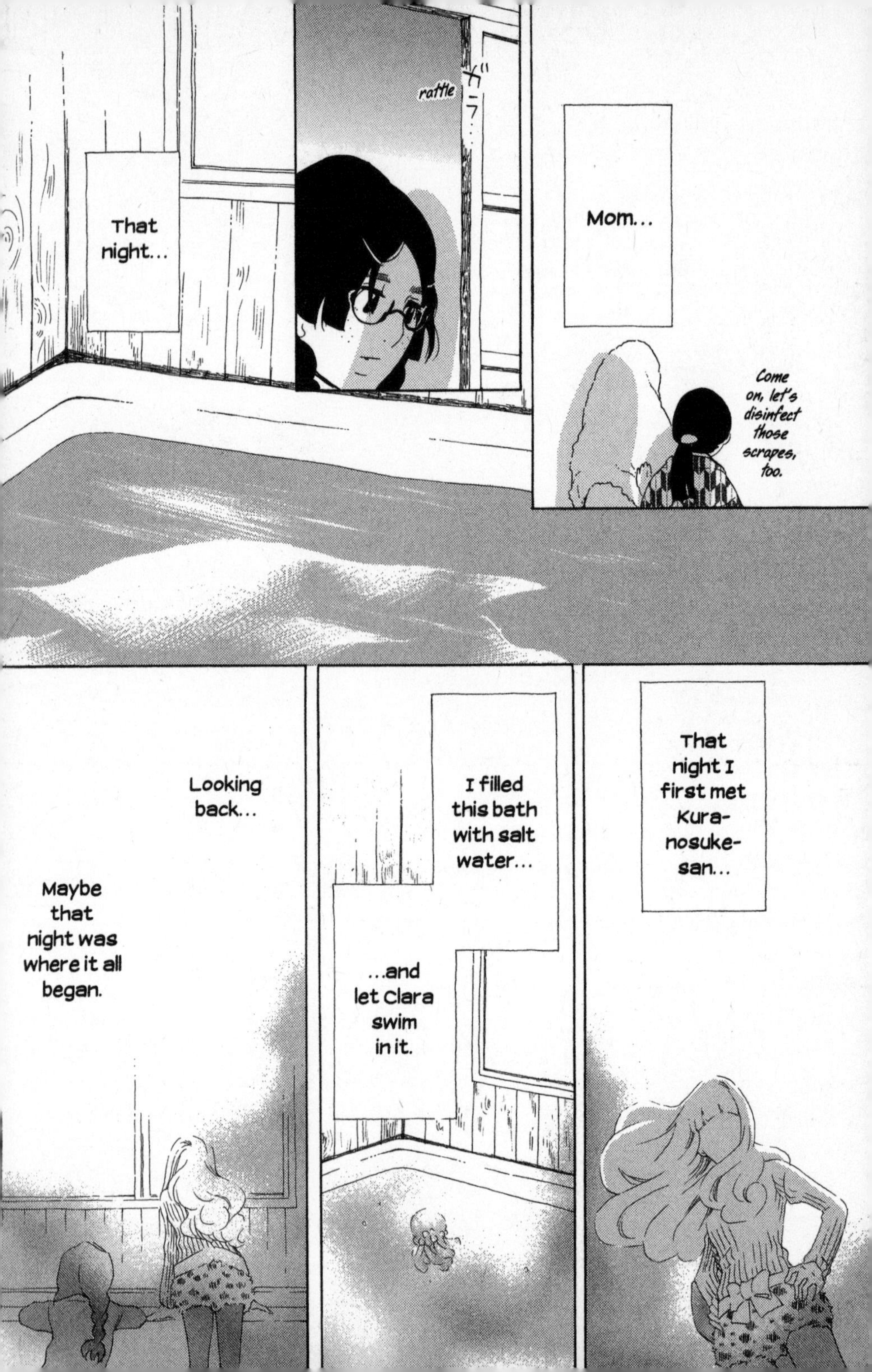
Mom...
Come on, let's disinfect those scrapes, too.
rattle
That night...
That night I first met Kura-nosuke-san...
I filled this bath with salt water...
...and let Clara swim in it.
Looking back...
Maybe that night was where it all began.

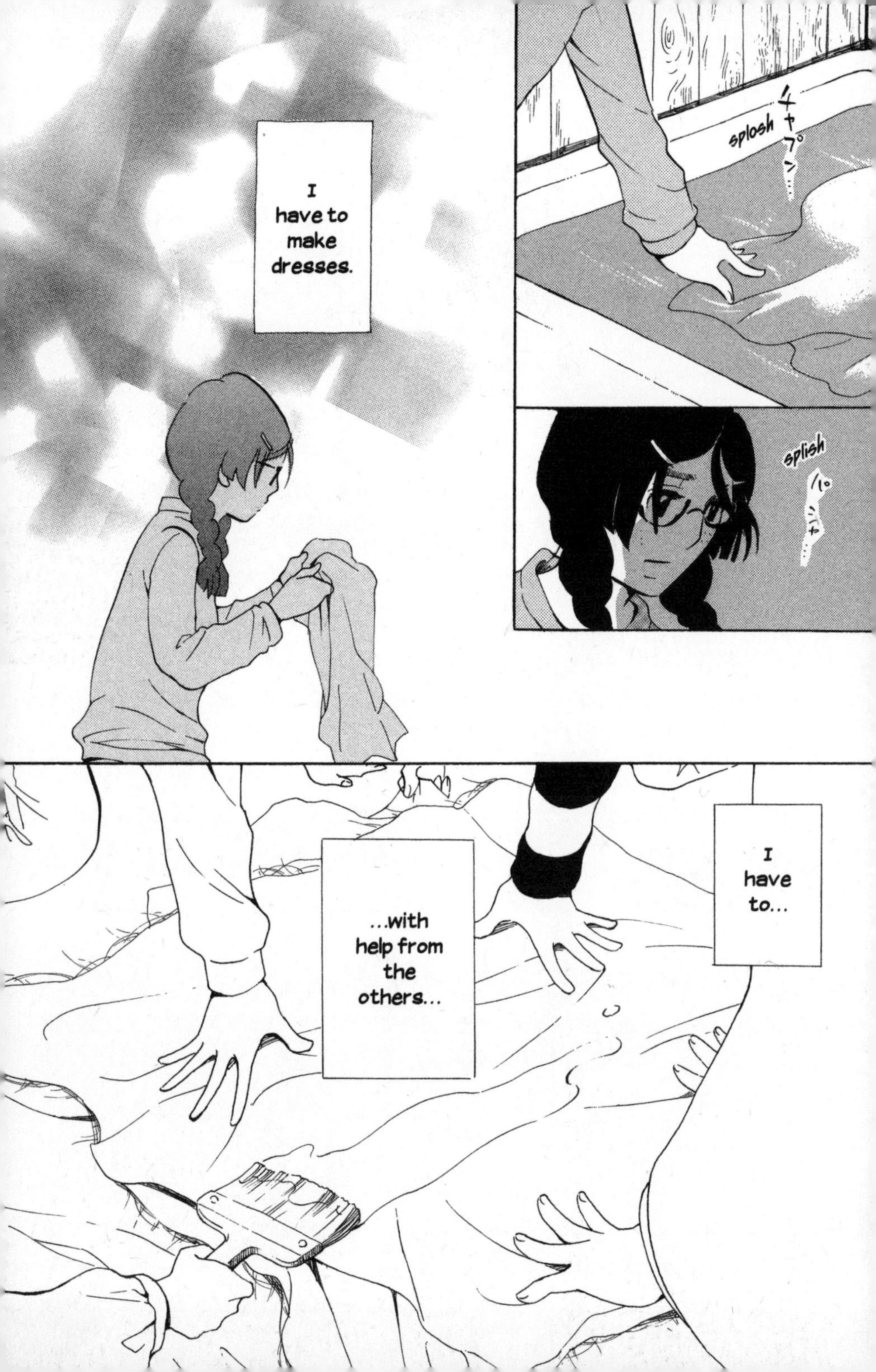
splosh
チャプン…
splosh
パシャ…
I have to make dresses.
I have to…
…with help from the others…

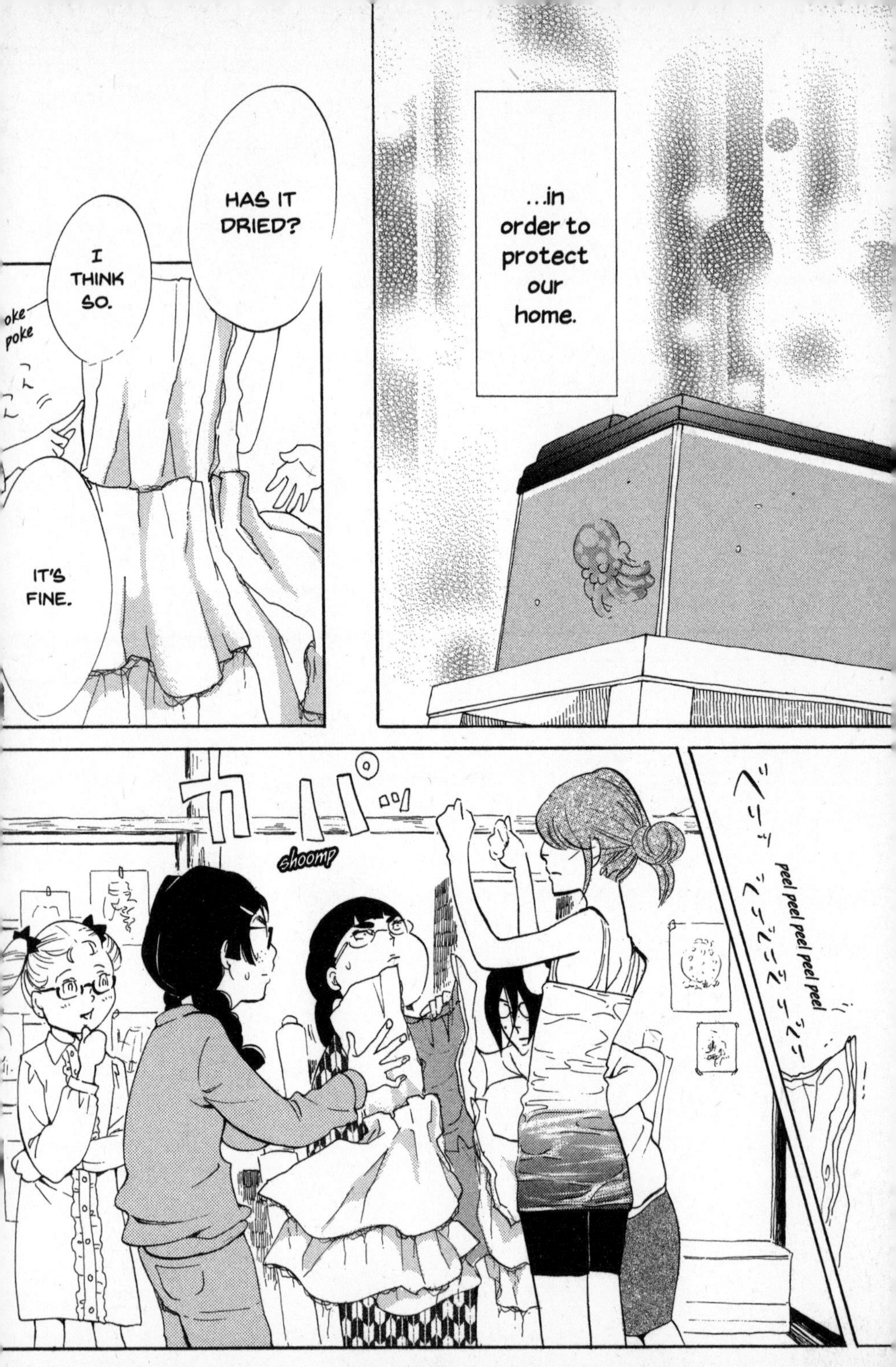
...in order to protect our home.
HAS IT DRIED?
I THINK SO.
oke poke
IT'S FINE.
peel peel peel peel peel
shoomp

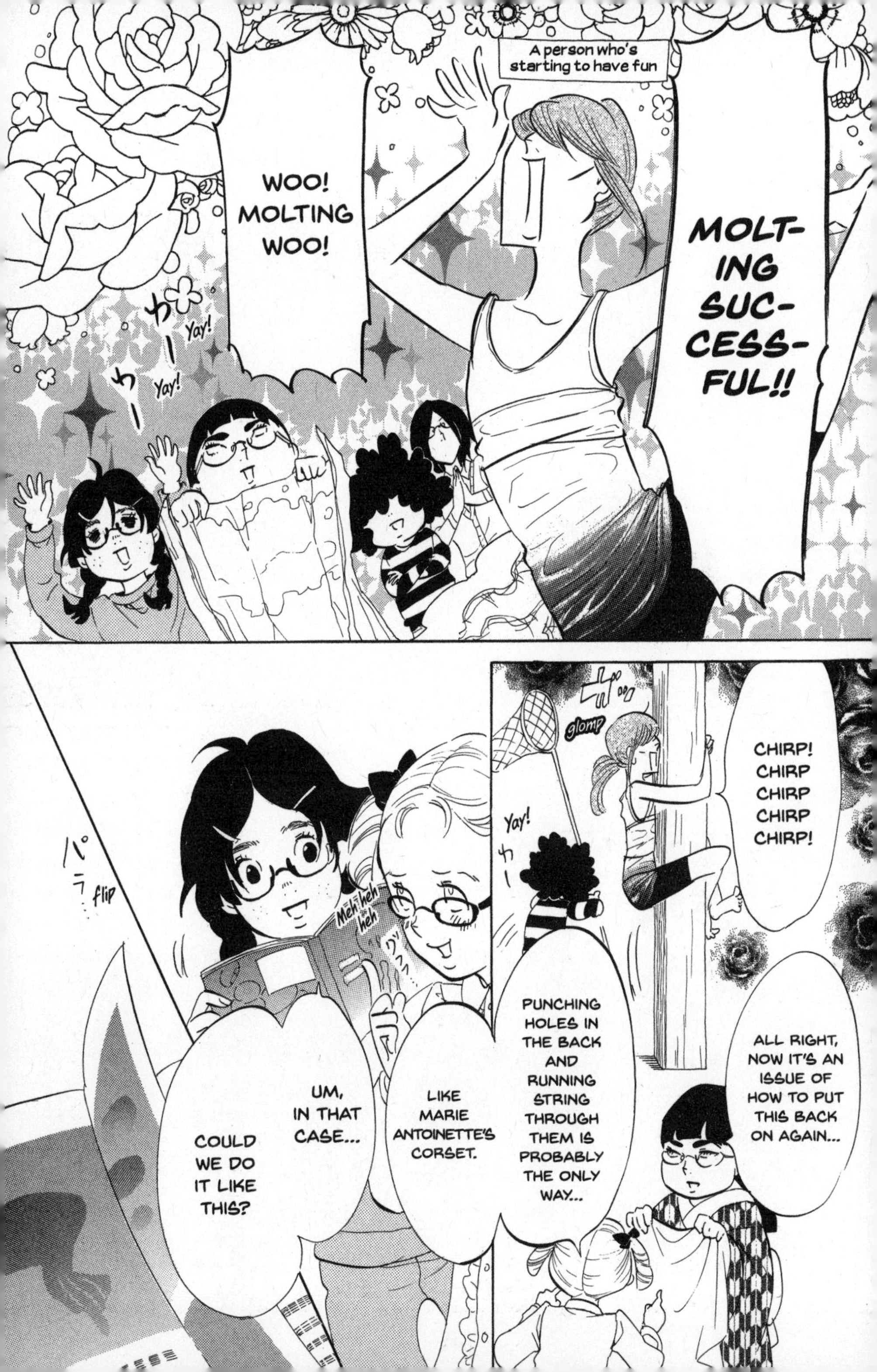
A person who's starting to have fun
MOLTING SUCCESSFUL!!
WOO! MOLTING WOO!
Yay!
Yay!
glomp
CHIRP! CHIRP CHIRP CHIRP CHIRP!
Yay!
ALL RIGHT, NOW IT'S AN ISSUE OF HOW TO PUT THIS BACK ON AGAIN...
PUNCHING HOLES IN THE BACK AND RUNNING STRING THROUGH THEM IS PROBABLY THE ONLY WAY...
Meh heh heh
LIKE MARIE ANTOINETTE'S CORSET.
UM, IN THAT CASE...
COULD WE DO IT LIKE THIS?
flip

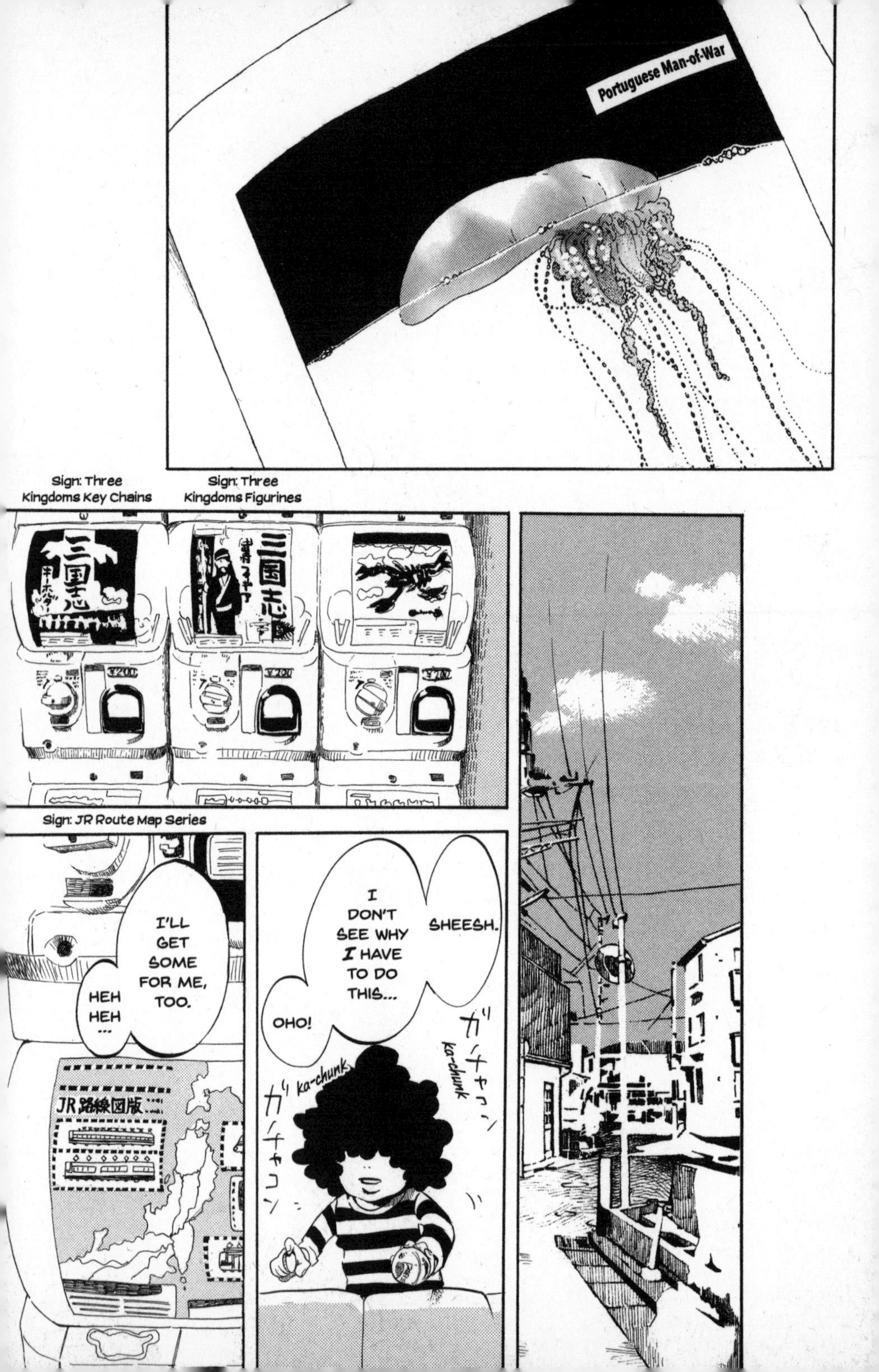
Portuguese Man-of-War
Sign: Three Kingdoms Figurines
Sign: Three Kingdoms Key Chains
Sign: JR Route Map Series
SHEESH.
I DON'T SEE WHY *I* HAVE TO DO THIS...
OHO!
ガチャコン
ka-chunk
ガチャコン
ka-chunk
I'LL GET SOME FOR ME, TOO.
HEH HEH ...
JR路線図版

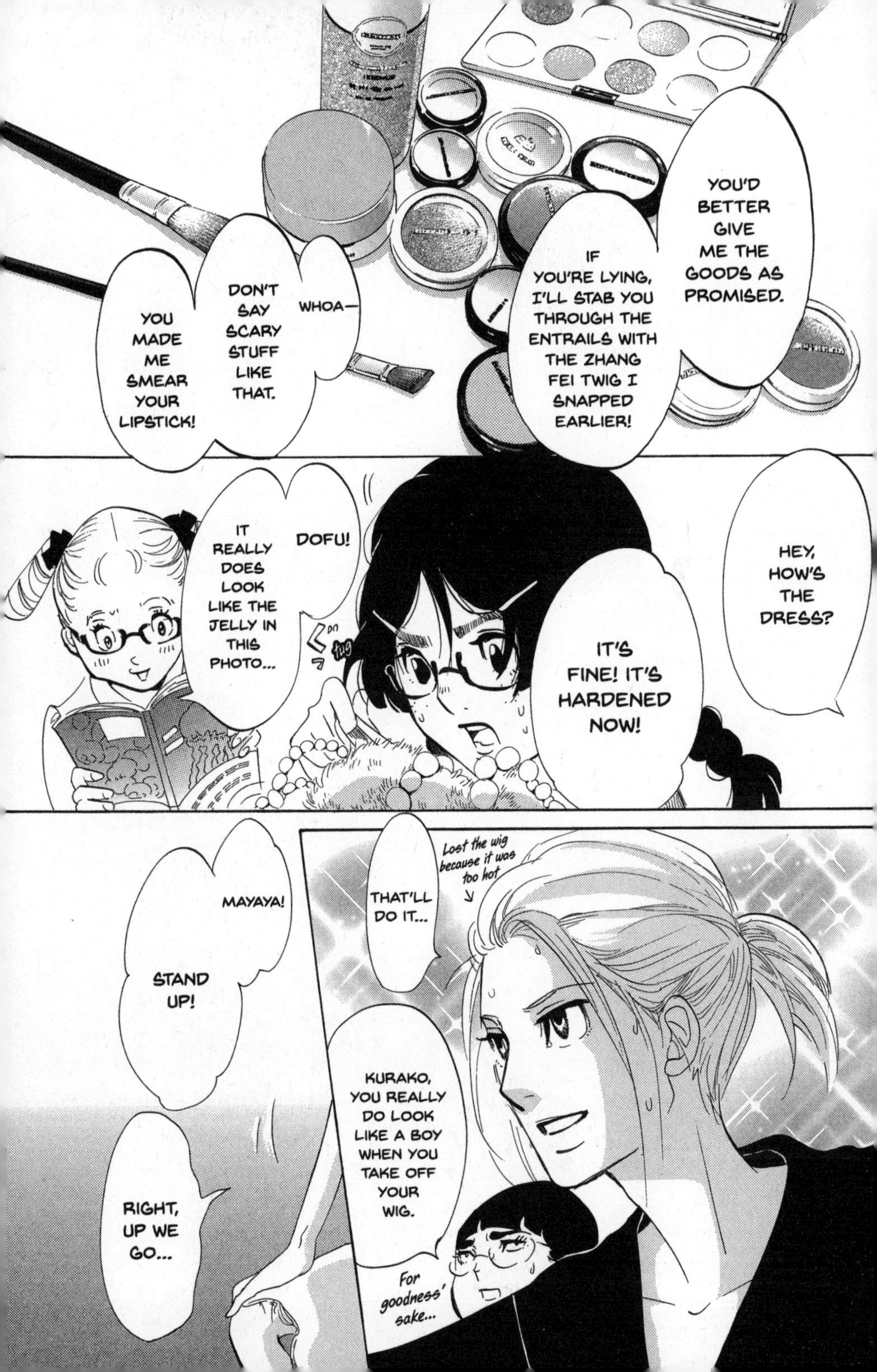
YOU'D BETTER GIVE ME THE GOODS AS PROMISED.
IF YOU'RE LYING, I'LL STAB YOU THROUGH THE ENTRAILS WITH THE ZHANG FEI TWIG I SNAPPED EARLIER!
WHOA—
DON'T SAY SCARY STUFF LIKE THAT.
YOU MADE ME SMEAR YOUR LIPSTICK!
HEY, HOW'S THE DRESS?
IT'S FINE! IT'S HARDENED NOW!
DOFU!
IT REALLY DOES LOOK LIKE THE JELLY IN THIS PHOTO...
THAT'LL DO IT...
Lost the wig because it was too hot
KURAKO, YOU REALLY DO LOOK LIKE A BOY WHEN YOU TAKE OFF YOUR WIG.
For goodness' sake...
MAYAYA!
STAND UP!
RIGHT, UP WE GO...

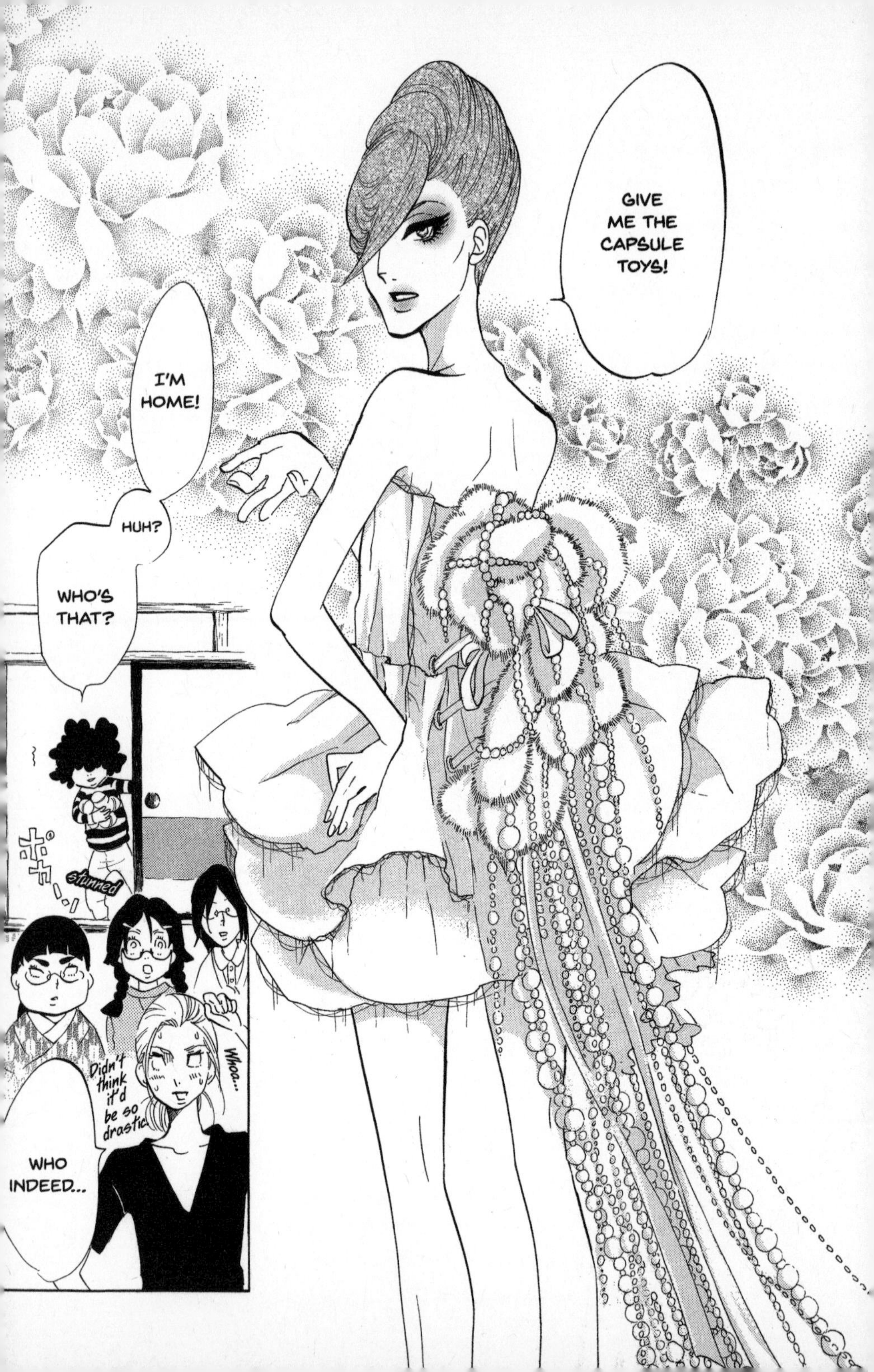
GIVE ME THE CAPSULE TOYS!
I'M HOME!
HUH?
WHO'S THAT?
stunned
Whoa...
Didn't think it'd be so drastic
WHO INDEED...

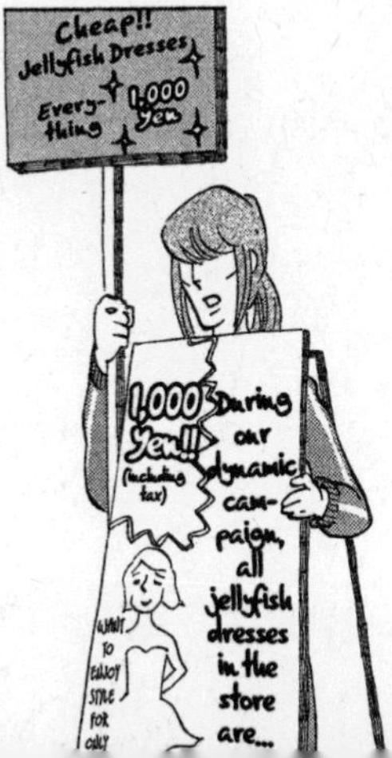
Cheap!! Jellyfish Dresses Every-thing 1,000 Yen
1,000 Yen!! (including tax)
During our dynamic cam-paign, all jellyfish dresses in the store are...
WANT TO ENJOY STYLE FOR ONLY

Episode 34
Party Monster

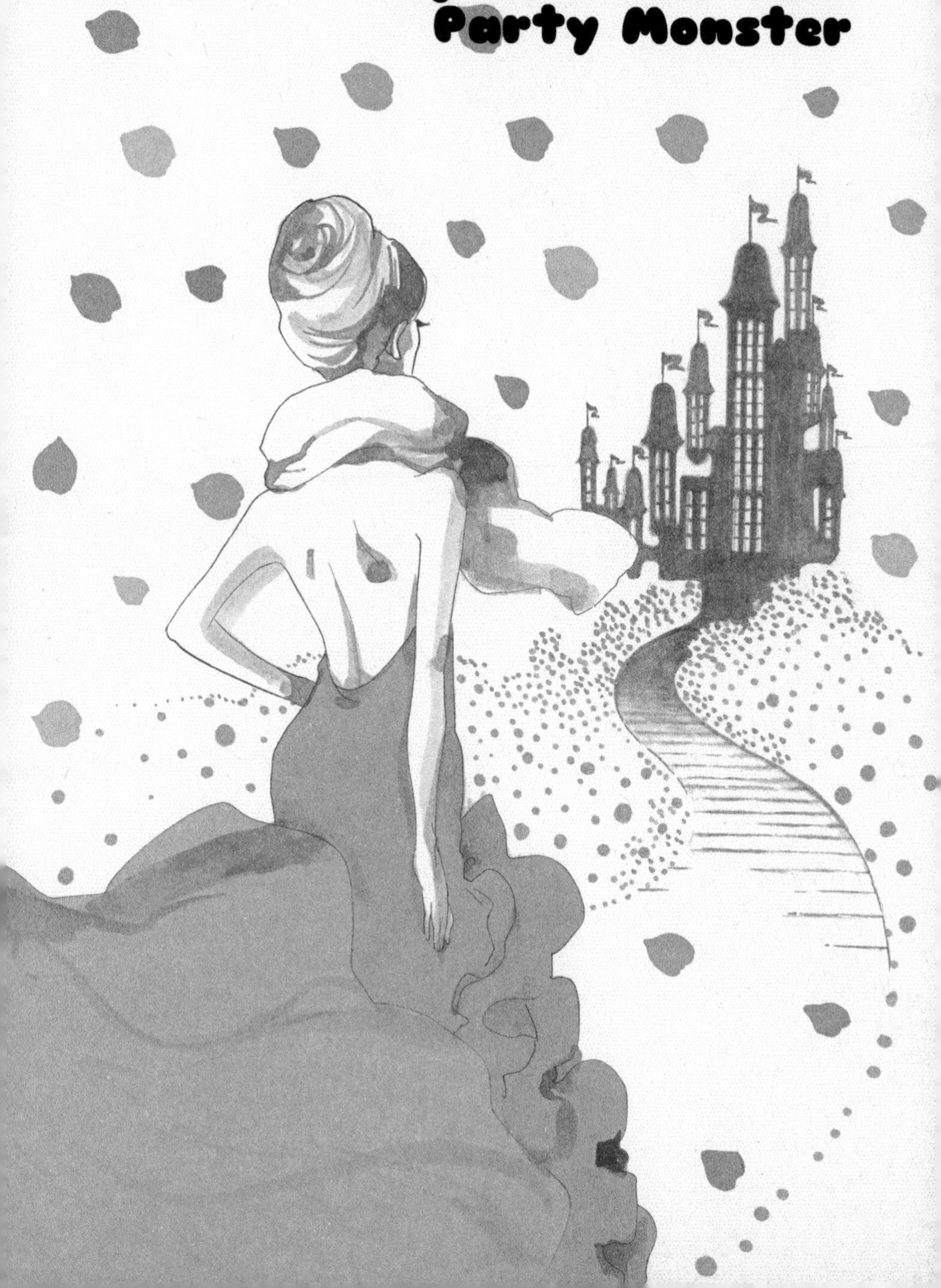

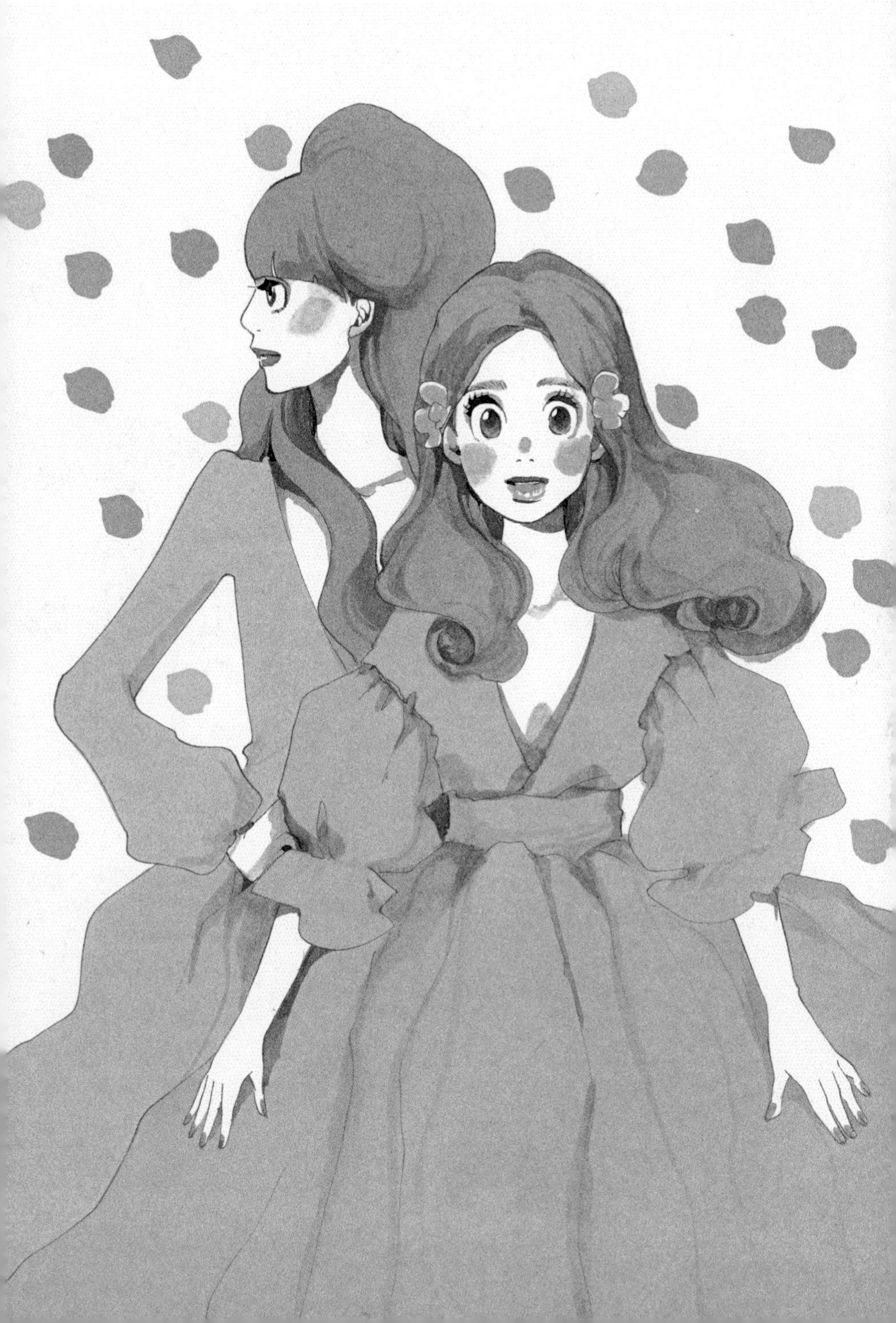

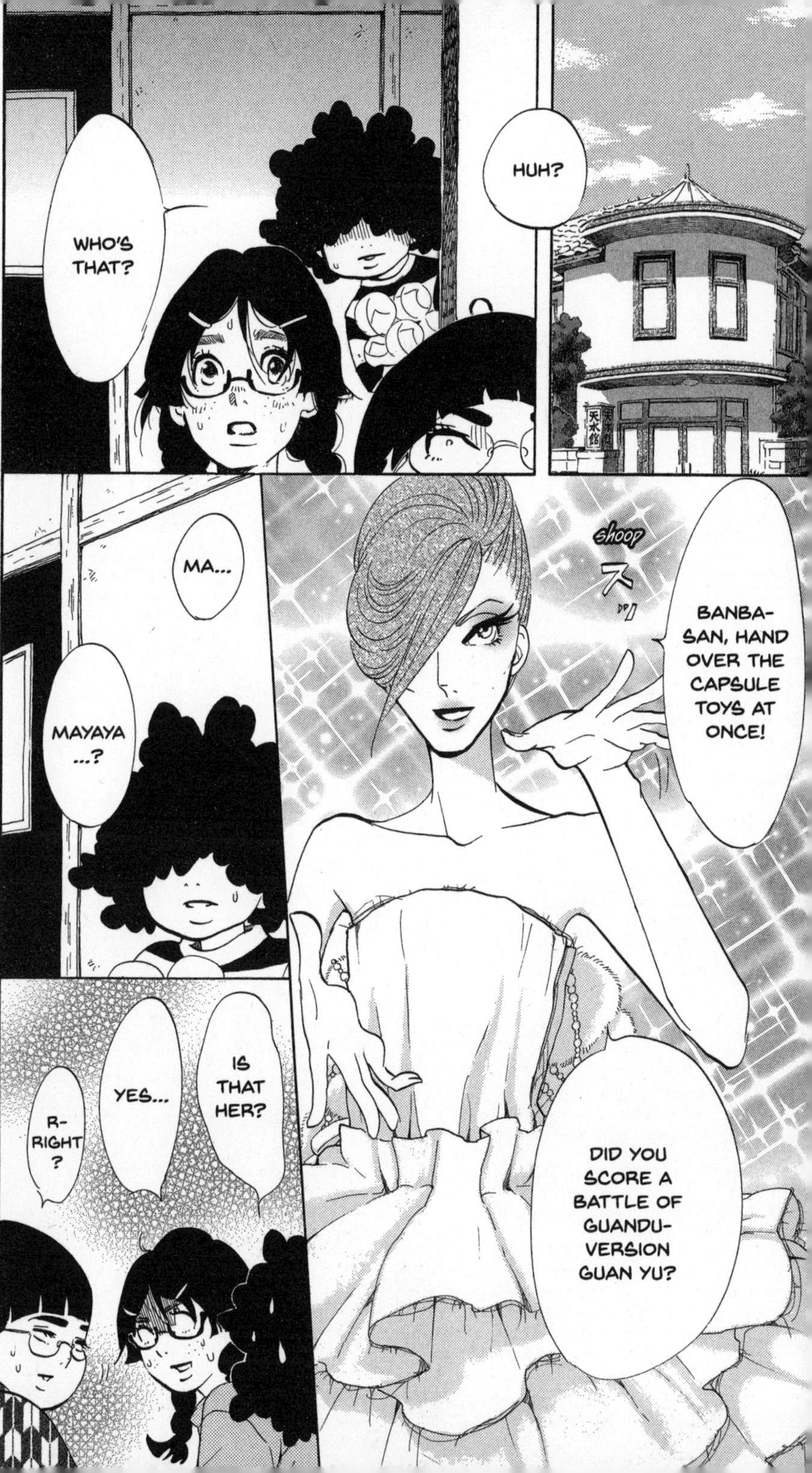
HUH?
WHO'S THAT?
shoop
ス
BANBA-SAN, HAND OVER THE CAPSULE TOYS AT ONCE!
DID YOU SCORE A BATTLE OF GUANDU-VERSION GUAN YU?
MA...
MAYAYA ...?
IS THAT HER?
YES...
R-RIGHT?

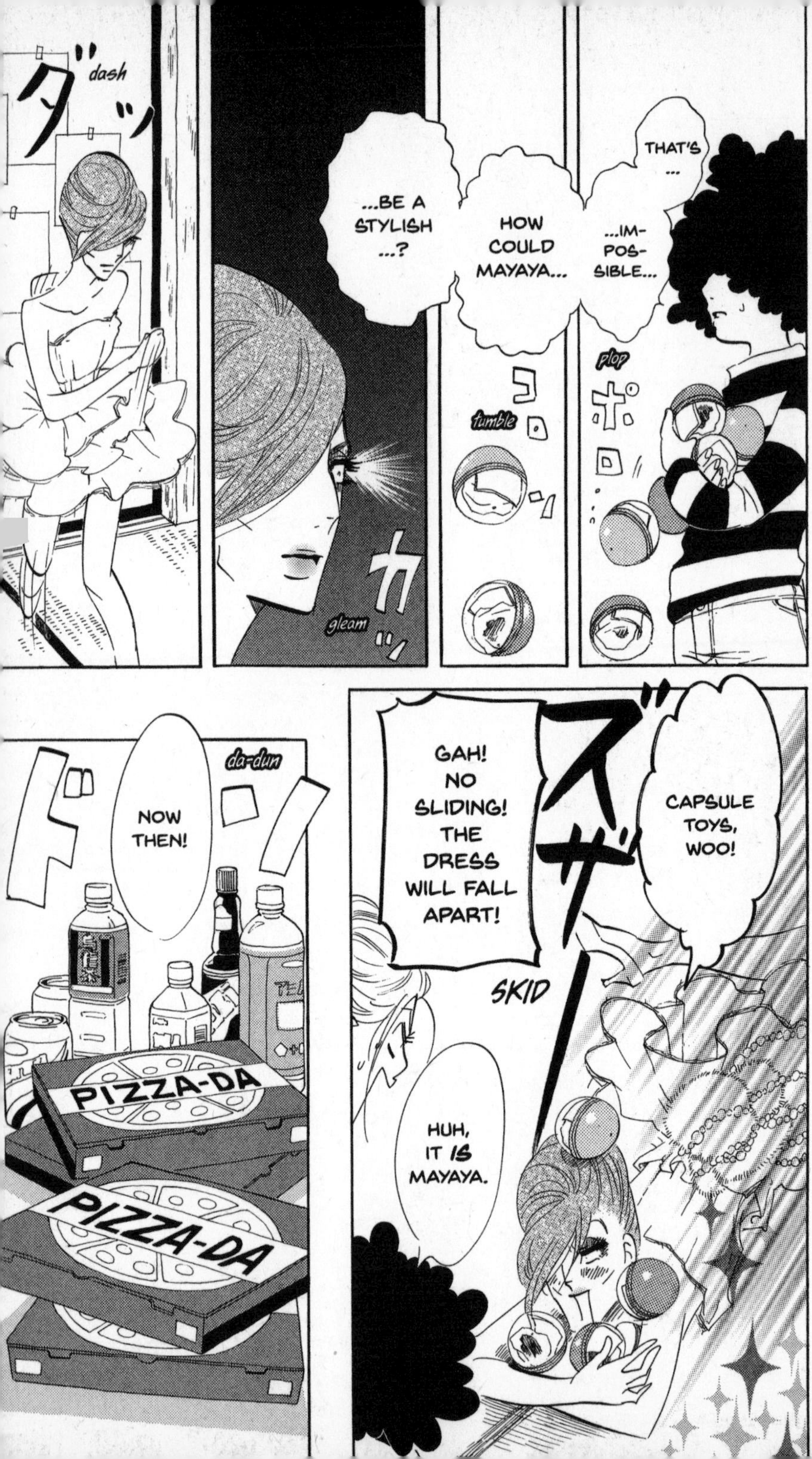
THAT'S ...
...IM-POS-SIBLE...
plop
HOW COULD MAYAYA...
...BE A STYLISH ...?
tumble
gleam
dash
CAPSULE TOYS, WOO!
GAH! NO SLIDING! THE DRESS WILL FALL APART!
SKID
HUH, IT IS MAYAYA.
da-dun
NOW THEN!
PIZZA-DA
PIZZA-DA

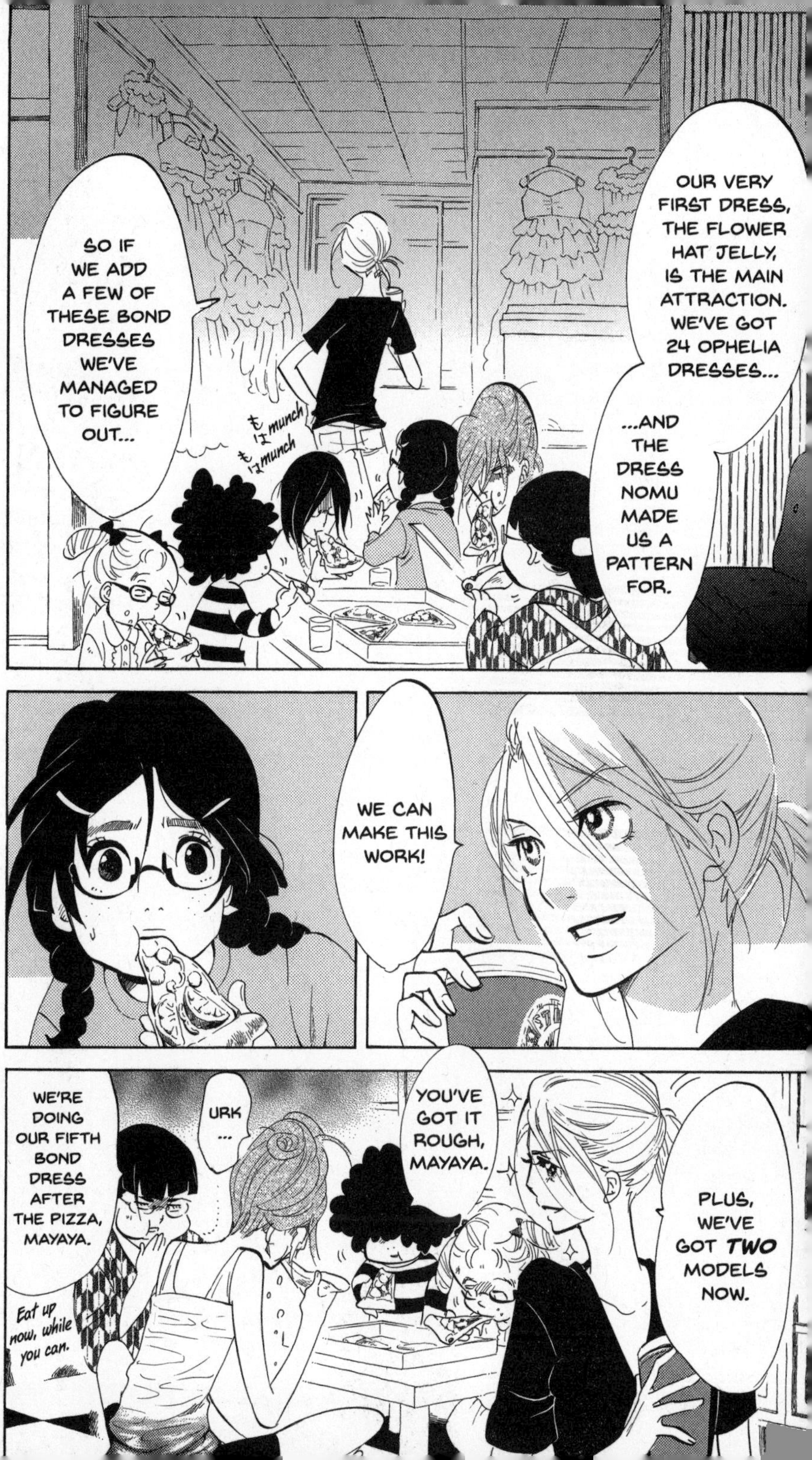
OUR VERY FIRST DRESS, THE FLOWER HAT JELLY, IS THE MAIN ATTRACTION. WE'VE GOT 24 OPHELIA DRESSES...
...AND THE DRESS NOMU MADE US A PATTERN FOR.
SO IF WE ADD A FEW OF THESE BOND DRESSES WE'VE MANAGED TO FIGURE OUT...
もは munch
もは munch
WE CAN MAKE THIS WORK!
PLUS, WE'VE GOT **TWO** MODELS NOW.
YOU'VE GOT IT ROUGH, MAYAYA.
URK ...
WE'RE DOING OUR FIFTH BOND DRESS AFTER THE PIZZA, MAYAYA.
Eat up now, while you can.

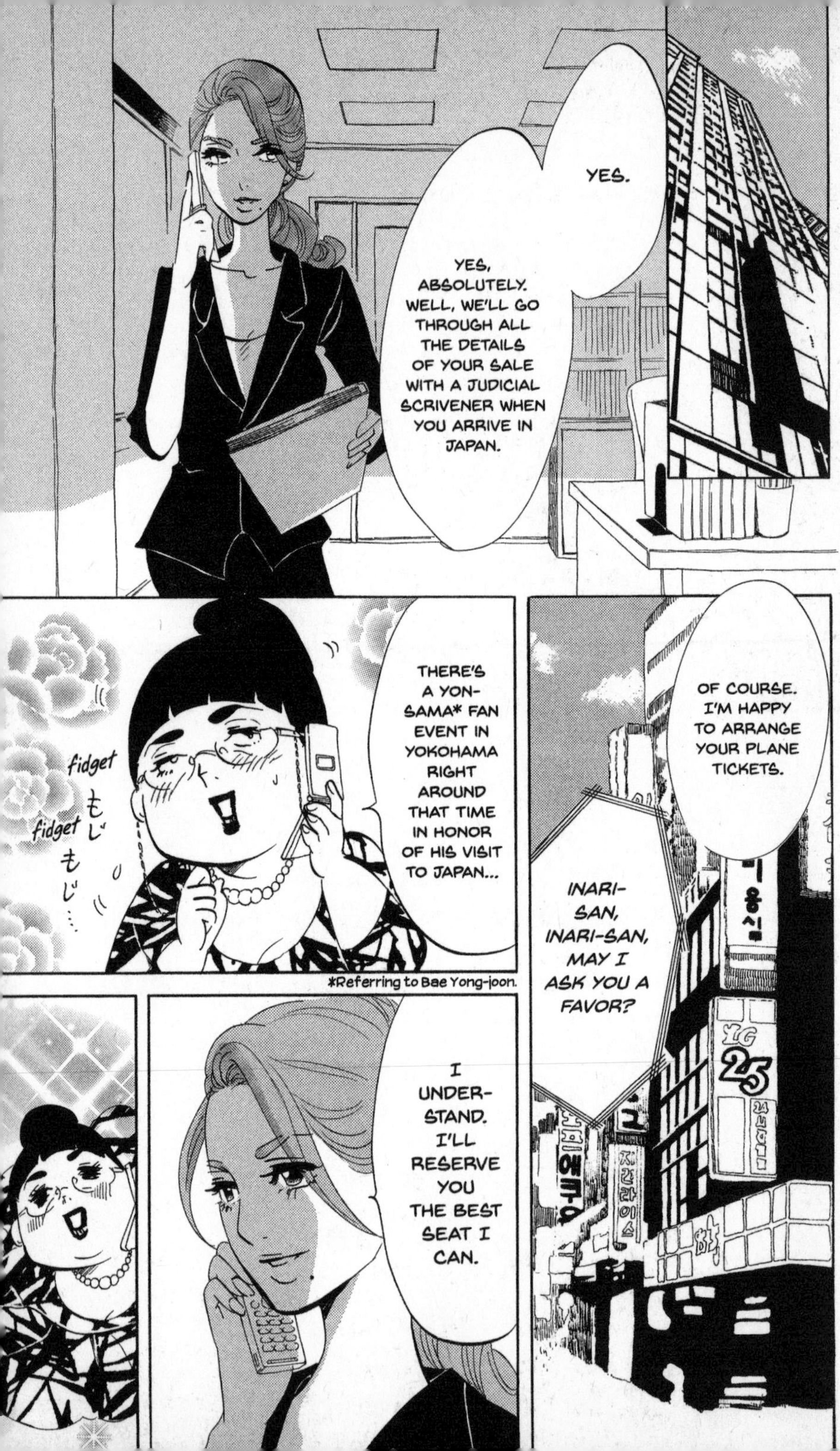
YES.
YES, ABSOLUTELY. WELL, WE'LL GO THROUGH ALL THE DETAILS OF YOUR SALE WITH A JUDICIAL SCRIVENER WHEN YOU ARRIVE IN JAPAN.
OF COURSE. I'M HAPPY TO ARRANGE YOUR PLANE TICKETS.
INARI-SAN, INARI-SAN, MAY I ASK YOU A FAVOR?
YG 25
THERE'S A YON-SAMA* FAN EVENT IN YOKOHAMA RIGHT AROUND THAT TIME IN HONOR OF HIS VISIT TO JAPAN...
fidget もじ
fidget もじ...
*Referring to Bae Yong-joon.
I UNDERSTAND. I'LL RESERVE YOU THE BEST SEAT I CAN.

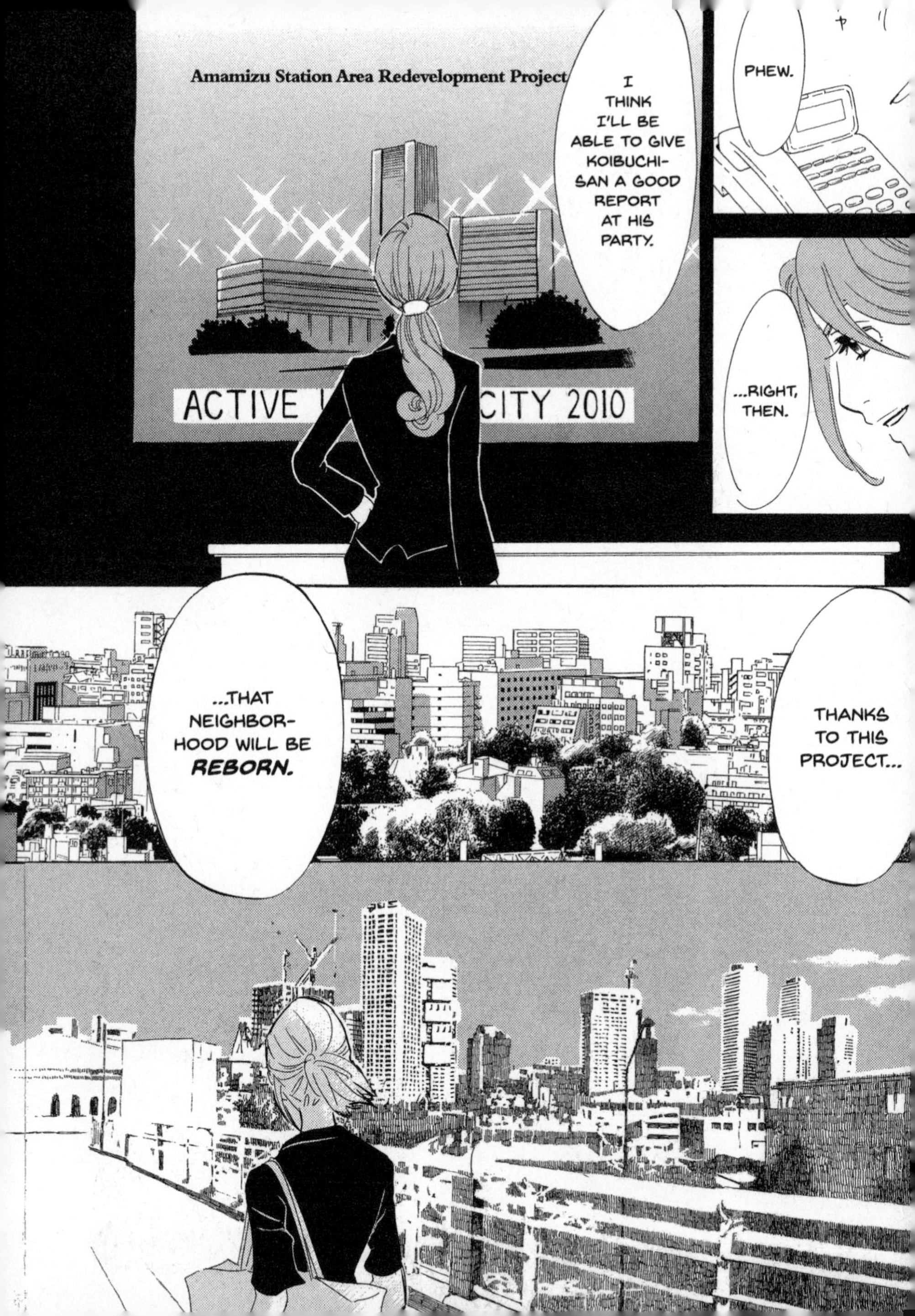
PHEW.
...RIGHT, THEN.
Amamizu Station Area Redevelopment Project
ACTIVE
CITY 2010
I THINK I'LL BE ABLE TO GIVE KOIBUCHI-SAN A GOOD REPORT AT HIS PARTY.
THANKS TO THIS PROJECT...
...THAT NEIGHBOR-HOOD WILL BE REBORN.

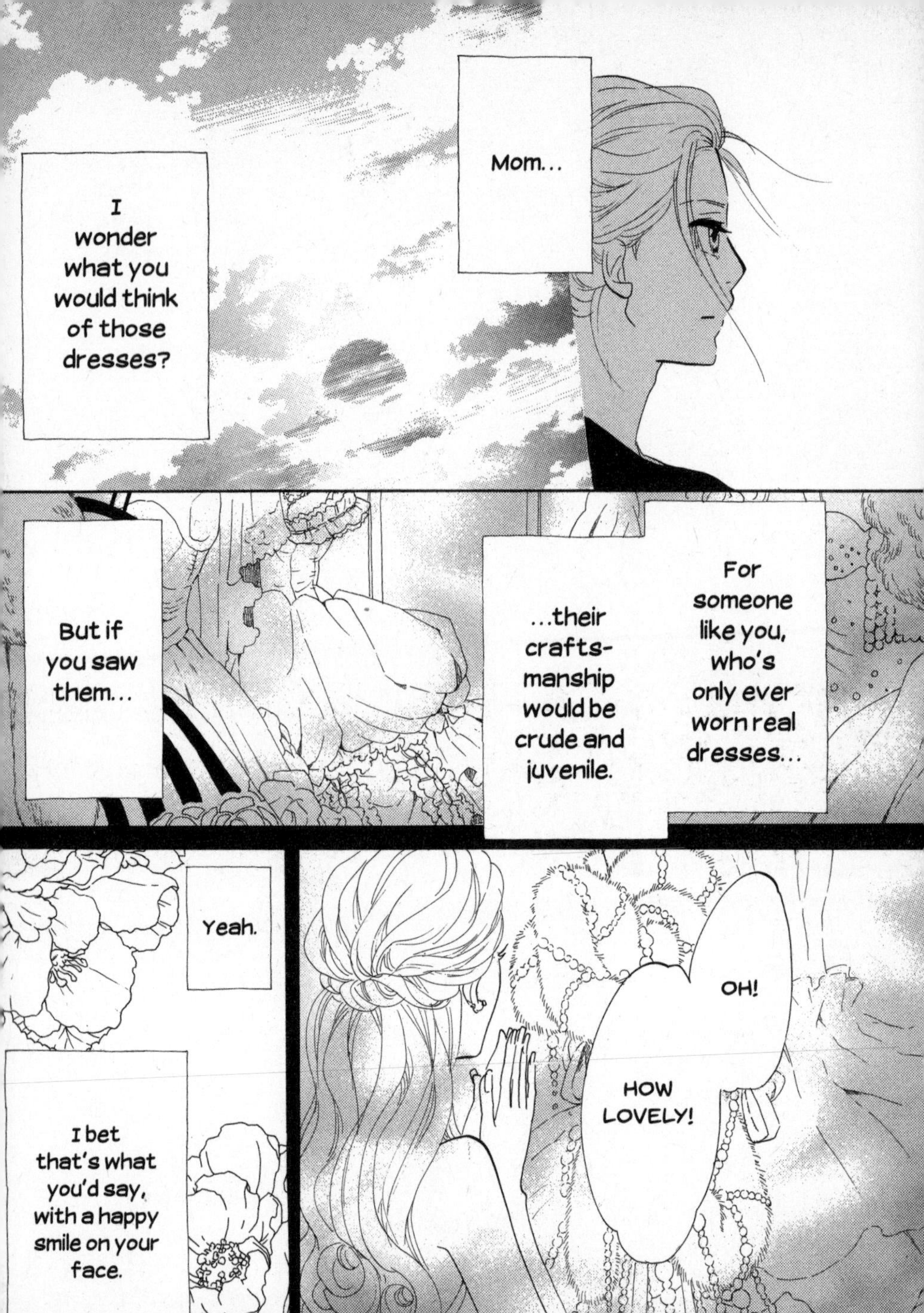

Mom...
I wonder what you would think of those dresses?
For someone like you, who's only ever worn real dresses...
...their crafts-manship would be crude and juvenile.
But if you saw them...
OH!
HOW LOVELY!
Yeah.
I bet that's what you'd say, with a happy smile on your face.

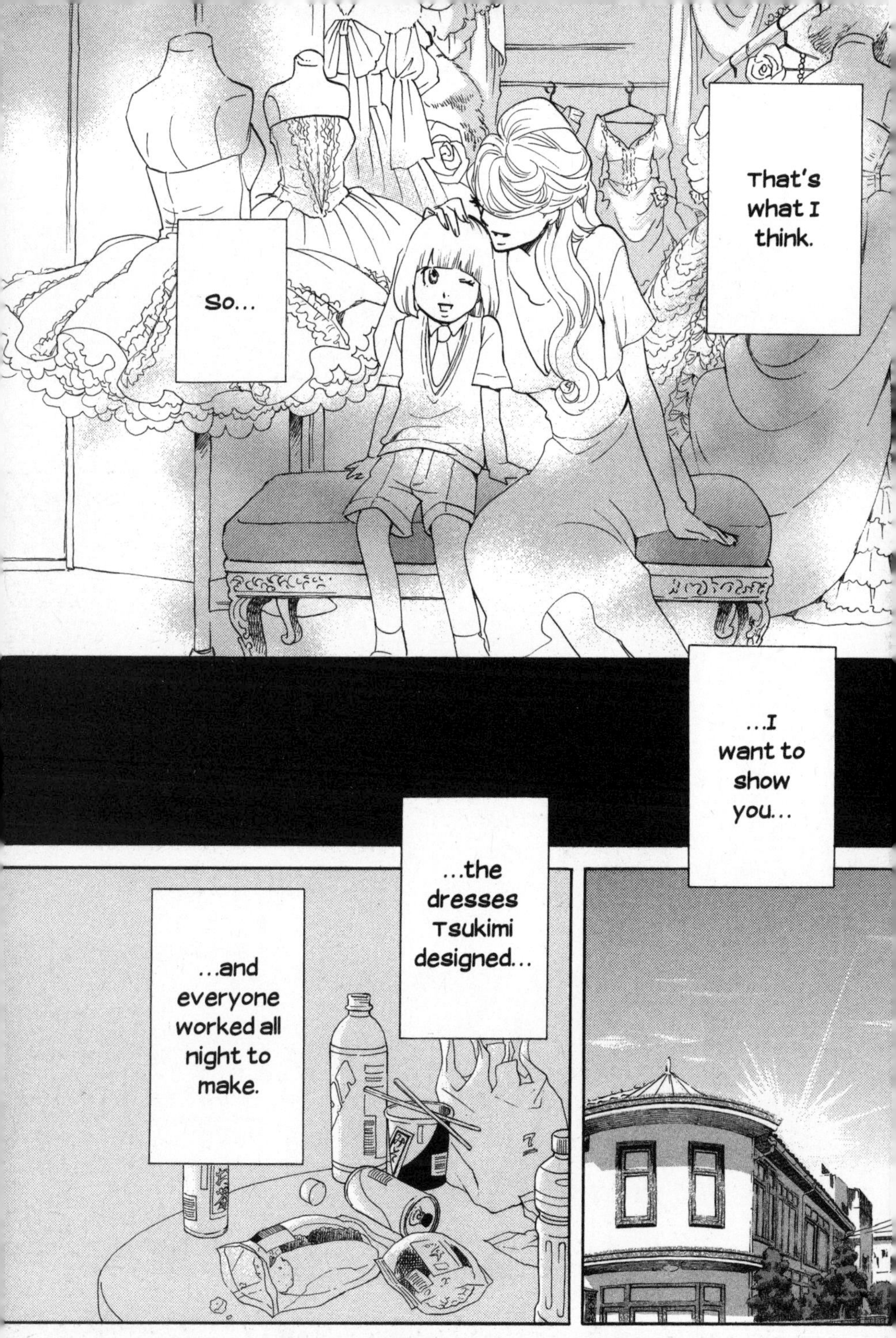
That's what I think.
So...
...I want to show you...
...the dresses Tsukimi designed...
...and everyone worked all night to make.

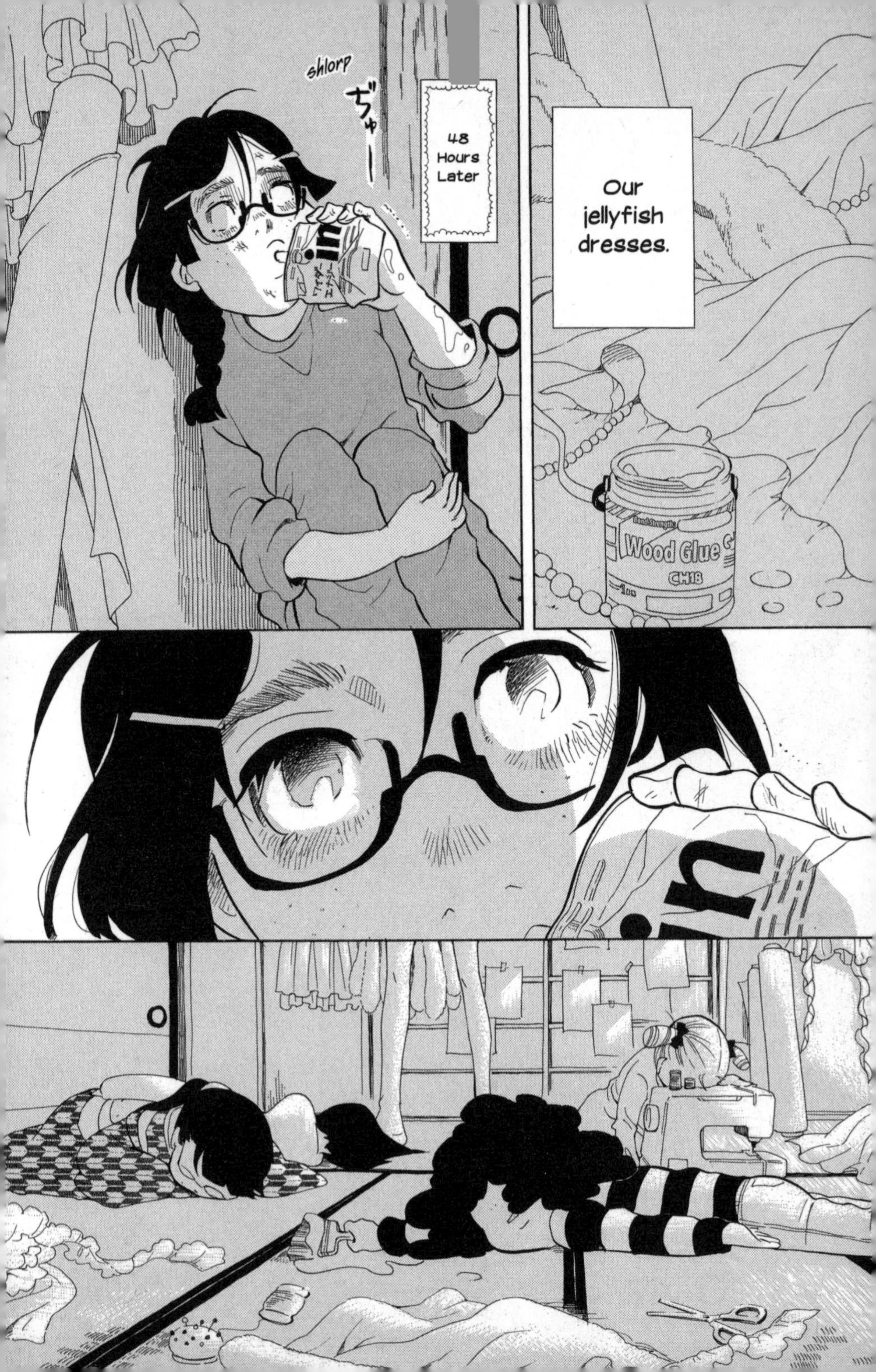
Our jellyfish dresses.
Wood Glue
CH18
48 Hours Later
shlorp
ぢゅー

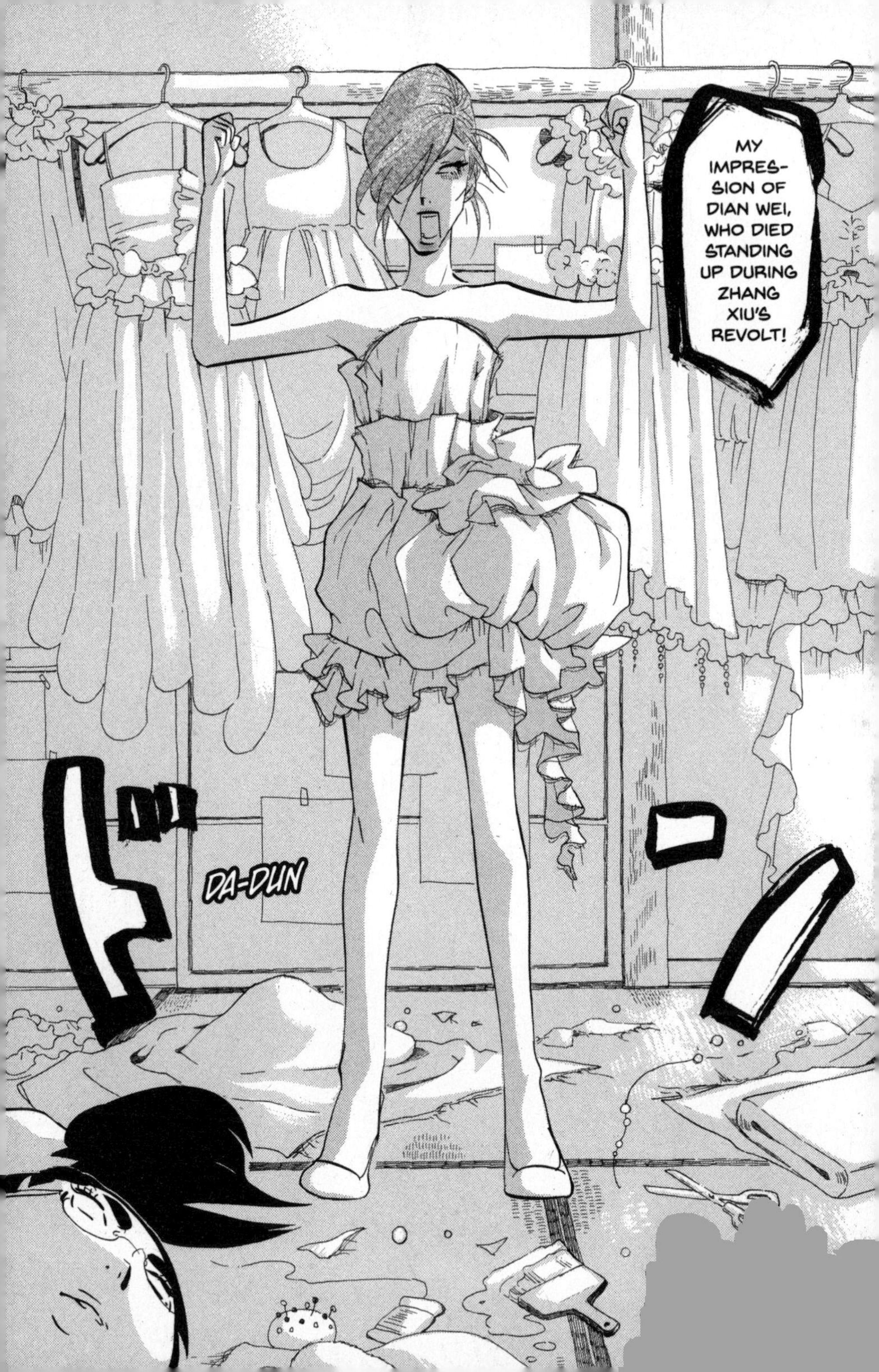
MY IMPRES-SION OF DIAN WEI, WHO DIED STANDING UP DURING ZHANG XIU'S REVOLT!
DA-DUN

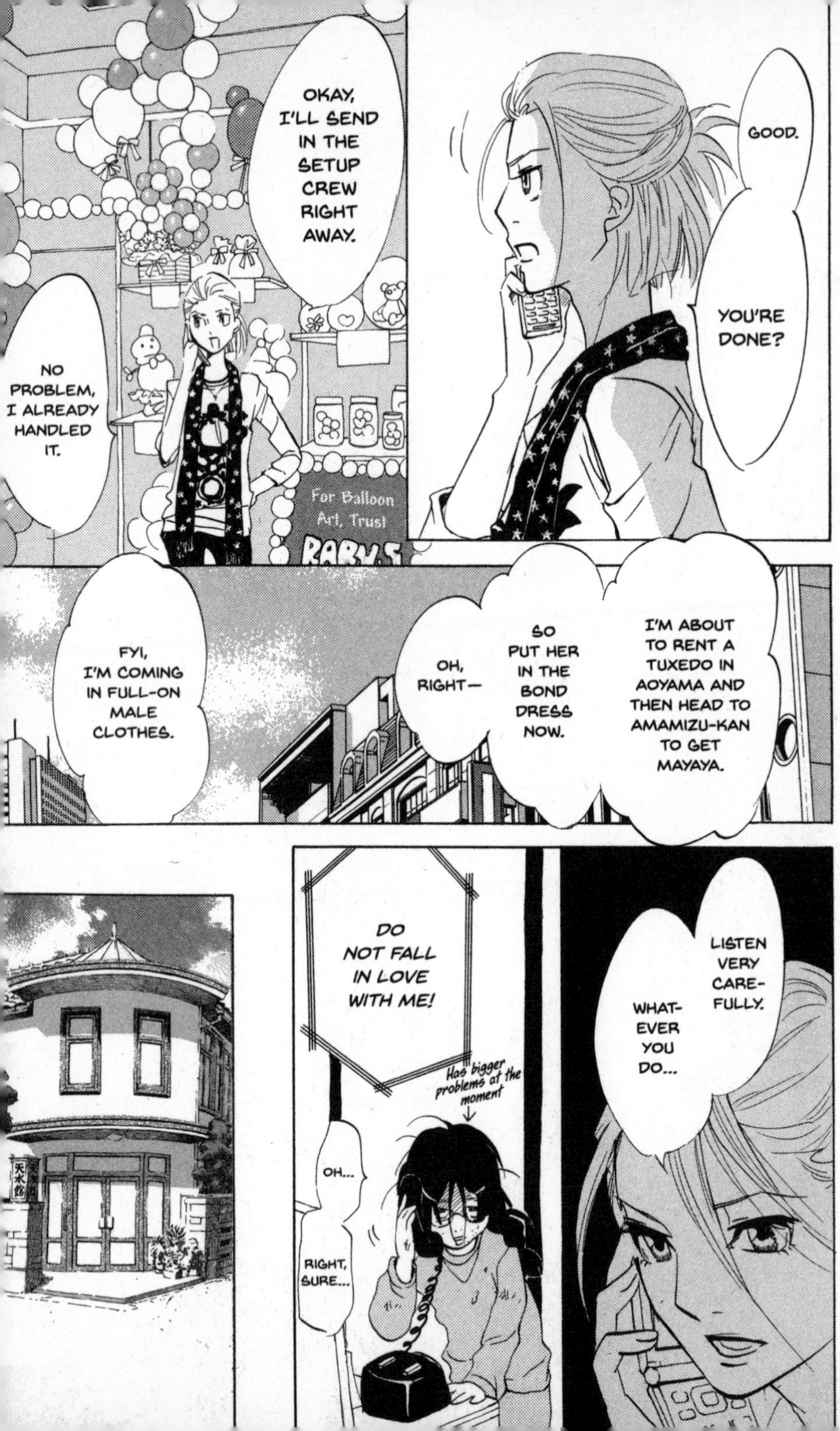
GOOD.
YOU'RE DONE?
OKAY, I'LL SEND IN THE SETUP CREW RIGHT AWAY.
NO PROBLEM, I ALREADY HANDLED IT.
For Balloon Art, Trust
I'M ABOUT TO RENT A TUXEDO IN AOYAMA AND THEN HEAD TO AMAMIZU-KAN TO GET MAYAYA.
SO PUT HER IN THE BOND DRESS NOW.
OH, RIGHT—
FYI, I'M COMING IN FULL-ON MALE CLOTHES.
LISTEN VERY CARE-FULLY.
WHAT-EVER YOU DO...
DO NOT FALL IN LOVE WITH ME!
Has bigger problems at the moment
OH...
RIGHT, SURE...

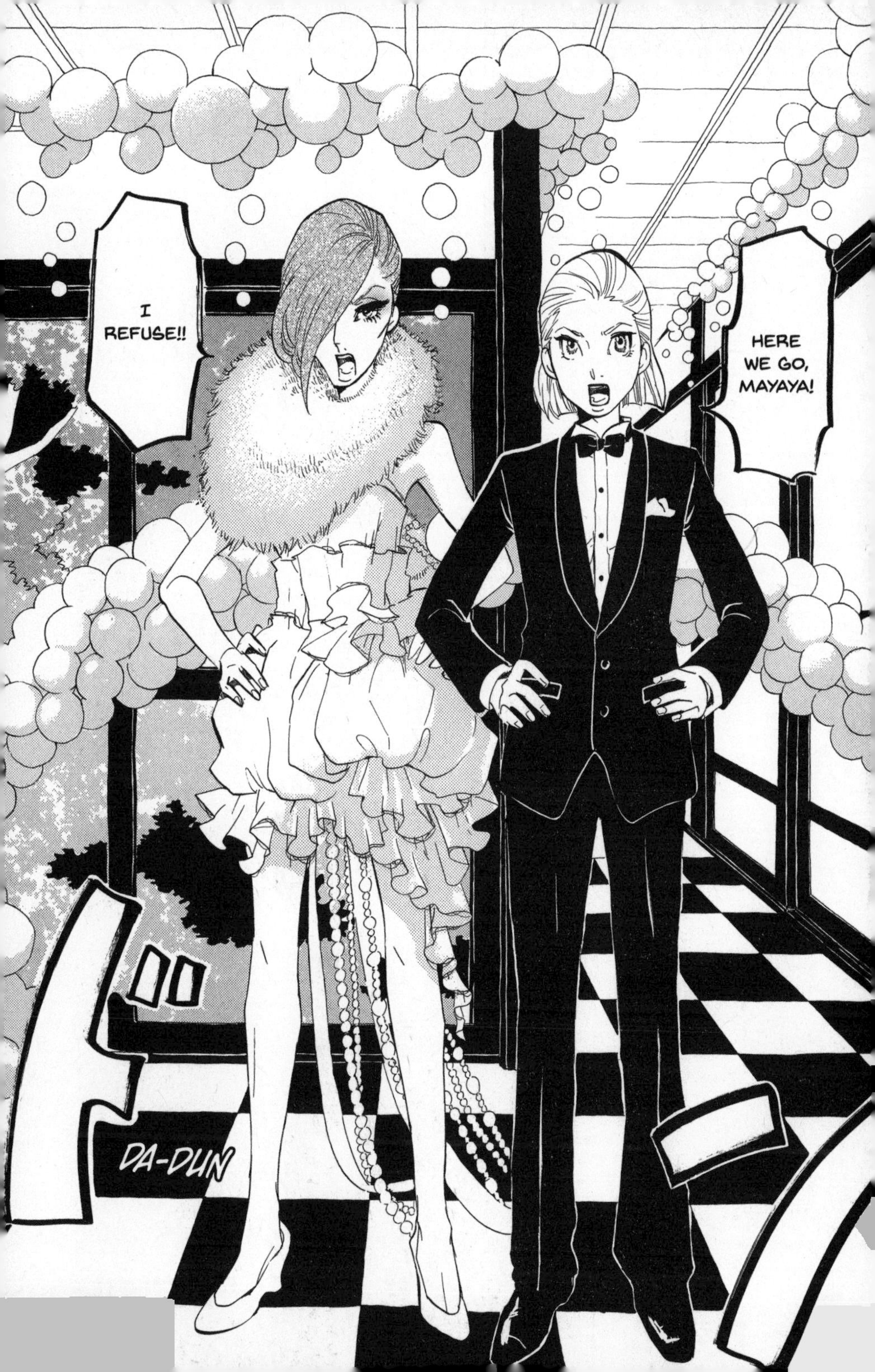
HERE WE GO, MAYAYA!
I REFUSE!!
DA-DUN

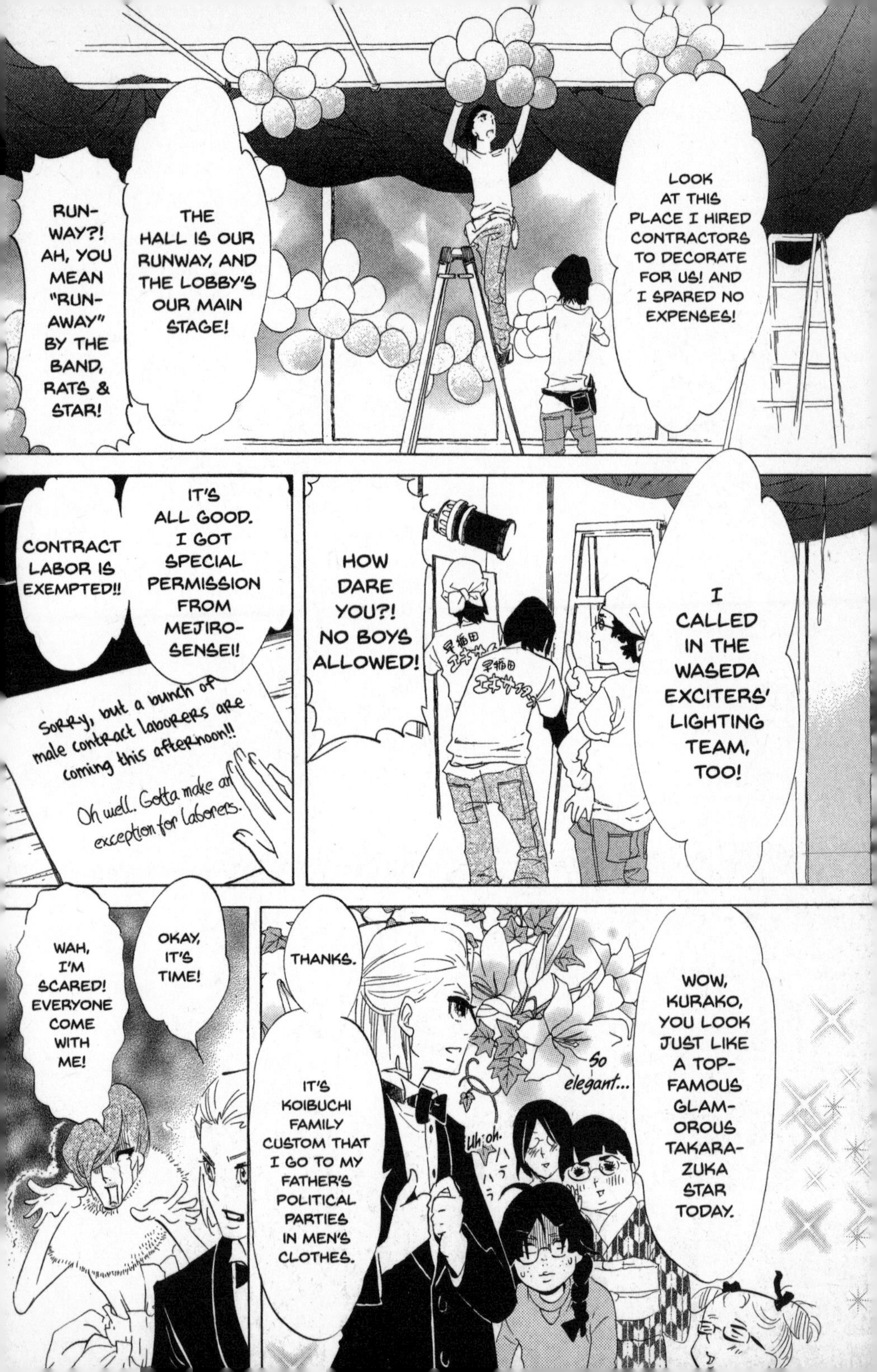
LOOK AT THIS PLACE I HIRED CONTRACTORS TO DECORATE FOR US! AND I SPARED NO EXPENSES!
THE HALL IS OUR RUNWAY, AND THE LOBBY'S OUR MAIN STAGE!
RUN-WAY?! AH, YOU MEAN "RUN-AWAY" BY THE BAND, RATS & STAR!
I CALLED IN THE WASEDA EXCITERS' LIGHTING TEAM, TOO!
HOW DARE YOU?! NO BOYS ALLOWED!
IT'S ALL GOOD. I GOT SPECIAL PERMISSION FROM MEJIRO-SENSEI!
CONTRACT LABOR IS EXEMPTED!!
Sorry, but a bunch of male contract laborers are coming this afternoon!!
Oh well. Gotta make an exception for laborers.
WOW, KURAKO, YOU LOOK JUST LIKE A TOP-FAMOUS GLAM-OROUS TAKARA-ZUKA STAR TODAY.
So elegant...
Uh oh.
THANKS.
IT'S KOIBUCHI FAMILY CUSTOM THAT I GO TO MY FATHER'S POLITICAL PARTIES IN MEN'S CLOTHES.
OKAY, IT'S TIME!
WAH, I'M SCARED! EVERYONE COME WITH ME!

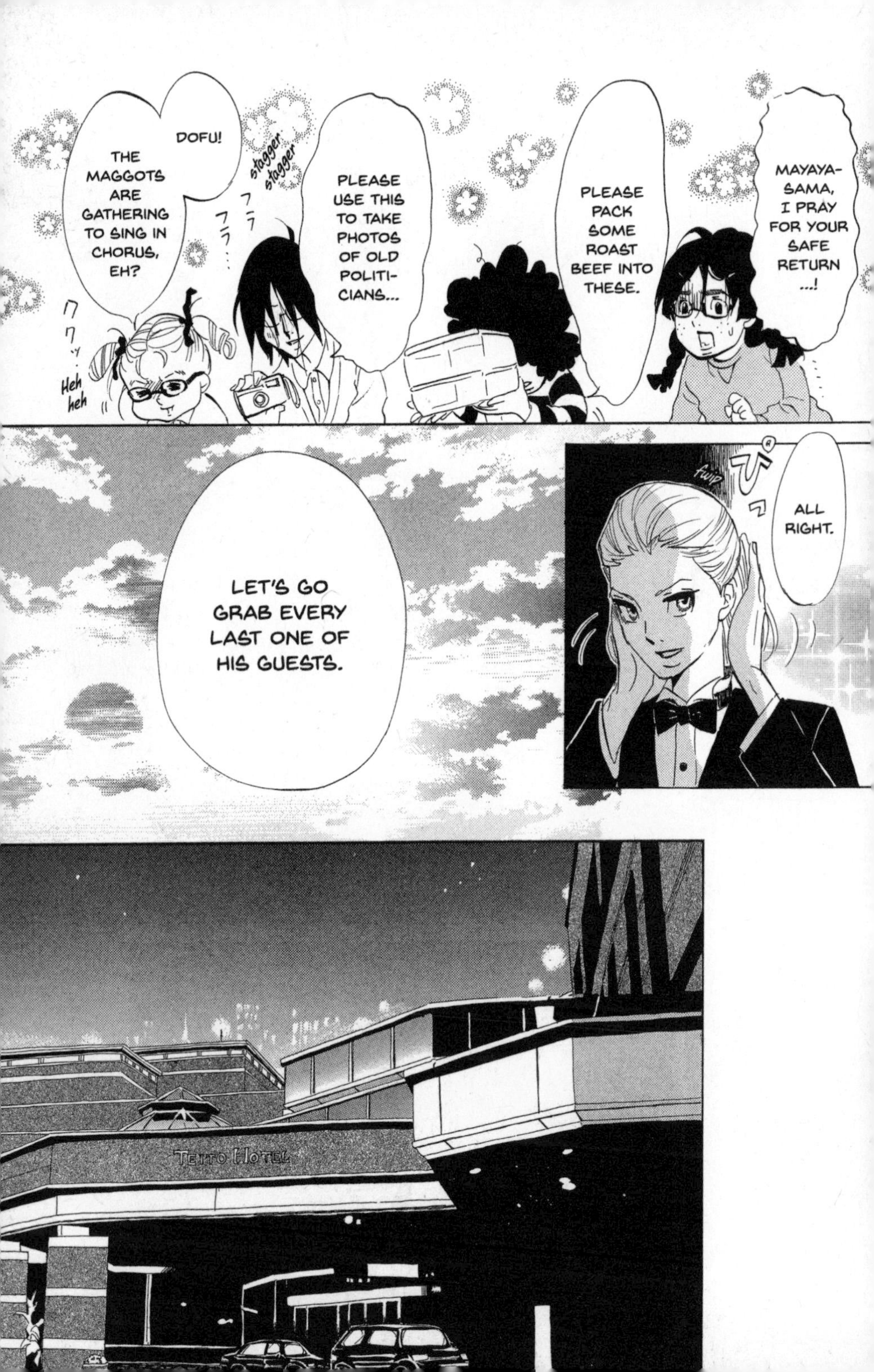
MAYAYA-SAMA, I PRAY FOR YOUR SAFE RETURN ...!
PLEASE PACK SOME ROAST BEEF INTO THESE.
PLEASE USE THIS TO TAKE PHOTOS OF OLD POLITICIANS...
stagger stagger
DOFU! THE MAGGOTS ARE GATHERING TO SING IN CHORUS, EH?
Heh heh
fwip
ALL RIGHT.
LET'S GO GRAB EVERY LAST ONE OF HIS GUESTS.
TEITO HOTEL

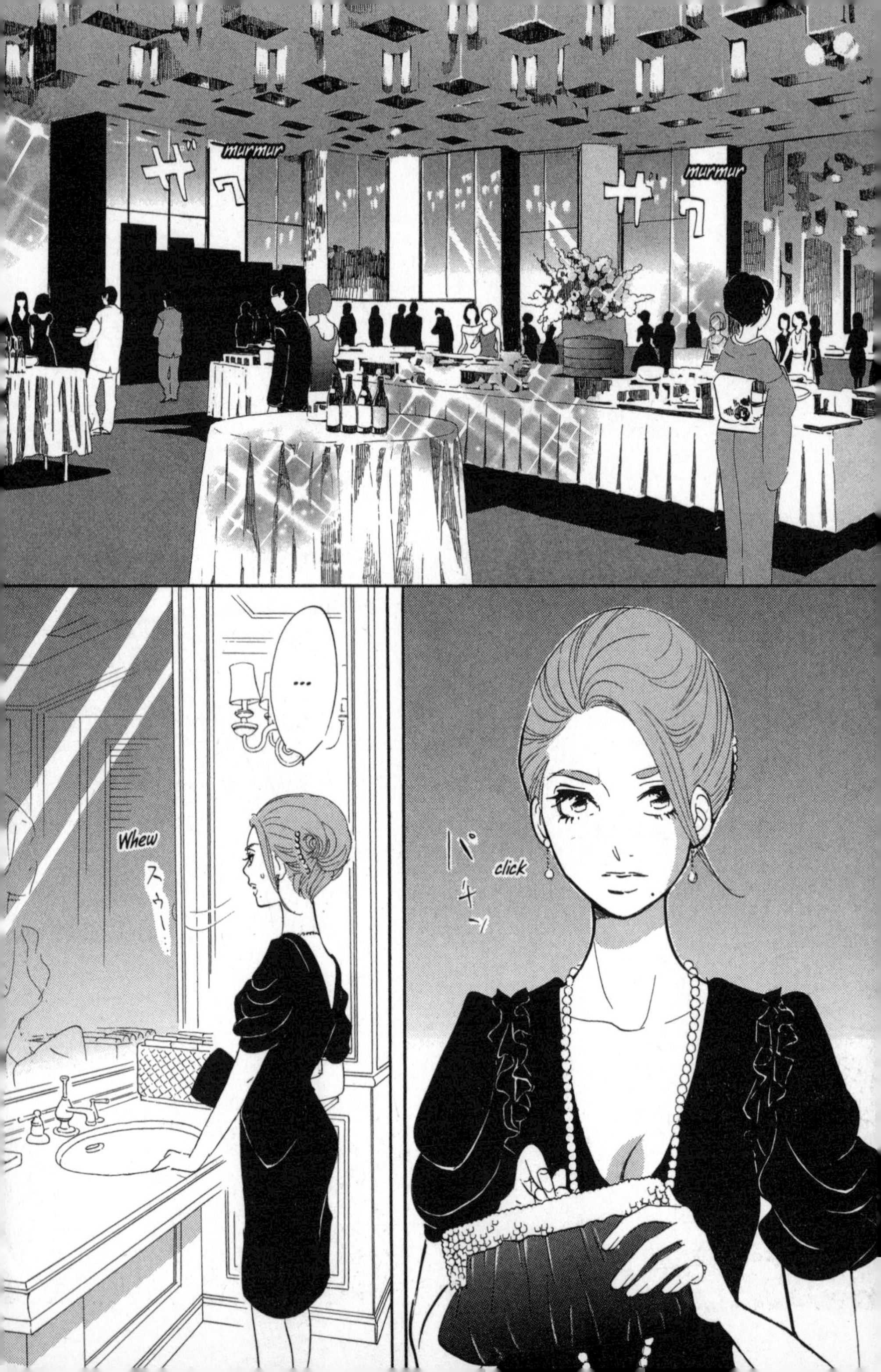
ザワ
murmur
ザワ
murmur
パキッ
click
...
Whew
スゥー…

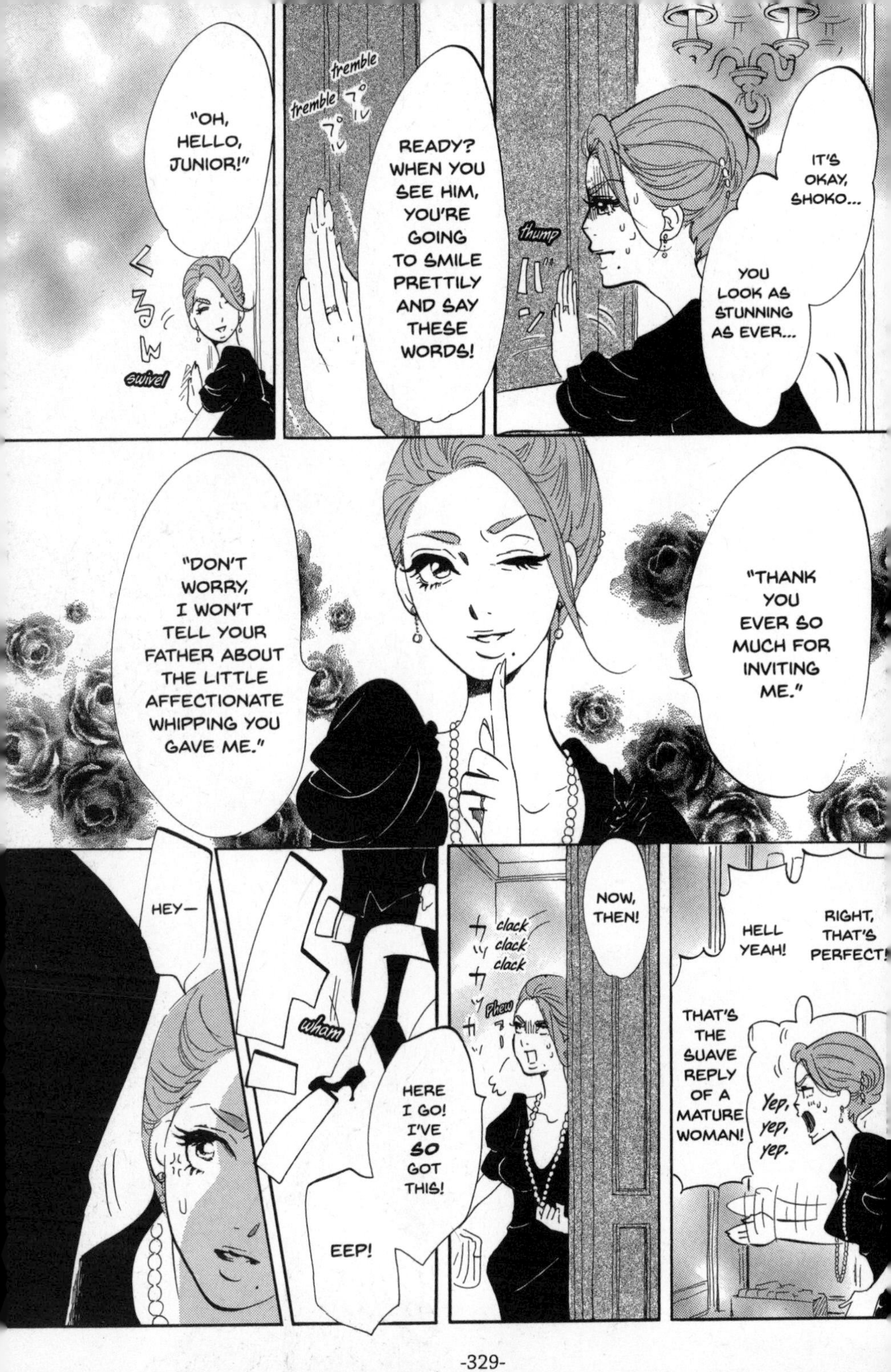
thump
IT'S OKAY, SHOKO...
YOU LOOK AS STUNNING AS EVER...
tremble tremble
READY? WHEN YOU SEE HIM, YOU'RE GOING TO SMILE PRETTILY AND SAY THESE WORDS!
"OH, HELLO, JUNIOR!"
swivel
"THANK YOU EVER SO MUCH FOR INVITING ME."
"DON'T WORRY, I WON'T TELL YOUR FATHER ABOUT THE LITTLE AFFECTIONATE WHIPPING YOU GAVE ME."
RIGHT, THAT'S PERFECT!
HELL YEAH!
THAT'S THE SUAVE REPLY OF A MATURE WOMAN!
Yep, yep, yep.
NOW, THEN!
clack clack clack
Phew
HERE I GO! I'VE SO GOT THIS!
wham
HEY—
EEP!

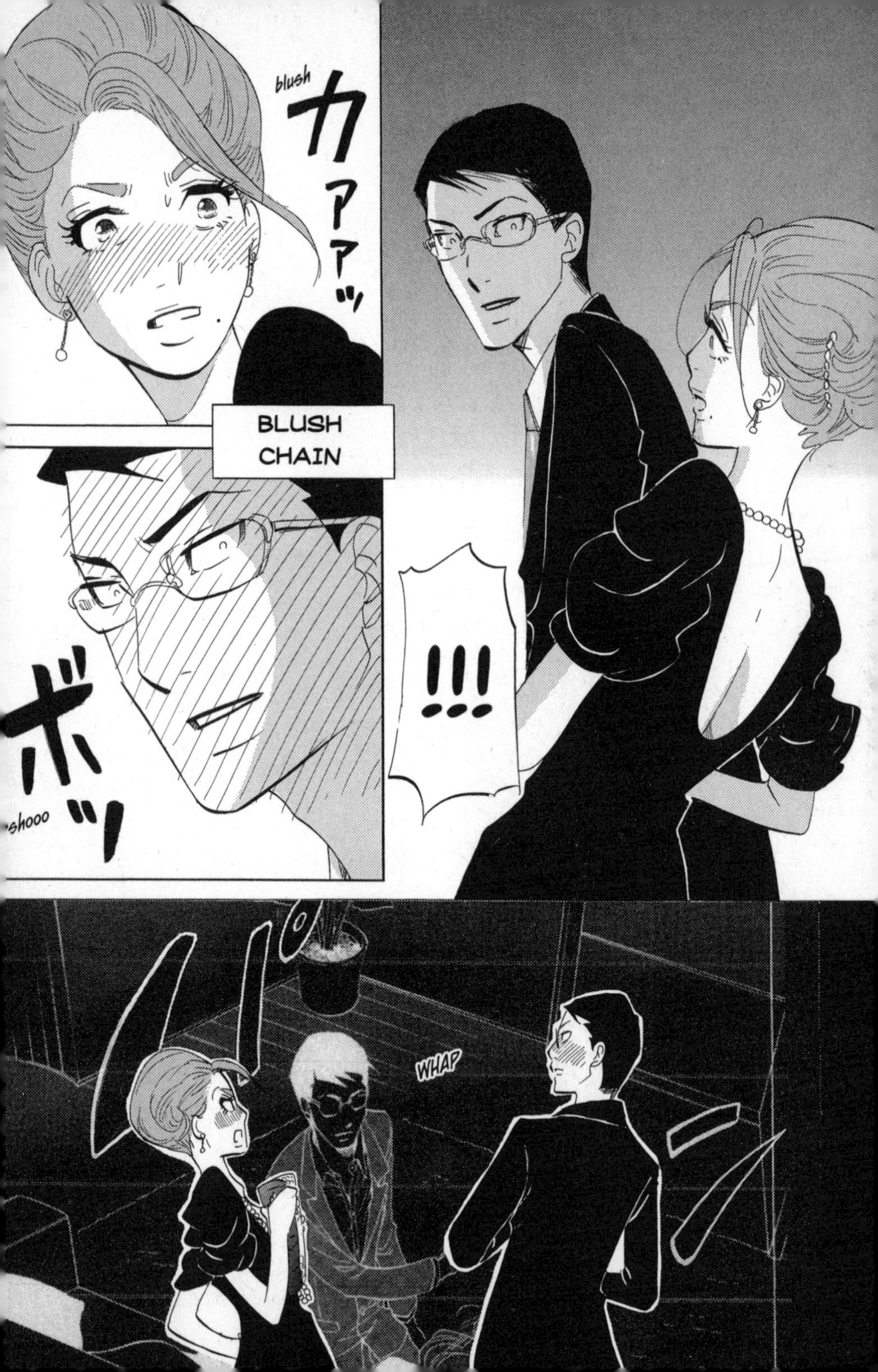
!!!
blush
カアアッ
BLUSH CHAIN
ボッ
shooo
WHAP

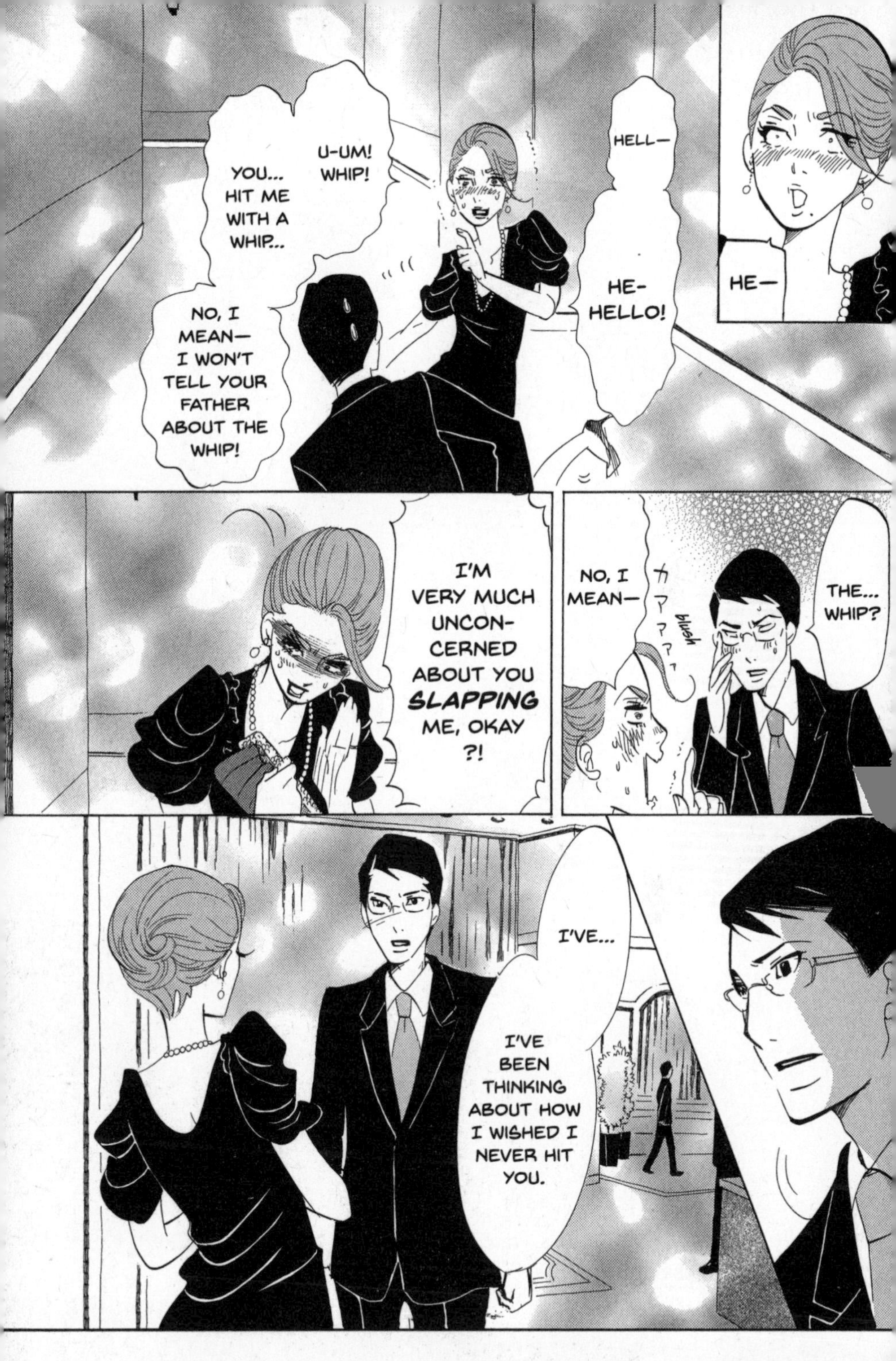
HE—
HELL—
HE- HELLO!
U-UM! WHIP!
YOU... HIT ME WITH A WHIP...
NO, I MEAN— I WON'T TELL YOUR FATHER ABOUT THE WHIP!
THE... WHIP?
blush
NO, I MEAN—
I'M VERY MUCH UNCONCERNED ABOUT YOU SLAPPING ME, OKAY?!
I'VE...
I'VE BEEN THINKING ABOUT HOW I WISHED I NEVER HIT YOU.

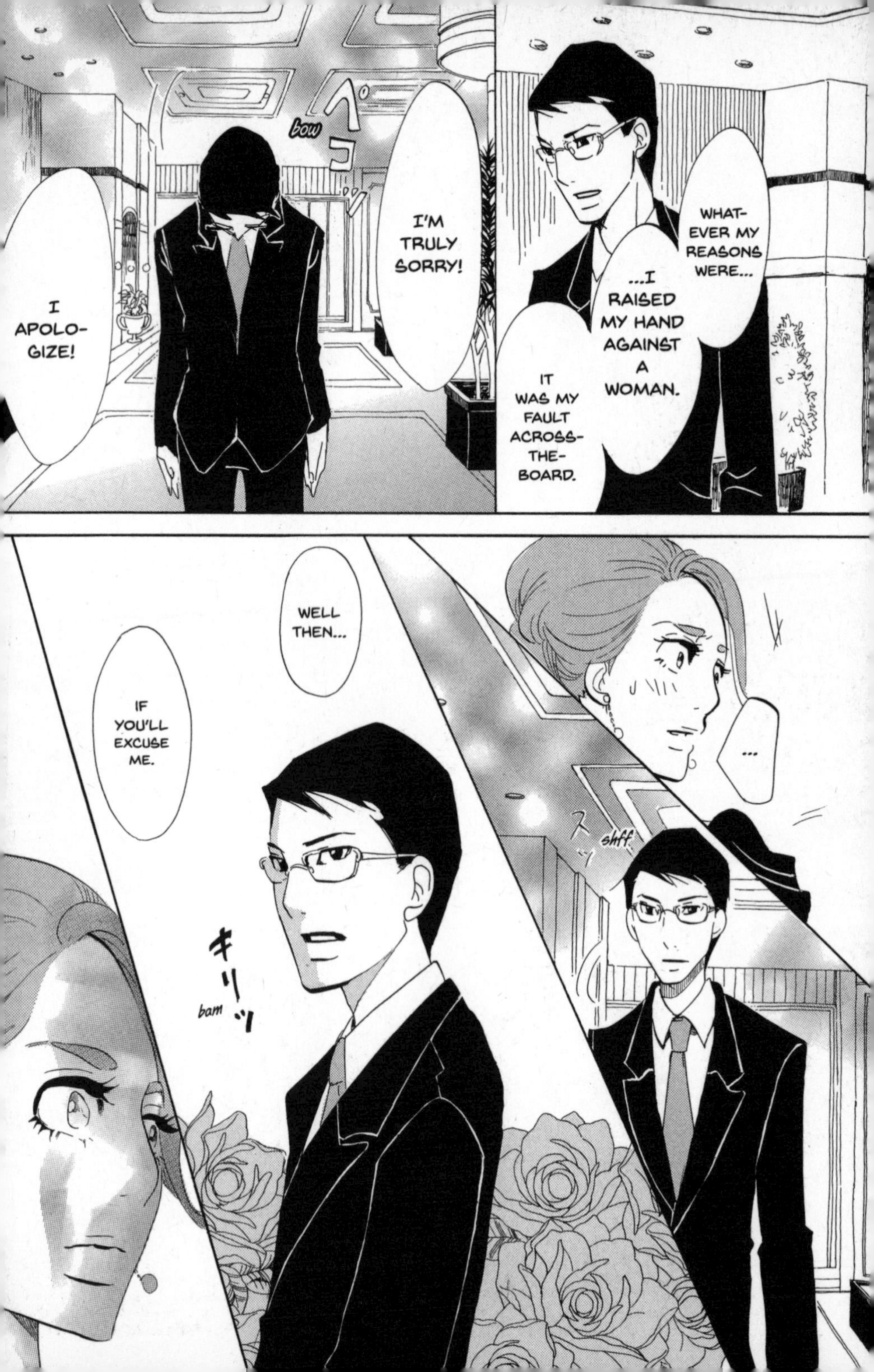
WHAT-EVER MY REASONS WERE...
...I RAISED MY HAND AGAINST A WOMAN.
IT WAS MY FAULT ACROSS-THE-BOARD.
I'M TRULY SORRY!
bow
I APOLOGIZE!
...
shff
WELL THEN...
IF YOU'LL EXCUSE ME.
bam

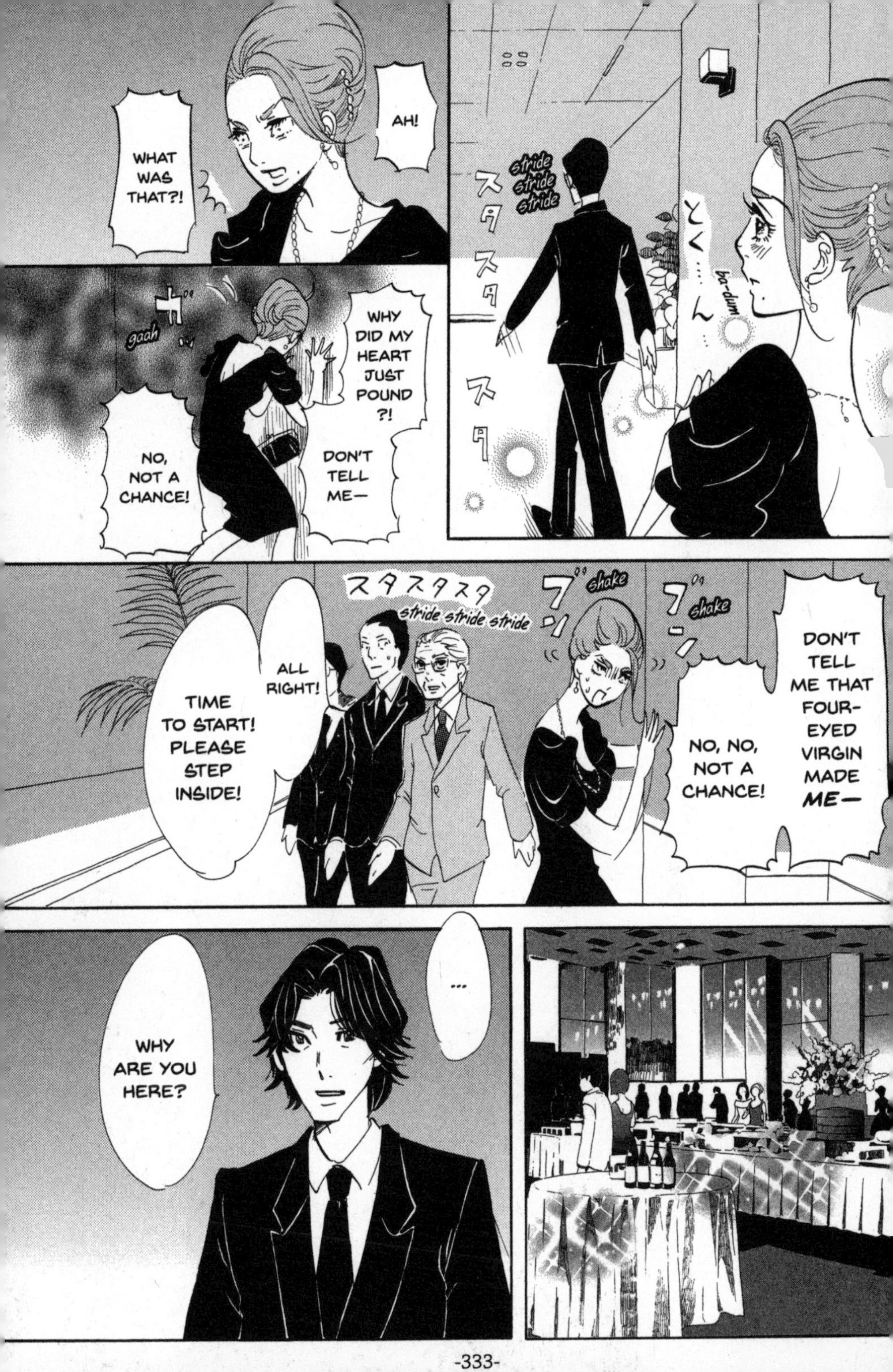
スタスタ
stride stride stride
とく…ん…
ba-dum
AH!
WHAT WAS THAT?!
WHY DID MY HEART JUST POUND?!
DON'T TELL ME—
NO, NOT A CHANCE!
gaah
DON'T TELL ME THAT FOUR-EYED VIRGIN MADE ME—
NO, NO, NOT A CHANCE!
shake
shake
スタスタスタ
stride stride stride
ALL RIGHT!
TIME TO START! PLEASE STEP INSIDE!
...
WHY ARE YOU HERE?

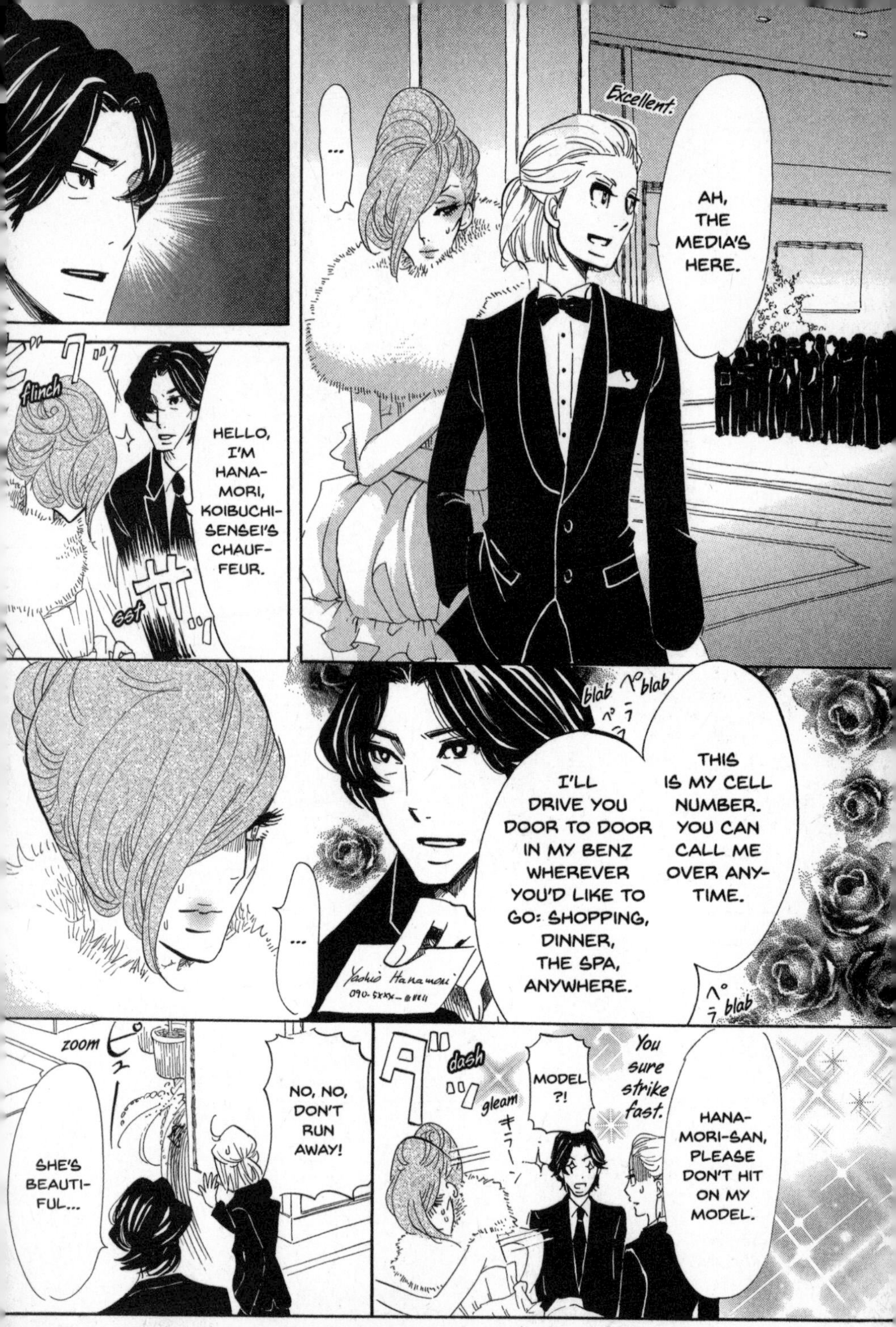
Excellent.
AH, THE MEDIA'S HERE.
...
HELLO, I'M HANA-MORI, KOIBUCHI-SENSEI'S CHAUF-FEUR.
flinch
sst
blab blab
THIS IS MY CELL NUMBER. YOU CAN CALL ME OVER ANY-TIME.
I'LL DRIVE YOU DOOR TO DOOR IN MY BENZ WHEREVER YOU'D LIKE TO GO: SHOPPING, DINNER, THE SPA, ANYWHERE.
blab
...
HANA-MORI-SAN, PLEASE DON'T HIT ON MY MODEL.
You sure strike fast.
MODEL ?!
gleam
dash
NO, NO, DON'T RUN AWAY!
zoom
SHE'S BEAUTI-FUL...

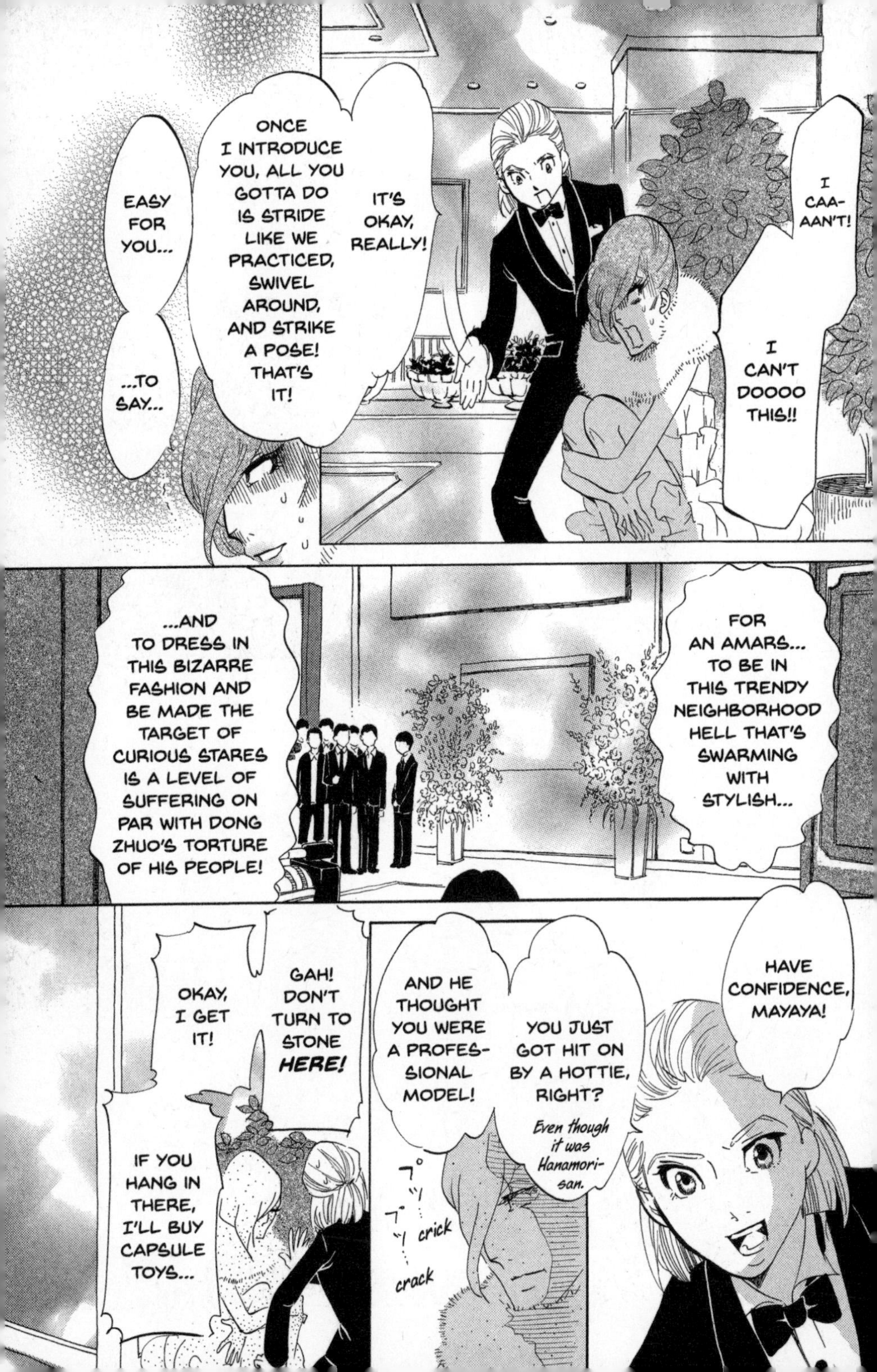
I CAA-AAN'T!
I CAN'T DOOOO THIS!!
IT'S OKAY, REALLY!
ONCE I INTRODUCE YOU, ALL YOU GOTTA DO IS STRIDE LIKE WE PRACTICED, SWIVEL AROUND, AND STRIKE A POSE! THAT'S IT!
EASY FOR YOU...
...TO SAY...
FOR AN AMARS... TO BE IN THIS TRENDY NEIGHBORHOOD HELL THAT'S SWARMING WITH STYLISH...
...AND TO DRESS IN THIS BIZARRE FASHION AND BE MADE THE TARGET OF CURIOUS STARES IS A LEVEL OF SUFFERING ON PAR WITH DONG ZHUO'S TORTURE OF HIS PEOPLE!
HAVE CONFIDENCE, MAYAYA!
YOU JUST GOT HIT ON BY A HOTTIE, RIGHT?
Even though it was Hanamori-san.
AND HE THOUGHT YOU WERE A PROFES-SIONAL MODEL!
crick
crack
GAH! DON'T TURN TO STONE HERE!
OKAY, I GET IT!
IF YOU HANG IN THERE, I'LL BUY CAPSULE TOYS...

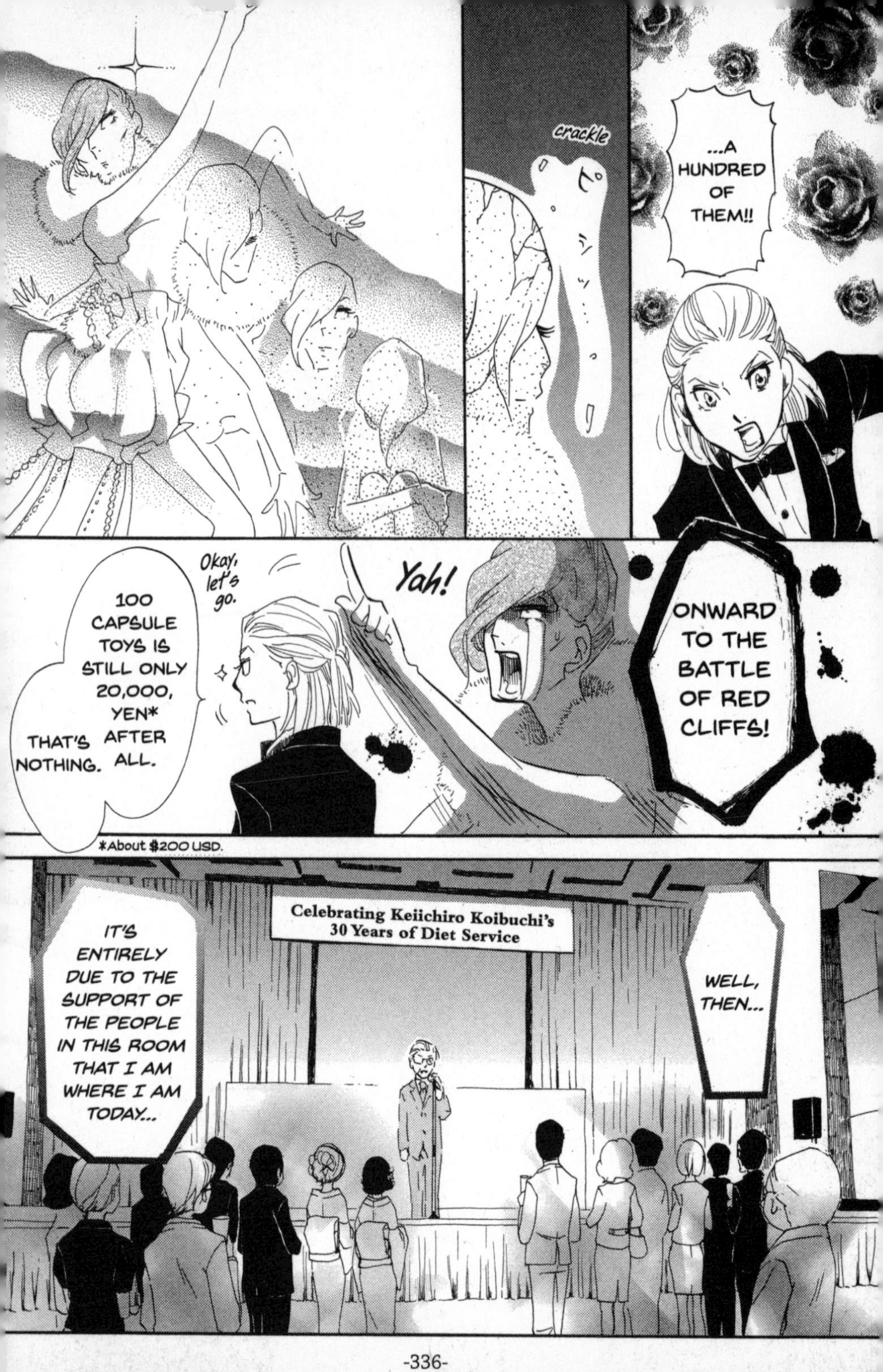
...A HUNDRED OF THEM!!
crackle
ONWARD TO THE BATTLE OF RED CLIFFS!
Yah!
Okay, let's go.
100 CAPSULE TOYS IS STILL ONLY 20,000, YEN* AFTER ALL.
THAT'S NOTHING.
WELL, THEN...
Celebrating Keiichiro Koibuchi's 30 Years of Diet Service
IT'S ENTIRELY DUE TO THE SUPPORT OF THE PEOPLE IN THIS ROOM THAT I AM WHERE I AM TODAY...

*About $200 USD.

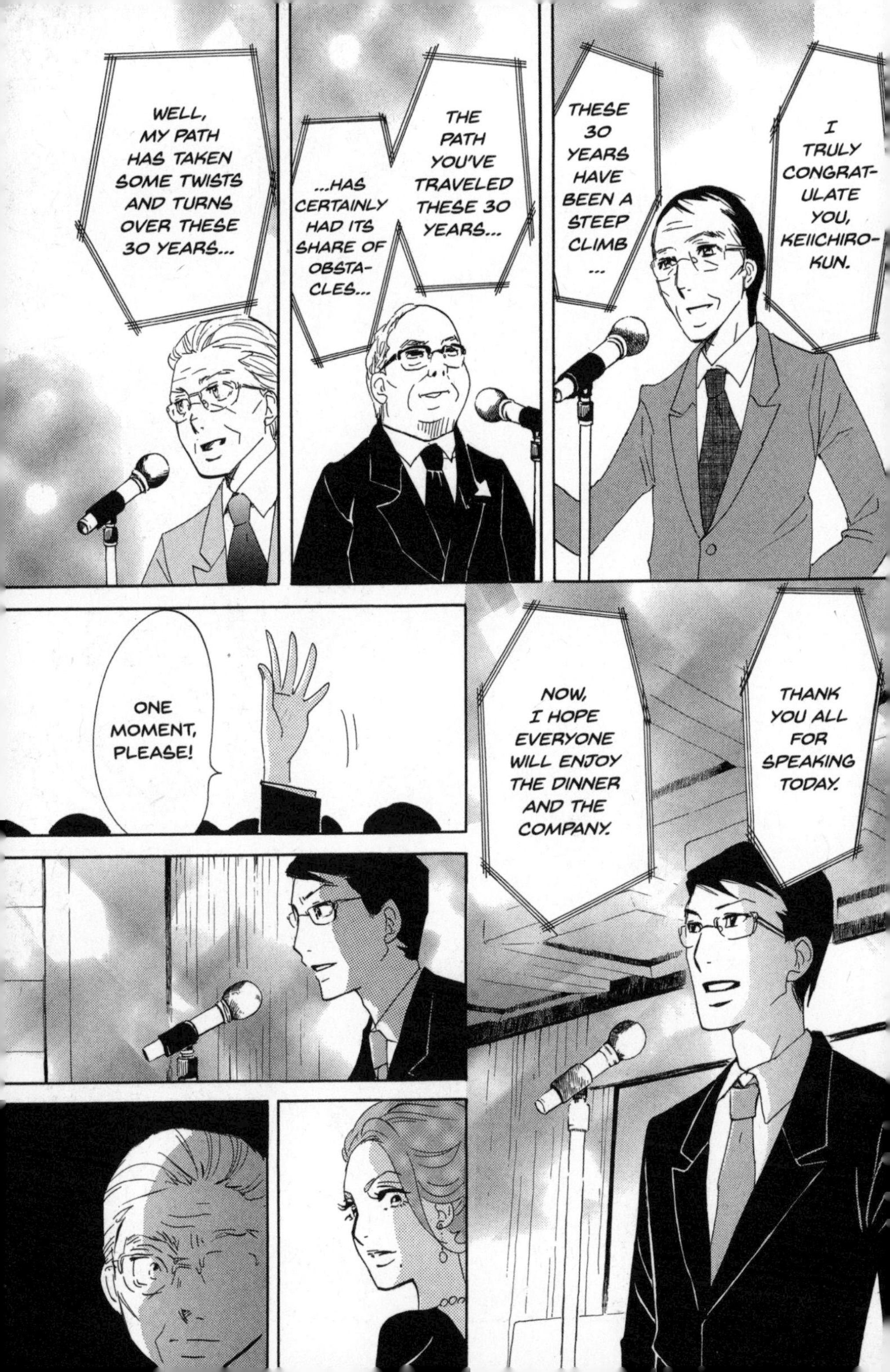
I TRULY CONGRATULATE YOU, KEIICHIRO-KUN.
THESE 30 YEARS HAVE BEEN A STEEP CLIMB...
THE PATH YOU'VE TRAVELED THESE 30 YEARS...
...HAS CERTAINLY HAD ITS SHARE OF OBSTACLES...
WELL, MY PATH HAS TAKEN SOME TWISTS AND TURNS OVER THESE 30 YEARS...
THANK YOU ALL FOR SPEAKING TODAY.
NOW, I HOPE EVERYONE WILL ENJOY THE DINNER AND THE COMPANY.
ONE MOMENT, PLEASE!

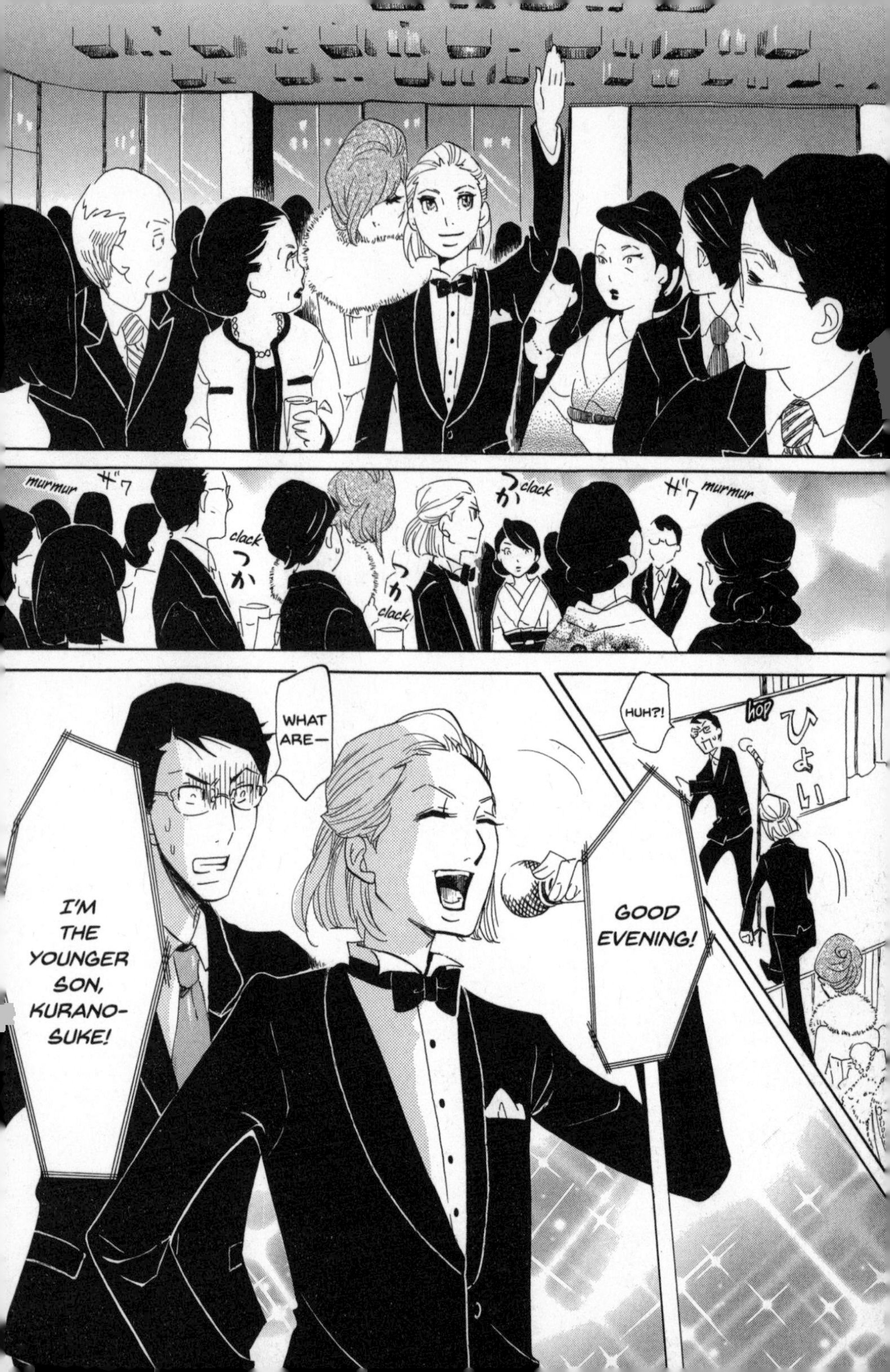
ザワ
murmur
つか
clack
つか
clack
clack
つか
murmur
ザワ
HUH?!
hop
ひょい
WHAT ARE—
GOOD EVENING!
I'M THE YOUNGER SON, KURANO-SUKE!

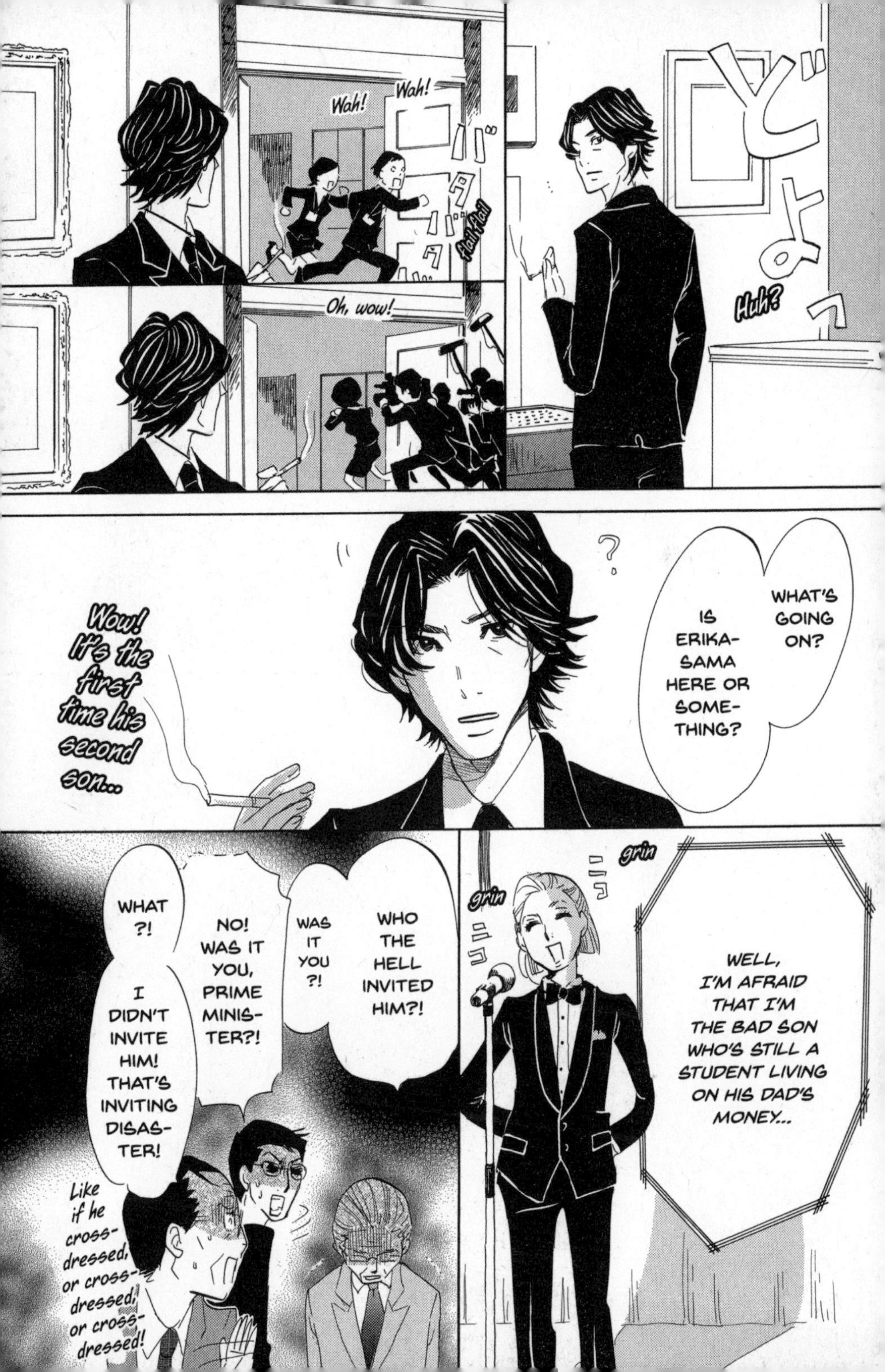
どよっ
Huh?
Wah!
Wah!
バタバタ
flail flail
Oh, wow!
WHAT'S GOING ON?
IS ERIKA-SAMA HERE OR SOME-THING?
?
Wow! It's the first time his second son...
grin
grin
WELL, I'M AFRAID THAT I'M THE BAD SON WHO'S STILL A STUDENT LIVING ON HIS DAD'S MONEY...
WHO THE HELL INVITED HIM?!
WAS IT YOU?!
NO! WAS IT YOU, PRIME MINIS-TER?!
WHAT?!
I DIDN'T INVITE HIM! THAT'S INVITING DISAS-TER!
Like if he cross-dressed, or cross-dressed, or cross-dressed!

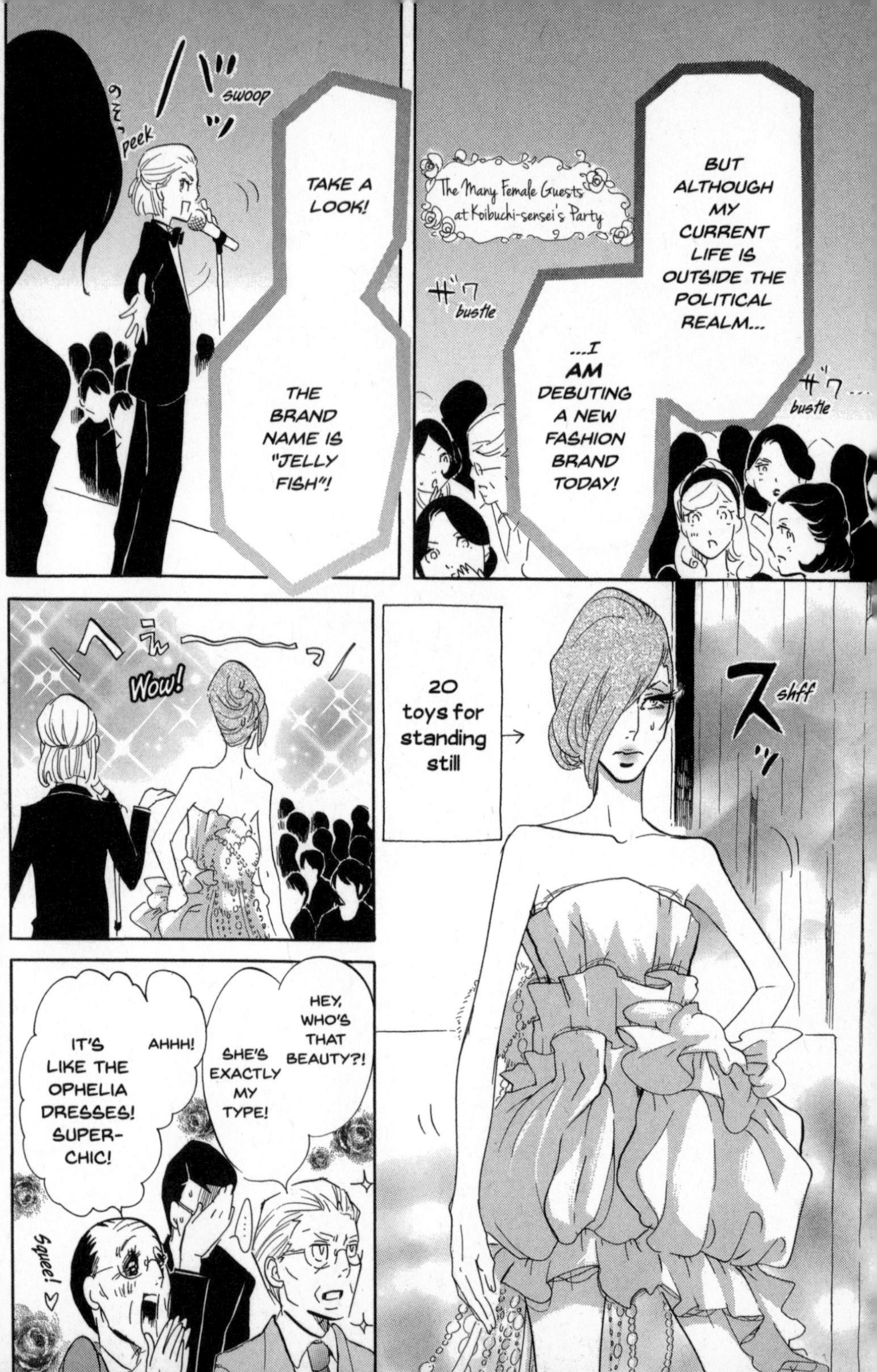

BUT ALTHOUGH MY CURRENT LIFE IS OUTSIDE THE POLITICAL REALM...
bustle
The Many Female Guests at Koibuchi-sensei's Party
bustle
...I AM DEBUTING A NEW FASHION BRAND TODAY!
swoop
peek
TAKE A LOOK!
THE BRAND NAME IS "JELLY FISH"!
shff
20 toys for standing still
Wow!
HEY, WHO'S THAT BEAUTY?!
SHE'S EXACTLY MY TYPE!
AHHH!
IT'S LIKE THE OPHELIA DRESSES! SUPER-CHIC!
Squee! ♥
...

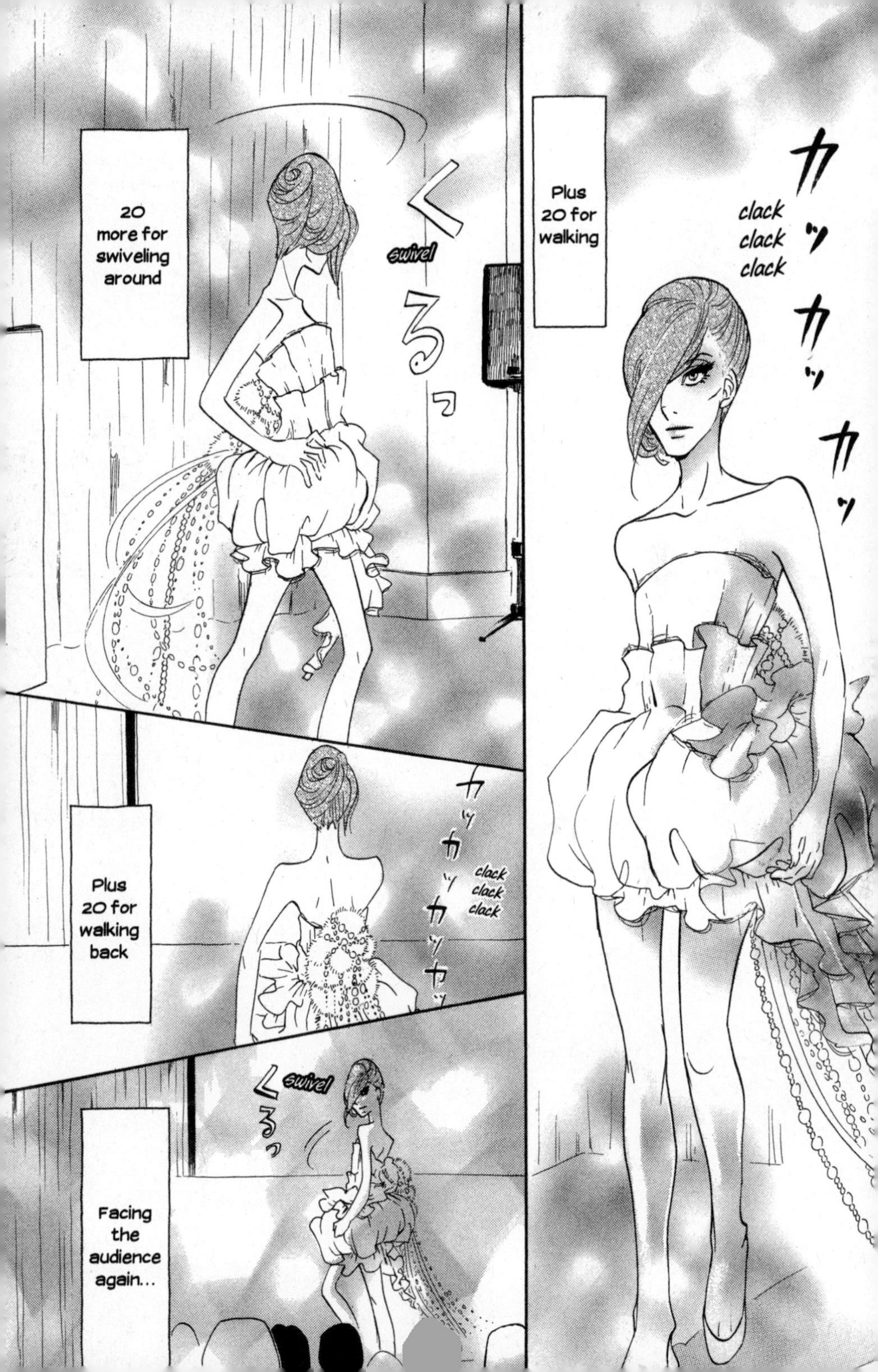
Plus 20 for walking
カッカッカッ
clack clack clack
20 more for swiveling around
くるっ
swivel
Plus 20 for walking back
カッカッカッカッ
clack clack clack
Facing the audience again...
くるっ
swivel

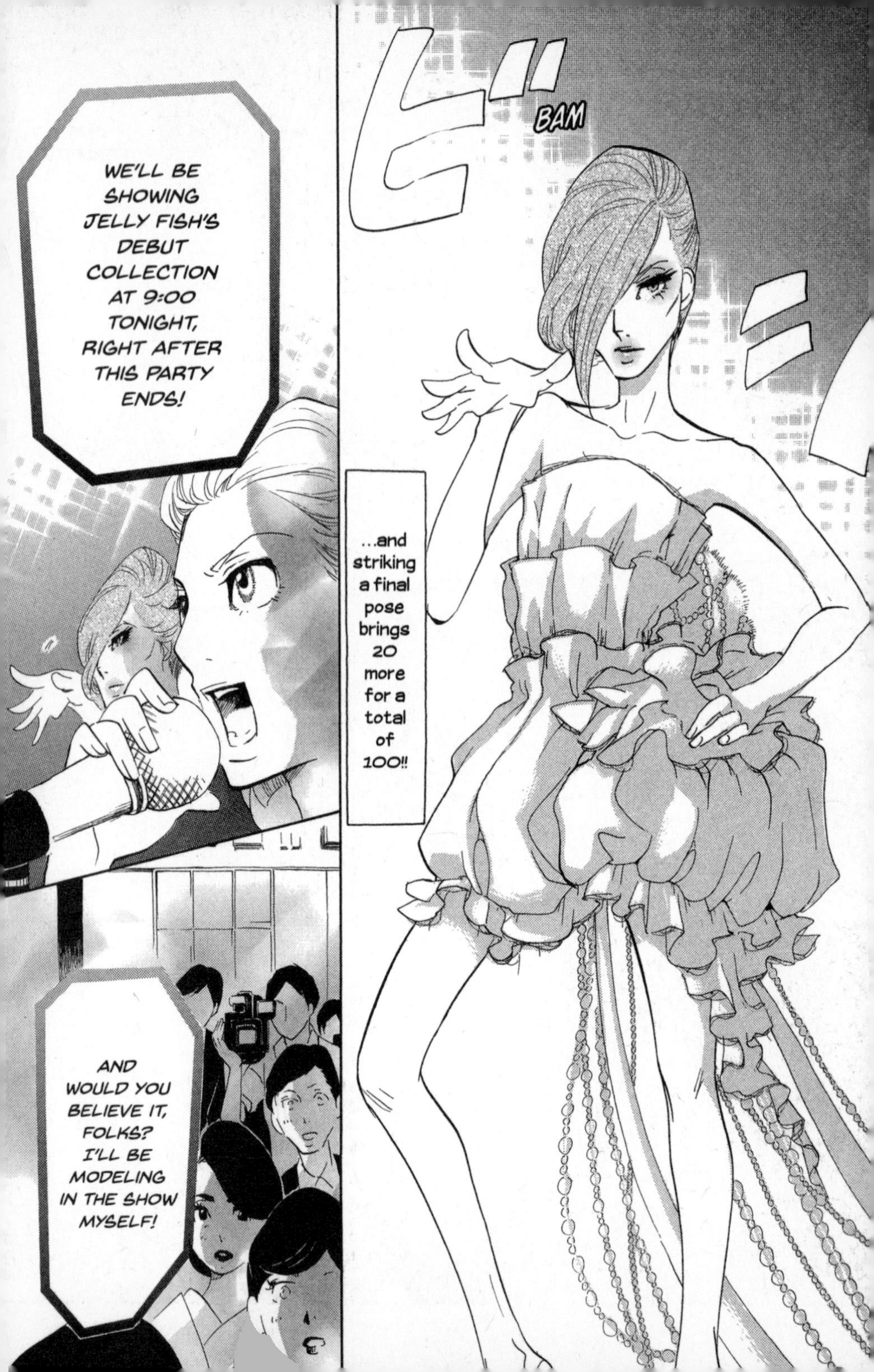
BAM
...and striking a final pose brings 20 more for a total of 100!!
WE'LL BE SHOWING JELLY FISH'S DEBUT COLLECTION AT 9:00 TONIGHT, RIGHT AFTER THIS PARTY ENDS!
AND WOULD YOU BELIEVE IT, FOLKS? I'LL BE MODELING IN THE SHOW MYSELF!

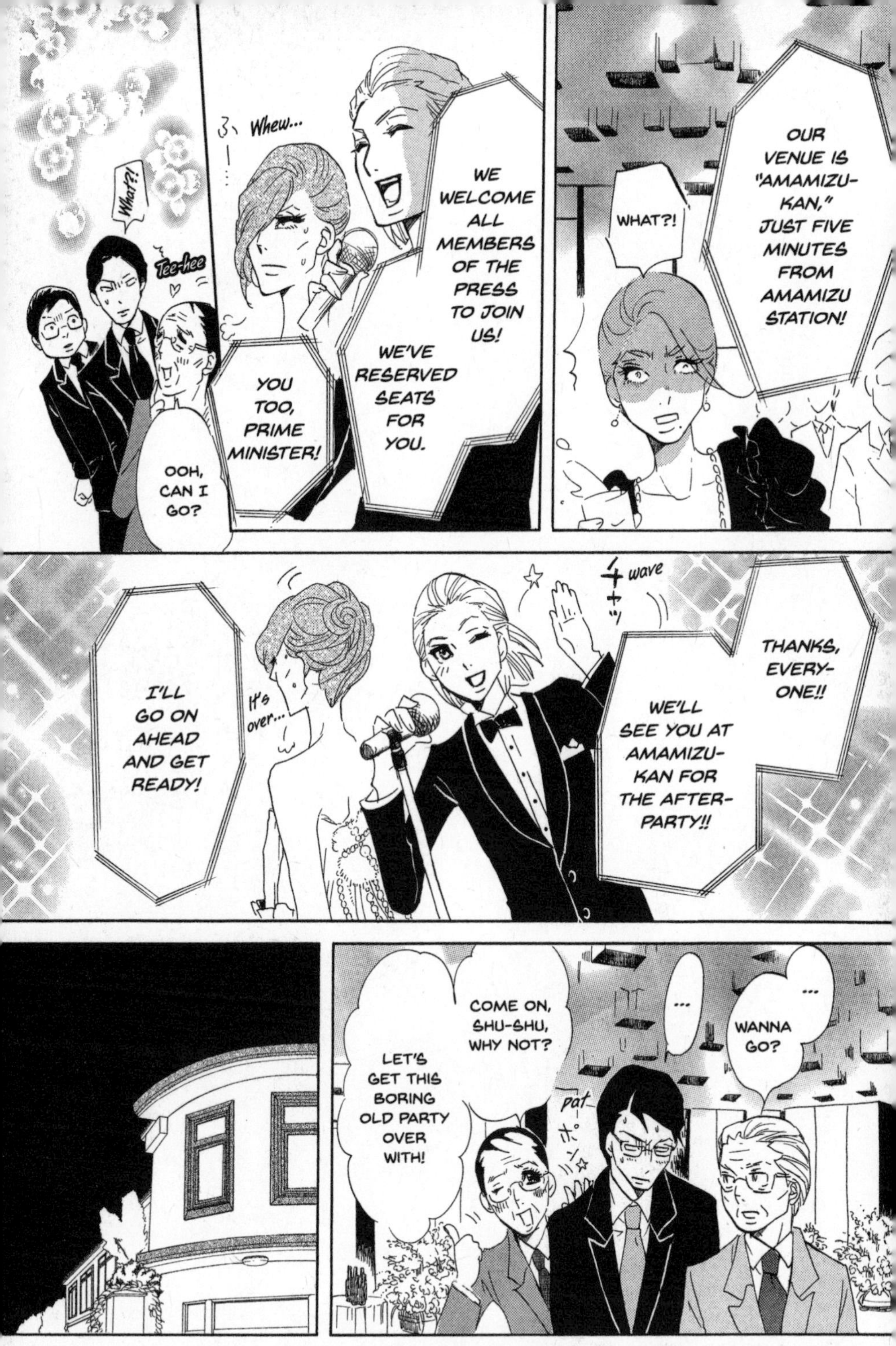
OUR VENUE IS "AMAMIZU-KAN," JUST FIVE MINUTES FROM AMAMIZU STATION!
WHAT?!
WE WELCOME ALL MEMBERS OF THE PRESS TO JOIN US!
WE'VE RESERVED SEATS FOR YOU.
YOU TOO, PRIME MINISTER!
Whew...
What?!
Tee-hee
OOH, CAN I GO?
wave
THANKS, EVERY-ONE!!
WE'LL SEE YOU AT AMAMIZU-KAN FOR THE AFTER-PARTY!!
It's over...
I'LL GO ON AHEAD AND GET READY!
...
WANNA GO?
...
COME ON, SHU-SHU, WHY NOT?
pat
LET'S GET THIS BORING OLD PARTY OVER WITH!

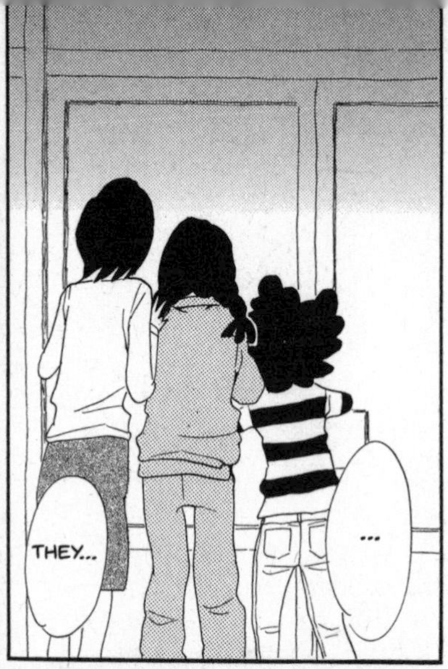
...
THEY...

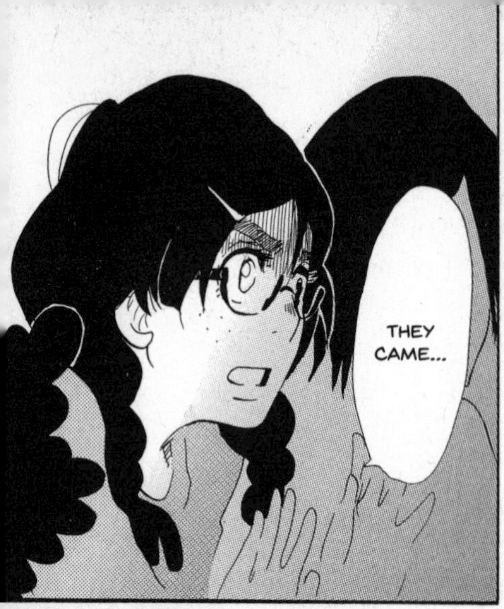
THEY CAME...

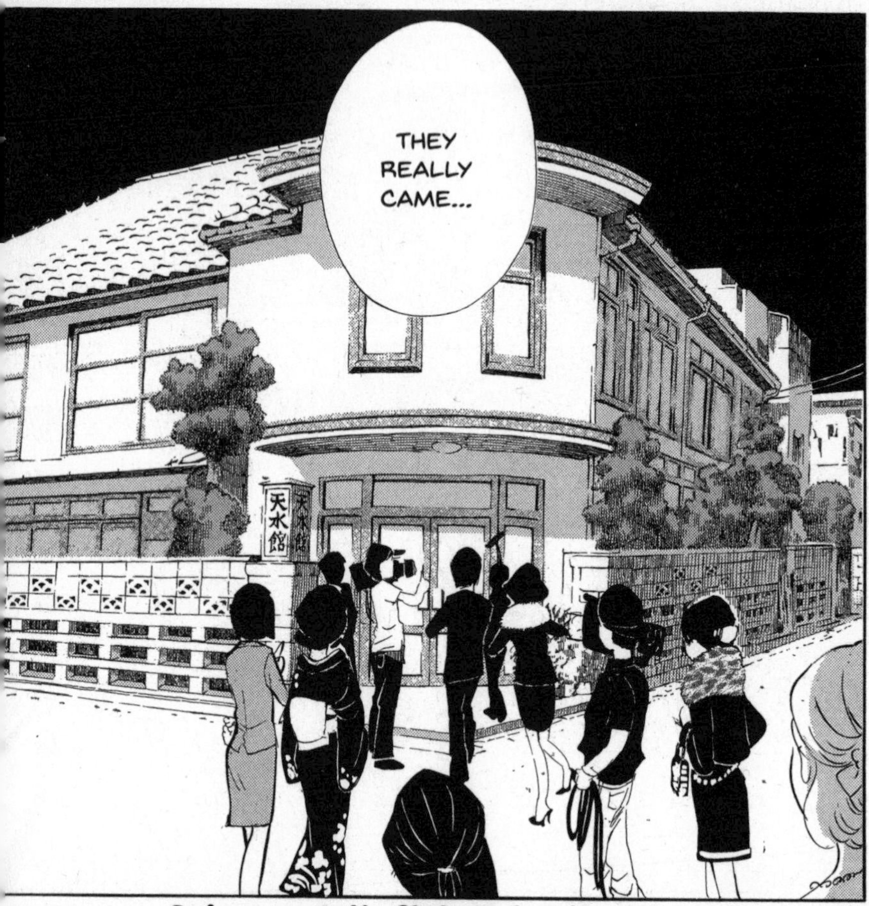
THEY REALLY CAME...

Princess Jellyfish Vol. 3/End

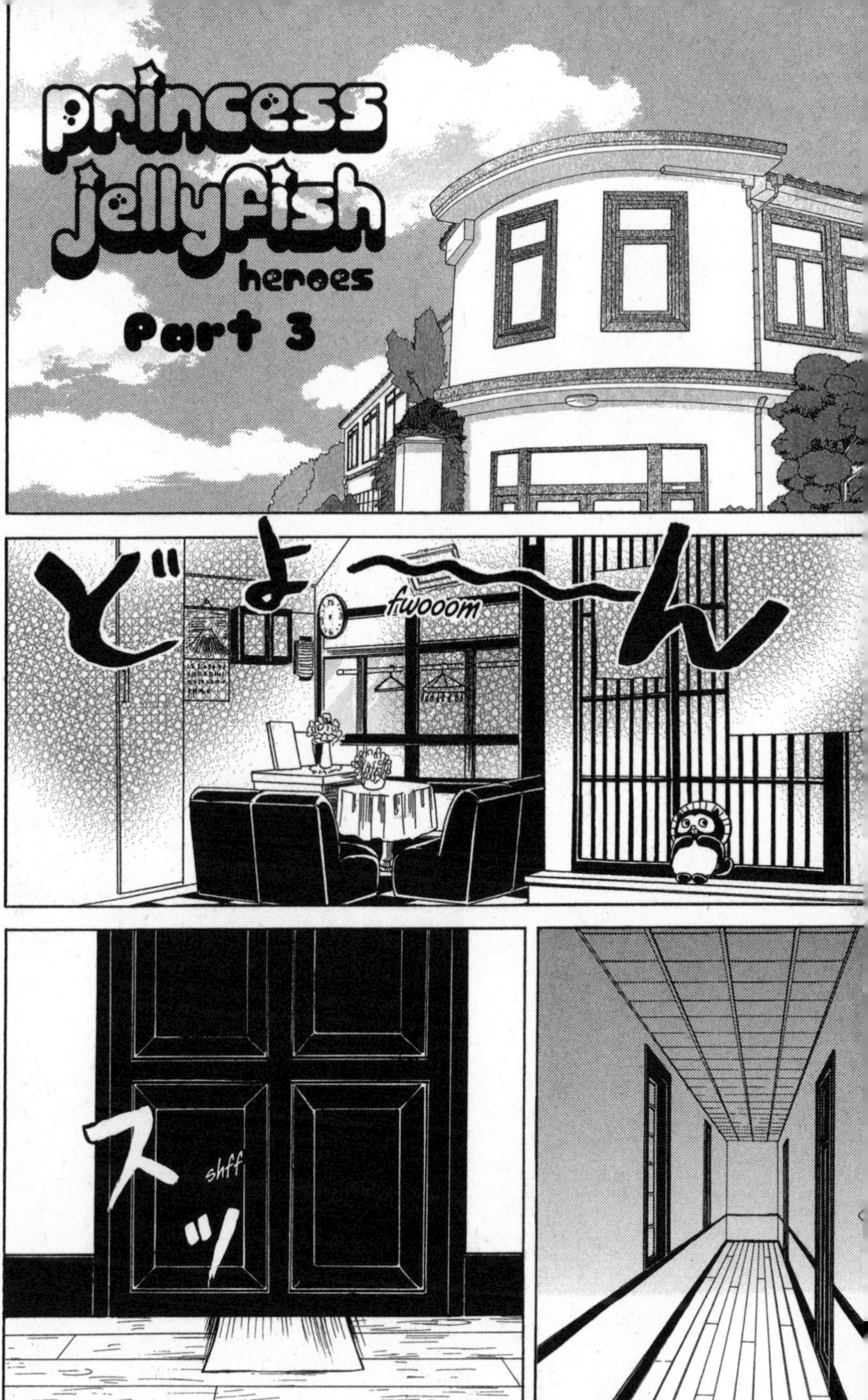
princess jellyfish
heroes
Part 3
どよ〜〜ん
fwooom
スッ
shff

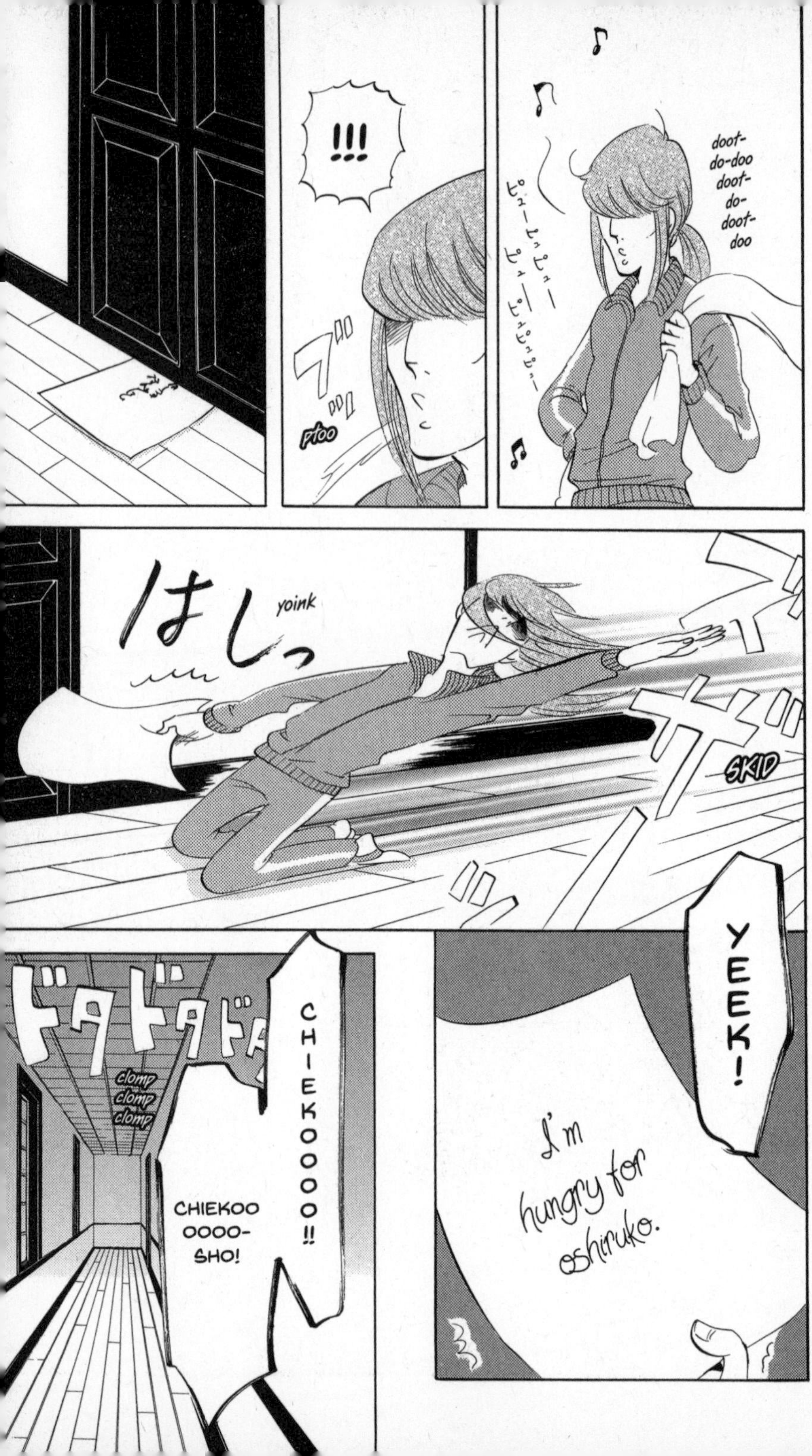
doot-do-doo doot-do-doot-doo
!!!
ptoo
SKID
はしっ
yoink
YEEK!
I'm hungry for oshiruko.
CHIEKOOOOO!!
CHIEKOO OOOO-SHO!
clomp clomp clomp

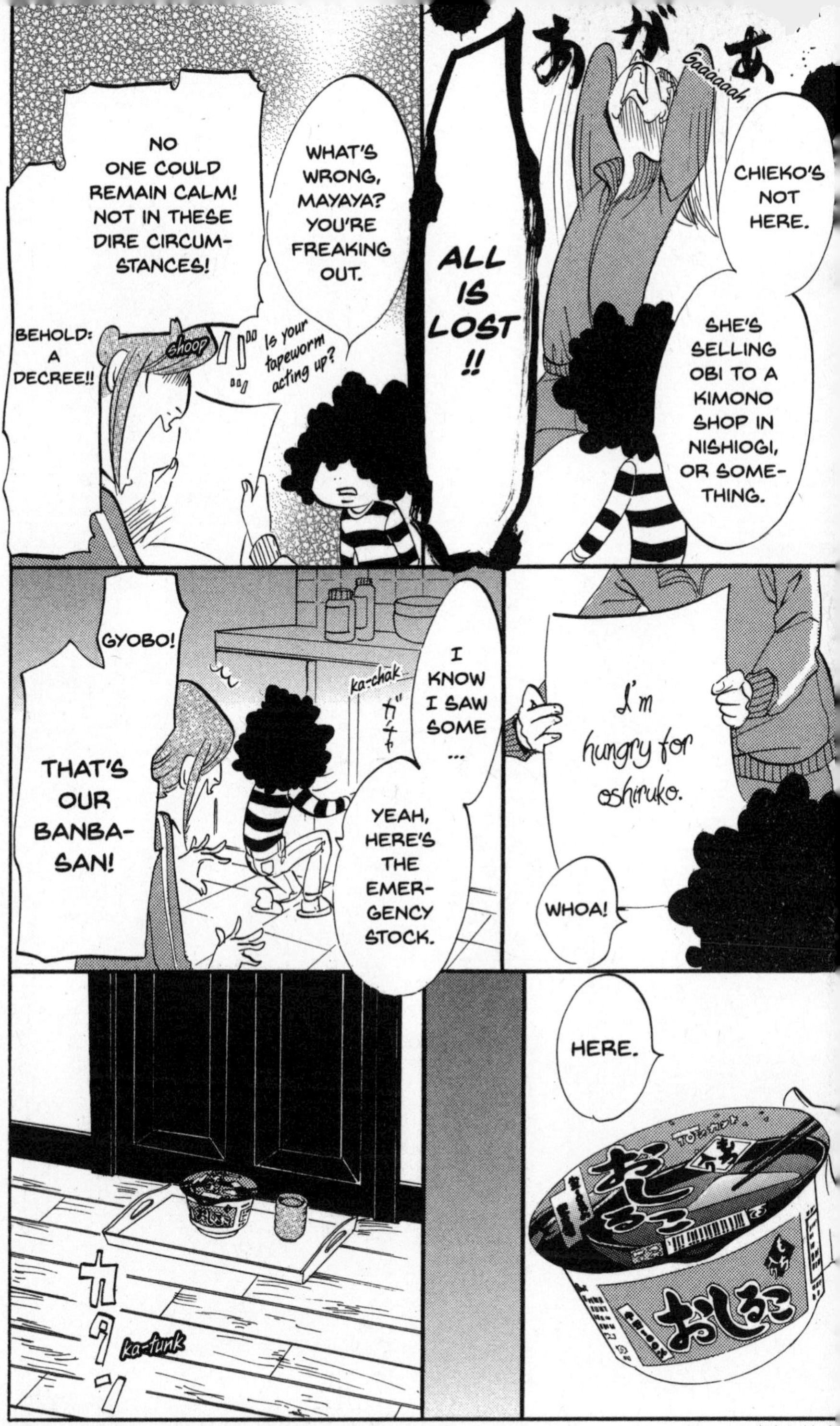
Gaaaaaah
CHIEKO'S NOT HERE.
SHE'S SELLING OBI TO A KIMONO SHOP IN NISHIOGI, OR SOMETHING.
ALL IS LOST !!
WHAT'S WRONG, MAYAYA? YOU'RE FREAKING OUT.
Is your tapeworm acting up?
NO ONE COULD REMAIN CALM! NOT IN THESE DIRE CIRCUMSTANCES!
shoop
BEHOLD: A DECREE!!
I'm hungry for oshiruko.
WHOA!
I KNOW I SAW SOME ...
ka-chak
YEAH, HERE'S THE EMERGENCY STOCK.
GYOBO!
THAT'S OUR BANBA-SAN!
HERE.
ka-tunk

Label: Oshiruk

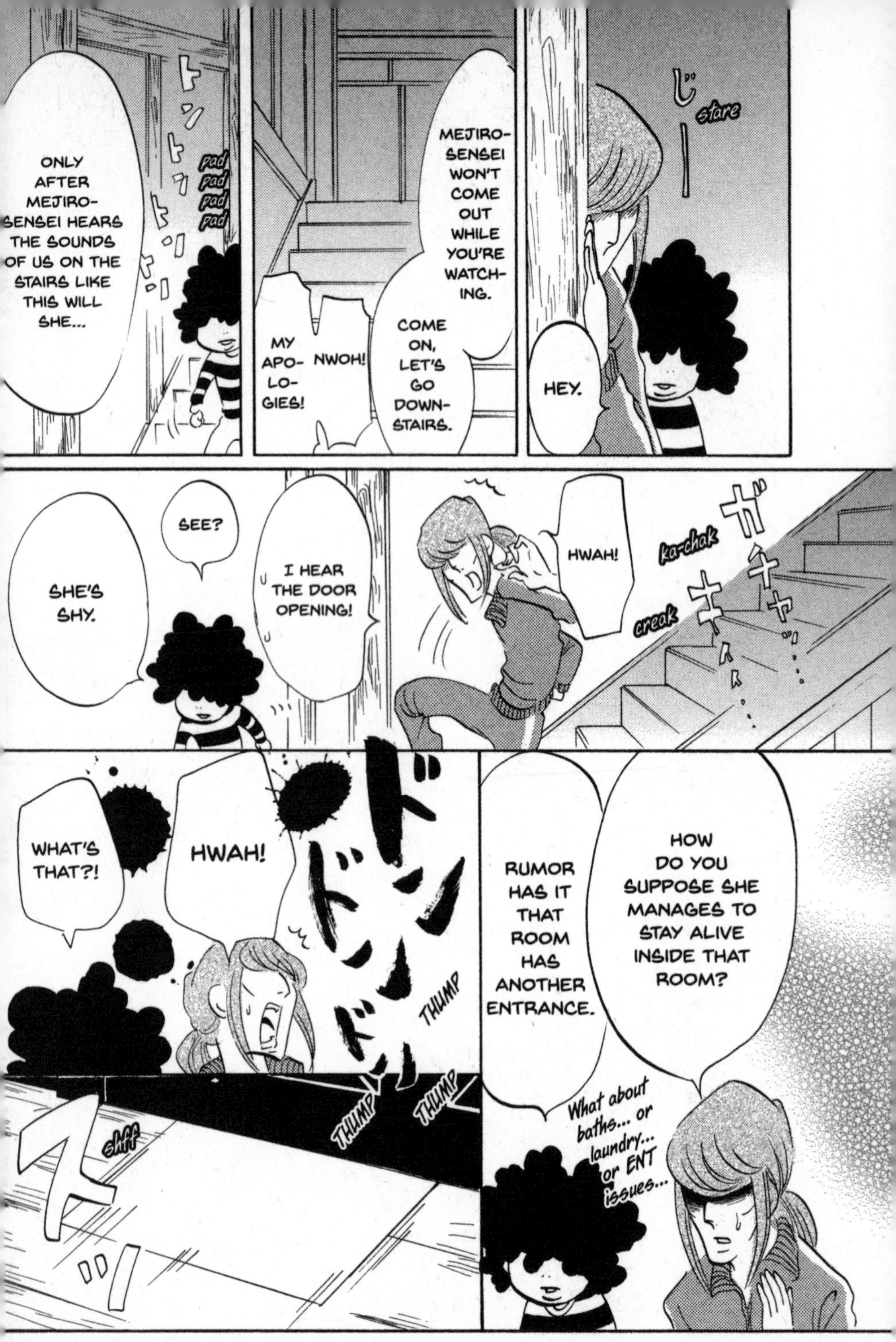
stare
HEY.
MEJIRO-SENSEI WON'T COME OUT WHILE YOU'RE WATCHING.
COME ON, LET'S GO DOWNSTAIRS.
NWOH!
MY APOLOGIES!
pad pad pad pad
ONLY AFTER MEJIRO-SENSEI HEARS THE SOUNDS OF US ON THE STAIRS LIKE THIS WILL SHE...
ka-chak
creak
HWAH!
I HEAR THE DOOR OPENING!
SEE?
SHE'S SHY.
HOW DO YOU SUPPOSE SHE MANAGES TO STAY ALIVE INSIDE THAT ROOM?
RUMOR HAS IT THAT ROOM HAS ANOTHER ENTRANCE.
What about baths... or laundry... or ENT issues...
THUMP
THUMP
THUMP
THUMP
HWAH!
WHAT'S THAT?!
shff

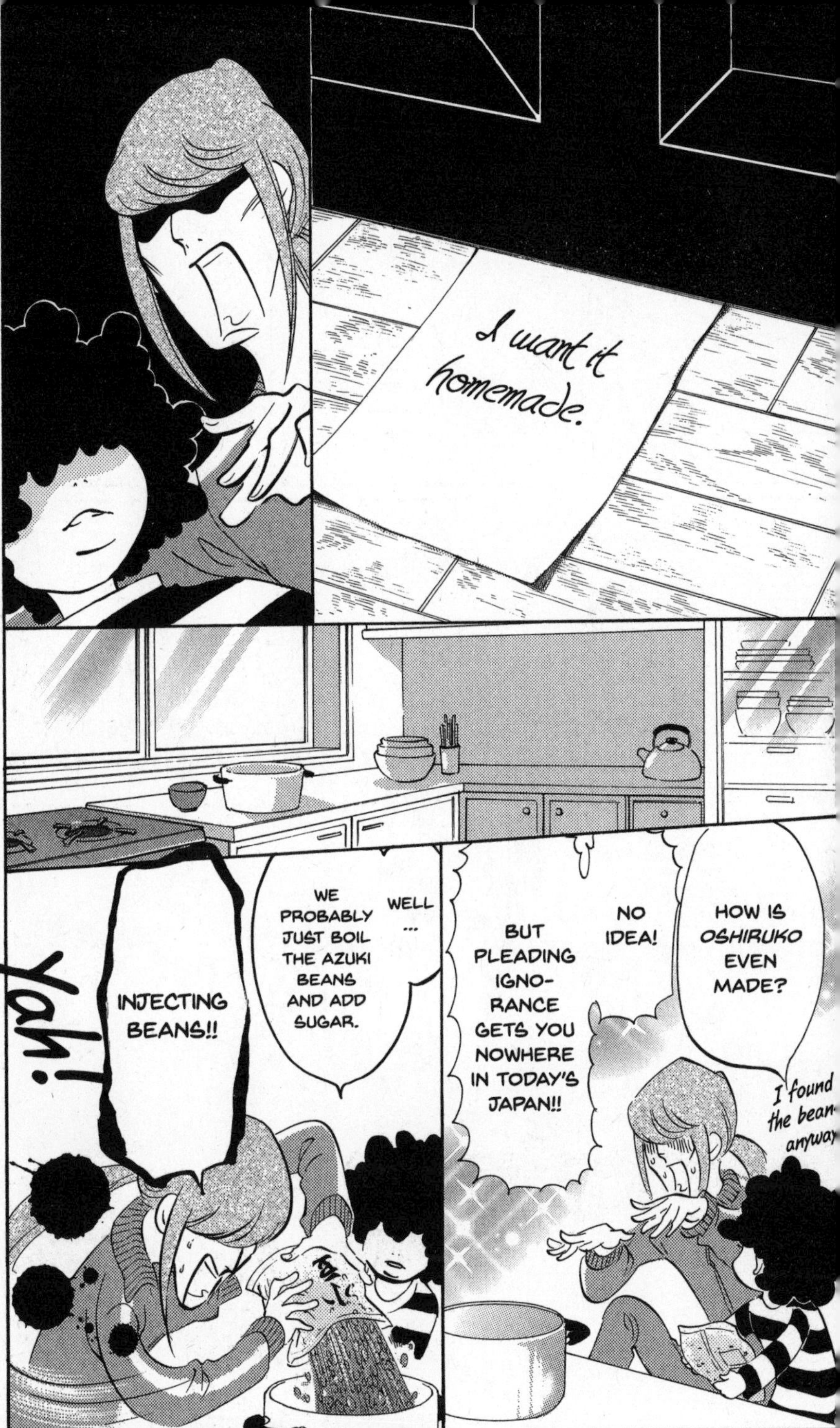

I want it homemade.
HOW IS OSHIRUKO EVEN MADE?
NO IDEA!
BUT PLEADING IGNORANCE GETS YOU NOWHERE IN TODAY'S JAPAN!!
I found the bean anyway
WELL ...
WE PROBABLY JUST BOIL THE AZUKI BEANS AND ADD SUGAR.
INJECTING BEANS!!
Yah!

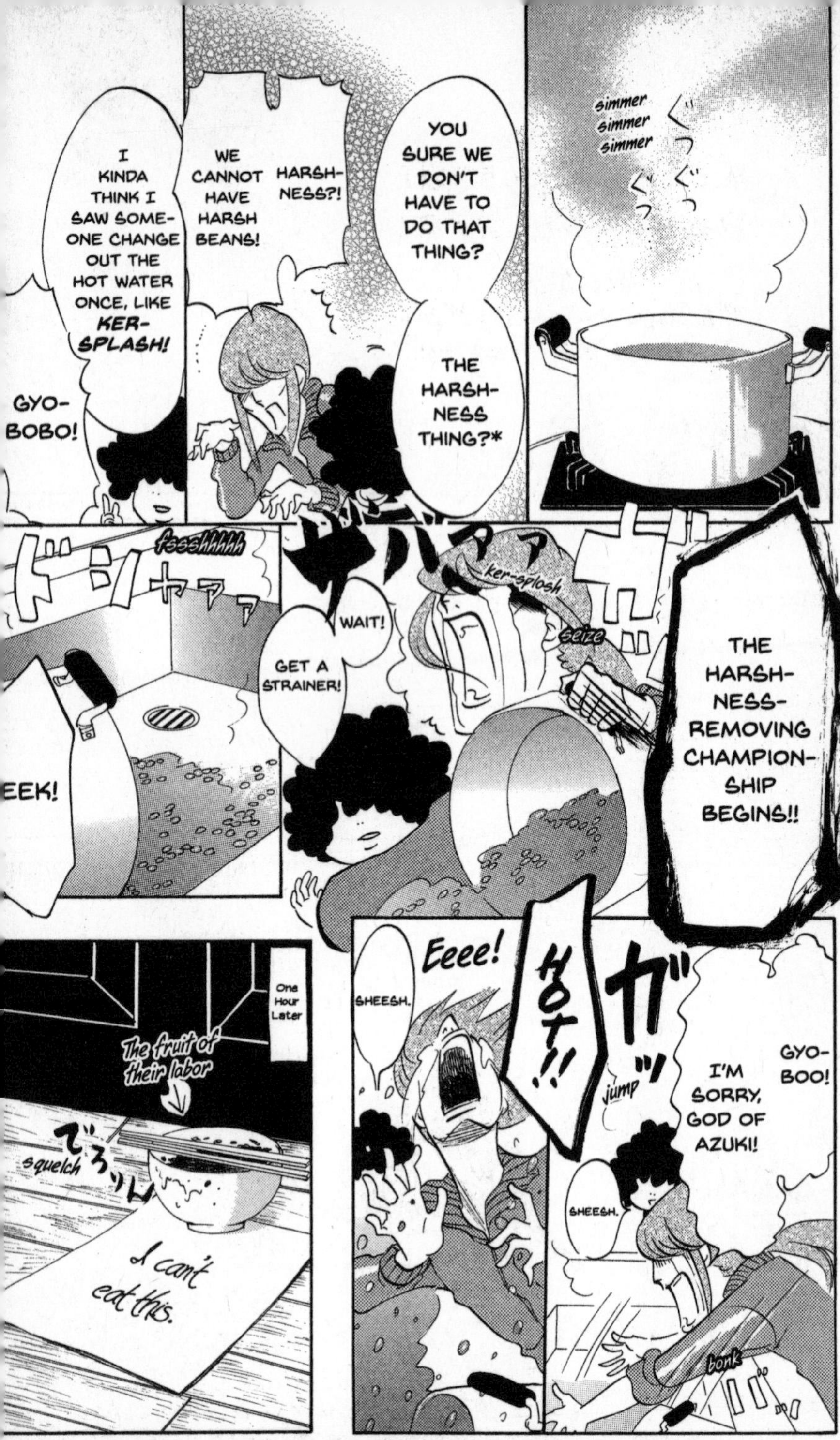
simmer simmer simmer
ぐつぐつぐつ
YOU SURE WE DON'T HAVE TO DO THAT THING?
THE HARSHNESS THING?*
HARSHNESS?!
WE CANNOT HAVE HARSH BEANS!
I KINDA THINK I SAW SOMEONE CHANGE OUT THE HOT WATER ONCE, LIKE KER-SPLASH!
GYO-BOBO!
THE HARSHNESS-REMOVING CHAMPIONSHIP BEGINS!!
seize
ker-splosh
WAIT!
GET A STRAINER!
fssshhhhh
EEK!
GYO-BOO!
I'M SORRY, GOD OF AZUKI!
jump
HOT!!
Eeee!
SHEESH.
SHEESH.
bonk
One Hour Later
The fruit of their labor
squelch
I can't eat this.

*Aku-nuki, or literally "harshness removal." A Japanese cooking method to remove bitterness from raw foods.

Princess Jellyfish Heroes Part 3-End

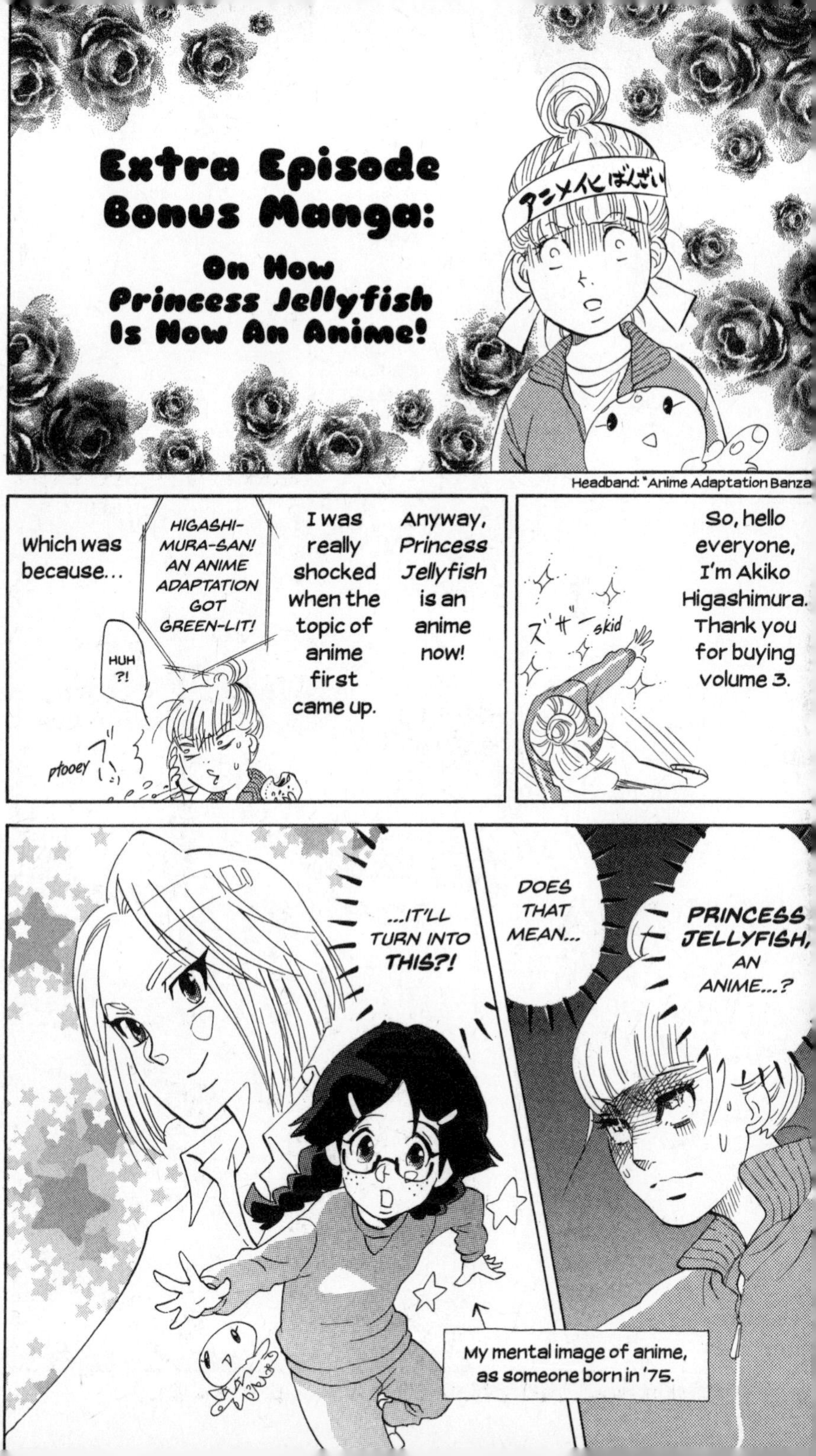
Extra Episode Bonus Manga:
On How *Princess Jellyfish* Is Now An Anime!
アニメ化ばんざい
So, hello everyone, I'm Akiko Higashimura. Thank you for buying volume 3.
ズザー skid
Anyway, *Princess Jellyfish* is an anime now!
I was really shocked when the topic of anime first came up.
HIGASHI-MURA-SAN! AN ANIME ADAPTATION GOT GREEN-LIT!
HUH?!
Which was because...
ptooey
PRINCESS JELLYFISH, AN ANIME...?
DOES THAT MEAN...
...IT'LL TURN INTO THIS?!
My mental image of anime, as someone born in '75.
Headband: "Anime Adaptation Banza

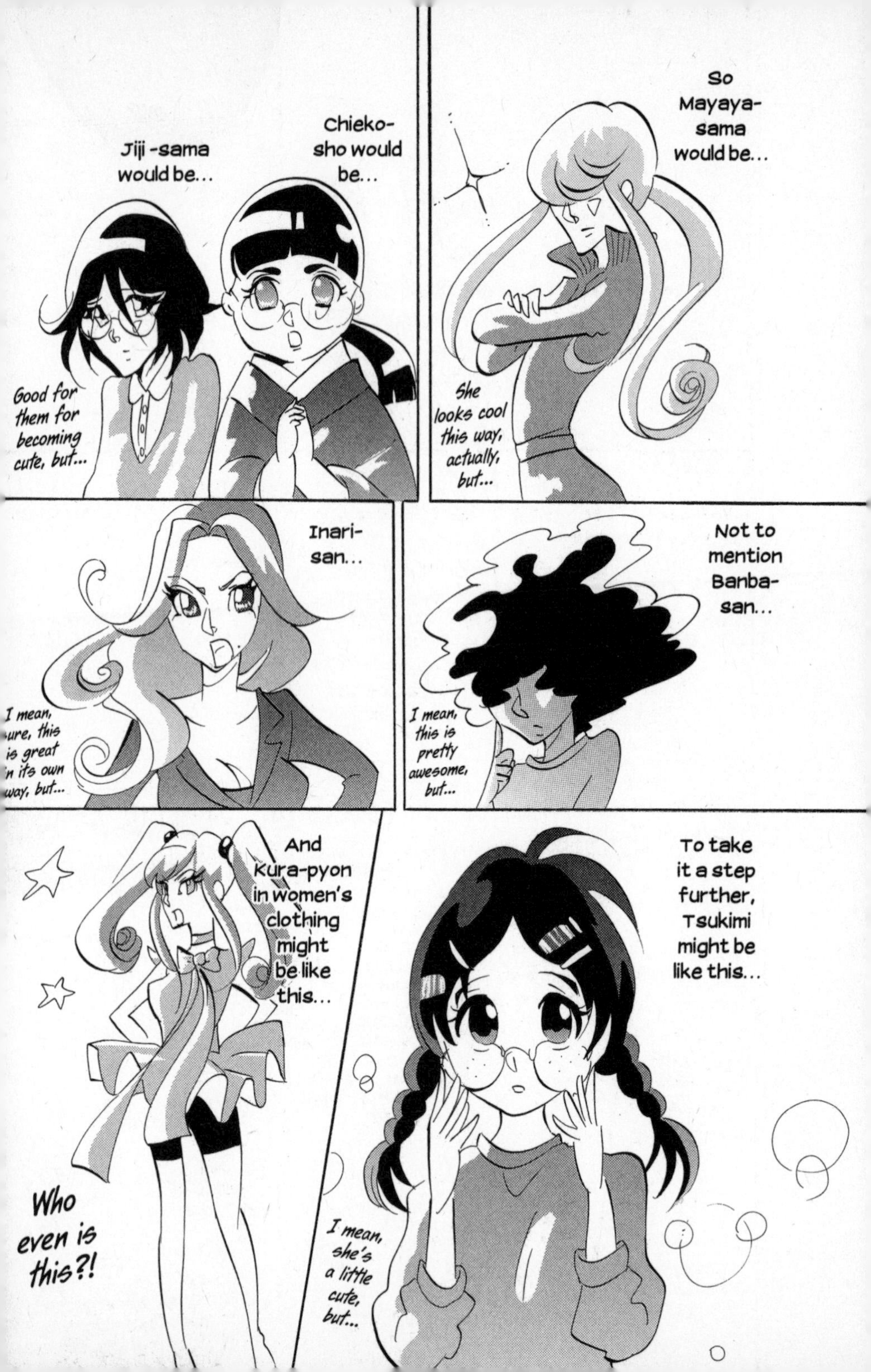
So Mayaya-sama would be...
She looks cool this way, actually, but...
Chieko-sho would be...
Jiji-sama would be...
Good for them for becoming cute, but...
Not to mention Banba-san...
I mean, this is pretty awesome, but...
Inari-san...
I mean, ure, this is great n its own way, but...
To take it a step further, Tsukimi might be like this...
I mean, she's a little cute, but...
And Kura-pyon in women's clothing might be like this...
Who even is this?!

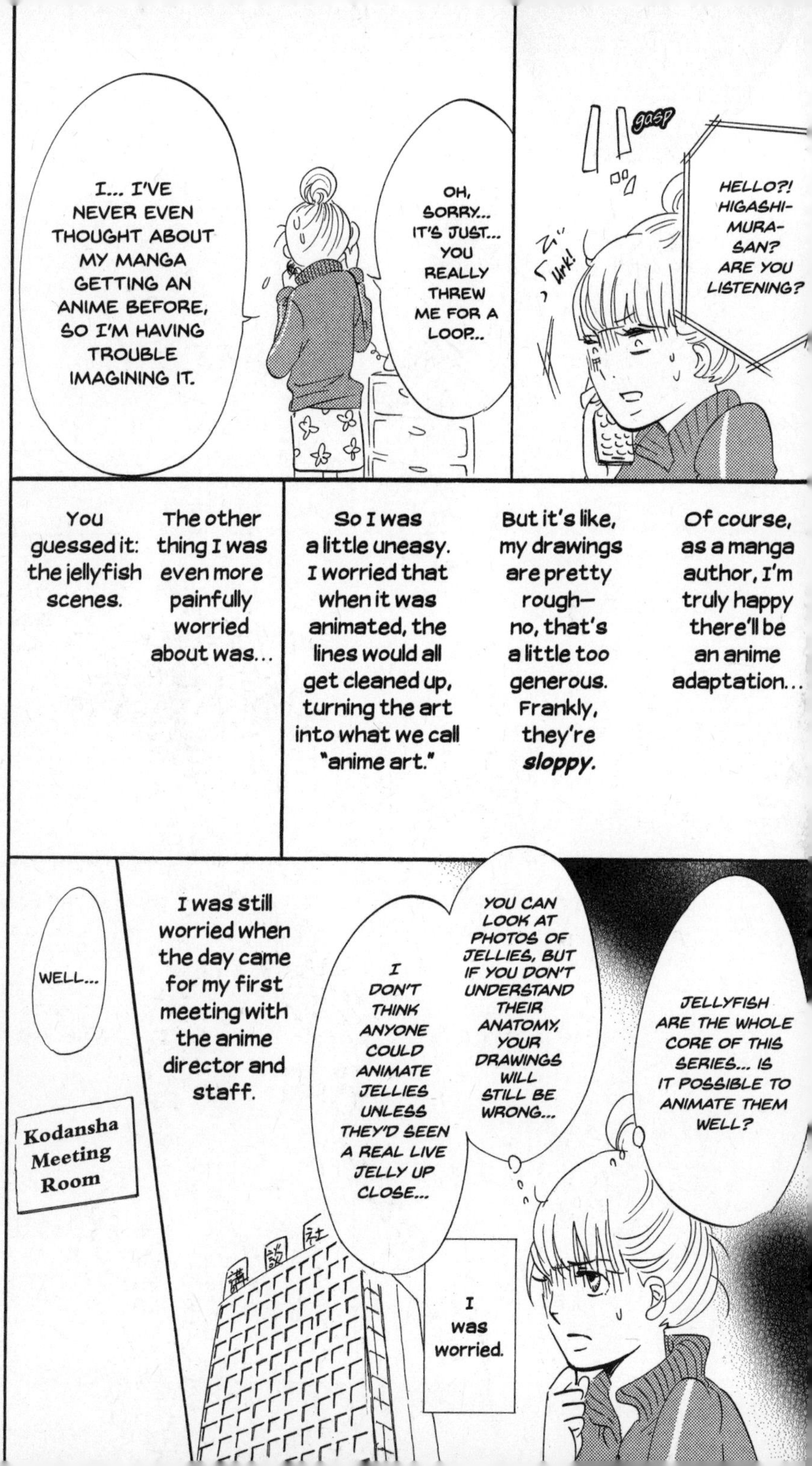
gasp
Urk!
HELLO?! HIGASHI-MURA-SAN? ARE YOU LISTENING?
OH, SORRY... IT'S JUST... YOU REALLY THREW ME FOR A LOOP...
I... I'VE NEVER EVEN THOUGHT ABOUT MY MANGA GETTING AN ANIME BEFORE, SO I'M HAVING TROUBLE IMAGINING IT.
Of course, as a manga author, I'm truly happy there'll be an anime adaptation...
But it's like, my drawings are pretty rough—no, that's a little too generous. Frankly, they're *sloppy*.
So I was a little uneasy. I worried that when it was animated, the lines would all get cleaned up, turning the art into what we call "anime art."
The other thing I was even more painfully worried about was...
You guessed it: the jellyfish scenes.
I was still worried when the day came for my first meeting with the anime director and staff.
JELLYFISH ARE THE WHOLE CORE OF THIS SERIES... IS IT POSSIBLE TO ANIMATE THEM WELL?
YOU CAN LOOK AT PHOTOS OF JELLIES, BUT IF YOU DON'T UNDERSTAND THEIR ANATOMY, YOUR DRAWINGS WILL STILL BE WRONG...
I DON'T THINK ANYONE COULD ANIMATE JELLIES UNLESS THEY'D SEEN A REAL LIVE JELLY UP CLOSE...
I was worried.
WELL...
Kodansha Meeting Room

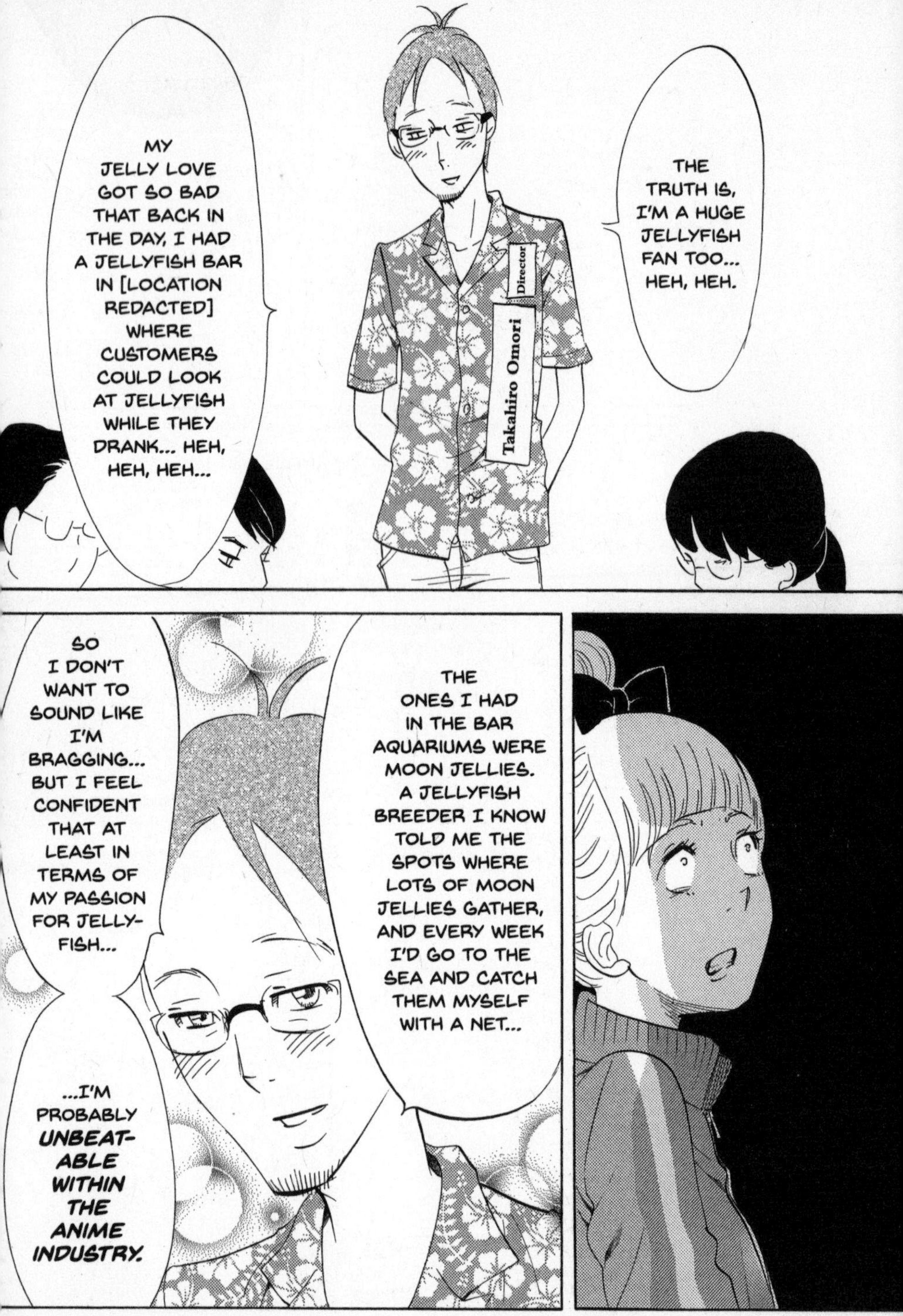
THE TRUTH IS, I'M A HUGE JELLYFISH FAN TOO... HEH, HEH.
Director
Takahiro Omori
MY JELLY LOVE GOT SO BAD THAT BACK IN THE DAY, I HAD A JELLYFISH BAR IN [LOCATION REDACTED] WHERE CUSTOMERS COULD LOOK AT JELLYFISH WHILE THEY DRANK... HEH, HEH, HEH...
THE ONES I HAD IN THE BAR AQUARIUMS WERE MOON JELLIES. A JELLYFISH BREEDER I KNOW TOLD ME THE SPOTS WHERE LOTS OF MOON JELLIES GATHER, AND EVERY WEEK I'D GO TO THE SEA AND CATCH THEM MYSELF WITH A NET...
SO I DON'T WANT TO SOUND LIKE I'M BRAGGING... BUT I FEEL CONFIDENT THAT AT LEAST IN TERMS OF MY PASSION FOR JELLY-FISH...
...I'M PROBABLY *UNBEAT-ABLE WITHIN THE ANIME INDUSTRY.*

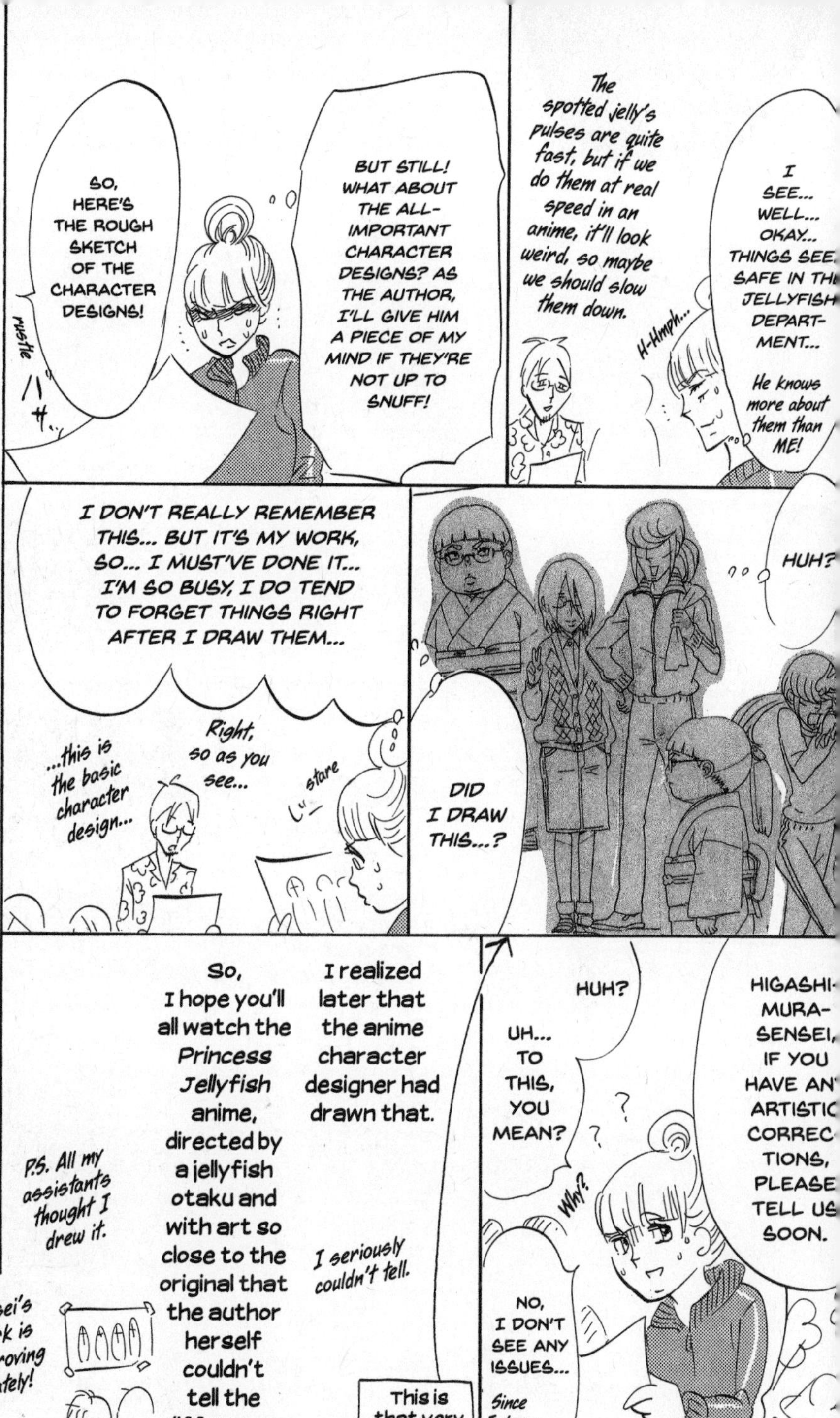
The spotted jelly's pulses are quite fast, but if we do them at real speed in an anime, it'll look weird, so maybe we should slow them down.
H-Hmph...
I SEE... WELL... OKAY... THINGS SEE SAFE IN TH JELLYFISH DEPARTMENT...
He knows more about them than ME!
BUT STILL! WHAT ABOUT THE ALL-IMPORTANT CHARACTER DESIGNS? AS THE AUTHOR, I'LL GIVE HIM A PIECE OF MY MIND IF THEY'RE NOT UP TO SNUFF!
SO, HERE'S THE ROUGH SKETCH OF THE CHARACTER DESIGNS!
rustle
HUH?
DID I DRAW THIS...?
I DON'T REALLY REMEMBER THIS... BUT IT'S MY WORK, SO... I MUST'VE DONE IT... I'M SO BUSY, I DO TEND TO FORGET THINGS RIGHT AFTER I DRAW THEM...
Right, so as you see...
stare
...this is the basic character design...
HIGASHI-MURA-SENSEI, IF YOU HAVE AN ARTISTIC CORREC-TIONS, PLEASE TELL US SOON.
HUH?
UH... TO THIS, YOU MEAN?
Why?
NO, I DON'T SEE ANY ISSUES...
Since I drew this...
I realized later that the anime character designer had drawn that.
So, I hope you'll all watch the Princess Jellyfish anime, directed by a jellyfish otaku and with art so close to the original that the author herself couldn't tell the difference!
I seriously couldn't tell.
P.S. All my assistants thought I drew it.
Sensei's work is improving lately!
This is that very drawing.

Translation Notes

Deception, page 184
The Japanese release title for *Deception* was *Kare ga Nido Aishita S*, or "S, Whom He Loved Twice." The Japanese title of this chapter is *"Kare ga Nido Aishita T."*

Are you the marionette in the mirror?!, page 193
This is a reference to the song "Marionette" by the Japanese band BOØWY.

Go, Mayaya! You're the Shiko Munakata of eraser stamps!, page 195
Shiko Munakata (1903-1975) is considered one of the most important modern Japanese artists. Though he worked in different mediums over the course of his career, he's particularly well known for woodblock prints, the medium he fell in love with. His distinctive style is very different from the *ukiyo-e* prints one may already be familiar with.

We'll be forced to work for room and board at a hot spring in the mountains... Like in Haru-chan..., page 200
Haru-chan was the name of a 1980s manga & TV drama. The title character did indeed work as a waitress at a hot spring *ryokan* (a *ryokan* is a traditional Japanese-style inn).

Mizushima and The Burmese Harp, page 201
Kon Ichikawa's 1956 film *The Burmese Harp* is set during the Burma Campaign in World War II. Private Mizushima becomes a harpist in a group of soldiers who play music. When Mizushima goes missing, his captain believes he is still alive somewhere. In order to find him, the captain trains a parrot to say, "Mizushima, let's go home to Japan together!" Later, Mizushima responds that although the war is over, he cannot leave Burma until he finishes burying those who have fallen.

For the color dress, I thought I'd go with pink to match her hair, page 228
In some Asian countries, the bride changes dresses multiple times during the course of the wedding festivities. In Japanese, this specific type of dress change is called a "color change," and a "color dress" is a dress in a striking color or colors that one might wear to one's reception after the white wedding dress at the ceremony.

The Dragon King's palace, page 241
The Dragon King, divine king of the sea, rules from a palace at the bottom of the ocean. This figure of Japanese mythology and his palace appear in many folktales, including the tale of *Urashima Taro*, the boy who rode to the palace on the back of a turtle he rescued.

Dor**mon, page 246
Doraemon is the title character from the famous children's show of the same name. He is a robot companion to a boy named Nobita, and often helps the child overcome obstacles with special gadgets. Doraemon has a gadget called Big Light, which is a flashlight that can make items bigger. Kuranosuke and Amars could've really used his help with those dresses!

Amars: Countdown to Destruction, page 248
Alpha Dog was released as *Alpha Dog: Countdown to Destruction* in Japan, which is where this chapter draws its title from.

♫ Amars woooorked late at night.
Seeeewing clothes fooor maggots ♫, page 254,
They're riffing on "*Kaasan no Uta*," or "Mother's Song," which is actually a song about a mother staying up late at night to knit mittens for her child.

This technique is frequently used on antique dolls, such as what we call "French dolls.", page 286
The dolls known as "French dolls" in Japan are not necessarily dolls from France, which is why Nomu phrases it like this. The term has been generalized over the years to refer to a European-styled porcelain doll, regardless of what country the doll was originally produced in. The dresses most often associated with "French dolls" are frilly and evocative of aristocratic fashions in late 19th-century France.

Master Ima Kuruyo, page 290
Ima Kuruyo was part of the comedy duo Ima Ikuyo Kuruyo before Ikuyo passed away in May 2015, several years after this manga chapter was written. She was known as the plump one of the duo, with Ikuyo being the super skinny one. She's also famous for her flamboyant outfits, many of which were off the shoulder and heavily ruffled like Chieko's in this panel.

Pigmon, page 290
Pigmon is one of the monsters in the *Ultraman* franchise. Appearing in various *Ultraman* works, he is a friendly monster who has no problems with humans. We're sure the Banba version would be pretty friendly, too, if the humans had beef.

Shannel? De-oil? What are they supposed to be, friends of Noi-Coi?, page 292
Noi-Coi is the nickname for the comedy group Showa Noiru Coiru. Since L and R sound the same in Japanese, "Chanel" and "Dior" both end in a -*ru* sound, just like Noiru and Coiru.

Ryotaro Sugi, page 301

Ryotaro Sugi is a prolific Japanese actor and singer. Out of makeup his eyes don't look much like Mayaya's, but when he's in his makeup for one of his many samurai or kabuki-style roles, there is a fierce resemblance.

Nobuyo Ohyama, page 302

Nobuyo Ohyama is an actor and voice actor, and was the voice of Doraemon for over two decades, making her a household name. Chieko does in fact bear some resemblance to her, and since Ms. Ohyama is from the same generation as Amars's grandmothers would be, part of what this means is that Chieko has looked older than her age since childhood.

We'll go through all the details of your sale with a judicial scrivener when you arrive in Japan., page 318

The judicial scrivener is a part of the Japanese legal system that doesn't exist in the United States. These legal professionals assist clients with things like registering real estate, starting new businesses, and dealing with adult guardianship matters.

Ah, you mean "Runaway" by the band, RATS & STAR!, page 326

When their debut single "Runaway" came out in 1980, this Japanese band was called CHANELS, a reference to The Channels, an American doo-wop group from the 1950s. In 1983, their name changed to RATS & STAR. After spending time performing in a Los Angeles bar, the band became famous for their upbeat music and performances in blackface. "Blackface" refers to a practice where performers who are not of African descent apply black makeup imitating caricatures of Black people. Up to the mid-20th century, blackface was perceived by white Americans and many others as wholesome entertainment, and it spread harmful stereotypes about Black people around the world. Commodore Matthew Perry brought blackface to Japan on his fateful voyage aimed at "opening up" Japan to Western influence, presenting a performance by white members of his crew. As more and more Western popular culture was imported into Japan, blackface became just as widely accepted there as it was in the United States at the time. Many Americans have acknowledged the insidious stereotypes spread by blackface performance, and it has largely disappeared from the U.S., but in Japan, where Black people make up a small fraction of 1 percent of the population, it has proved difficult to educate the public about the pain caused by such a practice. Recently, a collaboration between RATS & STAR and an idol group, Momoiro Clover Z, was canceled before it could air on television because of the controversy caused by both groups' use of blackface. Bands including The Gospellers and Puffy AmiYumi have also collaborated with RATS & STAR. RATS & STAR stopped recording new music about two decades ago, but never officially disbanded.

What's going on? Is Erika here or something?, page 339
The Erika that Hanamori imagines here is the renowned actress and singer Erika Sawajiri.

Oshiruko, page 346
Oshiruko is a sweet dessert porridge made of red azuki beans.

You sure we don't have to do that thing? The harshness thing?, page 350
The "harshness thing" Banba's talking about is *aku-nuki*, or "harshness removal." It's a common step in many Japanese recipes, and its purpose is to remove *aku*, or natural bitterness or astringency, from vegetables and other foods. It's a process other countries use, too, just not for as many types of foods. For example, if your cookbook tells you to boil something for a while and then scrape off any scum that rises to the top of the water, that's *aku-nuki*. Essentially, this process removes some of the sharp notes from an ingredient's flavor, bringing out more of the sweetness. Although the *aku* in *aku-nuki* doesn't mean "evil," it's a homophone of the Japanese word for "evil." Which is why Mayaya is particularly dramatic in this scene.

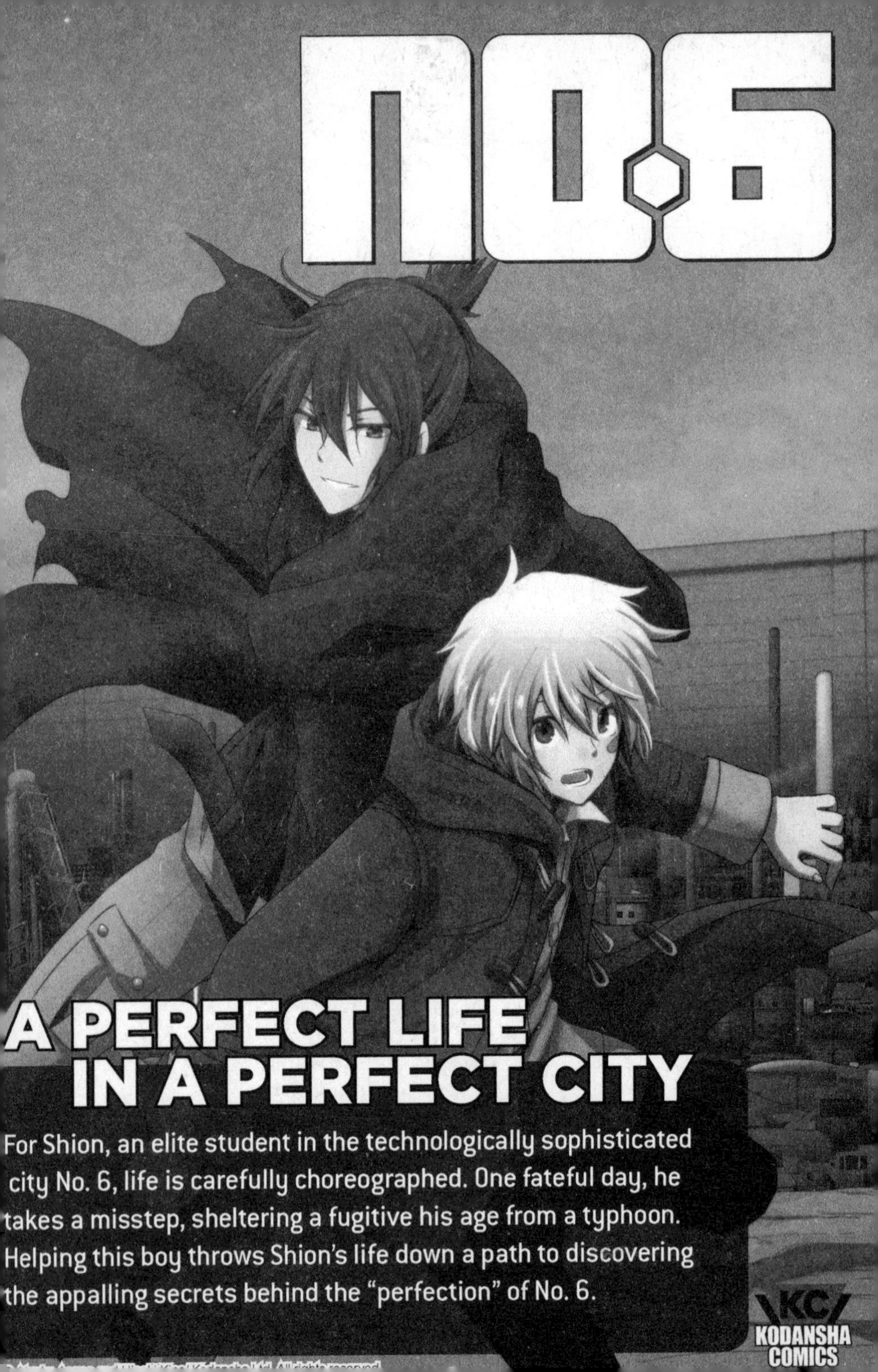
NO.6
A PERFECT LIFE
IN A PERFECT CITY
For Shion, an elite student in the technologically sophisticated city No. 6, life is carefully choreographed. One fateful day, he takes a misstep, sheltering a fugitive his age from a typhoon. Helping this boy throws Shion's life down a path to discovering the appalling secrets behind the "perfection" of No. 6.
KC
KODANSHA
COMICS

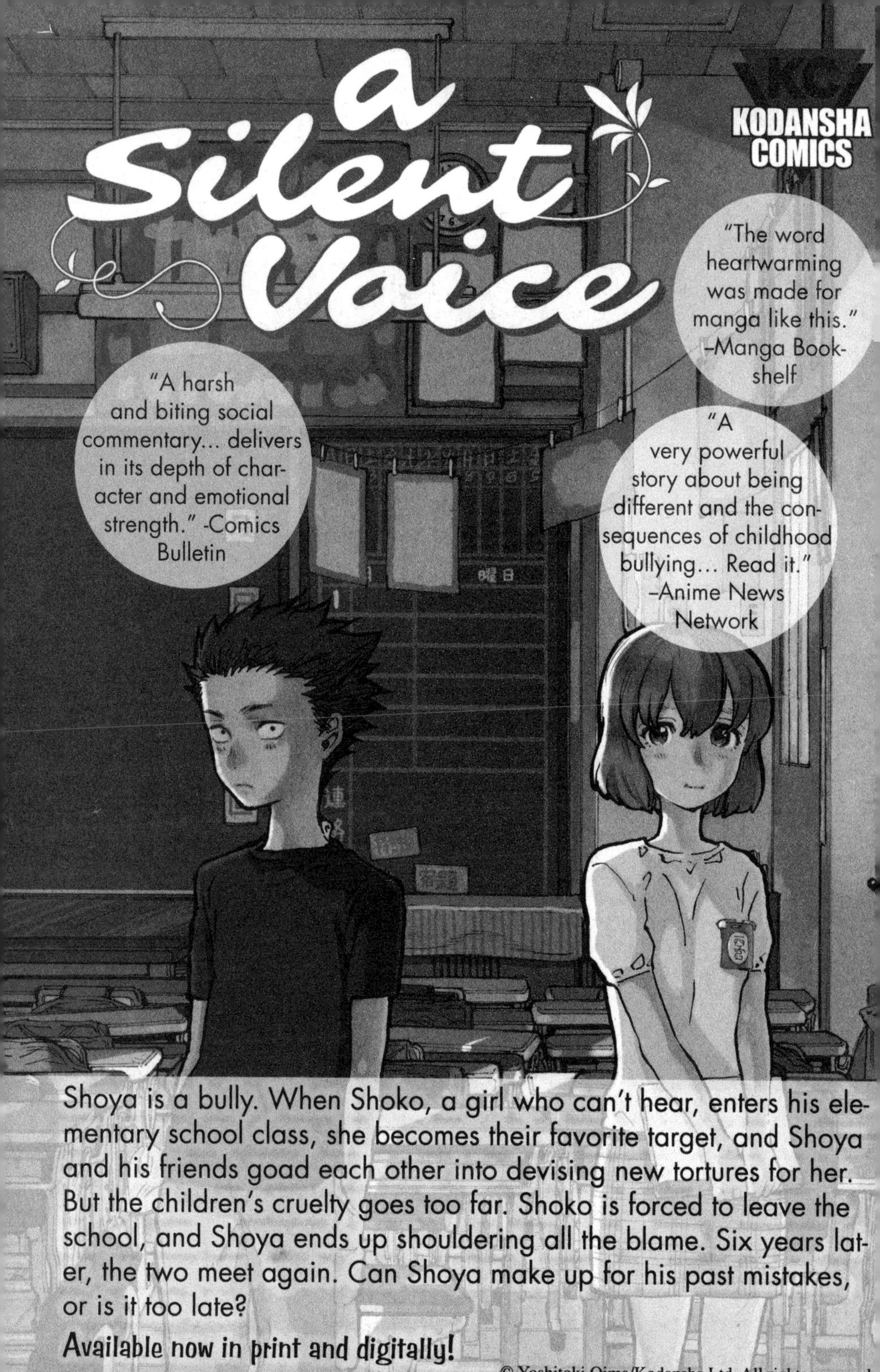
a Silent Voice
KODANSHA COMICS
"The word heartwarming was made for manga like this." –Manga Bookshelf
"A harsh and biting social commentary... delivers in its depth of character and emotional strength." -Comics Bulletin
"A very powerful story about being different and the consequences of childhood bullying... Read it." –Anime News Network
Shoya is a bully. When Shoko, a girl who can't hear, enters his elementary school class, she becomes their favorite target, and Shoya and his friends goad each other into devising new tortures for her. But the children's cruelty goes too far. Shoko is forced to leave the school, and Shoya ends up shouldering all the blame. Six years later, the two meet again. Can Shoya make up for his past mistakes, or is it too late?
Available now in print and digitally!

A Kodansha Comics Trade Paperback Original.

Published in the United States by Kodansha Comics,
an imprint of Kodansha USA Publishing, LLC, New York.

Publication rights for this English edition arranged through Kodansha Ltd., Tokyo.

First published in Japan in 2010 by Kodansha Ltd., Tokyo,
as *Kuragehime* volumes 5 & 6.

ISBN 978-1-63236-230-8

Printed in the United States of America.

www.kodanshacomics.com

9 8 7 6 5 4 3 2 1

Translation: Sarah Alys Lindholm
Lettering: Carl Vanstiphout
Additional Layout: Belynda Ungurath
Editing: Haruko Hashimoto
Kodansha Comics Edition Cover Design: Phil Balsman